Child Psychology

Child Psychology

Edited by Harry Winkler

CLANRYE INTERNATIONAL
www.clanryeinternational.com

Clanrye International,
750 Third Avenue, 9th Floor,
New York, NY 10017, USA

ISBN: 978-1-63240-722-1

Cataloging-in-Publication Data

Child psychology / edited by Harry Winkler.
p. cm.
Includes bibliographical references and index.
ISBN 978-1-63240-722-1
1. Child psychology. 2. Child development. 3. Developmental psychology. 4. Psychology.
5. Social psychology. I. Winkler, Harry.
BF721 .C45 2018
155.4--dc23

For information on all Clanrye International publications
visit our website at www.clanryeinternational.com

CLANRYE INTERNATIONAL

Printed in China.

Contents

Preface

Child psychology refers to the study of the change happening in the human brain. It is an intricate subject that deals with the development and growth of children, infants and, adolescences. The topics included in this vast field are identity formulation, social change, development of motor skills, moral understanding, self-concept, personality and language acquisition, etc. The various studies that are constantly contributing towards evolution of this field are examined in detail in this book. It is a compilation of chapters that discuss the most vital concepts and emerging trends in the field of child psychology. This book will serve as a reference to a broad spectrum of readers.

This book is a result of research of several months to collate the most relevant data in the field.

When I was approached with the idea of this book and the proposal to edit it, I was overwhelmed. It gave me an opportunity to reach out to all those who share a common interest with me in this field. I had 3 main parameters for editing this text:

1. Accuracy - The data and information provided in this book should be up-to-date and valuable to the readers.

2. Structure - The data must be presented in a structured format for easy understanding and better grasping of the readers.

3. Universal Approach - This book not only targets students but also experts and innovators in the field, thus my aim was to present topics which are of use to all.

Thus, it took me a couple of months to finish the editing of this book.

I would like to make a special mention of my publisher who considered me worthy of this opportunity and also supported me throughout the editing process. I would also like to thank the editing team at the back-end who extended their help whenever required.

Editor

1

Child-caregiver interaction in two remote Indigenous Australian communities

Jill Vaughan[1], Gillian Wigglesworth[1], Deborah Loakes[1], Samantha Disbray[2] and Karin Moses[3]*

[1] School of Languages and Linguistics, University of Melbourne, Parkville, VIC, Australia, [2] Northern Institute, Charles Darwin University, Alice Springs, NT, Australia, [3] Student Learning, La Trobe University, Bendigo, VIC, Australia

This paper reports on a study in two remote multilingual Indigenous Australian communities: Yakanarra in the Kimberley region of Western Australia and Tennant Creek in the Barkly region of the Northern Territory. In both communities, processes of language shift are underway from a traditional language (Walmajarri and Warumungu, respectively) to a local creole variety (Fitzroy Valley Kriol and Wumpurrarni English, respectively). The study focuses on language input from primary caregivers to a group of preschool children, and on the children's productive language. The study further highlights child-caregiver interactions as a site of importance in understanding the broader processes of language shift. We use longitudinal data from two time-points, approximately 2 years apart, to explore changes in adult input over time and developmental patterns in the children's speech. At both time points, the local creole varieties are the preferred codes of communication for the dyads in this study, although there is some use of the traditional language in both communities. Results show that for measures of turn length (MLT), there are notable differences between the two communities for both the focus children and their caregivers. In Tennant Creek, children and caregivers use longer turns at Time 2, while in Yakanarra the picture is more variable. The two communities also show differing trends in terms of conversational load (MLT ratio). For measures of morphosyntactic complexity (MLU), children and caregivers in Tennant Creek use more complex utterances at Time 2, while caregivers in Yakanarra show less complexity in their language at that time point. The study's findings contribute to providing a more detailed picture of the multilingual practices at Yakanarra and Tennant Creek, with implications for understanding broader processes of language shift. They also elucidate how children's language and linguistic input varies diachronically across time. As such, we contribute to understandings of normative language development for non-Western, non middle-class children in multilingual contexts.

Edited by:
Carmel O'Shannessy, University of Michigan, USA

Reviewed by:
Jennifer Smith, University of Glasgow, UK
Ian Grenville Malcolm, Edith Cowan University, Australia (retired)

***Correspondence:**
Gillian Wigglesworth, School of Languages and Linguistics, University of Melbourne, Darling Street, Parkville, VIC 3010, Australia
gillianw@unimelb.edu.au

Specialty section:
This article was submitted to Language Sciences, a section of the journal Frontiers in Psychology

Keywords: child language acquisition, language input, language shift, Walmajarri, Fitzroy Valley Kriol, Warumungu, Wumpurrarni English

Introduction

Indigenous children in Australia grow up in a range of diverse language settings. In the cities and metropolitan areas, particularly along the populated coastlines of Australia, which were settled early by Europeans, traditional languages have long ceased to be spoken as the primary means of day-to-day communication. Instead, local varieties of Aboriginal English are spoken as in-community and in-family codes. "Aboriginal English" is an umbrella term, covering a range of varieties in different sociolinguistic and geographic settings (see Malcolm and Kaldor, 1991). Aboriginal English is largely mutually intelligible with standard Australian English, and in its "lightest" styles differs only in minor ways from the standard, usually in pronunciation, lexis, grammatical patterns, speech pragmatics and conceptualization (see e.g., Kaldor and Malcolm, 1982; Malcolm and Kaldor, 1991; Eades, 1996; Malcolm and Sharifian, 2002, 2007; McGregor, 2004; Sharifian, 2005; Butcher, 2008).

In more remote locations, particularly in central and northern Australia, the picture is more complex. In some places, traditional languages continue to be acquired as first languages by the current generation of children, and in other places, language shift to contact varieties, including mixed languages and local creole varieties, has taken place, or is in process (see e.g., McConvell and Thieberger, 2001). Creole varieties on mainland Australia are referred to as *Kriol*, the name being based on the word *creole*[1]. There are a number of locally named varieties of Kriol, for example in Yakanarra (one of our field sites), the variety is called Fitzroy Valley Kriol (or Kimberley Kriol) (see e.g., Hudson, 1985), henceforth FVKriol. Another example is Roper River Kriol spoken in the Ngukurr region. In Tennant Creek (our second field site) the creole is referred to as Wumpurrarni English, henceforth WE, and varies from acrolectal (more like English) to basilectal (a heavy creole) (see e.g., Disbray and Simpson, 2004; Disbray, 2009)[2].

Recent research into such language settings in Australia is providing descriptions of children's language acquisition in diverse and dynamic contexts (see, for example, the variety of papers in Simpson and Wigglesworth, 2008). Other research focuses on the rapidly changing language environments and the emergence of new contact varieties (e.g., Bavin and Shopen, 1985 for Yuendumu Warlpiri; McConvell and Meakins, 2005; Meakins, 2011 for Gurindji Kriol; O'Shannessy, 2005 for Light Warlpiri and McConvell, 2008 for general discussion of mixed languages in Indigenous Australia).

This study is an investigation of language use amongst Indigenous caregivers and their young children in two remote communities in Australia. There are two themes to the paper. The first regards child language development, and the second compares how this manifests in two communities of Indigenous people that are in many ways comparable (remote, multiple codes spoken, community language endangerment, and shift) but are markedly different in terms of the sociolinguistic setting and the mixture of languages that children are exposed to.

Our own work has looked in some detail at the language situation in Indigenous Australia. The work is associated with The Aboriginal Child Language Acquisition (ACLA1) study[3], carried out from 2004 to 2007, which focused on child-directed speech, as well as language use by children, in three Indigenous Australian communities (for more information on ACLA1 see Wigglesworth and Simpson, 2008)—Yakanarra, Tennant Creek and Kalkaringi[4]. This is particularly interesting because of the relative dearth of information on how non-Western children acquire language, and also because these particular children live in multilingual societies which are undergoing rapid language shift. We address prior research in this area further below.

Studies of Child-Directed Speech

We have looked, for example, at the way Yakanarra children deal with questions in an informal setting (Moses and Yallop, 2008), at the language codes children receive from different aged interlocutors (Loakes et al., 2013), and children's knowledge of their traditional language (Loakes et al., 2012). From this, we know that Indigenous children in Yakanarra frequently experience questions and respond to questioning, debunking earlier views that Indigenous Australians are not familiar with question-answer routines (Moses and Yallop, 2008). We know that children speak and hear FVKriol predominantly, but are also exposed to the traditional language Walmajarri, especially from older community members. As far as Walmajarri is concerned, we also know that children have relatively good receptive knowledge when it comes to nouns (Loakes et al., 2012), and we also know that their traditional language knowledge goes beyond this, because they may respond to Walmajarri utterances from an elder entirely (and appropriately) in FVKriol (examples shown in Loakes et al., 2013).

In Tennant Creek we have investigated interactions between caregivers and children during joint picture-book viewing (Disbray, 2008). In these interactions we saw that caregivers of the children aged between 18 months and 5 years of age were sensitive to the child's level of attention at different ages, and that through questioning and prompting, and through repetition and elaboration, they collaboratively "built" a rich narrative. This study also established common patterns of use of Warumungu features in WE, further explored as a factor of the age of the adult speaker in Morrison and Disbray (2008). These studies have shown that children hear full Warumungu only from elderly speakers, and that in the WE speech of younger adults, some common Warumungu nouns and fewer Warumungu verbs are used, a bilingual speech pattern which children also later develop (Disbray, 2009). Additionally, semantic case-markers, derived from Warumungu, have been incorporated into WE, and are used variably (Disbray and Simpson, 2004; Morrison and Disbray, 2008).

We know that, in general, children have acquired most of the skills needed for adult-like language proficiency by the time they attend primary school (Hoff, 2001), and spend their school years mastering more complex grammatical and phonological features. However, studies of the development of grammaticality in Indigenous Australian children have only recently gained

[1] In the Torres Strait Islands off Northern Queensland, the creole variety spoken is referred to as "Torres Strait Creole." The spelling Kriol stems from the orthography developed for Roper River Kriol (Sandefur, 1979).

[2] See Harris (1993) for a discussion of the development of Kriol in Australia, and more information about the varieties spoken.

[3] http://languages-linguistics.unimelb.edu.au/past-projects/acla1

[4] See Moses (2009), Disbray (2009), and Meakins (2011) respectively.

momentum. Malcolm (1996) reports on development of the verb phrase in Aboriginal English spoken in a remote Indigenous region, and concludes that there is evidence that language development may be ongoing for bilingual/bidialectal Indigenous children even between 5 and 10 years of age. Disbray (2009) investigated the development of discourse competence among 5–14 year old WE-speaking children, demonstrating that the children pass through similar developmental stages to children speaking other languages to create a cohesive text. A great deal of further research is needed to understand language development amongst Indigenous Australian children.

Previous studies of child-directed speech have noted that parental speech to children can involve utterances that are shorter, morphosyntactically simpler, and more redundant than speech directed at adults (e.g., Snow, 1972, 1977; Sachs et al., 1976; Ferguson, 1977). These findings contributed to the idea that simplified language input may help children's language development (e.g., Snow, 1972), often referred to as the "motherese hypothesis." In the 2–5 year old age range, as in the present study, language development is characterized by a move from simple two- and three-word combinations to the production of more grammatically sophisticated utterances, as children become skilled at using most of the requisite grammatical morphemes and begin to construct complex multiclause sentences (Hoff, 2001; Berko Gleason, 2005).

Snow (1972) observed that maternal speech to 2-year olds is simpler and more redundant than speech directed at 10-year-olds, and other studies focusing on younger children in the fundamental stages of language acquisition have demonstrated that caregivers make fine adjustments to the complexity of their speech according to the age of the child (e.g., Vosoughi, 2010). Kaye (1980), Philips (1973) and Rondal (1980) all observed markedly shorter, simpler, and more repetitive utterances to infants than to toddler-aged children. A more recent study by Huttenlocher et al. (2007) with children aged 14–30 months reinforces these early findings; their analysis of the speech used by English-speaking parents with their children at 4-month intervals revealed that caregivers made substantial adjustments to the syntactic complexity and diversity of their speech over the 16-month time period. In the sample of 50 parents, Huttenlocher et al. also found individual differences in input patterns related to caregiver education level, and noted that caregivers maintained their idiosyncratic input patterns at the same time as making incremental adjustments to their speech depending on the age of their child interlocutor. The researchers suggest that this consistent adjustment indicates caregiver sensitivity to the language levels of young children, while providing the children with a progressively broader set of language models.

Other studies incorporating child production data have demonstrated that longer and more complex utterances from caregivers correlate with more advanced morphosyntactic development in children. Hoff-Ginsberg (1998), in a study of maternal speech to children based on birth order, found that first-born children showed "more precocious lexical and grammatical development than later borns" (Hoff-Ginsberg, 1998, p. 626), and that this correlated with longer and more complex utterances from their mothers. Huttenlocher et al. (2002) looked at the production of multiclause utterances by 4-year olds in relation to parental input at home, and teacher input at pre-school, and found that the style of parental input was the major predictor of syntactic complexity in children's speech. In addition, various studies have shown the complexity, quantity, and lexical diversity of caregiver speech to have strong correlations with children's vocabulary development (Huttenlocher et al., 1991; Hart and Risley, 1995; Bornstein et al., 1998; Naigles and Hoff-Ginsberg, 1998; Hoff and Naigles, 2002; Hoff, 2003; Pan et al., 2005; Rowe, 2008).

Recent studies of the acquisition of sociolinguistic variation (e.g., Foulkes et al., 1999, 2005; Díaz-Campos, 2005; Smith et al., 2007, 2013; O'Shannessy, 2011) emphasize that child-directed speech plays a central role in socializing children into the appropriate use and the social-indexical values of variables (Foulkes et al., 2005, p. 177). For example, in their study of 29 child/caregiver pairs in a small Scottish fishing village, Smith et al. showed that patterns of variation are acquired at a very early age in tandem with language acquisition more generally, but that the nature of this process may vary according to the variable in question (2013, p. 321). Foulkes et al. (2005), in their study of child-directed speech among 39 mothers in North East England, found that phonetic variants used in this register differed markedly from inter-adult speech, and further noted effects with regard to the gender of the children in the dyads: speech to girls contained more standard variants than speech to boys, which contained higher rates of vernacular variants. This effect was more apparent for younger children in the sample.

Studies of Cross-Cultural Language Input

Cross-culturally, children have different early language experiences, and the existing research on non-Western cultural groups indicates that there is a great deal of variation in the type and amount of direct language input children receive in the preschool years (Hoff, 2006). Various studies have observed that in some non-Western cultures, young children are not seen as communicative partners, and receive very little child-directed speech as infants, in contrast to the patterns observed for North American and European caregivers. This been noted for Gusii mothers in Kenya (Richman et al., 1992; LeVine, 2004), Gapuners in Papua New Guinea (Kulick, 1992), the Kaluli in Papua New Guinea (Ochs and Schieffelin, 1994), Samoans in Western Samoa (Ochs and Schieffelin, 1994), the Warlpiri of central Australia (Bavin, 1992), K'iche' Maya speakers in Guatemala (Pye, 1992), Tzeltal speakers in Mexico (Brown, 2001), Javanese speakers in East Java (Smith-Hefner, 1998), and African-Americans in South Carolina (Heath, 1983). In many of these studies (e.g., Ochs and Schieffelin, 1994), the researchers suggest that a large amount of early language learning must be based on overheard, rather than child-directed, language, and that minimal direct speech to children may correlate with relatively late language development (Brown, 2001).

However, there is very little research describing language input in these non-Western societies on occasions when input *is* provided by caregivers, and even less looking at child language development in relation to input, beyond the body of research on the acquisition of language-specific grammatical and phonological features. In Indigenous Australia, a number of researchers have observed the use of "baby talk" registers (Laughren, 1984; Lee, 1987; Bavin, 1992, 1993; Kral and Ellis, 2008; Jones and Meakins, 2013; Turpin et al., 2014). This register is typically characterized by such features as phonological simplification, semantic simplification (for some groups of vocabulary items), repetition, slower speech rate and falling prosodic contour.

Outside the Australian context, Harkness' (1977) cross-sectional study found that Kipsigis caregivers in Kenya modified the length and complexity of their utterances as a function of their child interlocutor's MLU, adjusting their speech to the developmental stage of the child, leading Harkness to observe that "mothers and children in cultures far removed from our own modify their speech to children learning to talk in the same way that Americans do" (1977: 315). In contrast, there are claims that when caregivers in some other cultures talk to children, they do not use "baby talk"; for example, Ochs and Schieffelin (1994) observe that Kaluli and Samoan caregivers, though they may use pitch manipulation, do not engage in the morphosyntactic simplification synonymous with child-directed speech. Despite this, "Kaluli and Samoan children become fluent speakers within the range of normal developmental variation" (Ochs and Schieffelin, 1994, p. 494). Crago et al. (1997) have similarly found that of the minimal language input received by children in Inuktitut-speaking communities in Quebec, very little is morphosyntactically modified, but the children still achieve the major language development milestones at ages comparable to those for Western children. In reviewing the literature on child-directed speech, Lieven (1994) argues that the child-centered style of speaking may be one way of enabling children to learn and use their mother tongue, "but it is clearly not essential" (1994: 72), and concludes that children worldwide tend to learn language at around the same time, despite the diverse ways of speaking to (and around) children.

A further important aspect of the linguistic socialization of Indigenous children in Australia pertains to the high level of input children receive from interactants other than adults. In many Indigenous communities, children spend a great deal of their time playing and interacting with other children, with older children often taking on caregiving roles. Hamilton's (1981) observations in Arnhem Land describe how from the age of two, children are absorbed into a peer group of related children for support and learning experiences. These groups may develop into more structured "kid mobs" common for children from 5 to 9 years of age, resulting in less frequent interaction with adults. After-school and weekend activities may take place in kid mob groupings, which are largely determined by common linguistic and kinship ties. The linguistic consequences may be significant, with the "kid mob" a potentially dominant force in community language shift whereby younger speakers may even socialize adults in language choice (see Luykx, 2005 and Gafaranga, 2010). O'Shannessy (2012, 2013) has shown that children can play a significant role in language change, partly due to their spending time in peer groups, and partly due to the kind of input they receive. Loakes et al. (2013) addressed this aspect of community language shift in Yakanarra by investigating the input received from different-aged interlocutors with regard to code choice and found that less traditional language is found in children's interactions with younger interlocutors. These young interlocutors also use markedly more talk than older interactants.

While there is some research into normative language development for non middle-class, non-Western children, this area remains poorly understood, particularly in situations where the children grow up in multilingual communities. Research suggests that bi- or multilingual children progress through linguistic developmental stages at similar rates to monolingual children (Pearson et al., 1993; Paradis and Genesee, 1996; De Houwer, 2005), and in particular that when *all* the child's linguistic resources are considered (i.e., their knowledge of both/all languages), multilingual children have similar vocabulary sizes and grammatical abilities to monolingual children (Pearson and Fernandez, 1994; Nicoladis and Genesee, 1997; Patterson, 1998; Patterson and Pearson, 2004). However, in assessing children's abilities in each separate language, some research suggests that at comparable ages, bi- or multilingual children may have less developed vocabularies and grammatical abilities in each individual language than monolingual children in their sole language (Bialystok and Feng, 2011; Hoff et al., 2012). Other research indicates that language development progresses language-specifically (Marchman et al., 2004; Conboy and Thal, 2006). Language development for multilingual children is also clearly tied in with the issue of language dominance, which in turn is closely related to the type and quantity of language input children receive from carers (Lanza, 1997; De Houwer, 1999, 2007; Hoff et al., 2012). As for other areas of acquisition research, knowledge about language socialization in multilingual families tends to be based on research in Western cultures. Some research has investigated language socialization in language contact settings (Garrett and Baquedano-López, 2002; Luykx, 2005; Makihara, 2005; Gafaranga, 2010; O'Shannessy, 2011) including creole contexts (Garrett, 2005; Paugh, 2005), and it is clear that these non-Western contexts encompass an extremely diverse range of language learning environments, with many unique and context-specific factors that need to be considered in investigations of child language development.

We cannot assume that current understandings of child language input and language development hold true for children in linguistically diverse non-Western settings, and there is still a large amount of research to be done on the nature of the language received and produced by children in these settings, as well as the language development patterns that are normal for them. As Saxton (2009, 2010) points out, many non-Western language socialization studies are anthropological in nature, rather than designed specifically to investigate child language input and acquisition, particularly those cited as evidence of minimal or non-modified child directed speech.

There is evidently a need for targeted exploration of caregiver input behavior and child language production cross-culturally and cross-linguistically, and the present study contributes to this by providing input and production data for two Indigenous Australian communities: Yakanarra in the Kimberley area of Western Australia, and Tennant Creek in the Barkly region of the Northern Territory. The study focuses on language input by primary caregivers to a group of preschool children, and also focuses on the children's productive language. We use longitudinal data from two time-points, approximately 2 years apart, to describe changes in adult input over time and developmental patterns in the children's speech.

Profiles of the Communities

Both communities in this study are located in remote desert regions of Australia. Yakanarra is in the far north of the state of Western Australia, and Tennant Creek is centrally located in the Northern Territory.

Yakanarra

Yakanarra consists of about 30 houses 110 km south-east of Fitzroy Crossing in the Kimberley region. Yakanarra is typical of a remote rural Indigenous community in Australia, with the majority of residents being Indigenous, and the few non-Indigenous residents working in the school, community center, or shop. Yakanarra was established in 1989 by Walmajarri people, the oldest of whom had left their traditional country and hunter-gatherer way of life in the 1950s.

The traditional language of Yakanarra is Walmajarri, but by 2006, when Moses was carrying out fieldwork, FVKriol had displaced Walmajarri as the language of everyday talk, although Walmajarri was still spoken to some degree by the older members of the community (see especially Loakes et al., 2013). Some Standard Australian English is spoken in limited circumstances, typically in formal contexts, and with non-Indigenous people (see e.g., Wigglesworth and Simpson, 2008, p. 20).

Tennant Creek

Tennant Creek is a remote, urban township in the Barkly region of Central Australia. It is a small town with a population of approximately 3000, half of whom are Indigenous. The township is located on Warumungu country, the traditional language of the area. The local Kriol variety, Wumpurrarni English (see Disbray, 2009), is the main language of everyday communication for most Warumungu people. This local variety shares features with other Kriol varieties spoken in Indigenous Australia, but has a number of local features, including the use of Warumungu-source features, such as insertional code-switches and semantic case-marking (Morrison and Disbray, 2008).

Like many contact settings, there is substantial variation in the way people in Tennant Creek use the contact variety Wumpurrarni English, with the speech varieties best understood as occupying a continuum from "lighter" or more acrolectal to "heavier" or more basilectal styles. Similarly to the situation in Yakanarra, Warumungu has undergone significant language shift, and is spoken as a full code only by a small number of elders, with younger adult speakers tending to be partial speakers (Morrison and Disbray, 2008).

Comparing Yakanarra and Tennant Creek

Yakanarra and Tennant Creek are both located in desert regions of Australia. Yakanarra is a remote and relatively closed community with little outside influence, while Tennant Creek is a larger town on a major highway, with a greater variety of people from varied language backgrounds.

Aims

As discussed earlier, our previous work in both Yakanarra and Tennant Creek has shown that language shift is occurring rapidly, and children hear a variety of different input codes, with FVKriol in Yakanarra and Wumpurrani English in Tennant Creek being the main codes used. The input they hear varies along a continuum from more acrolectal to more basilectal determined by various factors including the person, the setting and the interlocutor. This study therefore examines both features of input to the children, and features of the production of the children at two points in time 2 years apart, when the children were approximately two and four.

The specific research questions we address are:

(1) What are the characteristics of the children's language use at ages two and four in terms of MLT and MLU?
(2) What are the characteristics of the caregivers' language use at the two time points in terms of MLT and MLU?
(3) In these two communities, what kinds of multilingual practices can be observed in the children's and the caregivers' language use?

While analysis of Time 1 compared to Time 2 is sometimes considered a gross measure of development (c.f. Snow, 1995), we argue that it is a crucial first step to understanding longitudinal changes in child language in these communities. Given the lack of understanding about normative language development in Indigenous Australian communities generally, and particularly in areas undergoing rapid language shift, we hope that results of the current study will be used as a reference sample for other researchers working in this area.

In general, ongoing work in Indigenous Australian communities is largely a response to the fact that language acquisition in monolingual (especially English-speaking) communities is well-understood, yet language acquisition in multilingual Indigenous societies such as those in Australia is understudied (see for example the discussion in Wigglesworth and Simpson, 2008, p. 14). Additionally, it is a response to the need for basic, language-specific work on developmental patterns before a full theory of child language acquisition can be attained (see e.g., Slobin, 1997).

Method

Participants

For both communities there are four child participants in the study, as well as their main caregiver, who were their mothers in all cases but one—BM is Belinda's great-grandmother[5]. This gives four interactional pairs and eight participants in each community, with sixteen participants in total. Information about the participants is shown in **Table 1** below. This includes pseudonyms which refer to the children, their sex, the code for their caregiver, the children's ages at Time 1 and 2, and the age difference across the time-points. The caregiver code corresponds to the first initial of the child and the initial "M" for mother, so for example the mother of the first child in the table, Natalie, is referred to as NM.

[5] It is not unusual to have a great grandmother in an Indigenous community.

TABLE 1 | Participant details.

Community	Child	Sex	Caregiver	Child age time 1	Child age time 2	Time 2-time 1
Tennant creek	Natalie	F	NM	2;7	4;7	2;0
Tennant creek	Melanie	F	MM	2;7	4;3	1;8
Tennant creek	Sarah	F	SM	1;8	3;7	1;11
Tennant creek	Belinda	F	BM	2;2	4;2	2;0
Yakanarra	Katherine	F	KM	3;6	5;6	2;0
Yakanarra	Olivia	F	OM	2;7	4;7	2;0
Yakanarra	Andrew	M	AM	2;2	4;7	2;5
Yakanarra	Emily	F	EM	2;6	4;6	2;0

All participants were female with the exception of Andrew in Yakanarra. At Time 1, they ranged in age from 1;8 to 3;6, and at time 2 from 3;7 to 5;6. The age range between the two time periods varied from 1;8 to 2;5, (average 2;0) with five children having exactly 2 years between the two times. The average age of the children in Tennant Creek at time 1 was 2;3 and 4;2 at Time 2; in Yakanarra it was 2;8 at time 1 and 4;10 at time 2. The caregivers range from being in their early twenties to early thirties, while BM is in her early seventies.

The fact that age is not balanced across the sessions is a limitation, but a reflection of the reality of data collection in Indigenous communities. In Indigenous Australia, people tend to be highly mobile. Communities are small and members are often traveling between different communities, visiting family and taking part in local events across a region. Following participants to record them in other locations is not feasible, given the remoteness of the communities and the distance that would need to be covered. As such, we have had to make compromises as far as exact comparability of child ages and difference between sessions is concerned. Furthermore, in Indigenous Australia, caregiving is shared by a range of older kin, including older children (i.e., the "kid mob" Hamilton, 1981; Andrews, 2008), grandparents and great grandparents and children therefore receive language input from a diverse group of speakers. To achieve maximal comparability, we have limited our study to four dyads in each location, and to child-caregiver interactions. This poses limitations to the breadth of representation of the range of participants and speech styles in such inherently dynamic speech settings. Despite this, we expect that results will be an important contribution to knowledge in the field of child language generally, with data from rarely studied locations which are undergoing rapid language shift, and where little is known about how children acquire language.

Procedure

The corpus for this study comprises sixteen transcripts transcribed into CLAN[6]. Transcripts were based on video and audio-recorded interactions between the eight focus children and their primary caregivers, at the two different time periods. All transcripts are of equal length, with 100 lines being chosen for commensurability. Participants were primarily engaged in two types of tasks: prompted play (for example using toy cash registers, a doctor's kit or building with wooden blocks) and picture book-prompted story telling (Egan, 1986; O'Shannessy, 2004).

The data are a subset of materials collected in the first phase of a longitudinal study, The Australian Child Language Acquisition project (ACLA)[7], now in its second phase. The first phase of the project focused on caregiver input to young Indigenous children, who were between the ages of 18 months and two and a half years at the beginning of the project. Language data were collected from children and caregivers every 6-months over a 4-year period. While data were collected in three remote Australian communities, this paper focuses only on Yakanarra and Tennant Creek.

In the transcripts, each morpheme was coded as either the local contact variety, or as the traditional language. It was not always straightforward to determine which words have been incorporated as loan words (and so should be coded as Kriol), and which are simply the product of code-switching (and so should be coded as traditional language). This is in part because no definitive description of the Kriol lexicon exists in either location. However, we were able to consistently apply our analysis across the data, with work on the Kriol lexicon in Yakanarra by Hudson (1985), and with Sandefur (1979) and Lee (2004) guiding our transcription, glossing and, in some areas, description of both the Tennant Creek and Yakanarra data. Words were coded as traditional language when the phonological and semantic structure matched that of the traditional language. All other cases were coded as the contact variety. In the extracts given throughout this paper, tokens identified as Walmajarri or Warumungu are underlined. Standard English, while certainly used in some instances in these communities, was not found in the child-caregiver interactions that we recorded.

For this study, we have collapsed acrolectal and basilectal Kriol forms into one category, despite the fact that speakers vary considerably along a continuum with respect to this. Separating out these varieties is, in practice, next to impossible as many elements are shared across the continuum and variation occurs in relation

[6] http://childes.psy.cmu.edu/

[7] The first phase of this project is described in greater detail in Wigglesworth and Simpson(2008, see esp. pp. 19–27). The second phase of the project, currently underway, is investigating issues faced by Indigenous children as they enter the formal school system where they encounter Standard Australian English, of which they often have little knowledge, as well as significant cultural differences.

to interlocutor and topic as well as age and idiolect. Since distinguishing Kriol varieties is not a central concern of this study, we have not attempted such a categorization. While the resultant procedure is broad, and potentially limiting in terms of over-representing the traditional language, this exact coding procedure worked well for the Yakanarra data analyzed by Loakes et al. (2013). In that study, we were able to demonstrate distinct differences across age-groups in terms of language use with the contact variety, FVKriol, used as the main language by all speakers when interacting with young children. However, the traditional language Walmajarri, while rarely used by younger people, was used about a third of the time by speakers over the age of 50.

The following quantitative measures were used:

- Mean length of turn (MLT)
- MLT ratio
- Mean length of utterance (MLU)

This battery of measures illustrates the overall utterance length (MLT), conversational load (MLT ratio) and sentence complexity (MLU). Mean length of turn is the ratio of words to turn, where a turn is "a sequence of utterances spoken by a single speaker" (McWhinney, 2012, p. 92). MLT ratio is a related measure, calculated by dividing the focus child MLT over interlocutor MLT. Where the value is below 1.0 the interactant has a greater conversational burden, and greater than 1.0 means the child has a greater share (see McWhinney, 2012, p. 40).

Mean length of utterance is a measure of morphosyntactic complexity and consists of the ratio of morphemes to utterances, where an utterance can range from a single token to a full clause. MLU has not been without its critics, but has been widely used to measure children's language development despite criticisms relating to its lack of sensitivity to social context, and the unrepresentativeness of the early populations sampled by psycholinguists (e.g., Geneshi and Glupczynski, 2006). As one of a battery of measures though, it remains a valid technique.

While we acknowledge that these measures are limited in their depth of analysis, the approach has been chosen to provide an initial comparison of language use to and by children in the communities. It is by no means exhaustive. But to date, there has been no quantitative, longitudinal study of children's language development in these indigenous communities: this study is, thus, a first step in that direction.

Results

Language Use

In both communities, the local Kriol variety was used overwhelmingly at T1 and T2 by both children and caregivers—well over 90% of morphemes. The exceptions were at T1 where Belinda used the Warumungu words *karnanti* ("mother"), *kampaju* ("father"), and *kupunta* ("burn"), repeatedly, and Melanie uttered only four morphemes, one of which was in Warumungu. Belinda's great-grandmother, BM, is a fluent Warumungu speaker who uses Warumungu frequently, including in her interactions with children. Similarly in Yakanarra, children and their caregivers use the traditional language at very low rates overall, although there are small increases in its use between T1 and T2. This is commensurate with our findings in Yakanarra (i.e., Loakes et al., 2013), where we saw that the older people in the community were more likely to use the traditional language in their interactions with children than younger adults were, as a result of which children used more traditional language in response. Similarly children sometimes responded entirely in Kriol when spoken to by older people entirely in the traditional language (Loakes et al., 2013)—a case of "receptive multilingualism" (see e.g., ten Thije and Zeevaert, 2007; ten Thije et al., 2012), or "two-way" conversation (Elwell, 1982). Meakins (2008) made similar observations in Kalkaringi for Gurindji and Gurindji Kriol.

A more detailed examination of the *nature* of the interaction between the codes may provide some insights about the ongoing pragmatic and interactional role of traditional languages. In Extract 1, where Melanie is looking at a picture book with her mother, the turn is predominantly in Wumpurrarni English, but with Warumungu (underlined) used occasionally. The Warumungu-usage which priviledges nouns (e.g., *julaka* "bird") and case-markers (such as the possessive *-kayi*) is typical.

Extract 1: ***Melanie 4;3 and mother MM, T2.***

MM: dat lil julaka bin go na
DET little bird PST go LOC
im-kayi mami na
3S POSS mother now
the little bird went to its mother.

MM: yu luk deya
2S look there
see there.

MM: im-kayi mami i bin kraiin fo
3S POSS mother 3S PST cry for
im
3S
his mother was crying for him.

MM: i bin ran wai dumuj i bin
3S PST run away because 3S PST
git los
get lost
he ran away from because he got lost.

Similarly, in Yakanarra, in Extract 2 Olivia and her mother are sharing a book and code-switching between FVKriol and Walmajarri (underlined).

Extract 2: ***Olivia 2;7 and mother OM,*** **T1.**

OM: hu dijan?
Who this one
Who's this one?

Olivia: pirla
ghost

```
OM:       na parri det parri parri parri
          No boy  DEM boy  boy  boy
          no boy, that's a boy, boy, boy.

Olivia:   ei parri
          Yes boy
          yeah boy
```

Again, it is typically nouns that elicit Walmajarri. Indeed, Loakes et al. (2012) demonstrated that children in Yakanarra have a relatively good receptive knowledge of Walmajarri nouns related to the presence of these words in their input. Nouns are not the only targets of switching however. The traditional language is also used frequently for tag questions (e.g., *payi* "is that OK?" as in Extract 6 below). And in the following example, Emily's mother (EM) issues her command first in Walmajarri and then in Kriol. This use of both languages in parallel utterances has also been documented in Tennant Creek speech styles (Disbray, 2008):

Extract 3: *EM's direction to Emily* 2;6, T1.

```
EM:       yutanti
          Sit-down-IMP
          sit down

EM:       sidan
          Sit   down
          sit down.
```

Receptive multilingualism, i.e., the use of one language per participant in an interaction is known to be a common practice in these communities (see e.g., the example in Loakes et al. (2013, p. 700) where a child speaks FVKriol to her grandmother and is responded to in Walmajarri). In Yakanarra it appears to be largely an intergenerational practice, and so perhaps is a product of language shift, but this is not the case in all communities (e.g., in Maningrida, Arnhem Land—see Elwell, 1982). Indeed, this kind of code-switching is known to have been a stable linguistic practice traditionally with distinct pragmatic and social functions (Wilkins and Nash, 2008; Singer and Harris, forthcoming).

Code-switching raises a number of issues and questions for our analysis and for research of this kind more generally. Firstly, it presents a challenge for data analysis in that while it is uncontroversial in theory that code-switching differs from lexical borrowing (i.e., where a foreign word has been fully adapted into a host language), it is not always clear in practice (Poplack, 2004). For example, if the surface form is uninflected, if it occupies a slot shared by both languages, and/or if phonological cues are absent or unclear, the task is by no means a straightforward one. The challenge is mitigated to some extent by the fact that the researchers know the communities well and are able to make judgments based on their knowledge of the standard adult language and common community linguistic practices. Furthermore, the methodological issue begs a larger question regarding the social reality of code distinction: are speakers attending to the difference between codes? If not, should the researcher?[8]

[8] See work on code-mixing and "translanguaging" for further exploration of these points, especially (García, 2007; Creese and Blackledge, 2010; García and Wei, 2014).

TABLE 2 | MLT observations for focus children and caregivers, Tennant Creek.

Tennant Creek	Child (T1)	Child (T2)	CG (T1)	CG (T2)
Natalie and NM	2.0	1.4	4.1	24.6
Melanie and MM	2.0	4.3	6.3	26.3
Sarah and SM	1.8	5.5	6.6	35.3
Belinda and BM	1.9	5.2	8.3	15.1
Average	1.9	4.1	6.3	25.3

TABLE 3 | MLT ratios, Tennant Creek.

	Time 1	Time 2
Natalie and NM	0.48	0.06
Melanie and MM	0.32	0.16
Sarah and SM	0.27	0.16
Belinda and BM	0.23	0.35
Average	0.33	0.18

Of course in cases of multilingual language acquisition there is the added complication that young children may not yet have learnt to discriminate between codes as the adult target does. This is not a question we will dwell on here, but it is important to acknowledge that the necessity of distinguishing codes for the purpose of quantitative analysis can obfuscate the social reality in terms of how speakers actually understand and manipulate codes.

As we have seen, the contact varieties of Wumpurrarni English and FVKriol are the preferred languages for communication, but the traditional languages, Warumungu and Walmajarri, have a continued presence in interaction through a range of multilingual practices. Both communities appear to demonstrate similar uses of the traditional language in terms of the linguistic interaction of codes. However, an understanding of the social aspects of code use will require further research. In the next section we focus on *how* children's productive language develops across the time periods.

Developmental Measures

Mean Length of Turn (MLT)

The MLT provides an impression of overall utterance length, while the related measure, MLT ratio, reflects the conversational load of each interactant. MLT is the average of the number of words used per turn, while conversational load is the ratio of child MLT over caregiver MLT.

MLT values and the associated MLT ratios are shown in **Tables 2, 3** below for Tennant Creek.

As might be expected, the Tennant Creek children use slightly more than double the number of words per turn at T2 compared to T1. At T1 the children all appear to be at a similar stage, with results ranging from 1.8 to 2.0 words per turn on average. At Time 2, all of the children, except Natalie, have a marked increase in words usage, ranging from 4.3 to 5.5 words per turn. And as we see below, Natalie's results may be task based.

For the caregivers, MLT values are always higher than the children's, especially at Time 2. At Time 1, the average MLT was 6.3 with a range of 4.1–8.3. However, the most striking result from this table is the average length of utterances used by the caregivers at Time 2, with an average of 25.3 words per turn, equating to four times as many words per turn on average than used at Time 1. Results for individual speakers range from 15.1 for Belinda's great-grandmother to 35.3 for Sarah's mother.

Extract 4 is from Sarah's mother at T2 and clearly shows the relatively monologic nature of her talk. She is telling a story and is not often interrupted by Sarah. This type of narration routine was observed in a previous study of Tennant Creek child-caregiver interaction (Disbray, 2008). Here adults tended to tell "elaborate" stories possibly as a strategy to maintain the children's attention and to model story-telling.

Extract 4: ***SM's interaction with Sarah 3;6, Time 2.***

```
SM:      iya  damob      bin jeis-im  na
         Here that group PST chase-TR now
         luk
         look
         here, that group were chasing it,
         now look.

SM:      dubala bin jeis-im  bat    im
         2 NOM  PST chase-TR QUANT⁹ 3S
         na
         now
         two of them were chasing it now.

Sarah:   na  na  dat dat
         Now now DEM DEM
         now now, that that.

SM:      stik  bin pok-im  im
         Stick PST poke-TR 3S
         the stick poked him.

SM:      luk  what kain pants
         Look what kind pants
         look what kind of pants.

SM:      stik  bin pok-im  im
         Stick PST poke-TR 3S
         the stick poked him.

SM:      im, gad, im still gad shangayi
         3S  got  3S still got shanghai
         he's got, he's still got the
         shanghai (sling-shot).

SM:      wan bala jeis-im
         One 3NOM chase-TR
         one of them chases it.

SM:      deya  im-kayi mami   na
         There 3S POSS mother now
         there's it's mother now
```

In Extract 5, Natalie is playing with blocks, and her mother provides a series of requests and explanations. She draws the child's attention to the construction depicted on the box containing the blocks, encouraging the child to build a similar construction. The especially long number of words per turn is typical of this session, yet markedly different to the length of utterance for the same speaker at T1. In this particular case, NM uses 32 words before Natalie's one word response.

Extract 5: ***NM's interaction with Natalie 4;7, Time 2.***

```
NM:        yu gid dat pitja   deya  luk
           2S get Dem picture there look
           you get that picture there, look.

NM:        si  deya
           See there
           see there.

NM:        yu trai du dat
           2S try  do that
           you try to do that

NM:        luk, dem deya
           Look 3Pl there
           look, them there.

NM:        yu kin meik haus
           2S can make house
           you can make a house.

NM:        kasel
           castle
           castle.

NM:        si  tivi an  bed yu kin meik im
           See TV   and bed 2S can make 3S
           see the TV and bed, you can make
           them

NM:        kwik
           quickly
           quickly.

NM:        weya  dat  Harvey?
           Where that Harvey
           where's that Harvey?

Natalie:   dawan
           That  one
           that one.
```

The related MLT ratio (child/caregiver MLT) or conversational load is one way of representing the proportion of the utterance attributable to each speaker. We can expect this to be low at T2 given the long caregiver utterances as shown in **Table 3**[10].

These data suggest the conversational burden rests mostly with the caregivers in all instances, although T2 is more variable

[9] "bat" is an event quantifier indicating the event is not performed once by one individual.

[10] A ratio of 1 would indicate equality in conversational load, and any value less than 1 means the caregiver has a greater conversational burden than the child.

TABLE 4 | MLT observations for focus children and caregivers, Yakanarra.

	Child (T1)	Child (T2)	CG (T1)	CG (T2)
Katherine and KM	5.3	2.5	10.2	7.6
Olivia and OM	3.1	5.2	7.6	8.9
Andrew and AM	2.3	5.1	27.3	14.8
Emily and EM	4.7	4.7	5.1	3.3
Average	3.9	4.4	12.6	8.7

TABLE 5 | MLT ratios, Yakanarra.

	Time 1	Time 2
Katherine and KM	0.52	0.33
Olivia and OM	0.41	0.58
Andrew and AM	0.08	0.34
Emily and EM	0.92	1.42
Average	0.48	0.67

than T1 with a low MLT for Natalie and her mother, reflective of Natalie's minimal talk during the wooden block play, as seen in Extract 5 above. Melanie and Sarah have the same MLT ratio at T2 and Belinda is the only child to take on more of the conversational load at T2 compared to T1 increasing from 0.23 to 0.35 (still relatively low).

The picture at Yakanarra is different, with more variability amongst participants, as shown in **Table 4** which presents the MLT.

For the Yakanarra child participants, there is little difference between T1 and T2, on average. At T1, their average MLT is around double the average of the Tennant Creek children (at 1.9), and at T2 their MLT of 4.4 is only marginally higher than at Time 1, and than the Tennant Creek children's MLT at T2 (4.1). Thus, while Yakanarra children have a much higher average MLT at T1, by T2 they are very similar. It is likely that the MLT difference between Tennant Creek and Yakanarra children at T1 is linked to the difference in the average age between participants, since the Tennant Creek children are younger. At T1, the Yakanarra children's MLT values correlate with their age: Katherine is the oldest participant and has an MLT of 5.3, but Andrew, the youngest only averages 2.3. At Time 2 however, Katherine has the lowest MLT.

There is considerable variation in Yakanarra. Two children increase in MLT from T1 to T2 (Olivia and Andrew), and two do not—Katherine's MLT is lower at T2, while Emily's is the same. Thus, the range of values for MLT is quite broad at both times, between 2.3 and 5.3 words per turn at T1, and 2.5–5.2 at T2. This differs from the Tennant Creek results where the MLT fitted within a narrow range at each time period.

For the caregivers, results are also different from Tennant Creek. At T1, the Yakanarra children have twice the average words per turn than Tennant Creek children, and this is also true for caregivers, where the average 12.6 words per turn is double those for Tennant Creek. At T2, Yakanarra caregivers have a lower MLT than at T1, while in Tennant Creek they were four times higher. Additionally, MLT values for the Tennant Creek caregivers fall within a relatively narrow range of values, whereas for the Yakanarra caregivers there is a wide range from 5.1 to 27.3 at T1 and from 3.3 to 14.8 at T2. Finally, three Yakanarra caregivers have similar MLT values to their children; the exception is Andrew and AM, with AM having exceptionally high MLT values (27.3 at T1, and 14.8 at T12). This is reflected in the MLT ratio, as shown in **Table 5**.

Yakanarra children have, on average, a higher MLT than the Tennant Creek children at both time periods. This indicates that the Yakanarra children generally have a greater share of the conversation when interacting with their caregivers compared to the Tennant Creek children in these sessions. While neither group is approaching an equal conversational load, the Yakanarra children have a higher MLT ratio at T1 than the Tennant Creek children had at both T1 and T2, and they increase their conversational share at T2.

A brief note about individual variation is important given these results. At T1, Andrew's ratio is especially low at 0.08 indicating that he barely contributes, verbally, to the interaction. Emily, on the other hand, has an MLT ratio approaching 1.0 suggesting equal conversational load between her and her mother. At T2, Katherine and Andrew have similar, relatively low, MLT ratios although this is an increase for Andrew, but a decrease for Katherine. Emily is the only participant with a higher conversational burden than her mother. Emily's input remains the same at T1 and T2, but her mother's changes, with less input at T2 (see Extract 10 for an example of this pair's interaction).

Extracts 6 and 7 from Olivia's interaction with OM are from an identical task where a book is being read. At T1, Olivia averaged three words per turn on average, and five at T2. OM averaged 7.6 words per turn at T1 and 9 at T2 yielding a slightly greater conversational load for Olivia at T2.

Extract 6: ***OM's interaction with Olivia 2;7, Time 1.***

OM:	en wat i bin du? And what 3S PST do *And what has it done?*
OM:	luk wat i bin du? Look what 3S PST do *look, what has it done?*
OM:	i bin fol dan, payi? 3S PST fall down isn't it *It's fallen down, hasn't it?*
Olivia:	ye yes *yeah.*
OM:	oi i bin fol dan Oh 3S PST fall down *oh, it's fallen down.*
Olivia:	no i rait. No 3S right *no its OK.*

M: en we det jikjik la is
And where the chicken LOC 3S
mami, payi?
mother isn't it
and where is that chicken's - its at his mother's isn't it?

Olivia: im iya
3S here
it's here.

At T2, the development in Olivia's interactional capability is clear. Here she has more, and longer turns, than at T1.

Extract 7: ***OM's interaction with Olivia 4;7, Time 2.***

OM: en we dijan fo shanghai?
And where Dem for shanghai
and where is the shanghai (sling-shot).

Olivia: de
there
there

Olivia: den dei tjeis-im bat im tjeis
Then 3Pl chase-TR QUANT 3S chase
then they chase it, chase

Olivia: im bat im tjeis-im bat im
3S but 3S chase-TR QUANT 3S
it, chased it.

OM: a pupala
Ah poorthing
ah poor thing.

Olivia: ye
yes
yeah.

OM: dei bin ged im hepi
3PL PST get 3S happy
They were happy.

Olivia la nes i bin bi
LOC nest 3S PST be
it was in the nest

Olivia: we is mami wan?
Where POSS mother Det
where is its mother?

Olivia: de?
there
there?

OM: na is mami bin go ged-im
No POSS mother PST go get-TR
no its mother has gone
bat mangarri bla im
QUANT food for him
to get food for it.

Recall that Andrew is the youngest child in the Yakanarra cohort, and his interaction with his mother patterned somewhat differently to others. In Extract 8, they are looking at figurines, and the reasons for Andrew's comparatively low MLT (5.1 to AM's 14.8) as well as relatively low conversational load (0.38), are clear.

Extract 8: ***AM's interaction with Andrew 4;7, Time 2.***

AM: ei dis da mami wan fo det
Hey Dem is mother NOM for Dem
beibi
baby
hey this is the mother for that baby,
si i garra bodul.
See 3S get bottle
see it's got a bottle.

Andrew: hu detwan?
Who that one
who's that?

AM: ai dono hu det
1S don't know who Dem
I don't know who that is.

Andrew: xxx ting.
Xxx thing
[unintelligible word] thing

AM: ye lil skul gel
Yes little school girl
yeah it's a little school girl.

AM: en diswan god lil
And this one got little
mobailfon
mobile phone
and this one has got a little mobile phone.

AM: yu luk-im lil mobailfon
2S look-TR little mobile phone
you look, a little mobile phone.

Andrew: ye ai garram iya
Yes 1S got here
yeah I've got it here.

In this section, we have seen that utterance length is used differently in each of the two communities analyzed. In Tennant Creek, both children and caregivers tend to have an increase in MLT over time. As illustrated, the caregivers use exceptionally long utterances at Time 2, and this impacts on conversational load where we saw that Tennant Creek children take on less of the overall conversational burden at Time 2. The Yakanarra caregivers, by contrast, use shorter utterances on average at Time 2, while the children have slightly longer utterances. In Yakanarra, the children's conversational burden is generally greater at Time 2, and one of the children actually has a higher conversational load than her caregiver.

The caregivers in the two communities seem to respond differently with respect to quantity of talk. Tennant Creek caregivers use more talk at Time 2 perhaps recognizing their children's increased receptive capacity, while the Yakanarra participants use less talk on average perhaps making room for their children's productive capacity. It may be the age difference of the children, with the children older at Yakanarra, that elicits this response.

MLU

MLU is a measure of morphological complexity, reflecting the ratio of morphemes to utterances, and is generally considered useful for comparing development across time points. MLU is often compared to standardized values, but this is not possible here as there are no standardized MLU values for Kriol and the traditional languages featured. However, values can be used comparatively across the corpus. In this study, MLU is measured using morphemes primarily from Kriol, with some traditional language morphemes also included in the analysis. This is justified because, as seen earlier, the number of traditional language morphemes used by participants was very minimal. MLU values for Tennant Creek are presented in **Table 6** below.

All children and their caregivers use morphologically more complex utterances at T2 with the children having the greatest increase from 1.7 to 5.3. At T2, both groups have a similar average MLU (5.3 and 5.6), reflecting similar grammatical complexity despite the marked differences in utterance length described earlier. At T1 the caregivers tend to have a much higher MLU than their children (besides Natalie and NM), but at T2 they are almost at parity. The exception is Melanie and MM, with MM having a higher MLU than Melanie.

As with MLT, the Tennant Creek data again falls within a relatively narrow range, although Natalie and NM have somewhat lower MLUs, and Melanie and MM slightly higher values. Extract 5 gave an example of Natalie and NM's interaction at T2 and Extract 9 is an example from Melanie and MM's (see also Extract 1). Verbal morphemes (preceded by an underscore) help to explain the higher MLU. Both participants use relatively long utterances providing a useful illustration of average turn length.

Extract 9: ***MM's interaction with Melanie 4;3, Time 2.***

```
MM:       an  dei bin keriy im,
          And 3Pl Pst carry 3S
          and they were carrying it,

          keriy-im bat   im na   dat nes,
          carry-TR QUANT 3S from Dem nest
          carrying it from that nest -

          i  bin jamp of  fom  dat nes
          3S Pst jump off from Dem nest
          it jumped off from that nest

Melanie:  an  dei gada   gid im na
          And 3Pl got to get 3S now
          ini?
          isn't it
          and they have to get it now,
          don't they?
```

Yakanarra results for MLU are shown below.

In Yakanarra, MLU is narrower than Tennant Creek between 2.4 and 4.4, with caregivers having a higher MLU than the children at both times. Emily and EM are the exception to this, with Emily's MLU at T2 slightly higher than EM's. MLU increases at T2 for the children, and decreases slightly for the caregivers. Individual variation is fairly minimal as with the other measures analyzed in this study.

Average values point to an increase in child MLU across the time periods, with three of the four children showing higher MLU values at Time 2 (an increase of 1.2 in each case). Katherine is the exception here, with a slightly higher MLU at Time 1 (3.0 compared with 2.6). For the caregivers, average MLU decreased slightly across the time periods. Results in **Table 7** show that this is the case for all except OM, who has a slightly higher MLU at Time 2 (4.4 compared with 5.0).

Examples of Olivia (and OM's) speech are given in extracts 2, 6, and 7. Extracts 6 (T1) and 7 (T2) in particular illustrate Olivia's increase in morpho-syntactic complexity across the time periods. Extract 10 shows Emily interacting with EM, which demonstrates EM's relatively low MLU T2, given the demonstrably low morpho-syntactic complexity of her turn (it is also indicative of the pair's MLT ratio, as discussed earlier).

Extract 10: ***EM's interaction with Emily 4;6, Time 2.***

```
Emily:    en  de  det beed
          And Dem Dem bird
          and there, that bird.

EM:       yu  luk  det nes
          2Pl look Dem next
          you look, that nest.

Emily     en  det nes
          And Dem nest
          and that nest.
```

TABLE 6 | MLU, Tennant Creek.

	Child (T1)	Child (T2)	CG (T1)	CG (T2)
Natalie and NM	1.8	3.7	1.4	3.5
Melanie and MM	2	6.3	3.9	7.5
Sarah and SM	1.5	5.4	4	5.6
Belinda and BM	1.6	5.9	4.1	5.9
Average	1.7	5.3	3.4	5.6

TABLE 7 | MLU, Yakanarra.

	Child (T1)	Child (T2)	CG (T1)	CG (T2)
Katherine and KM	3	2.6	5.1	4.4
Olivia and OM	2.6	3.8	4.4	5
Andrew and AM	2.1	3.3	4.8	4.3
Emily and EM	2	3.2	3.1	2.7
Average	2.4	3.2	4.4	4.1

```
Emily:      en  de    i  flaiing
            And there 3S flying
            and there it's flying.
```

These MLU results indicate that in both communities the children use grammatically more complex utterances at T2. At both times, caregivers use more complex utterances than their children, but in Yakanarra the caregivers use less complex utterances at T2 than at T1. In other words, while children's language is developing over the 2-year period, as would be expected, caregiver responses pattern differently in each community.

Discussion and Conclusion

This study compared language use in two remote Indigenous Australian communities. Reflecting a loss of the traditional languages of the area, creole varieties—Wumpurrarni English and Fitzroy Valley Kriol, respectively—are used predominantly by the child-caregiver pairs studied in Tennant Creek and Yakanarra. The individual variation in language use observed was consistent with our previous study in Yakanarra where traditional language tends to be reserved for use by, and with, older participants aged 50+ (e.g., Loakes et al., 2013). McConvell (2008) also discusses a general trend for language shift in Indigenous Australia, where children appear to be largely monolingual (speaking a variety of Kriol). This compares to the situation previously in Australia, where community members tended to be multilingual in two or more traditional languages as well as English (e.g., Brandl and Walsh, 1982; Singer and Harris, forthcoming).

While our results point to a general decline in multilingualism and its attendant linguistic practices in Indigenous Australia, we have noted a range of uses for the surviving elements of the traditional languages featured. Code-switching and receptive multilingualism have important social and pragmatic functions, even, or perhaps especially, in cases of language change. Indeed, it can be the case that low-frequency linguistic forms carry significant pragmatic force (i.e., contributing to "markedness"). McConvell (2008) notes that such uses of traditional languages may have strong social meaning as "acts of identity" (see also Le Page and Tabouret-Keller, 1985).

As found in the early studies of caregiver talk (e.g., Snow, 1972, 1977; Sachs et al., 1976; Ferguson, 1977) for the caregivers in Tennant Creek, speech increases in MLT with age, reflecting similar patterns of development and we may assume, consequently, that caregivers make similar adjustments in terms of fine-tuning to their speech as those found in previous studies such as Vosoughi (2010) and that this is a function of the child's age. In contrast, the Yakanarra caregivers tend to use shorter and fewer turns at T2, and may respond to their children's language development by making room for their productive language capacity. For caregivers then, the main difference across the communities is the *quantity* of talk used.

In both Tennant Creek and Yakanarra we observed the general developmental characteristics of focus children using data collected approximately 2 years apart. The children displayed more developed language skills at T2, an unsurprising result given that they were on average 2 years older than at T1. While productive language capacity was not clear for Tennant Creek when we analyzed MLT and MLT ratio, we might infer that the especially long turns used by their caregivers is a response to their greater receptive knowledge at T2.

While not an explicit focus of this study, work on Baby Talk registers in Australian languages formed part of the theoretical grounding of register (see Laughren, 1984; Bavin, 1992, 1993; Kral and Ellis, 2008; O'Shannessy, 2011; Jones and Meakins, 2013; Turpin et al., 2014). We are, thus, able to reflect on the language input to the children in our study with this work in mind. Certain features noted in previous studies were observable in our data (largely use of repetition (see, e.g., Extract 2) and slower speech rate), but not the full range of features described in the studies above. Further research is required to fully investigate the existence and nature of this register in Tennant Creek and Yakanarra.

As discussed in the introduction, relatively little is known about child language development outside middle-class Western societies, and measures of analysis have tended to develop from languages spoken in these environments. As such, it is worth reflecting on our results to determine the validity of the measures we used for analysing contact varieties. One measure in particular, MLU, was used in this study in quite broadly and language types were grouped together (i.e., both Kriol and the traditional language) in calculating it. However, use of the traditional language was quantitatively minimal and so this is unlikely to have had much impact on results.

A crucial issue, which warrants further investigation, is that of variation. Heavy Kriol varieties have a more complex morphology and use grammatical and case-marking morphemes not used in English. At T1, where children ranged between 1;8 and 3;6, there was little evidence that they used such morphology. However, the children use a wider variety of verbal and nominal morphemes, and more of them, at T2 as reflected in the higher MLU for both cohorts. This could be for a number of reasons—the data may indicate acquisition of morphology, but it may also be an indication that children are using a heavier style of Kriol at T2. Semantic case-marking is also an optional feature, often occurring with relatively low frequency, so it may simply be that case-marking did not appear in the T1 data. In future work, it will be important for researchers to analyse individual speaker styles closely, and to relate them to children's stylistic use. Cross-sectional data from older children in Tennant Creek show use of complex morphology, through the use of transitive marking on verbs, and semantic case-marking (Disbray, 2009), particularly in heavy WE styles. These results are useful for contributing to knowledge on the types of values to expect for Kriol varieties where MLU is concerned, and a more detailed analysis, beyond the scope of this paper, may throw further light on this. The results of this study support those of Hoff (2006) who observed considerable variation in type and amount of direct language input children in these age groups received. These communities are undergoing, or have undergone in recent year, sizeable shifts in the languages spoken, commensurate with increasing variability in the input the children receive (see Loakes et al. (2013) for further discussion of this phenomenon).

This study has provided an initial insight into child-caregiver interaction in two remote Indigenous communities. Despite the different community structures—with Yakanarra being relatively closed, and Tennant Creek having more varied demographics—results are similar in terms of general developmental patterns, and the language types used. The creole variety local to each community is the preferred language of communication at both time points. For measures of morphosyntactic complexity (MLU), children in both communities use more complex utterances at T2 than at T1, and child-caregiver averages are similar to each other at T2. For measures of utterance length (MLT), there are more notable differences between the two communities for both children and caregivers at T2; for children in Tennant Creek, MLT doubled on average between T1 and T2, while in Yakanarra children were more variable. Strikingly, caregivers' MLT quadrupled between T1 and T2 in Tennant Creek, while in Yakanarra caregivers' MLT was lower at T2 than T1. We note, however, that the samples used here were convenience samples, and very small ones with only four dyads in each community. We may attribute some of the different results also to the fact that the children in Tennant Creek were younger at the start of the study than those in Yakanarra.

In tandem with Loakes et al.'s (2013) findings for Yakanarra, this research has contributed to a depiction of both language input to children, as well as their own language production. The former study elucidated how this language varies synchronically (according to interlocutor age), while the current study has focused on how children's language varies diachronically across time points 2 years apart. These results are a start in developing a picture of how children acquire language in these two multilingual Indigenous Australian communities.

Acknowledgments

We would like to thank all the participants, children and adults who contributed data to this study. Thanks also to the anonymous reviewers for their insightful comments, and to Jane Simpson for assistance with the interlinear glossing. The study was supported by Australian Research Council Discovery Grants (DP0343189 and DP0877762).

References

Andrews, J. (2008). "Bringing up our yorta yorta children," in *Contexts of Child Development: Culture, Policy and Intervention*, eds G. Robinson, U. Eickelkamp, J. Goodnow, and I. Katz (Darwin: Charles Darwin University Press), 23–35.

Bavin, E. (1992). "The acquisition of Warlpiri," in *The Crosslinguistic Study of Language Acquisition*, Vol. 3, ed D. I. Slobin (Hillsdale, NJ: Lawrence Erlbaum), 309–371.

Bavin, E. (1993). "Language and culture: socialization in a Warlpiri community," in *Language and Culture in Aboriginal Australia*, eds M. Walsh and C. Yallop (Canberra, ACT: Aboriginal Studies Press), 85–96.

Bavin, E., and Shopen, T. (1985). "Warlpiri and English: language in contact," in *Australia, Meeting Place of Languages*, ed M. Clyne (Canberra, ACT: Pacific Linguistics), 81–94.

Berko Gleason, J. (eds.). (2005). *The Development of Language, 6th Edn.* Boston: Pearson/Allyn & Bacon.

Bialystok, E., and Feng, X. (2011). "Language proficiency and its implications for monolingual and bilingual children," in *Language and Literacy Development in Bilingual Settings*, eds A. Durgunogle and C. Goldenberg (New York, NY: Guilford), 121–138.

Bornstein, M. H., Haynes, M. O., and Painter, K. M. (1998). Sources of child vocabulary competence: a multivariate model. *J. Child Lang.* 25, 367–394. doi: 10.1017/S0305000998003456

Brandl, M. M., and Walsh, M. (1982). Speakers of many tongues: toward understanding multilingualism among Aboriginal Australians. *Int. J. Sociol. Lang.* 36, 71–81.

Brown, P. (2001). "Learning to talk about motion UP and DOWN in Tzeltal: is there a language-specific bias for verb learning?" in *Language Acquisition and Conceptual Development*, eds M. Bowerman and S. C. Levinson (Cambridge: Cambridge University Press), 512–543.

Butcher, A. R. (2008). Linguistic aspects of Australian Aboriginal English. *Clin. Linguist. Phon.* 22, 625–642. doi: 10.1080/02699200802223535

Conboy, B. T., and Thal, D. J. (2006). Ties between the lexicon and grammar: cross-sectional and longitudinal studies of bilingual toddlers. *Child Dev.* 77, 712–735. doi: 10.1111/j.1467-8624.2006.00899.x

Crago, M. B., Allen, S. E. M., and Hough-Eyamie, W. P. (1997). "Exploring innateness through cultural and linguistic variation: an Inuit example," in *The Biological Basis of Language*, ed M. J. Gopnik (Oxford: Oxford University Press), 70–90.

Creese, A., and Blackledge, A. (2010). Translanguaging in the bilingual classroom: a pedagogy for learning and teaching? *Mod. Lang. J.* 94, 103–115. doi: 10.1111/j.1540-4781.2009.00986.x

De Houwer, A. (1999). "Environmental factors in early bilingual development: the role of parental beliefs and attitudes," in *Bilingualism and Migration*, eds G. Extra and L. Verhoeven (New York, NY: Mouton de Gruyter), 75–96.

De Houwer, A. (2005). "Early bilingual acquisition: focus on morphosyntax and the separate development hypothesis," in *Handbook of Bilingualism: Psycholinguistic Approaches*, eds J. F. Kroll and A. M. B. De Groot (Oxford: Oxford University Press), 30–48.

De Houwer, A. (2007). Parental language input patterns and children's bilingual use. *Appl. Psycholinguist.* 28, 411–424. doi: 10.1017/S0142716407070221

Díaz-Campos, M. (2005). "The emergence of adult-like command of sociolinguistic variables: a study of consonant weakening in Spanish-speaking children," in *Studies in the Acquisition of the Hispanic Languages: Papers from the 6th conference on the acquisition of Spanish and Portuguese as* first *and* second *languages*, ed D. Eddington (Somerville, MA: Cascadilla), 56–65.

Disbray, S. (2008). "Story-telling styles: a study of adult-child interactions in narrations of a picture book in Tennant Creek," in *Children's Language and Multilingualism: Indigenous Language Use at Home and School*, eds J. Simpson and G. Wigglesworth (London: Continuum International Press), 56–98.

Disbray, S. (2009). *More than One Way to Catch a Frog: Children's Discourse in a Contact Setting.* Ph.D. dissertation, The University of Melbourne.

Disbray, S., and Simpson, J. (2004). The expression of possession in Wumpurrarni English, Tennant Creek. *Monash Univ. Linguist. Papers* 4, 65–86.

Eades, D. (1996). "Aboriginal english," in *Atlas of Languages of Intercultural Communication in the Pacific, Asia, and the Americas*, eds S. A. Wurm, P. Mühlhäusler, and D. T. Tryon (Berlin; New York: Mouton de Gruyter), 133–141.

Egan, A. (1986). *Pintaru-kurlu "The Quail".* Yuendumu, NT: Bilingual Resources Development Unit.

Elwell, V. M. R. (1982). Some social factors affecting multilingualism among Aboriginal Australians: a case study of Maningrida. *Int. J. Soc. Lang.* 36, 83–103. doi: 10.1515/ijsl.1982.36.83

Ferguson, C. A. (1977). "Baby talk as a simplified register," in *Talking to Children: Language Input and Acquisition*, eds C. E. Snow and C. A. Ferguson (New York, NY: Cambridge University Press), 219–235.

Foulkes, P., Docherty, G. J., and Watt, D. (1999). Tracking the emergence of structured variation: realisations of (t) by Newcastle children. *Leeds Work. Pap. Linguist. Phon.* 7, 1–25.

Foulkes, P., Docherty, G. J., and Watt, D. (2005). Phonological variation in child-directed speech. *Language* 81, 177–206. doi: 10.1353/lan.2005.0018

Gafaranga, J. (2010). Medium request: talking language shift into being. *Lang. Soc.* 39, 241–270. doi: 10.1017/S0047404510000047

García, O. (2007). "Foreword," in *Disinventing and Reconstituting Languages,* eds S. Makoni and A. Pennycook (Clevedon: Multilingual Matters), xi-xv.

García, O., and Wei, L. (2014). *Translanguaging: Language, Bilingualism and Education.* New York, NY: Palgrave Macmillan.

Garrett, P. B. (2005). What a language is good for: language socialization, language shift, and the persistence of code-specific genres in St. Lucia. *Lang. Soc.* 34, 327–361. doi: 10.1017/S0047404505050128

Garrett, P. B., and Baquedano-López, P. (2002). Language socialization: reproduction and continuity, transformation and change. *Annu. Rev. Anthropol.* 31, 339–361. doi: 10.1146/annurev.anthro.31.040402.085352

Geneshi, C., and Glupczynski, T. (2006). "Language and literacy research: multiple methods and perspectives," in *Handbook of Complementary Methods in Education Research,* eds J. L. Green, G. Camilli, and P. B. Elmore (Mahwah, NJ: Lawrence Erlbaum), 657–680.

Hamilton, A. (1981). *Nature and Nurture: Aboriginal Child-rearing in North-central Arnhem Land.* Canberra, ACT: Australian Institute of Aboriginal Studies.

Harkness, S. (1977). "Aspects of the social environment and first language acquisition in rural Africa," in *Talking to Children: Language Input and Acquisition,* eds C. E. Snow and C. A. Ferguson (New York, NY: Cambridge University Press), 309–318.

Harris, J. (1993). "Losing and gaining a language: the story of Kriol in the Northern Territory," in *Language and Culture in Aboriginal Australia,* eds M. Walsh and C. Yallop (Canberra, ACT: Aboriginal Studies Press), 155–168.

Hart, B., and Risley, T. R. (1995). *Meaningful Differences in the Everyday Experience of Young American Children.* Baltimore, MD: Brookes.

Heath, S. B. (1983). *Ways With Words: Language, Life and Work in Communities and Classrooms.* Cambridge: Cambridge University Press.

Hoff, E. (2001). *Language Development.* Belmont, CA: Wadsworth.

Hoff, E. (2003). The specificity of environmental influence: socioeconomic status affects early vocabulary development via maternal speech. *Child Dev.* 74, 1368–1378. doi: 10.1111/1467-8624.00612

Hoff, E. (2006). How social contexts support and shape language development. *Dev. Rev.* 26, 55–58. doi: 10.1016/j.dr.2005.11.002

Hoff, E., Core, C., Place, S., Rumiche, R., Señor, M., and Parra, M. (2012). Dual language exposure and early bilingual development. *J. Child Lang.* 39, 1–27. doi: 10.1017/S0305000910000759

Hoff, E., and Naigles, L. (2002). How children use input to acquire a lexicon. *Child Dev.* 73, 418–433. doi: 10.1111/1467-8624.00415

Hoff-Ginsberg, E. (1998). The relation of birth order and socioeconomic status to children's language experience and language development. *Appl. Psycholinguist.* 19, 603–629. doi: 10.1017/S0142716400010389

Hudson, J. (1985). *Grammatical and Semantic Aspects of Fitzroy Valley Kriol.* Darwin, Summer Institute of Linguistics.

Huttenlocher, J., Haight, W., Bryk, A., Seltzer, M., and Lyons, T. (1991). Early vocabulary growth: relation to language input and gender. *Dev. Psychol.* 27, 236–248. doi: 10.1037/0012-1649.27.2.236

Huttenlocher, J., Vasilyeva, M., Cymweman, E., and Levine, S. (2002). Language input at home and at school: relation to child syntax. *Cogn. Psychol.* 45, 337–374. doi: 10.1016/S0010-0285(02)00500-5

Huttenlocher, J., Vasilyeva, M., Waterfall, H. R., Vevea, J. L., and Hedges, L. V. (2007). The varieties of speech to young children. *Dev. Psychol.* 43, 1062–1083. doi: 10.1037/0012-1649.43.5.1062

Jones, C., and Meakins, F. (2013). The phonological forms and perceived functions of janyarrp, the Gurindji "baby talk" register. *Lingua* 134, 170–193. doi: 10.1016/j.lingua.2013.07.004

Kaldor, S., and Malcolm, I. (1982). "Aboriginal English in country and remote areas: a Western Australian perspective," in *English and the Aboriginal Child,* eds R. D. Eagleson, S. Kaldor, and I. Malcolm (Canberra, ACT: Curriculum Development Centre), 75–112.

Kaye, K. (1980). Why we don't "baby talk" to babies. *J. Child Lang.* 7, 498–507. doi: 10.1017/S0305000900002804

Kral, I., and Ellis, E. M. (2008). "Children, language and literacy in the Ngaanyatjarra lands," in *Children's Language and Multilingualism,* eds J. Simpson and G. Wigglesworth (London: Continuum), 154–172.

Kulick, D. (1992). *Language Shift and Cultural Reproduction. Socialization, Self and Syncretism in a Papua New Guinean Village.* Cambridge: Cambridge University Press.

Lanza, E. (1997). *Language Mixing in Infant Bilingualism: A Sociolinguistic Perspective.* Oxford: Clarendon Press.

Laughren, M. (1984). Warlpiri Baby Talk. *Aust. J. Linguist.* 4, 73–88. doi: 10.1080/07268608408599321

Lee, J. (1987). *Tiwi Today: A Study of Language Change in a Contact Situation.* Canberra, ACT: Pacific Linguistics.

Lee, J. (2004). *Kriol-Ingglish Dikshenri.* SIL Darwin: Summer Institute of Linguistics.

Le Page, R., and Tabouret-Keller, A. (1985). *Acts of Identity: Creole-Based Approaches to Language and Ethnicity.* Cambridge: Cambridge University Press.

LeVine, R. A. (2004). "Challenging expert knowledge: findings from an African study of infant care and development," in *Childhood and Adolescence: Cross-Cultural Perspectives and Applications,* eds U. P. Gielen and J. Roopnarine (Westport, CT: Praeger), 149–165.

Lieven, E. V. M. (1994). "Crosslinguistic and crosscultural aspects of language addressed to children," in *Input and Interaction in Language Acquisition,* eds C. Galloway and B. J. Richards (Cambridge: Cambridge University Press), 56–73.

Loakes, D., Moses, K., Simpson, J., and Wigglesworth, G. (2012). Developing tests for the assessment of traditional language skill: a case study in an Indigenous Australian community. *Lang. Assess. Q.* 9, 311–330. doi: 10.1080/15434303.2011.653918

Loakes, D., Moses, K., Wigglesworth, G., Simpson, J., and Billington, R. (2013). Children's language input: a study of a remote multilingual Indigenous Australian community. *Multilingua* 32, 683–711. doi: 10.1515/mult-2013-0032

Luykx, A. (2005). "Children as socializing agents: family language policy in situations of language shift," in *Proceedings of the 4th International Symposium on Bilingualism,* eds J. Cohen, K. T. McAlister, K. Rolstad, and J. MacSwan (Somerville, MA: Cascadilla), 1407–1414.

Makihara, M. (2005). Rapa Nui ways of speaking Spanish: language shift and socialization on Easter Island. *Lang. Soc.* 34, 727–762. doi: 10.1017/S004740450505027X

Malcolm, I. (1996). Observations on the variability in the verb phrase in Aboriginal English. *Aust. J. Linguist.* 16, 145–165. doi: 10.1080/07268609608599536

Malcolm, I., and Kaldor, S. (1991). "Aboriginal English – an overview," in *Language in Australia,* ed S. Romaine (Cambridge: Cambridge University Press), 67–83.

Malcolm, I. G., and Sharifian, F. (2002). Aspects of Aboriginal English oral discourse: an application of cultural schema theory. Discourse Stud. 4, 169-181.

Malcolm, I. G., and Sharifian, F. (2007). "Multiwords in Aboriginal English," in *Phraseology and Culture in English,* ed P. Skandera (Berlin, New York: Mouton De Gruyter).

Marchman, V., Martinez-Sussman, C., and Dale, P. S. (2004). The language-specific nature of grammatical development: evidence from bilingual language learners. *Dev. Sci.* 7, 212–224. doi: 10.1111/j.1467-7687.2004.00340.x

McConvell, P. (2008). "Language mixing and language shift in Indigenous Australia," in *Children's Language and Multilingualism: Indigenous Language use at Home and School,* eds J. Simpson and G. Wigglesworth (London: Continuum International Press), 237–260.

McConvell, P., and Meakins, F. (2005). Gurindji Kriol: a mixed language emerges from code-switching. *Aust. J. Linguist.* 25, 9–30. doi: 10.1080/07268600500110456

McConvell, P., and Thieberger, N. (2001). *State of Indigenous Languages in Australia – 2001. Australia State of the Environment Technical Paper Series (Natural and Cultural Heritage), Series 2.* Canberra, ACT: Department of the Environment and Heritage.

McGregor, W. B. (2004). *The Languages of the Kimberley, Western Australia.* London: Routledge.

McWhinney, B. (2012). *The Childes Project: Tools for Analyzing Talk, Vol. 1, 3rd Edn*. New York; East Sussex: Psychology Press.

Meakins, F. (2008). "Unravelling languages: multilingualism and language contact in Kalkaringi," in *Children's Language and Multilingualism: Indigenous Language use at Home and School*, eds J. Simpson and G. Wigglesworth (London: Continuum), 283–382.

Meakins, F. (2011). *Case-marking in Contact: The Development and Function of Case Morphology in Gurindji Kriol*. Amsterdam: John Benjamins Publishing Company.

Morrison, B., and Disbray, S. (2008). "Warumungu children and language in Tennant Creek," in *Warra wiltaniappendi = Strengthening languages. Proceedings of the Inaugural Indigenous Languages Conference (ILC) 2007* (Adelaide, SA: Australia), 107–111.

Moses, K. (2009). *How do Dinosaurs hug in the Kimberley? The Use of Questions by Aboriginal Caregivers and Children in a Walmajarri Community*. Ph.D. dissertation, University of Melbourne.

Moses, K., and Yallop, C. (2008). "Questions about questions," in *Children's Language and Multilingualism: Indigenous Language use at Home and School*, eds J. Simpson and G. Wigglesworth (London: Continuum International Press), 30–55.

Naigles, L., and Hoff-Ginsberg, E. (1998). Why are some verbs learned before other verbs? Effects of input frequency and structure on children's early verb use. *J. Child Lang.* 25, 95–120. doi: 10.1017/S0305000997003358

Nicoladis, E., and Genesee, F. (1997). Language development in preschool bilingual children. *J. Speech Lang. Pathol. Audiol.* 21, 258–270.

O'Shannessy, C. (2005). Light warlpiri: a new language. *Aust. J. Linguist.* 25, 31–57. doi: 10.1080/07268600500110472

O'Shannessy, C. (2011). "Young children's social meaning making in a new mixed language," in *Growing Up in Central Australia: New Anthropological Studies of Aboriginal Childhood and Adolescence*, ed U. Eickelkamp (New York, NY; Oxford: Berghan Books), 131–155.

O'Shannessy, C. (2012). The role of code-switched input to children in the origin of a new mixed language. *Linguistics* 50, 305–340. doi: 10.1515/ling-2012-0011

Ochs, E., and Schieffelin, B. B. (1994). "Language acquisition and socialization: three developmental stories and their implications," in *Language, Culture and Society: A Book of Readings, 2nd Edn.*, ed B. G. Blount (Prospect Heights, IL: Waveland Press Inc.), 470–512.

O'Shannessy, C. (2004). *The Monster Stories: A Set of Picture Books to Elicit Overt Transitive Subjects in Oral Texts*. Nijmegen: Max Planck Institute for Psycholinguistics.

O'Shannessy, C. (2013). The role of multiple sources in the formation of an innovative auxiliary category in Light Warlpiri, a new Australian mixed language. *Language* 89, 328–354. doi: 10.1353/lan.2013.0025

Pan, B. A., Rowe, M. L., Singer, J. D., and Snow, C. E. (2005). Maternal correlates of growth in toddler vocabulary production in low-income families. *Child Dev.* 76, 763–782. doi: 10.1111/1467-8624.00498-i1

Paradis, J., and Genesee, F. (1996). Syntactic acquisition in bilingual children: autonomous or interdependent? *Stud. Second Lang. Acquis.* 18, 1–25. doi: 10.1017/S0272263100014662

Patterson, J. L. (1998). Expressive vocabulary development and word combinations of Spanish-English bilingual toddlers. *Am. J. Speech Lang. Pathol.* 7, 46–56. doi: 10.1044/1058-0360.0704.46

Patterson, J. L., and Pearson, B. Z. (2004). "Bilingual lexical development: influences, contexts and processes," in *Bilingual Language Development and Disorders in Spanish-English Speakers*, ed B. A. Goldstein (Baltimore: Brookes), 77–104.

Paugh, A. L. (2005). Multilingual play: children's code-switching, role play, and agency in Dominica, West Indies. *Lang. Soc.* 34, 63–86. doi: 10.1017/S0047404505050037

Pearson, B. Z., and Fernandez, S. C. (1994). Patterns of interaction in the lexical development in two languages of bilingual infants. *Lang. Learn.* 44, 617–653. doi: 10.1111/j.1467-1770.1994.tb00633.x

Pearson, B. Z., Fernandez, S. C., and Oller, D. K. (1993). Lexical development in bilingual infants and toddlers: comparison to monolingual norms. *Lang. Learn.* 43, 93–120. doi: 10.1111/j.1467-1770.1993.tb00174.x

Philips, J. R. (1973). Syntax and vocabulary of mothers' speech to young children: age and sex comparisons. *Child Dev.* 44, 182–185. doi: 10.2307/1127699

Poplack, S. (2004). "Code-Switching," in *Sociolinguistics. An International Handbook of the Science of Language and Society, 2nd Edn.*, eds U. Ammon, N. Dittmar, K. J. Mattheier, and P. Trudgill (Berlin: Walter de Gruyter), 589–596.

Pye, C. (1992). "The acquisition of K'iche' (Maya)", in *The Crosslinguistic Study of Language Acquisition*, Vol. 3, ed D. I. Slobin (Hillsdale, NJ: Lawrence Erlbaum), 221–308.

Richman, A. L., Miller, P. M., and LeVine, R. A. (1992). Cultural and educational variations in maternal responsiveness. *Dev. Psychol.* 28, 614–621. doi: 10.1037/0012-1649.28.4.614

Rondal, J. A. (1980). Fathers' and mothers' speech in early language development. *J. Child Lang.* 7, 353–369. doi: 10.1017/S0305000900002671

Rowe, M. L. (2008). Child-directed speech: relation to socioeconomic status, knowledge of child development and child vocabulary skill. *J. Child Lang.* 35, 185–205. doi: 10.1017/S0305000907008343

Sachs, J., Brown, R., and Salerno, R. A. (1976). "Adults' speech to children," in *Baby Talk and Infant Speech*, eds W. von Raffler-Engel and Y. Lebraun (Lisse: Swets & Zeitlinger), 240–245.

Sandefur, J. R. (1979). *An Australian Creole in the Northern Territory: A Description of Ngukurr-Bamyili Dialects Part 1. Work Papers of SIL-AAB Series B*, Vol. 3, Darwin: Summer Institute of Linguistics - Australian Aborigines Branch.

Saxton, M. (2009). "The inevitability of child-directed speech," in *Language Acquisition*, ed S. H. Foster-Cohen (London: Palgrave Macmillan), 62–86.

Saxton, M. (2010). *Child Language: Acquisition and Development*. London: Sage.

Sharifian, F. (2005). Cultural conceptualisations in English words: a study of Aboriginal children in Perth. *Lang. Educ.* 19, 74–88. doi: 10.1080/09500780508668805

Simpson, J., and Wigglesworth, G. (2008). *Children's Language and Multilingualism: Indigenous Language use at Home and School*. London: Continuum International Press.

Singer, R., and Harris, S. (forthcoming). What practices and ideologies support small-scale multilingualism? A case study of unexpected language survival in an Australian Indigenous community. *J. Socioling.*

Slobin, D. (eds.). (1997). *The Crosslinguistic Study of Language Acquisition*, Vol. 4. Hillsdale, NJ: Lawrence Erlbaum.

Smith, J., Durham, M., and Fortune, L. (2007). Community, caregiver and child in the acquisition of variation in a Scottish dialect. *Lang. Var. Change* 19, 63–99. doi: 10.1017/S0954394507070044

Smith, J., Durham, M., and Richards, H. (2013). The social and linguistic in the acquisition of sociolinguistic norms: caregivers, children, and variation. *Linguistics* 51, 285–324. doi: 10.1515/ling-2013-0012

Smith-Hefner, N. J. (1998). The linguistic socialization of Javanese children in two communities. *Anthropol. Linguist.* 30, 166–198.

Snow, C. E. (1972). Mothers' speech to children learning language. *Child Dev.* 43, 549–565. doi: 10.2307/1127555

Snow, C. E. (1977). "Mothers' speech research: from input to interaction," in *Talking to Children: Language Input and Acquisition*, eds C. E. Snow and C. A. Ferguson (New York, NY: Cambridge University Press), 31–49.

Snow, C. E. (1995). "Issues in the study of input: fine-tuning, universality, individual and developmental differences, and necessary causes," in *Handbook of Child Language*, eds P. Fletcher and B. MacWhinney (Oxford: Blackwell), 180–193.

ten Thije, J. D., Rehbein, J., and Verschik, A. (2012). *Receptive Multilingualism—Introduction. Int. J. Biling.* 16, 245–247. doi: 10.1177/1367006911426468

ten Thije, J. D., and Zeevaert, L. (eds.). (2007). *Receptive Multilingualism: Linguistic Analyses, Language Policies and Didactic Concepts*. Amsterdam: John Benjamins.

Turpin, M., Demuth, K., and Campbell, A. N. (2014). "Phonological aspects of Arandic baby talk," in *Language Description Informed by Theory*, eds R. Pensalfini, M. Turpin, and D. Guillemin (Amsterdam: John Benjamins), 49–80.

Vosoughi, S. (2010). *Interactions of Caregiver Speech and Early Word Learning in the Speechome Corpus: Computational Explorations*. Cambridge, MA. Massachusetts Institute of Technology MSc thesis.

Wigglesworth, G., and Simpson, J. (2008). "The language learning environment of preschool children in Indigenous communities," in *Children's Language and Multilingualism: Indigenous Language use at Home and School*, eds J. Simpson and G. Wigglesworth (London: Continuum International Press), 13–29.

Wilkins, D. P., and Nash, D. (2008). "The European "discovery" of a multilingual Australia: the linguistic and ethnographic successes of a failed expedition," in

The History of Research on Australian Aboriginal languages, ed W. McGregor (Canberra, ACT: Pacific Linguistics), 485–507.

Conflict of Interest Statement: The authors declare that the research was conducted in the absence of any commercial or financial relationships that could be construed as a potential conflict of interest.

2

A Commentary on Parent–Child Cognitive Learning Interaction Research: What Have We Learned from Two Decades of Research?

Yvette R. Harris and Seham Almutairi*

Department of Psychology, Miami University, Oxford, OH, USA

The role of family influences on preschool and school age cognitive development has received considerable empirical attention from cognitive developmental psychology researchers in the last few decades. As a result of the interest, investigators have focused their attention on developing coding/observational systems to capture the interactions occurring between mothers and their young children. This paper reviews a select body of research on parent–child cognitive learning interactions with the goal of determining how the researchers have operationalized the behaviors that occur within learning interactions. The paper concludes with a discussion of the suggestions on next steps for conducting parent–child cognitive learning interaction research in the future.

Keywords: coding strategies, parent–child interaction, memory problem solving book reading

Edited by:
Jessica S. Horst, University of Sussex, UK

Reviewed by:
Yoshifumi Ikeda, Joetsu University of Education, Japan
Jeffrey Coldren, Youngstown State University, USA

****Correspondence:***
Yvette R. Harris
harrisyr@miamioh.edu

Specialty section:
This article was submitted to Developmental Psychology, a section of the journal Frontiers in Psychology

INTRODUCTION

The role of family influences on preschool and school age cognitive development has occupied the discourse and the research of cognitive developmentalists for more than half a century (Hunt, 1961; Bloom, 1964). One reason for this interest is the realization by scholars of the primacy of the family environment in shaping, facilitating or constraining immediate and long term cognitive and intellectual competencies in young children.

The ways in which family influences have been operationalized and measured can be conceptualized as representing three empirical waves of research (see **Figure 1**). Each wave posits a different set of questions and at some level is framed from different theoretical and empirical orientations.

For example, research conducted during wave one, examines the question of how parental status variables are linked to global measures of preschool and school age intellectual performance. Researchers operationalize status variables as parental educational level, parental socioeconomic status and parental race. This work is motivated by the classic debate surrounding the relative and independent influence of nature versus nurture to children's intellectual competence (Gottfried, 1984). Numerous studies conducted in the 1960's and the 1970's explore the various ways parental socioeconomic status, parental race, and parental educational level predict children's intellectual functioning (Caldwell and Richmond, 1967; Golden and Birns, 1968; Wachs et al., 1971; Willerman, 1979). **Figure 2** provides an illustration of that relationship.

The second empirical wave concentrates on assessing specific aspects of the home environment (i.e., provision of play materials and parent–child stimulation), and correlating those aspects of the home environment with global measures of children's cognitive performance

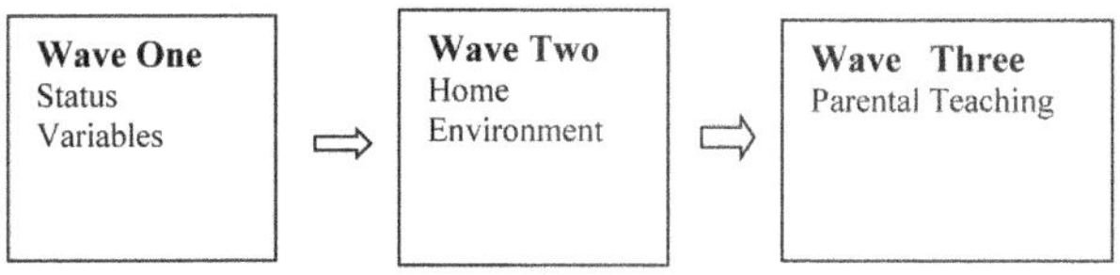

FIGURE 1 | Conceptual model of family influences on young children's cognitive and intellectual competencies.

FIGURE 2 | Conceptual model of early work examining the link between status variables and child cognitive outcomes.

(Bradley and Caldwell, 1978). Researchers argue that exploring status variables provide little specificity in illuminating precisely how the home environment provides stimulation to developing children. This work is influenced by the theoretical frame and empirical work of Hunt (1961) and Bloom (1964). Consequently measurements of the home environment were constructed with the goals of identifying and quantifying the overall quality of the home environment for learning (i.e., Bradley and Caldwell, 1981; Caughy et al., 2002). Parental socioeconomic status, education level, and race were put forward as moderators of the relationship between the home environment and child cognitive outcomes. This relationship is shown in **Figure 3**.

Wave three, developed out of the growing interesting amongst scholars in exploring specific patterns of teaching occurring between parents and children in formal and informal settings. Much of this research is framed from a Vygotsky (1978) theoretical perspective, which acknowledges the important role of social interaction in supporting the development of children's cognitive skills. Family influences are operationalized as parental teaching behaviors and coding systems are used to capture parental teaching strategies. In this case, investigators are explicitly interested in examining the strategies (e.g., questions, comments), parents use during formal and informal learning activities and exploring how those strategies are linked to children's concurrent and long-term cognitive competence. This research also focuses on identifying the moderating role of culture, ethnicity and educational level (Rogoff, 1993; Harris et al., 1999). See **Figure 4**.

The three empirical waves summarized above describe the extensive ways family influences are defined, and discuss the different approaches taken with regard to measuring the impact of family influences on child cognitive outcomes and performance. In addition, this body of research, collectively, is influential in shaping a new narrative on the role of family influences on preschool and school age intellectual and cognitive development; and is instrumental in moving interaction researchers beyond a dichotomous view of the contribution of the role of the family on preschool and school age cognitive and intellectual competence.

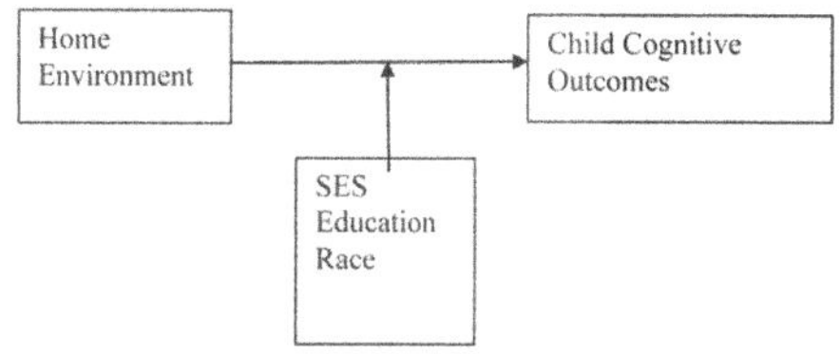

FIGURE 3 | Conceptual model of research examining the link between home environment and child cognitive outcomes with SES, education race as moderators.

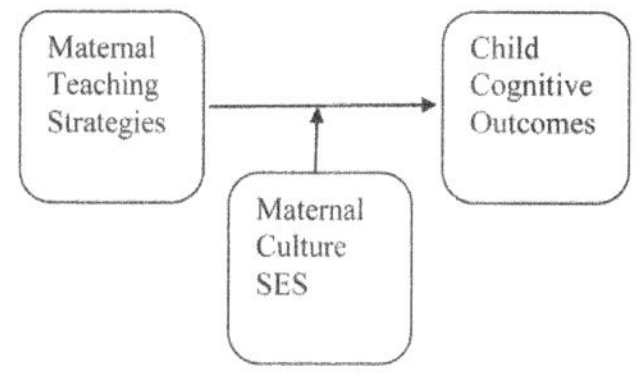

FIGURE 4 | Conceptual model on research exploring the link between maternal teaching strategies and child cognitive competence with maternal culture and SES as moderators.

For this paper, we chose to review a select body of work on parent–child cognitive learning interactions (PCCLI) conducted in the past 20 years (1994–2014) for two reasons. One, during the latter part of the 20th century, the bulk of the work on family influences on children's cognitive and intellectual performance centers on PCCLI. Two, our research on PCCLI, is informed by the theoretical frame of Vygotsky (1978), and the empirical work of PCCLI researchers.

We had three objectives in mind when assembling this paper. First, we wanted to learn how PCCLI are conceptualized. More specifically, how are PCCLI operationalized, defined, and coded? Second, we wanted to address the broader issue of identifying the critical cognitive skills children learn as a result of interacting with their parents. Third, we wanted to pinpoint the gaps in the literature and offer suggestions for future directions in the field.

SEARCH PROCESS

In order to find articles for inclusion in this paper, electronic databases such as PsycLIT, ERIC and Mendeley were searched for articles on parent-child cognitive learning interactions. Key words such as parent-child learning, parent-child cognitive development and parent–child interaction were used as the terms to identify articles. The reference lists of the selected articles were then scanned to find additional relevant publications. Twenty four papers published from 1994 to 2014 on parent–child cognitive interactions were finally selected for inclusion in this paper.

The research reviewed here exemplifies some of the major ways in which PCCLI have been studied over the last 20 years. Not every relevant line of research is included in this paper nor are studies of social development, as well as discussions of intervention programs.

SUMMARY OF MAJOR FINDINGS

Selection Results

Twenty percent (5) of the articles reviewed focus on parental associations with young children's memory skills; 33% (8) on shared book reading; and 48% (11) on general cognitive skills.

Measuring Parent–Child Cognitive Learning Interactions

Multiple coding systems have been employed to measure PCCLI. The studies reported in this paper, differ with respect to the number of coding categories (i.e., a low of three to a high of 25 coding categories). Some studies employ frequency counts, while others convert frequency counts to portions, and some researchers use Likert type scales to capture parent and child behavior. Furthermore, there is a great deal of diversity to the extent to which researchers code the children's performance. That is, some researchers code the children's concurrent performance (i.e., questions, off task comments) while others code their independent performance using standardized tests, or global scores.

Memory Skills

The bulk of the research in this area highlights parental influences on children's memory for past experiences or past events, with specific attention given to the strategies mothers use to elicit those memories from their children. The studies differ significantly in the number of discussions that mothers engage in with their children about past events and differ with reference to the recency of those events. For example, Melzi et al. (2011) had mothers select six events that the children had recently experienced; Cleveland and Reese (2005) had parents' select four shared and unshared past events to discuss with their children, whereas Tulviste et al. (2015) had mothers' select two conversations about past events to discuss with their children. Haden et al. (2009), observed mothers engaging in past conversations with their children ranging from two–three events depending on the child's age and Chang (2003) had mothers select one event that children had recently experienced. The studies also diverge in terms of how elicitation strategies are defined, and how children's use of strategies in recalling past events are assessed. These studies also differ in exploring the relationship between maternal elicitation strategies and the children's performance and their inclusion of mothers and children from diverse socioeconomic, and cultural and racial backgrounds.

MATERNAL ELICITATION STYLES

A few of the studies concentrate on maternal elicitation or reminiscing styles, and address how those styles change overtime and pinpoint how they are linked to children's recall of past events. For example, Haden et al. (2009), identifies two distinct elicitation/reminiscing styles in a sample of Caucasian middle class mothers as they are engaged in memory conversations when their children were 18, 24, and 30 months. Three general categories of maternal memory conversations are scored. *Elaborations* (questions, statements requesting the child to provide new information about the event), *Repetitions* (requests for children to restate information), and *Confirmations* (acknowledging children's correct responses). From these three categories, two maternal elicitation styles are identified. High eliciting mothers ask more questions, repeat information from their narratives, and affirm the child's responses. On the other hand, Low eliciting mothers mostly provide new information to their children and this new information is significantly different from the original event. High eliciting mothers overtime, increase their use of questions, continue to provide new information and repeat old information if requested to do so by their children.

The children's concurrent performance is determined by their use of memory elaborations (provision of new information about the past event), and their use of memory placeholders (repeating mothers comments). The children are also given the Preschool Language Scale-3. Children of high eliciting mothers increase their memory elaborations comments (providing more information) as well as their use of memory placeholders overtime.

Cleveland and Reese (2005) had the central goals of identifying maternal elicitation styles in a sample of New Zealand middle class mothers. Like Haden et al. (2009) they also address how those styles change over time (at 45 and 65 months) and explore how those styles are linked to the children's performance. They identified four different maternal styles in their research. Mothers are classified as either High Structure/Controlling. These mothers corroborate the children's recall of the past event, but they may change the topic of discussion. Some mothers are classified as High Structure/Autonomy Supporting. These mothers also validate their children's recall of the past event, however, they allow their children to assume a larger role in re-telling the story. A few mothers are classified as Low Structure/Controlling. These mothers fail to validate their children's recall of the event, and they control the discussion of the events, as their children are not given the freedom to tell the story. Lastly there are mothers who are classified as Low Structure/Autonomy support. Like mothers in the previous category, these mothers do not validate their children's recollection of the past event, yet, they do permit their children to re-tell the past events with little interruption. According to Cleveland and Reese (2005), maternal elicitation style is fairly stable across time, and children of mothers classified as High Structure/Autonomy Support recall significantly more detail about the memory events at both 45 and 65 months than children of mothers from the other styles.

Likewise, Melzi et al. (2011) look at how maternal narrative styles of middle class American mothers and the narrative styles of middle class Peruvian mothers are linked to children's recall of past experiences at one time point. In this particular study, mothers' elicitation styles are classified into two categories. There are mothers identified as *Elicitors,* who use comments to primarily elicit information from their children. This style is mainly adopted by the Peruvian mothers. In contrast there are mothers who are identified as *Constructors* and this style is predominantly characteristic of the U.S. mothers. These mothers elicit recall of past events from their children by requesting information, and provide information to assist their children in re-telling the story.

Children's concurrent contribution to the interaction is assessed by their use of questions, independent contributions, and their requests for assistance from their mothers to aid in their recall of past events. Children of *Elicitors* offer more independent information about the past event than do children of *Constructors*.

SPECIFIC NARRATIVE/ELICITATION STRATEGIES

Chang (2003) examines how the narrative strategies employed by middle class Chinese mothers used to discuss past events with their change over the course of a year. She codes both maternal narrative strategy use and child narrative strategy use along two dimensions. *Narrative Structure* which includes references to actions, events, discussions of the location of the event, references to character dialog, and discussions of how the events ended. *Interaction Coding* which assesses: Topic introduction (questions or statements introducing the past event), Questions (soliciting more detail about the event, repeating previously asked questions or soliciting yes/no responses from the child). Memory prompts (statements requiring more information) Clarification (asking for explanation), and Associative talk (comments connecting past events to present events). Chang (2003) found that mothers decrease their use of such as yes/no focused questions overtime and children increase their contribution to the interaction in the form of associate talk overtime.

Tulviste et al. (2015) examine the elicitation strategies that mothers from diverse cultural backgrounds (German, Swedish, Estonian, and Cameroonian-Nso) use as they engage their children in conversations about two past events. Two separate coding systems are used to capture those conversations. One system examines the structure of the conversations, and includes measures of the Total number of independent clauses, (complete sentences and words) Statement elaborations (comments that provide detail about the past event) and Opened ended questions (probing questions to elicit more detail) and Maternal Conversational Dominance (mother controls the discussion of past events). The second classifies the content of the conversations and includes eight categories. (1) Child (number of times the child is referenced as the focus of the past event) (2) Co agency (the number of times both the mother and children are mentioned as the focus of the event), (3) Mother (references to the mothers as the focus of the event), (4) Non-social content (references to the past event with no mention of person), (5) Social Content (referring to other people in the past event), (6) Actions or external behavior references to specific behavior), (7) Mental states (reference to thoughts or feelings during the event), and (8) Physical characteristics (references to clothing, appearance).

Their principal findings reveal that German mothers use more complete sentences and words in structuring the conversation and similar to Swedish mothers use more statement elaborations. Mothers from Estonia ask more open ended questions and mothers from Cameroonian-Nso exert more maternal dominance. In terms of the content of the conversations, Cameroonian-Nso mothers make their children and other people the center of the past event with a specific focus on actions of the actors. Conversely, Estonian mothers, include themselves and their children as central characters in the event, and make references to how they are feeling and thinking about the event. German mothers, on the other hand, emphasize past events that do not include naming specific people, but their stories contain references to such physical states as what people were wearing (clothing) or what they look like (appearances). The children's narrative strategies also vary by culture. Similar to their mothers, Cameroonian-Nso children include in their stories references to themselves and others as central characters of the event; and German children make references to Non-social content. Unlike their mothers, Co-agency content is higher amongst Swedish children.

Shared Book Reading

The studies in this domain vary considerably with reference to number of books used during the interaction, mention of socioeconomic status, and inclusion of parents and children from diverse racial and cultural backgrounds. They also differ to the extent to how parent strategies and child strategies are defined and measured and coded.

UTTERANCES

Robertson and Reese (2015) focus on the types of extra textual utterances used by middle class Caucasian mothers as they are involved in reading two books to their children, a narrative book *Hemi's Pet* (DeHamel, 1985a,b) and an expository book, *What is a Fish* (Tu akoi, 2007). Extratextual utterances are defined as *Descriptions* (naming or labeling); *Predictions and Inferences* (infer motives or causality), *Relating to Self* (connecting material to life experiences), *Print Talk* (sounding out words), *Evaluations* (likability of the book), *Confirmation* (acknowledging child's contribution), *Correction/Clarification* (asking for clarity, redirecting the child), *Metacomments* (expression lack of clarity with the text to the child). Three concurrent child strategies were coded- *Child book related initiated* (child interrupts with question), Child book related (child makes a comment about the text) and *Child non-book related* (not related to book). Children were also administered independent language and literacy measures (Test of Early Language Development, Dynamic Indicators of Early Literacy Skills, Letter Naming), as well as concurrent literacy measures (story comprehension and story re-telling tasks).

Their central findings suggest that maternal use of Prediction and Inferences when reading the narrative book correlate with the children's story comprehension and letter naming performance; whereas, their use of descriptives when reading the expository book correlated with the children's expressive vocabulary scores.

In a somewhat similar study, Deckner et al. (2006) explore the utterances middle class Caucasian mothers employ while engaged in reading three books with their children—*Clifford: Where is the Big Red Dog* (Bridwell, 1998); *Mice Squeak We Speak* (DePaola, 1997) and *Biscuit's Picnic* (Capucilli, 1998). In this study utterances are coded as on task and off task. On task utterances are defined as reading or discussing the book, and discussion utterances are further coded into non-metalingual or metalingual utterances. Non-metalingual discussion utterances include requests from the mothers for the child to point to information in the text (referential points) to turn the page (behavioral directives) and to respond to questions. Metalingual discussion utterances are coded as *Prompts* (asking the child to generate a comment), *Responses* (answering the child request for more information), *Recasting* (repeating or expanding upon what children say) *Scripting* (reading the text with pauses), *Vocabulary Introduction* (emphasizing new words), and *References to Print Elements* (comments about the text). Off tasks utterances are considered those comments with no relevance to the reading interaction.

Three levels of the children's contribution are assessed as well. Level one, their level of interest, availability, affect, and active participation during the book reading interaction on a 5 point Likert type scale (0 = low interests; 5 = high interest). Level two, their independent language performance measured by the Mullen Scales of Early Learning, (administered to the children at 18 months), the Peabody Picture Vocabulary Test-III and the Expressive Vocabulary Test (administered when the children were 30 and 42 months of age). Level three, their emergent literacy skills (Clay's Concept's About Print) assessed at 42 months.

Their most important finding shows that mothers employ more metalingual utterances than non-metalingual utterances, regardless of book type, and those utterances are predictive of the children's affect, and active participation in the reading interaction. Furthermore the utterances correlate with children expressive vocabulary scores at 30 and 42 months.

Correspondingly, Chang and Huang (2015), observe the utterances that mothers and their children of varying socioeconomic levels express while reading the book, *Good Dog Carl* (Day, 1985). Maternal utterances and child utterances are classified into four general coding categories. (1) *Interaction coding* includes requests for provision of information, questions, evaluation of the situation, attention, clarification, turn taking, and feedback. (2) *Immediate Talk* includes information about the location of the story, naming objects in the story, and solicitations for sequential information. (3) *Non-Immediate Talk* captures maternal inferences about the story, predictions about what will happen in the story, emphasis on real life experiences, emphasis on vocabulary, and general knowledge. (4) *Opportunity Education* –consists of maternal comments about issues of morality and right and wrong behavior.

Their major results indicate that mothers from higher socioeconomic levels in contrast to mothers from lower socioeconomic status groups, are more likely to use book reading utterances that make requests for information about the book from their children; and request their children's sustained attention during the book reading interaction. They also elaborate more in the form of questions about the text of book and unlike mothers from low ses backgrounds offer inferences about the characters in the books, and describe possible outcomes (predictions). In contrast, mothers from low ses backgrounds are more likely than mothers from high ses groups to use the opportunity of the book reading interaction to instruct their children on issues of morality.

Children from higher ses backgrounds are more likely than children from lower ses backgrounds to provide information about the story when requested to do so by their mothers; while children from lower ses backgrounds are more likely to obey commands to return their attention to the text, than are children from higher ses backgrounds.

STRATEGIES

Moving beyond looking at utterances, Vandermaas-Peeler et al. (2009) examine the types of guidance strategies and the engagement strategies that mothers from middle class and from lower socioeconomic status levels use while reading two books with their children, *Bunny Cakes* (Wells, 2002) and *Bunny Money* (Wells, 2000).

Guidance strategies are coded as *Teaching* (asking questions, sharing information), *Commands* (directing the child's behavior), *Praise* (acknowledging the child's performance), *Social connections* (asking the child questions about preference), and *Building bridges* (connecting the story book information to real life experiences). Engagement strategies, are assessed on a three point Likert type scale where 1 equal's low engagement and 3 equal's high engagement. Children's concurrent performance is coded as child initiated (comments child makes to begin the reading activity).

The researchers found middle class mothers use more teaching strategies overall, and more praise in contrast to mothers from the lower ses level. Whereas, mothers from low ses background use more commands. Mothers and children from middle class background are rated as being more engaged in the reading interaction, than are mothers and children from lower class backgrounds.

McDonnell et al. (2003) look at the discourse strategies that middle class Caucasian mothers use when engaged in reading the book *Show and Tell Day* (Rockwell, 1997), with their children over a 3 weeks time frame. They were particularly interested in exploring how their use of discourse strategies change overtime.

Discourse strategies are operationalized as *Conversation Control* (initiations, responses), *Turn Control* (the extent to how long speakers take turns?), *Contextualization Control* (labeling, counting, paraphrasing, explanations, inferences, prediction, and real world connections), and *Lexical Diversity* (number of different words). The children are administered language (Peabody Picture Vocabulary and Expressive Vocabulary Test) and cognitive measures (Bayley Scales of Infant Development).

Their key results suggest that mothers decrease their activity in the book reading interaction overtime (using fewer Discourse Strategies) and the children become more active participants in terms of the increase in their use of Conversational Control strategies during the book reading interaction.

Using a somewhat different approach to capture maternal strategies and child strategies, Kuchirko et al. (2015) coded the types of questions that mothers from different ethnic backgrounds (African American, Dominican, and Mexican) pose to their 3, 4, and 5 years old children as they are engaged in reading *Frog Where are You?* (Mayer, 1969). Questions are coded as *Referential questions* (asks child for a description or label of book text), *Story specific questions* (child is asked to respond to a book specific question), and *Open-ended questions* (asks the child to make inferences and predictions about the story). Their focus in this research is on answering the questions of how maternal questions vary by ethnicity; how maternal questions change overtime and how those questions correlate with children's narrative contribution. Children's narrative contributions are assessed using a story grammar framework (references to settings, problems, internal responses, consequences, actions, and resolution), their responses to mothers' questions and their spontaneous contribution to the story.

Their work yields three major findings. One, mothers independent of cultural background ask more referential questions and open ended questions when engaging in the book reading activity with 3 years old children. Mothers direct more story specific questions to 4 and 5 years old children. Two, Mexican and Dominican mothers ask more referential questions than African American mothers. Whereas, African American mothers ask more story specific questions than Mexican and Dominican mothers. Three, maternal referential, and story specific questions are associated with children's narrative contributions at age three; maternal use of referential, and opened end questions are associated with children's narrative contributions at age four and at age five.

MATERNAL STYLES

A few of the studies in this domain examine stylistic differences in maternal book reading behavior and tie those stylistic differences to the children's performance. Britto et al.'s (2006) work, for instance, assesses the link between maternal story telling style and children's vocabulary and school readiness performance in a sample of low income African American mothers engaged in reading the book, *Sounds I Hear* (Gelbart, 1983) with their children. Mothers' behaviors are scored according to their use of *Timing of Maternal Talk* (how did mothers, introduce and conclude the book reading interaction), *Decontextualized Language* (going beyond the text) *Expressive language use* (questions, points real life experience); *Labeling questions* (requests the child to name an item in the book), and *Positive feedback* (acknowledgment of the child's performance). Children are administered a series of tests to tap their expressive and receptive vocabulary and their school readiness skills.

Two maternal story telling styles are identified: Story Readers (rarely talked, just read from text) and Story Tellers (make more decontextualized comments, use a number of different words, ask more labeling questions, and give more positive feedback). They found that children of mothers classified as Story tellers have higher expressive language scores in contrast to children of mothers identified as Story Readers.

Similarly, Caspe (2009) focusing exclusively on Latina mothers, also observed mothers reading *Frog Where are You* (Mayer, 1969) and coded mothers strategies into three storytelling styles. Story builders-labelers use strategies to request narrative information from their children; Storytellers, employ strategies that involve telling the story to their children and controlling the direction of the story. Abridged storytellers request concise information from their children. The children are administered concepts about print, letter identification, a narrative task to assess their independent performance. Measures of their concurrent performance include assessments of their referential, evaluative and advanced utterances.

The primary findings show that a Storytellers style significantly predicts children's concepts about print; and an Abridged story telling style negatively predicts children's evaluative comments during the interaction.

General Cognitive Skills Domain

The studies in the third cognitive domain, general cognitive skills is perhaps the most diverse of all of the areas. The cognitive tasks in this domain consist of numeracy (Anderson, 1997; Bjorklund et al., 2004; Susperreguy and Davis-Kean, 2015); problem solving (Kermani and Brenner, 2000; Jimerson and Bond, 2001; Eisenberg, 2002; Hustedt and Raver, 2002; Prudhomme, 2003; Tamis-LeMonda et al., 2004); dinner table conversations (Ely et al., 2001) and shared scientific thinking (Crowley et al., 2001).

The research varies along several different dimensions. First, according to number of interaction sessions. Anderson (1997), Kermani and Brenner (2000), Crowley et al. (2001), Ely et al. (2001), Eisenberg (2002), and Susperreguy and Davis-Kean (2015) observed parent–child interactions in one session. In contrast, Jimerson and Bond (2001), Hustedt and Raver (2002), Prudhomme (2003), Bjorklund et al. (2004), and Tamis-LeMonda et al. (2004) observe interactions over multiple sessions. Second, the studies differ in their operalization of strategies used by parents and children, their focus on culture, and socioeconomic status and whether they include measures of children's concurrent and independent performance.

NUMERACY

Using a microgenetic approach, Bjorklund et al. (2004) code the *General strategies* (e.g., prompt, prompting after an error, affirmation, disaffirmation, provide answer), and the *Cognitive directives* (e.g., modeling, instruction, and re-representation) that middle class mothers from diverse cultural backgrounds (Bahamas, Columbia, Germany, Great Britain South Africa, and U.S) use as they are engaged in a numeracy activity and game type activity (game board) with their children. Their major aim is to determine how maternal strategy use varies across activity, to determine how maternal strategy use changes overtime, and to identify the association between maternal strategy use and children's strategy use (e.g., counting, fact retrieval, guessing strategies).

Findings suggest that maternal use of such general strategies as prompting after the child makes an error, and their use of affirmation, correlate with children's guessing strategies when working on the math activity. In addition, maternal use of disaffirmation, predicts children's use of addition strategies, and their use of guessing during the game context.

In a somewhat similar study focusing on math, Anderson (1997) explore the type of math talk that occurs in the homes of middle class Caucasian families as they are involved in several different types of tasks (e.g., assembling blocks, and preschool math worksheets). They had a particular interest in assessing the degree to which both parents and children emphasize such strategies as *Counting, Naming Shapes, Estimating, Adding, Measuring,* and *Subtracting* across the tasks.

They found that both parents and children employ counting, naming numbers, estimating, and comparing size type strategies (e.g., which one is bigger or smaller) when engaging with the math worksheets; whereas, they use comparing sizes and adding as strategies (e.g., adding sums) when working with blocks.

Like Anderson (1997), Susperreguy and Davis-Kean (2015) examine the type of math talk that occur in the homes of a sample of middle class mothers and their children; however, their focus is on how math talk emerges in every day conversations and activities. The most common type of math talk centers on counting, time, ordinal numbers, and number games. They did not explore links between maternal behavior and child behavior.

PROBLEM SOLVING

Jimerson and Bond (2001) observe the strategies that low income mothers use when engaging their children in one free play and two problem tasks (working with Legos to build a structure assembling a puzzle) over two different sessions. The goal of their research is to identify how mothers "take turns" as they engage with their children in these problem solving tasks. Four coding steps are used to capture turn taking strategies. The first step codes *Conversational Turns,* which include verbal and non-verbal behavior acknowledging when one speaker finishes speaking. The second step, *Contingent Interaction* includes five major categories: (1) Uncodeable Turn (comments cannot be coded), (2) Relevant Turn (comments that focus on a mutual understanding of the task) (3) Irrelevant Turn (comments that are off task, and do not relate to the task), (4) Simultaneous Turn (mother and child speaking at the same time) and (5) Not Applicable Turn (turns that do not apply to the above codes). The third step codes *Length of Turn which includes (1)* Alternating Verbal Turns (back forth exchange between mother and child), (2) Long Verbal Turn (comments on the task by the same speaker), and (3) Non-verbal Turn (nods, handing objects to one another). The fourth step *Failure to leave time for a response* codes how long mothers paused to allow the child to respond. The fifth step codes *Interrupting the Child* (mother takes over before the child completes an activity). They found that across problem solving tasks, and sessions, both mothers and children engaged in taking turns equally. In addition, mothers respond to children in relevant ways, they alternate turns with their children and use fewer long verbal turns.

Tamis-LeMonda et al. (2004) explore how low income mothers of color and low income fathers of color engage their children in playing with a set of toys (e.g., teddy bear, large boat with animals) at 24 and 36 months. Six parenting behaviors such as *Sensitivity* (accurately perceives child's signals during the interaction), *Positive Regard* (parent demonstrates love and respect for the child during the interaction), *Cognitive Stimulation* (part teaches and expands child knowledge during the interaction), *Intrusiveness* (parent is controlling during the interaction), *Detachment* (parent is under involved), and *Negative Regard* (parent rejects the child) are coded on a seven point Likert type scale where 1 equals very low and 7 equals very high. The children are given the Mental Scale of the Bayley's' Scale of Infant Development at 24 and 36 months, and the Peabody Picture Vocabulary Test-III at 36 months.

Their major findings indicate that parental sensitivity increases across age, with a slight decrease in positive regard and cognitive stimulation at 36 months. Sensitivity, Positive Regard and Cognitive Stimulation correlate with child performance across time. Intrusiveness positively correlates with children's MDI scores at 24 months and their PPVT scores at 24 and 36 months.

A few of the studies turn their attention to exploring maternal scaffolding strategies. For instance, Kermani and Brenner (2000) look at scaffolding strategies that mothers from two cultural groups (American Middle Class mothers and Iranian Middle Class mothers) use as they are engaged in two problem solving tasks with their children. One task involves assembling a set of blocks and the second task involves free play.

Scaffolding strategies are coded as *Promotion of Independence* (child is encouraged to perform on their own) *Explanation* (mothers provide clarity to the task) *Inquiry* (mother asks child to perform an activity) *Verbal hints* (mother provides general suggestions), *Verbal Prompts* (mother provides a specific hint), *Instructional* Directives (mother instructs the child to perform a specific behavior), *Modeling* (mother demonstrated for the child), *Correction* (mother redirects child behavior to another solution) and *Physical Control* (mother performs the task on her own). The three child behaviors coded include Asking for help, Refusal of help and Independent Performance.

Their results indicate that independent of task, American mothers use more inquiry and verbal hints; whereas Iranian mothers use more verbal prompts, directives, modeling, correction and physical control. In terms of the children's behavior, the children, especially the Iranian children ask for more help. There were no reported correlations between the maternal behavior and the children's behavior.

Similarly, Hustedt and Raver (2002) focus on coding the scaffolding strategies that low income mothers employ on a problem solving task (inserting a straw into a juice box) and a free play task with their children. However, in their study scaffolding strategies are operationalized as *Strategy Support* (verbal hints and direction maintenance), *Manual Help* (mothers offer to help the child) *Modeling* (mother showed child how to insert straw), *Maternal solution* (mother complete the task), *Recruitment* (mothers focusing children's attention on the task), *Feedback*, (positive or negative comments), and *Off topic Speech* (comments about another subject not related to the task). Preschoolers' engagement in the activities are coded as: paying attention, solving the task, following directions, seeking help from mother.

The researchers clustered maternal scaffolding strategies into the five distinct categories ranging from Highly Involved mothers (use more verbal strategies overall) to Less involved mothers (who use fewer verbal strategies). Their key findings indicate that children of highly involved mothers pay more attention to the task and their mothers' directives, work consistently on the task, and avoid engaging in off task behaviors.

Some studies in this domain code maternal use of distancing strategies. The distancing strategies perspective advanced by Sigel (2002) argues that high level strategies, referred to as demands (such as questions, comments that require the child to plan, speculate infer and problem solve) facilitate cognitive growth and development. Using this framework, Prudhomme (2003) examines the link between maternal distancing strategies (e.g., low, medium, and high cognitive demands) and preschoolers' memory for events in a sample of middle and upper middle class mothers engaging in a free play activity. Mother's behaviors are coded according to level of distancing demands. *Low level Distancing Strategies* (the parent asks the child to watch, name or label an object), *Medium Level Distancing Strategies* (the parent asks yes/no questions, and makes general comments about the task), *High Level Distancing Strategies* (parents ask the child to complete the task while providing a series of questions, comments and prompts). Two features of the children's behavior are coded. Their immediate recall and delayed recall (tasks administered during the second visit) as assessed by their performance on the *Novel Enabling Sequences* (imitating making a rattle from two objects) and *Novel Arbitrary Sequences tasks* (imitating pulling a train, dressing and feeding a teddy bear).

Two chief findings emerge from her work. One, the majority of the mothers use low level distancing strategies when engaging their children in a problem solving activity. Two, maternal use of low level distancing strategies and medium level distancing strategies correlate with children's performance on the enabling sequence.

Using a distance model perspective to coding her data, Eisenberg (2002) investigates how Mexican American mothers from middle class and working class backgrounds engage their children in two problem solving tasks (building a model with blocks, and baking biscuits). The goals of her study are to identify social class and task differences in maternal use of distancing strategies and child use of distancing strategies. Distancing strategies are defined as: *Verbal Supports* (negative feedback, and positive feedback), *Task Structuring* (general directives to perform an act) and *Distancing Behaviors* (statements and questions). Mothers and children's behaviors are then classified into three mutually exclusive categories. *Low complexity* (labeling, describing, or demonstrating), *Intermediate complexity* (sequencing, classifying, or comparing) and *High complexity* (inferring casual relations, classifying, or comparing).

Her foremost findings reveal that middle class mothers in comparison to working class mothers offer more verbal support to their children in the form of positive feedback and use more intermediate and high complexity type strategies across tasks. In terms of the children's performance, children from working class backgrounds ask more questions and offer more task structuring comments, then do children from middle class backgrounds.

When looking at task differences, mothers independent of social class provide more positive feedback, ask more questions, and use low complexity type strategies while working on the block task, and use high complexity type strategies while engaged in the baking tasks. Children, ask more questions about baking biscuits, and use both low level and intermediate strategies while engaged in the baking activity with their mothers. She did not examine the link between maternal strategies and preschool strategies.

CONVERSATIONS AND COMMUNICATION IN NATURALISTIC SETTINGS

Crowley et al. (2001) explore how middle class parents engage their children in scientific thinking during a museum visit. Three types of parental behavior are coded (describing evidence, giving directions, and explanation) and their results suggest that parents use strategies that describe the evidence more so than they give directions, or provide explanations during a museum visit. The investigators offer no information on the children's contribution to the discussion during the museum visit.

Ely et al. (2001) examine the types of conversation strategies that middle class Caucasian families use to elicit dinner table conversation from their children. In this case conversation strategies are coded as *Terms*, (list of words they used during the dinner table conversation) and *Pragmatic strategies* which include Control (speaker attempts to control who speaks) Clarification (listener requests explanation), Elicitation (speaker asks child to recount days activities), and Specification (speaker specifies the content of what they would like the other speaker to say). *Metalinguistic codes* are scored as: Emphasis (speaker explains a comment) Comment (makes a comment on words used during the dinner table conversation), Comment about past speech (speaker makes a comment on past speech), Labeling (speaker labels objects, names), Reported speech (speaker requests compliance with good dinner table behavior), and Inanimate speech (speaker makes reference to previous objects), *Literacy codes* which are Literacy (speaker makes reference to engaging in a written activity) and Incomplete (uncodeable).

Several major findings emerge from this work. First, reported speech, comments, and literacy talk are far more common that other forms of speech occurring during the dinner table conversations. Second, mother talk correlates with children's talk.

That is mothers' use of language focused terms predicts children's use of language focused terms during dinner table conversations.

DISCUSSION

The goal of this paper was to present a selected review of research conducted on PCCLI in the last 20 years. We were specifically interested in answering three questions. (1) How do the researchers operationalize and define parent strategies and children strategies? (2) What critical cognitive skills might children "learn" as a result of interacting with their parents? (3) Lastly, what are the gaps in the research and what are next steps?

Operationalization of Strategies

Overall, the studies, regardless of cognitive domain, identify what might be considered the essential pedagogical strategies that parents use to structure, guide, maintain, and conclude learning interactions with their children. However, they differ to the extent to which they emphasize each of the pedagogical strategies in their research; and how they define those pedagogical strategies.

It appears that collectively for research in the memory skills domain, prominence is placed on how parents' guide the interaction (i.e., orientation, location statements, and repetition) and maintain the interaction (i.e., confirmation, future talk, and correction) as they elicit narratives of past events from their children. It also seems that the varied ways in which maternal behaviors have been operationalized in this domain cohere into two distinct categories. Those categories are maternal styles, and specific narrative strategies. Thematically it could be argued that mothers are viewed as information processing supports for their children.

In the book reading domain, the shared variance" among the studies is their observation of how parents' guide the shared book reading interaction (e.g., provision of information, labels, correction, evaluation, and questions), and how they maintain the interaction (e.g., general knowledge, prompts, personal experiences, and building bridges). Similar to the maternal behaviors identified in the memory skills domain there are stylistic differences that predict children's active engagement and contribution to the shared book reading activity. Thematically the case can be made that mothers serve a coaches for their children as they find ways to involve them in the book reading interactions.

The studies in the third cognitive domain, general cognitive skills are perhaps the most diverse of all of the areas. In contrast to the other areas, these studies stress the way in which parents initially structure the interaction. In this case structure is operationalized as scaffolding (i.e., strategies to promote independence, verbal statements, directions and modeling, contingency analysis, cognitive assistance). The researchers also give attention to how parents' guide the interaction (i.e., give directions, explanation, labeling, and describe evidence), and how they maintain the interaction (i.e., number games or songs, sensitivity, turn taking, clarification, and general knowledge). Thematically, mothers and fathers in some instances, serve in the role as co- creators as they engage their children in problem solving, and numeracy related activities.

What Are the Critical Cognitive Skills That Children "Learn" from Interacting with Their Parents?

We can only speculate that children "learn" a vast array of cognitive skills as a result of engaging in interactions with their mothers. On the one hand, they develop important book reading skills, such as learning ways to comment on text, to elaborate information presented in the text by linking characters with real life experiences, and to develop their vocabulary. Or they learn what Tamis -Lemonda and Song (2013) refer to as the *initiation -reply-evaluation- sequence*. In addition, they learn ways of sharing narratives about past events with others, and in doing so learn the social pragmatics of sharing those events (i.e., turn taking). Lastly, they learn how to allocate their attention, ask complex questions and infer causality as they engage with their parents in dinner table conversations, visits to museums, and other problem solving activities. All of these skills are critical and important cognitive skills as they lay the foundation for later learning in formal academic settings.

What Are the Gaps in the Research and What Are the Next Steps for This Body of Research?

First, a major gap in the research is the lack of consistent inclusivity and diversity in observations of dyads from racially and economically diverse groups. At present, based on the available research, we know little about the pedagogical skills of parents from diverse cultural and economic backgrounds as they engage their children in cognitive tasks involving museum visits, dinner table conversations, and naturalistic math talk. Thus an important next step and future direction in this line of research is to continue to explore patterns of teaching in economically, racially, and culturally diverse dyads in those cognitive areas. Especially with an explicit focus on looking at within cultural group variation. It could be argued that parents and children from the same cultural communities differ significantly in terms of their patterns of cognitive learning interactions.

Second, the assortment and sheer number of coding systems should be re-evaluated. Few of the coding systems are explicitly grounded in theory and many appear too complicated to replicate. Thus an important next step may involve simplification of existing coding/observation systems. This might necessitate communication and collaboration among researchers to achieve consensus on operationalization of behaviors, and the metrics used to code those behaviors, especially within cognitive domains. Doing so might assist with the translational potential of PCCLI research for parents, teachers and social policy makers.

As we move forward in the future, it may fitting for PCCLI researchers to expand the focus of their questions. For example, those contemporary questions could address:

(1) **Intraindividual differences**. That is, when and how do children benefit from PCCLI's? Furthermore, how in the context of interacting with their parents, do they *discover* new strategies?

How stable are those strategies, and when and how do those strategies become part of their learning repertoire? Microgenetic designs (Siegler, 2016) might be effective in addressing those questions. (2) **Digital Technology**. How do parents engage their children in using digital technology? There are too few studies in this area, thus it is certainly ripe for future work. The small body of available literature suggests that parents use a set of different strategies when engaging their children in technology based book reading activities versus traditional book reading (Lauricella et al., 2014) and **(3) STEM related activities.** While the research is growing is this area, the major limitation is there is a lack of attention given to children and parents from economically and racially diverse backgrounds. Thus a focus of future work chould be to address how parents from these diverse groups involve their children in daily STEM related conversations and activities.

AUTHOR CONTRIBUTIONS

All authors listed, have made substantial, direct and intellectual contribution to the work, and approved it for publication.

ACKNOWLEDGMENT

The authors would like to acknowledge the contribution of Virginia Hollatz and Lakia Kidd for their assistance in retrieving articles for this publication.

REFERENCES

Anderson, A. (1997). Families and mathematics: a study of parent-child interactions. *J. Res. Math. Educ.* 28, 484–511. doi: 10.2307/749684

Bjorklund, D., Hubertz, M., and Reubens, A. (2004). Young children's arithmetic strategiesin social context: how parents contribute to children's strategy development whileplaying games. *Int. J. Behav. Dev.* 28, 347–357. doi: 10.1080/01650250444000027

Bloom, B. S. (1964). *Stability and Change in Human Characteristics*. New York, NY: Wiley.

Bradley, R., and Caldwell, B. (1978). Screening the environment. *Am. J. Orthopsychiatry.* 48, 114–129. doi: 10.1111/j.1939-0025.1978.tb01293.x

Bradley, R., and Caldwell, B. (1981). The home inventory, a validation of the preschool scale for black children. *Child Dev.* 52, 708–710.

Bridwell, N. (1998). *Clifford: Where is the Big Red Doggie?*. New York, NY: Cartwheel Books.

Britto, P., Brooks-Gunn, J., and Griffin, T. (2006). Maternal reading and teachingpatterns: association with school readiness in low-income African Americanfamilies. *Read. Res. Q.* 41, 68–89. doi: 10.1598/RRQ.41.1.3

Caldwell, B., and Richmond, J. (1967). Social class level and the stimulation potential of the home. *Except. Infant* 1, 453–466.

Capucilli, A. S. (1998). *Biscuits' Picnic*. New York, NY: Harper Collins Publishers.

Caspe, M. (2009). Low income Latino mothers' book sharing styles and children's emergent literacy development. *Early Child. Res. Q.* 24, 306–324. doi: 10.1016/j.ecresq.2009.03.006

Caughy, M., Randolph, S., and O'Campo, P. (2002). The Africentric home environment inventory: an observational measure of racial socialization feature of the home environment for African American Preschool Children. *J. Black Psychol.* 28, 37–52. doi: 10.1177/0095798402028001003

Chang, C. (2003). Talking about the past: how do Chinese mothers elicit narratives from their young children across time. *Narrat. Inq.* 13, 99–126. doi: 10.1075/ni.13.1.04cha

Chang, C., and Huang, C. (2015). Mother-child talk during joint book reading in two social classes in Taiwan: interaction strategies and information types. *Appl. Psycholinguist.* 24, 1–24.

Cleveland, E., and Reese, E. (2005). Maternal structure and autonomy support in conversations about the past: contributions to children's autobiographical memory. *Dev. Psychol.* 2, 376–388. doi: 10.1037/0012-1649.41.2.376

Crowley, K., Callanan, M., Jipson, J., Galco, J., Topping, K., and Shrager, J. (2001). Shared scientific thinking in everyday parent-child activity. *Inform. Sci.* 85, 712–732.

Day, A. (1985). *Good Dog, Carl*. New York, NY: Simon & Schuster.

DeHamel, J. (1985a). *Hemi and the Shortie Pajamas*. London: Puffin Books.

De Hamel, J. (1985b). *Hemi's Pet*. London: Reed Methuen.

Deckner, D., Adamson, L., and Bakeman, R. (2006). Children and maternal contributions to shared reading: effects on language and literacy development. *Appl. Dev. Psychol.* 27, 31–41. doi: 10.1016/j.appdev.2005.12.001

DePaola, T. (1997). *Mice Squeak We Speak*. New York, NY: G.P. Putnam's Sons.

Eisenberg, A. (2002). Maternal talk with families of mexican descent: influences of taskand socioeconomic status. *Hisp. J. Behav. Sci.* 24, 206–224. doi: 10.1177/0739986302024002006

Ely, R., Berko Gleason, J., MacGibbon, A., and Zaretsky, E. (2001). Attention to language: lessons learned at the dinner table. *Soc. Dev.* 10, 355–373. doi: 10.1111/1467-9507.00170

Gelbart, O. (1983). *Sounds I Hear*. Jerusalem: Hippy USA.

Golden, M., and Birns, B. (1968). Social class and cognitive development in infancy. *Merrill Palmer Q.* 14, 139–149.

Gottfried, A. (1984). "Issues concerning the relationship between Home Environment and Early Cognitive Development," in *Home Environment and Early Cognitive Development: Longitudinal Research*, ed. A. W. Gottfried (New York, NY: Academic Press), 1–4.

Haden, C., Orstein, P., Rudek, D., and Cameron, D. (2009). Reminiscing in the early years: patterns of maternal elaborativeness and children's remembering. *Int. J. Behav. Dev.* 32, 118–130. doi: 10.1177/0165025408098038

Harris, Y. R., Terrell, D., and Allen, G. (1999). The influence of maternal beliefs on the teaching behaviors of African American mothers. *J. Black Psychol.* 24, 490–503. doi: 10.1177/0095798499025004002

Hunt, J. (1961). *Intelligence and Experience*. New York, NY: Ronald Press Co.

Hustedt, J., and Raver, C. (2002). Scaffolding in low income mother-child dyads: relations with joint attention and dyadic reciprocity. *Int. J. Behav. Dev.* 26, 113–119. doi: 10.1080/01650250042000636

Jimerson, T., and Bond, L. (2001). Mothers' epistemologies, turn taking and contingent interaction with preschoolers'. *Appl. Dev. Psychol.* 22, 379–396. doi: 10.1016/S0193-3973(01)00079-X

Kermani, H., and Brenner, M. (2000). Maternal scaffolding in the child's zone of proximal development across tasks: cross cultural perspective. *J. Res. Child. Educ.*. 15, 30–52. doi: 10.1080/02568540009594774

Kuchirko, Y., Tamis-LeMonda, C., Luo, R., and Liang, E. (2015). What happened next?: developmental changes in mothers' questions to children. *J. Early Child. Lit.* doi: 10.1177/1468798415598822

Lauricella, A. R., Barr, R., and Calvert, S. (2014). Parent–child interactions during traditional and computer storybook reading for children's comprehension: implications for electronic storybook design. *Int. J. Child Comput. Interact.* 2, 17–25.

Mayer, M. (1969). *Frog Where are you?* New York, NY: Dial Books.

McDonnell, S., Friel-Patti, S., and Rollins, P. (2003). Patterns of change in maternal-childdiscourse behaviors across repeated storybook readings. *Appl. Psycholinguist.* 24, 323–341. doi: 10.1017/S0142716403000171

Melzi, G., Schick, A., and Kennedy, J. (2011). Narrative elaboration and participation: two dimensions of maternal elicitation style. *Child Dev.* 82, 1282–1296. doi: 10.1111/j.1467-8624.2011.01600.x

Prudhomme, N. (2003). Maternal distancing and event memory at 20 months. *Infant Child Dev.* 12, 369–385. doi: 10.1002/icd.317

Robertson, S., and Reese, E. (2015). The very hungry caterpillar turned into a butterfly: children's and parents' enjoyment of different book genres. *J. Early Child. Lit.* doi: 10.1177/1468798415598354

Rockwell, A. (1997). *Show and Tell Day*. New York, NY: Harper Collins.
Rogoff, B. (1993). "Guided participation and appropriation," in *Development in Context: Acting and Thinking in Specific Environment*, eds R. Wozniak and K. Fischer (Mahwah, NJ: Lawrence Erlbaum Associates), 121–153.
Siegler, R. (2016). Continuity and change in the field of cognitive development and the perspectives of one cognitive developmentalist. *Child Dev. Perspect.* 10, 128–133. doi: 10.1111/cdep.12173
Sigel, I. (2002). The psychological distancing model. *A* study of socialization of cognition. *Cult. Psychol.* 8, 189–214. doi: 10.1177/1354067X02008002438
Susperreguy, M., and Davis-Kean, P. E. (2015). Socialization of maths in the home environment: using recordings to study math talk. *Stud. Psychol.* 36, 643–655. doi: 10.1080/02109395.2015.1078555
Tamis -Lemonda, C., and Song, L. (2013). "Parent infant communicative interactions in cultural contexts," in *Handbook of Psychology:Developmental Psychology*, Vol. 6, eds R. M. Lerner, M. Ann Easterbrooks, and J. Mistry (Hoboken, NJ: John Wiley & Sons), 143–170.
Tamis-LeMonda, C., Shannon, J., Cabrera, N., and Lamb, M. (2004). Fathers and mothers play with their 2 and 3 year olds: contributions to language and cognitive development. *Child Dev.* 75, 1806–1820. doi: 10.1111/j.1467-8624.2004.00818.x
Tu akoi, F. (2007). *What is a Fish?* Auckland: Scholastic.
Tulviste, T., Tougu, P., Keller, H., Schroder, L., and De Geer, B. (2015). Children's and mothers' contribution to joint reminiscing in different sociocultural context. Who speaks and what is said. *Infant Child Dev.* 25, 43–63.
Vandermaas-Peeler, M., Nelson, J., Bumpass, C., and Sassine, B. (2009). Social contexts of development: parent-child interactions during reading and play. *J. Early Child. Lit.* 9, 295–317. doi: 10.3389/fpsyg.2016.01078
Vygotsky, L. S. (1978). *Mind in Society: The Development of Higher Psychological Processes*. Cambridge, MA: Harvard University Press.
Wachs, T., Uzgiris, I., and Hunt, J. (1971). Cognitive development in infants from different age levels and environmental backgrounds: an explanatory investigation. *Merrill Palmer Q.* 17, 283–317.
Wells, R. (2000). *Bunny Money*. New York,NY: Penguin Books.
Wells, R. (2002). *Bunny Cakes*. New York, NY: Penguin Books.
Willerman, L. (1979). Effects of families on intellectual development. *Am. Psychol.* 34, 923–948. doi: 10.1037/0003-066X.34.10.923

Conflict of Interest Statement: The authors declare that the research was conducted in the absence of any commercial or financial relationships that could be construed as a potential conflict of interest.

3

The Agreement between Parent-Reported and Directly Measured Child Language and Parenting Behaviors

Shannon K. Bennetts[1,2,3], Fiona K. Mensah[1,2,4], Elizabeth M. Westrupp[1,2,3], Naomi J. Hackworth[2,3] and Sheena Reilly[1,2,4,5]*

[1] Department of Paediatrics, The University of Melbourne, Parkville, VIC, Australia, [2] Murdoch Childrens Research Institute, Parkville, VIC, Australia, [3] Judith Lumley Centre, La Trobe University, Melbourne, VIC, Australia, [4] The Royal Children's Hospital, Parkville, VIC, Australia, [5] Menzies Health Institute Queensland, Griffith University, Gold Coast, QLD, Australia

Edited by:
Ann Dowker,
University of Oxford, UK

Reviewed by:
Catherine M. Sandhofer,
University of California, Los Angeles, USA
Ewa Haman,
University of Warsaw, Poland

***Correspondence:**
Shannon K. Bennetts
shannon.bennetts@mcri.edu.au

Specialty section:
This article was submitted to Developmental Psychology, a section of the journal Frontiers in Psychology

Parenting behaviors are commonly targeted in early interventions to improve children's language development. Accurate measurement of both parenting behaviors and children's language outcomes is thus crucial for sensitive assessment of intervention outcomes. To date, only a small number of studies have compared parent-reported and directly measured behaviors, and these have been hampered by small sample sizes and inaccurate statistical techniques, such as correlations. The Bland–Altman Method and Reduced Major Axis regression represent more reliable alternatives because they allow us to quantify fixed and proportional bias between measures. In this study, we draw on data from two Australian early childhood cohorts (N = 201 parents and slow-to-talk toddlers aged 24 months; and N = 218 parents and children aged 6–36 months experiencing social adversity) to (1) examine agreement and quantify bias between parent-reported and direct measures, and (2) to determine socio-demographic predictors of the differences between parent-reported and direct measures. Measures of child language and parenting behaviors were collected from parents and their children. Our findings support the utility of the Bland–Altman Method and Reduced Major Axis regression in comparing measurement methods. Results indicated stronger agreement between parent-reported and directly measured child language, and poorer agreement between measures of parenting behaviors. Child age was associated with difference scores for child language; however, the direction varied for each cohort. Parents who rated their child's temperament as more difficult tended to report lower language scores on the parent questionnaire, compared to the directly measured scores. Older parents tended to report lower parenting responsiveness on the parent questionnaire, compared to directly measured scores. Finally, speaking a language other than English was associated with less responsive parenting behaviors on the videotaped observation compared to the parent questionnaire. Variation in patterns of agreement across the distribution of scores highlighted the importance of assessing agreement comprehensively, providing strong evidence that simple correlations are grossly insufficient for method comparisons. We discuss implications for researchers and clinicians, including guidance for measurement selection, and the potential to reduce financial and time-related expenses and improve data quality. Further research is required to determine whether findings described here are reflected in more representative populations.

Keywords: agreement, bias, Bland–Altman Method, Reduced Major Axis regression, measurement, parent-report, child language, parenting

INTRODUCTION

The success of early intervention programs relies on accurate and sensitive measurement of intervention processes and outcomes. It is surprising then, that research comparing agreement between different types of measurement methods has been extremely limited. There has been increasing attention over the past decade on early intervention programs targeting parenting behaviors in order to improve children's language outcomes. Language delay affects around one in five children at age four (e.g., Reilly et al., 2010) and persistent difficulties can impact upon future academic success, employment prospects and socio-emotional functioning (Campbell and Ramey, 1994; Stothard et al., 1998). Parenting characterized by warm, positive and responsive interactions can facilitate language development in the early years (Sim, 2012; Cartmill et al., 2013), serving as a buffer against the above-mentioned risks. Understanding how to identify language concerns and intervene early relies upon accurate and reliable measurement. This paper uses existing data from two early childhood cohorts to examine agreement between parent-reported and directly measured child language and parenting behaviors, and the socio-demographic predictors of the difference between measures.

Research focused on understanding complex child developmental and family processes requires highly sensitive assessment tools. Two primary options for researchers seeking to quantify constructs related to child language and parenting behaviors are parent-reported measures and direct (observational or standardized) measures. Both possess notable strengths and limitations, yet there is a lack of comparable data to help researchers identify the circumstances in which one or both methods should be employed. Parents are uniquely positioned to report on their children's behavior retrospectively and across multiple settings (Gartstein and Marmion, 2008). Parent-reported data is relatively straightforward and inexpensive to collect and analyze (Hawes and Dadds, 2006), making it an appealing measurement approach in large-scale trials where time and cost are significant considerations. However, parents' unique set of experiences, opinions and attitudes (both explicit and implicit) can contribute to response bias. For example, parents may vary in their interpretation of key terms (Aspland and Gardner, 2003); psychological difficulties can color parents' perceptions of their children's behavior (Hayden et al., 2010); or responses can be influenced by social desirability (Law and Roy, 2008). In contrast, direct measures permit the collection of data which is more objective (Wysocki, 2015). For this reason, direct measures are often considered the "gold standard" for assessing both parenting behaviors (Hawes and Dadds, 2006) and child language (Sachse and Von Suchodoletz, 2008). However, collection of such measures requires considerable time and financial resources (Gardner, 2000), and generalizability to other time points and settings has been questioned (Gardner, 1997).

Myriad factors can affect observed behavior or parent-reported responses. Direct measures can be influenced by the presence of the observer or assessor, illness, tiredness, or distractions. Parent-reported measures may be biased by factors associated with a parent's background. Parents from low socio-economic backgrounds (e.g., low income, low education) have been shown to over- or under-estimate children's vocabulary on the Communicative Development Inventory (Roberts et al., 1999; Feldman et al., 2000), suggesting that caution in interpretation is required. Furthermore, acquiescence or "yea-saying" (i.e., the tendency to agree with items irrespective of their content) may be a particularly important consideration when administering parent-reported measures with socially disadvantaged populations (Meisenberg and Williams, 2008). It has also been suggested that less educated parents may be less able than well-educated parents to discriminate between expressive and receptive items on a vocabulary checklist, thus providing an inflated estimate of their child's language abilities (Reese and Read, 2000). Child characteristics such as temperament and gender have similarly been shown to affect parent responses or parent behaviors (Hayden et al., 2010; Olino et al., 2013).

In light of these relative strengths and limitations of parent-reported and direct measures, it is important to establish the extent to which these measurement methods concur and for whom. This information will allow researchers to make more informed decisions about the most appropriate and cost-effective measurement option, given the specific context of their study and finite study resources. For example, given evidence of strong agreement between parent-reported and direct measures, researchers may opt to administer only parent-report; whereas evidence suggesting weak agreement may require researchers to administer multiple methods or only the agreed "gold standard" method.

Few studies have investigated agreement between parent-reported and directly measured behaviors. Of those that have, two primary limitations can be identified. Firstly, these studies tend to employ small sample sizes (in the range of $N = 50$–70). While understandable given the expense associated with using direct measures, small samples reduce the power of the study to identify the limits of agreement with precision. Secondly, these studies typically employ correlational analyses to quantify agreement between measures. For example, moderate correlations have been reported between parent-reported and directly measured child language (e.g., Ring and Fenson, 2000; Sachse and Von

Suchodoletz, 2008) and weak to negligible correlations between parent-reported and directly measured parenting behaviors (e.g., Arney, 2004). The use of correlations is problematic because correlations provide a single figure representing the strength of the association between two related variables; they do not assess agreement (Eadie et al., 2014). That is, correlations do not allow for differences in agreement to be examined *across* the spectrum, and they do not account for bias which may be present between two measures, including fixed bias (i.e., bias which is constant across the distribution) or proportional bias (i.e., bias which varies proportionally across the distribution) (see Bland and Altman, 1986; Carstensen, 2010; Bennetts et al., in press). We agree with Stolarova et al. (2014) that greater awareness of the difference between agreement and correlation will lead to the use of more appropriate statistical methods.

Methods such as the Bland–Altman Method (Bland and Altman, 1986) or Reduced Major Axis (RMA) regression (Ludbrook, 2010) represent appropriate alternatives for assessing agreement, allowing researchers to quantify fixed and proportional bias, respectively. These techniques are commonly used for method comparisons in fields such as medicine and chemistry, but are seldom applied in psychology due to a lack of awareness and paucity of literature in the field (Miles and Banyard, 2007). The Bland-Altman Method involves plotting the mean of two measures against the difference between two measures (Altman and Bland, 1983). This provides a visual means of examining the variation in agreement across the spectrum of scores. RMA regression is particularly helpful for identifying proportional bias between measures (Ludbrook, 1997). Execution of this technique involves minimizing the sum of the vertical and horizontal residuals. RMA is suitable for contexts in which measurement error is present in both x and y, as would be expected in the current study.

This study used data from two cohorts of parents and their children aged 6–36 months to: (1) quantify the agreement between parent-reported and directly measured child language and parenting behaviors, and to (2) determine the association between a range of socio-demographic factors and the difference between parent-reported and direct measures.

MATERIALS AND METHODS

Participants

Data were drawn from two randomized controlled trials of early childhood parenting interventions; (1) a community-based sample of parent–child dyads participating in the Language for Learning program for slow-to-talk toddlers aged 24 months ($N = 201$), and (2) parent–child dyads participating in the Early Home Learning Study; an evaluation of a community-based program to support disadvantaged parents to provide a rich home learning environment for their children aged 6–36 months ($N = 218$). Parents and children completed a suite of assessments, including parent-reported and direct measures of child language and parenting behaviors.

Language for Learning participants were recruited by maternal and child health nurses in three local government areas in Victoria, Australia. All children residing in these areas were recruited at 12 months of age. Children were excluded if there was a known cognitive delay, a major medical condition, or if parents were unable to complete written questionnaires. At child age 18 months, parents completed the Sure Start Language Measure. Children falling below the 20th percentile were invited to participate in the current study of slow-to-talk toddlers.

Early Home Learning Study participants were recruited by child and family service workers and maternal and child health nurses within twenty local government areas in Victoria, Australia. Eligibility criteria included: living within the geographical boundaries of a trial locality; having at least one child aged 6–36 months; and evidence of at least one risk indicator for social disadvantage including: low family income; receipt of government benefits (e.g., Health Care Card for low income families); single, socially isolated or young parent (<25 years); and culturally and linguistically diverse background. Parents were not eligible if they were aged less than 18 years, did not speak English, or were receiving intensive support or child protection services.

Measures

A summary of parent-reported and direct measures administered for each cohort is provided in **Table 1**. Both cohorts completed parent-reported and direct measures of child language. Direct measures included a standardized language assessment for the Language for Learning cohort, and a videotaped observation for the Early Home Learning Study cohort. Participants in the Early Home Learning Study also completed a videotaped observation of parent–child interaction, as well as parent-reported measures of parenting behaviors.

Parent-Reported Measures

MacArthur-Bates Communicative Development Inventories

The CDI is a brief, reliable and commonly used measure of children's language skills (Fenson et al., 2000). One of three versions was used depending on the child's age in months. The CDI Short-Form Level I was used for children up to 18 months, consisting of an 89-word list, resulting in a total score from 0 to 89. Parents were asked to indicate if their child "understands" or "understands and says" each word. Parents of children aged 19–30 months completed the Short-Form Level II. Parents were

TABLE 1 | Parent-reported and direct measures.

	Parent-reported measures	Direct measures
Child language	• Sure Start Language Measure (SSLM)[a] • Ages and Stages Questionnaire (ASQ)[a,b] communication subscale • Macarthur-Bates Communicative Development Inventory (Short-Form, CDI)[b]	• Preschool Language Scale (PLS-4)[a] • Early Communication Indicator (ECI)[b]
Parenting behaviors	• Parental Verbal Responsivity (PVR)[b] • Home Activities with Child (HAC)[b]	• Indicator of Parent-Child Interactions (IPCI)[b]

[a]*Language for Learning;* [b]*Early Home Learning Study.*

asked to report whether their child 'says' 100 listed words resulting in a total score from 0 to 100 for word production and a single item assessing word combinations. Parents of children aged 31 months and above completed the CDI III, consisting of a 100-word vocabulary checklist, 12 sentence pairs to evaluate complexity of language use, and 12 yes/no items assessing language comprehension, resulting in a total score from 0 to 124. Minor changes in word items were made for the Australian context, in-line with other Australian studies (Reilly et al., 2009; Skeat et al., 2010). Scores were standardized for each of the three age-appropriate versions.

Sure Start Language Measure

Children's expressive vocabulary was assessed with the Sure Start Language Measure (SSLM) 100-word checklist (Roy et al., 2005). The SSLM was developed based on the commonly used MacArthur-Bates Communicative Development Inventory, with some items adjusted for the United Kingdom, rather than American context. Parents were asked to indicate whether their child could say 100 words, (e.g., "meow," "finish" or "happy") and whether their child was combining words "not yet," "sometimes" or "often" to produce a total score out of 100.

Ages and Stages Questionnaire (ASQ-3) communication subscale

The ASQ allows for developmental and social-emotional screening of children, aged between 1 and 66 months (Squires et al., 2009). Questionnaires comprise five sub-scales: communication, gross motor, fine motor, problem solving, and personal-social, with six items in each subscale, plus an additional 8 open-ended questions addressing overall child development. Only the communication subscale is reported here. Parents were asked to indicate whether their child performs a specific activity using three response categories: 'yes,' 'sometimes' or 'not yet' across six items, each scored as 10, 5, or 0 for 'yes,' 'sometimes' or 'not yet' respectively (e.g., "Does your child correctly use at least two words like "me," "I," "mine" and "you"?). Scores were summed to give a total score ranging from 0 to 60. Higher scores indicated stronger communicative abilities. Fourteen age-appropriate versions were administered; therefore scores were standardized within age bands to derive z-scores.

Parental Verbal Responsivity

The four-item PVR subscale from the StimQ-Toddler (Dreyer et al., 1996) measures how verbally responsive the parent is in interactions with their child on a dichotomous "yes"/"no" scale. To detect greater variability, an alternative 4-point Likert scale was used, where 1 = not at all and 4 = every day (e.g., "I talk about the day while my child is eating"). Scores were summed to produce a total score between 4 and 16, with higher scores indicating greater Parental Verbal Responsivity.

Home Activities with Child

The five-item "Home Activities with Child" scale (Nicholson et al., 2008) assessed the frequency with which parents engage in developmentally important activities with their child in a typical week. The scale is administered on 4-point Likert scale, where 1 = not at all, and 4 = every day (e.g., "How often do you involve your child in everyday activities at home, such as cooking or caring for pets?"). Item scores were summed to produce a total score between 5 and 20, with higher scores indicating greater frequency of home activities between the parent and child.

Direct Measures

Preschool Language Scale, Fourth Edition

The PLS-4 (Zimmerman et al., 2002a) is a standardized and norm-referenced instrument to evaluate children's receptive and expressive language skills from birth to 6 years and 11 months. This assessment can be used as a screening tool for a range of developmental delays such as problems with language, articulation, connected speech, social communication skills, stuttering, or voice disorders. Although this measure is normed on a US, rather than Australian sample, (n = 1564) (Zimmerman et al., 2009), it is one of the most widely used, directly assessed, standardized tools for assessing language ability in very young children. The PLS-4 has been used in other Australian studies with young children (e.g., Ching et al., 2013). This study reports only on the PLS standard score for expressive language.

Early Communication Indicator

The ECI (Carta et al., 2010) aims to assess early communicative development of children aged 6–36 months across four key domains: vocalizations; single words; multiple words; and gestures. Parents were asked to play with their child with a standardized set of toys for 6 min while being videotaped. Accredited expert coders scored video data according to standardized protocols. Frequencies for each of the four domains were recorded at 1-min intervals. A total communication composite score was generated by weighting single words by two and multiple words by three, before summing all four domain scores. Inter-rater agreement on 20% of observations independently coded by both assessors was 93.9%, consistent with previously reported figures (Greenwood et al., 2010). Families from a non-English speaking background were not instructed to speak English. Rather, all families were asked to "do what they normally do." Videos featuring families who spoke a language other than English could not be coded due to the need to employ interpreters; only families who chose to interact in English are included in this analysis.

Indicator of Parent–Child Interactions

The IPCI (Carta et al., 2010) was used to quantify the frequency of specific parent and child behaviors during a set of four common early childhood activities: free play (4 min); looking at books (2 min); distraction (2 min); and getting dressed (2 min). The distraction task required parents to keep their child on a small blanket without the child touching a small musical device which was placed within reach. This activity was not administered to children less than 12 months of age. The activities are designed to elicit natural interactions which would typically occur between the parent and child. Activities were videotaped, resulting in a total of 8–10 min' footage. Accredited expert coders scored video data according to standardized protocols by counting the frequency of interactions for each activity across six parent domains: conveys acceptance and warmth; uses descriptive language; follows child's lead; maintains or extends child's focus; uses criticism or harsh voice; uses restrictions or intrusions. For each activity, a relative frequency was allocated to each domain based on a 4-point scale where 0 = never; 1 = rarely; 2 = sometimes or inconsistently; 3 = often or consistently. After each activity was rated, a domain percentage score was calculated by summing all activity scores and dividing by the total number of possible points for that domain. This study reports on the total positive caregiver score only, which captures the frequency of responsive parenting behaviors occurring during the videotaped observation. This total score was generated by summing the percentage scores for the first four domains listed above. Inter-rater agreement on 20% of observations independently coded by both assessors was 87.4%, consistent with previously reported figures (Baggett and Carta, 2006). As described above, all families were asked to "do what they normally do." However, videos featuring families who spoke a language other than English could not be coded due to the need to employ interpreters.

Socio-Demographic Factors

Variables available for both cohorts included: parent age, child age, child gender, parent education, household income, household unemployment, language other than English and socio-economic disadvantage. Socio-economic disadvantage was assessed with the Socio-Economic Indexes for Areas Disadvantage indicator (Australian Bureau of Statistics, 2011), which summarizes the economic and social circumstances for people and households in a particular area ($m = 1000$; $SD = 100$). Lower scores indicate greater disadvantage. A single-item indicator of child temperament was included for both cohorts (higher scores indicated more difficult temperament). Additional variables were included in the Early Home Learning Study analysis due to availability of data, and evidence that these factors may affect parent responses or behavior: global parenting self-efficacy, assessed using a single-item indicator ("Overall, as a parent, do you feel that you are ..." not very good at being a parent; a person who has some trouble being a parent; an average parent; a better than average parent; a very good parent); psychosocial distress assessed with the K6 (Kessler et al., 2002); and health-related quality of life evaluated with the SF-12 UK version (Jenkinson and Layte, 1997).

Procedure

Language for Learning: Children identified as slow-to-talk at 18 months were assessed at 24 months by a trained research assistant. Researchers visited families at home to collect parent-reported data and to administer a standardized child language assessment. *Early Home Learning Study:* Prior to intervention, trained research assistants videotaped parents and children at home during play activities to examine child language development and parent–child interactions. Parents also completed a brief measure of child language during the visit. A 30-min parent questionnaire was administered via computer-assisted telephone interview.

Ethical approval for the Language for Learning study was granted by the Royal Children's Hospital Human Research Ethics Committee (EHRC #26028) and The University of Melbourne (#0829736). All parents provided written informed consent. Ethical approval to access existing Language for Learning data for the current study was covered under the Centre for Excellence in Child Language and approved by the Royal Children's Hospital Human Research Ethics Committee (HREC #32261 B). Ethical approval for the Early Home Learning Study was granted by the Victorian Government Department of Health (HREC 08/10). All parents provided written informed consent. Ethical approval to access existing Early Home Learning Study data for the current study was granted by The University of Melbourne Human Research Ethics Committee (ID 1543863.1).

Statistical Analyses

All analysis was conducted using Stata/IC Version 13.0 (StataCorp, 2013). Prior to analyses, two fathers were excluded from the *Language for Learning* dataset and nine from the Early Home Learning Study dataset, given that parent gender has been found to contribute to differences in data collection (Olino et al., 2013) and the inclusion of such small numbers of fathers was considered insufficient to identify differences between mothers and fathers. A total of nine measures were examined across the two cohorts. Between these measures, nine comparisons were conducted: six compared parent-reported and directly measured behaviors, and three compared parent-reported and parent-reported behaviors. Histograms of the differences were examined for all nine comparisons, followed by scatterplots with a line of best fit to examine linear association. Both Pearson's Correlation Coefficients and Spearman Rank Correlation Coefficients were calculated for each comparison. Pearson's is reported here to enable cross-study comparisons with existing literature, and Spearman's is also reported to account for non-normality of distributions. The Concordance Correlation Coefficient (CCC) was also computed using the Stata "-concord" command. Developed by Lin (1989) as a measure of agreement, the CCC quantifies the degree to which pairs of observations fall on the 45° line through the origin. It contains a measure of precision using the Pearson's Correlation Coefficient, as well as a bias correction for accuracy.

Z-scores were derived for each of the outcome variables to enable cross-measure comparisons on the same scale. Bland–Altman plots were then generated using the Stata "-concord" command (Cox and Steichen, 2007) for all nine comparisons. This plots the mean of the measures against the difference between the measures, as well as the line of mean difference and the 95% limits of agreement. RMA regression (or "ordinary least products" regression) was conducted using the Stata "–concord" command.

The associations between a range of socio-demographic factors and the difference between *z*-scores were estimated using unadjusted and adjusted linear regression. Difference scores were calculated by subtracting one *z*-score from the other, and these were then used as the outcome variables for the regressions. Unadjusted associations were examined, before the adjusted models were tested. Only variables associated with the outcome at $p \leq 0.1$ were included in the adjusted models. All continuous variables were screened for evidence of multicollinearity ($r \geq 0.70$); none were excluded. Factors included in the adjusted models for both cohorts included parent age, child age, child gender, parental education, household income, household unemployment, SEIFA disadvantage score, language other than English and a single-item indicator of child temperament. Additional variables included in the analyses from the Early Home Learning Study dataset were parenting self-efficacy, psychosocial distress, and health-related quality of life. The Stata "-mixed" command was used for this cohort, to account for the cluster-RCT study design and Intraclass Correlation Coefficients were examined.

Finally, quantile regressions were conducted to determine whether the association between the socio-demographic factors and the difference scores varied across the distribution of the difference scores. Associations were examined across the 25th, 50th, and 75th quantiles. Each model was compared to the standard ordinary least squares output and a test for heteroscedasticity was used to determine whether there was evidence against the null hypothesis of constant variance across the quantiles.

Sample Size

Bland (2004) provides a formula to evaluate the precision of the sample size to accurately assess agreement between measures. Bland advises that the 95% confidence interval around the limits for agreement may be estimated as $\pm 1.96\sqrt{\frac{3}{n}}s$ where s is the standard deviation of the differences between measurements by the two methods, and n is the sample size. Bland recommends that a sample size of 100 is adequate for method comparisons. Applying this formula provides excellent precision for the Language for Learning cohort of $N = 201$ (± 0.24 s). For the Early Home Learning Study, direct measures were only available for a subset of the cohort (Early Communication Indicator, $N = 100$; and Indicator of Parent–Child Interactions, $N = 163$) providing adequate precision for comparisons involving these measures (± 0.34 s and ± 0.27 s, respectively).

TABLE 2 | Sample characteristics for participants in each cohort.

Variable	Language for Learning ($n = 201$)	Early Home Learning Study ($n = 218$)
Parent age, years, mean *(SD)*	35.3 (4.4)	32.6 (5.1)
Child age, months, *mean (SD)*	24.4 (1.1)	16.2 (9.3)
Child female, *n (%)*	95 (47.0)	113 (51.8)
Parent marital status n, (%)		
Single/separated/divorced	11 (5.5)	17 (7.8)
Married/de facto	190 (94.5)	201 (92.2)
Household unemployment *n (%)'*	10 (5.0)	18 (8.3)
Parent education, *n (%)*		
Higher education	93 (46.7)	112 (51.4)
No higher education	106 (53.3)	106 (48.6)
LOTE, *n (%)ˆ*	19 (9.5)	46 (21.1)
Household income p/a, *n (%)**		
<$46,800	38 (19.3)	–
$46,800–$70,200	69 (35.0)	–
>$70,200	90 (45.7)	–
<$36,400	–	26 (12.0)
$36,400–51,999	–	36 (16.6)
≥ $52,000	–	147 (67.7)
SEIFA#, *mean (SD)*	1026.6 (54.1)	984.2 (57.9)

*'Single parent unemployed or both parents unemployed; ˆLanguage other than English; *Different categories of income were administered for each sample; #Socio-Economic Index for Areas (SEIFA) Disadvantage score is an indicator of relative disadvantage, based on postcode of residence, accounting for low income, low educational attainment and high unemployment. Lower index scores indicate greater disadvantage.*

RESULTS

Sample

Sample characteristics for each study are summarized in **Table 2**. *Language for Learning*: Nearly half of the parents had completed higher education and fewer than one in 10 families spoke a non-English language. There were approximately equal proportions of male and female children, and more than three-quarters of parents were married. Most parents reported earning a mid to high range household income, with one in five reporting a low income. *Early Home Learning Study*: Similar characteristics were observed in terms of education, marital status and child gender compared to families in the Language for Learning study. However, Early Home Learning Study parents were more likely to be younger, to speak a language other than English, and to live in a household without an employed person. Language for Learning participants were on average, less disadvantaged compared with the Australian mean ($m = 1026.6$) and Early Home Learning Study participants were slightly more disadvantaged ($m = 984.2$); however, there was also a large degree of variation in scores (ranges: 888.2–1117.5 and 816.7–1105.9, respectively).

Descriptive Statistics

The means, standard deviations and ranges for the parent-reported and directly measured behaviors are presented in **Table 3**. Alpha coefficients indicate excellent internal consistency for the SSLM and Preschool Language Scale, consistent with figures reported elsewhere (Zimmerman et al., 2002b; Roy et al., 2005; Zubrick et al., 2007). There was poorer internal consistency for Parental Verbal Responsivity and the Home Activities with Child scales, which is typically expected for measures with few items (Gliem and Gliem, 2003). Children's expressive language standard scores on the Preschool Language Scale ($m = 91.2$, $SD = 12.3$) indicate that, on average, children were performing below the 50th percentile. As shown, direct measures were only available for a sub-sample of participants in the Early Home Learning Study cohort. Due to the financial expenses associated with video coding, the data used in this paper represents a sub-sample of a larger dataset; this sub-sample was selected at random.

Correlations

The strongest correlations were obtained for comparisons involving two parent-reported measures, with moderate positive associations (see **Table 4**). The strongest correlation for any parent-reported and direct comparison was between the

TABLE 3 | Descriptives for parent-reported and directly measured behaviors.

	M (SD)	Range	α	*N* Missing from Total Sample *N*
Child language				
Sure Start Language Measure[a]	35.0 (22.7)	0 to 98	0.97	7/201
Ages and Stages Questionnaire[a*]	0 (1)	−2.8 to 1.1	n/a	1/201
Ages and Stages Questionnaire[b*]	0 (1)	−3.0 to 1.7	n/a	1/218
Communicative Development Inventory[b]	100.4 (9.7)	81.0 to 160.7	n/a	5/218
Preschool Language Scale[a]	91.2 (12.3)	64 to 135	0.86	2/201
Early Communication Indicator[b]	10.1 (7.3)	0.3 to 32.3	n/a	118/218
Parenting behaviors				
Parental Verbal Responsivity[b]	12.9 (2.21)	6 to 16	0.40	0/218
Home Activities with Child[b]	17.1 (2.52)	9 to 20	0.49	0/218
Indicator of Parent–Child Interactions[b]	200.1 (55.3)	50 to 370	n/a	55/218

[a]*Language for Learning;* [b]*Early Home Learning Study;* **Z-Scores were derived to account for different age-appropriate versions.*

TABLE 4 | Pearson's (*r*), Spearman's Rank (ρ) and Lin's Concordance (ρ_c) correlation coefficients for each of the nine comparisons.

	r	ρ	ρ_c
Child language			
(1) Ages and Stages Questionnaire vs. Sure Start Language Measure	0.70***	0.73***	0.70***
(2) Ages and Stages Questionnaire vs. Preschool Language Scale	0.61***	0.59***	0.61***
(3) Sure Start Language Measure vs. Preschool Language Measure	0.56***	0.60***	0.56***
(4) Ages and Stages Questionnaire vs. Communicative Development Inventory	0.44***	0.48***	0.001***
(5) Ages and Stages Questionnaire vs. Early Communication Indicator	0.12	0.16	0.01
(6) Communicative Development Inventory vs. Early Communication Indicator	0.32**	0.33**	0.01**
Parenting behaviors			
(7) Parental Verbal Responsivity vs. Home Activities with Child	0.45***	0.45***	0.17***
(8) Parental Verbal Responsivity vs. Indicator of Parent–Child Interaction	−0.03	−0.04	0.00
(9) Home Activities with Child vs. Indicator of Parent–Child Interaction	0.06	0.08	0.00

***$p \leq 0.001$; **$p \leq 0.01$; *$p < 0.05$.

Ages and Stages Questionnaire (communication subscale) and Preschool Language Scale (expressive language), with a moderate, positive correlation. Weaker associations were obtained for the remaining comparisons, with a moderate positive correlation between the Communicative Development Inventory and the Early Communication Indicator, and a weak non-significant correlation between the Ages and Stages Questionnaire and the Early Communication Indicator. Associations between measures of parenting behaviors were much weaker than the child language comparisons, with near-negligible associations between parent-reported and direct measures. In contrast to the Pearson's and Spearman's coefficients, which produced similar coefficients for each comparison, the Lin's CCC produced markedly smaller correlations for several comparisons. This suggests that, although the measures are associated, the level of *agreement* is much poorer. Lin's correlation line passes through the origin, with a slope of one. Thus, it provides a measure of correspondence between measures, rather than association. As shown in **Table 4**, the Lin's coefficient for two comparisons was close to zero, yet highly significant. The confidence intervals for these comparisons were very narrow, hence the significant *p*-values.

Agreement between Methods

Application of the Bland–Altman Method requires the differences between measures to be approximately normally distributed (Bland and Altman, 2003). Histograms of the differences showed approximate normality, with slight negative skewness evident for the ASQ-ECI and ASQ-CDI, and positive skewness for the PVR-HAC. The association between each of the nine comparisons was examined using scatterplots with a fitted line of equality. Scatterplots suggested a positive, approximately linear relationship whereby higher scores on one measure correspond with increasing scores on the other measure. Exceptions were the PVR-IPCI and HAC-IPCI scatterplots, which did not provide evidence of a linear association. Bland–Altman Plots were generated for each of the nine comparisons (**Figures 1–3**). In each plot, the solid horizontal line represents the mean difference between the measures and the dotted lines represent the 'limits of agreement' within which 95% of data points lie. The overall bias (mean difference) was close to zero for most comparisons, reflecting the scaling of the measures to *z*-scores; we therefore focus on the limits of agreement and patterns of agreement across the range of scores.

Child Language

Figure 1 shows the three Language for Learning comparisons. Plot A shows the agreement between the parent-reported ASQ and the standardized language measure, PLS. The points are widely dispersed around the mid-section, indicating poorer agreement for children with average language abilities. Points are closest to $y = 0$ at the lower end, indicating the strongest agreement for children with the poorest language abilities. Vertical reference lines at $x = -1$ and $x = 1$ have been included for ease of interpretation. At the upper end of the spectrum (scores > 1 on the x axis), points are all below $y = 0$, indicating that the parent-reported ASQ is systematically underestimating children's language, compared to the direct measure (PLS). The limits of agreement tell us that 95% of the points lie between −1.75 and 1.73 standard deviations. Plot B shows the agreement between the parent-reported SSLM and the

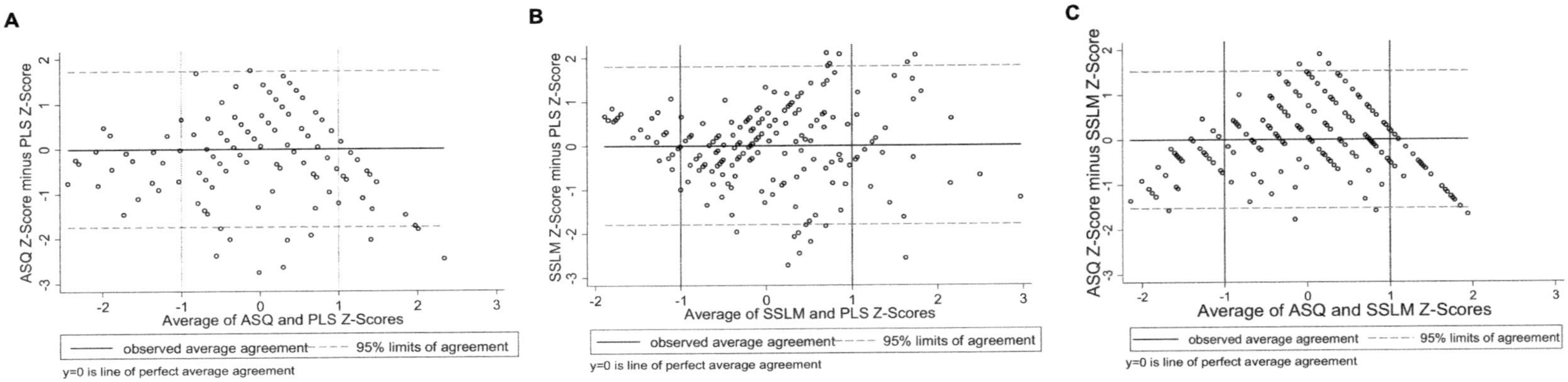

FIGURE 1 | Bland-Altman Plots: (A) Ages and Stages Questionnaire and Preschool Language Scale [95% limits of agreement: −1.75 to 1.73]; **(B)** Sure Start Language Measure and Preschool Language Scale [95% limits of agreement: −1.80 to 1.80]; **(C)** Ages and Stages Questionnaire and Sure Start Language Measure [95% limits of agreement: −1.52 to 1.53].

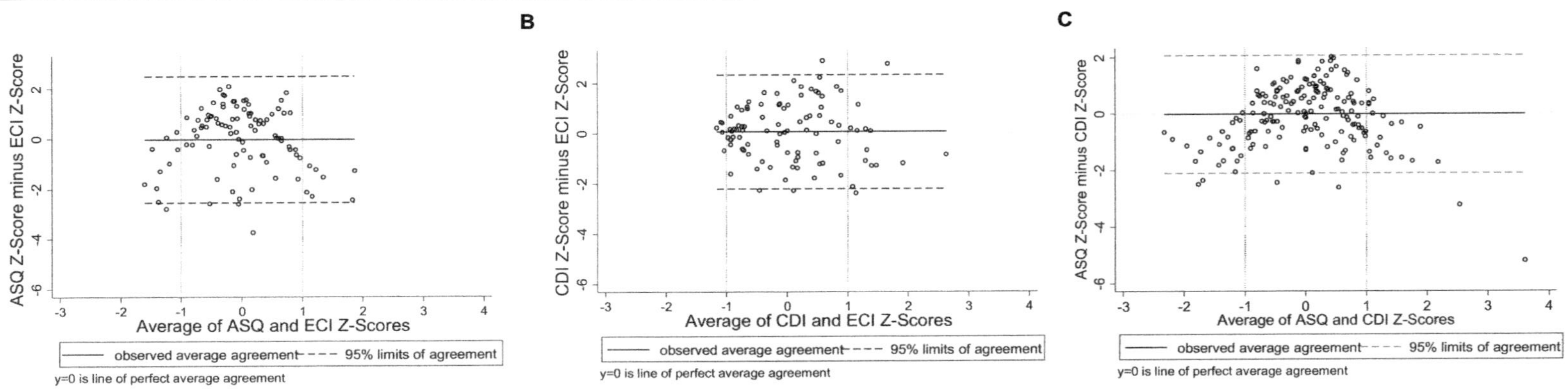

FIGURE 2 | Bland–Altman Plots: (A) Ages and Stages Questionnaire and Early Communication Indicator [95% limits of agreement: −2.55 to 2.48]; **(B)** Communicative Development Inventory and Early Communication Indicator [95% limits of agreement: −2.21 to 2.33]; **(C)** Ages and Stages Questionnaire and Communicative Development Inventory [95% limits of agreement: −2.10 to 2.06].

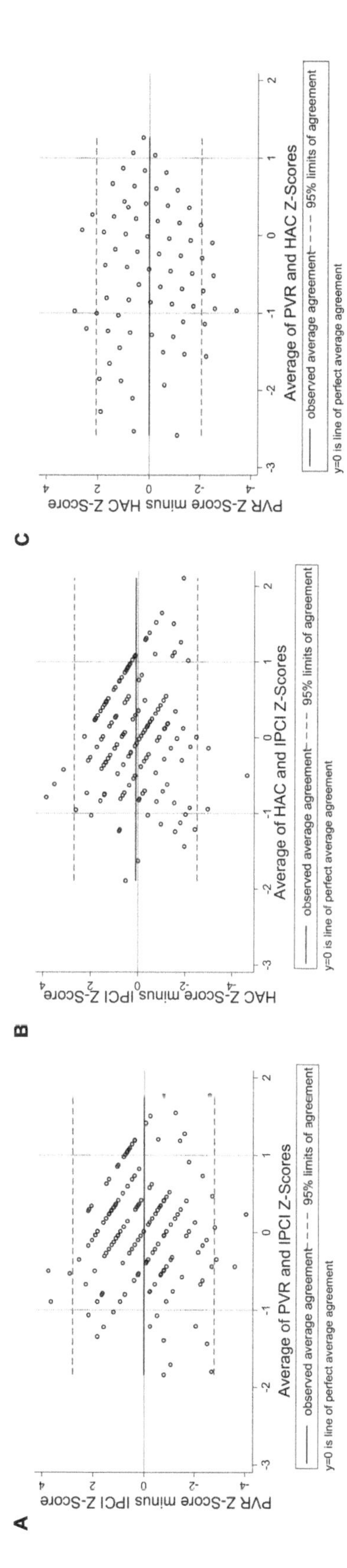

FIGURE 3 | Bland–Altman Plots: (A) Parental Verbal Responsivity and Indicator of Parent–Child Interactions [95% limits of agreement: −2.78 to 2.80]; **(B)** Home Activities with Child and Indicator of Parent–Child Interactions [95% limits of agreement: −2.52 to 2.70]; **(C)** Parental Verbal Responsivity and Home Activities with Child [95% limits of agreement: −2.06 to 2.06].

standardized language measure, the PLS. At the lower end (scores below $x = -1$) points are more tightly clustered around the line $y = 0$, indicating stronger agreement between these measures for children with poorer language abilities. Agreement then appears to deteriorate across the spectrum, as children's average language abilities increase. This is shown by the much wider dispersion of points from $x = 0$ and above. The limits of agreement tell us that 95% of the points lie between −1.80 and 1.80 standard deviations. The strongest agreement of all nine comparisons was found for two parent-reported language measures, the ASQ and the SSLM (Plot C), with the narrowest limits of agreement (−1.53 to 1.53 standard deviations). For children with average language abilities (scores between −1 and 1 on the x-axis) parents both underestimate and overestimate on the ASQ, compared to the SSLM. For children with poorer language abilities (below −1 on the x-axis) and higher average language abilities (above 1 on the x-axis), the ASQ produces lower scores than the SSLM.

Figure 2 shows the three Early Home Learning Study comparisons. Plot A shows the agreement between the parent-reported ASQ and the direct videotaped observation, the ECI. For children with average language abilities, parents are over- and under-estimating their children's language abilities on the ASQ, compared to scores from the directly measured ECI. For children with poorer language abilities (scores below −1 on the x-axis) and stronger language abilities (scores above 1 on the x-axis), most points are positioned below the line $y = 0$. This suggests that parents of children with very poor or very strong average language abilities are underestimating on the ASQ, compared to the directly measured ECI. The limits of agreement tell us that 95% of the points lie between −2.55 and 2.48 standard deviations. A different pattern of agreement is evident between the parent-reported CDI and the ECI (Plot B), whereby the strongest agreement occurred for children with the poorest language ability, and agreement progressively deteriorated as children's language ability improved (95% limits of agreement: −2.21 to 2.33 standard deviations). Not surprisingly, the strongest agreement of the six Early Home Learning Study comparisons was between the two parent-reported measures, the ASQ and the CDI (Plot C) (95% limits of agreement: −2.10 to 2.06 standard deviations). However, the distribution of points suggests that the poorest agreement between the measures is for children with average language abilities (scores between −1 and 1 on the x-axis). For children with poorer average language abilities (scores < -1 on the x-axis) and stronger average language abilities (scores > 1 on the x-axis), the ASQ is underestimating, compared to the SSLM.

Parenting Behaviors

Figure 3 shows poorer agreement between measures of parenting behaviors compared to the child language measures. Plot A presents agreement between the parent-reported PVR and the direct videotaped observation, the IPCI. The more dispersed scatter of points around the mid-section reveals that the poorest agreement is for parents of average responsiveness (95% limits of agreement: −2.78 to 2.80 standard deviations). Parents with poorer average responsiveness (scores < -1 on the x-axis) and parents with stronger average responsiveness (scores > 1 on the

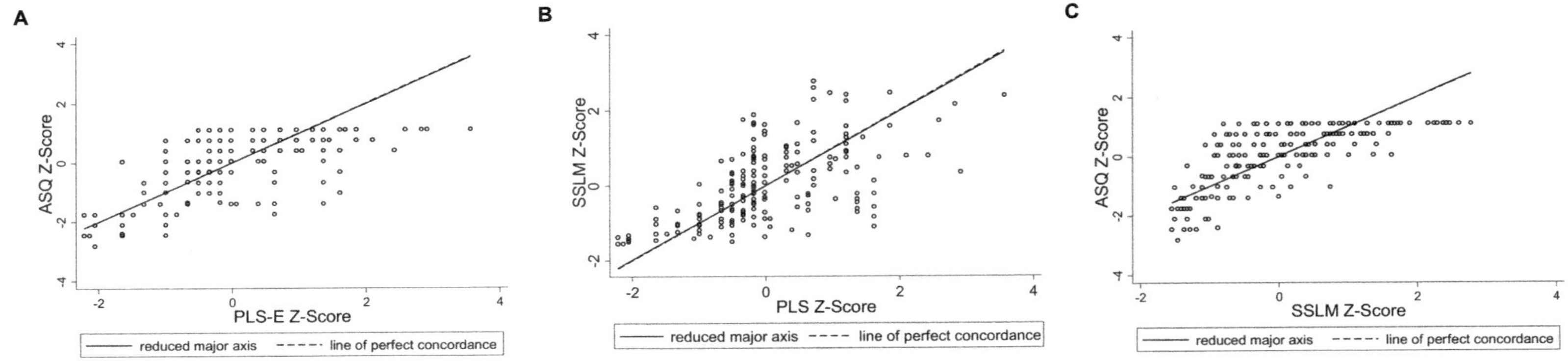

FIGURE 4 | RMA plots: (A) Ages and Stages Questionnaire and Preschool Language Scale, Slope = 0.996; Intercept = −0.009; **(B)** Sure Start Language Measure and Preschool Language Scale, Slope = 0.990; Intercept = −0.001; **(C)** Ages and Stages Questionnaire and Sure Start Language Measure, Slope = 1.005; Intercept = 0.002.

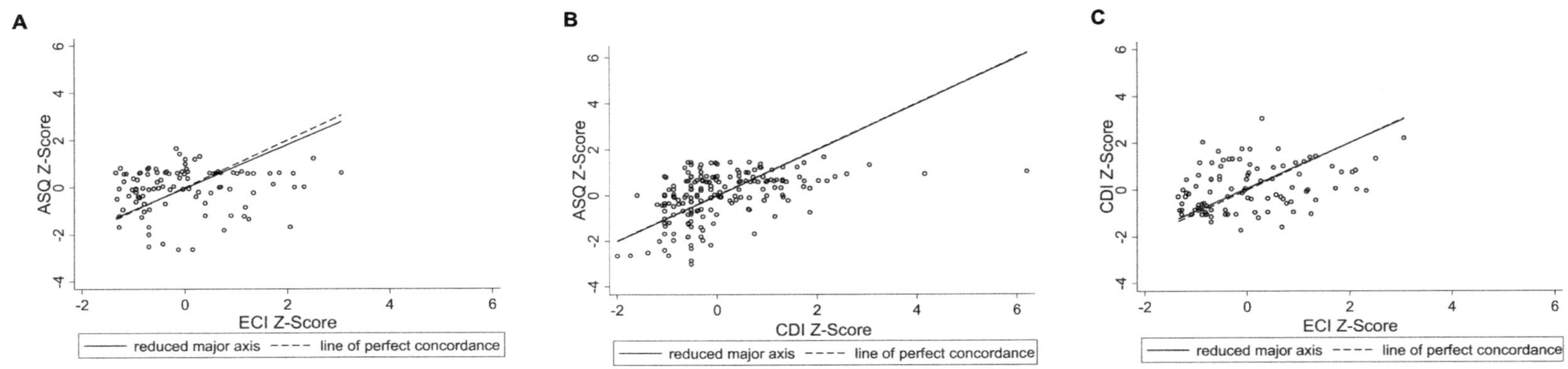

FIGURE 5 | RMA plots: (A) Ages and Stages Questionnaire and Early Communication Indicator, Slope = 0.924; Intercept = −0.036; **(B)** Ages and Stages Questionnaire and Communicative Development Inventory, Slope = 1.000; Intercept = −0.020; **(C)** Communicative Development Inventory and Early Communication Indicator, Slope = 0.967; Intercept = 0.064.

x-axis) tend to underestimate their responsiveness on the PVR, compared to scores on the IPCI. A similar pattern can be seen between the parent-reported HAC and the IPCI (Plot B), with slightly stronger agreement indicated by narrower 95% limits of agreement (−2.52 to 2.70 standard deviations). As shown with the child language comparisons, the strongest agreement between measures of parenting behaviors was between the two parent-reported measures, the PVR and the HAC (Plot C), whereby 95% of the points lie between −2.06 and 2.06 standard deviations. The horizontal scatter of points indicates that the bias between these measures is relatively fixed across the distribution of scores.

Identification of Proportional Bias

Figures 4–6 present the RMA regression plots to identify the presence of proportional bias. As shown in **Figure 4**, the Language for Learning language measures show very minimal proportional bias, evidenced by the slopes which are close to one and the intercepts which are close to zero. The three Early Home Learning Study child language comparisons also show minimal proportional bias; however, **Figure 5A** shows a degree of bias between the parent-reported ASQ and the directly measured videotaped observation, the ECI, indicated by the slight divergence of lines. **Figure 6** shows the three parenting behavior comparisons. Substantial proportional bias is evident between the parent-reported PVR and the directly measured videotaped observation, the IPCI (**Figure 6A**). This is shown by the strong divergence of lines in the plot. The slope of around −1 indicates that for lower PVR scores, IPCI scores are relatively higher, and for lower IPCI scores, PVR scores are relatively higher. Only slight proportional bias can be seen between the parent-reported HAC and the IPCI (**Figure 6B**). **Figure 6C** indicates the absence of proportional bias between the parent-reported PVR and the parent-reported HAC.

Socio-Demographic Factors and Agreement

The results of the adjusted linear regressions are presented in **Table 5** for the Language for Learning cohort and **Tables 6** and **7** for the Early Home Learning cohort (See Supplementary Tables for unadjusted models). Non-significant variables at the unadjusted level ($p > 0.1$) were excluded from the adjusted analyses. The outcome variables in all regression analyses are difference scores, calculated by subtracting one *z*-score from another. The intraclass correlations from the multilevel mixed-effects linear regression for each outcome measure (Early Home Learning Study cohort) ranged from 0.00 to 0.22. This reflected the cluster randomized controlled trial design and was accounted for in the regression models.

Child Language (Language for Learning Cohort)

Child age was a significant predictor of difference scores for this cohort. Parents of older children tended to report higher child language scores on the parent-reported ASQ and SSLM, compared to scores generated by the directly measured PLS. Older child age was also associated with lower scores on the ASQ, compared with the SSLM. The included predictors explained nearly twice the amount of variance in difference scores for the

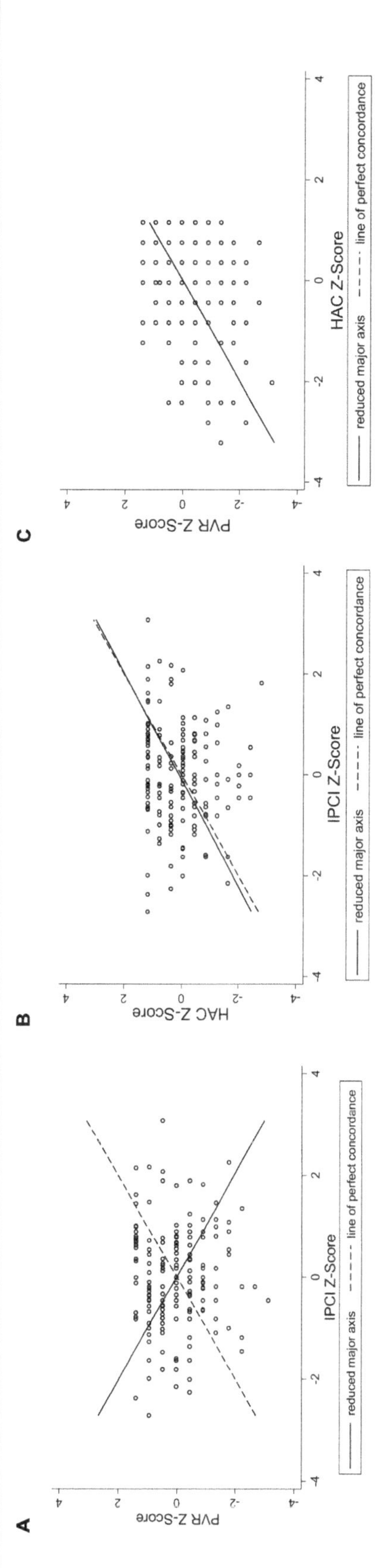

FIGURE 6 | RMA plots: (A) Parental Verbal Responsivity and Indicator of Parent–Child Interactions, Slope = −0.98; Intercept = 0.012; **(B)** Home Activities with Child and Indicator of Parent–Child Interactions, Slope = 0.94; Intercept = 0.09; **(C)** Parental Verbal Responsivity and Home Activities with Child, Slope = 1.00; Intercept = 0.00.

TABLE 5 | Adjusted analysis for Language for Learning difference scores and socio-demographic factors.

	ASQ vs. PLS-E			SSLM vs. PLS-E			ASQ vs. SSLM		
	Coefficient	*p*	95% CI	Coefficient	*p*	95% CI	Coefficient	*p*	95% CI
Parent age (years)	*	*	*	*	*	*	0.03	0.05	0.00, 0.05
Child age (months)	0.23	<0.001	0.12, 0.34	0.35	<0.001	0.23, 0.46	−0.13	0.02	−0.24, −0.02
Child gender (female)	*	*	*	0.18	0.14	−0.06, 0.42	*	*	*
Single parent	*	*	*	0.37	0.24	−0.24, 0.98	*	*	*
Household unemployment	*	*	*	*	*	*	−0.20	0.50	−0.79, 0.38
No higher education	*	*	*	*	*	*	*	*	*
Income									
Low vs. mid	*	*	*	−0.22	0.25	−0.59, 0.16	0.27	0.12	−0.07, 0.61
Low vs. high	*	*	*	−0.33	0.08	−0.70, 0.04	0.38	0.02	0.06, 0.71
SEIFA/100 (less disadvantage)	−0.23	0.05	−0.46, 0.00	−0.15	0.22	−0.39, 0.09	*	*	*
LOTE	*	*	*	*	*	*	0.29	0.15	−0.11, 0.69
Difficult child temperament	*	*	*	*	*	*	−0.18	0.02	−0.33, −0.03
	$R^2 = 0.09$			$R^2 = 0.19$			$R^2 = 0.10$		

**Excluded due to p > 0.1 at univariate level; LOTE, Language other than English. ASQ = Ages and Stages Questionnaire, communication subscale; PLS-E = Preschool Language Scale, expressive language score; SSLM = Sure Start Language Measure.*

TABLE 6 | Adjusted analysis for the Early Home Learning Study difference scores and socio-demographic factors (child language measures).

	ASQ vs. ECI			CDI vs. ECI			ASQ vs. CDI		
	Coefficient	*p*	95% CI	Coefficient	*p*	95% CI	Coefficient	*p*	95% CI
Parent age (years)	*	*	*	*	*	*	*	*	*
Child age (months)	−0.09	<0.001	−0.12, −0.06	−0.07	<0.001	−0.10, −0.04	*	*	*
Child gender (female)	0.24	0.24	−0.16, 0.64	*	*	*	*	*	*
Single parent	*	*	*	*	*	*	*	*	*
Household unemployment	*	*	*	*	*	*	*	*	*
No higher education	*	*	*	*	*	*	*	*	*
Income									
Low vs. mid	*	*	*	*	*	*	*	*	*
Low vs. high	*	*	*	*	*	*	*	*	*
SEIFA/100 (less disadvantage)	*	*	*	*	*	*	*	*	*
LOTE	*	*	*	*	*	*	0.31	0.08	−0.04, 0.66
Difficult child temperament	−0.50	0.05	−0.99, −0.01	−0.51	0.02	−0.95, −0.07	*	*	*
High parenting self-efficacy	0.06	0.63	−0.18, 0.30	*	*	*	*	*	*
Poor health-related quality of life	−0.07	0.54	−0.29, 0.15	−0.10	0.34	−0.31, 0.11	*	*	*
Greater psychological distress	*	*	*	*	*	*	*	*	*
	$R^2 = 0.40$			$R^2 = 0.33$			$R^2 = 0.01$		

**Excluded due to p > 0.1 at univariate level; LOTE, Language other than English. ASQ = Ages and Stages Questionnaire, communication subscale; ECI = Early Communication Indicator; CDI = Communicative Development Inventory.*

SSLM and PLS ($R^2 = 0.19$, 19%), compared to the ASQ and PLS (9%) and the ASQ and SSLM (10%).

Child Language (Early Home Learning Study Cohort)

Child age and temperament predicted the difference scores between the parent-reported ASQ and the directly measured ECI, as well as the parent-reported CDI and ECI. For both comparisons, older child age was associated with lower scores on the ASQ and CDI, compared to the ECI. Parents who perceived their child as more difficult also tended to report lower scores on the ASQ and CDI, compared with the ECI. The included predictors explained negligible variance in difference scores between the two parent-reported measures, the ASQ and the CDI ($R^2 = 0.01$, 1%), but explained substantial variance between the ASQ and ECI (40%) and the CDI and ECI (33%).

Parenting Behaviors (Early Home Learning Study Cohort)

The differences between measures of parenting behaviors were associated with parent age and English language status. Parents who spoke a language other than English were more likely than native English speakers to report greater parental responsiveness on a parent questionnaire (PVR or HAC), compared to scores

TABLE 7 | Adjusted analysis for the Early Home Learning Study difference scores and socio-demographic factors (parenting behavior measures).

	PVR vs. IPCI			HAC vs. IPCI			PVR vs HAC		
	Coefficient	*p*	95% CI	Coefficient	*p*	95% CI	Coefficient	*p*	95% CI
Parent age (years)	−0.04	0.07	−0.08, 0.00	−0.04	0.02	−0.08, 0.00	*	*	*
Child age (months)	−0.01	0.32	−0.04, 0.01	*	*	*	−0.02	<0.01	−0.04, −0.01
Child gender (female)	*	*	*	−0.47	0.02	−0.85, −0.09	*	*	*
Single parent	*	*	*	*	*	*	*	*	*
Household unemployment	*	*	*	*	*	*	*	*	*
No higher education	0.53	0.01	0.12, 0.93	*	*	*	*	*	*
Income									
Low vs. mid	*	*	*	*	*	*	*	*	*
Low vs. high	*	*	*	*	*	*	*	*	*
SEIFA/100 (less disadvantage)	*	*	*	*	*	*	*	*	*
LOTE	1.23	<0.001	0.66, 1.79	1.09	<0.001	0.56, 1.62	*	*	*
Difficult child temperament	−0.43	0.11	−0.96, 0.10	*	*	*	−0.10	0.59	−0.46, 0.26
Low parenting self-efficacy	0.17	0.16	−0.07, 0.40	*	*	*	*	*	*
Poor health-related quality of life	*	*	*	*	*	*	*	*	*
Greater psychological distress	*	*	*	*	*	*	*	*	*
	$R^2 = 0.18$			$R^2 = 0.14$			$R^2 = 0.05$		

**Excluded due to p > 0.1 at univariate level; LOTE, Language other than English. PVR = Parental Verbal Responsivity scale; IPCI = Indicator of Parent-Child Interactions, positive caregiver score; HAC = Home Activities with Child scale.*

generated from the directly measured IPCI. Older parents were also more likely to report less parent responsiveness on the parent-reported PVR and HAC, compared with scores on the IPCI. The included predictors explained minimal variance in difference scores: PVR and IPCI ($R^2 = 0.18$, 18%); HAC and IPCI: (14%); PVR and HAC (5%).

Socio-Demographic Factors across Quantiles of Agreement

Quantile regression analyses provided scant evidence that the association between the socio-demographic factors and the difference scores varied across the distribution of the difference scores. The Breusch–Pagen/Cook–Weisberg test for heteroscedasticity provided non-significant *p*-values for eight of the nine comparisons (Language for Learning: ASQ-PLS, $p = 0.40$; SSLM-PLS, $p = 0.16$; ASQ-SSLM, $p = 0.31$ and Early Home Learning Study: ASQ-ECI, $p = 0.20$; ASQ-CDI, $p = 0.12$; CDI-ECI, $p = 0.87$; PVR-IPCI, $p = 0.87$; PVR-HAC, $p = 0.11$). This suggests that the standard Ordinary Least Squares regression is sufficient for quantifying these associations. However, associations did vary across the distribution of difference scores for the HAC-IPCI comparison ($p = 0.03$). Closer inspection of the HAC-IPCI comparison revealed that income (low vs. mid income), varied across the quantiles of difference (25th quantile: coefficient = 0.27, $p = 0.68$; 50th quantile: coefficient = −0.64, $p = 0.30$; 75th quantile: coefficient = −1.44, $p = 0.01$). That is, participants with a low income were more likely to have a large difference between HAC and IPCI scores, compared to participants with a mid-range income. This finding should be interpreted with caution; given the number of comparisons made, it is potentially attributable to chance.

DISCUSSION

This is the first study to specifically examine agreement between parent-reported and directly measured behaviors using the Bland–Altman Method and RMA regression. Nine comparisons were conducted using data from two independent Australian cohorts (six child language and three parenting behaviors). Although correlational findings were consistent with extant literature, Bland–Altman plots revealed substantial variation in agreement between parent-reported and directly measured child language and parenting behaviors across the distribution of scores. Agreement was generally stronger for children with poorer or exceptional language abilities, and weaker for children with average language abilities. Particularly for comparisons involving the ASQ, parents tended to underestimate their children's language abilities, when children's language was either poor or exceptional. Agreement between measures of parenting behaviors was slightly weaker than child language. Proportional bias between child language measures was minimal, but considerable bias was evident between parent-reported and directly measured parenting behaviors. Differences between child language measures were associated with child age and temperament, and differences between parenting behavior measures were associated with parent age and speaking a language other than English. Findings provide strong evidence that simple correlations are grossly insufficient for method comparisons.

Child Language

Findings suggest that parent-reported measures are most accurate for children who display either language difficulties or exceptional language abilities. Overall, the strongest agreement was observed for children with the poorest language. This may reflect parental concern and a tendency to more closely observe and monitor child development. Children at either end of the language spectrum may "stand out" from their peers. Reflecting the phenomenon identified in Festinger's (1954) Social Comparison Theory, parents may rely on social comparisons to inform their decision about their children's development. Children whose abilities reflect the norm may not generate the same close attention from their parents as children at either end of the spectrum. The variability in child language in the early years is well-established (Ukoumunne et al., 2012), however, it is possible that children at the extreme ends of the spectrum are more stable in their language over time, supporting more accurate measurement for these groups. Whereas parent-reported measures may be sufficient to identify children with very poor or very strong language skills, multiple or gold standard direct measures would be necessary to delineate the language skills of children across the mid ranges of child language.

It should be noted that for comparisons involving the ASQ (**Figures 1A,C** and **2A,C**) parents tended to underestimate children's language abilities for children with very poor or exceptional language. This may reflect the limited variability captured by the ASQ, given that it is a six-item measure scored on a 3-point scale. For comparisons involving the CDI or the UK version of the CDI (SSLM), a different pattern emerged, whereby agreement with direct measures was stronger for children with poorer language ability and progressively worsened as children's language abilities strengthened. This may reflect a ceiling effect for this commonly used parent-reported measure of expressive vocabulary, where variation in children with exceptional skills cannot be accurately captured. Indeed, the potential for ceiling effects on the CDI for children aged 27 months and above has been reported elsewhere, particularly for children with more advanced language (Fenson et al., 2000). Together, these findings suggest that accurately capturing the full spectrum of language abilities using parent-reported measures with a small number of items may be problematic.

The strongest agreement between child language measures was for the Language for Learning cohort. This may reflect the study sample of slow-to-talk toddlers, as well as the use of a standardized language assessment for this cohort, compared with the videotaped observational measure used in the Early Home Learning Study cohort. Some disagreement between measures may be attributable to differences in the constructs captured using each measure. While the SSLM, Communicative Development Inventory, and Preschool Language Scale specifically measure children's expressive language, the Early Communication Indicator and Ages and Stages Questionnaire include some aspects of non-verbal communication. For example, the Early Communication Indicator includes the frequency of a child's communicative gestures, as well as vocalizations, single words and multiple words. The Ages and Stages communication subscales include items which measure both expressive and receptive language. The RMA plots provided a clear means of identifying the presence of proportional bias; the six child language plots showed minimal proportional bias, suggesting that any bias between the measures was relatively consistent across the distribution of scores.

The strongest predictor of the difference between language measures was child age; however, the direction of this association varied for each cohort. Parents of older children in the Language for Learning cohort tended to report higher scores on parent-reported measures, whereas parents of older children in the Early Home Learning Study cohort tended to report higher scores on the direct measure. Previous research has shown that parents' ability to accurately report on their child's language development may deteriorate as children grow older and their vocabulary expands and language use becomes more complex (Law and Roy, 2008). Differences between these cohorts may also be attributable to the child age ranges (24 months and 6–36 months, respectively), as well as the nature of the selected measures. For example, parents of children aged less than 18 months participating in the Early Home Learning Study were asked about receptive as well as expressive vocabulary. In addition, the Early Communication Indicator only assessed *observable* features, such as gestures, vocalizations, single and multiple words. Regardless, it is remarkable that child age was such a highly significant predictor for the Language for Learning cohort, given the narrow range of child ages ($M = 24.4$ months; $SD = 1.1$ months). At this young age, language develops rapidly and a small amount of time can result in quite different language scores. This finding highlights the complexity of measuring language in young children, as well as the importance of selecting measures specific to child age in years and months.

Temperament also emerged as a predictor of child language difference scores, particularly for the Early Home Learning Study cohort. Perhaps surprisingly, more difficult child temperament was generally associated with less discrepancy between language measures. This may be due to parents of children with challenging behaviors having greater awareness of their child's behavior and development, permitting greater accuracy in parent-reported measures. Again, this could be more apparent through parents' use of social comparison with the child's peers. It is also possible that children with behavioral difficulties are the children with poorer language abilities, for whom the strongest agreement was evident. Indeed, there is evidence that language and behavioral difficulties can occur comorbidly (Carpenter and Drabick, 2011). The nature of the assessment – structured assessment or videotaped observation – as well as the presence of the researcher in the home, may also contribute to differences between measures of children's expressive language.

Parenting Behaviors

Slightly poorer agreement was observed between measures of parenting behaviors compared to the language measures. We found relatively strong agreement between the parent-reported Home Activities with Child and the Indicator of Parent–Child Interactions Positive Caregiver Score, compared with the parent-reported Parental Verbal Responsivity and the IPCI. As a four-item measure, the PVR performed more poorly as an indicator of parental responsiveness, whereby a ceiling effect led to restricted variation in scores. This measure also showed low internal consistency, making it a less reliable measure.

Both the PVR and HAC showed a tendency to underestimate parental responsiveness at the lower and upper extremes. Overall, our findings suggest that a brief parent-reported measure of the frequency of engagement in parent-child activities in the home (HAC) may represent a reliable indicator of parental responsiveness and engagement, which shows relatively good agreement with a comprehensive observational measure. For studies with limited resources, the HAC could be a feasible alternative to time-intensive and costly observation required for the IPCI. It should be acknowledged that some disagreement between the measures of parenting behaviors could be explained by differences in the construct being measured or coded. For example, the PVR measures parents' *verbal* responsiveness specifically, whereas the HAC assesses parent engagement and responsiveness more broadly, including both verbal and non-verbal behaviors. Both the PVR and HAC ask parents about the frequency with which they engage in everyday activities, such as reading books or talking about the day during mealtimes. The Positive Caregiver Total score derived from the IPCI captured the frequency of both verbal and non-verbal parenting behaviors, such as using descriptive language, and following the child's lead (i.e., quantity and quality of parenting behaviors).

Language other than English was the strongest explanatory factor of the difference between parent-reported and directly measured parenting behaviors. Families with a non-English speaking background tended to report lower scores on the directly measured videotaped observation, the IPCI, and higher scores on both the PVR and HAC. This may be attributable to potential acquiescence (i.e., consistently indicating positive responses). Acquiescence has been shown to vary cross-culturally, for example, strong cultural preferences to avoid uncertainty can lead to a tendency to select more extreme values (Smith, 2004). Findings may also reflect cultural differences in the frequency with which parents and children engage in the activities being measured (e.g., HAC: "telling stories to your child" or PVR: "playing peek-a-boo or hide-and-seek"). It is also possible that parents and children with a non-English speaking background felt less comfortable than native English speakers during the videotaped activities. Furthermore, these differences could be attributable to difficulties understanding the verbal instructions of the videotaped activities, or difficulties in coding parent utterances during these activities. Lastly, we acknowledge that parents' English proficiency may vary to that of the child, particularly in early childhood when children have not yet been exposed to English in the school environment.

The small proportion of variance explained by the socio-demographic factors for parenting behaviors suggests that other unmeasured factors may be responsible for differences between these measures. The current study was limited by the data collected in the two datasets analyzed; it is possible that other factors may have greater explanatory power than variables assessed in these studies. For example, the parent or child's unique and subjective experience of the assessments, understanding of the task requirements or the questionnaire items, cultural factors affecting parent–child interactions, discomfort during the assessment, rapport with the assessor, experiences of fatigue or illness at the time of the assessment or external factors causing stress or distraction may have been more relevant predictors of agreement. Quantile regression analyses revealed that the associations between the socio-demographic factors and the difference scores remained stable across the quantiles of agreement. The only exception was the comparison between the parent-reported HAC and the directly measured videotaped observation, the IPCI. Greater discrepancy between these measures was associated with parents with a lower income. The five HAC items refer to everyday parent–child activities; however, many of these activities require resources such as books and toys, which may be less readily available for parents who have a very low income. Indeed, this link between families of a lower socio-economic status and the provision of a less stimulating home environment is well-established (e.g., Davis-Kean, 2005).

Implications

This study provides evidence to guide the selection of appropriate measures for parents and their children aged 6–36 months. Method comparisons such as this are critical for supporting the collection of high data quality and the appropriate allocation of limited resources. Our data suggest that brief parent-reported measures of child language may be used with reasonable confidence for children up to 3 years of age. Particularly for children who are slow-to-talk, parent-reported measures may provide an accurate and cost-effective means of monitoring development over time. Findings indicate that agreement between measures of parenting behaviors is generally poorer than child language measures. Parenting behaviors can be difficult to accurately measure, given that social desirability can cause parents to consciously or unconsciously change the way they respond on parent-reported questionnaires (Zaslow et al., 2006; Law and Roy, 2008), or the way they behave during observations (Arney, 2004). It is also conceivable that parents are more able to objectively report on their child's language but are less objective when evaluating their own behaviors (e.g., parenting responsiveness). Despite this, the parent-reported Home Activities with Child measure showed relatively strong agreement with the direct videotaped observation, the Indicator of Parent–Child Interactions, with minimal proportional bias. This suggests that measuring the frequency of developmentally beneficial activities such as reading, story-telling, singing, or involving the child in everyday tasks at home, provides a valid indication of parents' general level of engagement and responsiveness.

When selecting measures, it is important to consider the purpose for which the data is being generated; a brief parent-reported measure of children's expressive language or communicative development such as the SSLM, Communicative Development Inventory or Ages and Stages Questionnaire may be sufficient for large-scale studies where time and resources are limited and a large pool of data is required. Whereas a clinician making decisions about treatment options for a young child may be best to draw on both direct and parent-reported measures to ensure a comprehensive assessment.

The study has significant implications for the analysis of method comparisons. We demonstrate how the Bland–Altman Method and RMA regression permit a comprehensive assessment of agreement across the distribution of scores. While correlational analyses reported here were comparable to those reported elsewhere for similar constructs, analyses using the Bland–Altman Method and RMA regression clearly show how correlations have the potential to be misleading. Correlations represent a single figure which summarizes association across the spectrum of scores, whereas agreement may vary between higher and lower scores. The level of detail generated by these more comprehensive techniques is crucial for identifying groups of children or parents for whom one method may be sufficient (in the case of strong agreement), or for whom multiple methods or an agreed "gold standard" measure may be necessary (in the case of poor agreement).

Strengths and Limitations

To our knowledge, this is the first study to apply the Bland–Altman Method to a comparison of parent-reported and directly measured behaviors. This technique permitted the identification of patterns of bias across the distribution of scores. As a result, we were able to identify groups of children or parents for whom multi-method administration may be necessary, or for whom one method of measurement may be permissible. Rarely used in non-medical fields, the Bland–Altman method represents a relatively simple and visually appealing technique. The approach lends itself to other comparisons such as parent-, teacher-, and child-report of the same questionnaire (e.g., Gabbe et al., 2010; Stolarova et al., 2014), or comparisons of the same measure across time points (e.g., Eadie et al., 2014). Another strength is the use of RMA regression to identify the magnitude of proportional bias between methods. Together, Bland–Altman and RMA regression plots represent powerful visuals for comparing measures which can be executed and interpreted with relative ease. The use of quantile regression analyses also allowed us to determine whether associations between socio-demographic factors and agreement varied across quantiles of agreement, which is not possible using standard ordinary least squares regression.

We acknowledge that we were limited to the measures available within existing datasets, and therefore cannot presume agreement findings are generalizable to other measures of child language and parenting behaviors. Despite this, our measures are commonly used and well-validated. It should be noted that the PLS-4 was only normed on US data at the time of data collection; no Australian norms were available. Data also pertained to a sample of toddlers identified as "slow-to-talk" at age 18 months, and another sample of families experiencing social disadvantage; different populations may yield different results. We also recognize that each of the measures used in this study will, naturally, capture slightly different aspects of child language or parental responsiveness. As with any method comparison, total agreement is not expected, nor is it feasible to strive for this; some degree of measurement error is inevitable (Bland and Altman, 1999). Regardless, method comparisons are critical for determining whether measures are potentially interchangeable, and may contribute to more effective allocation of limited resources and strengthened data quality.

Future Research

We suggest that researchers consider applying these techniques to method comparisons of other commonly used early childhood language measures, such as Clinical Evaluation of Language Fundamentals (CELF), and with larger sample sizes where possible to ensure greater precision around the limits of agreement. Our future research will employ qualitative methodologies to determine how parents' unique and subjective experiences of assessments may further explain and contextualize agreement findings. This is particularly important given that a broad range of socio-demographic factors explained little variability in the difference scores for a number of measures. It is possible that parents and children vary in their level of comfort when behaviors are being measured directly (i.e., videotaped observations or standardized assessments), especially for participants who are not native English speakers. Exploring this qualitatively could go some way to understanding agreement and supporting data collection methods which optimize the validity of parent and child data.

CONCLUSION

This study demonstrates how well-established statistical techniques from non-psychology disciplines can be applied to method comparisons in the field of psychology. The Bland–Altman Method is a useful visual technique for detecting bias and for determining potential interchangeability between measurement methods, which can be used in combination with RMA regression to identify the presence of both fixed and proportional bias. Although we found correlations which were consistent with previous comparisons of child language and parenting behaviors, agreement varied substantially across the distribution of scores, demonstrating the need for these more comprehensive techniques. On the whole, poorer agreement was observed for children with average expressive language abilities, and stronger agreement was observed for children with very poor or more advanced language abilities. Slightly poorer agreement was observed between measures of parenting behaviors, with the weakest agreement seen for parents of average responsiveness. As would be expected, stronger agreement was observed between comparisons of two parent-reported measures. Further research is required to determine agreement between other commonly used measures and how the participant experience may explain agreement between parent-reported and directly measured behaviors. We recommend that journal editors encourage the use of the Bland–Altman Method and RMA regression techniques and discourage the use of correlations for method comparisons.

AUTHOR CONTRIBUTIONS

SB was responsible for leading the preparation of this manuscript. SB, FM, EW, NH, and SR all made substantial contributions to the study design, analysis, interpretation, writing and revision of the manuscript. All authors provided approval for publication.

ACKNOWLEDGMENTS

We thank the Language for Learning and Early Home Learning Study project teams and all participating families, and acknowledge the support of the NHMRC-funded Centre of Research Excellence in Child Language (#1023493). The Early Home Learning Study was funded by the Department of Early Education and Childhood Development (DEECD) and conducted by the Parenting Research Centre. The authors gratefully acknowledge the support of the Parenting Research Centre in providing access to this data. We also thank A/Prof Kathleen Baggett, A/Prof Jay Buzhardt and research staff at The University of Kansas for coding the videotaped data collected for the Early Home Learning Study. SB is a Ph.D. Candidate, supported by the NHMRC-funded Centre of Research Excellence in Child Language (#1023493), FM is a Biostatistician supported by an NHMRC Early Career Fellowship (#1037449) and Career Development Fellowship (#1111160), SR is supported by an NHMRC Practitioner Fellowship (#1041892) and SB, EW, and NH are supported by Australian Communities Foundation through the Roberta Holmes Transition to Contemporary Parenthood Program (Coronella sub-fund) at La Trobe University. The contents of the published material herein are the sole responsibility of the authors and do not reflect the views of the NHMRC. Research at the Murdoch Childrens Research Institute is supported by the Victorian Government's Operational Infrastructure Support Program.

REFERENCES

Altman, D., and Bland, M. (1983). Measurement in medicine: the analysis of method comparison studies. *Statistician* 32, 307–317. doi: 10.2307/2987937

Arney, F. (2004). *A Comparison of Direct Observation and Self-Report Measures of Parenting Behaviour*. Ph.D. thesis, Adelaide University, Adelaide, SA.

Aspland, H., and Gardner, F. (2003). Observational measures of parent-child interaction: an introductory review. *Child Adolesc. Ment. Health* 8, 136–143. doi: 10.1111/1475-3588.00061

Australian Bureau of Statistics (2011). *Socio-Economic Indexes for Areas (SEIFA)*. Available at: http://www.abs.gov.au/ausstats/abs@.nsf/mf/2033.0.55.001 [accessed May 5, 2016]

Baggett, K., and Carta, J. (2006). Using assessment to guide social-emotional intervention for very young children: an individual growth and development indicator (IGDI) of parent-child interaction. *Young Except. Child. Monogr. Ser.* 8, 67–76.

Bennetts, S. K., Mensah, F. K., Westrupp, E. M., Hackworth, N., Nicholson, J. M., and Reilly, S. (in press). Establishing agreement between parent-reported and directly measured behaviours. *Aust. J. Early Child.*

Bland, M. (2004). *How Can I Decide the Sample Size for a Study of Agreement between Two Methods of Measurement?*. Available at: https://www-users.york.ac.uk/~mb55/meas/sizemeth.htm [accessed May 19, 2016].

Bland, M., and Altman, D. (1986). Statistical methods for assessing agreement between two methods of clinical measurement. *Lancet* 327, 307–310. doi: 10.1016/S0140-6736(86)90837-8

Bland, M., and Altman, D. (1999). Measuring agreement in method comparison studies. *Stat. Methods Med. Res.* 8, 135–160. doi: 10.1177/096228029900800204

Bland, M., and Altman, D. (2003). Applying the right statistics: analyses of measurement studies. *Ultrasound Obstet. Gynecol.* 22, 85–93. doi: 10.1002/uog.122

Campbell, F., and Ramey, C. (1994). Effects of early intervention on intellectual and academic achievement: a follow-up study of children from low-income families. *Child Dev.* 65, 684–698. doi: 10.2307/1131410

Carpenter, J. L., and Drabick, D. A. G. (2011). Co-occurrence of linguistic and behavioural difficulties in early childhood: a developmental psychopathology perspective. *Early Child Dev. Care* 181, 1021–1045. doi: 10.1080/03004430.2010.509795

Carstensen, B. (2010). *Comparing Clinical Measurement Methods: A Practical Guide*. Chichester: John Wiley & Sons Ltd.

Carta, J., Greenwood, C., Walker, D., and Buzhardt, J. (2010). *Using IGDIs: Monitoring Progress and Improving Intervention for Infants and Young Children*. Baltimore, MD: Brookes Publishing Company.

Cartmill, E., Armstrong, B., Gleitman, L., Goldin-Meadow, S., Medina, T., and Trueswell, J. (2013). Quality of early parent input predicts child vocabulary 3 years later. *Proc. Natl. Acad. Sci. U.S.A.* 110, 11278–11283. doi: 10.1073/pnas.1309518110

Ching, T. Y., Leigh, G., and Dillon, H. (2013). Introduction to the longitudinal outcomes of children with hearing impairment (LOCHI) study: background, design, sample characteristics. *Int. J. Audiol.* 52(Suppl. 2), S4–S9. doi: 10.3109/14992027.2013.866342

Cox, N., and Steichen, T. J. (2007). *CONCORD: Stata Module for Concordance Correlation*. Available at: https://ideas.repec.org/c/boc/bocode/s404501.html

Davis-Kean, P. E. (2005). The influence of parent education and family income on child achievement: the indirect role of parental expectations and the home environment. *J. Fam. Psychol.* 19:294. doi: 10.1037/0893-3200.19.2.294

Dreyer, B. P., Mendelsohn, A. L., and Tamis-LeMonda, C. S. (1996). Assessing the child's cognitive home environment through parental report; reliability and validity. *Early Dev. Parent.* 5, 271–287. doi: 10.1002/(SICI)1099-0917(199612)5:4<271::AID-EDP138>3.3.CO;2-4

Eadie, P., Nguyen, C., Carlin, J., Bavin, E., Bretherton, L., and Reilly, S. (2014). Stability of language performance at 4 and 5 years: measurement and participant variability. *Int. J. Lang. Commun. Disord.* 49, 215–227. doi: 10.1111/1460-6984.12065

Feldman, H., Dollaghan, C., Campbell, T., Kurs-Lasky, M., Janosky, J., and Paradise, J. (2000). Measurement properties of the MacArthur communicative development inventories at ages one and two years. *Child Dev.* 71, 310–322. doi: 10.1111/1467-8624.00146

Fenson, L., Pethick, S., Renda, C., Cox, J. L., Dale, P. S., and Reznick, S. J. (2000). Short-form versions of the MacArthur communicative development inventories. *Appl. Psycholinguist.* 21, 95–116. doi: 10.1017/S0142716400001053

Festinger, L. (1954). A theory of social comparison processes. *Hum. Relat.* 7, 117–140. doi: 10.1177/001872675400700202

Gabbe, B., Simpson, P., Sutherland, A., Palmer, C., Butt, W., Bevan, C., et al. (2010). Agreement between parent and child report of health-related quality of life: impact of time postinjury. *J. Trauma Acute Care Surg.* 69, 1578–1582. doi: 10.1097/TA.0b013e3181f8fd5f

Gardner, F. (1997). Observational methods for recording parent-child interaction: how generalisable are the findings? *Child Adolesc. Ment. Health* 2, 70–74. doi: 10.1111/j.1475-3588.1997.tb00049.x

Gardner, F. (2000). Methodological issues in the direct observation of parent–child interaction: do observational findings reflect the natural behavior of participants? *Clin. Child Fam. Psychol. Rev.* 3, 185–198. doi: 10.1023/A:1009503409699

Gartstein, M., and Marmion, J. (2008). Fear and positive affectivity in infancy: convergence/discrepancy between parent-report and laboratory-based indicators. *Infant Behav. Dev.* 31, 227–238. doi: 10.1016/j.infbeh.2007.10.012

Gliem, J. A., and Gliem, R. R. (2003). Calculating, interpreting, and reporting Cronbach's alpha reliability coefficient for Likert-type scales. *Paper presented at the Midwest Research-to-Practice Conference in Adult, Continuing, and Community Education*, Ohio State University, Columbus, OH.

Greenwood, C. R., Walker, D., and Buzhardt, J. (2010). The Early Communication Indicator for infants and toddlers: early Head Start growth norms from two states. *J. Early Interv.* 32, 310–334. doi: 10.1177/1053815110392335

Hawes, D., and Dadds, M. (2006). Assessing parenting practices through parent-report and direct observation during parent-training. *J. Child Fam. Stud.* 15, 554–567. doi: 10.1007/s10826-006-9029-x

Hayden, E., Durbin, E., Klein, D., and Olino, T. (2010). Maternal personality influences the relationship between maternal reports and laboratory measures of child temperament. *J. Pers. Assess.* 92, 586–593. doi: 10.1080/00223891.2010.513308

Jenkinson, C., and Layte, R. (1997). Development and testing of the UK SF-12. *J. Health Serv. Res.* 2, 14–18. doi: 10.1177/135581969700200105

Kessler, R. C., Andrews, G., Colpe, L. J., Hiripi, E., Mroczek, D. K., Normand, S. L., et al. (2002). Short screening scales to monitor population prevalences and trends in non-specific psychological distress. *Psychol. Med.* 32, 959–976. doi: 10.1017/S0033291702006074

Law, J., and Roy, P. (2008). Parental report of infant language skills: a review of the development and application of the communicative development inventories. *Child Adolesc. Ment. Health* 13, 198–206. doi: 10.1111/j.1475-3588.2008.00503.x

Lin, L. I. (1989). A concordance correlation coefficient to evaluate reproducibility. *Biometrics* 45, 255–268. doi: 10.2307/2532051

Ludbrook, J. (1997). Comparing methods of measurements. *Clin. Exp. Pharmacol. Physiol.* 24, 193–203. doi: 10.1111/j.1440-1681.1997.tb01807.x

Ludbrook, J. (2010). Linear regression analysis for comparing two measurers or methods of measurement: but which regression? *Clin. Exp. Pharmacol. Physiol.* 37, 692–699. doi: 10.1111/j.1440-1681.2010.05376.x

Meisenberg, G., and Williams, A. (2008). Are acquiescent and extreme response styles related to low intelligence and education? *Pers. Individ. Dif.* 44, 1539–1550. doi: 10.1016/j.paid.2008.01.010

Miles, J., and Banyard, P. (2007). *Understanding and Using Statistics in Psychology: A Practical Introduction.* London: SAGE Publications Ltd.

Nicholson, J. M., Berthelsen, D., Abad, V., Williams, K., and Bradley, J. (2008). Impact of music therapy to promote positive parenting and child development. *J. Health Psychol.* 13, 226–238. doi: 10.1177/1359105307086705

Olino, T., Durbin, E., Klein, D., Hayden, E., and Dyson, M. (2013). Gender differences in young children's temperament traits: comparisons across observational and parent-report methods. *J. Pers.* 81, 119–129. doi: 10.1111/jopy.12000

Reese, E., and Read, S. (2000). Predictive validity of the New Zealand MacArthur communicative development inventory: words and sentences. *J. Child Lang.* 27, 255–266. doi: 10.1017/S0305000900004098

Reilly, S., Bavin, E. L., Bretherton, L., Conway, L., Eadie, P., Cini, E., et al. (2009). The Early Language in Victoria Study (ELVS): a prospective, longitudinal study of communication skills and expressive vocabulary development at 8, 12 and 24 months. *Int. J. Speech Lang. Pathol.* 11, 344–357. doi: 10.1080/17549500903147560

Reilly, S., Wake, M., Ukoumunne, O., Bavin, E., Prior, M., Cini, E., et al. (2010). Predicting language outcomes at 4 years of age: findings from the early language in victoria study. *Pediatrics* 126, e1530–e1537. doi: 10.1542/peds.2010-0254

Ring, E., and Fenson, L. (2000). The correspondence between parent report and child performance for receptive and expressive vocabulary beyond infancy. *First Lang.* 20, 141–159. doi: 10.1177/014272370002005902

Roberts, J., Burchinal, M., and Durham, M. (1999). Parents' report of vocabulary and grammatical development of African American preschoolers: child and environmental associations. *Child Dev.* 70, 92–106. doi: 10.1111/1467-8624.00008

Roy, P., Kersley, H., and Law, J. (2005). *The Sure Start Language Measure Standardisation Study.* Available at: http://tna.europarchive.org/20070101101348/http://www.dfes.gov.uk/research/programmeofresearch/projectinformation.cfm?projectid=14628&resultspage=1

Sachse, S., and Von Suchodoletz, W. (2008). Early identification of language delay by direct language assessment or parent report? *J. Dev. Behav. Pediatr.* 29, 34–41. doi: 10.1097/DBP.0b013e318146902a

Sim, S. (2012). *Supporting Children's Language and Literacy skills: The Effectiveness of Shared Book Reading Intervention Strategies with Parents.* Ph.D. thesis, Queensland University of Technology, Brisbane, QLD.

Skeat, J., Eadie, P., Ukoumunne, O., and Reilly, S. (2010). Predictors of parents seeking help or advice about children's communication development in the early years. *Child Care Health Dev.* 36, 878–887. doi: 10.1111/j.1365-2214.2010.01093.x

Smith, P. B. (2004). Acquiescent response bias as an aspect of cultural communication style. *J. Cross Cult. Psychol.* 35, 50–61. doi: 10.1177/0022022103260380

Squires, J., Twombly, E., Bricker, D., and Potter, L. (2009). *ASQ-3 User's Guide.* Baltimore, MD: Brookes Publishing Co. Inc.

StataCorp. (2013). *Stata Statistical Software: Release 13.* College Station, TX: StataCorp LP.

Stolarova, M., Wolf, C., Rinker, T., and Brielmann, A. (2014). How to assess and compare inter-rater reliability, agreement and correlation of ratings: an exemplary analysis of mother-father and parent-teacher expressive vocabulary rating pairs. *Front. Psychol.* 5:509. doi: 10.3389/fpsyg.2014.00509

Stothard, S., Snowling, M., Bishop, D., Chipchase, B., and Kaplan, C. (1998). Language-impaired preschoolers: a follow-up into adolescence. *J. Speech Lang. Hear. Res.* 41, 407–418. doi: 10.1044/jslhr.4102.407

Ukoumunne, O., Wake, M., Carlin, J., Bavin, E., Lum, J., Skeat, J., et al. (2012). Profiles of language development in pre-school children: a longitudinal latent class analysis of data from the early language in victoria study. *Child Care Health Dev.* 38, 341–349. doi: 10.1111/j.1365-2214.2011.01234.x

Wysocki, T. (2015). Introduction to the special issue: direct observation in pediatric psychology research. *J. Pediatr. Psychol.* 40, 1–7. doi: 10.1093/jpepsy/jsu104

Zaslow, M., Weinfield, N., Gallagher, M., Hair, E., Ogawa, J., Egeland, B., et al. (2006). Longitudinal prediction of child outcomes from differing measures of parenting in a low-income sample. *Dev. Psychol.* 42, 27–37. doi: 10.1037/0012-1649.42.1.27

Zimmerman, I. L., Steiner, V. G., and Pond, R. E. (2002a). *Preschool Language Scale*, 4th Edn. San Antonio, TX: Psychcorp.

Zimmerman, I. L., Steiner, V. G., and Pond, R. E. (2002b). *Preschool Language Scale Fourth Edition: Examiner's Manual.* San Antonia, TX: Harcourt Assessment.

Zimmerman, I. L., Steiner, V. G., and Pond, R. E. (2009). *Technical Report: Preschool Language Scale*, 4th Edn. San Antonio, TX: The Psychological Corporation.

Zubrick, S. R., Taylor, C. L., and Rice, M. L. (2007). Late language emergence at 24 months: an epidemiological study of prevalence, predictors, and covariates. *J. Speech lang. Hear. Res.* 50, 1562–1592. doi: 10.1044/1092-4388(2007/106)

Conflict of Interest Statement: The authors declare that the research was conducted in the absence of any commercial or financial relationships that could be construed as a potential conflict of interest.

4

Child abuse predicts adult PTSD symptoms among individuals diagnosed with intellectual disabilities

Claudia Catani and Iris M. Sossalla*

Department of Psychology, Bielefeld University, Bielefeld, Germany

Prior research has shown that people with intellectual disabilities (ID) are more likely to experience child abuse as well as other forms of traumatic or negative events later in life compared to the general population. Little is known however, about the association of these experiences with adult mental health in intellectually disabled individuals. The present study aimed to assess whether child abuse in families and institutions as well as other types of adverse life events, were associated with current posttraumatic stress disorder (PTSD) and depression symptoms in individuals with ID. We conducted clinical interviews which included standardized self-report measures for childhood abuse, PTSD, and depression in an unselected sample of 56 persons with a medical diagnosis of ID who were attending a specialized welfare center. The frequency of traumatic experiences was very high, with physical and emotional child abuse being the most common trauma types. 87% of the persons reported at least one aversive experience on the family violence spectrum, and 50% of the sample reported a violent physical attack later in adulthood. 25% were diagnosed with PTSD and almost 27% had a critical score on the depression scale. Physical and emotional child abuse was positively correlated with the amount of institutional violence and the number of general traumatic events, whereas childhood sexual abuse was related to the experience of intimate partner violence in adult life. A linear regression model revealed child abuse in the family to be the only significant independent predictor of PTSD symptom severity. The current findings underscore the central role of child maltreatment in the increased risk of further victimization and in the development of mental health problems in adulthood in intellectually disabled individuals. Our data have important clinical implications and demonstrate the need for targeted prevention and intervention programs that are tailored to the specific needs of children and adults with intellectual disability.

Edited by:
Alessandra Simonelli, University of Padova, Italy

Reviewed by:
Maicon R. Albuquerque, Universidade Federal de Viçosa, Brazil
Andrew E. Rasmussen, Fordham University, USA

***Correspondence:**
Claudia Catani
claudia.catani@uni-bielefeld.de

Specialty section:
This article was submitted to Psychopathology, a section of the journal Frontiers in Psychology

Keywords: child abuse, victimization, intellectual disabilities, trauma, PTSD

INTRODUCTION

There is growing evidence that individuals with disabilities constitute a particularly vulnerable group with regard to likelihood of abusive experiences during childhood as well as later in life. Two recent meta-analyses have reported alarming prevalence rates of violence against disabled adults (Hughes et al., 2012) and children (Jones et al., 2012). The increased risk of having experienced violence in the last year in adults with disabilities compared to the healthy population is approximately 50% (Hughes et al., 2012). Children with disabilities are more than three times more likely to have experienced violence in their lives than non-disabled children. More specifically, children with mental or intellectual impairments seem to have a higher prevalence and risk of violence than do children with other types of disability (Jones et al., 2012). This finding is consistent with studies showing that adults with intellectual disabilities (ID) have the highest population rates of violence compared with both the general population and persons with other disability types (Lin et al., 2009; Rand and Harrell, 2009).

Even though there is a widespread view that disability increases the likelihood for children to be abused by parents or other caretakers (Spencer et al., 2005), there is still a paucity of research examining specific types of child abuse (e.g., neglect vs. physical violence vs. emotional violence) and their association with specific types of disability (e.g., physical vs. intellectual). Many studies are methodologically weak and rely on medical or school records or information from caretakers or social workers rather than subjective information provided directly by the disabled individuals. A population-based study by Sullivan and Knutson (2000a) assessed the prevalence of abuse and neglect among children with and without disabilities by relating specific types of disabilities to specific types of abuse. The analysis of school records and official databases revealed a 31% maltreatment rate (including sexual, physical, emotional abuse, and neglect) among children with disabilities compared to a 9% rate in non-disabled children. Neglect was the predominant form of maltreatment, followed by physical abuse, emotional abuse and sexual abuse. The maltreatment risk was particularly high for children with mental retardation and learning disabilities, when compared to children with physical impairments.

A number of studies show that violence in the lives of people with disabilities usually does not end in childhood but rather continues throughout the life span with intimate partner violence (IPV) being a very frequent phenomenon. Women with disabilities (physical and intellectual) are more likely to be abused by their partners than women without disabilities, and for longer periods of time (Nosek et al., 2001; Smith and Strauser, 2008; Hughes et al., 2011; Scherer et al., 2014). In addition to experiencing subtle forms of abuse that exploit aspects of disability, such as withholding medication or denying needed supports (Lund, 2011), they are also more often victims of severe forms of physical partner violence, including being kicked or punched (Brownridge, 2006). Even though women in general are substantially more likely to experience severe domestic or dating violence (Black et al., 2011), men with disabilities are also vulnerable to victimization by their partners. Two population-based studies have examined IPV against men with disabilities and showed a greater prevalence of lifetime and past-year IPV victimization amongst disabled men compared to non-disabled men (Cohen et al., 2006; Mitra and Mouradian, 2014). The high rates of child abuse in disabled individuals, together with the resulting psychological problems, can be assumed to be potential contributing factors to the frequent experience of IPV. In fact, research with non-disabled samples has repeatedly shown that abusive experiences in early childhood increase the likelihood of being re-victimized by a spouse or dating partner in adult life (Desai et al., 2002; Bensley et al., 2003).

Most of the existing studies on traumatic experiences in the lives of disabled individuals have focused on child abuse or domestic violence whereas only limited research has addressed other types of traumatic events or life adversities in this specific population. The National Crime Victimization Survey (Rand and Harrell, 2009) investigated the frequency of non-fatal violent crimes (e.g., rape, robbery, aggravated assault) and property crimes (e.g., household burglary, property theft) in persons aged 12 or older with physical or cognitive disabilities. Results showed that persons with disabilities were 1.5 times more likely to experience a violent crime and two times more likely to be sexually assaulted than persons without disabilities. Other evidence shows that most of the violence takes place within the social environment of the victim and that individuals with disabilities are most often victimized by someone close to them or by service providers (Sullivan and Knutson, 2000b; Reiter et al., 2007). It has been suggested, that disabled persons often become victims because they are considered to be vulnerable, helpless and not able to report the crime (Sobsey, 1994). In addition, an early study has shown that, even when crimes are reported by individuals with disabilities, there are lower rates of police follow-up, prosecution and convictions as well as lighter sentences when convictions do occur (Sobsey and Doe, 1991).

In sum, despite a number of gaps in the research, there is evidence that individuals with disabilities have a higher probability of experiencing adverse life experiences, particularly child abuse committed by family members or other caretakers. However, a critical question that remains unanswered is whether disabled children and adults are also vulnerable to the disruptive effects of trauma on mental health and psychosocial functioning. Amongst non-disabled individuals, the long-term detrimental consequences of childhood abuse and other early traumatic experiences are well documented. Childhood trauma has been repeatedly associated with poor mental health in adults, especially with a higher risk for depression (Heim et al., 2008; Nanni et al., 2012) and posttraumatic stress disorder (PTSD; Koenen et al., 2007; Sugaya et al., 2012). An increased risk of physical problems later in life has also been demonstrated (Knudsen et al., 2006; Tischler et al., 2006; Shonkoff et al., 2012). However, little systematic research has explored whether the consequences of violence against individuals with disabilities are quantitatively or qualitatively different from non-disabled persons. Individuals with ID might be more likely to develop psychological disorders in the aftermath of exposure to trauma. In addition to reduced cognitive coping mechanisms, external factors such as an increased dependency on others, early institutionalization, limited social support (Martorell et al., 2009) or being surrounded by a high risk peer network (Kepper et al., 2014) might play a role in increasing the vulnerability of this group.

However, the empirical evidence linking childhood trauma and mental ill-health and specifically PTSD in individuals with ID is very limited even though studies from the general population suggest an association between PTSD risk and intelligence. For instance, a prospective study following children over a time interval of 11 years found that higher levels of intelligence were associated with a decreased conditional risk for PTSD (Breslau et al., 2006). Consistent with this, research with combat veterans showed that lower levels of intelligence were linked to a greater risk of developing PTSD symptoms (Macklin et al., 1998). Different results were yielded by a very recent study with Israeli civilians with ID (Berger et al., 2015) exposed to war violence (missile attacks). Similar to the research findings for non-disabled people, war exposure in this group was related to Posttraumatic symptoms and functioning problems, but the rate of mental health impairments was low compared to the general exposed Israeli population. However, study results might be questionable since they were exclusively based on an assessment of the professional caretaker.

Taken together, evidence from studies with disabled and non-disabled individuals suggest that survivors of child abuse with ID have an elevated risk for developing PTSD compared to non-abused samples. However, it remains unclear whether this risk is different from that of non-disabled individuals who experienced child abuse (Mevissen and de Jongh, 2010). In addition, very little is known about potential risk factors associated with PTSD in adults with ID. Based on studies with the general population and high-risk populations without disabilities, it can be assumed that the amount of traumatic experiences of different types (child abuse, IPV) plays a critical role for the development of PTSD (Gilbert et al., 2009; Catani and Ruck, 2012). Recent evidence has proven that institutional child abuse, too, has a negative impact on the mental health of adult survivors (Fitzpatrick et al., 2010) and is related to a diagnosis of PTSD in adult life (Lueger-Schuster et al., 2014). Yet, there is no research addressing the relationship between institutional child abuse and PTSD in intellectually disabled people.

The current study aimed to assess child abuse and later traumatic life events as well as current PTSD and depressive symptoms in an unselected sample of individuals with ID. We hypothesized that the amount of different types of violent and adverse experiences including childhood maltreatment in families or institutions and IPV, would be associated with PTSD symptom severity. In addition, we assumed that participants with many experiences of child abuse would report a greater severity of current depression symptoms compared to individuals without or with less abuse.

MATERIALS AND METHODS

Sample

The sample consisted of 56 persons who were attending a welfare center that specialized in the care and support of people with ID. Because of concerns related to participants' burden and due to logistical reasons, a formal IQ testing could not be carried out. Instead, we used the presence of a formal diagnosis of intellectual disability (ID) in the participant's medical records as primary inclusion criterion. In addition, participants had to be aged over 18 to be eligible for this study. Exclusion criteria were the presence of cognitive problems that were too severe to allow for an adequate understanding of interview contents, current psychotic disorder or acute suicide ideation. We invited the social workers working at the center to inform all of their clients who met the inclusion criteria about the study. We also instructed the social workers to document the number of persons they had informed and the reason for failing to inform some of their cases. Since some social workers opted out of the study, we did not obtain any information for 30% of the approximately 140 users of the welfare center. Another 20 persons were not informed about the study because their social workers had the impression they were too stressed or burdened with daily hassles to participate in the interview. In total, 88 persons with ID attending the center were informed about the study and asked to participate. Out of those, 17 refused to take part and 71 persons opted in. Reasons for not participating were mainly "no interest" or "being afraid to talk to strangers." We were able to interview 56 people within the available time period. **Table 1** provides an overview of the socio-demographic characteristics of the final group of participants.

TABLE 1 | Sociodemographic and other characteristics of participants (*N* = 56).

Gender, % male (*n*)	54(30)
Age, *M* (SD)	41.5 (13, 3)
Nationality, % German (*n*)	96.4 (54)
Family status, % (*n*)	
Single	46.4 (26)
Not married, but stable partner	32.1 (18)
Married	8.9 (5)
Other	12.5 (7)
Degree of education, % (*n*)	
No degree	35.2 (19)
Certification from a special-needs school	37.0 (20)
Certificate of secondary education	18.5 (10)
Other (higher) degrees	8.9 (5)
Unknown	3.6 (2)
Current employment status, % (*n*)	
Working in protected environments (specifically for people with ID)	73.2 (41)
Unemployed	5.4 (3)
Retired	7.1 (4)
Other	14.3 (8)
Part of childhood spent in a child care center, % yes (*n*)	32.1 (18)

Procedure

Participants who volunteered to take part in the study arranged individual appointments through their personal social worker who accompanied them to the interview. All interviews took place in a quiet and private room at the welfare center and were conducted by one of the authors. Participants were invited to choose whether they wanted their social worker to be present during the interview or not. All but one ($n = 55$) participants wanted their social workers to stay. Before the interview started, aim and content of the study, procedure, risks, the right to withdraw and confidentiality were explained and written consent was obtained. The clinical examination was conducted as a standardized interview. We also included self-report questionnaires that were all administered as a face-to-face interview in order to enhance clarity and to adapt questions to the cognitive capabilities of the respective participant, if needed. Interviews lasted on average 60 min. The study was approved by the Ethical Review Board of the University of Bielefeld.

Instruments

Sociodemographic and Clinical Information

The first part of the interview comprised of a series of questions about individual sociodemographic characteristics and clinical information related to the type of disability, medical and psychiatric diagnoses, current or past psychiatric or psychological treatments, intake of medication, acts of self-injury, and suicide attempts.

Adverse Childhood Experiences and Intimate Partner Violence

For the assessment of adverse childhood experiences we created a 22—item checklist by selecting items from a questionnaire that had previously been used with children in various cultural contexts (Catani et al., 2008). Following discussions with clinical experts and social workers involved in the daily work with persons with ID, the most suitable items for this specific group of people were chosen and wording was adapted if needed. The final checklist consists of five items asking about physical abuse, e.g., "Have you been hit with an object?", three items addressing sexual abuse, e.g., "Have you been forced to have sexual intercourse with a family member (a teacher/child care worker)?", four items asking about emotional abuse, e.g., "Have you been told that you are stupid or ugly?", and four items addressing neglect, e.g., "Were you not given enough to eat or drink?". Two additional items ask about witnessing violence, e.g., "Have you seen your mother being hit at home?". For each item, participants were asked whether they had experienced the specific event type as a child either in their family environment or in a children's home or daycare institution or school. Two further questions explored whether the participants had injuries (e.g., bruises, broken bones) or needed medical treatment as a consequence of the experienced violence. An index of the severity of childhood abuse was established by counting the numbers of event types reported by the participants, separately for incidences that had happened at home/in the family (*family abuse*) and those that took place in a particular institutional setting (*institutional abuse*).

At the end of the questionnaire, participants were asked whether they had ever been beaten by an intimate partner.

Posttraumatic Stress Disorder

DSM-IV diagnosis and severity of PTSD were assessed using the German version of the Posttraumatic Stress Diagnostic Scale (PDS; Steil and Ehlers, 2000) carried out in interview form. The PDS is a DSM-IV-based self-report measure and includes a checklist of 12 traumatic events as well as 17 symptom items for the assessment of past-month PTSD symptoms. The number of experienced or witnessed traumatic events is determined by counting every positive response to the event checklist. Frequency of each of the 17 symptoms items is coded on a 4-point Likert-type scale ranging from 0 (never or only once in the past month) to 3 (almost daily in the past month). The symptom severity score for each symptom cluster is obtained by summing scores of the respective items for cluster B, C, and D. A sum score for overall PTSD severity score is provided by the total score of all symptom items (range: 0–51). Symptom severity was rated based on the cut-offs provided in the original manual (Foa, 1995). A diagnosis of PTSD was made on the basis of DSM-IV criteria. The PDS has previously been adapted and used for the assessment of PTSD in individuals with ID (Mitchell et al., 2006; Brackenridge, 2010).

Depression and Substance Use

We employed the German Version (Glaesmer et al., 2014) of the 15-item depression section (DHSCL) of the Hopkins Symptom Checklist (HSCL) to measure current symptoms of depression. The DHSCL uses a 4-point Likert scale ranging from 0 ("not at all") to 3 ("extremely"). The severity of depression symptom was calculated on the basis of the total scale mean score. The presence of clinically relevant depression symptoms was derived using the internationally accepted cutoff score of 1.75 (Derogatis et al., 1974; Mollica et al., 1987).

To assess participants' level of alcohol use, we employed four questions asking (1) whether the participants drank alcohol, (2) how often they drank alcohol, (3) whether they had tried and failed to stop drinking in the past 12 months, and (4) whether a relative, friend or health worker had been concerned about their drinking. In addition, participants were asked whether they consume any other substance.

Data Analysis

All statistical analyses were carried out using STATISTICA, Version 8.0 (StatSoft, 2007). Associations between different types of adverse and traumatic experiences were explored using Spearman rank correlations. In order to identify risk factors for severity of PTSD symptoms, we conducted a linear regression analysis on the PDS sum score. The model was adjusted for gender and age. We entered exposure to IPV, the number of traumatic events, the amount of family violence, and the number of experiences related to institutional violence as predictor variables in the model. Spearman's rho was calculated for continuous predictor variables and point-biserial correlations for dichotomous predictor variables. The linear regression model was adjusted for gender and age. To compare clinical outcomes between subgroups of the sample, the Student's t-test for unpaired samples was used whereas chi-square tests were employed for categorical variables.

RESULTS

Childhood Abuse

Forty-nine (87.5%) of the participants reported at least one type of abusive event as a child in their family and still 28 (50%) had experienced four or more different types. 76.8% of the sample reported at least one form of emotional abuse, 73.2% reported physical abuse, 39.3% reported experiences of neglect and 12.5% had experienced at least one incidence of sexual violence in their families. 48.2% of the participants had witnessed their mother or siblings being beaten at home. On average, participants reported 5.2 (SD = 4.2) out of 18 possible different types of child abuse experiences happening in their families. **Figure 1** illustrates the frequency of the most common types of events described by the participants.

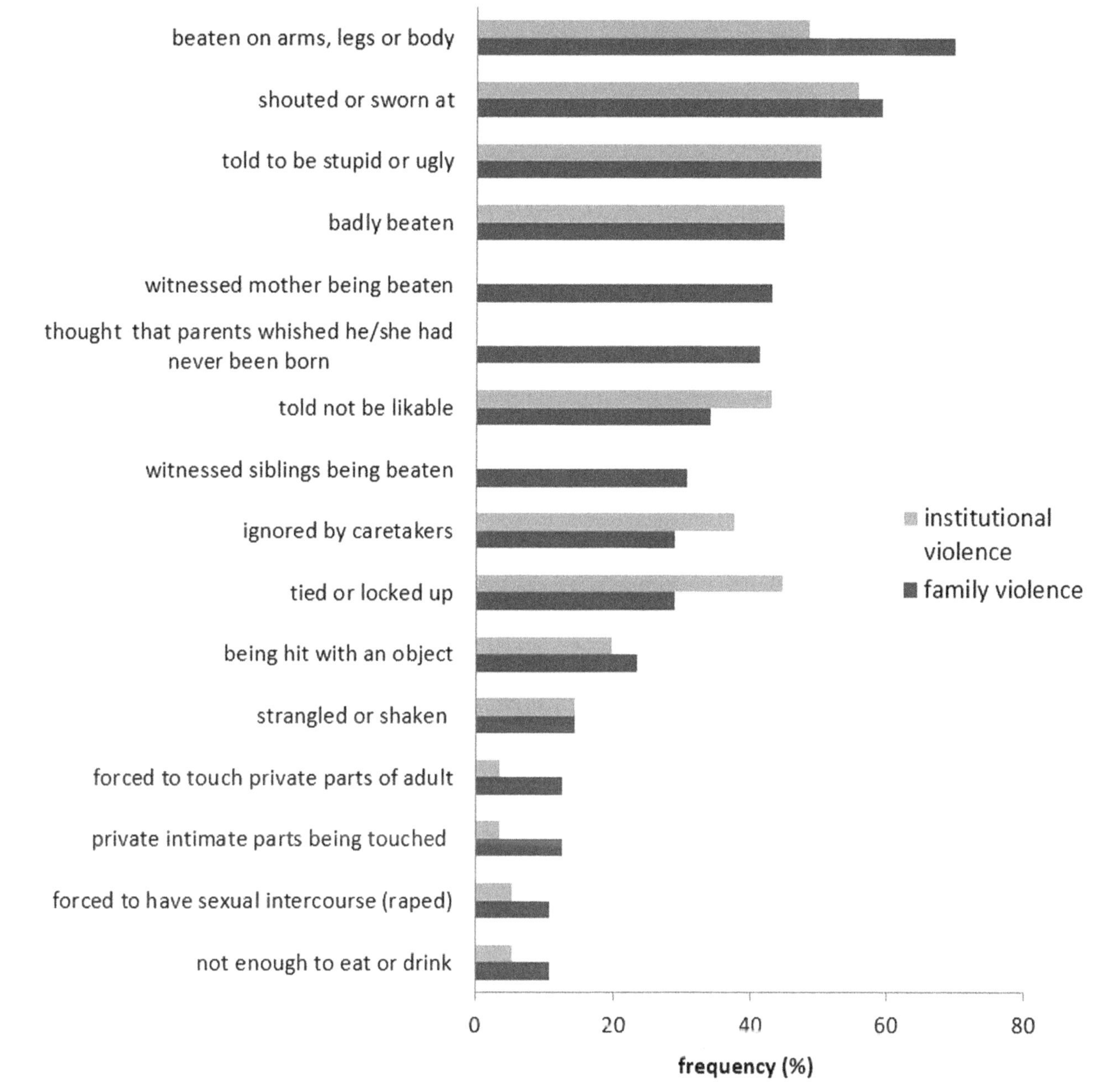

FIGURE 1 | Frequency (%) of types of abusive experiences reported most often by the participants (separately for events experienced at home and in children's homes, school, or daycare institutions).

The majority of the sample also reported a variety of child abuse experiences that had happened in a particular institution (see **Figure 1**), e.g., in a children's home, a daycare unit or at school. 45 participants (80.4%) had experienced at least one form of institutional abuse and 55.4% reported four or more different types. 69.6% of the sample reported at least one type of emotional abuse, 76.8% reported physical abuse, 42.9% reported experiences of neglect and 5.3% had experienced at least one incidence of sexual violence in a child care or educational institution. On average, participants reported four (SD = 3.1) different types of institutional abuse experienced as a child.

Regarding the consequences of these abusive experiences, 42.9% of the participants had suffered at least one injury because of the violent experiences at home or in institutions and 17.9% of them had needed medical treatment on at least one of those occasions.

Trauma Exposure

Fifty-two participants (92.9%) reported at least one traumatic event on the PDS event checklist. On average, they reported 3.6 (SD = 2.1) different events. The most frequently mentioned traumatic experiences were non-sexual assaults by a family

TABLE 2 | Spearman rank correlations between different types of childhood abuse and traumatic experiences.

	Physical abuse (family)	Emotional abuse (family)	Neglect (family)	Sexual abuse (family)	Witnessing family violence	Institutional Violence (total)	Intimate Partner violence (y/n)	Number of traumatic events
Physical abuse (family)	–	0.66**	0.01	0.36**	0.39**	0.49**	0.07	0.50**
Emotional abuse (family)	–	–	−0.07	0.35**	0.56**	0.78**	−0.02	0.54**
Neglect (family)	–	–	–	0.06	−0.11	−0.06	0.14	0.04
Sexual abuse (family)	–	–	–	–	0.18	0.14	0.35**	0.24+
Witnessing family violence	–	–	–	–	–	0.43**	−0.01	0.20
Institutional violence (total)	–	–	–	–	–	–	−0.19	0.47**

***Indicate correlations significant on $p < 0.01$. +Indicates a statistical trend on $p < 0.08$.*

member or someone known (53.6%, $n = 30$), non-sexual assaults by strangers (50%, $n = 28$), serious accidents (50%, $n = 28$), and a life-threatening illness (48.2%, $n = 27$). 14.3% ($n = 8$) of the sample reported a sexual assault by a family member or someone known. 41.1% ($n = 26$) stated they had experienced something described as "other traumatic events." Examples for this category were "*Surgery in my childhood*," "*stillbirth*," "*sudden death of my husband*."

The question "*Have you ever been beaten by an intimate partner*" was answered positively by 10.7% of the male participants ($n = 3$) and 45.8% ($n = 12$) of the females.

Association Between Different Types of Adverse and Traumatic Experience

As shown in **Table 2**, there were a number of significant correlations between the different types of adverse experiences in childhood and adult life. Physical and emotional abuse in the family were significantly associated with every other form of abuse and trauma except for neglect. Institutional violence significantly correlated with abusive experiences in the family, i.e., physical and emotional abuse and the witnessing of family violence.

PTSD, Depressive Symptoms and Alcohol Use

Thirty-nine participants (69.6%) reported an event that fulfilled the trauma criterion A according to the DSM-IV. In 30.4% ($n = 17$) of the cases, the most upsetting event was related to an assault (sexual or physical) by a family member or someone known, in another 16.1% ($n = 9$) it was an aggressive act by a stranger. 30.4% ($n = 17$) of the participants reported an event in the category "any other traumatic event" as being their most upsetting.

The prevalence for current PTSD was high, with 25% of the participants ($n = 14$) fulfilling DSM-IV criteria for the disorder. **Table 3** provides an overview on number of trauma symptoms and severity scores.

Mean depression score on the HSCL was 1.55 (SD = 0.43). 26.8% ($n = 15$) of the sample scored above the cut-off score for clinically relevant depression. Applying the available norms for the German general population (Glaesmer et al., 2014), 50% ($n = 28$) of the participants had normal depression scores, 14.3% ($n = 8$) had marginally abnormal scores, 5.4% ($n = 3$) had strongly abnormal scores, and 30.4% ($n = 17$) had extremely abnormal

TABLE 3 | PTSD prevalence and trauma symptom severity.

PTSD diagnosis, *n* (%)	14 (25.0)
Mean PTSD severity score *for participants with PTSD (SD)*	19.14 (5.79)
Moderate severity, *n* (%)	8 (57.2)
Moderate to severe severity, *n* (%)	6 (42.9)
Mean number of PTSD symptoms *for participants with PTSD (SD)*	12.57 (2.14)
Mean number of impaired areas of psychosocial functioning *for participants with PTSD (SD)*	4.93 (1.77)

depression scores on the HSCL. Ten participants (18.2%) reported a suicide attempt in the past.

Asked about their drinking habits, 35.7% ($n = 20$) of the sample reported that they did not drink alcohol at all or less than once a month. 14.3% ($n = 8$) of the participants reported drinking two to four times a month and another 14.3% ($n = 8$) stated to drink two to four times a week. Four individuals (7%) reported to drink four or more times a week. The same number of participants had tried to stop drinking at least once in the past 12 months. Six individuals (11% of the sample) reported that a relative, friend or health worker had expressed concern about their drinking. Only one participant reported consumption of any other substance.

Associations Between Child Abuse and Psychopathology

Predictors of PTSD were established by calculating a linear regression model on the PDS symptom severity score (see **Table 4**). An analysis of standard residuals was carried out, which showed that the data contained no outliers (Std. Residual Min = −1.73, Std. Residual Max = 2.94). Additional tests and visual inspection of data distribution revealed that the data met the assumptions of collinearity, independent errors, normal distribution of the standardised residuals, homogeneity of variance, and linearity.

The regression analysis showed that the amount of child abuse experiences in the family (family violence) was the only significant predictor for PTSD symptom severity.

To further investigate the link between the amount of family violence and psychopathology, we subdivided the sample into two groups based on a median split for the total amount of different types of child abuse experiences that had happened in the family (high abuse >4; low abuse ≤4). A Chi-square test was used to verify the difference in percentage of PTSD diagnosis between the two subgroups. Differences on the HSCL depression score were

TABLE 4 | Prediction of PTSD symptom severity: standardized beta coefficients and zero-order correlation coefficients resulting from a linear regression model on PDS symptom severity score.

Predictor	β	Zero-order correlation
Age	0.08	−0.19
Gender (female)	0.07	−0.11
Exposure to intimate partner violence (yes)	0.08	0.02
Number of traumatic events	0.23	0.47**
Amount of family violence	0.50**	0.65**
Amount of institutional violence	0.05	0.49**

*Full model's adjusted $R^2 = 0.40$; $F(6.44) = 6.63$, $p < 0.0001$. Zero-order correlation is represented by Spearman's Rho for continuous predictor variables and point-biserial correlation for dichotomous predictor variables. **Indicate correlations significant on $p < 0.01$.*

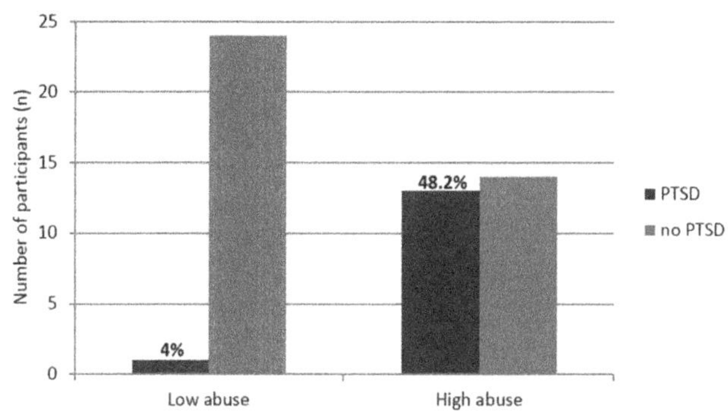

FIGURE 2 | Frequency (*n*) of PTSD diagnosis for participants in the "high abuse" and "low abuse" group.

analyzed by the Student's two-tailed t-test for unpaired samples. As illustrated in **Figure 2**, PTSD prevalence of participants with a high amount of child abuse experiences in their families ("high abuse") was significantly higher ($\chi^2 = 12.86$; $p < 0.001$) compared to the "low abuse" group.

In addition, the "high abuse" subgroup reported a significantly higher score ($t = 2.54$; $p < 0.05$) on the HSCL depression scale ($M = 1.69$; SD $= 0.47$) compared to the "low abuse" group ($M = 1.41$; SD $= 0.15$).

DISCUSSION

By examining adverse and traumatic life experiences and PTSD symptoms in an unselected sample of adults with ID, the present study revealed high rates of child maltreatment related to both family abuse and victimization in an institutional setting. The prevalence rate for current PTSD was very high with 25% of the participants fulfilling DSM-IV criteria for the disorder. A key finding was that the amount of child abuse in the family emerged as an independent predictor of current PTSD symptom severity, suggesting an enduring impact of early maltreatment experiences on adult mental health in individuals with ID.

The majority of the participants (87.5%) described a least one type of abusive experience occurring in their families, with emotional and physical abuse being almost equally common (76.8 vs. 73.2%). Experience of severe physical violence such as being badly beaten (44.6%) and being beaten hit with an object (23.2%) were frequently reported. These numbers substantially exceed child abuse prevalence rates from the general population, which range from 12 to 14% for physical abuse and 10–15% for emotional abuse and neglect (Finkelhor et al., 2005; Häuser et al., 2011; Iffland et al., 2013). Childhood experience of sexual violence was reported by 12.5% of the individuals in the present study, which is also elevated compared to data from the non-disabled population. This finding is in agreement with prevalence rates for child sexual abuse reported in prior research examining adults and children with (intellectual) disabilities (Sullivan and Knutson, 2000a; Jones et al., 2012). Physical abuse and neglect are reported more frequently in the present study when compared to previous findings in disabled populations; however, a direct comparison is difficult due to differences in the operationalization of "maltreatment" and an often inadequate specification of the disability type (Mikton and Shakespeare, 2014). Nevertheless, based on the results of the present study, specifically that 43% of the participants reported having suffered at least one injury and almost one in five (18%) had needed medical treatment because of the abuse, we can conclude that the level of childhood exposure to family violence was exceptionally high. In addition, it seems that violence was not exclusively directed toward the child with ID as 43% of the participants reported that they had witnessed their mother being beaten and 30% stated that their siblings were also beaten. This finding challenges the view that violence by caretakers is specifically directed toward the disabled child because increased rates of conduct, attention or compliance problems (Larzelere, 2000; Alizadeh et al., 2007) increase parents' stress and lead to frustrated or angry reactive parenting behavior (Hendricks et al., 2014). Rather, it appears that the level of intrafamilial violence in general is increased when one child is affected by ID as this condition often places greater emotional, economic and social demands on the family as a whole. This concords with the finding that in the presence of adverse circumstances, different risk factors tend to accumulate (Rutter, 1985). Family characteristics such as unemployment, social isolation, financial difficulties and interparental violence have all been associated with a higher risk of child maltreatment (Edleson, 1999; Hamilton-Giachritsis and Browne, 2005).

Based on the present findings, we can assume that violence against people with ID is not only limited to the family context, but also takes place within institutions intended to protect and educate disabled children such as in schools, daycare units or children's homes. Around 80% of the present sample reported at least one abusive experience in institutions, with physical abuse being the most frequent from of institutional violence (reported by 77%). We are unable to classify the severity of the abuse in the present study as we did not use a questionnaire with validated cut-offs for the presence of abuse. However, the fact that almost 45% of the individuals stated that they had been badly beaten by caretakers in their institutions hints at the alarming magnitude of the problem. Unfortunately, to date there is little valid data available about the frequency of institutional violence committed against children with disability, particularly in relation to non-residential institutions. Based on analysis of historical records of residential facilities, it is clear that a residential placement is a major risk factor for experiencing sexual or physical abuse for disabled children (Sullivan, 2009). In sum, the present retrospective data indicate elevated rated of institutional abuse toward children with disabilities and highlight the need for more thorough research on the prevalence and nature of this phenomenon and its consequences for child and adult mental health.

There were numerous intercorrelations between the various forms of victimization experiences. Physical and emotional child abuse was positively correlated with the amount of institutional violence and the number of general traumatic events, whereas childhood sexual abuse was related to the experience of IPV in adult life. Both results are in agreement with the well-known finding in non-disabled persons that prior exposure to violence constitutes an important risk factor for re-victimization (Widom et al., 2008). 45.8% of the females (compared to 10.7% of men) stated that they had experienced physical violence in an intimate relationship. In addition, more than half of the sample had been physically assaulted by a stranger. These results demonstrate that individuals with ID (and particularly women) are at high risk of experiencing interpersonal violence, not only during childhood but also later in life. This is consistent with the findings of a study exploring the prevalence of violent crimes against persons with disabilities (Rand and Harrell, 2009). It has been suggested that individuals with ID might be especially vulnerable to re-victimization because of their impairments in judgment, social skills and communication (Weiss et al., 2011) and due to the fact that they are often socially isolated and therefore less likely to seek help and report assaults to others. The elevated risk for sexual assault in women with ID might also be related to a lack of knowledge about appropriate sexual behavior and inadequate self-protective strategies against abuse (Sobsey, 1997). The present findings point to the need for targeted interventions aimed at both reducing the adverse effects of abuse in children with ID and also promoting effective prevention strategies against further victimization in adulthood.

The consequences of the extensive amount of abusive experiences reported by the present sample are reflected in a high PTSD prevalence (25%) as well as an elevated occurrence of clinically relevant symptoms of depression (27%). It is not possible to compare these findings with others because of the absence of studies investigating prevalence of mental illness such as PTSD in samples of persons with ID. However, outcomes in the present study are similar to the prevalence rates of mental health disorders that have been published for non-disabled adult survivors of child abuse (Widom, 1999; Scott et al., 2012). Our initial assumption of a cumulative effect of different stressors on current PTSD was confirmed only on a correlational level whereas a regression analysis revealed the amount of child abuse in the family to be the only significant independent predictor of PTSD symptom severity. Again, as there are no comparable studies with individuals with ID, we can only discuss this finding based on the evidence that has been described for the general population or non-disabled samples. The relationship between child abuse and adult PTSD is well established (Widom, 1999; Stovall-McClough and Cloitre, 2006; Heim and Nemeroff, 2015) and a number of factors have been proposed to account for this association. For instance, child abuse may alter attachment patterns as well as neurobiological developmental processes (Watts-English et al., 2006) including interactions with genetic factors (Mehta and Binder, 2012) thereby enhancing the risk of subsequent development of PTSD. The presence of ID might further increase this vulnerability since previous longitudinal studies have revealed that a lower IQ in young children heightened their risk for PTSD in response to subsequent traumatic events (Breslau et al., 2006; Koenen et al., 2007).

All but one individual with a PTSD diagnosis had experienced a high incidence of abuse, thereby validating the importance of child abuse in subsequent development of PTSD during adulthood as well as in symptom severity. A number of studies have shown that childhood maltreatment is a key determinant for the development of depression (Anda et al., 2002; Norman et al., 2012). Similarly in the present study, individuals who had experienced more severe levels of child abuse also reported higher levels of depressive symptoms. The extent of child abuse in the family was related to both a higher number of adverse and traumatic experiences as well as to adult mental health problems, highlighting how essential family factors and particularly parenting practices are for the development of children with ID. In fact, whilst experiences of institutional violence, IPV, and aggression by strangers were frequent in our sample, none of these adversities was associated with current PTSD symptom severity if the amount of childhood family violence was taken into account. These findings underscore the urgent need to support families with children with ID and to promote supportive and non-violent ways of parenting in order to reduce the risk for later re-victimization and to encourage healthy development in intellectually disabled individuals.

Limitations

The current study contributes new insight into the association between child abuse and adult mental health in individuals with ID. However, several limitations have to be acknowledged. Firstly, the sample size is small and participants were not tested with a formal IQ test to validate the diagnosis of ID. In addition, the sample was recruited through a welfare center that specialized in the care of individuals with mostly mild and moderate forms of ID. Thus, findings cannot be generalized to the entire population of people with ID. Despite efforts to obtain an unselected sample within the welfare center, a number of individuals refused to take part. This might have biased our results. However, the fact that the most common reasons for refusal were fear of talking to strangers or being too burdened might give rise to the assumption that disproportionately many individuals with a particularly high stress load were among the people who did not take part in the study. We might therefore assume that the present findings were biased more likely toward an underestimation the frequency of abusive and stressful experiences and current mental health problems. In addition, we cannot rule out that the presence of the social worker during the interview might have influenced the participants' answers.

Furthermore, our cross-sectional design does not allow for verification of hypothesized causal relationships. In fact, the potential for reverse causation, i.e., disability arises as a result of child abuse (Govindshenoy and Spencer, 2007), cannot be ruled out, even though many participants reported that their disabilities occurred from birth or soon afterward. Longitudinal studies are necessary in order to clarify whether (intellectual) disabilities are a risk factor or rather an outcome of child abuse, or both. Longitudinal designs would have the additional advantage of avoiding potential report bias in adults regarding retrospective events.

One of the most important limitations of the present study is the fact that, we did not assess peer victimization and bullying experiences. The evidence that people with ID have an increased risk of being victimized by their peers (Jones et al., 2012) together with the recent knowledge about long-term consequences of peer bullying for adult mental health (Lereya et al., 2015) may give rise to the assumption that such experiences might have an additional impact in the present sample. Future research should address the frequency of peer victimization and related consequences for the development of children and youth with ID.

CONCLUSION

Child maltreatment seems to play a decisive role for the development of mental health problems and exposure to further trauma amongst intellectually disabled individuals. The current study indicates high prevalence of child maltreatment, which is strongly associated with other forms of victimization, such as institutional abuse or IPV, and is an independent risk factor for the severity of adult PTSD, a disorder diagnosed in a quarter of the participants. In order to reduce the frequent victimization of intellectually disabled people across different contexts, intervention and prevention programs should start at the family level. Parent training programs should be tailored to the specific needs of families with an intellectually disabled child and should teach parents non-violent and supportive ways of educating their children. In addition, targeted preventive measures should be designed to empower children with ID to recognize abuse and grooming and to effectively seek help. Finally, given the high PTSD rate in populations with intellectual impairments, further research is required to see whether current therapeutic approaches with proven efficacy in non-disabled populations are also effective in this group, or whether adaptations to current treatments are required.

AUTHOR CONTRIBUTIONS

CC conceived the study, developed the design, participated in and supervised data acquisition, performed the statistical analysis and drafted the manuscript. IS carried out clinical interviews, entered the data, and revised the manuscript critically for important intellectual content. Both authors gave their final approval of the current version of the manuscript. The authors agree to be accountable for all aspects of the work in ensuring that questions related to the accuracy or integrity of any part of the work are appropriately investigated and resolved.

ACKNOWLEDGMENTS

We are grateful to all participants who took part in the study. We would like to thank Kathrin Bücker and her committed staff members at Gemeinsam Wohnen e.V. for their continuous support in initiating and conducting the study. We also thank Dr. Katy Robjant for editing. Furthermore, we acknowledge support for the Article Processing Charge by the Deutsche Forschungsgemeinschaft and the Open Access Publication Fund of Bielefeld University.

REFERENCES

Alizadeh, H., Applequist, K. F., and Coolidge, F. L. (2007). Parental self-confidence, parenting styles, and corporal punishment in families of ADHD children in Iran. *Child Abuse Negl.* 31, 567–572. doi: 10.1016/j.chiabu.2006.12.005

Anda, R. F., Whitfield, C. L., Felitti, V. J., Chapman, D., Edwards, V. J., Dube, S. R., et al. (2002). Adverse childhood experiences, alcoholic parents, and later risk of alcoholism and depression. *Psychiatr. Serv.* 53, 1001–1009. doi: 10.1176/appi.ps.53.8.1001

Bensley, L., Van Eenwyk, J., and Simmons, K. W. (2003). Childhood family violence history and women's risk for intimate partner violence and poor health. *Am. J. Prev. Med.* 25, 38–44. doi: 10.1016/S0749-3797(03)00094-1

Berger, R., Gelkopf, M., Versano-Mor, K., and Shpigelman, C.-N. (2015). Impact of exposure to potentially traumatic events on individuals with intellectual disability. *Am. J. Intellect. Dev. Disabil.* 120, 176–188. doi: 10.1352/1944-7558-120.2.176

Black, M. C., Basile, K. C., Breiding, M. J., Smith, S. G., Walters, M. L., Merrick, M. T., et al. (2011). The National Intimate Partner and Sexual Violence Survey (NISVS): 2010 Summary Report. Atlante, GA: National Center for Injury Prevention and Control, Centers for Disease Control and Prevention.

Brackenridge, I. (2010). Trauma and post-traumatic stress disorder (PTSD) in a high secure forensic learning disability population: future directions for practice. *Health (San Francisco)* 4, 49–57. doi: 10.5042/amhid.2010.0544

Breslau, N., Lucia, V. C., and Alvarado, G. F. (2006). Intelligence and other predisposing factors in exposure to trauma and posttraumatic stress disorder: a follow-up study at age 17 years. *Arch. Gen. Psychiatry* 63, 1238–1245. doi: 10.1001/archpsyc.63.11.1238

Brownridge, D. A. (2006). Partner violence against women with disabilities: prevalence, risk, and explanations. *Violence Against Women* 12, 805–822. doi: 10.1177/1077801206292681

Catani, C., Jacob, N., Schauer, E., Kohila, M., and Neuner, F. (2008). Family violence, war, and natural disasters: a study of the effect of extreme stress on children's mental health in Sri Lanka. *BMC Psychiatry* 8:33. doi: 10.1186/1471-244X-8-33

Catani, C., and Ruck, B. (2012). Misshandelte Frauen: Zusammenhänge zwischen Kindesmissbrauch, Beziehungsgewalt und Posttraumatischer Belastungsstörung. *Trauma Gewalt* 6, 16–29.

Cohen, M. M., Forte, T., Du Mont, J., Hyman, I., and Romans, S. (2006). Adding insult to injury: intimate partner violence among women and men reporting activity limitations. *Ann. Epidemiol.* 16, 644–651. doi: 10.1016/j.annepidem.2005.12.005

Derogatis, L. R., Lipman, R., Rickels, K., Uhlenhuth, E. H., and Covi, L. (1974). "The Hopkins Symptom Checklist (HSCL): a measure of primary symptom dimensions," in *Psychological Measurements in Psychopharmacology, Modern Problems in Pharmacopsychiatry*, ed. P. Pichot (Basel: Karger), 79–110.

Desai, S., Arias, I., Thompson, M. P., and Basile, K. C. (2002). Childhood victimization and subsequent adult revictimization assessed in a nationally representative sample of women and men. *Violence Vict.* 17, 639–653. doi: 10.1891/vivi.17.6.639.33725

Edleson, J. L. (1999). The overlap between child maltreatment and woman battering. *Violence Against Women* 5, 134–154. doi: 10.1177/107780129952003

Finkelhor, D., Ormrod, R., Turner, H., and Hamby, S. L. (2005). The victimization of children and youth: a comprehensive, national survey. *Child Maltreat.* 10, 5–25. doi: 10.1177/1077559504271287

Fitzpatrick, M., Carr, A., Dooley, B., Flanagan-Howard, R., Flanagan, E., Tierney, K., et al. (2010). Profiles of adult survivors of severe sexual, physical and emotional institutional abuse in Ireland. *Child Abuse Rev.* 19, 387–404. doi: 10.1002/car.1083

Foa, E. B. (1995). *Posttraumatic Stress Diagnostic Scale Manual.* Minneapolis, MN: National Computer Systems, Inc.

Gilbert, R., Widom, C. S., Browne, K., Fergusson, D., Webb, E., and Janson, S. (2009). Burden and consequences of child maltreatment in high-income countries. *Lancet* 373, 68–81. doi: 10.1016/S0140-6736(08)61706-7

Glaesmer, H., Braehler, E., Grande, G., Hinz, A., Petermann, F., and Romppel, M. (2014). The German Version of the Hopkins Symptoms Checklist-25 (HSCL-25)—factorial structure, psychometric properties, and population-based norms. *Compr. Psychiatry* 55, 396–403. doi: 10.1016/j.comppsych.2013.08.020

Govindshenoy, M., and Spencer, N. (2007). Abuse of the disabled child: a systematic review of population-based studies. *Child Care Health Dev.* 33, 552–558. doi: 10.1111/j.1365-2214.2006.00693.x

Häuser, W., Schmutzer, G., Brähler, E., and Glaesmer, H. (2011). Maltreatment in childhood and adolescence. [Results from a survey of a representative sample of the German population]. *Dtsch. Arztebl. Int.* 108, 287–294. doi: 10.3238/arztebl.2011.0287

Hamilton-Giachritsis, C. E., and Browne, K. D. (2005). A retrospective study of risk to siblings in abusing families. *J. Fam. Psychol.* 19, 619–624. doi: 10.1037/0893-3200.19.4.619

Heim, C., and Nemeroff, C. B. (2015). The role of childhood trauma in the neurobiology of mood and anxiety disorders: preclinical and clinical studies. *Biol. Psychiatry* 49, 1023–1039. doi: 10.1016/S0006-3223(01)01157-X

Heim, C., Newport, D. J., Mletzko, T., Miller, A. H., and Nemeroff, C. B. (2008). The link between childhood trauma and depression: insights from HPA axis studies in humans. *Psychoneuroendocrinology* 33, 693–710. doi: 10.1016/j.psyneuen.2008.03.008

Hendricks, C., Lansford, J. E., Deater-Deckard, K., and Bornstein, M. H. (2014). Associations between child disabilities and caregiver discipline and violence in low- and middle-income countries. *Child Dev.* 85, 513–531. doi: 10.1111/cdev.12132

Hughes, K., Bellis, M. A., Jones, L., Wood, S., Bates, G., Eckley, L., et al. (2012). Prevalence and risk of violence against adults with disabilities: a systematic review and meta-analysis of observational studies. *Lancet* 379, 1621–1629. doi: 10.1016/S0140-6736(11)61851-5

Hughes, R. B., Lund, E. M., Gabrielli, J., Powers, L. E., and Curry, M. A. (2011). Prevalence of interpersonal violence against community-living adults with disabilities: a literature review. *Rehabil. Psychol.* 56, 302–319. doi: 10.1037/a0025620

Iffland, B., Brahler, E., Neuner, F., Hauser, W., and Glaesmer, H. (2013). Frequency of child maltreatment in a representative sample of the German population. *BMC Public Health* 13:980. doi: 10.1186/1471-2458-13-980

Jones, L., Bellis, M. A., Wood, S., Hughes, K., McCoy, E., Eckley, L., et al. (2012). Prevalence and risk of violence against children with disabilities: a systematic review and meta-analysis of observational studies. *Lancet* 380, 899–907. doi: 10.1016/S0140-6736(12)60692-8

Kepper, A., van den Eijnden, R., Monshouwer, K., and Vollebergh, W. (2014). Understanding the elevated risk of substance use by adolescents in special education and residential youth care: the role of individual, family and peer factors. *Eur. Child Adolesc. Psychiatry* 23, 461–472. doi: 10.1007/s00787-013-0471-1

Knudsen, E. I., Heckman, J. J., Cameron, J. L., and Shonkoff, J. P. (2006). Economic, neurobiological, and behavioral perspectives on building America's future workforce. *Proc. Natl. Acad. Sci. U.S.A.* 103, 10155–10162. doi: 10.1073/pnas.0600888103

Koenen, K. C., Moffitt, T. E., Poulton, R., Martin, J., and Caspi, A. (2007). Early childhood factors associated with the development of post-traumatic stress disorder: results from a longitudinal birth cohort. *Psychol. Med.* 37, 181–192. doi: 10.1017/S0033291706009019

Larzelere, R. (2000). Child outcomes of nonabusive and customary physical punishment by parents: an updated literature review. *Clin. Child Fam. Psychol. Rev.* 3, 199–221. doi: 10.1023/A:1026473020315

Lereya, S. T., Copeland, W. E., Costello, E. J., and Wolke, D. (2015). Adult mental health consequences of peer bullying and maltreatment in childhood: two cohorts in two countries. *Lancet Psychiatry* 2, 524–531. doi: 10.1016/S2215-0366(15)00165-0

Lin, L. P., Yen, C. F., Kuo, F. Y., Wu, J. L., and Lin, J. D. (2009). Sexual assault of people with disabilities: results of a 2002–2007 national report in Taiwan. *Res. Dev. Disabil.* 30, 969–975. doi: 10.1016/j.ridd.2009.02.001

Lueger-Schuster, B., Kantor, V., Weindl, D., Knefel, M., Moy, Y., Butollo, A., et al. (2014). Institutional abuse of children in the Austrian Catholic Church: types of abuse and impact on adult survivors' current mental health. *Child Abuse Negl.* 38, 52–64. doi: 10.1016/j.chiabu.2013.07.013

Lund, E. M. (2011). Community-based services and interventions for adults with disabilities who have experienced interpersonal violence: a review of the literature. *Trauma Violence Abuse* 12, 171–182. doi: 10.1177/1524838011416377

Macklin, M. L., Metzger, L. J., Litz, B. T., McNally, R. J., Lasko, N. B., Orr, S. P., et al. (1998). Lower precombat intelligence is a risk factor for posttraumatic stress disorder. *J. Consult. Clin. Psychol.* 66, 323–326. doi: 10.1037/0022-006X.66.2.323

Martorell, A., Tsakanikos, E., Pereda, A., Gutiérrez-Recacha, P., Bouras, N., and Ayuso-Mateos, J. L. (2009). Mental health in adults with mild and moderate intellectual disabilities: the role of recent life events and traumatic experiences across the life span. *J. Nerv. Ment. Dis.* 197, 182–186. doi: 10.1097/NMD.0b013e3181923c8c

Mehta, D., and Binder, E. B. (2012). Gene × environment vulnerability factors for PTSD: the HPA-axis. *Neuropharmacology* 62, 654–662. doi: 10.1016/j.neuropharm.2011.03.009

Mevissen, L., and de Jongh, A. (2010). PTSD and its treatment in people with intellectual disabilities. A review of the literature. *Clin. Psychol. Rev.* 30, 308–316. doi: 10.1016/j.cpr.2009.12.005

Mikton, C., and Shakespeare, T. (2014). Introduction to special issue on violence against people with disability. *J. Interpers. Violence* 29, 3055–3062. doi: 10.1177/0886260514534531

Mitchell, A., Clegg, J., and Furniss, F. (2006). Exploring the meaning of trauma with adults with intellectual disabilities. *J. Appl. Res. Intellect. Disabil.* 19, 131–142. doi: 10.1111/j.1468-3148.2005.00235.x

Mitra, M., and Mouradian, V. E. (2014). Intimate partner violence in the relationships of men with disabilities in the United States: relative prevalence and health correlates. *J. Interpers. Violence* 29, 3150–3166. doi: 10.1177/0886260514534526

Mollica, R. F., Wyshak, G., de Marneffe, D., Khuon, F., and Lavelle, J. (1987). Indochinese versions of the Hopkins Symptom Checklist-25: a screening instrument for the psychiatric care of refugees. *Am. J. Psychiatry* 144, 497–500. doi: 10.1176/ajp.144.4.497

Nanni, V., Uher, R., and Danese, A. (2012). Childhood maltreatment predicts unfavorable course of illness and treatment outcome in depression: a meta-analysis. *Am. J. Psychiatry* 169, 141–151. doi: 10.1176/appi.ajp.2011.11020335

Norman, R. E., Byambaa, M., De, R., Butchart, A., Scott, J., and Vos, T. (2012). The long-term health consequences of child physical abuse, emotional abuse, and neglect: a systematic review and meta-analysis. *PLoS Med.* 9:e1001349. doi: 10.1371/journal.pmed.1001349

Nosek, M. A., Foley, C. C., Hughes, R. B., and Howland, C. A. (2001). Vulnerabilities for abuse among women with disabilities. *Sex. Disabil.* 19, 177–189. doi: 10.1023/A:1013152530758

Rand, M. R., and Harrell, E. (2009). National crime victimization survey: crime against people with disabilities, 2007. *Bur. Justice Stat. Spec. Rep.* NCJ227814, 1–12. Washington, DC: U.S. Department of Justice.

Reiter, S., Bryen, D. N., and Shachar, I. (2007). Adolescents with intellectual disabilities as victims of abuse. *J. Intellect. Disabil.* 11, 371–387. doi: 10.1177/1744629507084602

Rutter, M. (1985). Resilience in the face of adversity. Protective factors and resistance to psychiatric disorder. *Br. J. Psychiatry* 147, 598–611. doi: 10.1192/bjp.147.6.598

Scherer, H. L., Snyder, J. A., and Fisher, B. S. (2014). Intimate partner victimization among college students with and without disabilities prevalence of and relationship to emotional well-being. *J. Interpers. Violence* 1–32. doi: 10.1177/0886260514555126

Scott, K. M., McLaughlin, K. A., Smith, D. A. R., and Ellis, P. M. (2012). Childhood maltreatment and DSM-IV adult mental disorders: comparison of prospective and retrospective findings. *Br. J. Psychiatry* 200, 469–475. doi: 10.1192/bjp.bp.111.103267

Shonkoff, J. P., Garner, A. S., Siegel, B. S., Dobbins, M. I., Earls, M. F., Garner, A. S., et al. (2012). The lifelong effects of early childhood adversity and toxic stress. *Pediatrics* 129, e232–e246. doi: 10.1542/peds.2011-2663

Smith, D. L., and Strauser, D. R. (2008). Examining the impact of physical and sexual abuse on the employment of women with disabilities in the United States: an exploratory analysis. *Disabil. Rehabil.* 30, 1039–1046. doi: 10.1080/09637480701539542

Sobsey, D. (1994). *Violence and Abuse in the Lives of People with Disabilities: The End of Silent Acceptance?* Baltimore, MD: Paul H. Brooks Publishing Co.

Sobsey, D. (1997). Iatrogenic mechanisms for abuse of children with disabilities? *Child Abuse Negl.* 21, 819–821. doi: 10.1016/S0145-2134(97)00043-4

Sobsey, D., and Doe, T. (1991). Patterns of sexual abuse and assault. *Sex. Disabil.* 9, 243–259. doi: 10.1007/BF01102395

Spencer, N., Devereux, E., Wallace, A., Sundrum, R., Shenoy, M., Bacchus, C., et al. (2005). Disabling conditions and registration for child abuse and neglect: a population-based study. *Pediatrics* 116, 609–613. doi: 10.1542/peds.2004-1882

StatSoft. (2007). *STATISTICA (data analysis software)*, version 8.0.

Steil, R., and Ehlers, A. (2000). *Posttraumatische Diagnoseskala*. Jena: Universität Jena.

Stovall-McClough, K. C., and Cloitre, M. (2006). Unresolved attachment, PTSD, and dissociation in women with childhood abuse histories. *J. Consult. Clin. Psychol.* 74, 219–228. doi: 10.1037/0022-006X.74.2.219

Sugaya, L., Hasin, D. S., Olfson, M., Lin, K.-H., Grant, B. F., and Blanco, C. (2012). Child physical abuse and adult mental health: a national study. *J. Trauma Stress* 25, 384–392. doi: 10.1002/jts.21719

Sullivan, P. M. (2009). Violence exposure among children with disabilities. *Clin. Child Fam. Psychol. Rev.* 12, 196–216. doi: 10.1007/s10567-009-0056-1

Sullivan, P. M., and Knutson, J. F. (2000a). Maltreatment and disabilities: a population-based epidemiological study. *Child Abuse Negl.* 24, 1257–1273. doi: 10.1016/S0145-2134(00)00190-3

Sullivan, P. M., and Knutson, J. F. (2000b). The prevalence of disabilities and maltreatment among runaway children. *Child Abuse Negl.* 24, 1275–1288. doi: 10.1016/S0145-2134(00)00181-2

Tischler, L., Brand, S. R., Stavitsky, K., Labinsky, E., Newmark, R., Grossman, R., et al. (2006). The relationship between hippocampal volume and declarative memory in a population of combat veterans with and without PTSD. *Ann. N. Y. Acad. Sci.* 1071, 405–409. doi: 10.1196/annals.1364.031

Watts-English, T., Fortson, B. L., Gibler, N., Hooper, S. R., and De Bellis, M. D. (2006). The psychobiology of maltreatment in childhood. *J. Soc. Issues* 62, 717–736. doi: 10.1111/j.1540-4560.2006.00484.x

Weiss, J. A., MacMullin, J., Waechter, R., and Wekerle, C. (2011). Child maltreatment, adolescent attachment style, and dating violence: considerations in youths with borderline-to-mild intellectual disability. *Int. J. Ment. Health Addict.* 9, 555–576. doi: 10.1007/s11469-011-9321-x

Widom, C. S. (1999). Posttraumatic stress disorder in abused and neglected children grown up. *Am. J. Psychiatry* 156, 1223–1229.

Widom, C. S., Czaja, S. J., and Dutton, M. A. (2008). Childhood victimization and lifetime revictimization. *Child Abuse Negl.* 32, 785–796. doi: 10.1016/j.chiabu.2007.12.006

Conflict of Interest Statement: The authors declare that the research was conducted in the absence of any commercial or financial relationships that could be construed as a potential conflict of interest.

5

An Evidence-Based Education Program for Adults about Child Sexual Abuse ("*Prevent It!*") That Significantly Improves Attitudes, Knowledge, and Behavior

Erin K. Martin and Peter H. Silverstone *

Department of Psychiatry, University of Alberta, Edmonton, AB, Canada

Here we describe the development of an evidence-based education program for adults about childhood sexual abuse (CSA), called *Prevent It!* Uniquely, the primary goal of this program was to change the behavior of participants, as well as to increase knowledge about CSA and positive attitudes toward it. A comprehensive review shows no previous similar approach. The program includes a detailed manual to allow standardized administration by trained facilitators, as well as multiple video segments from CSA survivors and professionals. A total of 23 program workshops were run, with 366 adults participating. Of these, 312 (85%) agreed to take part in the study. All completed baseline ratings prior to the program and 195 (63% of study sample) completed follow-up assessments at 3-months. There were no significant differences between the demographic make-up of the baseline group and the follow-up group. Assessments included demographic data, knowledge, attitudes, and several measures of behavior (our primary outcome variable). Behavioral questions asked individuals to select behaviors used in the previous 3-months from a list of options. Questions also included asking "how many times in the previous 3-months" have you "talked about healthy sexual development or Child sexual abuse (CSA) with a child you know"; "suspected a child was sexually abused"; "taken steps to protect a child"; or "reported suspected sexual abuse to police or child welfare"? The majority of attendees were women, with the commonest age group being between 30 and 39 years old. Approximately 33% had experienced CSA themselves. At 3-month follow-up there were highly statistically significant improvements in several aspects of behavior and knowledge, and attitudes regarding CSA. For example, the number of subjects actively looking for evidence of CSA increased from 46% at baseline to 81% at follow-up, while the number of subjects who actively took steps to protect children increased from 25% at baseline to 48% at follow-up. For general public adults, this is the first program designed using the current evidence base for effective training in CSA examining longer-term outcomes and the first to focus on actual behavioral outcomes. The results suggest it is highly effective and support its widespread use.

Keywords: child, sexual, abuse, adult, education, prevention, program, evaluation

Edited by:
Jesus De La Fuente, University of Almeria, Spain

Reviewed by:
Ricardo Tejeiro, University of Liverpool, UK
Maite Garaigordobil, University of the Basque Country, Spain

***Correspondence:**
Peter H. Silverstone
peter.silverstone@ualberta.ca

Specialty section:
This article was submitted to Educational Psychology, a section of the journal Frontiers in Psychology

INTRODUCTION

Child sexual abuse (CSA) is common (Finkelhor, 1994; Pereda et al., 2009), with as many as 1 in 6 girls and 1 in 12 boys currently experiencing sexual abuse involving bodily contact (Martin and Silverstone, 2013). It is uncertain if there are changes in the rates of CSA in the United States (Finkelhor, 2009) or Canada (Collin-Vézina et al., 2010), particularly given the increase in use of internet pornography (Diamond et al., 2011; Livingstone and Smith, 2014). Adults who experienced CSA have higher rates of psychopathology (Chen et al., 2010) and are at higher risk of a range of medical, psychological, behavioral, and sexual disorders (Maniglio, 2009) than those who have not been sexually abused. It is possible that these impacts are mediated through changes in brain structures and functions (Anda et al., 2006; Kaffman, 2009; Belsky and de Haan, 2011), as well as neurobiological stress systems, with "child maltreatment (being) a preventable contributor to child psychopathology, cognitive impairment, and developmental difficulties" (Watts-English et al., 2006).

Because of the frequent long-term impacts of CSA, preventing it is of great importance. One method is to include a range of people in prevention efforts including parents, professionals, and the general public (Wurtele, 2009). Toward this end, it is likely that adults who interact with children may be in the best position to reduce children's vulnerability to CSA, as well as to reduce their vulnerability to negative impacts associated with CSA. This is of value as positive adult support may improve outcomes, helping children experience fewer negative impacts than others (Yancey et al., 2011). It should also be recognized that previous research into the possible effectiveness of adult training programs has provided insight into knowledge gain, attitude change, and behavioral *intentions* (Rheingold et al., 2007; Self-Brown et al., 2008), but not on the key issue of actual behavior *changes* in regards to CSA preventative behaviors.

There is great variety in the types of prevention programs that exists, their target groups, the methods, and their specific contexts (Zollner et al., 2014). Despite this variety, there are few CSA prevention programs targeting general public adults that have been developed using a research informed approach, and none to our knowledge that reflect recent research findings. All such programs do need to be based on current theoretical understandings of healthy child development (Zeuthen and Hagelskjær, 2013). Furthermore, evidence-based approaches that include policy, legislation, and services are also currently lacking (Collin-Vézina et al., 2010). For this reason, we believe that development of a novel program is required, and here we report on such a program, titled: *Prevent It!* Taking Action to Stop Child Sexual Abuse (*Prevent It!*). In the current publication we describe the current research background, the theoretical background, methodology of development of the program, and the first study into it's effectiveness. In particular, we examined the extent to which a classroom-based CSA prevention program for adults can change participant's longer-term behaviors, as well as attitudes and knowledge.

MATERIALS AND METHODS

Ethical and Personal Impact Consideration

This study was approved by the Ethics Board of the University of Alberta. All participants completed informed consent prior to any involvement in the program. All individuals were given a unique study number, and this was the only identifier used to collect all study-related information at a secure on-line site. To ensure confidentiality for participants in a group setting we only used first names, and also included a section in the introduction of the program where the facilitator asks participants to respect and maintain each other's confidentiality.

Additionally, there is potential for the program to be emotionally upsetting, and have a personal impact particularly for those individuals who have themselves experienced CSA. We therefore took several steps to address this concern. Firstly, all participants were provided with a 24-h crisis line resource to access, should they want to talk to someone outside their own support system or get more information about professional services. Secondly, the facilitators discussed this issue at the start of the program, letting each participant know that the program could be upsetting to them, or could bring up thoughts and feelings that are difficult to manage. Thirdly, participants were encouraged to use their own support system, if needed, and were reminded of this at the start and end of the program.

Program Development and Literature Review

We reviewed literature related to CSA topics in order to determine program content using the databases PubMed, PsycINFO, and ERIC. In order to obtain an overview of the topic we searched the databases using the following search terms: "sexual abuse," "rates," "occurrence," "epidemiology," "impact," "signs," "indicators," "victim," "survivor," "offenders," "perpetrators," "disclosure," "education," "prevention," "reporting," "parents," "children," "caregivers," and "teachers."

Current Situation

School-based, child targeted prevention programs have been widely used in CSA education (Zwi et al., 2007; Wurtele, 2009; Walsch et al., 2015). Accessing children directly through schools allows educators to reach children from a wide range of socio-economic and ethnic backgrounds (Wurtele, 2009). Targeting children at school rather than relying on parents to provide the information helps ensure children who are being abused in their homes still have access to CSA education. The extent to which schools are currently using this type of approach is yet to be assessed in a systematic way (Wurtele, 2009). Literature reviews (MacMillan et al., 2009; Fryda and Hulme, 2015) and meta-analysis (Davis and Gidycz, 2000; Zwi et al., 2007; Walsch et al., 2015) indicate child-targeted programs can increase children's knowledge, self-protective behaviors, and reporting behaviors (MacMillan et al., 2009). While child-targeted CSA education plays an important role in CSA prevention, adults may also be a useful target group (Wurtele, 2009; Zeuthen and Hagelskjær, 2013).

Of the adult-targeted education, research on caregivers is most common (Berrick, 1988; Hébert et al., 2002; Rheingold et al., 2007; Self-Brown et al., 2008; Kenny, 2009). Caregivers may be in positions where they can rapidly identify CSA situations and help at-risk or affected children (Hébert et al., 2002). It should be noted that children's disclosure of abuse is often a process rather than a one-time event (Alaggia, 2004; Jenson et al., 2005), and their caregivers can be in ideal positions to respond to these disclosures. Nonetheless, a caregiver may also be involved in perpetrating abuse (Public Health Agency of Canada, 2010), making it necessary for adults outside the home to also receive CSA education. In part for this reason, it has been suggested (Wurtele, 2009) that non-caregiver adults should also have CSA education, although these adults remain the least studied group. Teachers have received slightly more attention than other non-caregiver adults (Walsch et al., 2012), and the potential effectiveness of media campaigns on general adult populations has also been examined (Self-Brown et al., 2008). The focus of many adult-targeted education programs has been on changing knowledge and attitudes about CSA (Bowman et al., 2010; Walsch et al., 2012), as well as behavioral *intentions* with regard to responding to suspected CSA (Hébert et al., 2002; Self-Brown et al., 2008). To our knowledge, there are no previous studies that have examined actual changes in behavior after training programs.

Adult-targeted CSA education programs use a variety of formats to teach adults about CSA. One randomized controlled study measured attitudes, knowledge, and behavioral intentions after being exposed to media-based CSA materials founding a significant increase in knowledge scores after exposure but no significant change in attitude (Rheingold et al., 2007). Another study used survey and focus group methods to evaluate the effectives of public service announcements on knowledge and likelihood of behavioral change, but while they found a very short-term increase in knowledge, participants agreed this approach was not enough to change behavior (Self-Brown et al., 2008). The results from these studies suggest that a brief exposure to CSA educational materials may increase knowledge in the short-term, but not be sufficient to change behavior. One online version of a CSA education program shows that professionals (i.e., teachers, psychologist, and social workers) who interact with children and youth regularly had significant gains in CSA related empathy in the 6 months after taking the online program (Man-Ging et al., 2015). Similarly, other classroom-based studies show an increase in short-term knowledge as well as increase appropriate behavioral intentions (Hébert et al., 2002; Kenny, 2009; Bowman et al., 2010; Rheingold et al., 2012). However, only one of these studies included follow-up assessment beyond 1 month (Rheingold et al., 2015), and thus the longer-term effectiveness of previous adult-targeted classroom-based education is promising but far from certain. It is also unclear if repeated information sessions, rather than a single exposure, alters the effectiveness of education (Davis and Gidycz, 2000; Rheingold et al., 2007). According to the results of a multi-site, randomized control trail study, adult-targeted CSA education programs designed for childcare professionals can increase knowledge and self-reported use of prevention behaviors in both classroom and online versions (Rheingold et al., 2015). There are no studies that show an increase in knowledge over more than a 1-month period, and none that have examined actual behavioral changes in general public adults. Given increasing literature and knowledge about the most effective types of adult education (Petty and Thomas, 2014; Taylor and Laros, 2014), we developed a novel program education program targeting general population adults (*Prevent It!*) to address this issue. We also evaluated the program, with our primary outcome measure focusing on behavior changes over a 3-month period.

Consultation and Theoretical Grounding

Taking into consideration the current situation, we consulted with topic experts in order to assess current needs (and potential gaps) in CSA education with a wide group of individuals. These included members of the Police Services involved with all aspects of CSA, psychologists working in the field of CSA, charities involved in training, and with sexual assault centers. Because our main outcome goal for the program was behavior change, it was important to structure the program utilizing methodology previously demonstrated to maximize likelihood of subsequent behavioral changes. Although some studies have shown changes in behavior *intentions* after taking an adult-targeted CSA education program (Hébert et al., 2002; Rheingold et al., 2007; Self-Brown et al., 2008; Paranal et al., 2012) and one study measured self-report behavior change in childcare professionals (Rheingold et al., 2015) we are unaware of any studies measuring actual behavior changes in general public adults. The lack of research means that little is known about the key components required to change participant's behavior in regards to sexual prevention. For these reasons, we used previously well-established models, namely the Transtheoretical Model of change (TTM) (Diclemente et al., 1991; Diclemente and Prochaska, 1998) and the Experiential Learning Cycle (Kolb, 1975) to develop the program.

The TTM approach to understanding behavior change combines all components into a single cohesive theory (Diclemente and Prochaska, 1998). Although initially developed to understand behavior in regards to addictions, the TTM is useful in helping understand how adults change their behavior. According to the TTM model, adults cycle through five stages when changing their behavior. In (1) *pre-contemplation,* adults are not yet considering the behavior change in question, while in (2) *contemplation,* the person considers change but has not yet decided to make the change. In (3) *preparation,* the person prepares for, and plans for, making the change and in (4) *action,* the individual starts making the change. Finally, in (5) *maintenance,* the change has is made and is continued over a longer period of time. The program was therefore designed to facilitate the movement of participants through each subsequent stage, and to assist them to reach the action (stage 4) and maintenance (stage 5) phases of change.

The activities in the program were structured utilizing methodology described in the Experiential Learning Cycle (ELC) (Kolb, 1975). The ELC can be considered as a tool used to create movement through the TTM. This cycle has 4 components: (1) concrete experience, (2) reflective observation, (3) abstract conceptualization, and (4) action/active experimentation. First, the facilitator introduced a structured experience, such as playing a video clip segment or directing participants to an activity in the program. Experiences engage participants in ways that relate to the program's desired outcomes. They also provide participants with a common base for discussion. Second, the facilitator guides participants to reflect on the previous concrete experience encouraging then to personalize the experience by exploring their feelings about, reactions to, and observations of the activity. Third, the facilitator poses "*so what*" and "*now what*" questions to help participants look for personal lessons and future applications. In this step participants make real-world meaning of the activity by utilizing more general principals. Finally, the facilitator helps participants explore ways in which they can implement their learning in their own lives and organizations. They are encouraged to think creatively about the ways in which these leanings can be applied in their unique situations as well as consider possible barriers to implementing changes. Utilizing the well-validated TTM and the ELC ensured the strong theoretical foundation for the program.

Content and Program Guides

Program content was determined after the detailed consultation process, combined with regular communication and contact with the range of stakeholders and also with experienced trainers. A detailed "program guide" was developed, including the rationale for each section, presented in an easy to understand format written for a general audience. It provides all necessary background information for the program content and approach. The program guide is an 80-page document and was made available to program staff.

A briefer "information book" was also developed for all program participants, derived directly from the program guide, to be used by all participants during the program, and subsequently by them as reference material. During the program, facilitators directed participants to the relevant sections of the information books to engage in exercises throughout the program, and used this to guide participants through the exercises.

The program includes a significant video component, with the group facilitator showing video segments throughout the program. The facilitator introduces each section before showing it, and after viewing each segment, there was a guided exercise aimed to increase personal and critical reflection on the material. Video sections include overall narration, interviews with experts in the area, survivors of sexual abuse, and professionals who work in related fields.

The survivor interviews provide personal accounts of sexual abuse as well some of the impact of CSA on them in both the shorter-term and longer-term. These interviews helped to highlight the personal toll of CSA and remind participants that CSA significantly impacts of range of different people in multiple ways. In order to reduce the potential for harm to people that might regret their decision to tell their story in the educational video format, only CSA survivors who were already publicly sharing their stories were approached to be involved. All survivors were told in advance about the types of questions they would be asked in the interview, and were told that they were in control of the question answering process. They did not need to answer all the questions if they did not want to, and they were reminded that they could change their mind and decide not to participate at any point in time during the video production phase or subsequently.

Professionals working in fields related to sexual abuse were also interviewed. Effort was taken to have a wide range of professional voices represented. Interviews featured in the film, in addition to CSA victims, include a psychologist and Traumatologist, an experienced police detective involved in many cases of CSA, a defense attorney, and a psychiatrist.

Facilitator Guide

The facilitator guide explained what was expected from the facilitator at each point in the program workshop, with information grouped around several themes. **Table 1** outlines program themes and topics. The program workshops were designed to be given by community volunteers, rather than specialists, to allow it to be generalizable. For this reason, the Facilitator Guide was written in non-specialist language. Additionally, this model allows for volunteers from a range of communities to be trained and to return to their own communities (and surrounding areas) to provide the program. We believe this model can increase access to the program for individuals in many areas, is scalable, and also practical for use in remote and rural areas. In order to allow for volunteers to facilitate the program consistently we created a highly detailed guide for them to follow. The guide outlines what to say to introduce each video segment and the subsequent exercises. It also provides questions to prompt participant reflection, and identifies key points that are to be emphasized or summarized at the end of each exercise. In the present study we utilized two individuals who received funding for running the program workshops, and who had significant experience doing this previously. To ensure fidelity across sessions, facilitators were instructed to follow the script and guide closely during each program workshop.

Program Evaluation

The target group was adults who interact with children, including caregivers, teachers, coaches for sports and recreation activities, youth group leaders, and religious leaders. This study evaluated the effectiveness of the *Prevent It!* program at changing adult participant's behaviors 3-months after the training session (the primary outcome goal), as well as improving attitudes toward CSA and knowledge about this. A priori hypotheses were that participants who took the workshop would: (1) decrease adherence to problematic myths about CSA (referred to as negative attitudes), (2) increase accurate knowledge about CSA, and (3) increase their use of individual and organizational prevention behaviors to reduce risk of CSA and identify this early. One explicit long-term goal, not studied in the current program, was that this program will help with early identification, and appropriate interventions, of CSA when it occurs. We hope to explore this issue in subsequent research.

TABLE 1 | Content of the adult-targeted child sexual abuse education program.

Section	Topics
General Information	• Definitions • Rates • Offenders • Internet
Talking with Children	• Being a good listener • HSD[a] • Talking with children about HSD • Talking with children about CSA[b]
Observing children and adults	• Possible signs of distress in children • Possible signs of CSA • Grooming • Concerning signs in other adults
Preparing for Action	• Disclosures of CSA • Reporting CSA • Suspicions of CSA • Individual prevention strategies • Organizational best practices • Individualized goal setting

General sections and the topics included within the sections for the Prevent It! child sexual abuse education program.
[a]HSD, healthy sexual development.
[b]CSA, child sexual abuse.

Sampling Strategy and Setting

We wanted to measure the effectiveness of the program based on the population that it will be serving. To do this, we used a convenience sample of adults who registered to take educational programs with a charity that provides this (Little Warriors).

Recruitment

Study participants were recruited from people that enrolled to take the program. While registering for the program, each person was informed in general terms about the study, and asked if he/she could be contacted with more information. Individuals who agreed to find out more were provided with information and the informed consent form. If they agreed to take part they were then given a unique user number, and information about how to use this to access the secure on-line site where information was collected at baseline. The only required inclusion criteria, other than agreeing to take part in the training session and study, was that they were aged 18 or older. There were no additional exclusion criteria for this study.

Program Implementation

There were a total of 23 program workshops, involving 366 participants, carried out during the final 3-months of 2014 in 14 communities in Western Canada. The individual who facilitated the vast majority of groups had no previous expertise in this, and no background in medicine or allied professions, to allow some approximation toward the anticipated outcomes when given by other similar individuals. Groups who participated in program workshops included those offered to the general public (14), child/youth serving organizations (5), community groups (2), a mother's group (1), and a group of individuals attending a conference regarding youth issues (1).

Measurement of Effectiveness and Research Design

Participants were given pre-test (baseline) measurements to assess attitudes, knowledge, and behaviors related to CSA during the 7-days prior to the program workshop. Three months after their participation in the program workshop they were asked to complete follow-up questionnaires. Each participant's post-test results were compared to baseline results to assess the amount of change that occurred. The main hypothesis being tested was that, at 3-months post-training, participation in the *Prevent It!* program would increase behaviors to reduce children's vulnerability to CSA.

Procedures

During the 7-days prior the program workshops, participants completed baseline questionnaires via the secure online site. Participants then took part in the 3-h program workshop. Three months after completion of the program, study participants were contacted and asked to complete the follow-up questionnaire online. This process involved contact (via phone or email—at the choice of the participant). A maximum of three attempts were made for each individual who did not complete the follow-up questionnaire.

Sample and Demographics

Participants were asked to self-report their gender, age, highest education level completed, level of previous CSA training received, and if they had experienced any type CSA themselves during their childhood. Before being asked about their own experience of sexual abuse, each participant was reminded of the confidentiality of their responses and of the reason for collecting the information. Participants were able to skip demographic details if they chose.

The sample consisted of 312 adults who took the program and completed the informed consent and pre-test questionnaire. Of these, 209 individuals (67%) also completed the 3-month follow-up questionnaire. However, of these a total of 12 questionnaires were not usable due to incomplete identifying information, while one individual with the same identifying information completed the questionnaire twice and both versions were therefore excluded. Thus the final study sample consisted of 195 individuals (63%) for whom there was study data, although some individuals did not complete every section as specified below. Demographic details for the 3 month follow-up group are shown in **Table 2**.

It is important to note that we have baseline demographic data on 312 individuals, but detailed follow-up data only 195 individuals. However, a Wilcoxon signed-rank test showed no statistically significant demographic differences between these groups.

Knowledge, Attitudes, and Behavioral Change

Previous studies demonstrate increased accurate knowledge and positive attitudes after exposure to a CSA education program (Hébert et al., 2002; Rheingold et al., 2007; Self-Brown et al., 2008; and Bowman et al., 2010). Consequently, we measured these

TABLE 2 | Demographics of Study Participants ($n = 195$).

Demographic Information	N (%)
GENDER	
Male	21 (11%)
Female	174 (89%)
AGE	
18–29	57 (29%)
30–39	64 (33%)
40–49	41 (21%)
50–59	21 (11%)
60 and older	12 (6%)
LEVEL OF EDUCATION COMPLETED	
High school	25 (13%)
Post-secondary	139 (71%)
Graduate studies	31 (16%)
PREVIOUS CSA[a] TRAINING	
None	105 (54%)
Some	80 (41%)
Extensive	10 (5%)
PREVIOUS PERSONAL HISTORY OF CSA	
Yes	62 (32%)
No	115 (59%)
Unsure	14 (7%)
Did not answer	4 (2%)

Demographic make-up of the post-test sample. There was no significant difference between the sample at baseline and the sample at 3-month-follow up.
[a]CSA, child sexual abuse.

TABLE 3 | Measurement of knowledge and attitude.

Measure	Statement[a]
Knowledge	Children are most commonly sexually abused by people who are known to the child and the child's family.
	When a child tells an adult he/she was sexually abused, it is important for the adult to determine whether or not the abuse happened.
	If I suspect that a child is being sexually abused, I have a legal obligation to report this abuse to child social services or police.
Attitude	Children who act in a seductive manner are not to blame if an adult responds to them in a sexual way.
	Sexual contact between an adult and a child that does not involve actual or attempted sexual intercourse is unlikely to have serious psychological consequences for the child.
	Children who do not report ongoing sexual abuse must want the sexual contact to continue.

[a]Measured using a 5-point Likert scale: Strongly disagree (coded 4), disagree (coded 3), not sure (coded 2), agree (coded 1), strongly agree (coded 0).

constructs briefly. Knowledge was measured using three Likert scale items. To measure attitudes we utilized three items from the *Child Abuse Myth Scale* (Collings, 1997). Participants were asked to indicate the extent to which they agreed with the statements (**Table 3**) using Likert scale answers.

To measure behavioral change we created questions based upon current best knowledge about how to decrease children's vulnerability to CSA (Martin and Silverstone, 2013). We measured behaviors related to four major categories: talking about CSA and healthy sexual development (HSD); suspecting and reporting CSA; individual action strategies; and organizational action strategies. We assessed participant's use of behavioral strategies by asking them to select the number of times they had used the strategy in the previous 3-months as well as to select all of the specific items they used from provided checklists. **Table 4** details the format, measurement, and coding of each question.

Statistical Analysis

In order to assess change from pre-test to 3-month follow-up we computed scores for several of the measures. To assess attitude and knowledge change, each Likert scale response was scored using the ideal responses with higher scores representing more ideal responses. Each participant was given an attitude score and a knowledge score at baseline and at pre-test with higher scores representing more ideal responses. These scores were used to determine attitude and knowledge change.

We assessed behavior change in several ways. First, the measures for the number of times talking about CSA and HSD, the number of times suspecting CSA, and the number of times reporting CSA were compared directly between baseline measurement and post-test measurement. Total scores for CSA and HSD related topics, individual action strategies, and organizational action strategies were computed by adding together each strategy selected. We then computed an overall behavior score for each participant at baseline and post-test by summing the scores for CSA/HSD related topics talked about, individual action strategies, and organizational action strategies used to produce a single total score for each participant. Note that for participants who selected *not applicable* for organizational action strategies were excluded from the organizational strategies analysis.

We used the Wilcoxon signed rank test to determine within-subject statistically significant change from baseline measurements to post test measurements, given that the Wilcoxon test is appropriate for use with non-parametric data and related groups. Note that we did not apply a Bonferroni correction for multiple comparisons since, while a Bonferroni correction can be useful for reducing the risk of Type I errors in multiple comparisons, it also creates a loss of power to detect changes that are present making its usefulness disputed in studies such as the current one (Keppel, 1991; Perneger, 1998; Divine et al., 2013). Effect sizes were calculated using the standardized *z*-score from the results of the Wilcoxon signed Rank test divided by the square root of "n" (Field, 2009). Effect sizes were understood using Cohen's (1992) guidelines: $r = 0.010$ (small effect), $r = 0.30$ (medium effect), $r = 0.50$ (large effect). Statistical significance was defined as $p < 0.05$. Spearman's correlation was used to determine associations between demographic variables and dependent variables. Missing values due to lack of response to individual questions were excluded from analysis.

TABLE 4 | Measurement and coding of behavior.

Behavioral Measures	Measurement	Codes
TALKING ABOUT CSA AND HEALTHY SEXUAL DEVELOPMENT		
In the past 3-months, how many times have you talked about healthy sexual development or child sexual abuse with children that you know?	0 times 1–2 times 3–4 times 5 or more times	0 1 2 3
In the past 3-months, which of the following have you talked about with a child you know? Select all that apply. • Boundaries • Identifying a range of emotions • Internet safety • Proper names for genitals • Using the word "surprise" for things like birthday presents rather than "secret" • Definition of sexual abuse • Grooming techniques adults might use • Children are never to blame if they are sexually abused • What to do if you are sexually abused • How to tell someone if you are sexually abused • Saying "no" is allowed	Total score between 0 and 11	0 = No 1 = Yes
SUSPECTING AND REPORTING CSA		
In the past 3-months, how many times have you suspected a child you know might have been sexually abused?	0 times 1–2 times 3–4 times 5 or more times	0 1 2 3
In the past 3-months, how many times have you reported a child who you suspected was sexually abused to child social services or police?	0 times 1–2 times 3–4 times 5 or more times	0 1 2 3
INDIVIDUAL ACTION STRATEGIES		
In the past 3-months, what things have you done individually? Select all that apply. • Watched for signs of abuse in children • Taken steps to protect children from sexual abuse • Been a responsible role model for other adults in your interaction with children	Total score between 0 and 3	0 = No 1 = Yes
ORGANIZATIONAL ACTION STRATEGIES		
In the past 3-months, what things has your organization done with adults who interact with or want to interact with children? Select all that apply. • Does not apply to me[a] • Criminal record checks • Child welfare checks • Screening interviews • Reference checks • Provide written policy outlining appropriate conduct with children • Monitoring one-on-one time between adults and children • Provide written policy for handling suspicions of abuse • Provide written policy for handling disclosure of abuse • Provide written policy for identifying and handling inappropriate comments and behaviors by adults	Total score between 0 and 8	0 = No 1 = Yes

[a]*Participants who selected does not apply to me were excluded from this analysis.*

RESULTS

Knowledge and Attitude

Measurements of knowledge and attitude had statistically significantly increases from pre-test to 3-month follow-up (**Figure 1**). A total of 174 study participants completed both baseline and 3-month follow-up questionnaires in the knowledge section of the questionnaire. A Wilcoxon signed-rank test determined a highly statistically significant median increase in knowledge score from pre-test (9) to 3-month follow-up (11), $Z = 7.463$, $p < 0.001$ (**Table 5**). Of the 174 participants, 108 had higher scores. 44 had no change, and 22 had a decrease. A total of 189 study participants completed both baseline and 3-month follow-up questionnaires in the attitude section of the questionnaire. A Wilcoxon signed-rank test also showed a highly statistically significant median increase in attitude score from pre-test (10) to 3-month follow-up (12), $Z = 4.724$, $p < 0.001$ (**Table 5**). Of the 189 participants, 78 had increased scores, 86 had no change, and 25 had a decrease in scores.

Behavioral Measures

All 195 study participants completed at least one section of the behavioral questionnaire at both baseline and follow-up, while a total of 117 study participants completed both baseline and 3-month follow-up questionnaires on all sections of the behavioral questionnaire (including organizational—which didn't apply to many individuals). Results of a Wilcoxon signed-rank test found a highly statistically significant change between the median at baseline and 3-month follow-up, $Z = 5.322$, $p < 0.001$ (**Figure 1**). From the total number of 113 participants 77 scores increased, 7 scores did not change, and 29 scores decreased.

Suspecting Child Sexual Abuse

A total of 186 study participants completed both baseline and 3-month follow-up questionnaires in this section of the behavioral questionnaire. Results of a Wilcoxon signed-rank test found no statistically significant changes between the median at baseline and 3-month follow-up (**Table 6**). After the 3-month follow-up 22 participant's scores in regards to suspecting CSA increased, 141 stayed the same, and 23 decreased.

Reporting Child Sexual Abuse

A total of 180 study participants completed both baseline and 3-month follow-up questionnaires on this section of the behavioral questionnaire. Results of a Wilcoxon signed-rank test found no statistically significant changes between the median at baseline and 3-month follow-up (**Table 6**). After the 3-month follow-up, 13 participant's scores in regards to reporting CSA increased, 155 stayed the same, and 12 decreased.

Number of Times Talking about Child Sexual Abuse or Healthy Sexual Development

A total of 186 study participants completed both baseline and 3-month follow-up questionnaires in this section of the behavioral questionnaire. Results of a Wilcoxon signed-rank test found a statistically significant change between the median at baseline and 3-month follow-up (**Table 6**). From the total number of 186 participants 81 scores increased, 51 scored did not change, and 54 scores decreased.

Total Number of Topics Talked about

A total of 195 study participants completed both baseline and 3-month follow-up questionnaires on this section of the behavioral questionnaire. The median score at 3-month follow-up was higher than at pre-test. Results of a Wilcoxon signed-rank test found a highly statistically significant change between the median at baseline and 3-month follow-up (**Table 6**, **Figure 2**). From the total number of 195 participants there were 101 increased scores, 31 did not change, and 63 had decreased scores.

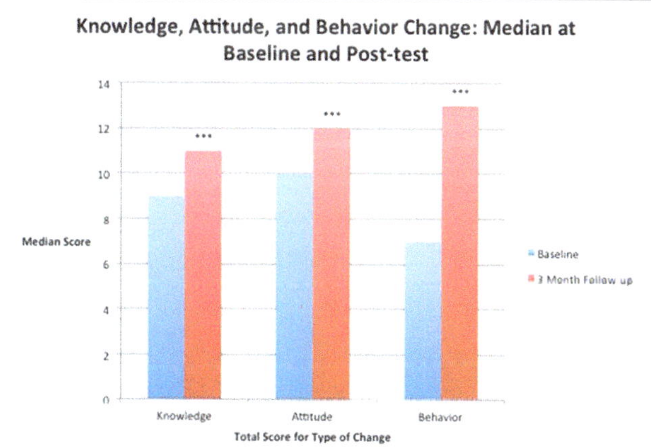

FIGURE 1 | Median score for attitude, knowledge, and behavior before taking the workshop (baseline) and at 3-months after taking the workshop (3-month follow-up). ***Results significant at $p < 0.001$.

Total Individual Prevention Strategies Used

A total of 194 study participants completed both baseline and 3-month follow-up questionnaires on this section of the behavioral questionnaire. Median score at 3-month follow-up was double that at pre-test (**Figure 2**). Results of a Wilcoxon signed-rank test found a statistically significant change between the median at baseline and 3-month follow-up (**Table 6**). Of the 194 participants that completed these measures, 101 had an increase in score, 49 scores did not change, and 44 scores decreased.

The individual action strategies are shown in **Figure 3** with each category being measured using the percentage of the sample that used each strategy both at baseline and at 3-month follow-up (**Table 7**). Results of a Wilcoxon signed-rank test found a statistically significant change for watching for signs of abuse between the median at baseline and 3-month follow-up (**Table 6**). Of the 194 participants that completed these measures, 72 had an increase in score, 105 scores did not change, and 17 scores decreased. The Wilcoxon signed-rank test also found statistically significant change for taking steps to protect children from baseline to 3-month follow-up. Of the 194 participants that completed these measures, 74 had an increase in score, 85 scores did not change, and 35 scores decreased. Statically significant change from pre-test to 3-months follow-up also occurred in being a responsible role model for other adult. Of the 194 participants that completed these measures, 74 had an increase in score, 85 scores did not change, and 35 scores decreased.

Total Organizational Prevention Strategies Used

A total of 124 study participants completed both baseline and 3-month follow-up questionnaires on this section of the behavioral questionnaire, with the rest stating this section of the questionnaire was not relevant to their role. Median scores at 3-month follow-up were three times higher than at pre-test (**Figure 2**). Results of a Wilcoxon signed-rank test found a highly statistically significant change between the median at baseline and 3-month follow-up (**Table 6**). Of these 124 individuals involved with organizations 79 had an increase in score, 9 scores did not change, and 37 scores decreased.

TABLE 5 | Results for attitude and knowledge change.

	Median		Range		*Z*-score	*p*-value	Effect size[a]
	Baseline	3 Month Follow-up	Baseline	3 Month Follow-up			
Total Knowledge Score	9	11	12	7	7.463	<0.0005***	0.57
Total Attitude Score	10	12	12	8	4.724	<0.0005***	0.34

[a]*Effect sizes based on Cohen's (1992), $r = 0.01$ (small effect), $r = 0.30$ (medium effect), $r = 0.50$ (large effect).*

****Results significant at $p < 0.001$.*

TABLE 6 | Behavior change results.

	Median		Range		*Z*-score	*p*-value	Effect Size[a]
	Baseline	3 Month Follow-up	Baseline	3 Month Follow-up			
Number of times talking about CSA and HSD	0	1	3	3	2.456	0.014*	0.18
Total number of topics discussed	2	4	11	11	3.204	0.001**	0.23
Number of times suspecting CSA	0	0	3	3	0.250	0.802	NS[b]
Number of times reporting CSA	0	0	2	2	0.179	0.858	NS
Total number of individual action strategies used	1	2	3	3	5.398	< 0.0005***	0.39
Being a responsible role model for other adults	1	1	1	1	2.926	0.003*	0.21
Watching for signs of abuse in children	0	1	1	1	5.830	< 0.001***	0.42
Taking steps to protect children	0	0	1	1	3.736	< 0.001***	0.27
total number of organizational action strategies used	2	6	9	9	4.165	< 0.0005***	0.37

CSA, child sexual abuse.
HSD, healthy sexual development.
[a]*Effect sizes based on Cohen's (1992), $r = 0.01$ (small effect), $r = 0.30$ (medium effect), $r = 0.50$ (large effect).*
[b]*NS = non-significant. Effect sizes were not calculated when results were non-significant.*
**Results significant at $p = 0.05$.*
***Results significant at $p = 0.001$.*
****Results significant at $p < 0.001$.*

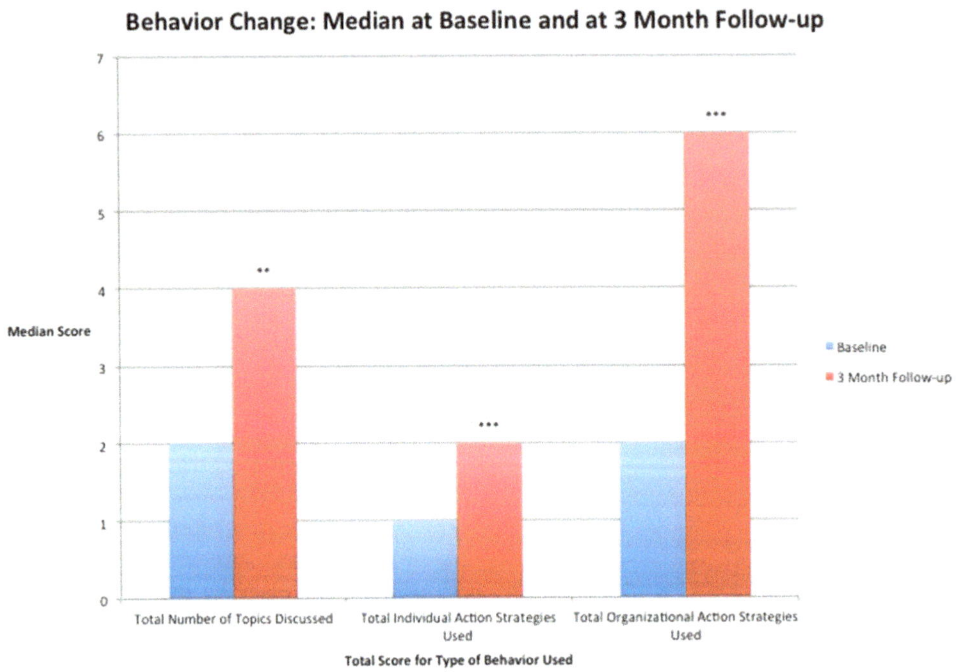

FIGURE 2 | Median score for specific behavior change categories before taking the workshop (baseline) and at 3-months after taking the workshop (3-month follow-up). **Results significant at $p = 0.001$. ***Results significant at $p < 0.001$.

Descriptive Statistics and Behavioral Change Measures

Behavioral measures were also separated into individual variable categories and looked at using percentages of the total sample (**Table 7**) in order to gain more insight into changes that occurred in the 3 months after taking the program. We ran statistical analysis on the variables included within individual action strategies (**Table 6**) because these variables were of particular interest. We did not run analysis to determine the statistical significance the remainder of these categories because of the high number of variables and associated increasing risk of Type I errors as more tests are run.

Correlations between Outcome Variables and Demographic Variables

Using a Spearman's rank correlation co-efficient test we examined potential correlations between demographic variables and changes in knowledge attitude, total topics talked about, total

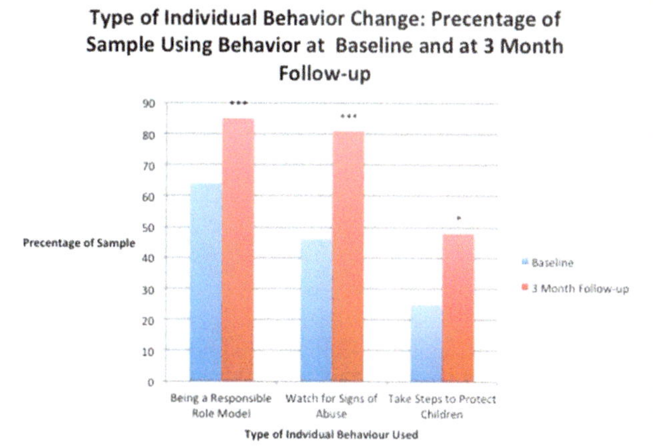

FIGURE 3 | Percentage of the sample that reported using each individual prevention strategy before taking the program (baseline) and after taking the program (3-month follow-up). *Results significant at $p < 0.05$. *** Results significant at $p < 0.001$.

individual action strategies used, total organizational strategies used, number of times suspecting CSA, or number of times reporting CSA. However, we found no statistically significant correlations between these variables and gender, age, highest level of education completed, or self-reported sexual abuse as a child other than a single negative relationship between having previous CSA training and change in use or organizational action strategies. There was a significant negative relationship between having previous CSA training and change in use or organizational action strategies, $r_s = -0.278$, $p = 0.002$.

Effect Sizes

Medium effect sizes were seen for individual and organizational behavior change and small effect sizes for measures related to talking with children about CSA and HSD (**Table 6**). Effect size for knowledge change was large (0.57) and medium for attitude (0.34) (**Table 5**).

DISCUSSION

The *Prevent It!* program workshops described in this study are a novel approach to create a program that can potentially help, or even reduce, the large numbers of individuals who experience CSA. This program was developed in a comprehensive manner and is unique compared to previous approaches. The goal was to develop an evidence-based program that can be administered by community volunteers adults involved with children, which will increase their knowledge and attitudes toward CSA. Perhaps even more importantly, the primarily outcome goal was that the *Prevent It!* program would improve the actual behaviors of the adults taking part. The results from the present study strongly support these intentions. The results clearly show that this program significantly improves knowledge, attitudes, and behaviors in adults that take the program.

Interestingly, while we found many changes overall, for the two items, "Suspecting CSA" and "Reporting CSA," there were

TABLE 7 | Behavioral measures expressed as percentages.

Behavioral Measures	Percentage of Sample	
	Baseline	3 Month Follow-up
NUMBER OF TIMES TALKING ABOUT CSA And HSD[a]*		
0 times	51.0	28.2
1–2 times	27.4	38.8
3–4 times	11.6	19.7
5 or more times	10.0	13.3
TYPES OF TOPIC DISCUSSED[b]**		
Boundaries	66.0	76.4
Identifying a range of emotions	44.6	56.4
Internet safety	31.4	41.5
Proper names for genitals	36.3	46.7
Using the word "surprise" for things like birthday presents rather than "secret"	15.1	40.5
Definition of sexual abuse	10.3	12.3
Grooming techniques adults might use	8.3	14.4
Children are never to blame if they are sexually abused	13.8	22.6
What to do if you are sexually abused	14.7	20.5
How to tell someone if you are sexually abused	14.1	17.9
Saying "no" is allowed	43.3	63.1
NUMBER OF TIMES SUSPECTING CSA[a, NS]		
0 times	84.8	86.1
1-2 times	11.6	11.8
3-4 times	1.6	1.1
5 or more times	1.9	1.1
Number OF TIMES REPORTING CSA[a, NS]		
0 times	92.7	92.5
1-2 times	6.9	7.0
3-4 times	0.3	0.5
5 or more times	0	0
INDIVIDUAL ACTION STRATEGIES USED[a]***		
Being a responsible role model for other adults	26.6	7.2
Watching for signs of abuse in children	30.4	14.4
Taking steps to protect children	24.7	36.6
ORGANIZATIONAL ACTION STRATEGIES USED[b]***		
Criminal record checks	55.9	88.5
Child welfare checks	40.7	63.9
Screening interviews	30.8	58.2
Reference checks	41.7	72.1
Provide written policy outlining appropriate conduct with children	23.1	55.4
Monitoring one-on-one time between adults and children	20.8	48.4
Provide written policy for handling suspicions of abuse	24.4	47.5
Provide written policy for handling disclosure of abuse	24.0	47.5
Provide written policy for identifying and handling inappropriate comments and behaviors by adults	18.6	45.1

This table shows descriptive data for each behavioral measure separated into individual variables using the percentage of the total sample at baseline and at 3 month follow-up.
[a]Participants were asked to select all that applied therefore percentages in these categories total more than 100.
[b]Participants were able to select only one answer therefore percentages in these categories equal 100.
*Results significant at $p = 0.05$.
**Results significant at $p = 0.001$.
***Results significant at $p < 0.001$.

no statistically significant changes. However, we believe the likely reason for this lack of change was that 3-months was not enough time for individuals to be in situations where they may have come across CSA. To answer such a question, a 12-month follow-up may help determine if the *Prevent It!* program changes these behaviors over the longer-term, and we anticipate such longer-term research in the future.

Our findings contribute to a small and growing field of research regarding adult-targeted CSA prevention. Results support previous studies that have found classroom-based teaching of adults about CSA can improve knowledge, attitudes, and behavioral intentions. However, one drawback of classroom-based training is the cost involved, and therefore internet based approaches are now starting to be considered because they are more cost-effective and can increase accessibility (Wurtele, 2009). It is uncertain about differential effectiveness of in-person training with a facilitator (Paranal et al., 2012; Rheingold et al., 2012) although results from one novel study suggest that an online version can be as effective as a classroom version for childcare professionals (Rheingold et al., 2015). Ideal future research will involve comparisons with an internet-based version of *Prevent It!* to assess if this is true for general public adults as well. For these reasons, we are developing this, and plan to study its effectiveness in future research. Additionally, although the program is designed to be facilitated by community volunteers, the present study utilized experienced staff, and therefore further research should compare the outcomes when such volunteers are facilitators.

Nonetheless, despite the positive findings from the present study, there are some methodological matters that should be considered as potential limitations. Firstly, we utilized a within-subject design comparing baseline to 3-month follow-up, with studies suggesting that attitudes and behavioral intentions are persistent over time (Deblinger et al., 2010). Nonetheless, for further certainty that all these positive findings were due to the program and not other factors, a randomized wait-list control study could be carried out. Secondly, our study population only consisted of 63% of those who took the program and completed baseline demographic data. However, there were no statistically significant differences in demographics between those who completed follow-up and those who did not, and we therefore believe that the results reflect the wider group, not just the responders. Thirdly, only a small number of men ($n = 22$) took part in the program, and therefore the impact of this program on men is less certain. This is a problem that is common in studies in this area (i.e., Rheingold et al., 2012, 2015), and it has also been suggested that there may be less support regarding the issue of CSA in some male-dominated organizations (Parent and Demers, 2009). It is possible that subsequent focus group research involving men may help address this issue. Fourthly, next steps in this field of research are to address challenges associated with the limitations of the measurement tools used. Cronbach's alpha may be a useful measure of internal consistency moving forward and some assessment of reliability and validity of the measurement tools will the generalizability of results in this study and others. Also, because self-report measures of behaviors were used, results may be biased by social desirability. The anonymous online questionnaire format of the measures may help to reduce the impact of social desirability in this study.

In conclusion, the purpose of this study was to determine the effectiveness of a CSA prevention program. Previous research has demonstrated the ability of programs such as this to change knowledge and increase participant's likelihood of using preventative behaviors. This is the first study to measure general public adult's self-reported use of preventative behaviors. Compared to baseline, at the 3-month follow up, participants who took the program were talking about CSA and healthy sexual development twice as much, were using twice as many individual action strategies, and were utilizing three times as many organizational strategies. Knowledge and positive attitude also increased significantly. The results suggest that the *Prevent It!* program is highly effective, and strongly support it's more widespread use.

AUTHOR CONTRIBUTIONS

PS and EM designed and performed all aspects of the study.

ACKNOWLEDGMENTS

We wish to thank Shannon Phelan for her invaluable on-site support and help with data collection. Both Shannon Phelan and Bronwyn Petersen provided extensive support while running and organizing the program workshops. Funding for this program was provided, in part, by the Center for Effective Business Management of Addiction Treatments (CEBMAT) at the University of Alberta, and also by Little Warriors, a charity devoted to reducing the frequency of child sexual abuse and to treating survivors. Previously, PS has been a non-paid volunteer on the Governance Board of Little Warriors. EM carried out most of this work as part of her submission for her Ph.D. in Psychiatry at the University of Alberta. We wish to also acknowledge the significant contribution from Global Creative (Edmonton, Canada) in supporting production of the video segments of the program. Neither author has any financial interest in the *Prevent It!* program.

REFERENCES

Alaggia, R. (2004). Many ways of telling: expanding conceptualizations of child sexual disclosure. *Child Abuse Neglect* 28, 1213–1227. doi: 10.1016/j.chiabu.2004.03.016

Anda, R. F., Felitti, V. J., Bremner, J. D., Walker, J. D., Whitfield, C., Perry, B. D., et al. (2006). The enduring effects of abuse and related adverse experiences in childhood: a convergence of evidence from neurobiology and epidemiology. *Eur. Arch. Psychiatry Clin. Neurosci.* 256, 174–189. doi: 10.1007/s00406-005-0624-4

Belsky, J., and de Haan, M. (2011). Annual research review: parenting and children's brain development: the end of the beginning. *J. Child Psychol. Psychiatry* 52, 409–428. doi: 10.1111/j.1469-7610.2010.02281.x

Berrick, J. D. (1988). Parental involvement in child abuse prevention training: what do they learn? *Child Abuse Neglect* 12, 543–553. doi: 10.1016/0145-2134(88)90071-3

Bowman, R. A., Scotti, J. R., and Morris, T. L. (2010). Sexual abuse prevention: a training program for developmental disabilities service providers. *J. Child Sex. Abus.* 19, 119–127. doi: 10.1080/10538711003614718

Chen, L. P., Murad, M. H., Paras, M. L., Colbenson, K. M., Sattler, A. L., Goranson, E. N., et al. (2010). Sexual abuse and lifetime diagnosis of psychiatric disorders: systemic review and meta-analysis. *Mayo Clinic Proceed.* 85, 618–629. doi: 10.4065/mcp.2009.0583

Cohen, J. (1992). A power primer. *Psychol. Bull.* 112, 155–159.

Collings, S. J. (1997). Development, reliability, and validity of the child sexual abuse myth scale. *J. Interpers. Violence* 12, 665–674. doi: 10.1177/088626097012005004

Collin-Vézina, D., Hélie, S., and Trocmé, N. (2010). Is child sexual abuse declining in Canada? An analysis of welfare data. *Child Abuse Neglect* 34, 807–812. doi: 10.1016/j.chiabu.2010.05.004

Davis, M. K., and Gidycz, C. A. (2000). Child sexual abuse prevention programs: a meta-analysis. *J. Clin. Child Psychol.* 29, 257–265. doi: 10.1207/S15374424jccp2902_11

Deblinger, E., Thakkar-Kolar, R. R., Berry, E. J., and Schoeder, C. M. (2010). Caregivers' efforts to educate their children about child sexual abuse. A replication study. *Child Maltreat.* 15, 91–100. doi: 10.1177/1077559509337408

Diamond, M., Jozifkova, E., and Weiss, P. (2011). Pornography and sex crimes in the Czech Republic. *Arch. Sex. Behav.* 40, 1037–1043; discussion 1045–1050. doi: 10.1007/s10508-010-9696-y

Diclemente, C. C., and Prochaska, J. O. (1998). "Toward a comprehensive, transtheoretical model of change: stages of change and addictive behaviors," in *Treating Addictive Behaviors 2nd Edn., Applied Clinical Psychology*, eds W. R. Miller, and N. Heather (New York, NY: Plenum Press), 3–24.

Diclemente, C. C., Prochaska, J. O., Fairhurst, S. K., Velicer, W. F., Velasque, M. M., and Rossi, J. S. (1991). Process of smoking cessation: an analysis of precontemplation, contemplation, and preparation stages of change. *J. Consult. Clin. Psychol.* 59, 295–304. doi: 10.1037/0022-006X.59.2.295

Divine, G., Norton, H. J., Hunt, R., and Dienemann, J. (2013). A review of analysis and sample size calculation considerations for Wilcoxon tests. *Econ. Educ. Policy* 117, 699–710. doi: 10.1213/ANE.0b013e31827f53d7

Field, A. (2009). *Discovering Statistics Using SPSS (and Sex and Drugs and Rock 'n' Roll)*. 3rd Edn. London: Sage Publications.

Finkelhor, D. (1994). The international epidemiology of child sexual abuse. *Child Abuse Neglect* 18, 409–417.

Finkelhor, D. (2009). The prevention of childhood sexual abuse. *Future Child.* 19, 169–194. doi: 10.1353/foc.0.0035

Fryda, C. M., and Hulme, P. A. (2015). School-based child sexual abuse prevention programs: an integrative review. *J. School Nurs.* 31, 167–182. doi: 10.1177/1059840514544125

Hébert, M., Lavoie, F., and Parent, N. (2002). An assessment of outcomes following parents' participation in a child abuse prevention program. *Violence Vict.* 17, 355–372. doi: 10.1891/vivi.17.3.355.33664

Jenson, T. K., Gulbrandsen, W., Mossige, S., Reichelt, S., and Tjersland, O. A. (2005). Reporting possible child sexual abuse: a qualitative study on children's perspectives and the context for disclosure. *Child Abuse Neglect* 29, 1395–1415. doi: 10.1016/j.chiabu.2005.07.004

Kaffman, A. (2009). The silent epidemic of neurodevelopmental injuries. *Biol. Psychiatry* 66, 624–626. doi: 10.1016/j.biopsych.2009.08.002

Kenny, M. C. (2009). Child sexual abuse prevention: psychoeducational groups for preschoolers and their parents. *J. Spec. Group Work* 34, 24–42. doi: 10.1080/01933920802600824

Keppel, G. (1991). *Design and Analysis: A Researchers' Handbook*. Englewood Cliffs, NJ: Prentice-Hall Inc.

Kolb, D. A. (1975). "Towards an applied theory of experiential learning," in *Studies of Group Process*, ed C. Cooper (New York, NY: John Wiley), 33–57.

Livingstone, S., and Smith, P. K. (2014). Annual research review: harms experienced by child users of online and mobile technologies: the nature, prevalence and management of sexual and aggressive risks in the digital age. *J. Child Psychol. Psychiatry* 55, 635–654. doi: 10.1111/jcpp.12197

MacMillan, H., Wathen, C. N., Barlow, J., Fergusson, D. M., Lenethal, J. M., and Taussig, H. N. (2009). Interventions to prevent child maltreatment and associated impairment. *Lancet* 373, 250–266. doi: 10.1016/S0140-6736(08)61708-0

Man-Ging, C. I., Böhm, B., Fuchs, K. A., Witte, S., and Frick, E. (2015). Improving empathy in the prevention of sexual abuse against children and youngsters. *J. Child Sex. Abus.* 24, 796–815. doi: 10.1080/10538712.2015.1077366

Maniglio, R. (2009). The impact of child sexual abuse on health: a systematic review of reviews. *Clin. Psychol. Rev.* 29, 647–657. doi: 10.1016/j.cpr.2009.08.003

Martin, E. K., and Silverstone, P. H. (2013). How much Child Sexual Abuse is "below the surface," and can we help adults identify it early? *Front. Psychiatry* 4:58. doi: 10.3389/fpsyt.2013.00058

Paranal, R., Washington, T. K., and Derrick, C. (2012). Utilizing online training for child sexual abuse prevention: benefits and limitations. *J. Child Sex. Abus.* 21, 507–520. doi: 10.1080/10538712.2012.697106

Parent, S., and Demers, G. (2009). Sexual abuse in sport: a model to prevent and protect athletes. *Child Abuse Rev.* 20, 120–133. doi: 10.1002/car.1135

Pereda, N., Guilera, G., Forns, M., and Gómez-Benito, J. (2009). The international epidemiology of child sexual abuse: a continuation of Finkelhor (1994). *Child Abuse Neglect* 33, 331–342. doi: 10.1016/j.chiabu.2008.07.007

Perneger, T. V. (1998). What's wrong with Bonferroni adjustments. *BMJ* 316, 1236–1238. doi: 10.1136/bmj.316.7139.1236

Petty, T., and Thomas, C. C. (2014). Approaches to a successful adult education program *Coll. Stud. J.* 3, 473–480.

Public Health Agency of Canada (2010). *Canadian Incidence Study of Reported Child Abuse and Neglect, – 2008: Major Findings*. Ottawa, ON.

Rheingold, A. A., Campbell, C., Self-Brown, S., de Arellano, M., Resnick, H., and Kilpatrick, D. (2007). Prevention of child sexual abuse: evaluation of a community media campaign. *Child Maltreat.* 12, 352–363. doi: 10.1177/1077559507305994

Rheingold, A. A., Zajac, K., Chapman, J. E., Patton, M., de Arellana, M., Saunders, B., et al. (2015). Child sexual abuse prevention training for childcare professionals: an independent multi-site randomized controlled trail of Stewards of Children. *Prev. Sci.* 16, 374–385. doi: 10.1007/s11121-014-0499-6

Rheingold, A. A., Zajac, K., and Patton, M. (2012). Feasibility and acceptability of a child sexual abuse prevention program for childcare professionals: comparison of a web-based and in-person training. *J. Child Sex. Abus.* 21, 422–436. doi: 10.1080/10538712.2012.675422

Self-Brown, S., Rheingold, A. A., Campbell, C., and de Arellano, M. A. (2008). A media campaign prevention program for child sexual abuse: community members' perspectives. *J. Interpers. Violence* 23, 728–743. doi: 10.1177/0886260507313946

Taylor, E. W., and Laros, A. (2014). Researching the practice of fostering transformative learning: lessons learned from the study of andragogy. *J. Transformative Educ.* 12, 134–147. doi: 10.1177/1541344614548589

Walsch, K., Rassafiani, M., Mathews, B., Farell, A., and Butler, W. (2012). Assessment and prevention: exploratory factor analysis and psychometric evaluation of the teacher reporting attitude scale of child sexual abuse. *J. Child Sex. Abus.* 21, 489–506. doi: 10.1080/10538712.2012.689423

Walsch, K., Zwi, K., Woolfenden, S., and Shlonsky, A. (2015). School-based education programmes for the preventions of child sexual abuse. *Cochrane Database Syst. Rev.* 4, 1361–6137. doi: 10.1002/14651858.CD004380.pub3

Watts-English, T., Fortson, B. L., Gibler, N., Hooper, S. R., and De Bellis, M. D. (2006). The psychobiology of maltreatment in childhood. *J. Soc. Issues* 62, 717–736. doi: 10.1111/j.1540-4560.2006.00484.x

Wurtele, S. K. (2009). Preventing sexual abuse of children in the twenty-first century: preparing for challenges and opportunities. *J. Child Sex. Abus.* 18, 1–18. doi: 10.1080/10538710802584650

Yancey, C. T., Hansen, D. J., and Naufel, K. Z. (2011). Heterogeneity of individuals with a history of child sexual abuse: an examination of children presenting to treatment. *J. Child Sex. Abus.* 20, 111–127. doi: 10.1080/10538712.2011.554341

Zeuthen, K., and Hagelskjær, M. (2013). Prevention of child sexual abuse: analysis and discussion of the field. *J. Child Sex. Abus.* 22, 742–760. doi: 10.1080/10538712.2013.811136

Zollner, H. S. J., Fuchs, K. A., and Fegert, J. M. (2014). Preventions of sexual abuse: improved information is crucial. *Child Adolesc. Psychiatry Ment. Health* 8, 1–9. doi: 10.1186/1753-2000-8-5

Zwi, K., Woolfenden, S., Wheeler, D. M., O'Brien, T., Tait, P., and Williams, K. J. (2007). School-based education programmes for the prevention of child sexual abuse. *Cochrane Database Syst. Rev.* 3:CD004380. doi: 10.1002/14651858.CD004380.pub2

Conflict of Interest Statement: Previously, PS has been a non-paid volunteer on the Governance Board of Little Warriors. Neither author has any financial interest in the *Prevent It!* program.

The other author declares that the research was conducted in the absence of any commercial or financial relationships that could be construed as a potential conflict of interest.

6

"No more a child, not yet an adult": studying social cognition in adolescence

Adelina Brizio [1,2], *Ilaria Gabbatore* [3]*, *Maurizio Tirassa* [1,4] *and Francesca M. Bosco* [1,4]

[1] Department of Psychology and Center for Cognitive Science, University of Turin, Turin, Italy, [2] Faculty of Communication Science, Università della Svizzera Italiana, Lugano, Switzerland, [3] Faculty of Humanities, Child Language Research Center, University of Oulu, Oulu, Finland, [4] Department of Psychology and Neuroscience Institute of Turin, Turin, Italy

There are several reasons why adolescence is interesting. It is in this phase that an individual finds herself fully facing the external world: basically equipped with the kind of social cognition that s/he has acquired at home, at school and through the media during childhood, s/he has now to meet a host of other, diverse views of what "reasonable," "appropriate," or "expected" courses of thought and emotions are, in the wild with friends and peers, romantic or sexual partners, teachers and employers, and the society at large. Furthermore, she is also expected, both at home and in the external world, to have a wholly new degree of control over such courses. While the idea that the development of social cognition still progresses after infancy (and possibly throughout the life span) is clearly gaining consensus in the field, the literature building on it is still scarce. One of the reasons for this probably is that most tests used to study it focus on its basic component, namely theory of mind, and have been mostly devised for us with children; therefore, they are not suitable to deal with the hugely increasing complexity of social and mental life during adolescence and adulthood. Starting from a review of the literature available, we will argue that the development of social cognition should be viewed as a largely yet-to-be-understood mix of biological and cultural factors. While it is widely agreed upon that the very initial manifestations of social life in the newborn are largely driven by an innate engine with which all humans are equally endowed, it is also evident that each culture, and each individual within it, develops specific adult versions of social cognition.

Keywords: adolescence, social cognition, theory of mind, mindreading, metacognition, self-reflection, development

Edited by:
Antonella Marchetti, Università Cattolica del Sacro Cuore, Italy

Reviewed by:
Giulia Cavalli, Università eCampus, Italy
Tuula M. Hurtig, University of Oulu, Finland
Paolo Bertrando, Università eCampus, Italy

***Correspondence:**
Ilaria Gabbatore, Faculty of Humanities, Child Language Research Center, University of Oulu, P.O. Box 1000, 90014 Oulu, Finland
ilaria.gabbatore@oulu.fi, ilariagabbatore@gmail.com

Specialty section:
This article was submitted to Cognitive Science, a section of the journal Frontiers in Psychology

Introduction

There are several reasons why adolescence—and, more to the point, social life and social cognition in adolescence—is scientifically interesting. It is during this period that an individual finds herself[1] fully facing the external world: basically equipped with the social competences that she has acquired at home, at school and through the media during childhood, she has now to meet a host of other,

[1] Throughout the paper we will use either the feminine or the masculine when referring to unspecified human beings. This is only made for the sake of readability and is not meant to convey any gender-related position or the idea that there may or may not be differences in social cognition between genders. However important, such themes are simply not relevant on the level of abstraction on which our arguments are cast.

views of what "reasonable," "appropriate," or "expected" courses of thought and emotions are, *in the wild* with friends and peers, romantic or sexual partners, teachers and employers, and the society at large. Furthermore, she is also expected, both at home and in the external world, to have a new degree of control over such courses.

Substantially analogous considerations hold when social cognition is viewed in its reflective aspects, that is as a means of self-knowledge. Again, adolescence is a crucial phase in the development of an individual's understanding of herself, of her own feelings and desires, her own ways of reasoning, her own reactions to external as well as internal situations, etc. And, again, both the need and the actual ability to control these courses of thought and emotions change greatly during this period.

However, the literature on social cognition in adolescence is scarce and scattered, particularly if compared with other ages of life, like infancy and childhood, or other domains of cognition: few empirical studies are available and there is no unitary theoretical framework within which to understand them.

Yet, a better understanding of adolescence would be crucial, if only because a quantitatively impressive part of human kind currently falls within such period. The present generation of people aged 10–24 years is the largest in history: at 1.8 billion, it comprises a quarter of the world's population. Nearly 90% of them live in low- or middle-income countries where, due to higher fertility rates, they constitute a far greater proportion of the population than in high-income countries (WHO, 2009).

Still another reason of interest is that several disorders—first and foremost, schizophrenia or substance abuse, but also mood and anxiety-related dysfunctions—have their onset or witness an increase during adolescence and early adulthood.

This makes it all the more interesting to understand what social cognition is in this phase of life, at least within the widely diffused theoretical framework that views a crucial aspect of social cognition, namely *theory of mind (ToM)*, as crucially involved in these disorders (Frith, 1992; for reviews, see Bosco et al., 2009a, and respectively, Bosco et al., 2014a).

This paper will discuss social cognition in adolescence. We will include both a review of the literature available and a theoretical discussion. We are aware that adolescence is, at least in part, a social construction, and that its features may vary between different sociocultural and historical therefore, we will do our best to keep our arguments on a sufficiently general level to allow for these differences. Yet, we are also aware that we are Western researchers, like most of our peers, and that this puts inescapable biases in our analyses.

From Childhood to Adolescence

The social world is the most important realm of interaction of human beings, that within which we spend the whole of our lives. Even when we are alone with ourselves, be it at home or during a walk in the mountains, we are immersed in an environment which is more or less completely made of social artifacts and products; even more crucially, our thoughts and feelings, as well as our actions, are largely shaped by (and generally aimed at) the social world (Clancey, 1997).

Unsurprisingly, a great deal of effort has been devoted within the psychological sciences to investigating into the nature of human social cognition, its evolution in the species and its development in the individual.

As far as phylogeny is concerned, starting from pioneering research on so-called "Machiavellian intelligence" (e.g., Humphrey, 1976; Byrne and Whiten, 1985; Dunbar, 1993), it has been claimed that social cognition is at the very root of the particular evolution of the primates' mind. Technology and a sophisticated use of artifacts would have played less important a role, at least until the appearance of the first hominins, since when the evolution of material cognition appears to have paralleled a further evolution of social cognition. The social life of humans, like that of the other great apes, is highly complex: they form long-term social relationship with others, understand the social relationship among third parties, and recognize that the actions of individuals are driven by their goals and by their perception of the situation (Tomasello and Vaish, 2013).

The phrase *social cognition* generally refers to "the various psychological processes that enable individuals to take advantage of being part of a social group" (Frith, 2008, p. 2033). It is crucial to put an emphasis on words like *cognition* and phrases like *to make sense*, which allow to keep social cognition proper as distinct from the mere influence that an individual's behavior may or may not have on the behavior of other individuals (Bara and Tirassa, 2010), something which instead is universal in animals and even in plants.

An important facet of social cognition in primates is the ability to understand the mental states of other individuals, including their intentions, desires and beliefs, i.e., what is called *ToM*, *mentalizing*, or *folk psychology* (Davies and Stone, 1995; Nichols and Stich, 2003; Goldman, 2006; Blakemore et al., 2007; Hutto et al., 2011). Together with other sophisticated cognitive competences like social emotional processing (Burnett et al., 2009), this capacity enables an individual to understand, explain and predict another individual's actions and thus also allows for the negotiation of complex interpersonal decisions (Crone, 2013). Social cognitive processes include also basic perceptual processes such as face processing (Farroni et al., 2005), biological motion detection (Pelphrey and Carter, 2008), and joint attention (Carpenter et al., 1998).

It is not completely understood if, or to what extent, this particular type of social cognition belongs to species other than ours (Heyes, 1998): it appears, however, that ToM-like competences are more widely diffused among primates than what is commonly thought (Tomasello, 2014). What can safely be said is that, while the social life of great apes is mainly about competition, human societies are vastly more and distinctively structured around and for cooperation (Tomasello and Vaish, 2013), which of course founds on the further evolution of peculiar cognitive competences, among which our special kind of social cognition. In a word, the social life of humans is largely a matter of *intersubjectivity* or *sharedness* (Premack and Premack, 1994; Tirassa, 1999; Tirassa and Bosco, 2008).

As regards ontogeny, there is now a remarkable amount of empirical literature in psychology describing the first years of development of social cognition and mindreading. This body of literature is far from yielding a univocal sense of what a child's social cognition is or how it develops: rather, it appears to be a multidimensional, highly complex patchwork of different subareas, different theoretical or empirical approaches, and, necessarily, different results.

Most proposals in this area subscribe to a common philosophical framework defined by a set of core assumptions, namely, as stated above, that the primary function of social cognition is to predict, explain, and control the actions of the others, which is made possible by the attribution, and hence the representation, of their mental states. The big issue is whether such attributions are achieved by means of theoretical inference, simulative analogy, or a bit of both (Gallagher and Hutto, 2008; Hutto et al., 2011).

Furthermore, as Hutto et al. (2011) argue, most theories tacitly assume that human adults entertain a fully developed mindreading; consequently, the main question concerns the extent to which the mentalizing abilities of infants (if and when they indeed have any) might compare to those of the adult. However, there is a substantial lack of cognitive models of mindreading in adults (see the review in Apperly, 2013) or of what the phrase *a fully developed mindreading* could precisely mean.

Gallagher (2006) notes that ToM approaches to the explanation of how we come to understand others typically are abstract (third-person when they need to be second-person), mentalistic (starting with the supposition that there are things like minds, beliefs, desires that we have no access to in others, and sometimes even in ourselves), and biased toward theoretical reason (when practical, situated reason is a better way to go: see also Bosco et al., 2009b). Overly intellectualizing what is involved in our basic encounters with others, they tend to forget emotion and our ability to read it not in the minds of others, but on their faces, as well as in their gestures and expressive movements. Yet, if the basic ontology of human social competence is the same from the very beginning of mental life (as has been claimed, e.g., by Tirassa et al., 2006a,b), a more situated, more embodied approach to social cognition should be developed, allowing the more rationally sophisticated abilities to be a precious tool that comes into play when it is necessary rather than the only nature of human intersubjectivity.

These problems notwithstanding, there can be little doubt that crucial advancements in our understanding of the ontogeny of social cognition have been achieved in the last few decades from which knowledge is likely to proceed further, though probably still without a unitary theoretical framework in the foreseeable future.

Much less is known about the ways and directions in which social cognition develops after infancy: despite the increasing interest in social cognition beyond childhood (e.g., Valle et al., 2015) knowledge of how it works in the adult or possibly decays in the elderly still is scarce and scattered. There are several possible explanations for this situation (Dumontheil et al., 2010). Firstly, the tasks that have been used to test ToM in early development are not appropriate for testing older children and adolescents. Since most ToM tasks are passed by 5-years-olds, ceiling effects might be obscuring the observation of any further development. Secondly, tasks typically enquire directly children's representations of another person's mental states; they do not tap into how ToM is used to drive decisions and actions in everyday life.

When a situated framework is adopted, further problems pop up. One is that only one-to-one interactions are normally studied, and even these are framed in terms of a subject who is asked to observe and explain another individual's behavior, rather than truly encountering him; that is, only a third-person perspective, instead of a second-person one, is adopted in practice. Another problem is that only real-time (vs. retrospective), status-free, culture-free interactions are taken into account, thus obliterating most of the complexities of real social life. Not only does the study of ToM in adolescence and early adulthood constitute a methodological challenge, insofar as it requires the creation of new empirical tasks fit to capture age differences (Henry et al., 2013; Moran, 2013; Valle et al., 2015): it also calls for a radical enrichment of the underlying theoretical frameworks.

Still another problem is that the ToM tasks that are normally used with children tend to impose rigid requirements on what the "right" answer is. This might be a reasonable choice, insofar as it can be assumed that all children—or, at least, all children of Western heritage—will basically follow the same developmental trajectories. It is less obvious, however, that the same may be the case of adults. Here, it might be said, "mindreader is as mindreader does": there is no need to assume that a plateau should exist as the final state of the ontogeny of social cognition, and even less to assume that such plateau should be the same for all individuals in all historical contexts.

In line with at least part of the current literature (e.g., Apperly, 2012; Blakemore, 2012; Bosco et al., 2014b), our stance is that the ontogeny of social cognition does not end with childhood; instead, it continues through adolescence and the different ages of adulthood, as biological, social, cultural, educational, autobiographical, reflective, and retrospective changes accrue and become ever more intertwined and stratified.

The whole issue is further complicated by the fact that the psychological literature on adolescence in its turn offers an overwhelmingly ample (and still growing), but fractured, picture. This makes it difficult to achieve a deeper and coherent understanding of it (Moshman, 2005).

In principle, and roughly stated, there can exist three possible frameworks for understanding adolescence, namely as the exit from childhood, the entrance into adulthood, or a distinct stage of human life, a bridge between what comes before and after it but (comparatively) autonomous with respect to both. While each of these views has its merit, we argue that the second is preferable: adolescence as the beginning of adulthood (in agreement with Moshman, 2005).

Of course, this is not meant to imply that there can exist a divide between childhood and adolescence/adulthood: instead, the adoption of a life-course perspective promotes understanding that the factors affecting the individual during childhood can cumulatively affect her as an adolescent and an adult. At the same time, both normative and maladaptive patterns during adolescence shape future trajectories (Sawyer et al., 2012), extending the development of (social) cognition to include issues apparently unrelated like active aging, early determinants of health and risk factors.

Physical and mental health is affected by a complex interplay of individual and social factors at personal, family, community, and national levels (Viner et al., 2012), as well as by individual differences in cognitive abilities (e.g., Romer et al., 2011), attachment history (Bowlby, 1988), and personality traits. As we are discussing throughout this paper, all these factors undergo dramatic modifications during adolescence that tend to slow down and stabilize as the individual becomes an adult—better yet, that adultness begins when these factors begin to slow down and stabilize. Given this framework, it is all too obvious that physical and mental health "leaks" heavily from adolescence into adult life.

The onset of schizophrenia, for example, typically occurs in late adolescence or early adulthood (Häfner and an der Heiden, 1997; van Os and Kapur, 2009; WHO, 2015). Also, the incidence of mood and anxiety-related dysfunctions increases during adolescence (Hankin and Abramson, 2001; Costello et al., 2002).

Adolescence, however, also presents risks and disorders of its own. For example, during this age individuals are probably the fastest, the strongest and the most resistant to disease that they will ever be; at the same time, their chances of dying from putting themselves at risk—through aggression, crime, promiscuity, reckless driving, and drug use—also peak. It follows that precisely such behaviors are the first cause of death in this age group (Casey and Caudle, 2013).

Risk behaviors appear to be caused by diminished self-control, sensation-seeking behaviors and peer pressure. Their determinants are frequently searched in the brain development and neuronal connections (e.g., Steinberg, 2008; Telzer et al., 2013). Several authors have also found a peak in risk taking as evaluated by laboratory tasks involving emotions (Figner et al., 2009; Cauffman et al., 2010) and decision making (Wolf et al., 2013).

A better understanding of adolescence and its features in terms of social cognition would thus have profound implications for protection and prevention. To relate scientific researches and methodologies to real-life issues appears to be crucial in the study of adolescence. Yet, a more critical analysis of the frequency and the contexts of occurrence of risk-taking behaviors in adolescence (Willoughby et al., 2013), an articulated model to understand the evolutionary functions of adolescence (Ellis et al., 2012), and a sound theoretical framework for social cognition during this age, are still needed to complete the picture (and then to develop its implications for protection and prevention).

What is Adolescence?

The rough definition of an adolescent as an individual who is no longer a child but not yet a true adult might seem poor and fuzzy from a scientific point of view, but it is probably the most effective in capturing the complexity and contextual dependence of the phenomenon called adolescence (e.g., Moshman, 2005; Hopkins, 2014).

In discussing adolescence, indeed, not only do we have to consider the high variability between individuals, but we also have to take into account that different societies define adolescence in terms of ages and social roles with comparatively little consistency (Sawyer et al., 2012). Furthermore, most societies throughout human history have not acknowledged the existence of an age called "adolescence," at least as we understand it (e.g., Kett, 1977; Hine, 1999; Hopkins, 2014). Many of the 1.8 billion youngsters mentioned above are likely not, or not fully, considered adolescents within their social contexts.

The beginning of adolescence is commonly identified with puberty, that is a complex biological transition which is universal in the human species, although the age at which it occurs may vary depending on features of both the individual and the context.

The decrease in the age of puberty onset that has taken place since the twentieth century in high-income countries (Sawyer et al., 2012) demonstrates the role of contexts in shaping individual trajectories, whereby the improvement in economic and material conditions like childhood hygiene, nutrition, and health appears to play a major role. At the same time, in those countries, sociocultural conditions like a longer education, possible delays or difficulties in employment, late marriage and childbearing have extended the duration of adolescence and changed its shape (Sawyer et al., 2012).

Adolescence looks different when viewed from one boundary or the other: basically, its beginning depends on biological and material features of the context, while its end depends on cultural and social factors. This also entails that individual differences become more important with age, while the merely chronological data become less important.

Around and with puberty begins a multidimensional and multilayered dynamics that involves every aspect of the individual's life. The young members of several cultures undergo specific rites of passage that take puberty as the symbolic threshold beyond which a child becomes an adult. Many cultures set one or more later thresholds after which the individual will be legally considered an adult as far as her rights and duties of a political, juridical, military, work and otherwise formal nature are concerned.

However, these further thresholds are merely relevant to legal and social norms, so much so that Black's (1990) law dictionary defines adolescence as "the age which follows puberty and precedes the age of majority." Thus, an adult is anyone whom the state legislation says is an adult, by modifying the permissions, obligations and prohibitions that in different ways change her social contexts and spheres of interaction as a member of the community. However, there is no reason to think that these norms depend on clear changes in the individual's cognition, whether social or otherwise.

A chronologically based definition promotes an understanding, typical of Western societies, of adulthood as taking place within the individual, with no concern for the social context: the end of adolescence is determined by law, with exclusive reference to age and not to the individual's interaction with other people and events (Schwartz et al., 2010). We opt for an operational definition of adolescence, instead of a legal/chronological one. Of course, this might turn out to be hardly manageable at the empirical level, where researchers need to have well-defined groups of subjects available; yet, we think that, at least on the theoretical level, this is a more sensible approach.

In fact, there may be different formal threshold ages for the different facets of citizenship, and they may vary from nation to nation or from decade to decade according to the historical context.

In other words, there is no biological threshold after puberty as well as no psychological threshold in a strict sense: the body, including the brain, progressively changes until it slowly reaches a mature stage, but it cannot be said to achieve a literally steady state, nor a state which be clearly distinguishable from adolescence. Its development never really ceases: it just slows down after the fast-paced events ongoing during adolescence proper. The same, of course, holds for cognition in general, and for social cognition specifically.

This makes identifying an end to adolescence a particularly difficult task. A phrase like *coming to terms with adulthood* is vague enough to warrant widely (or even wildly) different interpretations; and anyway, as we have said, adulthood may be differently conceived of in historically different contexts or even in different domains of an individual's life. Thus, for example, in many an affluent country it is comparatively normal to witness a divergence between the age at which an individual is legally and psychologically capable of living an autonomous adult's life and the individual or contextual conditions—like a particularly prolonged education, or the prices of housing and living—that may make this socially or subjectively unaffordable (Sawyer et al., 2012). In other countries or in other socioeconomic situations, of course, things may be hugely different: think, for example, of the many areas, in affluent as well as in less protected environments, where youngsters may legally or illegally be employed or exploited as slave workers, prostitutes, soldiers, or even suicide bombers. In this sense adolescence may be viewed as socially constructed by a society that can and wants to afford it.

A definition of adolescence as *coming to terms with adulthood* may appear to imply that mental life during this age should be viewed as a precursor to that of full adulthood and thus exclusively or prevailingly understood in terms of the latter: the adolescent would then be nothing more than a "future adult." This merits a brief discussion.

There are indeed various ways in which a sort of teleology belongs to this framework. At least some of the environments in which the adolescent participates are explicitly or implicitly conceived and structured so to offer the cognitive, social and cultural tools that will help her to acquire the knowledge, the competencies and the other skills that will be required of her as an adult: schools, professional education, reformatories and military academies are, of course, the most visible, important and formally structured environments of this kind, but there may be others as well. These environments in which the adolescent participates require her to think and act like an adult: many such contexts will be tolerant of "adolescent behavior," but others will not, or not completely. So far, we have a sort of a later-age, probably less tolerant, equivalent of Vygotsky's notion of the Zone of Proximal Development (Vygotsky, 1978; Daniels et al., 2007).

On the other hand, it should be noted that the opposite process may also be at work, whereby typically in the affluent areas of the world adolescents are *teenagers*, that is a specific market segment with features of its own. Of course, this also requires selling the idea that adolescents are *not* adults, that they have a mental and social functioning all of their own, and so on. The coexistence of these two processes increases the complexity of the adolescent's mental and social life.

Furthermore, the adolescent represents herself at least partially in accordance with the psychological, social, and cultural coordinates in which she finds herself. For the first time, she entertains a visible temporal and ontogenic horizon which she may strive to achieve; that is, she represents her own future in a non-oneiric way and may make concrete choices that are, or at least aim to be, consequential. She thus oscillates between two centers of gravity. One such center is the awareness and the expectation that she is soon going to be an adult: she has an idea, however approximate, of what this means, and might work toward such end, e.g., by going to school or by learning the skills that (she thinks) will help her reach her goals as an adult. The other center of gravity is the fears and the other emotions that prospective adultness may ingenerate, and the desire to enjoy the space of freedom which society allows her, in the fear of losing it with passing years.

Thus, teleology in adolescence is different from what it could be during childhood. While in both periods the individual needs be considered in her present time, which she lives with the full autonomy that her age allows for, adolescence is characterized by internal as well as external pressures and tensions between such present and a future which is both the object of representations, expectations and positive and negative feelings, and a set of cognitive, social and cultural tools that offer a scaffolding (again in a Vygotskian sense) which the individual has available to govern her own future, in a circularity whose features are those of a partially self-fulfilling prophecy.

Summing up, adolescence begins with puberty and is characterized by the intertwining of several kinds of changes:

(i) biological and psychological changes that are universal, albeit occurring at different ages;
(ii) socio-cultural and psychological changes that are practically universal, at least in their abstract or symbolical form, called rites of passage;
(iii) socio-cultural and psychological changes that are local and contextual, varying from the status of a young soldier, slave or prostitute to that of a "teenager" in an affluent family;
(iv) the appearance of true autonomy and self-government, with a still budding ability to deal with them and their internal and external sources and consequences.

Adolescence has no precisely identifiable end; it slowly shifts into adulthood as the individual comes to terms with his new state. *Coming to terms with adulthood* may have many different meanings, depending on the groups and the society in which an individual finds himself, of the requests posed by his environment, the resources and the opportunities he finds available, and so on. While puberty is a necessary biological and psychological transition, adulthood is defined contextually; in certain contexts a reasonable level of adultness may be reached at different ages in different domains, and often many years after biological maturity, while in others a distorted adultness ends up to be superimposed on an individual who is not yet ready to cope with the ensuing set of activities and interactions. Each of this paths may be laden with problems and tensions, which may then relapse on the individual's psychological or social wellbeing.

What Adolescence Requires of Social Cognition

From the subjective point of view, at least in Western countries, adolescence is a time when an individual finds herself confronting the feeling, simultaneously endogenous and exogenous, of becoming an adult. When she has become reasonably able to come to terms with these feelings, this phase ends; or, better, it shifts seamlessly into "full adulthood."

To conceive of adolescence as the beginning of adulthood brings one to also view social cognition during this stage of life as remarkably different from what it used to be during (the various phases of) childhood and more akin to what it will be at later ages. So, what developments in an individual's social cognition characterize this phase?

Changes in social cognition during adolescence are both inward and outward. The latter may be summarized as a further opening toward the world.

Several studies show how social networks change across the life span. Interactions during infancy and childhood normally take place within the family or in quasi-familiar environments like primary school. The global social network grows during adolescence, when the individual gains emotional and behavioral autonomy from parents, and then tends to decrease throughout adulthood (for a meta-analysis, see Wrzus et al., 2013).

An adolescent's social network becomes wider but also more impersonal in some of its zones. Adolescents are involved in situations that require them to take a role in a strict sense, including, e.g., secondary school, working places and other social grounds characterized by formal and formally accountable expectations and behaviors. The types of norms that this requires them to handle are not, or not mainly, behavioral rules in the form of do's and don'ts like those that are learned during childhood; instead, they are complex systems of social positioning and reasoning that establish a certain worldview from which situated social actions should be derived moment by moment. Things are even more complicated, and more challenging for social cognition, insofar as formality often is only part of the situation, a sort of facade that belies complex informal interpersonal, social, and (largely speaking) political dynamics.

On a still more abstract level, this new conception of social worldviews, social grounds, and social roles typically expands to system-wide dynamics. The adolescent begins to interact with and within the society at large and its structures and institutions, e.g., in terms of understanding and dealing with citizenship, or of getting intellectually interested or materially involved in local, national or international politics or economics. This is the age when an individual may begin reading the news, taking a political stance, participating in demonstrations or, in more troubled contexts, more or less voluntarily carrying a weapon in a war. Actually, possibly fueled by a still partial understanding of the relevant dynamics and of their visible and hidden complexities, the civic and political fervor of this period will seldom be found again at later ages. Recent approaches to youth health and development have taken a turn from the traditional view of youths as victims or problems of society and passive recipients of adult-directed interventions to one that portrays them as powerful catalysts to community change by acting as resources and competent citizens in their communities (Makhoul et al., 2012).

We argue that these interests and activities fully engage social cognition insofar as they require understanding social habits and norms, the ways in which different individuals may follow, exploit or violate such norms, the positions that different individuals occupy in groups, organizations and the society at large, how they have reached there and how they tend to interpret such position, and so on.

Within areas more classically acknowledged as relevant to social cognition proper there are at least two other crucial realms that need be considered about social life in adolescence, namely interaction with peers and interaction with romantic or sexual partners. While neither of them appears, strictly speaking, in adolescence, both take on whole new nature and roles with respect to what they used to be in childhood.

Peers may happen to be other individuals, different groups of which the adolescent is or is not a member (including allied or various rival or antagonistic groups), other organizations of which she is or is not a member, and so on. In a different acceptation of interaction, peers may even be the *representations* of the peers that are projected by the various social and cultural contexts in which the adolescent participates, like her family, her friends, the media, or the society at large. Such projections may be descriptive or normative in different ways, ranging from the rules and expectations that are enforced by the family or the group of peers to narratives found in books and movies, marketing and advertising in the media, and so on.

Interactions with peers, like all interactions, require the adolescent to handle habits and norms, hierarchies and statuses, and to understand how arrays of other individuals do the same. At the same time, however, these interactions may be "hotter" than others to adolescents: they are less abstract, more situated, and more emotionally and intellectually compelling. Therefore, these immediate social dynamics cannot be handled with the tendentially formal rules with which the more removed ones discussed above are: dealing with peers thus tends to be *subjectively* more complex, more challenging, and more potentially awkward.

At least in several human societies, even more so may be the other crucial type of interaction that characterizes adolescence, namely the romantic and/or sexual, which may (at least in principle) address the individual toward the construction of a long-lasting relationship. This poses several problems. Courting someone, or letting someone court us, requires a complicated game of showing and concealing one's feelings and intentions. Even more importantly, it requires recognizing, labeling, and wording one's own feelings and emotions (like, "what is it that I feel? Is this what love is? or is it sexual desire?" and so on) as well as those of the partner's. All of this turmoil may often involve further persons on one or the other side of the actual or potential couple, giving rise to even more complicated problems about cheating, jealousy, rejection, and so on.

Even such a brief outline of the changes that characterize outward social life and social cognition during adolescence makes it clear why an analogously complex change in inward, that is reflective, social cognition is needed. Basically, the adolescent has to devise cognitive tools and ways to deal, on the one hand, with all that is happening in the highly complex, multidimensional space of her outbound social life and, on the other hand, with her own rapidly changing personal identity.

This requires her, among other things, to be able to monitor, understand, explain, predict, abstract from, and, first and foremost, *feel*, her own mental dynamics: the kind of questions she has to answer may take forms like "what is this that I feel? whence do these thoughts and emotions come? how do I explain them? where do they lead me? how do I judge them? are they good or are they bad? how do I control them? how do I share them with other individuals, and how should I choose these individuals?".

Internal tensions concerning this dynamics may easily ensue, due to the sheer difficulty of dealing with such complex questions, accepting their consequences for oneself and for various other persons, and accepting the continuous redefinition of personal identity that they propose. It is in this age that social dynamics as diverse as shame, pride, isolation, rage, rebellion, leadership and others thrive: in several senses, this is the end of innocence. It also comes as no surprise that adolescents are more at risk of deviant behavior as well as of becoming victims of hoaxes, deceits, and so on.

Summing up, an individual's social cognition during adolescence is asked to deal in increasingly complex ways with (and, circularly, her social cognition begins to provide her with the ability of dealing with) different types of contexts:

(i) her own mind;
(ii) other, specific individuals (family, friends, colleagues or classmates, romantic or sexual partners, and so on);
(iii) other, generic individuals (strangers);
(iv) groups and organizations and their individual members acting as such.

This requires an intertwining of social cognition with other "cognitive functions" like planning and organizing one's own actions and recognizing how others plan and organize theirs, processes of education, cultivation, and acculturation, an appropriate management of autobiographical memory, and so on.

Data From Developmental Psychology

ToM is generally considered a crucial part of social cognition and has been extensively studied in developmental psychology.

Children's ability to understand and reason about mental states has traditionally been investigated by testing their accuracy on mentalizing tasks, often based on false beliefs (Dennett, 1978), which are typically passed by 3 or 4 years olds (Wimmer and Perner, 1983; Wellman and Liu, 2004). As discussed above, these kinds of tests rapidly reach a ceiling effect as the subjects' age increases; a gap thus emerges in the literature after the pre-scholar period. Researches with children older than about four have used more complex ToM tasks (e.g., Happé, 1994; Baron-Cohen et al., 1999); however, precisely these methodological differences make it difficult to highlight continuities or discontinuities in development (Apperly et al., 2011).

In any case, it is hard to imagine that social cognition would not change with adolescence, if only because the individual's general cognitive abilities change, as well as her social experiences do (Blakemore and Choudhury, 2006). In comparison with the large amount of researches investigating mentalizing abilities during childhood, however, only few studies explored the development of these capacities in adolescence and their relations with other life-span developments (Colvert et al., 2008; Apperly et al., 2011; Harenski et al., 2012).

The ability to reason about the mental states of the others and to understand and take into consideration what they think, feel and believe appears to require the ability to take another individual's perspective, which in turn is crucial to successfully manage social communication. Perspective taking is related to first-order ToM, since it involves what another person is thinking; also, it requires the awareness of one's own mental states (first-person perspective) and the ability to ascribe mental states to other individuals (third-person perspective; Blakemore and Choudhury, 2006).

In a study by Choudhury et al. (2006), children, adolescents and adults were tested with a perspective-taking task requiring them to imagine which emotion they themselves (first-person perspective) or another person (third-person perspective) would feel in different scenarios. The results showed that the differences in reaction time between first- and third-person perspective-taking decreased with age, suggesting that proficiency at perspective-taking improves between childhood and adulthood.

Dumontheil et al. (2010) tested the ability of a large sample of children, adolescents and young adults (aged 7–27) to use information received about another person's point of view in a perspective-taking communicative task. Again, the ability to take another person's perspective into account turned out to grow from infancy through adolescence with further improvements in adulthood.

Fett et al. (2014) showed that a greater inclination to take the others' perspectives into account was associated with a stronger pro-social approach toward others and a stronger trust during cooperative interactions. In interactions with an unfair partner, this inclination was associated with a more drastic decrease of trust and less benevolent reciprocity.

Bosco et al. (2014b) assessed the ability to understand and manage mental states in pre-adolescence and adolescence using the ToM Assessment Scale (Th.o.m.a.s.: Bosco et al., 2009a; see also Laghi et al., 2014) and some well-known ToM tasks (namely a subset of the Strange Stories by Happé, 1994). Th.o.m.a.s. is a semi-structured interview organized along four scales, each focusing on one of the knowledge domains in which a person's ToM may manifest itself; it provides a detailed profile of different facets of ToM abilities, namely first- vs. second-order, first- vs. third-person, egocentric vs. allocentric perspective. It also explores different types of mental states involved in ToM, namely beliefs, desires, positive emotions, and negative emotions. The results were that the performance at Th.o.m.a.s. improves with age, confirming that the ontogeny of ToM continues at least through adolescence.

Furthermore, in agreement with Goldman's (1993) hypothesis that adolescents can better reason about their own mental states than about those of the others, the participants performed better at first-person than at third-person tasks. This appears consistent with the widely diffused perception that a typical feature of preadolescence and adolescence is a tighter focus on the attempt to understand oneself than the others. Also, again in agreement with previous literature (Wellman and Liu, 2004), the adolescents performed better at first-order than at second-order ToM tasks. No significant difference emerged, instead, between the allocentric and the egocentric viewpoint.

The performance at Strange Stories did not reveal any significant age-related difference; however, there is no evidence in the literature that there should be any. While Strange Stories are considered advanced ToM tasks, they were originally developed for children (Baron-Cohen, 1989; Happé, 1994) and thus they too are probably unfit for the study of mentalization at later ages.

Th.o.m.a.s. also investigates the ability to deal with different types of mental states (beliefs, desires, positive emotions, negative emotions). In Bosco et al. (2014b), the participants scored higher at negative emotions than at the others, a result that could be explained with the turbulent psychological and relational changes that characterize adolescence, together with a sort of existential confusion which is likely to lead a person to reflect more deeply on her own negative emotions.

The ability to make inferences about emotions is called *affective ToM* and may be conceptualized as the integration of *cognitive ToM* (inferences about knowledge and beliefs) and empathy (Shamay-Tsoory et al., 2010). In a study by Sebastian et al. (2011), adolescents made more errors than adults in choosing the appropriate ending of vignettes depicting a character's response to a companion's emotions. Vetter et al. (2013) used film clips depicting the manifestation of emotions to investigate affective ToM across adolescence, finding that it develops with age. They also found that it correlates with executive functions (specifically inhibition) throughout adolescence until young adulthood.

The phrase *executive functions* refers to the cognitive processes involved in goal-directed actions, such as those that allow an individual to control and coordinate his thoughts and behavior (Shallice, 1982). These are, for example, selective attention, working memory, decision-making, and inhibition. Several behavioral studies show that the ability to manage tasks like inhibitory control (Leon-Carrion et al., 2004), processing speed (Luna et al., 2004), working memory and decision-making (Hooper et al., 2004) continues to develop during adolescence. A correlation between affective ToM and inhibition has also been found in studies conducted with young adults (Bull et al., 2008; Ahmed and Miller, 2011). In pre-school children, executive functions have been shown to play an important role in ToM performance (Carlson and Moses, 2001), which suggests that they may play an important role in the subsequent developmental stages as well.

Another construct which is commonly held to be closely related to social cognition is metacognition, defined as the ability to think about thinking (Flavell, 1979). Semerari et al. (2003, 2007) view it as composed of an array of independent subfunctions that concur to its overall functioning, namely the abilities to recognize one's own thoughts and emotions, to relate them to the relevant interpersonal events, to understand the mental states of other persons and to keep them distinct from (and possibly different to) those of one's own, to acknowledge that mental states incorporate a point of view and therefore are fallible, to describe mental states modifications in a coherent narrative, and to control and adjust internal states (*mastery*: more about this later). Based on this theoretical elaboration, Semerari et al. (2012) built and validated a semi-structured interview called the Metacognition Assessment Interview (MAI), that has been administered to persons with schizophrenia or personality disorders. What is relevant to our current purposes is the notions that social cognition is a highly complex faculty, far from being reducible to simpler processes, even if complex in their own way like ToM, and that there can be individual or ontogenetic differences in the persons' capacity to handle it.

Metacognitive mastery has been correlated with quality of life (Lysaker et al., 2005) and the complexity of social functioning (Lysaker et al., 2010) in persons with schizophrenia. In general, metacognition appears to be able to influence several aspects of experience (Metcalfe, 1996) such as self-regulating learning (Efklides, 2009) and decision making (Weil et al., 2013). An impairment in the ability to reflect on and to use knowledge about the mental states of one's own and those of the others may hamper the ability to cope with complex psychological and relational challenges and thus lead to dysfunctional reactions to individual or interactional difficulties (Lysaker et al., 2010). Given the dramatic number of new experiences and transformations characterizing adolescence, these issues and their interplay may end up playing a significant role.

Demetriou and Bakracevic (2009) investigated metacognitive ability asking adolescents and adults to assess their own performance on propositional, spatial and social reasoning tasks; this self-evaluation was found to improve from adolescence to adulthood.

Weil et al. (2013) analyzed the development of metacognitive ability from adolescence to adulthood, during a visual task implying decision-making processes. Their results showed that the awareness of one's own perceptual decisions undergoes a prolonged developmental trajectory during adolescence, again suggesting that metacognitive ability significantly improves with age.

Somatic Changes and Brain Maturation

Adolescence brings with itself a vast array of bodily modifications. Some of these modifications, namely those in the brain, are not immediately available to the subject's awareness, while others are external and dramatically important from a subjective point of view.

Adolescence, for example, normally entails a sudden, rapid, and remarkable upgrowth. One finds herself watching the world from about the same level from which adults watch it, sometimes from an even higher one. This alone will obviously yield a difference in how one perceives social relations, hierarchies and statuses, power (whether social or crudely physical), dependability, and so on. Perspective taking here is laden with an experiential burden that makes it impossible to reduce it to a "cognitive" issue in the classic acceptation of such word. The growth of muscle mass and the increase in agility and physical strength add to this change of one's body image.

Even more the same holds for sex-related morphological changes, like the development of primary and secondary sex characteristics. To find oneself being the agent or the recipient of sexual attention, sexual desire and sex-related activities, as well as *not* being one despite one's desires or needs, has an obvious impact on one's social attitudes. To acquire and to come to terms with the relevant set of thoughts, feelings, emotions, habits and so on, both in oneself and in the others, is a seemingly impossible task that, nevertheless, needs be accomplished with reasonable speed and efficiency.

A completely different set of data and considerations is supplied by other, more classic areas of research.

Several authors suggest that the endocrine changes that characterize puberty influence brain development and restructuring during adolescence (Sowell et al., 2002; Lenroot et al., 2007; for reviews, see Peper et al., 2011; Peper and Dahl, 2013). Functional magnetic resonance imaging (fMRI) studies provide evidence of the plasticity of the adolescent's brain, characterized by a general structural development, a synaptic neuronal reorganization and increase in connectivity (Sowell et al., 2003). Social cognition, particularly the ability to mentalize, is associated with a network of brain regions commonly referred to as the "social brain" (Frith and Frith, 2003). This network appears to be the counterpart of the ability to recognize other persons' mental states like intentions, feelings, emotions, desires and beliefs, and to use such recognition to understand their behavior. The social brain includes several areas: the medial prefrontal cortex (mPFC), the anterior cingulate cortex (ACC), the inferior frontal gyrus, the superior temporal sulcus (STS), the amygdala and the anterior insula (Blakemore, 2008).

Several studies offer empirical evidence of the development of the social brain during the adolescence (for a review, see Blakemore, 2008). Recently this subject has received renewed interest. Mills et al. (2014) studied the structural development of the social brain from late childhood through adolescence and into adulthood. They found that gray matter volume and cortical thickness in the mPFC, the temporoparietal junction and the posterior STS decreased from childhood into the early twenties. The anterior temporal cortex increased in gray matter volume until adolescence and in cortical thickness until early adulthood. The surface area for each region peaks in pre-adolescence or early adolescence before decreasing into the early twenties. The authors suggested that the reductions in gray matter volume may reflect synaptic reorganization and concluded that the social brain network continues to develop structurally across adolescence before relatively stabilizing in the early twenties.

Klapwijk et al. (2013) analyzed the relations of a set of endocrine and somatic pubertal indicators with functional connectivity in the social brain (dorsomedial prefrontal cortex, right posterior STS and right temporoparietal junction) involved in emotion processing in girls aged 11–13 years. Their results suggest that the progress of puberty in girls is related to the functional maturation of the social brain.

Finally, Goddings et al. (2014) found that puberty has a important role in influencing the subcortical development of the brain. They analyzed data from longitudinal magnetic resonance imaging scans of individuals aged 7–20 years, finding an interactive puberty-by-age effect on the volume of the nucleus accumbens, the globus pallidus and the caudate: these regions are involved in reward-seeking behaviors and decision-making processes (Gottfried, 2011). Goddings et al. (2014) also found pubertal effects on the growth of the amygdala, which is involved in emotion processing. Pubertal changes include modifications in the neurobiology of stress and emotions, capable of shaping reactivity to stressors and affective stimuli (Spear, 2009). These modifications may precipitate the emergence of psychopathologies in vulnerable individuals and contribute to the emergence of psychological disorders (Dahl, 2004; Walker et al., 2004).

Globally considered, these modifications appear to be related to several aspects of mind functioning that characterize social cognitive ability (see also Moriguchi et al., 2007). It probably is no coincidence that many of the functions whose cerebral counterparts undergo such modifications are those in which adolescence looks more stormy and potentially unsafe. Yet, brain studies can hardly link brain modifications to a person's social and cultural experience. In this sense, the "social brain" should be viewed and studied as a feature not of the individual, but of the contexts in which the embedded, situated, and embodied individual participates.

Conclusion

Adolescence is an extremely interesting as well as challenging topic for the study of social cognition.

A first issue is that context-free studies can hardly be devised. The social, cultural, educational, economic, and autobiographical situations in which the individuals participate play too important a role in how they experience and enact their social life. For the same reason, it is likely impossible to devise empirical methodologies similar to those that are commonly employed in the study of other aspects of the functioning of the mind or of the social life in infancy and childhood. Not coincidentally, a comparatively advanced ToM task like the Strange Stories (Happé, 1994), differently to the false-belief tasks that are used with children, is built around a narrative infrastructure and its contents are culturally localized.

A second issue is that the empirical methodologies should be adjusted to keep into account the vast differences in social situations, cognition, and actions that exist between different contexts, between different individuals, and between the different domains and activities in which the same individual may participate.

A third issue is that the notions that are generally employed for the study of social cognition, like ToM, are probably insufficient to account for it. In a phenomenological approach such as that adopted, for example, by Gallagher (2006), the notion of a ratiomorphic, purely inferential ToM appears to be far too simplistic to account for the richness and the complexity of human social experience. The alternative proposed by Gallagher is in terms of a narrative competence, which in its turn would be grounded in the direct perceptual access to the intentions and the feelings of others: in this approach, second-person interactions would replace the more typically studied observations in the third-person; and, of course, the situated, embedded, embodied, autobiographically rich first person would be the center of gravity of the whole narrative.

Theory of mind would then intervene when a breakdown occurs, analogously to how theories in naïve (or non-naïve) physics intervene when our bodily experience, normally grounded in habits and choreographies, encounters a breakdown.

Thus, according to Gallagher and Hutto (2008), it is not the inner life or the mental life of the others that we attempt to access, but their life in its worldly contexts, which is best captured in a narrative form. Life events, including social interactions, happen as stories with a beginning, a development, and possibly an end, that take place in the world and in which we, and the others, may happen to play a part (see also Goffman, 1959).

Adolescence may then be viewed as an age in which the narratives change suddenly and profoundly, opening a world of new possibilities, new promises, new dangers. Cast abruptly in this new world, the adolescent has to wade through it, finding her own way to deal with the new situations in which she wants and needs to find herself. In this task, social life is simultaneously a huge source of problems, opportunities, and resources. That most of us survive this storm to find comparatively calmer waters is one of the most amazing feat of human kind.

Acknowledgments

This research was supported by Cassa di Risparmio di Torino (CRT) Foundation, Vivomeglio, 2013. Project: Rehabilitation of communicative deficit in patients with schizophrenia.

References

Ahmed, F. S., and Miller, L. S. (2011). Executive function mechanisms of theory of mind. *J. Autism Dev. Disord.* 41, 667–678. doi: 10.1007/s10803-010-1087-7

Apperly, I. A. (2012). What is "theory of mind"? Concepts, cognitive processes and individual differences. *Q. J. Exp. Psychol.* 65, 825–839. doi: 10.1080/17470218.2012.676055

Apperly, I. A. (2013). "Can theory of mind grow up? Mindreading in adults, and its implications for the development and neuroscience of mindreading," in *Understanding Other Minds: Perspectives from Developmental Social Neuroscience*, eds S. Baron-Cohen, H. Tager-Flusberg, and M. Lombardo (Oxford: Oxford University Press), 72–92.

Apperly, I. A., Warren, F., Andrews, B. J., Grant, J., and Todd, S. (2011). Developmental continuity in theory of mind: speed and accuracy of belief–desire reasoning in children and adults. *Child Dev.* 82, 1691–1703. doi: 10.1111/j.1467-8624.2011.01635.x

Bara, B. G., and Tirassa, M. (2010). A mentalist framework for linguistic and extralinguistic communication. *Linguist. Philos. Investig.* 9, 182–193.

Baron-Cohen, S. (1989). The autistic child's Theory of Mind: a case of specific developmental delay. *J. Child Psychol. Psychiatry* 30, 285–297. doi: 10.1111/j.1469-7610.1989.tb00241.x

Baron-Cohen, S., O'Riordan, M., Stone, V., Jones, R., and Plaistead, K. (1999). Recognition of faux pas by normally developing children and children with Asperger syndrome or high-functioning autism. *J. Autism Dev. Disord.* 29, 407–418. doi: 10.1023/A:1023035012436

Black, H. C. (1990). *Black's Law Dictionary*. St. Paul, MN: West Publishing Co.

Blakemore, S. J. (2008). The social brain in adolescence. *Nat. Rev. Neurosci.* 9, 267–277. doi: 10.1038/nrn2353

Blakemore, S. J. (2012). Imaging brain development: the adolescent brain. *Neuroimage* 61, 397–406. doi: 10.1016/j.neuroimage.2011.11.080

Blakemore, S. J., and Choudhury, S. (2006). Development of the adolescent brain: implications for executive function and social cognition. *J. Child Psychol. Psychiatry* 47, 296–312. doi: 10.1111/j.1469-7610.2006.01611.x

Blakemore, S. J., den Ouden, H., Choudhury, S., and Frith, C. (2007). Adolescent development of the neural circuitry for thinking about intentions. *Soc. Cogn. Affect. Neurosci.* 2, 130–139. doi: 10.1093/scan/nsm009

Bosco, F. M., Capozzi, F., Colle, L., Marostica, P., and Tirassa, M. (2014a). Theory of Mind deficit in subjects with alcohol use disorder: an analysis of mindreading processes. *Alcohol Alcohol.* 49, 299–307. doi: 10.1093/alcalc/agt148

Bosco, F. M., Gabbatore, I., and Tirassa, M. (2014b). A broad assessment of theory of mind in adolescence: the complexity of mindreading. *Conscious. Cogn.* 24, 84–97. doi: 10.1016/j.concog.2014.01.003

Bosco, F. M., Colle, L., De Fazio, A., Bono, S., Ruberti, S., and Tirassa, M. (2009a). Th.o.m.a.s.: an exploratory assessment of Theory of Mind in schizophrenic subjects. *Conscious. Cogn.* 18, 306–319. doi: 10.1016/j.concog.2008.06.006

Bosco, F. M., Colle, L., and Tirassa, M. (2009b). The complexity of Theory of Mind. *Conscious. Cogn.* 18, 323–324. doi: 10.1016/j.concog.2008.12.007

Bowlby, J. (1988). *A Secure Base: Parent-Child Attachment and Healthy Human Development*. New York, NY: Basic Books.

Bull, R., Phillips, L. H., and Conway, C. A. (2008). The role of control functions in mentalizing: dual-task studies of theory of mind and executive function. *Cognition* 107, 663–672. doi: 10.1016/j.cognition.2007.07.015

Burnett, S., Bird, G., Moll, J., Frith, C., and Blakemore, S. J. (2009). Development during adolescence of the neural processing of social emotion. *J. Cogn. Neurosci.* 21, 1736–1750. doi: 10.1162/jocn.2009.21121

Byrne, R. W., and Whiten, A. (eds). (1985). *Machiavellian Intelligence: Social Expertise and the Evolution of Intellect in Monkeys, Apes, and Humans*. Oxford: Clarendon Press.

Carlson, S. M., and Moses, L. J. (2001). Individual differences in inhibitory control and children's theory of mind. *Child Dev.* 72, 1032–1053. doi: 10.1111/1467-8624.00333

Carpenter, M., Nagell, K., Tomasello, M., Butterworth, G., and Moore, C. (1998). Social cognition, joint attention, and communicative competence from 9 to 15 months of age. *Monogr. Soc. Res. Child Dev.* 63, 1–143. doi: 10.2307/1166214

Casey, B. J., and Caudle, K. (2013). The teenage brain self control. *Curr. Dir. Psychol. Sci.* 22, 82–87. doi: 10.1177/0963721413480170

Cauffman, E., Shulman, E. P., Steinberg, L., Claus, E., Banich, M. T., Graham, S., et al. (2010). Age differences in affective decision making as indexed by performance on the Iowa Gambling Task. *Dev. Psychol.* 46, 193–207. doi: 10.1037/a0016128

Choudhury, S., Blakemore, S.-J., and Charman, T. (2006). Social cognitive development during adolescence. *Soc. Cogn. Affect. Neurosci.* 1, 165–174. doi: 10.1093/scan/nsl024

Clancey, W. J. (1997). "The conceptual nature of knowledge, situations, and activity," in *Human and Machine Expertise in Context*, eds P. Feltovich, R. Hoffmann, and K. Ford (Menlo Park, CA: The AAAI Press), 247–291.

Colvert, E., Rutter, M., Kreppner, J., Beckett, C., Castle, J., Groothues, C., et al. (2008). Do theory of mind and executive function deficits underlie the adverse outcomes associated with profound early deprivation? Findings from the English and Romanian adoptees study. *J. Abnorm. Child Psychol.* 36, 1057–1068. doi: 10.1007/s10802-008-9232-x

Costello, E. J., Pine, D. S., Hammen, C., March, J. S., Plotsky, P. M., Weissman, M. M., et al. (2002). Development and natural history of mood disorders. *Biol. Psychiatry* 52, 529–542. doi: 10.1016/S0006-3223(02)01372-0

Crone, E. A. (2013). Considerations of fairness in the adolescent brain. *Child Dev. Perspect.* 7, 97–103. doi: 10.1111/cdep.12022

Dahl, R. E. (2004). Adolescent brain development: a period of vulnerabilities and opportunities. Keynote address. *Ann. N. Y. Acad. Sci.* 1021, 1–22. doi: 10.1196/annals.1308.001

Daniels, H., Cole, M., and Wertsch, J. V. (eds). (2007). *The Cambridge Companion to Vygotsky*. New York, NY: Cambridge University Press.

Davies, M., and Stone, T. (1995). *Folk Psychology: The Theory of Mind Debate*. Chichester: Wiley.

Demetriou, A., and Bakracevic, K. (2009). Reasoning and self-awareness from adolescence to middle age: organization and development as a function of education. *Learn. Indiv. Dif.* 19, 181–194. doi: 10.1016/j.lindif.2008.10.007

Dennett, D. C. (1978). Beliefs about beliefs. *Behav. Brain Sci.* 1, 568–570. doi: 10.1017/S0140525X00076664

Dumontheil, I., Apperly, I. A., and Blakemore, S.-J. (2010). Online usage of theory of mind continues to develop in late adolescence. *Dev. Sci.* 13, 331–338. doi: 10.1111/j.1467-7687.2009.00888.x

Dunbar, R. I. M. (1993). Coevolution of neocortical size, group size and language in humans. *Behav. Brain Sci.* 16, 681–735. doi: 10.1017/S0140525X00032325

Efklides, A. (2009). The role of metacognitive experiences in the learning process. *Psicothema* 21, 76–82.

Ellis, B. J., Del Giudice, M., Dishion, T. J., Figueredo, A. J., Gray, P., Griskevicius, V., et al. (2012). The evolutionary basis of risky adolescent behavior: implications for science, policy, and practice. *Dev. Psychol.* 48, 598–623. doi: 10.1037/a0026220

Farroni, T., Johnson, M. H., Menon, E., Zulian, L., Faraguna, D., and Csibra, G. (2005). Newborns' preference for face-relevant stimuli: effects of contrast polarity. *Proc. Natl. Acad. Sci. U.S.A.* 102, 17245–17250. doi: 10.1073/pnas.0502205102

Fett, A. K. J., Shergill, S. S., Gromann, P. M., Dumontheil, I., Blakemore, S.-J., Yakub, F., et al. (2014). Trust and social reciprocity in adolescence—a matter of perspective-taking. *J. Adolesc.* 37, 175–184. doi: 10.1016/j.adolescence.2013.11.011

Figner, B., Mackinlay, R. J., Wilkening, F. E., and Weber, U. (2009). Affective and deliberative processes in risky choice: age differences in risk taking in the Columbia Card Task. *J. Exp. Psychol. Learn. Mem. Cogn.* 35, 709–730. doi: 10.1037/a0014983

Flavell, J. H. (1979). Metacognition and cognitive monitoring: a new area of cognitive-developmental inquiry. *Am. Psychol.* 34, 906–911. doi: 10.1037/0003-066X.34.10.906

Frith, C. D. (1992). *The Cognitive Neuropsychology of Schizophrenia*. Hillsdale, NJ: Lawrence Erlbaum Associates.

Frith, C. D. (2008). Social cognition. *Philos. Trans. R. Soc. B Biol. Sci.* 363, 2033–2039. doi: 10.1098/rstb.2008.0005

Frith, U., and Frith, C. D. (2003). Development and neurophysiology of mentalizing. *Philos. Trans. Biol. Sci.* 358, 459–473. doi: 10.1098/rstb.2002.1218

Gallagher, S. (2006). "The narrative alternative to theory of mind," in *Radical Enactivism: Intentionality, Phenomenology, and Narrative*, ed. R. Menary (Amsterdam: John Benjamins), 223–229.

Gallagher, S., and Hutto, D. (2008). "Understanding others through primary interaction and narrative practice," in *The Shared Mind: Perspectives on Intersubjectivity*, eds J. Zlatev, T. Racine, C. Sinha, and E. Itkonen (Amsterdam: John Benjamins), 17–38.

Goddings, A., Mills, K. L., Clasenc, L., Giedd, J. N., Viner, R. M., and Blakemore, S.-J. (2014). The influence of puberty on subcortical brain development. *Neuroimage* 88, 242–251. doi: 10.1016/j.neuroimage.2013.09.073

Goffman, E. (1959). *The Presentation of Self in Everyday Life*. New York, NY: Doubleday.

Goldman, A. I. (1993). The psychology of folk psychology. *Behav. Brain Sci.* 16, 15–28. doi: 10.1017/S0140525X00028648

Goldman, A. I. (2006). *Simulating Minds: The Philosophy, Psychology, and Neuroscience of Mindreading*. Oxford: Oxford University Press.

Gottfried, J. A. (2011). *Neurobiology of Sensation and Reward (Frontiers in Neuroscience)*. Boca Raton, FL: CRC Press.

Häfner, H., and an der Heiden, W. (1997). Epidemiology of schizophrenia. *Can. J. Psychiatry* 42, 139–151.

Hankin, B. L., and Abramson, L. Y. (2001). Development of gender differences in depression: an elaborated cognitive vulnerability-transactional stress theory. *Psychol. Bull.* 127, 773–796. doi: 10.1O37//O033-29O9.127.6.773

Happé, F. (1994). An advanced test of theory of mind: understanding of story characters' thoughts and feelings by able autistic, mentally handicapped, and normal children and adults. *J. Autism Dev. Disord.* 24, 129–154. doi: 10.1007/BF02172093

Harenski, C. L., Harenski, K. A., Shane, M. S., and Kiehl, K. A. (2012). Neural development of mentalizing in moral judgment from adolescence to adulthood. *Dev. Cogn. Neurosci.* 2, 162–173. doi: 10.1016/j.dcn.2011.09.002

Henry, J. D., Phillips, L. H., Ruffman, T., and Bailey, P. E. (2013). A meta-analytic review of age differences in theory of mind. *Psychol. Aging* 28, 826–839. doi: 10.1037/a0030677

Heyes, C. M. (1998). Theory of mind in nonhuman primates. *Behav. Brain Sci.* 21, 101–148. doi: 10.1017/S0140525X98000703

Hine, T. (1999). The rise and decline of the teenager. *Am. Herit.* 50, 71–8l.

Hooper, C. J., Luciana, M., Conklin, H. M., and Yarger, R. S. (2004). Adolescents' performance on the development of decision making and ventromedial prefrontal cortex. *Dev. Psychol.* 40, 1148–1158. doi: 10.1037/0012-1649.40.6.1148

Hopkins, J. R. (2014). *Adolescence: The Transitional Years*. New York: Academic Press.

Humphrey, N. K. (1976). "The social function of intellect," in *Growing Points in Ethology*, eds P. P. G. Bateson and R. A. Hinde (Cambridge: Cambridge University Press), 303–317.

Hutto, D. D., Herschbach, M., and Southgate, V. (2011). Social cognition: mindreading and alternatives (Editorial). *Rev. Philos. Psychol.* 2, 375–395. doi: 10.1007/s13164-011-0073-0

Kett, J. F. (1977). *Rites of Passage: Adolescence in America, 1790–Present*. New York, NY: Basic Books.

Klapwijk, E. T., Goddings, A. L., Heyes, S. B., Bird, G., Viner, R. M., and Blakemore, S.-J. (2013). Increased functional connectivity with puberty in the mentalising network involved in social emotion processing. *Horm. Behav.* 64, 314–322. doi: 10.1016/j.yhbeh.2013.03.012

Laghi, F., Cotugno, A., Cecere, F., Sirolli, A., Palazzoni, D., and Bosco, F. M. (2014). An exploratory assessment of theory of mind and psychological impairment in patients with bulimia nervosa. *Br. J. Psychol.* 105, 509–523. doi: 10.1111/bjop.12054

Lenroot, R. K., Gogtay, N., Greenstein, D. K., Wells, E. M., Wallace, G. L., Clasen, L. S., et al. (2007). Sexual dimorphism of brain developmental trajectories during childhood and adolescence. *Neuroimage* 36, 1065–1073. doi: 10.1016/j.neuroimage.2007.03.053

Leon-Carrion, J., Garcia-Orza, J., and Perez-Santamaria, F. J. (2004). The development of the inhibitory component of the executive functions in children and adolescents. *Int. J. Neurosci.* 114, 1291–1311. doi: 10.1080/00207450490476066

Luna, B., Garver, K. E., Urban, T. A., Lazar, N. A., and Sweeney, J. A. (2004). Maturation of cognitive processes from late childhood to adulthood. *Child Dev.* 75, 1357–1372. doi: 10.1111/j.1467-8624.2004.00745.x

Lysaker, P. H., Carcione, A., Dimaggio, G., Johannesen, J. K., Nicolò, G., Procacci, M., et al. (2005). Metacognition amidst narratives of self and illness in schizophrenia: associations with neurocognition, symptoms, insight and quality of life. *Acta Psychiatr. Scand.* 112, 64–71. doi: 10.1111/j.1600-0447.2005.00514.x

Lysaker, P. H., Dimaggio, G., Carcione, A., Procacci, M., Buck, K. D., Davis, L. W., et al. (2010). Metacognition and schizophrenia: the capacity for self-reflectivity as a predictor for prospective assessments of work performance over six months. *Schizophr. Res.* 122, 124–130. doi: 10.1016/j.schres.2009.04.024

Makhoul, J., Alameddine, M., and Afifi, R. A. (2012). 'I felt that I was benefiting someone': youth as agents of change in a refugee community project. *Health Educ. Res.* 27, 914–926. doi: 10.1093/her/cyr011

Metcalfe, J. (1996). *Metacognition: Knowing about knowing*. Cambridge, MA: MIT Press.

Mills, K. L., Goddings, A.-L., and Blakemore, S.-J. (2014). Drama in the teenage brain. *Front. Young Minds* 2:16. doi: 10.3389/frym.2014.00016

Moran, J. M. (2013). Lifespan development: the effects of typical aging on theory of mind. *Behav. Brain Res.* 237, 32–40. doi: 10.1016/j.bbr.2012.09.020

Moriguchi, Y., Ohnishi, T., Mori, T., Matsuda, H., and Komaki, G. (2007). Changes of brain activity in the neural substrates for theory of mind during childhood and adolescence. *Psychiatry Clin. Neurosci.* 61, 355–363. doi: 10.1111/j.1440-1819.2007.01687.x

Moshman, D. (2005). *Adolescent Psychological Development: Rationality, Morality, and Identity*, ed. Lawrence Erlbaum (Mahwah, NJ: Psychology Press.)

Nichols, S., and Stich, S. P. (2003). *Mindreading: An Integrated Account of Presence, Self-Awareness, and Understanding Other Minds*. Oxford: Oxford University Press.

Pelphrey, K. A., and Carter, E. J. (2008). Brain mechanisms for social perception. *Ann. N. Y. Acad. Sci.* 1145, 283–299. doi: 10.1196/annals.1416.007

Peper, J. S., and Dahl, R. E. (2013). Teenage brain: surging hormones—Brain-behavior interactions during puberty. *Curr. Dir. Psychol. Sci.* 22, 134–139. doi: 10.1177/0963721412473755

Peper, J. S., Hulshoff Pol, H. E., Crone, E. A., and van Honk, J. (2011). Sex steroids and brain structure in pubertal boys and girls: a mini-review of neuroimaging studies. *Neuroscience* 191, 28–37. doi: 10.1016/j.neuroscience.2011.02.014

Premack, D., and Premack, A. J. (1994). "Why animals have neither culture nor history," in *Companion Encyclopedia of Anthropology*, ed. T. Ingold (London: Routledge), 350–365.

Romer, D., Betancourt, L. M., Brodsky, N. L., Giannetta, J. M., Yang, W., and Hurt, H. (2011). Does adolescent risk taking imply weak executive function? A prospective study of relations between working memory performance, impulsivity, and risk taking in early adolescence. *Dev. Sci.* 14, 1119–1133. doi: 10.1111/j.1467-7687.2011.01061.x

Sawyer, S. M., Afifi, R. A., Bearinger, L. H., Blakemore, S. J., Dick, B., Ezeh, A. C., et al. (2012). Adolescence: a foundation for future health. *Lancet* 379, 1630–1640. doi: 10.1016/S0140-6736(12)60072-5

Schwartz, S. J., Unger, J. B., Zamboanga, B. L., and Szapocznik, J. (2010). Rethinking the concept of acculturation: implications for theory and research. *Am. Psychol.* 65, 237–251. doi: 10.1037/a0019330

Sebastian, C. L., Fontaine, N. M., Bird, G., Blakemore, S.-J., De Brito, S. A., McCrory, E. J., et al. (2011). Neural processing associated with cognitive and affective Theory of Mind in adolescents and adults. *Soc. Cogn. Affect. Neurosci.* 7, 53–63. doi: 10.1093/scan/nsr023

Semerari, A., Carcione, A., Dimaggio, G., Falcone, M., Nicolo, G., Procacci, M., et al. (2003). How to evaluate metacognitive functioning in psychotherapy? The Metacognition Assessment Scale and its applications. *Clin. Psychol. Psychother.* 10, 238–261. doi: 10.1002/cpp.362

Semerari, A., Carcione, A., Dimaggio, G., Nicolò, G., and Procacci, M. (2007). Understanding minds: different functions and different disorders? The contribution of psychotherapy research. *Psychother. Res.* 17, 106–119. doi: 10.1080/10503300500536953

Semerari, A., Cucchi, M., Dimaggio, G., Cavadini, D., Carcione, A., Battelli, V., et al. (2012). The development of the Metacognition Assessment Interview: instrument description, factor structure and reliability in a non-clinical sample. *Psychiatry Res.* 200, 890–895. doi: 10.1016/j.psychres.2012.07.015

Shallice, T. (1982). Specific impairments of planning. *Philos. Trans. R. Soc. Lond. B Biol. Sci.* 298, 199–209. doi: 10.1098/rstb.1982.0082

Shamay-Tsoory, S. G., Harari, H., Aharon-Peretz, J., and Levkovitz, Y. (2010). The role of the orbitofrontal cortex in affective theory of mind deficits in criminal offenders with psychopathic tendencies. *Cortex* 46, 668–77. doi: 10.1016/j.cortex.2009.04.008

Sowell, E. R., Peterson, B. S., Thompson, P. M., Welcome, S. E., Henkenius, A. L., and Toga, A. W. (2003). Mapping cortical change across the human life span. *Nat. Neurosci.* 6, 309–315. doi: 10.1038/nn1008

Sowell, E. R., Trauner, D. A., Gamst, A., and Jernigan, T. L. (2002). Development of cortical and subcortical brain structures in childhood and adolescence: a structural MRI study. *Dev. Med. Child Neurol.* 44, 4–16. doi: 10.1111/j.1469-8749.2002.tb00253.x

Spear, L. P. (2009). Heightened stress responsivity and emotional reactivity during pubertal maturation: implications for psychopathology. *Dev. Psychopathol.* 21, 87–97. doi: 10.1017/S0954579409000066

Steinberg, L. (2008). A social neuroscience perspective on adolescent risk-taking. *Dev. Rev.* 2, 78–106. doi: 10.1016/j.dr.2007.08.002

Telzer, E. H., Fuligni, A. J., Lieberman, M. D., and Galván, A. (2013). Ventral striatum activation to prosocial rewards predicts longitudinal declines in adolescent risk taking. *Dev. Cogn. Neurosci.* 3, 45–52. doi: 10.1016/j.dcn.2012.08.004

Tirassa, M. (1999). Communicative competence and the architecture of the mind/brain. *Brain Lang.* 68, 419–441. doi: 10.1006/brln.1999.2121

Tirassa, M., and Bosco, F. M. (2008). "On the nature and role of intersubjectivity in human 1103 communication," in *Emerging Communication: Studies in New Technologies and Practices in Communication,* 10, 81–95.

Tirassa, M., Bosco, F. M., and Colle, L. (2006a). Rethinking the ontogeny of mindreading. *Conscious. Cogn.* 15, 197–217. doi: 10.1016/j.concog.2005.06.005

Tirassa, M., Bosco, F. M., and Colle, L. (2006b). Sharedness and privateness in human early social life. *Cogn. Syst. Res.* 7, 128–139. doi: 10.1016/j.cogsys.2006.01.002

Tomasello, M. (2014). *A Natural History of Human Thinking*. Cambridge: Harvard University Press.

Tomasello, M., and Vaish, A. (2013). Origins of human cooperation and morality. *Annu. Rev. Psychol.* 64, 231–255. doi: 10.1146/annurev-psych-113011-143812

Valle, A., Massaro, D., Castelli, I., and Marchetti, A. (2015). Theory of mind development in adolescence and early adulthood: the growing complexity of recursive thinking ability. *Eur. J. Psychol.* 11, 112–124. doi: 10.5964/ejop.v11i1.829

van Os, J., and Kapur, S. (2009). Schizophrenia. *Lancet* 374, 635–645. doi: 10.1016/S0140-6736(09)60995-8

Vetter, N. C., Altgassen, M., Phillips, L., Mahy, C. E., and Kliegel, M. (2013). Development of affective theory of mind across adolescence: disentangling the role of executive functions. *Dev. Neuropsychol.* 38, 114–125. doi: 10.1080/87565641.2012.733786

Viner, R. M., Ozer, E. M., Denny, S., Marmot, M., Resnick, M., Fatusi, A., et al. (2012). Adolescence and the social determinants of health. *Lancet* 379, 1641–1652. doi: 10.1016/S0140-6736(12)60149-4

Vygotsky, L. S. (1978). *Mind in Society: The Psychology of Higher Mental Functions*. Cambridge, MA: Harvard University Press.

Walker, E. F., Sabuwalla, Z., and Huot, R. (2004). Pubertal neuromaturation, stress sensitivity, and psychopathology. *Dev. Psychopathol.* 16, 807–824. doi: 10.1017/S0954579404040027

Weil, L. G., Fleming, S. M., Dumontheil, I., Kilford, E. J., Weil, R. S., Rees, G., et al. (2013). The development of metacognitive ability in adolescence. *Conscious. Cogn.* 22, 264–271. doi: 10.1016/j.concog.2013.01.004

Wellman, H. M., and Liu, D. (2004). Scaling of theory-of-mind tasks. *Child Dev.* 75, 523–541. doi: 10.1111/j.1467-8624.2004.00691.x

WHO. (2009). *Global Health Risks: Mortality and Burden of Disease Attributable to Selected Major Risks*. Geneva: World Health Organization.

WHO. (2015). *Schizophrenia*. Available at: http://www.who.int/mental_health/management/schizophrenia/en [accessed June 6, 2015].

Willoughby, T., Good, M., Adachi, P. J., Hamza, C., and Tavernier, R. (2013). Examining the link between adolescent brain development and risk taking from a social–developmental perspective. *Brain Cogn.* 83, 315–323. doi: 10.1016/j.bandc.2013.09.008

Wimmer, H. M., and Perner, J. (1983). Beliefs about beliefs: representation and constraining function of wrong beliefs in young children's understanding of deception. *Cognition* 13, 103–128. doi: 10.1016/0010-0277(83)90004-5

Wolf, L. K., Wright, N. D., Kilford, E. J., Raymond, E. J., Dolanb, J., and Blakemore, S. J. (2013). Developmental changes in effects of risk and valence on adolescent decision-making. *Cogn. Dev.* 28, 290–299. doi: 10.1016/j.cogdev.2013.04.001

Wrzus, C., Hänel, M., Wagner, J., and Neyer, F. J. (2013). Social network changes and life events across the life span: a meta-analysis. *Psychol. Bull.* 139, 53–80. doi: 10.1037/a0028601

Conflict of Interest Statement: The Reviewer Tuula M. Hurtig declares that, despite being affiliated to the same institution as the author Ilaria Gabbatore, the review process was handled objectively and no conflict of interest exists. The authors declare that the research was conducted in the absence of any commercial or financial relationships that could be construed as a potential conflict of interest.

7

Profiles of Perfectionism and School Anxiety: A Review of the 2 × 2 Model of Dispositional Perfectionism in Child Population

Cándido J. Inglés[1], José Manuel García-Fernández[2], María Vicent[2], Carolina Gonzálvez[2] and Ricardo Sanmartín[2]*

[1] Department of Health Psychology, Miguel Hernandez University of Elche, Elche, Spain, [2] Department of Developmental Psychology and Didactics, University of Alicante, Alicante, Spain

The 2 × 2 model of dispositional perfectionism has been very well received by researchers of the topic, leading to the creation of new studies that have analyzed the way in which the four proposed subtypes are distinctly associated with measures of adaptation and maladjustment. The goal of this study was to determine the possible existence of four profiles of child perfectionism that are congruent with the subtypes proposed by the 2 × 2 model, and whether these subtypes are associated with school anxiety, in accordance with the hypotheses established by the model. The sample was composed of 2157 students from Spanish Primary Education aged between 8 and 11 years ($M = 9.60$, $SD = 1.24$). The *Child and Adolescent Perfectionism Scale* was used to assess Socially Prescribed Perfectionism and Self-Oriented Perfectionism, and the School Anxiety Inventory for Primary Education was used to measure school anxiety. The results of cluster analysis identified four differential groups of perfectionists similar to the subtypes defined by the 2 × 2 model: Non-Perfectionism, Pure Personal Standards Perfectionism (Pure PSP), Pure Evaluative Concerns Perfectionism (Pure ECP), and Mixed Perfectionism. The four groups presented a differentiable pattern of association with school anxiety, with the exception of Pure PSP and Pure ECP, which showed no significant differences. Participants classified as Non-perfectionists presented the most adaptive outcomes, whereas subjects included in the Mixed Perfectionism group scored significantly higher on school anxiety than the three remaining groups. To conclude, the results partially supported the hypotheses of the 2 × 2 model, questioning the consideration of Self-Oriented Perfectionism as a positive manifestation of perfectionism and showing that it is the combination of high scores in both perfectionist dimensions, Self-Oriented Perfectionism and Socially Prescribed Perfectionism that implies higher levels of school anxiety. These findings should be taken into account when generalizing the 2 × 2 model to child population.

Edited by:
José Carlos Núñez, University of Oviedo, Spain

Reviewed by:
Leandro S. Almeida, University of Minho, Portugal
María Del Mar Molero, University of Almeria, Spain

***Correspondence:**
Cándido J. Inglés
cjingles@umh.es

Specialty section:
This article was submitted to Educational Psychology, a section of the journal Frontiers in Psychology

Keywords: 2 × 2 model of perfectionism, school anxiety, cluster analysis, Primary Education, socially prescribed perfectionism, self-oriented perfectionism

---

Abbreviations: CAPS, Child and Adolescent Perfectionism Scale; EC, Evaluative Concerns; IAEP, Inventario de Ansiedad Escolar para Educación Primaria [School Anxiety Inventory for Primary Education]; FMPS, Multidimensional Perfectionism Scale of Frost et al. (1990); HMPS, Multidimensional Perfectionism Scale of Hewitt and Flett (2004); PS, Personal Standards; Pure ECP, Pure Evaluative Concerns Perfectionism; Pure PSP, Pure Personal Standards Perfectionism.

INTRODUCTION

Perfectionism is a complex personality trait of an intra- and interpersonal nature, without a unanimously accepted definition. In fact, the inherent complexity of the construct has led to the existence of multiple conceptualizations of it (Stairs et al., 2012), and there is an intense ongoing debate about the facets that compose it, as well as about its adaptive and/or maladaptive nature (e.g., Flett and Hewitt, 2006; Owens and Slade, 2008). Both perfectionism heads have important implications from an educational point of view, especially due to its differentiating association with motivational variables and achievement-related behaviors and beliefs (Bong et al., 2014).

In an attempt to integrate the conceptualizations of perfectionism, diverse studies (Frost et al., 1993; Dunkley et al., 2000; Stoeber and Otto, 2006) proposed to group the various dimensions attributed to perfectionism into two dimensions, called, predominantly, Personal Standards (PS) and Evaluative Concerns (EC), which have been associated with indicators psychological adaptation and maladjustment, respectively (Stoeber and Otto, 2006). Thus, EC integrates those perfectionist facets associated with fear and concern about making mistakes or being judged negatively by others, a tendency to react negatively to manifestations of imperfection, and with feelings of discrepancy between one's self-expectations and one's performance. On another hand, PS includes perfectionist traits such as the tendency to strive and be motivated by achieving perfection and setting excessively high performance standards (Stoeber, 2012). The consideration of these two perfectionist dimensions simplifies the complexity of perfectionism and allows us to compare studies that have used different scales to evaluate it.

Gaudreau and Thompson (2010) developed the 2 × 2 model of dispositional perfectionism, which postulates the existence of four prototypical subtypes of perfectionism, according to the possible combinations of high and low levels of EC and PS: Non-Perfectionism (low EC and low PS), Pure Evaluative Concerns Perfectionism (hereafter Pure ECP; high EC and low PS), Pure Personal Standards Perfectionism (hereafter Pure PSP; low EC and high PS), and Mixed Perfectionism (high EC and high PS). This model is based on the following hypotheses: compared with the Non-Perfectionism subtype, the Pure PSP subtype is associated with healthier results (Hypothesis 1a), with less healthy results (Hypothesis 1b), or alternatively, the results do not differ significantly (Hypothesis 1c); Pure ECP leads to the most maladaptive results of all the subtypes (Hypothesis 2); the Mixed Perfectionism subtype is related to better results than the Pure ECP subtype (Hypothesis 3); and lastly, the Mixed Perfectionism subtype is related to worse results than the Pure PSP subtype (Hypothesis 4). Gaudreau and Thompson (2010) tested their model in a sample of 397 Canadian university students with a mean age 20.39 years, using moderate hierarchical regression methodology. Perfectionism was evaluated using the reduced versions (Cox et al., 2002) of the two Multidimensional Perfectionism Scales (FMPS; Frost et al., 1990; HMPS; Hewitt and Flett, 2004). The results revealed that the Pure PSP subtype was significantly associated with higher academic self-determination, satisfaction, positive affect, and goal progress than the Non-Perfectionist subtype, supporting Hypothesis 1a. In contrast, and in consistency with Hypothesis 1c, no significant differences were found between the two subtypes in negative affect. Likewise, Hypotheses 2, 3, and 4 were also supported by the results of the study. The Mixed subtype was associated with higher levels of negative affect and lower levels of academic self-determination, satisfaction, positive affect, and goal progress than the Pure PSP subtype, and the opposite occurred in the Pure ECP subtype, which was associated with more negative results in terms of maladjustment.

The 2 × 2 model follows a multidimensional conceptualization of perfectionism and defends that the subtypes cannot be understood without taking into account the continuous distribution of the facets and dimensions of perfectionism. Nevertheless, this model attempted to offer a harmonious perspective between the categorical vs. the dimensional currents of research (Gaudreau, 2013). Thus, various studies have recently tested the hypotheses of the model, most of them with a dimensional approach, using either the moderate hierarchical regression analysis method (Gaudreau and Verner-Filion, 2012; Hill, 2013; Crocker et al., 2014; Damian et al., 2014; Hill and Davis, 2014; Mallison et al., 2014; Méndez-Giménez et al., 2014; Speirs-Neumeister et al., 2015) or structural equations (Franche et al., 2012), but also grouping approaches through cluster analysis (Cumming and Duda, 2012; Li et al., 2014). In addition, the possibility of grouping the perfectionist dimensions into two higher dimensions (EC and PS) has allowed researchers to test the hypotheses of the model using different measures of perfectionism. Thus, for example, we highlight the use of the HMPS (Franche et al., 2012; Gaudreau and Verner-Filion, 2012; Speirs-Neumeister et al., 2015) or its version for children and adolescents: the CAPS (Flett et al., 2000, un published; Damian et al., 2014), the FMPS (Cumming and Duda, 2012) or the simultaneous employment of both (Hill, 2013; Hill and Davis, 2014). In contrast, Li et al. (2014) used the Almost Perfect Scale-Revised (Slaney et al., 2001), whereas Mallison et al. (2014) employed the Sport Multidimensional Perfectionism Scale 2 (Gotwals and Dunn, 2009). Méndez-Giménez et al. (2014) used the *Inventario de Perfeccionismo Infantil* [Child Perfectionism Inventory] (Lozano et al., 2012).

As mentioned, diverse studies tested the hypotheses formulated by Gaudreau and Thompson (2010). Even though some of them use different terms to refer to the subtypes proposed by the model, in the present review, we decided to always use the original terminology proposed by Gaudreau and Thompson (2010) in order to facilitate the comparison of the investigations.

With a sample of 208 Canadian athletes aged between 14 and 28 years, Gaudreau and Verner-Filion (2012) compared the associations between the four perfectionist subtypes and positive affect, subjective vitality, and life satisfaction. The results supported Hypotheses 1c, 2, and 3. However, differences were only observed between the Pure PSP subtype and the Mixed subtype with regard to life satisfaction, partially supporting Hypothesis 4. Likewise, Cumming and Duda (2012), using 194 English dance students aged between 14 and 20 years, found that the participants classified as Pure PSP and the Non-perfectionists did not differ significantly in the levels of social anxiety, negative affect, physical symptoms, and physical and emotional exhaustion, in accordance with Hypothesis 1c but they did differ in positive affect, in favor of the Pure PSP group, thus supporting Hypothesis 1a. Pure PSP obtained significantly lower scores than the Mixed subtype in all the measures of maladjustment but not in positive affect, whose differences did not reach statistical significance, partially supporting Hypothesis 4. Lastly, the results did not support Hypotheses 2 and 3 because the Mixed group and the Pure ECP did not differ significantly in terms of adaptation and maladjustment. In a cross-cultural study, comparing 697 university Canadian students of Asian and European origin aged between 16 and 54 years, Franche et al. (2012) obtained support for Hypotheses 1a, 2, and 3 with regard to academic achievement. However, regarding the degree of school satisfaction, differences were found between the participants of Asian and European origin. Thus, whereas the results for the university students of European origin supported Hypotheses 1a, 2, 3, and 4, there were no significant differences between the Mixed prototype and Pure PSP, or between Pure ECP and Non-Perfectionism in the sample of Asian origin, contradicting Hypotheses 2 and 4.

Subsequently, in a sample of 171 English soccer players aged between 13 and 19, Hill (2013) found support for Hypotheses 1a, 2, 3, and 4 regarding the variables of burnout and a decreased feeling of sport achievement. With regard to physical exhaustion and the devaluation of sport, the results supported Hypotheses 1c and 2. Conversely, they found no differences in the association between the Pure ECP and the Mixed subtype and physical exhaustion, or between the PSP subtype and the devaluation of sport. Recently, Hill and Davis (2014) tested the 2 × 2 model in 238 English coaches aged between 18 and 69 years. The results showed that the Pure PSP subtype was associated with more adaptive results in cognitive reappraisal and control of anger expression, both control-out and control-in, in comparison with the Non-Perfectionism subtype. Conversely, no significant differences were observed in the way in which both subtypes were associated with expressive suppression. Hypotheses 2, 3, and 4 were supported by the comparisons between the perfectionist subtypes and the variables of control-out and -in anger expression; as was Hypothesis 2 in the case of cognitive reappraisal and Hypothesis 4 in the case of expressive suppression. No significant differences were found between the Pure ECP subtype and Non-Perfectionism, or between Non-Perfectionism and Pure PSP, in their relation with cognitive reappraisal, contradicting Hypotheses 2 and 4. Likewise, in the case of expressive suppression, no differences were found between the Pure ECP subtype and Non-Perfectionism. However, there were differences between Pure ECP and the Mixed subtype, but not in the expected direction because the Mixed subtype showed more maladaptive results, contradicting Hypothesis 3.

Subsequently, Crocker et al. (2014) evaluated the hypotheses of the 2 × 2 model by means of a longitudinal design composed of 179 Canadian university athletes aged between 17 and 24 years. They found that the Pure PSP subtype was significantly associated with higher levels than the Non-Perfectionism group in control, challenge and threat appraisal during a competition, as well as in positive affect and goal progress. In contrast, they found no significant differences between these two subtypes for the variables of coping and negative affect. In addition, it was observed that the Pure ECP group only obtained more maladaptive results in the variables of challenge and control appraisal and goal progress. Pure ECP also scored significantly higher than the Mixed group in the control and challenge appraisal, goal progress, and positive affect. Lastly, the Mixed subtype, except for the results for the variables of positive affect and problem- and emotion-focused coping, generally obtained significantly more maladaptive results than Pure PSP. In a study with 345 Chinese employees aged between 19 and 42, Li et al. (2014) found no differences in the total scores of burnout between the Non-perfectionists and the Pure PSP group, or between the Pure ECP and Mixed Perfectionism groups but they did find differences between the Mixed and the Pure PSP groups, thereby supporting only Hypotheses 1c and 4 of the 2 × 2 model. Also, Mallison et al. (2014), using 241 English athletes between 11 and 19 years, found evidence in favor of Hypotheses 1a, 2, 3, and 4 of the 2 × 2 model, about the interaction effects of the variables enjoyment, physical self-esteem, and for most of the dimensions of quality of sports friendship. However, for friendship conflicts, only Hypotheses 1c and 3 were confirmed, and for things in common and conflict resolution, the results only supported Hypotheses 1c, 2, and 3. In Romanian adolescent population aged between 15 and 19 years (N = 576), Damian et al. (2014) obtained results supporting Hypotheses 1a, 2, 3, and 4 with regard to positive affect. In contrast, the results for negative affect showed that the Pure PSP and the Non-perfectionist groups did not differ, nor did the Pure ECP group and the Mixed subtype, although differences were observed between the Mixed subtype and the Pure PSP group. Thus, only Hypotheses 1c and 4 were confirmed. In the context of Physical Education, using 331 Spanish adolescents, between 12 and 16 years, Méndez-Giménez et al. (2014) found support for Hypotheses 1a, 2, 3, and 4 regarding the dimensions of physical condition, physical skill, life satisfaction, and positive affect. Nevertheless, support was only found for Hypothesis 1a for group differences in the levels of physical self-concept. Likewise, with regard to general self-concept, the results supported Hypotheses 1c, 2, 3, and 4.

Recently, using 393 high-performing American university students (M_{age} = 19.7), Speirs-Neumeister et al. (2015) compared the predictive values of each perfectionist subtype for achievement goals. The results, in general, partially supported the hypotheses of the model. Thus, for example, only Hypotheses 1a and 3 were confirmed for approach goals, whereas for avoidance goals, support was only found for Hypothesis 1b, observing higher levels for the Pure PSP subtype than for Non-Perfectionism. Lastly, Gaudreau (2015) developed a measure called Self-Assessment of Perfectionism Subtypes (SAPS) to assess the four subtypes of perfectionism previously proposed by the 2 × 2 model. The correlational analyses supported Hypotheses 1a, 2, 3, and 4 of the model for the variables of self-determination, academic goal progress, and academic joy, as well as Hypotheses 1c, 2, 3, and 4 for life satisfaction.

The review of the scientific literature of the 2 × 2 model of dispositional perfectionism has revealed diverse limitations.

Firstly, regarding the participant's characteristics, the studies that have evaluated the 2 × 2 model have mainly used samples of university students (Gaudreau and Thompson, 2010; Franche et al., 2012; Crocker et al., 2014; Gaudreau, 2015; Speirs-Neumeister et al., 2015), although they also used athletes and coaches (Gaudreau and Verner-Filion, 2012; Hill, 2013; Hill and Davis, 2014; Mallison et al., 2014), dancers (Cumming and Duda, 2012), actively working adults (Li et al., 2014) and adolescents (Damian et al., 2014; Méndez-Giménez et al., 2014). However, the hypotheses of the model have not been contrasted in child population, an aspect that would be great interest because childhood is considered a key stage for the development of perfectionism (Flett et al., 2002). Also, with the exception of the works conducted by Damian et al. (2014), Li et al. (2014) and Méndez-Giménez et al. (2014) with Chinese, Romanian, and Spanish participants, respectively, the above-mentioned investigations employed American or English population. Nevertheless, diverse studies assert that perfectionism may be influenced by the culture of origin (Marten and Rendón, 2012). As a result, the 2 × 2 model might not be generalizable to other populations with different cultural traits, an aspect about which the work of Franche et al. (2012) cast some doubt.

Thirdly, the viability of the hypotheses of the 2 × 2 model has been proven by comparing the results obtained by the four perfectionist subtypes and diverse variables of adaptation and maladjustment, obtaining, in most cases, results that support the 2 × 2 model, although also some contradictory results. Therefore, further research is required to deepen our knowledge in this sense, analyzing the relation between the perfectionist subtypes and other variables of interest, in order to continue enriching the literature on model.

The present study aims to contribute to solving some of the limitations detected by examining the validity of the 2 × 2 model of Gaudreau and Thompson (2010) in a sample of Spanish students aged between 8 and 11 years. This objective is specified in two parts: (a) to determine whether it is possible to find four child perfectionism profiles that match the subtypes proposed by the 2 × 2 model and (b) to confirm the criterion validity of the identified profiles by contrasting the differences in the mean school anxiety scores reported by each profile. This second goal is of great interest because, although perfectionism has been considered an underlying process that can broadly contribute to the development of anxiety in child population (Affrunti and Woodruff-Borden, 2014), to our knowledge, there are no studies that have previously analyzed the relation between perfectionism and anxiety, specifically school anxiety, understood as a set of symptoms grouped into cognitive, psychophysiological, and motor responses emitted by an individual in school situations that are perceived as threatening and/or dangerous (García-Fernández et al., 2008; Inglés et al., 2015).

Based on prior empirical evidence, it is expected that (a) the results of cluster analysis will reveal the existence four perfectionist profiles characterized by combinations in the scores of Socially Prescribed Perfectionism and Self-Oriented Perfectionism equivalent to the four perfectionist subtypes proposed by the 2 × 2 model, in accordance with the works of Cumming and Duda (2012) and Li et al. (2014), which replicated the subtypes of the 2 × 2 model using cluster analysis. Likewise, regarding the second goal of this study, it is expected that (b) the comparisons of the mean score reported by each cluster in the different factors of school anxiety will support Hypotheses 1a, 2, 3, and 4 of the 2 × 2 model, in accordance with most of the studies that have tested the model of Gaudreau and Thompson (2010).

MATERIALS AND METHODS

Participants

The sample was selected through random cluster sampling, taking as primary units the geographical areas of the province of Alicante: central, north, south, east, and west; and as secondary units, the schools each area (selecting between one and three schools in each area with proportional random sampling). Lastly, the tertiary units were the classrooms. By means of this method, we selected a total 25 schools from urban and rural areas, 19 public schools and 6 private ones, from which four classrooms were randomly chosen, 1 for each course from 3rd to 6th grade of Primary Education, obtaining approximately 95 participants per school. We thereby recruited an initial sample of 2157 students, of whom 83(4.57%) were excluded from the study for not having the minimum reading level required to do the tests, 57 (3.14%) for being repeaters, 97 (5.34%) due to lack of parental consent, and 105 (5.79%) because of errors or omissions in the applied tests. Thus, the final sample was composed of 1815 students aged between 8 and 11 years ($M = 9.60$, $SD = 1.24$), enrolled from 3rd to 6th grade of Primary Education. The ethnic composition of the sample was: 87.65 Spaniards, 6.29% South American, 3.57% Arab, 2.14% European, and 0.35% Asian. The 50.36% of participants were males and the 49.64% females. Regarding the sample distribution across age, it was obtained that the 32.34, 27.99, 18.13% and the 21.54% of participants were 8, 9, 10, and 11 years old, respectively. The Chi-squared test showed the uniform frequency distribution of the eight groups by age and sex ($\chi^2 = 6.55$, $p = 0.08$).

Measures

Child and Adolescent Perfectionism Scale (CAPS; Flett et al., 2000, un published)

The CAPS was developed from the HMPS (Hewitt and Flett, 2004) and is a 22-item self-report measure of perfectionism in children and adolescents as of age 8. It has two dimensions, Self-Oriented Perfectionism, considered as the application of unrealistic performance standards to oneself and the motivation to be a perfectionist (e.g., "I get upset if there is even one mistake in my work," "I try to be perfect in everything I do"); and Socially Prescribed Perfectionism, which assesses the belief that your loved ones expect you to be perfect (e.g., "My teachers expect my work to be perfect"). The items are rated on a five-point Likert-type scale, with higher scores indicating more perfectionism.

In its original validation with a population of 247 Canadian students aged between 8 and 17, acceptable scores of internal consistency were found ($\alpha = 0.85$ for Self-Oriented Perfectionism and α = 0.81 for Socially Prescribed Perfectionism), as well as adequate indexes of temporal stability that ranged between 0.66 and 0.74 for the dimensions of Self-Oriented Perfectionism and Socially Prescribed Perfectionism, respectively. The concurrent and discriminant validity of the scale were also supported by the results of the correlations between the two perfectionist dimensions and diverse measures of adaptation and maladjustment (Flett et al., 2000, un published).

The CAPS is the most used measure of child perfectionism (García-Fernández et al., 2016). Moreover, the scale has been adapted for application in Scottish (O'Connor et al., 2009), Turkish (Uz-Baş and Siyez, 2010), French (Douilliez and Hénot, 2013), Portuguese (Bento et al., 2014), and Chinese (Yang et al., 2015) population. Castro et al. (2004) applied a Spanish translation of the scale in a clinical and non-clinical sample of female adolescents, obtaining adequate rates of internal consistency (α = 0.88 for Self-Oriented Perfectionism, α = 0.87 for Socially Prescribed Perfectionism, and α = 0.89 for the total scale) and temporal stability (*tr* = 0.83). Also, Vicent et al. (2016) obtained appropriate reliability rates for Socially Prescribed Perfectionism dimension (α = 0.88) in a study of 804 Spanish students aged between 8 and 11 years. However, as the scale still has not yet been validated in Spanish population, the Spanish version of the CAPS was established using the back-translation method. Firstly, the original English version of the CAPS was translated into Spanish by a Spanish interpreter with a college degree in English, who was familiar with the English culture. Then, the Spanish translation of the CAPS was back-translated into English by another native Spanish translator with a degree in English language and knowledge of both cultures. The original version was compared with the back-translation and the translators made corrections and drafted the final Spanish translation. No item was deleted or significantly changed during the translation process.

Internal consistency, Cronbach's alpha, calculated for the present study was 0.84, for the total CAPS, 0.78 for Socially Prescribed Perfectionism, and 0.71 for Self-Oriented Perfectionism.

Inventario de Ansiedad Escolar para Educación Primaria [Inventory of School Anxiety for Primary Education] (IAEP; García-Fernández et al., 2014)

The IAEP was developed from of the *Inventario de Ansiedad Escolar para alumnos de Educación Secundaria y Bachillerato* [Inventory of School Anxiety for Students of Secondary Education and High School] (García-Fernández et al., 2011) to assess school anxiety in children aged 8–11 years. It consists of 22 items about four school situations that can frequently cause anxiety, and 15 items that present diverse responses of school anxiety. The four situational factors are: (I) School Punishment Anxiety, measuring anxiety in situations of explicit punishment at school or situations that could lead to punishment (e.g., "The teacher asks for my homework and I did not do it"); (II) Victimization Anxiety, which assesses anxiety caused by situations in which the student feels physically or psychologically abused by peers (e.g., "They insult me or threaten me at school"); (III) Social Evaluation Anxiety, which reflects anxiety in anticipation of being negatively judged by others at school (e.g., "Going to the black board"); (IV) School Evaluation Anxiety, in reference to anxiety associated with exams (e.g., "When I'm taking an exam"). The three response scales present cognitive (e.g., "I feel guilty"), behavioral (e.g., "I cannot sit still"), and psychophysiological (e.g., "I breathe faster") anxiety responses.

García-Fernández et al. (2014) analyzed the validity of the scale by means of exploratory factor analysis (EFA) and confirmatory factor analysis (CFA) in a sample of 1003 Spanish children between 8 and 11 years, supporting the factor structure of the instrument. The levels of reliability were acceptable both for the total scale (α = 0.92) and for the four situational factors (α = between 0.85 and 0.90) and the three response scales (α = between 0.80 and 0.84).

Internal consistency, Cronbach's alpha, calculated for the present study was 0.92 for the total IAEP, 0.89 for Factors I (School Punishment Anxiety) and II (Victimization Anxiety), 0.87 for Factor III (Social Evaluation Anxiety), 0.88 for Factor IV (School Evaluation Anxiety), 0.74 for the Cognitive Scale, 0.71 for the Behavioral Scale, and 0.73 for the Psychophysiological Scale.

Procedure

A meeting was held with the headmasters of the selected schools to explain the purpose of our work and request their collaboration. All the headmasters of the selected schools agreed to participate in our work. After selecting the classrooms, we requested the parents' written informed consent. Subsequently, we administered the tests to the students during normal school hours, for approximately 40 min, in group format and under the supervision of at least one trained researcher. At the beginning of the administration session of the two instruments, the researcher explained the goal of the work to the participants, focusing on its voluntary and anonymous nature. The participants were treated at all times according to the ethical criteria that govern scientific research.

Statistical Analysis

We applied cluster analysis, using the non-hierarchical method of *quick cluster analysis*, which allows previously specifying the number of clusters to be formed, so that only one cluster solution is given, and it also permits moving subjects from one group to another during the grouping process in order to optimize the cluster solution (Clatworthy et al., 2005). In addition, this procedure is considered the most adequate to establish profiles if the sample of participants is sufficiently large (Hair et al., 1998).

The profiles of child perfectionism were defined based on the different combinations of the dimensions Socially Prescribed Perfectionism and Self-Oriented Perfectionism, which were taken as indicators of the two dimensions proposed by the 2 × 2 model (EC and PS, respectively) as in previous studies (Franche et al., 2012; Gaudreau and Verner-Filion, 2012; Damian et al., 2014; Speirs-Neumeister et al., 2015). Before cluster analysis, we standardized the raw scores because the two subscales did not contain the same number of items. In order to replicate the 2 × 2 model, we defined an initial solution of four clusters. According to the criterion of Nordin-Bates et al. (2011) and Cumming and

Duda (2012), *z* scores below −0.5 are considered to be low levels; *z* scores between −0.5 and +0.5 moderate, and *z* scores over +0.5 are considered high.

We then carried out various analyses of variance (*ANOVA*) to examine the differences between the four groups identified in the school anxiety dimensions, and thus verify the validity of the hypotheses posed by the 2 × 2 model. Subsequently, in those cases that were statistically significant, *post hoc* tests were performed (*Scheffé* method) to determine between which groups such differences were found. In addition, the effect size or standardized mean difference was calculated (*d* index) to obtain the magnitude of the observed differences, considering values between 0.20 and 0.49 indicators of a small effect size, between 0.50 and 0.79, medium or moderate effect, and values equal to or greater than 0.80 as indicators of a large effect size (Cohen, 1988). All the data analyses were carried out with the SPSS/IBM 22.0 statistical package.

RESULTS

Identification of Child Perfectionism Profiles

According to the above criteria, the first group, which included 470 subjects (25.90%), was characterized by high levels of Socially Prescribed Perfectionism and moderate levels of Self-Oriented Perfectionism. Consequently, this group was called Pure ECP. The second cluster was made up of 381 participants (20.99%) who scored low in the two assessed perfectionist dimensions. Therefore, we decided to call this group Non-Perfectionism. The third cluster included 516 students (28.43%) with moderate scores in Self-Oriented Perfectionism and low scores in Socially Prescribed Perfectionism. This group was called Pure PSP. Lastly, we found a fourth group containing 448 participants (24.68%) with high scores in both scales, which was labeled Mixed Perfectionism (see **Figure 1**).

Inter-group Differences in School Anxiety

The results of the *ANOVA* revealed the existence of statistically significant differences among the four groups of perfectionists in the mean scores for total school anxiety and in all the subscales. In all cases, the Non-Perfectionism group obtained the lowest means in school anxiety, whereas the Mixed Perfectionism group obtained the highest scores (see **Table 1**).

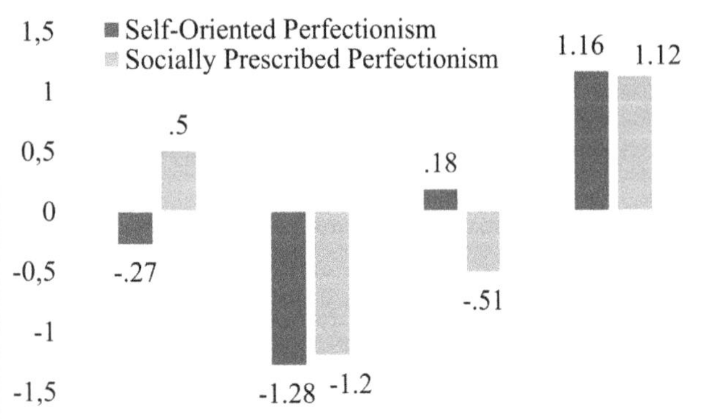

FIGURE 1 | Graphic representation of the profiles of child perfectionism through cluster analysis.

The *post hoc* tests (see **Table 2**) revealed statistically significant differences between the Pure ECP group and the Non-Perfectionist group in all the dimensions of school anxiety and in the total IAEP scores, with small effect sizes that ranged between $d = 0.25$ (for Victimization Anxiety) and $d = 0.43$ (for the total scale). The Pure ECP and Pure PSP groups did not differ significantly in school anxiety. In contrast, differences were observed between the Pure ECP cluster and Mixed Perfectionism, with small effect sizes (between $d = 0.20$ for Social Evaluation Anxiety and the Cognitive Scale, and $d = 0.28$, for School Punishment Anxiety). Likewise, the Non-Perfectionism and Pure PSP groups differed significantly, also with small effect sizes that varied between $d = 0.30$, for the Psychophysiological scale, and $d = 0.42$, for the School Punishment Anxiety scale. However, no significant differences were found between the two groups for Social Evaluation Anxiety and School Evaluation Anxiety. No differences were found between the Pure PSP and Mixed Perfectionism groups in the variable Victimization Anxiety, although differences were observed for the rest of factors and scales of school anxiety, with small effect sizes in all cases, ranging between $d = 0.23$ (Social Evaluation Anxiety, Cognitive and Behavioral Scales) and $d = 0.30$ (School Evaluation Anxiety). Lastly, we found the greatest differences between the Pure PSP cluster and Mixed Perfectionism (between $d = 0.40$, for Victimization Anxiety and $d = 0.67$ for School Punishment Anxiety), with moderate effect sizes for the variables of school anxiety.

DISCUSSION

The first goal of the present work was to analyze the existence of four profiles of child perfectionism in Spanish population and determine whether these profiles coincided with the perfectionist subtypes identified by Gaudreau and Thompson (2010). Accordingly, the results of the cluster analyses revealed four groups that were characterized by combinations of the scores in Socially Prescribed Perfectionism and Self-Oriented Perfectionism similar to the description of the four perfectionist subtypes proposed by the 2 × 2 model, and coherent with other previous studies of clusters that defined these same perfectionism profiles (Cumming and Duda, 2012; Li et al., 2014).

On another hand, the second goal of this investigation involved comparing the mean scores obtained by the four profiles identified in school anxiety, in order to support the hypotheses previously formulated by the 2 × 2 model. The results revealed statistically significant differences among the four groups, except for between the Pure ECP and Pure PSP clusters, comparing the mean scores obtained on the seven subscales and the total school anxiety score. However, these differences were not as expected. In fact, we found that the results did not support most of the hypotheses of the 2 × 2 model, as

TABLE 1 | Means and standard deviations obtained by the four groups, effect size for each dimension of school anxiety.

	Group 1 Pure ECP		Group 2 Non-Perfectionist		Group 3 Pure PSP		Group 4 Mixed Perfectionism		Statistical Significance		
Dimensions	***M***	***SD***	***M***	***SD***	***M***	***SD***	***M***	***SD***	$F_{(3,1811)}$	*p*	η^2
FI	25.43	14.11	19.47	14.19	25.63	14.97	29.77	16.33	29.240	<0.001	0.152
FII	15.13	14.29	11.75	12.26	16.20	14.36	17.64	16.46	11.057	<0.001	0.120
FIII	8.50	7.92	6.45	7.37	8.15	8.57	10.46	11.35	12.444	<0.001	0.123
FIV	14.06	8.91	11.28	7.93	12.56	8.68	15.26	9.63	14.366	<0.001	0.126
Cognitive Scale	29.48	13.29	23.43	14.16	29.01	14.34	32.45	16.04	24.506	<0.001	0.144
Behavioral Scale	14.85	10.60	11.01	9.69	15.17	10.80	17.88	12.43	24.237	<0.001	0.144
Psycho-physiogical Scale	19.74	14.01	15.41	12.70	19.66	15.12	23.76	16.77	19.334	<0.001	0.135
Total IAEP	63.14	33.46	48.96	32.38	62.55	36.39	73.14	41.15	27.544	<0.001	0.149

FI, School Punishment Anxiety; FII, Victimization Anxiety; FIII, Social Evaluation Anxiety; FIV, School Evaluation Anxiety.

TABLE 2 | *d* Cohen index to *post hoc* contrasts between the mean scores obtained and the four clusters in the factors of school anxiety.

	Pure ECP vs. Non-Perfectionist	Pure ECP vs. Pure PSP	Pure PSP vs. Mixed Perfectionism	Non-Perfectionist vs. Pure PSP	Non-Perfectionist vs. Mixed Perfectionism	Pure PSP vs. Mixed Perfectionism
FI	0.42	n.s	0.28	0.42	0.67	0.27
FII	0.25	n.s	n.s	0.33	0.40	n.s
FIII	0.27	n.s	0.20	n.s	0.41	0.23
FIV	0.33	n.s	n.s	n.s	0.45	0.30
Cognitive Scale	0.44	n.s	0.20	0.39	0.59	0.23
Behavioral Scale	0.38	n.s	0.26	0.40	0.61	0.23
Psycho-physiogical Scale	0.32	n.s	0.26	0.30	0.56	0.26
Total IAEP	0.43	n.s	0.27	0.39	0.65	0.27

FI, School Punishment Anxiety; FII, Victimization Anxiety; FIII, Social Evaluation Anxiety; FIV, School Evaluation Anxiety.

we had hypothesized. Specifically, we observed that the Pure PSP group obtained significantly higher scores in school anxiety than the Non-Perfectionism group, confirming Hypothesis 1b, except for the results for Factors III (Social Evaluation Anxiety) and IV (School Evaluation Anxiety), whose differences did not reach statistical significance (supporting Hypothesis 1c), and contradicting previous literature on the model, which had mainly found support for Hypothesis 1a (Gaudreau and Thompson, 2010; Franche et al., 2012; Crocker et al., 2014; Hill and Davis, 2014; Mallison et al., 2014; Méndez-Giménez et al., 2014; Gaudreau, 2015). These findings imply that Non-perfectionist students generally have lower levels of anxiety than students with high levels of PS and low levels of EC. In support of Hypothesis 4, we found that the Pure PSP group differed significantly from the Mixed group, with higher school anxiety scores in the latter group. These findings are in the line of prior works that supported the idea that the Pure PSP group is more adaptive than the Mixed subtype (Gaudreau and Thompson, 2010; Cumming and Duda, 2012; Hill, 2013; Crocker et al., 2014; Damian et al., 2014; Hill and Davis, 2014; Li et al., 2014; Mallison et al., 2014; Méndez-Giménez et al., 2014; Gaudreau, 2015). However, in contrast to Hypotheses 2 and 3, the Mixed Perfectionism group scored significantly higher in school anxiety. That is, contrary to the 2 × 2 model, which postulates that Pure ECP is the most harmful subtype (Gaudreau and Thompson, 2010; Franche et al., 2012; Gaudreau and Verner-Filion, 2012; Hill, 2013; Hill and Davis, 2014; Mallison et al., 2014; Méndez-Giménez et al., 2014; Gaudreau, 2015), the results of this study showed that the Mixed subtype is the most negative, in terms of maladjustment, for the specific case of school anxiety.

In general, the results found seem to indicate that Pure ECP and Pure PSP do not present a differentiable pattern of association with school anxiety, and both are more harmful than the Non Perfectionism group, which proved to be the most adaptive subtype of the four, whereas the combination of high levels in both dimensions (Self-Oriented Perfectionism and Socially Prescribed Perfectionism) is the most harmful manifestation of perfectionism. These results question the idea that Self-Oriented Perfectionism is a positive personality trait, at least regarding its relation with school anxiety. Certainly, taking into account that Self-Oriented Perfectionism is characterized by a tendency to set unrealistic and even impossible goals and a high motivation to pursue them, as well as the tendency to criticize oneself, it is not surprising that students who obtain moderate and high scores in this dimension (i.e., Pure PSP and Mixed Perfectionism clusters) experience higher levels of anxiety related to the academic setting. In fact, previous studies have also shown in child and youth population that this dimension is positively associated with diverse psychopathological variables such as anxiety (Hewitt et al., 2002; Essau et al., 2012; Nobel et al., 2012), depression (Hewitt et al., 2002; Castro et al., 2004; Christopher and Shewmaker, 2010; Nobel et al., 2012), eating disorders (Castro et al., 2004, 2007; Kirsh et al., 2007; Pamies and Quiles, 2014), a tendency toward shame and guilt (Choy and Drinnan, 2007), narcissisism (Freudenstein et al., 2012), and somatic symptoms (Jungyoon, 2012). Nevertheless, Self-Oriented Perfectionism has sometimes been shown to be associated with adaptive results. Thus, it has also been shown in students of diverse ages that Self-Oriented Perfectionism positively predicts academic achievement (Stoeber et al., 2015) and is positively related to academic self-efficacy and other motivational variables (Bong et al., 2014), to greater optimism about the probability of being successful (Eddington, 2014), and to adaptive problem-solving behaviors (Dry et al., 2015), among others aspects. This dual facet of Self-Oriented Perfectionism has meant that its construct validity has been questioned by diverse studies, which found that the factor structure of the CAPS has a better fit when Self-Oriented Perfectionism is divided into two differentiated scales, Self-Oriented Perfectionism-Efforts and Self-Oriented Perfectionism-Criticism, reflecting, respectively, the positive and negative side of perfectionist introspection (McCreary et al., 2004; O'Connor et al., 2009; Nobel et al., 2012). Therefore, if possible, we recommend replicating the perfectionist subtypes considering Self-Oriented Perfectionism-Efforts as a reflection of the PS dimension, and Self-Oriented Perfectionism-Criticism and Socially Prescribed Perfectionism as a reflection of the EC dimension, as well as analyzing the differences between the groups found, based on various measures of adaptation and maladjustment.

Limitations and Future Research

Some limitations identified and future lines of research should be mentioned before concluding this study. Firstly, given that perfectionism is multidimensional and lacks a unique definition, it should be taken into account that the use of one or another scale may involve subtle differences in the results. In our case, we chose the CAPS as being the most employed instrument to assess perfectionism in children and adolescents and because it evaluates the dimensions of Self-Oriented Perfectionism and Socially Prescribed Perfectionism, which have proven to be valid and reliable indicators of PS and EC (e.g., Frost et al., 1993; Dunkley et al., 2000; Bieling et al., 2004). Nevertheless, it would be interesting for future works to use other instruments validated in child population, for example, the Adaptative/Maladaptative Perfectionism Scale (Rice and Preusser, 2002; Rice et al., 2004), as the results may differ.

Secondly, only two previous studies have examined the 2 × 2 model through cluster analysis. However, these studies were carried out in very different populations from those employed in the present study. Thus, Cumming and Duda (2012) used English dance students aged between 14 and 20 years, whereas Li et al. (2014) focused on Chinese adults working in departments related to computer science. Therefore, as it has been suggested that perfectionism can vary in intensity and manifestation depending on the domain assessed (e.g., work, studies, physical appearance, sport...) (Stoeber and Stoeber, 2009), the results obtained by these works and by this study should be compared with caution.

Thirdly, regarding the methodological aspect, in this study, we chose by non-hierarchical method for the cluster analysis, as our goal was to replicate the four groups identified by the 2 × 2 model. However, it should be noted that small discrepancies were found with regard to the Pure PSP and Pure ECP groups. That is, whereas according to the 2 × 2 model, the Pure ECP group was characterized by high scores in EC and low scores in PS, and the opposite held true for Pure PSP, in our study, the Pure ECP group was characterized by high scores in EC and moderate scores in PS, and the Pure PSP group, by low scores in EC and moderate scores in PS. This could explain why the differences between these two subtypes in school anxiety did not reach statistical significance. Accordingly, we recommend future studies to determine whether another solution of profiles would better represent child perfectionism.

Fourthly, it is important to mention that, despite our sample size and sampling process guarantee the representability of Spanish students between 8 and 11 years old, it is important that future research consider as well relevant information like socioeconomically origin and previous academic performance, because they could play an important role in the relationship between perfectionism and academic anxiety.

Lastly, this study suggests that approximately one fourth of the child population has high scores in perfectionism and is at risk of presenting high levels of school anxiety. However, the cross-sectional design used limits the interpretation of the results about how perfectionism is associated with school anxiety. Therefore, it would be of interest for future works to solve this limitation by means of a longitudinal design that would allow establishing causal relations between the analyzed variables, as well as determining the negative consequences over time of belonging to one or another perfectionist subtype.

Despite the limitations, this is the first study that analyzes the 2 × 2 model in children from Primary Education (between 8 and 11 years), identifying four distinguishable child perfectionism profiles and comparing their association with school anxiety. The present investigation shows that students characterized by being perfectionists, either of an interpersonal or intrapersonal nature or presenting both forms concurrently, make up more than 70% of the students between 8 and 11 years. Therefore, a considerable number of perfectionist children present greater vulnerability for the development of psychological problems such as, for example, school anxiety. Educational institutions should pay more attention to this problem, intervening more actively. Thus, in the context of a society often characterized by a culture of the hyper-competitiveness (Fletcher et al., 2014), schools must take on the challenge of providing the students with the resilience required to be able to self-regulate, cope with adversity and failures, and to consider their errors as possibilities to improve and not as defects inherent to the person (Flett and Hewitt, 2014; Greenspon, 2014). In short, to form people who are capable of not allowing them to submit to the "tyranny of musts," that need of chimerical perfection that contributes to the development and maintenance a wide variety of psychiatric disorders (Egan et al., 2011).

AUTHOR CONTRIBUTIONS

CI has designed this research. He has also received the study in all its phases. JG-F has designed this research. He has also received the study in all its phases. MV has participated conducting a literature search and writing this manuscript. CG participated conducting a literature search and writing this manuscript. RS has participated performing statistical analyzes.

FUNDING

Part of this investigation is supported by the project "Assessment of school anxiety and its relation with psychoeducational variables in childhood. Study of the efficacy of a preventive program" (EDU2012-35124), awarded to JG-F, as well as by aid for the recruitment of pre-doctorate research staff, Program VALi+d (ACIF/2014/368) granted to MV, and by aid to contracts for the training of doctors -UA FPU 2013-5795 y 2015-5995, granted to CG and RS, respectively.

REFERENCES

Affrunti, N. W., and Woodruff-Borden, J. (2014). Perfectionism in pediatric anxiety and depressive disorders. *Clin. Child. Fam. Psychol. Rev.* 17, 299–317. doi: 10.1007/s10567-014-0164-4

Bento, C., Pereira, A. T., Saraiva, J. M., and Macedo, A. (2014). Children and adolescent perfectionism scale: validation in a Portuguese adolescent sample. *Psicol. Reflexão Crít.* 27, 228–232. doi: 10.1590/1678-7153.2014 27203

Bieling, P. J., Israeli, A. L., and Antony, M. M. (2004). Is perfectionism good, bad, or both? Examining models of the perfectionism construct. *Pers. Individ. Dif.* 36, 1373–1385. doi: 10.1016/S0191-8869(03) 00235-6

Bong, M., Hwang, A., Noh, A., and Sung-il, K. (2014). Perfectionism and motivation of adolescents in academic contexts. *J. Educ. Psychol.* 106, 711–729. doi: 10.1037/a0035836

Castro, J., Gila, A., Gual, P., Lahortiga, F., Saura, B., and Toro, J. (2004). Perfectionism dimensions in children and adolescents with anorexia nervosa. *J. Adolesc. Health* 35, 392–398. doi: 10.1016/j.jadohealth.2003. 11.094

Castro, J., Gual, P., Lahortiga, F., Gila, A., Casula, V., Fuhrmann, C., et al. (2007). Self-oriented perfectionism in eating disorders. *Int. J. Eat. Disord.* 40, 562–568. doi: 10.1002/eat.20393

Choy, G., and Drinnan, L. (2007). Perfectionism and self-evaluative emotions in primary school children. *Paper presented in the AARE Annual Conference*, Adelaidem, SA.

Christopher, M. M., and Shewmaker, J. (2010). The relationship of perfectionism to affective variables in gifted and highly able children. *Gifted Child Today* 33, 20–30. doi: 10.1177/107621751003300307

Clatworthy, J., Buick, D., Hankins, M., Weinman, J., and Horne, R. (2005). The use and reporting of cluster analysis in health psychology: a review. *Br. J. Health Psychol.* 10, 329–358. doi: 10.1348/135910705X 25697

Cohen, J. (1988). *Statistical Power Analysis for the Behavioral Sciences*. Hillsdale, NJ: Erlbaum.

Cox, B. J., Enns, M. W., and Clara, I. P. (2002). The multidimensional structure of perfectionism in clinically distressed and college student samples. *Psychol. Assess.* 14, 365–373. doi: 10.1037//1040-3590.14.3.365

Crocker, P. R. E., Gaudreau, P., Mosewich, A., and Kljajic, K. (2014). Perfectionism and the stress process in intercollegiate athletes: examining the 2 x 2 model of perfectionism in sport competition. *Int. J. Sport. Psychol.* 45, 325–348. doi: 10.7352/IJSP.2014.45.325

Cumming, J., and Duda, J. L. (2012). Profiles of perfectionism, body-related concerns, and indicators of psychological health in vocational dance students: an investigation of the 2 x 2 model of perfectionism. *Psychol. Sport. Exerc.* 13, 729–738. doi: 10.1016/j.psychsport.2012.05.004

Damian, L. E., Stoeber, J., Negru, O., and Baban, A. (2014). Positive and negative affect in adolescents: an investigation of the 2 x 2 model of perfectionism. *Cogn. Brain Behav.* 18, 1–16.

Douilliez, C., and Hénot, E. (2013). Mesures du perfectionnisme chez l'adolescent: validation des versions francophones de deux questionnairies. *Can. J. Behav. Sci.* 45, 64–71. doi: 10.1037/a0022686

Dry, S. M., Kane, R. T., and Rooney, R. M. (2015). An investigation into the role of coping in preventing depression associated with perfectionism in preadolescent children. *Front. Public Health* 3:190. doi: 10.3389/fpubh.2015. 00190

Dunkley, D. M., Blankstein, K. R., Halsall, J., Williams, M., and Winkworth, G. (2000). The relation between perfectionism and distress: hassles, coping, and perceived social support as mediators and moderators. *J. Couns. Psychol.* 47, 437–453. doi: 10.1037//0022-0167.47.4.437

Eddington, K. M. (2014). Perfectionism, goal adjustment, and self-regulation: a short-term follow-up study of distress and coping. *Self Identity* 13, 197–213. doi: 10.1080/15298868.2013.781740

Egan, J., Wade, T. D., and Shafran, R. (2011). Perfectionism as a transdiagnostic process: a clinical review. *Clin. Psychol. Rev.* 31, 203–212. doi: 10.1016/j.cpr.2010.04.009

Essau, C. A., Conradt, J., Sasagawa, S., and Ollendick, T. H. (2012). Prevention of anxiety symptoms in children: results from a universal school-based trial. *Behav. Ther.* 43, 450–464. doi: 10.1016/j.beth.2011.08.003

Fletcher, K. L., Speirs-Neumeister, K. L., and Flett, G. L. (2014). Introduction to the special issue: perfectionism in the school context. *Psychol. Sch.* 51, 897–898. doi: 10.1002/pits.21790

Flett, G. L., and Hewitt, P. L. (2006). Positive versus negative perfectionism in psychopathology. a comment on Slade and Owens's dual process model. *Behav. Modif.* 30, 472–495. doi: 10.1177/0145445506288026

Flett, G. L., and Hewitt, P. L. (2014). A proposed framework for preventing perfectionism and promoting resilience and mental health among vulnerable children and adolescents. *Psychol. Sch.* 51, 899–912. doi: 10.1002/pits.21792

Flett, G. L., Hewitt, P. L., Oliver, J. M., and Macdonald, S. (2002). "Perfectionism in children and their parents: a developmental analysis," in *Perfectionism: Theory, Research, and Treatment*, eds G. L. Flett and P. L. Hewitt (Washington, DC: American Psychological Association), 89–132.

Franche, V., Gaudreau, P., and Miranda, D. (2012). The 2 x 2 model of perfectionism: a comparison across Asian Canadians and European Canadians. *J. Couns. Psychol.* 59, 567–574. doi: 10.1037/a0028992

Freudenstein, O., Valevski, A., Apter, A., Zohar, A., Shoval, G., Nahshoni, E., et al. (2012). Perfectionism, narcissism, and depression in suicidal and nonsuicidal adolescent inpatients. *Compr. Psychiatry.* 53, 746–752. doi: 10.1016/j.comppsych.2011.08.011

Frost, R. O., Heimberg, R. G., Holt, C. S., Mattia, J. I., and Neubauer, A. L. (1993). A comparison of two measures of perfectionism. *Pers. Individ. Dif.* 14, 119–126. doi: 10.1016/0191-8869(93)90181-2

Frost, R. O., Marten, P., Lahart, C., and Rosemblate, R. (1990). The dimensions of perfectionism. *Cognit. Ther. Res.* 14, 449–468. doi: 10.1007/BF01172967

García-Fernández, J. M., Inglés, C. J., and Gómez-Núñez, M. I. (2014). *Inventario de Ansiedad Escolar Para Educación Primaria (IAEP). Manual Interno [Inventory of School Anxiety for Primary Education (IAEP). Internal manual]*. Alicante: Universidad de Alicante.

García-Fernández, J. M., Inglés, C. J., Martínez-Monteagudo, M. C., Marzo, J. C., and Estévez, E. (2011). Inventario de ansiedad escolar: validación en una muestra de estudiantes de educación secundaria [Inventory of school anxiety: validation in a sample of education secondary students]. *Psicothema* 23, 301–307.

García-Fernández, J. M., Inglés, C. J., Martínez-Monteagudo, M. C., and Redondo, J. (2008). Evaluación y tratamiento de la ansiedad escolar en la infancia y la adolescencia [Assessment and treatment of school anxiety in childhood and adolescence]. *Psicol. Conductual.* 16, 413–437. doi: 10.5093/ed2013a5

García-Fernández, J. M., Inglés, C. J., Vicent, M., Gonzálvez, C., Gómez-Núñez, M. I., and Poveda-Serra, P. (2016). Perfeccionismo durante la infancia y la adolescencia. Análisis bibliométrico y temático (2004-2014). [Perfectionism during childhood and adolescence. Bibliometric and thematic analysis (2004-2014)]. *Rev. Iberoam. Psicol. Salud* 7, 79–88. doi: 10.1016/j.rips.2016.02.001

Gaudreau, P. (2013). 2 x 2 model of perfectionism: commenting the critical comments and suggestions of Stoeber (2012). *Pers. Individ. Dif.* 55, 351–355. doi: 10.1016/j.paid.2012.04.029

Gaudreau, P. (2015). Self-assessment of the four subtypes of perfectionism in the 2 x 2 model of perfectionism. *Pers. Individ. Dif.* 84, 52–62. doi: 10.1016/j.paid2014.10.039

Gaudreau, P., and Thompson, A. (2010). Testing a 2 x 2 model of dispositional perfectionism. *Pers. Individ. Dif.* 48, 532–537. doi: 10.1016/j.paid.2009.11.031

Gaudreau, P., and Verner-Filion, J. (2012). Dispositional perfectionism and well-being: a test of the 2 x 2 model of perfectionism in the sport domain. *Sport Exerc. Perform. Psychol.* 1, 29–43. doi: 10.1037/a0025747

Gotwals, J. K., and Dunn, J. G. H. (2009). A multi-method multi-analytic approach to establish internal construct validity evidence: the sport multidimensional perfectionism scale 2. *Meas. Phys. Educ. Exerc. Sci.* 13, 71–92. doi: 10.1080/10913670902812663

Greenspon, T. S. (2014). Is there an antidote to perfectionism? *Psychol. Sch.* 51, 986–998. doi: 10.1002/pits.21797

Hair, J. F., Anderson, R. E., Tatham, R. C., and Black, W. C. (1998). *Multivariate Data Analysis*, 5th Edn. Upper Saddle River, NJ: Prentice-Hall.

Hewitt, P. L., Caelian, C. F., Flett, G. L., Sherry, S. B., Collins, L., and Flynn, C. A. (2002). Perfectionism in children: associations with depression, anxiety, and anger. *Pers. Individ. Dif.* 32, 1049–1061. doi: 10.1016/S0191-8869(01)00109-X

Hewitt, P. L., and Flett, G. L. (2004). *Multidimensional Perfectionism Scale (MPS): Technical Manual.* Toronto, ON: Multi-Health Systems.

Hill, A. P. (2013). Perfectionism and burnout in junior soccer players: a test of the 2 x 2 model of dispositional perfectionism. *Psychol. Sport Exerc.* 35, 18–29. doi: 10.1123/jsep.35.1.18

Hill, A. P., and Davis, P. A. (2014). Perfectionism and emotion regulation in coaches: a test of the 2 x 2 model of dispositional perfectionism. *Mot. Emot.* 38, 715–726. doi: 10.1007/s11031-014-9404-7

Inglés, C. J., Gonzálvez-Maciá, C., García-Fernández, J. M., Vicent, M., and Martínez-Montegudo, M. C. (2015). Current status of research on school refusal. *Eur. J. Educ. Psychol.* 8, 37–52. doi: 10.1016/j.ejeps.2015.10.005

Jungyoon, L. (2012). The relation between perfectionism and somatization among children: the moderating effect of stress-coping behaviors. *Korean J. Couns.* 13, 1029–1042. doi: 10.15703/kjc.13.2.201204.1029

Kirsh, G., McVey, G., Tweed, S., and Katzman, D. K. (2007). Psychosocial profiles of young adolescent females seeking treatment for an eating disorder. *J. Adolesc. Health* 40, 351–356. doi: 10.1016/j.jadohealth.2006.11.003

Li, X., Hou, Z. J., Chi, H. Y., Liu, J., and Hager, M. J. (2014). The mediating role of coping in the relationship between subtypes of perfectionism and job burnout: a test of the 2 x 2 model of perfectionism with employees in China. *Pers. Individ. Dif.* 58, 65–70. doi: 10.1016/j.paid.2013.10.007

Lozano, L. M., García, E., Martín, M., and Lozano, L. (2012). Desarrollo y validación del Inventario de Perfeccionismo Infantil (I.P.I.) [Development and validation of the Inventory of Child Perfectionism (I.P.I.)]. *Psicothema* 24, 149–155.

Mallison, S. H., Hill, A. P., Hall, H. K., and Gotwals, J. K. (2014). The 2 x 2 model of perfectionism and school -and community- based sport participation. *Psychol. Sch.* 51, 972–985. doi: 10.1002/pits.21796

Marten, P., and Rendón, M. J. (2012). A critical examination of the construct of perfectionism and its relationship to mental health in Asian and African Americans using a cross-cultural framework. *Clin. Psychol. Rev.* 32, 139–152. doi: 10.1016/j.cpr.2011.09.007

McCreary, B. T., Joiner, T. E., Schmidt, N. B., and Ialongo, N. S. (2004). The structure and correlates of perfectionism in African American children. *J. Clin. Child. Adolesc. Psychol.* 33, 313–324. doi: 10.1207/s15374424jccp3302_13

Méndez-Giménez, A., Cecchini-Estrada, J. A., and Fernández-Río, J. (2014). El modelo de perfeccionismo disposicional 2x2 en la adolescencia: una comprobación en el contexto de la Educación Física [The 2 x 2 dispositional model of perfectionism in adolescence: a confirmation in the Physical Education context]. *Univ. Psychol.* 13, 15–25. doi: 10.11144/Javeriana.UPSY13-4.mpda

Nobel, R., Manassis, K., and Wilansky-Traynor, P. (2012). The role of perfectionism in relation to an intervention to reduce anxious and depressive symptoms in children. *J. Ration. Emot. Cogn. Behav. Ther.* 30, 77–90. doi: 10.1007/s10942-011-0133-5

Nordin-Bates, S. M., Cumming, J., Aways, D., and Sharp, L. (2011). Imagining yourself dancing to perfection? Correlates of perfectionism among ballet and contemporary dancers. *J. Clin. Sport Psychol.* 5, 58–76. doi: 10.1123/jcsp.5.1.58

O'Connor, R. C., Dixon, D., and Rasmussen, S. (2009). The structure and temporal stability of the child and adolescent perfectionism scale. *Psychol. Assess.* 21, 437–443. doi: 10.1037/a0016264

Owens, R. G., and Slade, P. D. (2008). So perfect it's positively harmful? Reflections on the adaptiveness and maladaptiveness of positive and negative perfectionism. *Behav. Modif.* 32, 928–937. doi: 10.1177/0145445508319667

Pamies, L., and Quiles, Y. (2014). Perfeccionismo y factores de riesgo para el desarrollo de trastornos alimentarios en adolescentes españoles de ambos géneros [Perfectionism and risk factors for the development of eating disorders in Spanish adolescents of both genders]. *An. Psicol.* 30, 620–626. doi: 10.6018/analesps.30.2.158441

Rice, K. G., Kubal, A. E., and Preusser, K. J. (2004). Perfectionism and children's self-concept: further validation of the adaptive/maladaptive perfectionism scale. *Psychol. Sch.* 41, 279–290. doi: 10.1002/pits.10160

Rice, K. G., and Preusser, K. J. (2002). The adaptative/maladaptative perfectionism scale. *Meas. Eval. Couns. Dev.* 34, 210–222.

Slaney, R. B., Rice, K. G., Mobley, M., Trippi, J., and Ashby, J. S. (2001). The revised almost perfect scale. *Meas. Eval. Couns. Dev.* 34, 130–145.

Speirs-Neumeister, K. L., Fletcher, K. L., and Burney, V. H. (2015). Perfectionism and achievement motivation in high-ability students: an examination of the 2 x 2 model of perfectionism. *J. Educ. Gifted* 38, 215–232. doi: 10.1177/0162353215592502

Stairs, A. M., Smith, G. T., Zapolski, T. C. B., Combs, J. L., and Settles, R. E. (2012). Clarifying the construct of perfectionism. *Assessment* 19, 146–166. doi: 10.1177/1073191111411663

Stoeber, J. (2012). The 2 x 2 model of perfectionism: a critical comment and some suggestions. *Pers. Individ. Dif.* 53, 541–545. doi: 10.1016/j.paid.2012.04.029

Stoeber, J., Haskew, A. E., and Scott, C. (2015). Perfectionism and exam performance: the mediating effect of task-approach goals. *Pers. Individ. Dif.* 74, 171–176. doi: 10.1016/j.paid.2014.10.016

Stoeber, J., and Otto, K. (2006). Positive conceptions of perfectionism: approaches, evidence, challenges. *Pers. Soc. Psychol. Rev.* 10, 295–319. doi: 10.1207/s15327957pspr1004_2

Stoeber, J., and Stoeber, F. S. (2009). Domains of perfectionism: prevalence and relationships with perfectionism, gender, age and satisfaction with life. *Pers. Individ. Dif.* 46, 530–535. doi: 10.1016/j.paid.2008.12.006

Uz-Baş, A., and Siyez, D. M. (2010). Adaptation of the child and adolescent perfectionism scale to Turkish: the validity and reliability study. *Elem. Educ. Online* 9, 898–909.

Vicent, M., Inglés, C. J., Gonzálvez, C., Sanmartín, R., and García-Fernández, J. M. (2016). Perfeccionismo socialmente prescrito y los cinco grandes rasgos de la personalidad en niños. [Socially prescribed perfectionism and the Big Five personality traits in children]. *Eur. J. Invest. Health Psychol. Educ.* 6, 107–118. doi: 10.1989/ejihpe.v6i2.162

Yang, H., Hong, C., Tao, X., and Zhu, L. (2015). Revising the child and adolescent perfectionism scale: a test of the four-factor structure in a Chinese sample. *Meas. Eval. Couns. Dev.* 48, 192–203. doi: 10.1177/0748175615578733

Conflict of Interest Statement: The authors declare that the research was conducted in the absence of any commercial or financial relationships that could be construed as a potential conflict of interest.

8

A Values-Affirmation Intervention Does Not Benefit Negatively Stereotyped Immigrant Students in the Netherlands

Elisabeth M. de Jong, Francine C. Jellesma, Helma M. Y. Koomen and Peter F. de Jong*

Research Institute of Child Development and Education, University of Amsterdam, Amsterdam, Netherlands

Edited by:
Jesus De La Fuente,
University of Almería, Spain

Reviewed by:
Tobias Tempel,
University of Trier, Germany
Nina L. Powell,
National University of Singapore,
Singapore

***Correspondence:**
Elisabeth M. de Jong
e.m.dejong@uva.nl

Specialty section:
This article was submitted to
Educational Psychology,
a section of the journal
Frontiers in Psychology

Previous research showed that a values-affirmation intervention can help reduce the achievement gap between African American and European American students in the US. In the present study, it was examined if these results would generalize to ethnic minority students in a country outside the US, namely the Netherlands, where there is also an achievement gap between native and ethnic minority students. This type of intervention was tested in two separate studies, the first among first-year pre-vocational students ($n = 361$, 84% ethnic minority), and the second among sixth grade students ($n = 290$, 96% ethnic minority). Most minority participants had a Turkish-Dutch or Moroccan-Dutch immigrant background. In the second study, a third condition was added to the original paradigm, in which students elaborated on either their affirmation- or a control exercise with the help of a teaching assistant. We also examined whether values affirmation affected the level of problem behavior of negatively stereotyped ethnic minority youth. Contrary to what was expected, multilevel analyses revealed that the intervention had no effect on the school achievement or the problem behavior of the ethnic minority students. Possible explanations for these findings, mainly related to contextual and cultural differences between the Netherlands and the US, are discussed.

Keywords: stereotype threat, values-affirmation, immigrant students, school achievement, problem behavior

INTRODUCTION

In many countries around the world, there is a so-called 'achievement gap' between native and ethnic minority students. Ethnic minority students underperform in school in comparison to native students (Marks, 2005; Fryer and Levitt, 2006; Pásztor, 2008; Woolf et al., 2013). This gap remains even after controlling for differences in socio-economic status (SES; e.g., Pásztor, 2008; Azzolini et al., 2012; Woolf et al., 2013). It has been proposed that stereotype threat could be an important cause of this achievement gap. Stereotype threat can be defined as the experience of being at risk of confirming others' negative stereotypes about a group to which one belongs (Steele and Aronson, 1995). For example, in the US, African American students are negatively stereotyped in the academic domain. When these students find themselves in a situation in which the negative stereotype applies, they have been shown to underperform in comparison to students who are not negatively stereotyped in that situation (Steele and Aronson, 1995).

People under stereotype threat are assumed to worry about the personal and social consequences of obtaining poor test grades and, thereby, about confirming the negative group stereotype. These worries, in turn, place on them an extra cognitive and emotional burden that non-stereotyped individuals do not experience. This burden impairs concentration, and therefore, ironically, causes underperformance (Steele and Aronson, 1995; Aronson et al., 2002; Sherman, 2013). Indeed, studies have shown that stereotype threat can increase stress and reduce the working memory capacity that is needed to perform well on tests (see for an overview Schmader et al., 2008). Chronic experience of stereotype threat may lower feelings of belongingness at school (e.g., Cook et al., 2012), and might cause students to disidentify with the school domain. Once disidentified, school achievement is no longer a determinant of self-esteem and, consequently, motivation for school declines (Steele, 1997; Verkuyten and Thijs, 2004; Osborne and Walker, 2006; Owens and Massey, 2011). Because negative stereotypes continue to exist in society, stereotype threat is a chronic stressor for minority students and thereby contributes to the continuation of the achievement gap.

Stereotype threat has been shown to negatively affect the performance of many groups that are negatively stereotyped, including the school performance of Latino American students (Aronson and Salinas, 1997; Rodríguez, 2014), the mathematics performance of women (e.g., Spencer et al., 1999; see also Keller, 2002), the verbal performance of students with a low SES (Croizet and Claire, 1998), and the athletic and the golf performance of white males (Stone et al., 1999). It seems as though any group can be affected, provided that they are negatively stereotyped in a certain domain.

Although stereotype threat has been mostly investigated in the US, several studies have shown that the school performance of ethnic minority students in Europe can also suffer from stereotype threat. For example, Appel (2012) showed that adolescent immigrant students in Austria, including students with a Turkish background, underperformed on a culture fair intelligence test under stereotype threat. Furthermore, in France, young adult ethnic minority students' with a North-African or Arabic background (e.g., Moroccan) underperformed on a memory test (Berjot et al., 2011) and a test of verbal ability (Chateignier et al., 2009) under conditions of stereotype threat. Similar stereotype threat effects on performance have also been found for Turkish students in Germany (see Appel et al., 2015 for an overview of published and unpublished studies about stereotype threat effects among immigrant students).

To reduce the negative effects of stereotype threat on the school performance of African American middle school students, previous studies have used a values-affirmation intervention (e.g., Cohen et al., 2006b). Several longitudinal studies have shown that this type of intervention can reduce the achievement gap between non-stereotyped and stereotyped individuals (e.g., Cohen et al., 2006b, 2009; Miyake et al., 2010; Sherman et al., 2013; Harackiewicz et al., 2014).

Most research about stereotype threat and values affirmation has taken place in the United States. However, in other countries, there are also achievement gaps between native and negatively stereotyped ethnic minority students. The present study therefore examines whether a values-affirmation intervention can have the same positive effect on the performance of another group of students outside the US about whom similar negative stereotypes are thought to exist (e.g., Verkuyten and Thijs, 2000), namely ethnic minority students in the Netherlands. In addition to an achievement gap, in the Netherlands there are also differences in the levels of problem behavior of native and ethnic minority students (e.g., Stevens et al., 2003), although different informants (e.g., self-reporting, teacher, parent) do not always agree (Stevens and Vollebergh, 2008). As an extension of the original research (Cohen et al., 2006b), we also examine if a values-affirmation intervention has an effect on the level of problem behavior of these negatively stereotyped students.

Values-Affirmation Intervention

Values Affirmation and School Achievement

Values-affirmation interventions are based on self-affirmation theory (Steele, 1988). According to self-affirmation theory, people are motivated to maintain a sense of self-integrity or personal adequacy. When one is negatively stereotyped in a certain domain, such as academic ability, the sense of self-integrity can become threatened. Hence, one can experience stereotype threat in that domain. Values affirmation, which is a form of self-affirmation, helps to re-affirm self-integrity, presumably by giving individuals a broader perspective on the self (Sherman, 2013), and by taking the focus off of the threatened part of the identity (Sherman, 2013; Critcher and Dunning, 2014).

One of the first studies about stereotype threat and values affirmation was conducted by Cohen et al. (2006b). They conducted a large-scale longitudinal intervention study among seventh-graders in the US. In two randomized double-blind field experiments, African American and European American students were randomly assigned at the individual level to either the affirmation or the control condition. During school hours students received either one (Study 1) or two (Study 2) short writing assignments which took only 15 min to complete. In the affirmation condition, students were asked to choose from a list the two or three values that were *most* important to them (e.g., music, athletic abilities, relationships with friends and family) and to write a short paragraph about why those values were personally important to them. In the control condition, participants were asked to choose the two or three values that were *least* important to them and to write about why these values could be important to someone else (Cohen et al., 2006b).

Results showed that the values-affirmation intervention increased the academic performance of the negatively stereotyped African American students and reduced the achievement gap between African American and white students by 40% (i.e., average reduction over the two experiments; Cohen et al., 2006b). Furthermore, of the African Americans in the control condition, 20% scored a grade D or below in the targeted course, whereas in the affirmation condition, this was only the case for nine percent of the students. Results from a follow-up study revealed that the effects were even sustained over a 2-years period, after students had received several extra interventions over the course of the first year (Cohen et al., 2009). As expected, the intervention had no effect on the achievement of European American students.

According to Cohen et al. (2006b), the reason why such a seemingly small and simple intervention could have such a large impact is that the intervention disrupts a negative recursive cycle of stereotype threat and poor performance. They argue that re-affirmation of self-integrity probably causes a small reduction in psychological threat, which leads to a slightly better performance on the subsequent test. This effect can act as a self-fulfilling prophecy, interrupting a downward trend and instigating a more positive cycle. Indeed, African Americans in the control condition showed a significant downward linear trend in performance, whereas in the affirmation condition, this downward linear trend was absent. These results imply that the effects of a small intervention can be far-reaching. Especially when the intervention is planned early in the school year, before any negative recursive cycle can arise and when evaluative stress is assumed to be high, values affirmation has proven to be effective in improving performance (Cook et al., 2012).

After the study of Cohen et al. (2006b), several longitudinal replication studies have been conducted amongst negatively stereotyped groups other than African Americans, using a similar intervention paradigm. For example, Sherman et al. (2013) showed that a values-affirmation intervention had positive effects very similar to those found by (Cohen et al., 2006b, 2009) for Latino students, a group that differs from African American students at least in that most of them have a much more recent migration history (e.g., most of the parents of the students in the described study were first-generation immigrants), and many of them are not completely fluent in English (Sherman et al., 2013). Whereas (Cohen et al., 2006b, 2009) examined one racial group (i.e., African Americans), Sherman et al. (2013) combined Latino and Hispanic students from different countries into one ethnic minority group, arguing that they have a common social identity. Intervention effects were found for the combined group.

The studies described above were carried out at schools with a relatively even distribution of ethnic minority (i.e., African American, Latino) and majority (e.g., white) students. However, a study by Bowen et al. (2013) has shown that the intervention can have similar positive effects at schools where the student body consists mainly of ethnic minority students. To be able to compare their results to those of Cohen et al. (2006b), Bowen et al. (2013) focused their analyses on the African American and 'white' group in their sample. As opposed to the above described studies, the 'white' group in the study of Bowen et al. (2013) was much smaller, and consisted not only of white students, but also of Asian and mixed race students. Still, they assumed that all students at the examined school could experience some form of negative stereotyping, either because of their ethnic background or their low SES. Therefore, they hypothesized that the intervention would positively affect the performance of all participants. Indeed, this is what they found.

Another study, carried out by Harackiewicz et al. (2014), demonstrated that students with a relatively low SES can also benefit from the intervention. There is often an achievement gap between students who are the first in their family to go to college (usually coming from families with a low SES) and students who are not. Harackiewicz et al. (2014) showed that this gap can also be attenuated by a values-affirmation intervention. The authors describe two reasons why the intervention might have worked for these students. First, as in the previously described studies, first generation students could be suffering from stereotype threat, for example because of negative stereotypes regarding their low SES. Second, they argue that these students could also be experiencing a form of what they call 'cultural identity threat,' because of a conflict between their own interdependent motives to go to college and the independent norms of the college. These conflicting motives could lead to a lower sense of 'fit' or belonging in the academic context. Values affirmation has been shown to improve feelings of belongingness (e.g., Cook et al., 2012).

Yet another study that produced results very similar to those of Cohen et al. (2006b) was done by Miyake et al. (2010). They examined yet another negatively stereotyped group, namely women in the field of physics and mathematics. A values-affirmation intervention positively affected the performance of women in college physics, whereas this was not true for men. The gender gap was reduced by 61%. An earlier non-longitudinal experimental study had also shown the positive effect of values affirmation on the math performance of female introductory psychology students (Martens et al., 2006).

The studies described above were all performed in the US among middle school students (i.e., grades six to eight) or college students. All of these studies showed that the intervention had a positive effect on the achievement of the negatively stereotyped participants. However, it is unclear to what extent such effects would generalize to countries outside the US with, for example, different ethnic minority groups. One would expect similar results considering the variety of negatively stereotyped groups that have benefited from the intervention in the US. However, not many studies have examined effects outside the US.

One of the few studies is a non-longitudinal study among French female nursing students (Taillandier-Schmitt et al., 2012). For French nurses, mathematical skills are becoming increasingly important, while there is still a negative stereotype about women and mathematics. The researchers manipulated stereotype threat by using test instructions that either explicitly mentioned the negative stereotype or not. Thereafter, some students received a values-affirmation exercise, whereas others received a control exercise. The results showed that a values-affirmation intervention did indeed eliminate the negative effect of stereotype threat on the nurses' mathematical performance (Taillandier-Schmitt et al., 2012). It thus seems that the values-affirmation intervention can positively affect the performance of negatively stereotyped students outside the US as well. However, a disadvantage of this study was that there was no control group of male nurses included. Therefore, one cannot exclude the possibility that male nurses, who were not expected to suffer from stereotype threat, would have benefitted equally from the intervention.

The only longitudinal study about stereotype threat and values affirmation outside the US that we know of was carried out by Woolf et al. (2013). This study took place among native and ethnic minority medical students at a British medical school. The results were mixed. Woolf et al. (2013) examined the effects of the values-affirmation intervention on a written- and a clinical assessment. Against all expectations, they found that on the written assessment, white students in the affirmation condition performed worse than white students in the control condition, whereas there was no effect for ethnic minority students. On the clinical assessment they found that all students, white and ethnic minority, benefited from the intervention. Although, this study was presented as a direct replication of the studies of (Cohen et al., 2006b, 2009), it differed on at least two important aspects. First, the study was focused on an older population, namely university students. Second, the ethnic minority group that was studied (most had an Asian background) is not very comparable to the earlier described populations (e.g., Cohen et al., 2006b, 2009) in terms of being negatively stereotyped. Woolf et al. (2013) mention that stereotypes about these groups are, for example, that they are hardworking and do a lot of rote-learning. One could hardly call these negative stereotypes and could even consider these to be positive stereotypes. Therefore, one could question the applicability of the intervention in this situation.

In a recent meta-analysis, Appel et al. (2015) showed that stereotype threat effects are also found among immigrant students in Europe, and suggested that a values-affirmation intervention might benefit these immigrant students in the same way as it benefited ethnic minority students in the US. The present study focuses on examining to what extent the intervention effects would generalize to ethnic minority students (i.e., students with an immigrant background) in the Netherlands. Unlike the sample that was studied in the British study (Woolf et al., 2013), in the present study the ethnic minority students are more comparable to the students examined in the US intervention studies with regard to age as well as to negative stereotypes that exist about them in society. Furthermore, because ethnic minority students in the Netherlands are not only negatively stereotyped in the intellectual but also in the behavioral domain (e.g., Verkuyten and Thijs, 2000), we examine intervention effects on performance as well as on problem behavior.

Values Affirmation and Problem Behavior

Ethnic minority students are often negatively stereotyped in terms of problematic behavior (e.g., Verkuyten and Thijs, 2000, 2010; Nievers et al., 2010). However, to our knowledge, there are no studies examining the relationship between stereotype threat and problem behavior. For two reasons, we assume that stereotype threat can increase problem behavior and, therefore, that a values-affirmation intervention could also be suitable to reduce the level of problem behavior. First, previous research has shown that negative stereotypes about behavior can be directly related to problem behavior among the stereotyped individuals. Kamans et al. (2009) found that Moroccan-Dutch youth who felt negative about the native Dutch out-group and who felt personally stereotyped by them, were inclined to legitimize behavior in line with the negative stereotypes, such as loitering, aggressive and criminal behavior. When negatively stereotyped by a disliked out-group, desires to protect the in-group identity might thus ironically lead to an increase of problem behavior and a confirmation of the negative group stereotype.

One could argue that the process described above is a form of stereotype threat, because the identity threat stems from negative stereotypes and also leads to confirmation of the negative stereotype. Given that values affirmation is thought to relieve identity threats by making the individual aware of multiple sources of self-integrity (Sherman, 2013; Critcher and Dunning, 2014), one would expect that values affirmation could reduce such feelings of threat caused by negative stereotypes in the behavioral domain. Protecting the in-group identity by behaving negatively to out-group members (e.g., Kamans et al., 2009) would become less relevant, because values affirmation makes one aware that group membership is only one aspect of the self, and that one's self-integrity does not depend on this specific group membership only.

A second reason to expect that stereotype threat can increase problem behavior is that previous studies have shown that coping with stereotype threat in one domain (e.g., the intellectual domain), can deplete resources for self-control in subsequent (e.g., social) situations, unrelated to the stereotype (Inzlicht and Kang, 2010). Usually, aggressive impulses are regulated by self-control; the capacity that is needed to overcome environmental temptations and urges, emotions and automatic response tendencies (Baumeister and Heatherton, 1996). However, Inzlicht and Kang (2010) demonstrated that when self-control resources have been depleted by stereotype threat, this can reduce inner restraints against aggression.

Schmeichel and Vohs (2009) have shown that when self-control resources have been depleted in one situation, values affirmation can restore self-control resources for subsequent situations. In their first experiment, participants either did a task that depleted self-control resources or a control task. After the task, half of the participants did a values-affirmation exercise and half did a control exercise, comparable with the exercises used by Cohen et al. (2006b). Subsequently, participants did a task in which self-control was needed. The results showed that for the participants who had received the non-depleting first task, there was no difference in self-control on the second task between participants in the self-affirmation and control condition. However, for the participants who had done the depleting first task, self-affirmation had a positive effect on self-control on for the second task.

In the present study, we examine if a values-affirmation intervention can reduce problem behavior of negatively stereotyped ethnic minority students. We assume that when self-control resources are depleted by stereotype threat, value-affirmation could have similar positive effects on behavior as in the study of Schmeichel and Vohs (2009). Although, feelings of threat or the degree of the depletion of resources are not explicitly measured in the present study, we do examine if the values-affirmation intervention affects the level of problem behavior of ethnic minority students in the Netherlands.

Present Study

Two of the largest ethnic minority groups in the Netherlands are Moroccan and Turkish immigrants who came to Western Europe in the 20th century as guest workers to fill positions in the lower segments of the labor market. They mainly came from the lower socio-economic classes (Organisation for Economic Co-operation and Development [OECD], 2002). Turkish and Moroccan immigrants are negatively stereotyped in the Netherlands, in both the intellectual and the behavioral domain (e.g., Verkuyten and Thijs, 2000; Centraal Bureau Voor de Statistiek [CBS], 2005; Nievers et al., 2010). Moreover, they also experience negative stereotyping related to Muslim extremism (Kamans et al., 2009). Previous studies have shown stereotype threat effects on the performance of immigrant students of the same background (i.e., Moroccan and Turkish) in neighboring countries of the Netherlands (i.e., Germany, France, Austria; Chateignier et al., 2009; Berjot et al., 2011; Appel, 2012; see for an overview Appel et al., 2015), countries of which the cultures are similar to that of the Netherlands.

We expect the intervention to have positive effects on the school performance of ethnic minority students in the Netherlands similar to those seen in the US, because both are negatively stereotyped groups. Ethnic minority students in the Netherlands are probably most comparable to Latino American students in the US both in terms of their recent migration history and their second language fluency. For Latino American students, the intervention has been shown to have positive effects comparable with those found for African American students (Sherman et al., 2013). Moreover, apart from experiencing stereotype threat, ethnic minority students in the Netherlands could also be expected to experience cultural mismatch at school, as described in the study of Harackiewicz et al. (2014), or negative stereotyping because of their relatively low SES (Bowen et al., 2013; Harackiewicz et al., 2014). These are all additional reasons to expect the intervention to have the intended positive effect on these students. By means of two studies, the effects of a values-affirmation intervention on the school achievement and problem behavior of ethnic minority students (i.e., students with an immigrant background) in the Netherlands are examined. The aim of the first study was to examine if the findings of (Cohen et al., 2006b, 2009) would generalize to a sample of secondary school students outside the US with a comparable degree of negative stereotyping.

STUDY 1

This study was conducted among first-year pre-vocational students. In the Netherlands there are different levels of secondary education. Students make a transition to secondary school after sixth grade, and their level of performance at the end of primary school determines to which school level they go. Previous studies (e.g., Cohen et al., 2006b, 2009) have shown that poorly performing students benefited most from the values-affirmation intervention. Therefore, the present study was conducted at the lowest level of secondary education (pre-vocational education), directly after the transition to secondary school.

We hypothesized that the values-affirmation intervention would have similar positive effects on the school achievement of ethnic minority students in the Netherlands as in the US. For native students, our expectations were not clearly defined. On the one hand, one would expect native Dutch students not to benefit from the values-affirmation intervention because they are not negatively stereotyped in society on the basis of their ethnic background. However, native students in pre-vocational education often also have a relatively low SES, which could be related to experiencing negative stereotyping in the intellectual domain. If native students also experience a form of stereotype threat because of their low SES and supposedly low IQ, then one would expect the intervention to have a positive effect on this group as well (e.g., Bowen et al., 2013; Harackiewicz et al., 2014). Moreover, because girls are often negatively stereotyped in the science and mathematics domain and a values-affirmation has been shown to improve the performance of female students in science and mathematics (Martens et al., 2006; Miyake et al., 2010), in the present study we also examined if there were intervention effects on girl's mathematics performance.

Furthermore, the effects of the intervention on two underlying factors of the stereotype threat process, namely school belongingness (Cook et al., 2012) and identification with school (Steele, 1997; Osborne and Walker, 2006; Owens and Massey, 2011) were examined. In line with previous studies, we expected that the values-affirmation intervention would positively affect these two factors for ethnic minority students. Again, our expectations for the native Dutch group were not clearly defined.

We did not expect to find large achievement gaps between native and ethnic minority students at the beginning of the school year within classes, because students had already been subdivided into different school levels on the basis of their primary school performance. However, we assumed that being sent to the lowest level of education probably made students very aware of the fact that there are also students with higher performance levels.

As an extension to the study of Cohen et al. (2006b), we also examined the effects of the values-affirmation intervention on the level of problem behavior of ethnic minority students in the Netherlands. Our hypothesis was that the values-affirmation intervention would decrease the level of problem behavior amongst these students. For native Dutch students, we expected no intervention effects because they are not, or at least less, negatively stereotyped in the behavioral domain. We did not know whether to expect differences in problem behavior between native Dutch and ethnic minority students at the beginning of the school year. Although, previous studies have shown that teachers report more problem behavior for ethnic minority students than for native students (Stevens et al., 2003), we assumed that the level of problem behavior amongst native Dutch students at the lowest level of education might also be relatively high.

Materials and Methods

Participants

In total, 361 first year pre-vocational students (42.1% boys) participated in the present study (59 native Dutch and 302 ethnic minority). Ages ranged from 11.75 to 15.08 ($M_{age} = 12.90$ years, $SD = 0.58$). Students were assigned to the different conditions on the basis of a randomized controlled trial. Pairs of participants, matched on gender and ethnic background, were formed within classes. Of each pair, one participant was randomly assigned to the values-affirmation and the other to the control condition. Students for whom a match within the classroom was impossible because of an uneven number of students, were matched with students from another class. The assignment procedure is displayed in **Figure 1**.

The study took place in 17 classes from six pre-vocational secondary schools in the Netherlands. Schools were recruited in or near large cities in the western part of the Netherlands (Amsterdam, Rotterdam, The Hague), where percentages of ethnic minority students in secondary schools are high. Because the main focus of this research project was to examine the intervention effects on ethnic minority students, we explicitly recruited schools with a population of at least 45% ethnic minority students. Percentages of non-Western ethnic minority students per participating class ranged from 50 to 100%. With the exception of one school, all participating schools were located in areas with relatively high percentages of non-Western immigrants (between 32 and 74% of the total population of the area, versus 12% nationwide; CBS Statline, 2011). One school was not situated in an area with a high percentage of ethnic minority residents. However, this school was in a city that was easily accessible by bus from areas with high percentages of ethnic minority residents. Many students traveled from these areas to this school.

The ethnic background of the participants was determined by using the background information students provided during the first measurement occasion (e.g., country of birth, country of birth of parents and origin of the greater family). There were 19 students (6.3% of the ethnic minority students) with either incomplete background information or a Western ethnic minority background (e.g., Australia or France). It was decided to exclude these students from the analyses, because it was unclear if negative stereotypes existed about these groups. This left 342 students in the analyses, namely 59 native Dutch students (28 affirmation, 31 control) and 283 students with a non-Western ethnic minority background (146 affirmation, 137 control).

Of the 283 ethnic minority participants, 38.2% had a Moroccan background, 31.8% had a Turkish background and 12.0% had a Surinamese or Antillean background. These three groups were the largest ethnic minority groups in the sample, which corresponds to the largest ethnic minority groups in Dutch society. The remaining 18% of non-Western ethnic minority students in the sample had various ethnic backgrounds (e.g., Pakistan, Iraq, Indonesia, Somalia).

The ethnic minority students were mainly second generation immigrants, meaning that they were born in the Netherlands but had at least one parent born in a non-Western country. Thirty-two (11%) of the ethnic minority students indicated that they had

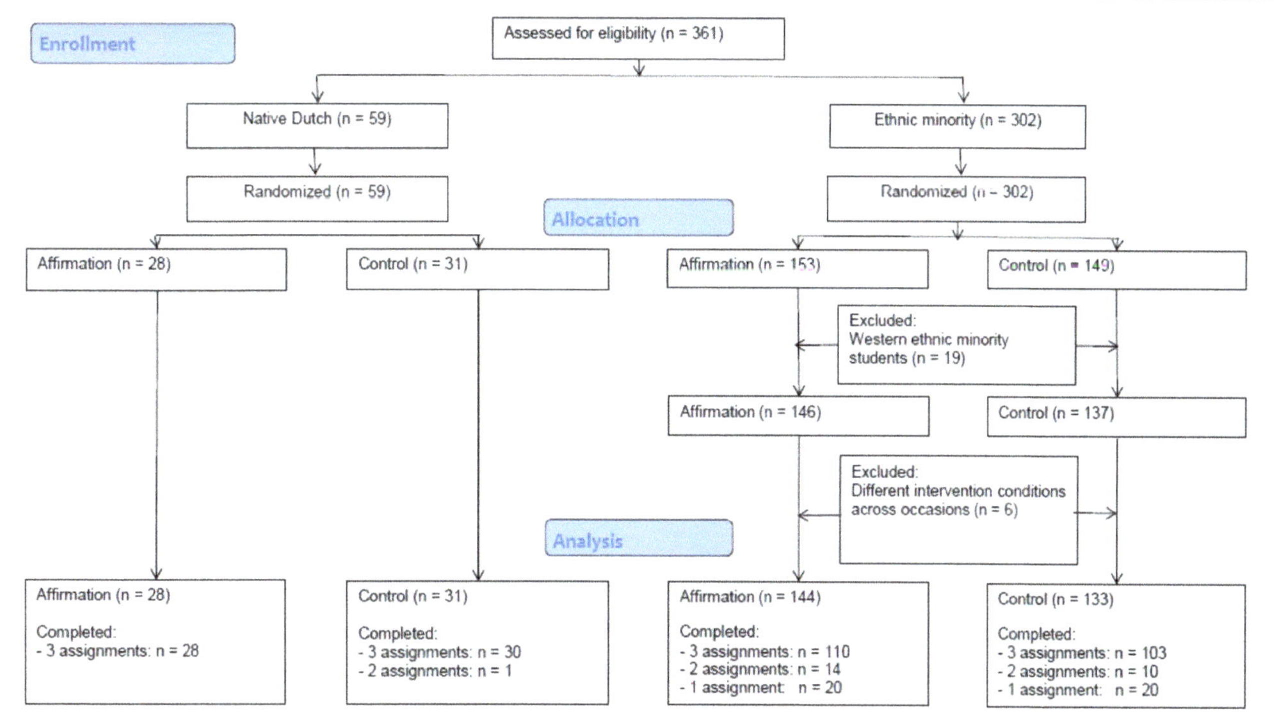

FIGURE 1 | Flowchart of the random assignment procedure of Study 1.

been born in the country of origin of the parents. However, these students resided in the Netherlands for on average 10.08 years ($SD = 2.19$). All other students were born in the Netherlands. No differences were found in the outcome measures between the group of students that was born in a non-Western country and the group that was born in the Netherlands. Therefore, the groups were combined.

Negative Stereotypes in the Netherlands

To examine if ethnic minority students in the Netherlands indeed experienced more negative stereotyping than native Dutch students, a study was conducted among another sample of seventh grade students ($N = 283$). Of these students, 49.8% had a native Dutch background, 19.8% had a Moroccan-Dutch background and 30.4% had a Turkish-Dutch background. Participants were asked to indicate if they did or did not experience the following negative stereotypes about their cultural group: dumb, unreliable, inhospitable, lazy, aggressive, greedy, not hard working, criminal, unable to understand things quickly. Two of the negative stereotypes (inhospitable and greedy) are negative stereotypes that were anticipated to exist about the Dutch. The other stereotypes were expected to exist about ethnic minority students in the Netherlands. Chi-square tests revealed that ethnic minority students thought significantly more often than native Dutch students that others saw their cultural group as dumb, untrustworthy, lazy, aggressive and criminal. On the other hand, native Dutch students more often thought that others saw their group as greedy than ethnic minority students. These results thus show that ethnic minority first-year pre-vocational students in the Netherlands experience negative stereotyping in the intellectual as well as the behavioral domain, and they experience negative stereotyping more often than native Dutch students.

Intervention

For the implementation of the intervention, we closely followed the procedures of (Cohen et al., 2006b, 2009; see also Sherman et al., 2013). The intervention consisted of three short writing assignments, spread out over a period of one school year. The writing assignments were adopted from (Cohen et al., 2006b, 2009) and translated into Dutch with the aid of a certified translator. Students in the values-affirmation condition received a list of 12 values (e.g., music, athletic ability, relationships with friends and family) and were asked to choose the two or three that were most important to them. Subsequently, they were asked to write a short paragraph about why these values were important to them. Students in the control condition received the same list of values, but were asked to select the two or three values that were least important to them. Their assignment was to write a short paragraph about why these values that were least important to them could be important to someone else. As a reinforcement of the manipulation, students were asked to indicate on a six-point scale how much they agreed with propositions concerning the chosen values. An example proposition in the affirmation condition was: 'I care about these values.' An example in the control condition was: 'Some people care about these values.'

Following the procedures of Cohen et al. (2006a; supporting online material), teachers were instructed to schedule the interventions directly before a school test. When this was not possible, the researchers either provided a standardized arithmetic test that teachers could give to their students directly before the intervention, or they instructed the teacher to have a short conversation with their students directly before the intervention took place. The topic of this conversation was school testing that would take place in the near future, and was also expected to raise evaluative stress. With the exception of two, all classes received the intervention at least one time before a school test or arithmetic test or after a conversation about school testing.

The first intervention round was timed as early in the school year as possible, because evaluative stress was expected to be high soon after the transition to secondary school and feelings of belongingness are still uncertain during such a transition. Furthermore, previous studies have shown that interventions timed early in the school year are more effective, because at that time they can still prevent the development of negative recursive cycles (Walton and Cohen, 2007; Cook et al., 2012).

Intervention assignments were administered by the teacher and were presented as a school task in order to prevent students from knowing that the interventions were part of a research project. To avoid expectancy effects, teachers were blind to the purpose of the writing assignments and were also unaware of the existence of different conditions. One or two weeks before the assignments were administered, teachers received information on how to administer the assignments, so that they could prepare. They received a document with standard instructions to introduce the assignments and were provided with standard answers to any potential questions that could be posed by students.

Most students received the assignments during Dutch class, since these were Dutch writing assignments. At one school (four classes), this was not possible and therefore students received the assignments during mentor supervision hours. Students received the assignments in white envelopes with their names on them. They were guided through the assignments via written instructions and completed the assignments independently. Students were instructed not to worry about spelling or grammar. The assignments took approximately 15 min to complete. After finishing, the participants were free to seal their envelopes. Teachers collected the assignments and resumed their lesson plans. The assignments were collected from the teachers by a member of the research team without the students knowing.

Procedure

Students received three interventions throughout the school year. Furthermore, belongingness, identification with school and problem behavior were measured by means of questionnaires before the first and after the third intervention (see **Figure 2**). The questionnaires were administered by a member of the research team, who gave a short introduction and was available for student questions. The teacher was also present. The questionnaires took approximately 40 min to complete. Pre- and post-intervention

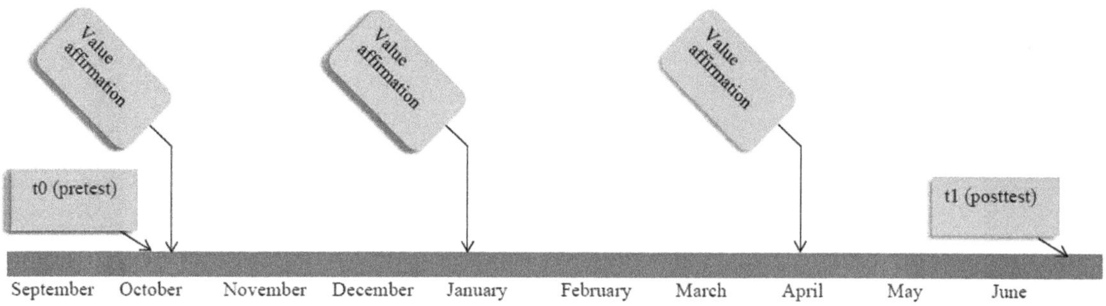

FIGURE 2 | Time schedule of the intervention Study 1.

school grades were obtained from the schools. The interventions were presented as a school task and were administered by the teachers. After the last questionnaire, participants received a small gift as a reward.

Ethics Statement

Before the onset of the study, the students' parents were informed about the project by letter and were asked to indicate whether they had any objections to the participation of their child (i.e., passive informed consent). One student did not receive parental permission and was given an alternative assignment while the rest of the class filled out the questionnaires. Because the intervention was presented as a school task and to prevent students from suspecting that the intervention was part of the research project, this student received the control writing exercises. No special approval from the department's Ethics Review Board needed to be requested at the start of the project, because the research was classified as 'standard' in our department: there was no reason to assume that the study would potentially have any negative effects on the participants, no physiological or health measures were taken, and the intervention assignments resembled a normal school task. Furthermore, consulting an Ethics Review Board was no standard procedure at our department at the time the study was to be conducted. Schools gave permission for the research project to take place within school hours. Data were analyzed anonymously. The students were requested to fill in their names on their questionnaires solely for the purpose of linking together their questionnaires from the different measurement occasions. The students were assured that their answers would be kept confidential and that no teacher nor school personnel nor others would read their answers, except for the researchers. After the first measurement occasion, all questionnaires were numbered. Names of the participants are kept in a separate file, which only the first author had access to. Identifying information was never used in any analyses.

Measures

School grades

School grades for the subjects Dutch, English, and mathematics were collected from the schools before the first and after the third intervention. In the Netherlands, students receive grades on a scale from 1 (very poor) to 10 (excellent). For a portion of the students (226 ethnic minority and 32 native Dutch), scores of the Cito test from sixth grade were available. The Cito test is a nationwide independent exam that is taken by all students at the end of sixth grade. It is a general assessment of what students have learned in primary school. The test consists of 290 multiple choice questions, divided over several modules, including language, arithmetic, world orientation (i.e., geography, history, science) and study skills. Students receive a standard score between 501 and 550. This score contributes to the recommendations teachers make with regard to which school level students should go after sixth grade. t-tests showed that both ethnic minority students, $t(226) = -8.64$, $p < 0.001$, as well as native Dutch students, $t(31) = -7.64$, $p < 0.001$, scored significantly lower than the national average on this test.

Problem behavior

Self-reported problem behavior was measured with items from the Dutch version of the Youth Self Report (YSR; De Groot et al., 1996). The items were selected from the subscales Rule Breaking Behavior and Aggressive Behavior (11 items, mean Cronbach's $\alpha = 0.78$ across measurement occasions; example items: 'I often skip classes at school' and 'I am mean to others'). All items were answered on a three-point scale, ranging from 'not true' to 'true.'

Belongingness

Feelings of belongingness at school were measured using two subscales of the School Attitude Questionnaire (Schoolvragenlijst; Smits and Vorst, 1990). These subscales were School Enjoyment (eight items, mean Cronbach's $\alpha = 0.73$ across measurement occasions) and Perceived Social Acceptance by Classmates (eight items, mean Cronbach's $\alpha = 0.78$ across measurement occasions). All items were answered on a three-point scale (i.e., that is not true, I don't know, that is true).

Identification with school

Identification with school was measured using four items about the perceived importance of performing well at school (mean Cronbach's $\alpha = 0.72$ across measurement occasions). There was one general item ("How important do you find it to receive good grades at school?") and three items that asked the same question for specific school subjects (Dutch, English, and mathematics). All items were answered on a three-point scale, ranging from 'important' to 'not important.'

Statistical Analyses

As data were gathered in different classes from different schools, they have a nested structure. Pupils nested within the same class are probably more equal to each other than pupils from other classes or from other schools. Therefore, multilevel or random coefficient models (Hox, 2010) were used. Multilevel analyses take into account dependencies among respondents from the same class (e.g., Snijders and Bosker, 2012). Multilevel analyses were conducted using SPSS Version 20.

Results

Data Preparation

Due to administrative errors, six participants were not included in the same intervention condition on all three intervention occasions and were therefore excluded from the analyses, leaving 336 students in the analyses, namely 59 native Dutch and 277 ethnic minority students (see **Figure 1**). Data are included in the Supplementary Materials (see Data Sheet 1). Of these 336 students, 271 students received all three intervention assignments. Due to absence during one or two intervention occasions, 24 students received only two assignments and 40 students received only one assignment (see also **Figure 1**). However, there were no significant differences between the values-affirmation and the control condition in the mean number of interventions completed, $F(1{,}334) = 0.002$, $p = 0.97$. Therefore, all 336 students remained in the analyses. There were 28 native Dutch students in the affirmation condition and 31 in the control condition. Of the ethnic minority students, there were 144 students in the affirmation condition and 133 in the control condition.

On both measurement occasions, data for school belongingness, school identification, and problem behavior were available. For all 17 classes, post-intervention school grades were also available. For one variable (i.e., pre-intervention school grades) there were some data missing. Because some schools did not provide information on the dates at which their school tests were administered, it was not possible to determine pre-intervention grades for all classes. Pre-intervention school grades were therefore only available for six (Dutch) or seven (English and mathematics) classes of the 17 classes. However, because these grades were missing for whole classes and not at the individual level, and students were randomized within classes, we expected no differences in background characteristics between students for whom grades on both measurement occasions were available and students for whom only post-intervention grades were available. An independent samples t-test showed that there were no age differences between the six classes with pre- and post-intervention Dutch grades available ($N = 123$) and the 11 classes ($N = 208$) with only post-intervention Dutch grades, $t(329) = -0.63$, $p = 0.53$. There were also no age differences between the seven classes with pre- and post-intervention English and mathematics grades available ($N = 143$) and the 10 classes ($N = 188$) with only post-intervention grades available, $t(329) = -1.85$, $p = 0.07$. School grades were missing for five students. Because post-intervention school grades were available for all classes, intervention effects on grades were first examined only on these post-intervention grades. Thereafter, analyses were performed in which we controlled for pre-intervention grades.

All predictor variables (i.e., gender, ethnic background, and condition), except pre-intervention grades and behavior, were added as dummy variables in the analyses. Gender was included in all models as a control variable. All outcome variables were standardized before they were entered into the analyses. In this way, the parameter estimates can be interpreted as effect sizes. For example, a coefficient of 0.5 corresponds to an increase of 0.5 *SD*.

For the analyses of the intervention effects, we followed the procedures of Cohen et al. (2006a, supporting online material). The only difference was that we used multilevel analyses to control for dependencies within classes, whereas Cohen et al. (2006b) used two dummy variables to control for the three different teachers in their study. Because our study included 17 different teachers, multilevel analyses were considered to be a more suitable solution.

Pre-intervention Differences between Native and Ethnic Minority Students

Before the effects of the intervention were analyzed, it was examined if there were differences in achievement (i.e., an achievement gap), and problem behavior between native Dutch and ethnic minority students. This was examined with multilevel analyses with two levels (students nested within classes) on pre-intervention school grades and problem behavior. Furthermore, it was also examined if there were pre-intervention differences in school belongingness, and identification with school.

Pre-intervention Achievement Gap and Differences in Problem Behavior

Multilevel models with two levels (students nested within classes) did not reveal a pre-intervention achievement gap in Dutch grades ($\beta = 0.03$, $p = 0.87$) or English grades ($\beta = -0.07$, $p = 0.65$), but there was one in mathematics grades ($\beta = 0.59$, $p < 0.01$). Native Dutch students had higher pre-intervention mathematics grades than ethnic minority students. There were no differences in pre-intervention self-reported problem behavior between native and ethnic minority students ($\beta = -0.13$, $p = 0.38$). As outlined in the introduction, an absence of differences in achievement or problem behavior within the class does not necessarily imply that the intervention cannot affect the achievement or behavior of ethnic minority students in the present study.

Pre-intervention Differences in Belongingness and Identification with School

There were no pre-intervention differences between native and ethnic minority students on the belongingness measures School Enjoyment ($\beta = -0.13$, $p = 0.42$), and Perceived Social Acceptance ($\beta = -0.20$, $p = 0.18$). There were also no pre-intervention differences on Identification with School ($\beta = -0.18, p = 0.23$).

Pre-intervention Differences between Girls and Boys on Mathematics Performance

There were no pre-intervention differences between boys and girls on mathematics performance ($\beta = -0.12, p = 0.44$).

Intervention Effects

Grades

Descriptives of post-intervention grades are displayed in **Table 1**. The outcomes of the multilevel analyses are presented in **Table 2**. Gender was included in all models as a control variable. Contrary to expectations, the intervention had no effect on post-intervention Dutch, English, or mathematics grades: there were no significant main effects of condition and the expected interaction effects between ethnic background and condition were also non-significant. There was a significant effect of gender on Dutch grades: boys performed worse than girls on this subjects. For mathematics, there was a significant effect of ethnic background. As seen in the pre-test, ethnic minority students performed lower on mathematics than ethnic majority students after the interventions.

Because the Moroccan-Dutch and the Turkish-Dutch groups are the largest ethnic minority groups in Dutch society, and because especially Moroccan-Dutch youth is very negatively stereotyped in the Netherlands, analyses were also conducted for these two groups separately, compared to the native Dutch group. The results of these analyses did not differ from those for the ethnic minority group as a whole.

Because we thought it possible that all participants (i.e., native and ethnic minority) could experience some form of stereotype threat, for example because of their low SES (e.g., Bowen et al., 2013), we also examined intervention effects on the group as a whole. Results of these analyses also did not reveal any intervention effects.

TABLE 2 | Effect sizes and standard errors of multilevel models for post-intervention Dutch, English, and mathematics grades Study 1.

	Grades		
	Dutch (*SE*)	English (*SE*)	Mathematics (*SE*)
Gender[a]	−0.53 (0.15)**	−0.13 (0.15)	−0.03 (0.14)
Ethnic Background[b]	−0.41 (0.23)	−0.03 (0.24)	−0.53 (0.23)*
Condition[c]	0.13 (0.14)	0.12 (0.14)	0.06 (0.13)
Ethnic background * Gender	−0.46 (0.27)	−0.22 (0.28)	−0.40 (0.26)
Gender * Condition	−0.05 (0.21)	−0.32 (0.21)	−0.04 (0.19)
Ethnic background * Condition	0.05 (0.26)	−0.11 (0.27)	0.06 (0.25)

**p < 0.05, **p < 0.01, ***p < 0.001. Parameter estimates (while controlling for effects of other parameters) can be interpreted as Cohen's d; [a]Girl = 0, Boy = 1; [b]Native Dutch = 0, Ethnic minority = 1; [c]Values-affirmation = 0, Control = 1.*

As mentioned before, we also conducted analyses in which we controlled for pre-intervention grades. The only difference of these results with the previous models was that pre-intervention achievement was a significant predictor of Dutch, English, and mathematics grades ($\beta = 0.51$, $p < 0.001$; $\beta = 0.77$, $p < 0.001$; and $\beta = 0.66$, $p < 0.001$, respectively). Gender was no longer a significant predictor of post-intervention grades after adding pre-intervention grades to the models.

Problem Behavior

Descriptives of pre- and post-intervention problem behavior are displayed in **Table 1**. Three extreme outliers (i.e., deviating more than 4 standard deviations from the mean) were left out of the analyses. In **Table 3** the outcome of the multilevel model is presented. We controlled for pre-intervention levels of problem behavior. Contrary to expectations, the

TABLE 1 | Descriptives of grades, problem behavior, belongingness, and identification with school for the different groups in Study 1.

	Native Dutch				Ethnic Minority			
	Control		Affirmation		Control		Affirmation	
	M	*SD*	*M*	*SD*	*M*	*SD*	*M*	*SD*
Dutch post-interventions	7.09	0.93	6.94	0.95	6.76	0.83	6.68	0.78
English post-interventions	6.90	1.29	7.00	1.22	6.95	1.28	6.96	1.05
Mathematics post-interventions	7.07	1.10	6.93	1.16	6.63	1.01	6.55	1.12
Problem behavior								
Pre-interventions	1.24	0.25	1.18	0.21	1.23	0.23	1.26	0.30
Post-interventions	1.26	0.31	1.31	0.30	1.28	0.27	1.28	0.30
School enjoyment								
Pre-interventions	2.59	0.34	2.64	0.33	2.54	0.36	2.48	0.39
Post-interventions	2.36	0.46	2.25	0.44	2.28	0.43	2.25	0.48
Perceived social acceptance								
Pre-interventions	2.81	0.33	2.84	0.28	2.78	0.32	2.76	0.29
Post-interventions	2.70	0.44	2.71	0.39	2.74	0.34	2.73	0.34
Identification with school								
Pre-interventions	2.72	0.29	2.80	0.28	2.88	0.24	2.87	0.32
Post-interventions	2.69	0.33	2.59	0.50	2.81	0.33	2.86	0.27

TABLE 3 | Effect sizes and standard errors of multilevel models for post-intervention problem behavior Study 1.

	Problem behavior (*SE*)
Gender[a]	0.09 (0.12)
Ethnic Background[b]	−0.24 (0.17)
Pre-intervention problem behavior	0.57 (0.05)***
Condition[c]	0.07 (0.11)
Ethnic Background * Gender	−0.03 (0.22)
Gender * Condition	0.05 (0.17)
Ethnic background * Condition	−0.30 (0.21)

**p* < 0.05, ***p* < 0.01, ****p* < 0.001. *Parameter estimates (while controlling for effects of other parameters) can be interpreted as Cohen's d;* [a]*Girl = 0, Boy = 1;* [b]*Native Dutch = 0, Ethnic minority = 1;* [c]*Values-affirmation = 0, Control = 1.*

intervention had no significant effect on the problem behavior of ethnic minority students. There was no significant main effect of condition and the expected interaction between ethnic background and condition was also non-significant. Pre-intervention problem behavior was the only significant predictor of problem behavior in this model. The positive parameter estimate of pre-intervention problem behavior indicates that higher levels of pre-intervention problem behavior correspond to higher levels of post-intervention problem behavior. Analyses were also conducted for the Turkish-Dutch and the Moroccan-Dutch group separately. In these models, again only pre-intervention problem behavior was a significant predictor of post-intervention problem behavior.

School belongingness and identification

Descriptives of school belongingness and identification are displayed in **Table 1**. In **Table 4**, outcomes of the multilevel models are presented. Results show that the only significant predictor of post-intervention school belongingness (i.e., school enjoyment and perceived social acceptance) is pre-intervention belongingness. The positive parameter estimates indicate that the higher the level of pre-intervention belongingness, the higher the level of post-intervention belongingness. For post-intervention identification, ethnic background and pre-intervention identification are significant predictors. Higher pre-intervention identification corresponds to higher post-intervention identification. Moreover, compared to native Dutch students, ethnic minority students report a higher level of identification with school. There was, however, no significant interaction between ethnic background and condition on school identification, which implies that this difference in identification is not related to the intervention.

TABLE 4 | Effect sizes and standard errors of multilevel models for post-intervention school belongingness and identification in Study 1.

	Belongingness		
	School enjoyment	Perceived social acceptance	Identification
Gender[a]	−0.03 (0.15)	−0.10 (0.16)	0.02 (0.16)
Ethnic Background[b]	0.11 (0.21)	0.27 (0.22)	0.63 (0.23)**
Pre-intervention belongingness or identification	0.56 (0.05)***	0.48 (0.06)***	0.33 (0.06)***
Condition[c]	−0.05 (0.14)	0.07 (0.15)	−0.25 (0.15)
Ethnic background * Gender	−0.34 (0.25)	0.22 (0.27)	−0.17 (0.28)
Gender * Condition	−0.06 (0.20)	−0.22 (0.21)	0.20 (0.22)
Ethnic background * Condition	0.34 (0.25)	0.04 (0.26)	0.54 (0.28)

**p* < 0.05, ***p* < 0.01, ****p* < 0.001. *Parameter estimates (while controlling for effects of other parameters) can be interpreted as Cohen's d;* [a]*Girl = 0, Boy = 1;* [b]*Native Dutch = 0, Ethnic minority = 1;* [c]*Values-affirmation = 0, Control = 1.*

Gender and mathematics performance

The mean post-intervention grade of girls in the affirmation condition was 6.67 ($SD = 0.79$), and of girls in the control condition it was 6.79 ($SD = 1.06$). For boys, the mean post-intervention mathematics grade was 6.54 ($SD = 0.91$) in the affirmation condition and 6.62 ($SD = 1.01$) in the control condition. As can be observed in **Table 2**, there was no effect of gender on post-intervention mathematics performance and the expected interaction between gender and condition was also not significant. When ethnic minority status was removed from the analyses, there was still no significant effect of gender ($\beta = -0.13$, $p = 0.45$) and no significant interaction between gender and condition ($\beta = 0.04, p = 0.87$).

Discussion

In contrast to earlier findings (Cohen et al., 2006b, 2009), our study did not show that a values-affirmation intervention has any effect on the school performance of ethnic minority students in the Netherlands. Furthermore, no intervention effects were found on school belongingness and identification, which have been assumed to be underlying factors in the process of stereotype threat in US studies (Cook et al., 2012; Sherman et al., 2013). In addition, we also examined whether the values-affirmation intervention would attenuate the level of problem behavior of ethnic minority students, who are often also negatively stereotyped in the behavioral domain. The values-affirmation intervention did not affect the level of problem behavior of these students either. These results are surprising, since intervention procedures were reproduced as closely as possible and ethnic minority students in the Netherlands were assumed to be negatively stereotyped in Dutch society in a manner comparable to African American or Latino American students in the US, and as immigrant students in other European countries, for whom stereotype threat effects have also been demonstrated (Appel et al., 2015). Furthermore, the intervention also did not have an effect on the mathematics performance of girls, who are often negatively stereotyped in the domain of science and mathematics.

Our results may suggest that the intervention simply does not work outside the US. Still, in the US, the intervention had been shown to work for many different negatively stereotyped groups from many different cultural backgrounds. Therefore, we expected that the results would generalize to negatively stereotyped groups outside the US. Furthermore, the previously described study among French nursing students Taillandier-Schmitt et al. (2012) showed that the intervention can have some effect on the performance of negatively stereotyped students outside the US. Also, a study by Thomaes et al. (2012) showed that a values-affirmation intervention can have an effect on the behavior of students in the Netherlands. Although, Thomaes et al. (2012) did not focus on ethnic minority students under stereotype threat, it did show that students who were qualified as antisocial showed elevated levels of prosocial behavior after having completed a self-affirmation exercise comparable to those used in the studies of (Cohen et al., 2006b, 2009).

For these reasons, we decided to test the intervention again, with a different group of students. A difference between previous studies and our first study was that our study took place at the lowest level of secondary education (seventh grade), whereas previous studies (described in the introduction) took place at schools where the performance levels of the students were more mixed. Therefore, we chose to conduct our second study in sixth grade, with students having different performance levels still in the same class. In addition, in Study 2, results of the Cito standardized nationwide test were used as a performance measure, to have a more objective measure of achievement. Furthermore, apart from using only self-reports of problem behavior, which may be subject to social desirability, teachers were asked to report on the problem behavior of a random selection of their students.

STUDY 2

Theoretically, it is believed that a values-affirmation intervention works because students are stimulated to reflect on values that are personally important to them. However, self-reflection is often more difficult for younger students. Since the students in our second study were relatively young, we decided to add a third condition to our intervention paradigm. In this condition, the students have a conversation with a teaching assistant after they finish their values-affirmation assignment. This assistant helps them to elaborate on their personally important values. To ensure that effects would still be attributable to the intervention and not simply to the extra attention these students receive, students in the original two conditions (i.e., the values-affirmation and control condition) also have a conversation with the teaching assistant, only their conversation is about a neutral, unrelated, assignment.

Our hypotheses for Study 2 were that the affirmation intervention would positively affect the school performance and the level of problem behavior of ethnic minority students. Furthermore, we expected that the joint elaboration condition would have a surplus effect.

Materials and Methods

Participants

In Study 2, 290 students (49.7% boys) participated (12 native Dutch and 278 ethnic minority). Ages ranged from 10 to 13 years ($M_{age} = 11.28$ years, $SD = 0.57$). Condition allocation procedures were the same as in Study 1, except that in the present study there were three conditions, namely an affirmation condition with elaboration on the affirmation assignment (AA), an affirmation condition with elaboration on a non-affirmative unrelated reading task (AR), and a control condition with elaboration on the same unrelated reading task (CR). The assignment procedure is displayed in **Figure 3**.

The study took place in 15 grade six classes at 13 primary schools in the Netherlands. There were two schools with two sixth grades, resulting in 15 participating classes. As our main group of interest were ethnic minority students, schools were again recruited in areas with many ethnic minority students. Percentages of non-Western ethnic minority students ranged between 58 AND 100%.

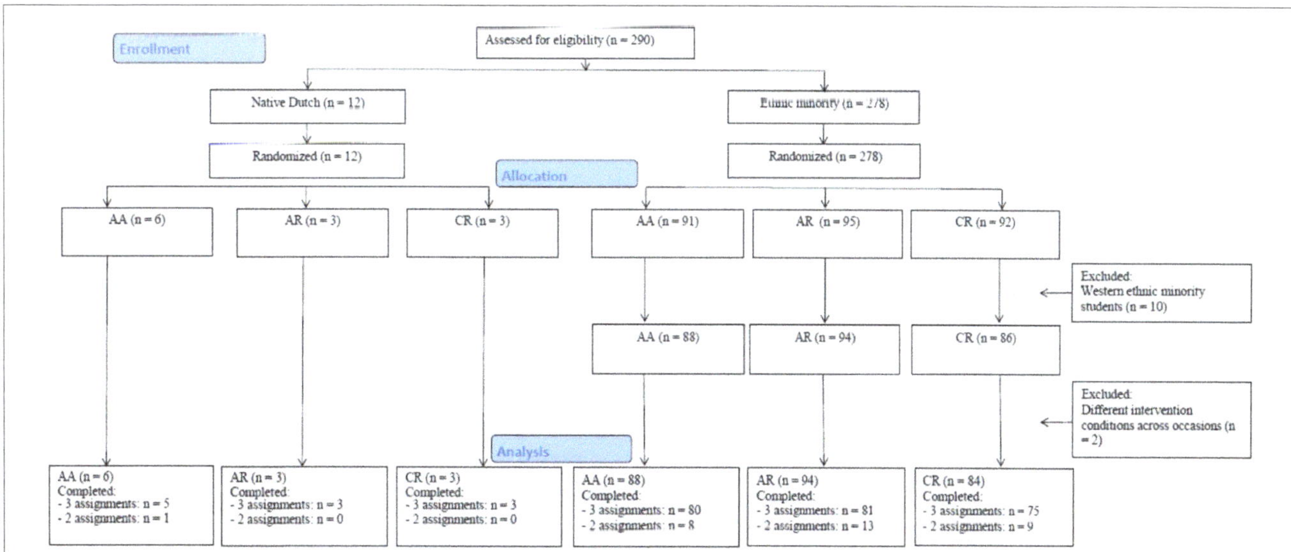

FIGURE 3 | Flowchart of the random assignment procedure of Study 2.

Of the 278 ethnic minority students, 10 (3.6%) had a Western ethnic minority background. As in Study 1, it was decided to leave these students out of the analyses, leaving 268 non-Western ethnic minority students (88 AA, 94 AR, 86 CR) and 12 native Dutch students (six AA, three AR, three CR) in the analyses. Of these 268 ethnic minority students, 38.8% had a Moroccan-Dutch background, 19.4% had a Turkish background, and 16.4% had a Surinamese or Antillean background. The remaining 25.4% had various backgrounds (e.g., Egypt, Pakistan, Ghana, China, India).

As in Study 1, most ethnic minority students were second generation immigrants (87%), meaning that their parents were born in the country of origin but the children themselves were born in the Netherlands. Thirty-four ethnic minority students (13%) were born in the country of origin of the parents. However, at the onset of the study they had lived in the Netherlands for an average of 7.77 years ($SD = 3.13$).

Negative Stereotypes in the Netherlands

To examine if sixth grade ethnic minority students in the Netherlands also experienced more negative stereotyping than native Dutch students, a study was conducted among another sample of fifth and sixth grade students ($N = 237$). Of these students, 47.3% had a native Dutch background, 11.8% had a Moroccan-Dutch background, 8.9% had a Turkish-Dutch background, 11.0% had a Surinamese or Antillean background and 21.1% had another ethnic minority background (eastern Europe, Iraq, Afghanistan, Africa, Asia, South America). Participants were asked to indicate on a three-point scale (yes, often – sometimes – no, never) to what extent they thought that others held the following negative stereotypes about their cultural group: lazy, untrustworthy, aggressive, greedy, dumb, always being late at appointments, done something wrong, criminal, love cheese and wooden shoes, unable to understand things quickly, not hardworking, stealing things, receiving bad grades at school, quickly starts to fight or scold, speaks Dutch badly. Items were rescored, so that a higher score indicated more experience with the stereotype. Multilevel analyses showed that ethnic minority students experienced significantly more often that others saw their cultural group as lazy, untrustworthy, aggressive, dumb, criminal, unable to understand things quickly, not hardworking, stealing things, quickly starts to fight or scold, and speaks Dutch badly. On the other hand, native Dutch students more often experienced that others saw their cultural group as people who all love cheese and wooden shoes. Moreover, when asked on a three-point scale how much they were bothered by the stereotypes that others hold about their group, ethnic minority students indicated to be significantly more often bothered by the negative stereotypes than native Dutch students. These results show that ethnic minority students in fifth and sixth grade thus experience negative stereotyping in the intellectual as well as the behavioral domain, and they feel bothered by these negative stereotypes more than native Dutch students do.

Intervention

As in Study 1, the students received three writing assignments throughout the school year. On Occasion 1 they received a writing assignment similar to the one used in Study 1. Because the students in Study 2 were relatively young, they received a simplified intervention on Occasions 2 and 3 (Sherman et al., 2013). On Occasion 2 students in the affirmation conditions again received the list of values and were asked to indicate only their most important value and to write about how that value would be important to them in the coming two winter months. For simplification, the reinforcing questions from Study 1 were removed. In the control condition, the students were asked to give a description of how they usually spend their afternoon, after school is out (e.g., How do you get home? How long does it take you to get home? Do you have a snack? At what time do you go to sleep?). On the third occasion students in the affirmation condition received a tailored writing assignment that stated which value they had chosen on Occasion 2, and asked them to write about why that value would again be important to them in the coming months. Because of an administrative error, there was one class for which the research team did not receive the writing assignments of Occasion 2 in time to prepare the tailored assignments. For these students a tailored assignment was made on the basis of the most important value from Occasion 1. In the control condition students were reminded that on the previous occasion they were asked to write something about how they usually spend their afternoon after they get home from school. Now, they were asked to write about what they had done in the morning, before they had come to school (e.g., At what time did you get up? How long did it take you to get ready? What, if anything, did you have for breakfast? How did you get to school?).

The writing assignments took approximately 15 min to complete. On Occasion 1, the students received an additional reading comprehension test after their writing assignment. They were asked to read a text about ice-cream and answer six questions about this text afterward. The two assignments together took approximately 25 min to complete.

On Occasion 1 all the students had a 10-min conversation with a trained member of our research team about one of their exercises. For participants to believe that the assignments were school exercises, the member of the research team presented herself as a trainee teacher. After the students had finished their assignments, the teaching assistant took the students out of the classroom one by one. In the AA condition, the teaching assistant spoke with the student about the values-affirmation writing assignment. In their writing assignment, students had chosen the two or three values that were most important to them. During the conversation, the students were asked to choose the most important of those two or three values and were asked, with standard questions, to elaborate on why that value was important to them. If there was still time left after discussing the most important value, the second most important value was also discussed. The teaching assistant helped the participant with self-reflection by paraphrasing and summarizing what the participant had said. In the AR and the CR conditions, the conversation was about the reading comprehension assignment. The teaching assistant reflected with the student on how they solved the questions that were part of the assignment and how they solve questions of reading comprehension assignments in general. In this condition, the researcher also paraphrased and summarized the answers of the student. Importantly, in none of the conditions did the teaching assistant give any evaluation of the performance of the student. The researcher made sure each conversation lasted for 10 min.

As in Study 1, Occasion 1 was timed as early in the school year as possible. On Occasions 2 and 3 the writing assignment was presented by the class teacher. Teachers were instructed to schedule the writing assignments directly before a school test. As in Study 1, teachers and students were blind to the purpose of the writing assignments and were unaware of the existence of different conditions.

Procedure

The procedure was similar to that of Study 1 and the time schedule is displayed in **Figure 4**. Five students did not receive parental permission. They received the control writing exercise and an alternative assignment during the measurement occasions.

Measures

School performance

Results of the Cito standardized test from the end of sixth grade were obtained from the school at the end of the school year. Some students also receive a standardized Cito test at the end of fifth grade, as a pre-indicator of their score on the test at the end of sixth grade. When possible, the schools also supplied the results of this test, to serve as a baseline performance indicator.

Problem behavior

Self-reported problem behavior was measured in the same way as in Study 1. Additionally, in this study, teachers also reported on the problem behavior of their students. They were asked to fill in the subscale 'Conduct problems' of the Dutch version of the Strengths and Difficulties Questionnaire (SDQ; Van Widenfelt et al., 2003). Because of the large workload of the teachers, we asked them to fill in these questionnaires for 12 randomly selected students from their class. Both student- and teacher-reported problem behavior were measured pre- and post-intervention. The teacher-reported problem behavior of the ethnic minority students in our study was compared to norm scores of the SDQ from 2013, which had been collected among a national sample of 2136 students in regular education, between the ages of 9 and 13 years (Diepenmaat et al., 2014). The percentages of ethnic minority students in the schools that participated in this national study were slightly higher than in the total population. The results showed that compared to the average of this norm population, the teachers in our study reported significantly higher levels of problem behavior for the ethnic minority students in our sample, $t(117) = 0.57$, $p < 0.01$. Since the native Dutch group in our sample was very small ($N = 12$), they were not compared to the norm group.

Statistical Analyses

Analytic procedures similar to those used in Study 1 were applied, with two differences. First, in the present study native Dutch students were left out of the analyses. This was done because the group of native Dutch students was very small ($N = 12$) and our main interest was to examine intervention effects for ethnic minority students. Secondly, since there were now three conditions, two dummy variables were created for condition instead of one.

Results

Data Preparation

Due to administrative errors, two participants did not receive the same intervention condition on all three occasions and were excluded from the analyses, leaving 266 ethnic minority students in the analyses (see **Figure 3**). Data are included in the Supplementary Materials (see Data Sheet 2). The majority of the students completed all three writing assignments. Due to administrative errors at one school, one class ($N = 15$) only completed the first and the third assignment. Most of those students who were absent during one occasion completed the assignment once they returned at school. Some students did not receive this opportunity from their teacher ($N = 16$) and completed only two out of three assignments. Only one student missed the first assignment. There were no differences between the three conditions in the mean number of interventions completed, $F(2,275) = 0.39$, $p = 0.68$. Therefore, all 266 ethnic minority students remained in the analyses. The distribution of the students across the three conditions is displayed in **Figure 3**.

For all classes, data on post-intervention school performance (i.e., Cito-scores) were available. For five of the 15 classes (79 ethnic minority students), pre-intervention performance information was available (i.e., the scores on the standardized Cito test from the end of fifth grade). Just as in Study 1, we expected no differences between the students for whom pre-intervention performance was available and those for whom it was unavailable, because the data was missing per class and not per individual student. Indeed, there were no age differences between the five classes for which the data on pre-intervention performance were available and the 10 classes for which these data were not available, $t(272) = -1.66$, $p = 0.10$.

Data on self-reported problem behavior were available for all classes. Three teachers were unable to report on problem behavior at either the first occasion or the second occasion. One class switched teachers three times during the school year. The 11 remaining teachers completed the questionnaires both on Occasions 1 and 2, resulting in teacher reports of problem behavior for 115 ethnic minority students (38 AF, 40 AN, 37 C).

Intervention Effects

School performance

Descriptives of pre- and post-intervention Cito-scores are displayed in **Table 5**. The outcomes of the multilevel analyses are displayed in **Table 6**. Gender was added as a control variable. Contrary to expectations, the intervention again had no effect on school performance. All other effects were also non-significant.

As in Study 1, we also examined intervention effects for the Moroccan-Dutch group and the Turkish-Dutch group separately. The effect was not significant for any of these groups. As in Study 1, we also examined intervention effects for the total

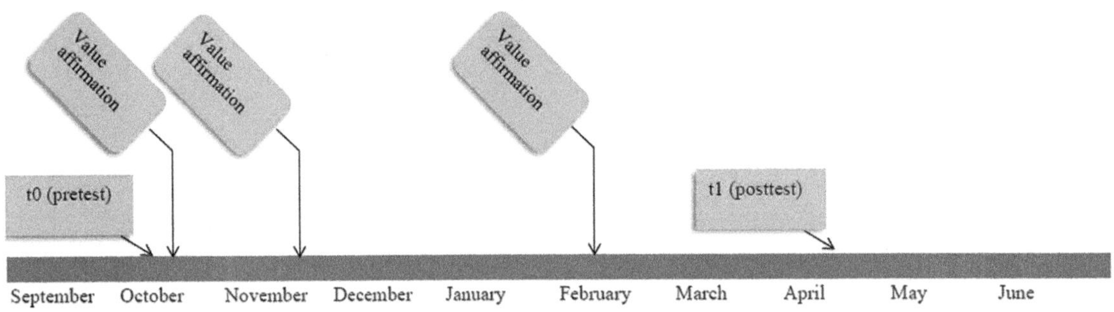

FIGURE 4 | Time schedule of the intervention Study 2.

group, including the native Dutch students. Again, there were no significant effects.

We also conducted analyses in which we controlled for pre-intervention performance. As mentioned before, these were available for five classes. The only difference was that pre-intervention performance was a significant predictor of post-intervention performance ($\beta = 0.89, p < 0.001$).

Problem behavior

Descriptives of pre- and post-intervention problem behavior are displayed in **Table 5**. The results of the multilevel analyses are displayed in **Table 7**. Gender and pre-intervention student-reported problem behavior were added as control variables. Again, the intervention did not have the expected effect on student-reported problem behavior. The only significant predictor of post-intervention problem behavior was pre-intervention problem behavior. The positive parameter indicates that the higher the level of pre-intervention problem behavior, the higher the level of post-intervention problem behavior.

Again, analyses were also conducted for the Moroccan-Dutch group and the Turkish-Dutch group, separately. As before, the only significant predictor in both groups was pre-intervention problem behavior. Analyses were also conducted for the native Dutch group and the ethnic minority group combined. Again, the only significant predictor was pre-intervention problem behavior.

As to teacher-reported problem behavior, there was also only a significant effect of pre-intervention teacher-reported problem behavior. Analyses were also performed for the Moroccan-Dutch and the Turkish-Dutch groups separately. The only difference from the results of the total ethnic minority group was that there was a significant main effect of gender for the Turkish-Dutch group, indicating that teachers reported higher levels of problem behavior for Turkish boys than for Turkish girls at the end of the school year. The analysis with the native Dutch and ethnic minority group combined also yielded the same results as the main analysis.

GENERAL DISCUSSION

The present study investigated whether the positive effects of a values-affirmation on the school performance of ethnic minority students found in earlier studies (e.g., Cohen et al., 2006b, 2009), would generalize to a negatively stereotyped minority group (i.e., immigrant students in the Netherlands) outside the US. With two double-blind field experiments, we examined if the intervention would reduce the negative effects of stereotype threat on the school achievement of ethnic minority students in the Netherlands. In contrast to findings of the previous studies discussed in the introduction, the values-affirmation intervention did not affect the school performance of the ethnic minority students included in our studies. In our second study, a third condition was added to the original paradigm, in which students received help in reflecting on their personally important values. This additional help with self-reflection did not improve their performance either. In addition, we applied stereotype threat theory to the problem behavior of ethnic minority students. We examined if the values-affirmation intervention would attenuate the level of problem behavior of ethnic minority students, who are often also negatively stereotyped in the behavioral domain. However, the values-affirmation intervention did not affect student problem behavior either. Finally, we also did not find that the intervention had an effect on school belongingness and identification, which have been identified as underlying factors in the process of stereotype threat in US studies (Cook et al., 2012; Sherman et al., 2013). These results were unexpected, since the intervention procedures were closely reproduced.

A possible explanation for the absence of intervention effects could be that there are certain preconditions that need to be fulfilled before the intervention can have the intended effect. Perhaps these preconditions were not met in the present study. Although not always explicitly mentioned, several possible preconditions can be deduced from previous studies. For example, a salient achievement gap seems to be necessary for the intervention to work. In most previous intervention studies, there was an achievement gap within the classrooms between the stereotyped and the non-stereotyped group, which was attenuated by the values-affirmation intervention (e.g., Cohen et al., 2006b; Sherman et al., 2013; Harackiewicz et al., 2014). In contrast, in our studies, one could argue that there was no salient achievement gap. In Study 1, there was no pre- or post-intervention gap in English or Dutch. In Study 2, the native Dutch group was very small ($N = 12$) and therefore, ethnic

TABLE 5 | Descriptives of grades, problem behavior, belongingness, and identification with school for the different groups in Study 2.

	Native Dutch						Ethnic minority					
	Affirmation + Feedback		Affirmation + Neutral		Control		Affirmation + Feedback		Affirmation + Neutral		Control	
	M	*SD*	*M*	*SD*	*M*	*SD*	*M*	*SD*	*M*	*SD*	*M*	*SD*
Cito scores Grade 6	530.50	11.36	527.33	5.69	531.33	8.08	530.43	11.24	529.80	10.26	530.21	11.71
Problem behavior												
SR pre-interventions	1.20	0.12	1.52	0.34	1.55	0.36	1.20	0.23	1.25	0.30	1.29	0.30
SR post-interventions	1.16	0.14	1.36	0.48	1.33	0.42	1.20	0.25	1.21	0.27	1.21	0.24
TR pre-interventions	1.70	0.81	1.53	0.50	1.55	0.35	1.28	0.45	1.26	0.34	1.33	0.44
TR post-interventions	1.50	0.50	1.20	0.00	1.60	0.57	1.29	0.44	1.30	0.39	1.30	0.43

SR, self-report; TR, teacher-report.

TABLE 6 | Effect sizes and standard errors of multilevel models for post-intervention Cito scores of sixth grade Study 2.

	Cito score (*SE*)
Gender[a]	0.25 (0.20)
Dummy 1: AA vs. CR[b]	0.17 (0.20)
Dummy 2: AR vs. CR[c]	0.15 (0.20)
Gender * Dummy 1	−0.15 (0.28)
Gender * Dummy 2	−0.28 (0.28)

**p < 0.05, **p < 0.01, ***p < 0.001. Parameter estimates (while controlling for effects of other parameters) can be interpreted as Cohen's d; [a]Girl = 0, Boy = 1; [b]CR = 0, AR = 0, AA = 1; [c]CR = 0, AA = 0, AR = 1.*

TABLE 7 | Effect sizes and standard errors of multilevel models for post-intervention problem behavior Study 2.

	Self-reported problem behavior (*SE*)	Teacher-reported problem behavior (*SE*)
Gender[a]	0.12 (0.17)	0.13 (0.21)
Pre-intervention problem behavior	0.59 (0.05)***	0.78 (0.06)***
Dummy 1: AA vs. CR[b]	0.15 (0.17)	−0.07 (0.21)
Dummy 2: AR vs. CR[c]	0.03 (0.17)	−0.06 (0.21)
Gender * Dummy 1	−0.23 (0.24)	−0.06 (0.29)
Gender * Dummy 2	0.08 (0.23)	−0.24 (0.29)

**p < 0.05, **p < 0.01, ***p < 0.001. Parameter estimates (while controlling for effects of other parameters) can be interpreted as Cohen's d; [a]Girl = 0, Boy = 1; [b]CR = 0, AR = 0, AA = 1; [c]CR = 0, AA = 0, AR = 1.*

minority students probably did not perceive a gap between their performance and that of the native Dutch students, at least not within the classroom. Could it be that the absence of a clear gap is the reason that the intervention did not have the intended effect in the present study?

An argument against this is that in Study 1, we did find an achievement gap in mathematics. If a salient achievement gap is necessary, then we would have expected at least an intervention effect on mathematics. However, this was not what we found. Furthermore, we believe that although achievement gaps might not have been salient within the classroom, the students most likely did perceive gaps between themselves and other students in broader society. For example, the students in Study 1 had just made the transition from primary to secondary school and were sent to the lowest level of secondary education. Because of this transition, the students were probably very aware of the fact that there are students with higher educational levels. Furthermore, the students in both the first and the second study scored significantly below the national average on nationwide standardized tests that are used to determine to which school level the student should go after sixth grade. Students spend a great amount of time training for these tests and they are most probably very well aware of their own score as well as of the national average. To conclude, we assume that the students in our sample were very aware of existing achievement gaps between themselves and other students. If perceiving a gap is a precondition for the efficacy of the intervention, we believe that this condition was satisfied in our studies.

On the other hand, the precondition of a salient achievement gap may not have been met for girls in mathematics. Within the classes, there was no pre-intervention achievement gap between girls and boys on mathematics performance. Furthermore, previous studies have shown that differences between girls and boys on mathematics performance have dramatically diminished in the past decades (e.g., Else-Quest et al., 2010). Whereas for ethnic minority students there are still plenty of clues that point to achievement gaps in broader society even though there is no gap within the classroom, for girls in mathematics even a gap in society is absent. This absence of a gap may have reduced the working of the intervention for girls in mathematics, even though they may still be negatively stereotyped in this domain.

Another possible precondition that can be deduced from previous research is that students should experience some form of stereotype threat or identity threat (e.g., Cohen et al., 2006b; Bowen et al., 2013; Sherman et al., 2013). One could argue that the intervention did not have the intended effect in the present study because the students in our studies perhaps did not experience stereotype threat, or that they experienced it to a lesser extent than for example African Americans or Latino Americans in the US. However, we have ample reason to believe that ethnic minority students in the Netherlands are pervasively negatively stereotyped in the same manner as the ethnic minorities in previous studies from the US. First, they are negatively stereotyped in the intellectual as well as the behavioral domain (e.g., Verkuyten and Thijs, 2000), and stereotype threat effects have been shown in immigrant students with similar ethnic backgrounds in neighboring European countries (i.e., France, Austria and Germany; Chateignier et al., 2009; Berjot et al., 2011; Appel, 2012; see Appel et al., 2015 for an overview). Furthermore, they also often have a low SES, which is also often accompanied by negative stereotypes (e.g., Croizet and Claire, 1998). Still, even though the level of negative stereotyping in the US and the Netherlands seems similar, it could be argued that the students in our studies *experienced* less stereotype threat than students in previous studies (e.g., Cohen et al., 2006b, 2009). One might, for example, expect that students in classes with an even distribution of ethnic minority and majority students experience more stereotype threat, because the out-group, and therefore also the negative stereotypes, are presumably more salient. Cohen et al. (2006b) for example used a school with a relatively even distribution of African Americans and European Americans. In contrast, in 11 of the 17 classes in our first study, the percentage of ethnic minority students was higher than 90%. The same was true for 13 of the 15 classes in Study 2. Perhaps this high percentage of ethnic minority students made these students experience less stereotype threat. If the experience of stereotype threat is indeed a precondition for the efficacy of the intervention, this could explain the absence of intervention effects. Yet, there are several arguments against this. Because in the present study there were more schools and classes included than in the study of (Cohen et al., 2006b, 2009), it was possible to examine intervention effects separately for the six classes with a relatively even distribution of ethnic minority and majority students (i.e., percentages of ethnic minority students ranging between 50 and 71%). There were still no intervention effects found. Furthermore, in the study of Bowen et al. (2013) the ethnic majority group was also very small and yet in their study the intervention did have the intended effect. The percentage of ethnic minority students in the classroom thus does not seem to determine the level of experienced stereotype threat. Rather, the level of negative stereotyping in broader society seems to matter.

In previous research, some moderators were identified that could potentially influence how much stereotype threat individuals experience. Based on the literature, gender-group identification and gender role orientation might moderate stereotype threat effects for women's mathematic performance (Schmader, 2002; Tempel and Neumann, 2015). With respect to stereotype threat for ethnic minority students, stigma consciousness might be of influence (Brown and Pinel, 2003). Additionally, individual vulnerability for stress responses, such as trait worry (Tempel and Neumann, 2014), has been shown to moderate stereotype threat effects. Although, it is recommendable that future studies include these potential moderators, we do not expect that they diminished the experience of stereotype threat in the present study. First, there was no reason for us to assume that trait worry would be different for ethnic minority students in the Netherlands than for ethnic minority students with the same background in France and Germany, where stereotype threat effects were found among immigrant students (Chateignier et al., 2009; Berjot et al., 2011; Appel, 2012). Second, previous research has shown that ethnic minority students in the Netherlands identify more strongly with their ethnic group than native Dutch students (e.g., Verkuyten and Thijs, 2001). Finally, because of the frequent negative media attention regarding ethnic minorities in the Netherlands, we expect that the students in the present study were highly aware of their stigmatized status.

Previous studies have merely assumed that experiencing stereotype threat is a necessary precondition for the intervention to work. A values-affirmation intervention is aimed at re-affirming self-integrity. Previous studies have shown that only negatively stereotyped students (e.g., African Americans; Cohen et al., 2006b) benefit from the intervention, whereas non-stereotyped individuals (e.g., European Americans) do not. The assumption is that this is because only negatively stereotyped students are in need of re-affirmation of their self-integrity. Although this assumption seems plausible, stereotype threat was never actually measured in any of these previous studies. Moreover, values-affirmation interventions have also been shown to have positive effects without stereotype threat being present (e.g., Thomaes et al., 2012; or after receiving negative feedback: Koole et al., 1999). Therefore, one cannot be certain that the experience of stereotype threat is indeed a precondition for the intervention to work. To our knowledge, no previous studies have found an adequate way to assess stereotype threat. Future studies should focus on this issue.

To conclude, previous research has provided clues as to what preconditions are important for the efficacy of the intervention. Our study seems to meet these criteria. This leads us back to the question as to why no intervention effects were found in the present study, whereas in previous research the intervention was very successful in improving the performance of negatively stereotyped students. We believe that there are also some broader, contextual, factors that could perhaps explain differences in intervention results between previous studies and the present study. One important difference is that in the present study, unlike in previous studies, most ethnic minority students had a Moroccan or Turkish background, which usually implied that they were Muslims. In their values-affirmation exercises, these students often selected 'religion' as one of their most important values. In Dutch society, Muslims are increasingly negatively stereotyped because there is growing media attention for extremism and terrorism which are often associated with Islam (e.g., Kamans et al., 2009). Writing about this value could therefore have increased instead of decreased their awareness of and worries about the negative stereotypes that exist about their group. Consequently, the intervention may have reduced instead of increased feelings of self-integrity.

Another important cultural difference is that the African American group differs from the Moroccan-Dutch and Turkish-Dutch group on one of the five cultural dimensions of Hofstede (2001), namely power distance. Power distance can be defined as the degree to which less powerful members of society accept and expect that power is distributed unequally. Cultures with a high power distance are characterized by hierarchical structures, with an emphasis on obedience and respect. The Moroccan and Turkish culture have a relatively high power distance (Hofstede et al., 2002), whereas African American culture has a moderately low power distance (Gibson, 2008), with the emphasis being more on social equality and equal opportunity. Perhaps being a member of a culture with a high power distance makes it difficult for Turkish-Dutch or Moroccan-Dutch students to believe that they can actually change their situation. In our first study for example, students presumably already perceived themselves as being at the lower end of the 'hierarchy,' because they are at the lowest level of secondary education. Perhaps these students perceive those who are placed higher in de hierarchy as more capable of inducing change in society than themselves. This view of themselves as not having the power to change their situation could impede the effectiveness of the intervention. Also, differences in power distance between US and Dutch ethnic minority students may have affected the types of values students selected as most important to them during the values-affirmation assignments. Students with a cultural background having a higher power distance (e.g., Moroccan, Turkish) may be inclined to choose values that are seen as important by their community or those higher in the hierarchy, whereas students from a culture with a low power distance (e.g., African American) may choose values that are more personally important to them. Choosing personally important values might be more related to intrinsic motivation, whereas choosing "community values" might be more related to extrinsic motivation. Extrinsic motivation refers to doing something because it leads to a separable outcome. Intrinsic motivation refers to doing things because they are inherently interesting and enjoyable (Ryan and Deci, 2000). As an example, many ethnic minority students in the affirmation condition chose religion as one of their most important values. When inspecting the motivations these students gave for choosing this value, it seemed that they often formulated relatively extrinsic motivations, such as 'you should do what is asked in Islam,' or 'because of my religion, I will go to paradise,' or 'everybody in my family is religious.' We hypothesize that the intervention would perhaps have been more effective if participants had chosen values that were more *personally* important to them, based on intrinsic motivation. More research is needed to explore if and how the choice of values and the motivation behind this influence intervention effects and if differences in power distance influence the efficacy of the intervention.

Apart from examining intervention effects on performance outside the US, the present study was also the first to examine if a values-affirmation intervention affects the level of problem behavior of negatively stereotyped ethnic minority students. However, it did not. The cultural factors described above that may have undermined the effect of the intervention on school achievement also apply to behavior. An additional explanation for the absence of intervention effects on behavior could be the timing of the intervention. In studies aimed at intervening in school results, self-affirmation is assumed to have the strongest effect when it is planned in a context in which the negative stereotype applies (Cohen et al., 2006a, supporting online material), for example just before a school test. To have an effect on problem behavior, however, timing the intervention in a context in which stereotypes about problem behavior are more salient could perhaps result in greater benefits (see for example Thomaes et al., 2012). More research is needed to examine the effects of a properly timed values-affirmation intervention on the problem behavior of negatively stereotyped ethnic minority students. Such research could perhaps best start in the US, where previous intervention effects were found on school achievement.

CONCLUSION

Values-affirmation interventions have had strong positive effects on negatively stereotyped ethnic minority students in previous studies (Cohen et al., 2006b, 2009), but the present study shows that these effects do not simply transfer to all negatively stereotyped ethnic minority groups. To cite Yeager and Walton (2011), social-psychological interventions 'are not magic.' They can be powerful, but their effects are dependent on the context in which they are used. In our opinion, there is a strong need to examine what the context-dependent conditions are under which values-affirmation interventions either succeed or fail to attain their goal.

AUTHOR CONTRIBUTIONS

The research grant was awarded to FCJ, HK, and PJ. All authors made substantial contributions. EJ, FCJ, HK, and PJ worked together on the design of the research project. Data collection, analysis, and writing of the article were carried out by EJ. FCJ, HK, and PJ critically revised the work. All authors gave their approval of the final version of the article.

ACKNOWLEDGMENT

This research project was funded by a grant from the Dutch Ministry of Education, grant OBD10035.

REFERENCES

Appel, M. (2012). Anti-immigrant propaganda by radical right parties and the intellectual performance of adolescents. *Polit. Psychol.* 33, 483–493. doi: 10.1111/j.1467-9221.2012.00902.x

Appel, M., Weber, S., and Kronberger, N. (2015). The influence of stereotype threat on immigrants: review and meta-analysis. *Front. Psychol.* 6:900. doi: 10.3389/fpsyg.2015.00900

Aronson, J., Fried, C. B., and Good, C. (2002). Reducing the effects of stereotype threat on African American college students by shaping theories of intelligence. *J. Exp. Soc. Psychol.* 38, 113–125. doi: 10.1006/jesp.2001.1491

Aronson, J., and Salinas, M. F. (1997). Stereotype threat: is low performance the proce of self-esteem for Mexican Americans? *Paper Presented to the Western Psychological Association Conference*, Seattle, WA.

Azzolini, D., Schnell, P., and Palmer, J. R. (2012). Educational achievement gaps between immigrant and native students in two "new" immigration countries Italy and Spain in comparison. *Ann. Am. Acad. Pol. Soc. Sci.* 643, 46–77. doi: 10.1177/0002716212441590

Baumeister, R. F., and Heatherton, T. F. (1996). Self-regulation failure: an overview. *Psychol. Inquiry* 7, 1–15. doi: 10.1207/s15327965pli0701_1

Berjot, S., Roland-Levy, C., and Girault-Lidvan, N. (2011). Cognitive appraisals of stereotype threat. *Psychol. Rep.* 108, 585–598. doi: 10.2466/04.07.21.PR0.108.2.585-598

Bowen, N. K., Wegmann, K. M., and Webber, K. C. (2013). Enhancing a brief writing intervention to combat stereotype threat among middle-school students. *J. Educ. Psychol.* 105:427. doi: 10.1037/a0031177

Brown, R. P., and Pinel, E. C. (2003). Stigma on my mind: individual differences in the experience of stereotype threat. *J. Exp. Soc. Psychol.* 39, 626–633. doi: 10.1016/S0022-1031(03)00039-8

CBS Statline (2011). Available at: http://Statline.cbs.nl

Centraal Bureau Voor de Statistiek [CBS] (2005). *Jaarrapport Integratie 2005.* Available at: http://www.cbs.nl/nl-NL/menu/themas/dossiers/allochtonen/publicaties/publicaties/archief/2005/2005-jaarrapport-integratie.htm

Chateignier, C., Dutrévis, M., Nugier, A., and Chekroun, P. (2009). French-Arab students and verbal intellectual performance: do they really suffer from a negative intellectual stereotype? *Eur. J. Psychol. Educ.* 24, 219–234. doi: 10.1007/BF03173013

Cohen, G. L., Garcia, J., Apfel, N., and Master, A. (2006a). *Supporting Online Material.* Available at: http://www.sciencemag.org/content/suppl/2006/08/29/313.5791.1307.DC1/Cohen.SOM.pdf

Cohen, G. L., Garcia, J., Apfel, N., and Master, A. (2006b). Reducing the racial achievement gap: a social-psychological intervention. *Science* 313, 1307–1310. doi: 10.1126/science.1128317

Cohen, G. L., Garcia, J., Purdie-Vaughns, V., Apfel, N., and Brzustoski, P. (2009). Recursive processes in self-affirmation: intervening to close the minority achievement gap. *Science* 324, 400–403. doi: 10.1126/science.1170769

Cook, J. E., Purdie-Vaughns, V., Garcia, J., and Cohen, G. L. (2012). Chronic threat and contingent belonging: protective benefits of values affirmation on identity development. *J. Pers. Soc. Psychol.* 102, 479–496. doi: 10.1037/a0026312

Critcher, C. R., and Dunning, D. (2014). Self-affirmations provide a broader perspective on self-threat. *Pers. Soc. Psychol. Bull.* 41, 3–18. doi: 10.1177/0146167214554956

Croizet, J. C., and Claire, T. (1998). Extending the concept of stereotype threat to social class: the intellectual underperformance of students from low socioeconomic backgrounds. *Pers. Soc. Psychol. Bull.* 24, 588–594. doi: 10.1177/0146167298246003

De Groot, A., Koot, H. M., and Verhulst, F. C. (1996). Cross-cultural generalizability of the youth self-report and teacher's report form cross-informant syndromes. *J. Abnorm. Child Psychol.* 24, 651–664. doi: 10.1007/BF01670105

Diepenmaat, A., Van Eijsden, M., Janssens, J., Loomans, E., and Stone, L. (2014). *Verantwoording SDQ Leerkrachtvragenlijst voor Gebruik Binnen het Onderwijs en in de zorg. [Accountability of the SDQ Teacher-Report Questionnaire for Usage in the Educational and Health Sector.].* Available at: http://www.hartenzielmonitor.nl/docs/hartenziel-cotan-verantwoording-sdq.pdf

Else-Quest, N. M., Hyde, J. S., and Linn, M. C. (2010). Cross-national patterns of gender differences in mathematics: a meta-analysis. *Psychol. Bull.* 136:103. doi: 10.1037/a0018053

Fryer, R. G., and Levitt, S. D. (2006). The black-white test score gap through third grade. *Am. Law Econ. Rev.* 8, 249–281. doi: 10.1093/aler/ahl003

Gibson, A. D. (2008). Cultural value differences and women-owned businesses in the United States: a preliminary exploration. *J. Appl. Bus. Econ.* 8, 23–34.

Harackiewicz, J. M., Canning, E. A., Tibbetts, Y., Giffen, C. J., Blair, S. S., Rouse, D. I., et al. (2014). Closing the social class achievement gap for first-generation students in undergraduate biology. *J. Educ. Psychol.* 106, 375–389. doi: 10.1037/a0034679

Hofstede, G. (2001). *Culture's Consequences; Comparing Values, Behaviours, Institutions and Organizations Across Nations.* California: Sage publications.

Hofstede, G. J., Pedersen, P., and Hofstede, G. (2002). *Exploring Culture: Exercises, Stories and Synthetic Cultures.* Maine: Intercultural Press.

Hox, J. J. (2010). *Multilevel Analysis. Techniques and Applications.* New York, NY: Routledge.

Inzlicht, M., and Kang, S. K. (2010). Stereotype threat spillover: how coping with threats to social identity affects aggression, eating, decision making, and attention. *J. Pers. Soc. Psychol.* 99, 467–481. doi: 10.1037/a0018951

Kamans, E., Gordijn, E. H., Oldenhuis, H., and Otten, S. (2009). What I think you see is what you get: influence of prejudice on assimilation to negative meta-stereotypes among Dutch Moroccan teenagers. *Eur. J. Soc. Psychol.* 39, 842–851. doi: 10.1002/ejsp.593

Keller, J. (2002). Blatant stereotype threat and women's math performance: self-handicapping as a strategic means to cope with obtrusive negative performance expectations. *Sex Roles* 47, 193–198. doi: 10.1023/A:1021003307511

Koole, S. L., Smeets, K., Van Knippenberg, A., and Dijksterhuis, A. (1999). The cessation of rumination through self-affirmation. *J. Pers. Soc. Psychol.* 77:111. doi: 10.1037/0022-3514.77.1.111

Marks, G. N. (2005). Accounting for immigrant non-immigrant differences in reading and mathematics in twenty countries. *Ethn. Racial Stud.* 28, 925–946. doi: 10.1080/01419870500158943

Martens, A., Johns, M., Greenberg, J., and Schimel, J. (2006). Combating stereotype threat: the effect of self-affirmation on women's intellectual performance. *J. Exp. Soc. Psychol.* 42, 236–243. doi: 10.1016/j.jesp.2005.04.010

Miyake, A., Kost-Smith, L. E., Finkelstein, N. D., Pollock, S. J., Cohen, G. L., and Ito, T. A. (2010). Reducing the gender achievement gap in college science: a classroom study of values affirmation. *Science* 330, 1234–1237. doi: 10.1126/science.1195996

Nievers, E. J., Andriessen, I., and Ross, J. A. (2010). *Discriminatiemonitor niet-westerse migranten op de arbeidsmarkt 2010. [Discrimination Minitor Non-Western Migrants at the Labor Market 2010].* Available at: http://www.scp.nl/Publicaties/Alle_publicaties/Publicaties_2010/Discriminatiemonitor_niet_westerse_migranten_op_de_arbeidsmarkt_2010

Organisation for Economic Co-operation and Development [OECD] (2002). *Trends in International Migration.* Available at: http://www.oecd.org/els/mig/trendsininternationalmigration-2002edition.htm

Osborne, J. W., and Walker, C. (2006). Stereotype threat, identification with academics, and withdrawal from school: why the most successful students of colour might be most likely to withdraw. *Educ. Psychol.* 26, 563–577. doi: 10.1080/01443410500342518

Owens, J., and Massey, D. S. (2011). Stereotype threat and college academic performance: a latent variables approach. *Soc. Sci. Res.* 40, 150–166. doi: 10.1016/j.ssresearch.2010.09.010

Pásztor, A. (2008). The children of guest workers: comparative analysis of scholastic achievement of pupils of Turkish origin throughout Europe. *Intercult. Educ.* 19, 407–419. doi: 10.1080/14675980802531598

Rodríguez, B. A. (2014). The threat of living up to expectations: analyzing the performance of Hispanic students on standardized exams. *J. Hispanic Higher Educ.* 13, 191–205. doi: 10.1177/1538192714531292

Ryan, R. M., and Deci, E. L. (2000). Intrinsic and extrinsic motivations: classic definitions and new directions. *Contemp. Educ. Psychol.* 25, 54–67. doi: 10.1006/ceps.1999.1020

Schmader, T. (2002). Gender identification moderates stereotype threat effects on women's math performance. *J. Exp. Soc. Psychol.* 38, 194–201. doi: 10.1177/0146167208318404

Schmader, T., Johns, M., and Forbes, C. (2008). An integrated process model of stereotype threat effects on performance. *Psychol. Rev.* 115, 336–356. doi: 10.1037/0033-295X.115.2.336

Schmeichel, B. J., and Vohs, K. (2009). Self-affirmation and self-control: affirming core values counteracts ego depletion. *J. Pers. Soc. Psychol.* 96:770. doi: 10.1037/a0014635

Sherman, D. K. (2013). Self-Affirmation: understanding the Effects. *Soc. Pers. Psychol. Compass* 7, 834–845. doi: 10.1111/spc3.12072

Sherman, D. K., Hartson, K. A., Binning, K. R., Purdie-Vaughns, V., Garcia, J., Taborsky-Barba, S., et al. (2013). Deflecting the trajectory and changing the narrative: how self-affirmation affects academic performance and motivation under identity threat. *J. Pers. Soc. Psychol.* 104, 591–618. doi: 10.1037/a0031495

Smits, J. A. E., and Vorst, H. C. M. (1990). *Schoolvragenlijst voor Basisonderwijs en Voortgezet Onderwijs: SVL. Handleiding voor Gebruikers. [School Attitude Questionnaire Secondary Education. Instruction Manual for Users]*. Nijmegen: Berkhout.

Snijders, T. A. B., and Bosker, R. J. (2012). *Multilevel Analysis: An Introduction to Basic and Advanced Multilevel Modeling*. London: Sage Publishers.

Spencer, S. J., Steele, C. M., and Quinn, D. M. (1999). Stereotype threat and women's math performance. *J. Exp. Soc. Psychol.* 35, 4–28. doi: 10.1006/jesp.1998.1373

Steele, C. M. (1988). "The psychology of self-affirmation: sustaining the integrity of the self," in *Advances in Experimental Social Psychology*, ed. L. Berkowitz (New York, NY: Academic Press), 261–302.

Steele, C. M. (1997). A threat in the air: how stereotypes shape intellectual identity and performance. *Am. Psychol.* 52, 613–629. doi: 10.1037/0003-066X.52.6.613

Steele, C. M., and Aronson, J. (1995). Stereotype threat and the intellectual test performance of African Americans. *J. Pers. Soc. Psychol.* 69, 797–811. doi: 10.1037/0022-3514.69.5.797

Stevens, G. W., and Vollebergh, W. A. (2008). Mental health in migrant children. *J. Child Psychol. Psychiatry* 49, 276–294. doi: 10.1111/j.1469-7610.2007.01848.x

Stevens, G. W. J. M., Pels, T., Bengi-Aslan, L., Verhulst, F. C., Vollebergh, W. A. M., and Crijnen, A. A. M. (2003). Parent, teacher and self-reported problem behavior in the Netherlands. Comparing Moroccan immigrant with Dutch and with Turkish immigrant children and adolescents. *Soc. Psychiatry Psychiatr. Epidemiol.* 38, 576–585. doi: 10.1007/s00127-003-0677-5

Stone, J., Lynch, C. I., Sjomeling, M., and Darley, J. M. (1999). Stereotype threat effects on black and white athletic performance. *J. Pers. Soc. Psychol.* 77, 1213–1227. doi: 10.1037/0022-3514.77.6.1213

Taillandier-Schmitt, A., Esnard, C., and Mokounkolo, R. (2012). Self-affirmation in occupational training: effects of the math performance of French women nurses under stereotype threat. *Sex Roles* 67, 43–57. doi: 10.1007/s11199-012-0157-z

Tempel, T., and Neumann, R. (2014). Stereotype threat, test anxiety, and mathematics performance. *Soc. Psychol. Educ.* 17, 491–501. doi: 10.1007/s11218-014-9263-9

Tempel, T., and Neumann, R. (2015). Gender role orientation moderates effects of stereotype activation on test performances. *Soc. Psychol.* doi: 10.1027/1864-9335/a000259

Thomaes, S., Bushman, B. J., de Castro, B. O., and Reijntjes, A. (2012). Arousing "gentle passions" in young adolescents: sustained experimental effects of value affirmations on prosocial feelings and behaviors. *Dev. Psychol.* 48, 103–110. doi: 10.1037/a0025677

Van Widenfelt, B. M., Goedhart, A. W., Treffers, P. D., and Goodman, R. (2003). Dutch version of the strengths and difficulties questionnaire (SDQ). *Eur. Child Adolesc. Psychiatry* 12, 281–289. doi: 10.1007/s00787-003-0341-3

Verkuyten, M., and Thijs, J. (2000). *Discriminatie, Zelfbeeld, Relaties en Leerprestaties in 'Witte' en 'Zwarte' Basisscholen*. Amsterdam: Thela Thesis.

Verkuyten, M., and Thijs, J. (2001). Ethnic and gender bias among Dutch and Turkish children in late childhood: the role of social context. *Infant Child Dev.* 10, 203–217. doi: 10.1002/icd.279

Verkuyten, M., and Thijs, J. (2004). Psychological disidentification with the academic domain among ethnic minority adolescents in The Netherlands. *Br. J. Educ. Psychol.* 74, 109–125. doi: 10.1348/000709904322848842

Verkuyten, M., and Thijs, J. (2010). Ethnic minority labeling, multiculturalism, and the attitude of majority group members. *J. Lang. Soc. Psychol.* 29, 467–477. doi: 10.1177/0261927X10377992

Walton, G. M., and Cohen, G. L. (2007). A question of belonging: race, social fit, and achievement. *J. Pers. Soc. Psychol.* 92:82. doi: 10.1037/0022-3514.92.1.82

Woolf, K., McManus, I. C., Potts, H. W. W., and Dacre, J. (2013). The mediators of minority ethnic underperformance in final medical school examinations. *Br. J. Educ. Psychol.* 83, 135–159. doi: 10.1111/j.2044-8279.2011.02060.x

Yeager, D. S., and Walton, G. M. (2011). Social-psychological interventions in education They're not magic. *Rev. Educ. Res.* 81, 267–301. doi: 10.3102/0034654311405999

Conflict of Interest Statement: The authors declare that the research was conducted in the absence of any commercial or financial relationships that could be construed as a potential conflict of interest.

9

First Steps into Language? Examining the Specific Longitudinal Relations between Walking, Exploration and Linguistic Skills

Ora Oudgenoeg-Paz, M(Chiel). J. M. Volman and Paul P. M. Leseman*

Department of Child, Family and Education Studies, Utrecht University, Utrecht, Netherlands

Recent empirical evidence demonstrates relationships between motor and language development that are partially mediated by exploration. This is in line with the embodied cognition approach to development that views language as grounded in real-life sensorimotor interactions with the environment. This view implies that the relations between motor and linguistic skills should be specific. Moreover, as motor development *initially* changes the possibilities children have to explore the environment, initial relations between motor and linguistic skills should become weaker over time. Empirical evidence pertaining to the duration and specificity of these relations is still lacking. The current study investigated longitudinal relations between attainment of walking and the development of several linguistic skills, and tested whether exploration through self-locomotion mediated these relations. Linguistic skills were measured at age 43 months, which is later than the age used in previous studies. Three hypotheses were tested: (1) the relations between walking and language found at younger ages will decrease over time (2) exploration through self-locomotion will remain an important predictor of spatial language (3) no relation will be found between walking, exploration and the use of grammatical and lexical categories and between exploration and general vocabulary. Thirty-one Dutch children took part in a longitudinal study. Parents reported about age of attainment of walking. Exploration through self-locomotion was measured using observations of play with a standard set of toys at age 20 months. Receptive vocabulary, spatial language and use of grammatical and lexical categories were measured at age 43 months using (standard) tests. Results reveal that age of walking does not directly predict spatial language at age 43 months. Exploration through self-locomotion does significantly and completely mediate the indirect effect of age of walking on spatial language. Moreover, neither age of walking nor exploration predict general vocabulary and the use of grammatical and lexical categories. Results support the idea that the initial relations between motor development and linguistic skills decrease over time and that these relations are specific and intrinsically dependent on the information children pick up through the execution of specific motor activities.

Keywords: motor milestones, independent walking, exploration, spatial language, language development, embodiment

Edited by:
Klaus Libertus,
University of Pittsburgh, USA

Reviewed by:
Sarah Berger,
College of Staten Island, USA
Jo Van Herwegen,
Kingston University, UK

****Correspondence:***
Ora Oudgenoeg-Paz
O.Oudgenoeg@uu.nl

Specialty section:
This article was submitted to Developmental Psychology, a section of the journal Frontiers in Psychology

INTRODUCTION

In recent years, an increasing number of theoretical and empirical papers have addressed the link between motor development and development in other domains. One of the central theoretical approaches stressing the role of movement and motor control in cognitive-linguistic development is the embodied cognition approach (e.g., Hockema and Smith, 2009; Iverson, 2010). According to this approach, cognitive skills (including linguistic skills) are softly assembled in real-time from elementary perception-action processes that are rooted in concrete real-life interactions (Thelen and Smith, 1994). Development of new motor skills, such as sitting, crawling and walking opens the door to new ways of interacting with the environment and fundamentally alters children's sensorimotor experiences by bringing new possibilities of exploring the environment (Gibson, 1988; Thelen and Smith, 1994; Soska and Adolph, 2014). The increased possibilities for exploring objects, relations between objects, and spatial layouts provide the cognitive basis for language learning. Therefore, the development of motor skills is expected to predict linguistic advances. The situated nature of cognitive skills (including linguistic skills) suggests highly specific relations between what is explored and the cognitive-linguistic skills that are grounded in these specific sensorimotor interactions. For example, exploring objects that can be stacked is expected to be related to the development of spatial concepts and related prepositions such as *'on'* and *'under,'* but not to the learning of food names or grammatical skills such as verb inflection. While in recent years increasing evidence is reported for a link between the development of motor skills and language development (e.g., Oudgenoeg-Paz et al., 2012; Walle and Campos, 2014; Libertus and Violi, 2016), evidence regarding the *specific* and *meaning-intrinsic* nature of these links, how they influence cognitive-linguistic development over longer periods of time and the role of exploration as a mediating process between motor skill development and cognitive-linguistic outcomes is still scarce. The current study focuses on the specific links between attainment of motor milestones and the development of several linguistic skills. By doing so we aim to study not only which linguistic skills are related to motor development, but also which skills are *not*. The linguistic skills examined in the current study include general and spatial vocabulary and the use of grammatical and lexical categories (e.g., determiners, subjects). In addition, the current study also examines the long-term associations between motor milestone attainment and cognitive-linguistic skills. Previous studies demonstrated mainly relations in the short term, but it is not clear how stable these relations are when examined longitudinally over longer periods of time. Finally, the current study examines the role of exploration behavior as a mediator of the relation between motor milestones attainment and linguistic skills.

In line with the embodied cognition approach, Hockema and Smith (2009) describe linguistic development as composed of recurrent outside-in processes (children perceive information from the environment) and inside-out processes (children act on the environment). For example, when learning semantic categories, children may draw on physical features of objects to categorize them (e.g., all round objects are balls), but children may also actively sort similar objects to the same spatial location, thus making it easier for them to perceive the similarities and construct a semantic category. This model of language learning is also in line with ecological psychology theory stressing the central role of recurrent perception-action processes in development. Children, on the one hand, perceive information to be processed, but on the other hand, they also act in their environment and thus change the information they can perceive (Gibson, 1979; Gibson and Pick, 2000). While the classical ecological approach does not mention cognition at all (Gibson, 1979), the embodied view of cognition as situated in the context of an agent interacting with the environment, is in full agreement with the notion of recurrent perception-action cycles in which increasingly complex affordances are detected and the skill to act upon these affordances is developed. This notion, that is central to the ecological approach, will here be referred to as exploration (Thelen and Smith, 1994; Gibson and Pick, 2000; Smith and Gasser, 2005). The knowledge about the world acquired through exploration forms the basis for the development of advanced cognitive (and linguistic) skills (Gibson and Pick, 2000; Smith and Gasser, 2005).

The attainment of motor milestones dramatically changes children's exploration possibilities and is therefore expected to contribute to further advances in their linguistic development. A major milestone in motor development is the attainment of independent walking. Exploration of the environment through self-locomotion enables children first of all to explore more complex spatial relations that require taking different positions in space or moving objects to different places in space. The exploration of these spatial relations is expected to relate to more complex spatial language (e.g., the prepositions 'behind,' 'between,' 'through'). Moreover, moving around initiates a shift from predominantly egocentric to allocentric view of spatial relations and therefore allows children to learn about different, dynamically changing perspectives of their environment. This shift has been related to advances in spatial cognition (Campos et al., 2000; Newcombe, 2002; Sheya and Smith, 2011). Thus, exploring objects while engaging in self-locomotion enables infants to experience the relationship between their own movement and changing position and the position and view of the object they are exploring (Thelen and Smith, 1994). In addition, walking enables children not only to carry objects from one location to another, but also to draw parents' attention to their exploratory behavior and to the objects they are engaged with. This implies that children that are able to walk independently are more likely to receive linguistic input pertaining to their current focus of attention (Clearfield, 2011; Karasik et al., 2011). Thus, attainment of independent walking is expected to facilitate language acquisition in general, and the acquisition of spatial language in particular, because walking specifically enables children to learn about spatial relationships. We further expect that the relation between the attainment of walking and acquisition of spatial language is mediated by children's exploration behavior as related to self-locomotion. Spatial language, as measured in the current study, includes locative prepositions (e.g., in, on) and verbs describing movement in a specific direction (e.g., push, climb; Landau and Jackendoff, 1993).

Empirical evidence provides support for a link between attainment of walking and advances in general vocabulary. A previous study with the same sample as in the current study has shown that attainment of independent walking predicted a quicker rate of growth in productive vocabulary between ages 16 and 28 months (Oudgenoeg-Paz et al., 2012). Two other studies have shown that the transition from crawling to walking predicted significant increases in both receptive and productive vocabularies in both the US and China (Walle and Campos, 2014; He et al., 2015). In addition, previous work with the current sample has shown that children who attained independent walking earlier than peers engaged more in exploration through self-locomotion at age 20 months. These children also showed better knowledge of spatial vocabulary at age 36 months. Exploration through self-locomotion at age 20 months, largely mediated this effect (Oudgenoeg-Paz et al., 2015).

Thus, previous work has found support for a link between attainment of walking and general and spatial vocabulary. Moreover, exploration through self-locomotion mediated the relation between walking attainment and spatial language at age 36 months. However, whether these early relations endure over longer time is not yet known. According to the embodied cognition approach the importance of motor development is that it facilitates exploration behavior. Therefore, when examined longitudinally, the initial relations between attainment of walking and linguistic skills are expected to decrease as variability in walking skill decreases as well and most children eventually learn to walk (in the current study all but one child before age 20 months). However, the initial individual differences in exploration behavior are expected to remain important for language development, because exploration provides the embodied conceptual basis for language learning. The mediating role of exploration found in previous work provides support for this hypothesis. As the studies regarding general vocabulary tested the relation between walking attainment and language development close to the onset of walking, it is not yet clear whether these relations also remain when language is measured at later ages. To test this hypothesis, the current study investigated the relation between attainment of walking and receptive general vocabulary and spatial vocabulary at age 43 months, that is at a later time and more distant from the actual attainment of independent walking compared to previous studies. Moreover, direct knowledge of the spatial vocabulary included in the current study (i.e., verbs and prepositions) only develops in the 3rd year of life (Pruden et al., 2004). Therefore knowledge of spatial vocabulary at age 43 months is expected to be more advanced and stable than at age 36 months (the age at which spatial vocabulary was measured in our previous study). To summarize, we hypothesize that the link between walking and general and spatial vocabulary seen at younger ages will be much smaller in magnitude and may even disappear when vocabulary is measured at age 43 months.

Previous studies did not examine the role of exploration through self-locomotion in general vocabulary development. We hypothesize that this kind of exploration is especially important for spatial vocabulary, as the kind of information this exploration provides is relevant for this linguistic domain. Therefore, we do not expect any relation between this kind of exploration and general vocabulary. In our previous work (Oudgenoeg-Paz et al., 2015) we have shown that exploration through self-locomotion mediated the relation between attainment of walking and spatial vocabulary. In the current study we expect to replicate this finding and show that while the initial direct effect of attainment of walking might be smaller (or even disappear completely), exploration through self-locomotion will still mediate the (indirect) relations between attainment of independent walking and spatial language at age 43 months.

If the hypotheses derived from the embodied cognition approach to development are taken too generally, they may imply that motor development is related (through exploration and other possible underlying mechanisms) to all areas of cognitive development. This might be taken by some to simply indicate a general maturation process or broad shifts in general developmental stages. However, the grounding of cognition in real-life experiences suggests that the developmental relationships between motor development, exploration and linguistic skills should be *specific* and intrinsically grounded in the information structures present in the environment and the actions these information structures afford (Thelen and Smith, 1994; Wilson, 2002). For example, exploration of nesting cups is expected to be related to the learning of concepts and words such as *'in,' 'out,' 'under,' 'on'* in addition to concepts and words related to colors and textures, but not to learning of concepts and words such as different tools used to work in the garden or grammatical knowledge about the use of determiners. Previous empirical work (e.g., Oudgenoeg-Paz et al., 2012; Walle and Campos, 2014) points to linguistic skills that are related to walking attainment, but fails to show which linguistic skills are *not* related to the attainment of walking. Therefore, in the current study, we attempted to distinguish between linguistic skills that are and are not related to motor development. By doing so, the study will contribute important evidence for the distinction between relations based on processes of general maturation and specific relations based on the nature of real-life experiences as suggested by the embodied cognition approach. More specifically, we hypothesize that attainment of independent walking and exploration through self-locomotion will *not* be related to the development of grammatical knowledge. We focus on the use of lexical and grammatical categories including the subject, determiner, auxiliaries and verbal prefix.

Empirical evidence suggests that the use of such lexical and grammatical categories is usually learned from linguistic input provided by the environment (Saffran, 2001). Types of input that seem to be of particular importance for the acquisition of these categories are infant directed speech (Shi et al., 1998), book reading (Naigles and Hoff-Ginsberg, 1998) and conversation eliciting questions in maternal speech (see Hoff, 2006 for a review). As previously discussed, attainment of walking and exploration through self-locomotion are likely to increase naming of objects by parents or prohibiting sentence (e.g., Gogate and Hollich, 2010; Karasik et al., 2011). However, we do not know of any study or theory linking independent walking and exploration through self-locomotion to linguistic input such as infant directed speech and book reading. Therefore, these types of linguistic input are not likely to be elicited by the attainment of walking and exploration through self-locomotion.

To summarize, in the current study three hypotheses were tested: (1) The relation between walking attainment and general and spatial vocabulary measured at age 43 months, will be weaker than the relations reported at earlier ages and may even completely disappear; (2) Exploration through self-locomotion is expected to mediate the (indirect) relation between attainment of walking and spatial language at age 43 months; (3) No relation is expected between attainment of independent walking and exploration through self-locomotion and the use of grammatical and lexical categories at age 43 months. Moreover, no relation is expected between exploration through self-locomotion and general vocabulary.

The current study included 31 Dutch children who took part in a longitudinal study. For the current analyses data were used from home visits at ages 20 and 43 months. Parental reports were obtained about the age of attainment of independent walking. Exploration through self-locomotion was measured using observations of children playing with a standard set of toys at age 20 months. This age was chosen as at this age (almost) all children are expected to be able to walk independently. Therefore, individual differences in exploration at this age do not merely reflect walking proficiency. In addition, in order to compare the magnitude of the relations with previous work, it is important to maintain the same age used in these studies (e.g., Walle and Campos, 2014; Oudgenoeg-Paz et al., 2015) for the predictors and only shift the outcome measures to a later age. Productive spatial language, receptive vocabulary, and command of grammatical and lexical categories were measured at age 43 months using (standard) tests.

MATERIALS AND METHODS

Participants

The sample is a subgroup of participants from a larger longitudinal study. The sample included 31 Dutch children (58% girls). Data of three additional children were excluded, as these children did not participate in the measurement wave at age 43 months. Participants were recruited through day-care centers in the municipality of Utrecht, The Netherlands, and surroundings and through an address list made available by the municipality. Most parents enjoyed medium to high educational and occupational levels. The children had no known developmental disabilities or delays at the time of recruitment. Informed consent was obtained from the parents for all of the children and the study was conducted in accordance with the ethical guidelines of Utrecht University. For the current study data were used from two measurement waves at the age of 20 months ($M = 20.75$, $SD = 0.61$) and at the age of 43 months ($M = 43.20$, $SD = 0.71$).

Procedure

Exploration behavior and linguistic skills were measured during home visits. Exploration through self-locomotion was measured at age 20 months. The children were filmed while allowed to explore a standard set of objects for 8 min. The set of objects included a hoop (70 cm diameter), a large foam dice (15 cm × 15 cm × 15 cm) and a play tunnel made of polyester (150 cm length and 45 cm diameter). See **Figure 1** for a photo of the objects used. The films of children's interaction with the objects were later edited to remove interruptions (such as stopping to drink). Exploration behavior was then scored based on the first 4 min of uninterrupted play. These 4 min started when the child first made contact with the objects. The duration of 4 min was selected based on pilot coding showing that this duration was both sufficient for most children to interact with all three objects and short enough to prevent children from getting bored and terminating their interaction with the objects. General vocabulary, spatial language and the use of grammatical and lexical categories were measured using playful (standard) tests administered by trained research assistants in a fixed order. The tests of grammatical and lexical categories were administered using a laptop computer. Parental reports were obtained regarding the age of attainment of independent walking. To thank the families for participation, the children were given a small gift at each measurement wave.

Measures

Age of Attaining Independent Walking

At the time of enrolment in the study (between ages 13 and 20 months for the current sample), parents were given the Parental Checklist of Developmental Milestones (Bodnarchuk and Eaton, 2004). Parents were asked to indicate for all milestones in the list at what age their child had attained this milestone. For milestones not yet attained, parents were asked to keep track of their child's development and note when these milestones were attained. A detailed description of each milestone was provided to help parents decide if their child had attained this milestone. For the current study, parental reports regarding age of independent walking were used. The description of this milestone given to the parents was: "The child is walking unsupported across the room; the child uses walking as the main means of moving around." Previous studies have shown that parents' reports using such descriptions are reliable (Bodnarchuk and Eaton, 2004; Berger et al., 2007; Adolph et al., 2011). When the milestone of independent walking was attained prior to enrolment in the study parents were asked to use the records kept by the Child and Infant Health Centre or their own records (such as diaries, blog entries, digital photos, or email communication) to determine the age of onset of independent walking. If parents had no such records, data were considered missing. This was the case for one child in the current sample.

Exploration

Children's exploration behavior was scored by trained observers based on the films of the first 4 min of exploration with the set of objects shown in **Figure 1**. The 4-min recordings were each divided in 24 intervals of 10 s each. Per interval, all the activities of

FIGURE 1 | Objects used in the observations.

the child and the duration of each activity in seconds were noted. In the current study we were interested in spatial exploration and specifically in exploration through self-locomotion. Therefore, the initial detailed scoring at the level of separate explorative activities (such as banging, carrying, and looking) was aggregated and activities were scored as either stationary (i.e., the child was exploring the objects from a stationary position), or engaged in self-locomotion (i.e., the child was changing location by self-movement, such as crawling or walking while exploring the objects). During the 4-min recordings, most children (over 86%) interacted with the objects for more than 96% of the time. The remaining four children interacted with the objects for a minimum of 20 intervals (i.e., 83% of the time), but most of these children interacted with the objects for longer periods. Thus, the coding represents children's posture while exploring the objects.

Examples of exploratory actions observed with the objects while in stationary position are: standing and banging on the tunnel, standing in the hoop, sitting in the tunnel, holding the dice and looking at it, holding and manipulating the dice in sitting position, sitting next to the hoop or dice and lifting it. Examples of exploratory actions observed with the objects while engaged in self-locomotion are: crawling through the tunnel with or without the dice, jumping in and out of the hoop, throwing or rolling the dice and running or crawling after it, walking while dragging the hoop or the tunnel, walking around the tunnel while looking at it, lifting the dice and transferring it toward the hoop and putting it into the hoop.

The objects used were all novel for the children and presented various action possibilities to learn about spatial relations. Therefore, all the actions children performed with the objects could be considered as exploration (Weisler and McCall, 1976; Schuetze et al., 1999; see for example also measurement of exploration used by Needham et al., 2002; Lobo and Galloway, 2013). It should be noted that in the current stud we are not referring to locomotor exploration in the sense of navigation and exploring the space, but rather to exploration of the three objects in a way that requires self-locomotion for exploring the spatial affordances of the objects (either separately or as a combination of objects) or for moving from one object to another (see also Cole et al., 2015). For example, when the infant attempts to crawl through the tunnel he or she explores the spatial affordance of 'moving- through-a-tube' and learns, among other things, about the size relations between aperture of the tunnel and the body and about the spatial relations of *in* the tunnel and *out* of the tunnel. The exploration of these spatial relations is only possible while engaging in self-locomotion. Similarly, when the infant picks the dice, walks with it and transfers it into the hoop it learns about moving objects in space and changing the spatial location of the dice (i.e., the dice can be lifted, carried and transferred to a different location) and it learns about the size relations enabling the hoop to contain the dice and about the relation of *in* and *out* of the hoop. Again, the learning of these complex affordances requires self-locomotion.

A total score was given to each interval based on the longest enduring activity. If both stationary (scored as 0) and engaged in self-locomotion (scored as 1) were present equally long within an interval, a score of 1 was given to the whole interval. Intervals that could not be scored for technical reasons (e.g., child's actions were not visible), were given a missing score. About 9% (three children) of the recordings had more than 50% of the intervals missing and were therefore excluded from the analyses. An additional 48% had less than 50% missing intervals and the majority of these recordings (14 out of the 15 children) had less than 25% missing intervals. Two coders independently scored about 22.6% of the films. The mean Cohen's kappa was 0.81 ($SD = 0.08$) and all kappa values were above 0.70. These values are considered satisfactory (Landis and Koch, 1977).

The total score on exploration through self-locomotion was the proportion of the intervals in which children explored the objects while engaging in self-locomotion at least as much as exploring from a stationary position. This score was preferred to a score based on the total time of self-locomotion, in order to control for the missing intervals.

Spatial Language

Productive knowledge of locative prepositions and verbs containing a direction was measured using two playful tasks. Knowledge of propositions was measured using a hand puppet of Ernie from the TV program Sesame Street and a set of small toys. The toys included furniture for a dollhouse and small objects that fit in and around the furniture. The experimenter and the child used the furniture and objects to build a house for Ernie, according to a photo showing where everything should be located in Ernie's house. The objects were placed so that they represented the entire range of spatial prepositions (e.g., *in* the closet, *between* two chairs). Following this, the child had to explain to Ernie where to find the different objects in the house, by using spatial prepositions to indicate the location of the objects. To prevent the children from pointing to the location, they were asked to talk to Ernie via a toy telephone. The task began with two practice items. During these items the experimenter reminded the children that Ernie cannot see them and that the instruction has to be given in words. When needed, the experimenter modeled the right answer. Children were then encouraged to repeat the right answer. Following the practice items, 10 test items were administered. Each item elicited a different locative preposition. If the child did not answer a question posed by Ernie, the experimenter repeated the question. If the child still did not answer, the experimenter pointed to the location of the object on the photo used to build the house and said: "look there is the [name of object], can you tell Ernie where the [name of object] is?" If the child still did not answer the experimenter provided the right answer. After an answer was given (either correct or wrong, by either the child or the experimenter), Ernie 'found' the object and thanked the child. Children were always given positive feedback for providing an answer, regardless if it was right or wrong.

Productive knowledge of spatial verbs was measured using small dolls of Dora and Boots from the cartoon film 'Dora the Explorer' and two large (A3) pictures. The pictures each depicted a trail leading to either a beach or a treasure chest. Along the trail different locations and objects were drawn. Dora and Boots were moved by the experimenter along the trail and stopped at each location. Whenever Dora and boots stopped the child was asked what they should do at that location. The answer always included a spatial verb. For example, when reaching a slide, Dora says she wants to go down the slide and asks the child how can she get up the slide. The answer should then include the word *climb*. Also in this test if children did not answer the question, the question was repeated. If the child still did not answer, the experimenter prompted the child by saying for example "how can Dora get up the slide? She has to..." If the child still did not answer, the experimenter provided the correct answer. Children were always given positive feedback for every answer they provided either right or wrong. After an answer was given (either correct or wrong, by either the child or the experimenter) Dora and Boots went on to do the activity and then proceeded on the trail. Each child completed the trails on both pictures. The task included 19 test items representing 19 spatial verbs.

The total score on each task (prepositions and verbs) was the number of words produced correctly. Scores on both tasks correlated strongly ($r = 0.70$, $p < 0.001$). A total score was computed by calculating the mean of the scores on the two tasks after Z-transformations were applied. Scores on these tasks correlated moderately ($r = 0.39$, $p = 0.04$ and $r = 0.38$, $p = 0.07$) with scores on a different task measuring receptive and productive knowledge of locative propositions and spatial verbs used at age 36 months (for a description of this task, see Oudgenoeg-Paz et al., 2015).

General Receptive Vocabulary

Receptive vocabulary was measured using the Dutch translation of the normed Peabody Picture Vocabulary Test-III (PPVT-III Dunn and Dunn, 2005). In this test the children are shown sets of four pictures each and are asked to point to the picture representing the word said by the experimenter. Each set contains 12 words. Difficulty level of the test varies with age and standard starting and stopping rules are applied. At age 43 months children always start on the third set and testing is stopped when children make nine or more errors within a specific set. Reliability and validity of this test are reported to be good (Dunn and Dunn, 2005).

Use of Grammatical and Lexical Categories

The use of grammatical and lexical categories was measured using a sentence repetition task developed by Wilsenach (2006). This task is an elicited imitation task following the rationale that in order for children to repeat a sentence containing a specific structure, this structure should be part of the child's grammatical skill. The children saw a robot on a laptop screen. The robot said a sentence and the children were then asked to repeat what the robot said. The test included three training items and 12 test items. During the training phase the children were asked to repeat the training sentences. In this phase the experimenter helped the children if needed by modeling the right answer and coaching them in order to avoid use of strategies such as only repeating the last word. The training items could be repeated as often as needed in order for the children to learn the task. In the test phase no coaching was provided. If, during the test phase, a child did not respond or repeated only one word, the stimulus from the robot was repeated once more. If the child repeated only one word also the second time, this was noted as the answer. If the child provided a response (correct or incorrect) a reward was visible. Rewards were various visual effects that appeal to young children, such as balloons flying across the screen. If the child did not provide a response, the next item was presented directly without first presenting the reward.

We used 12 of the 18 sentences included in the original task. In order to adjust the level of difficulty for the current age group we left out the sentences with distransitive verbs used in the original task. The experimenter noted which words were correctly repeated and which were omitted or incorrectly repeated. Scoring included the number of determiners correctly repeated (range 0–23) and the number of subjects, auxiliaries and verbal prefixes correctly repeated (all with a range of 0–12). A Total score was calculated by computing the mean of the scores on all scales after Z-transformations were applied. Wilsenach (2006) has shown that this task has good reliability. Items in the test with the current sample also showed good reliability with Crobnach's alpha of 0.99.

Statistical Analysis

All three research questions were analyzed using hierarchical regression models, following the steps defined by Baron and Kenny (1986) for testing mediation. First the main effects representing the relation between age of walking attainment and the three dependent variables (i.e., spatial language, general vocabulary and use of grammatical and lexical categories) were tested. Next, the relation between age of walking attainment and the mediator, exploration through self-locomotion, was tested. Third, the mediator was added to the hierarchical regression models. In models where the mediator significantly predicted the dependent variable, the Sobel-Goodman test was applied to test the significance of the mediation. Given the relatively small sample size, bootstrapping was applied in order to obtain more robust parameter estimates.

RESULTS

Descriptive Analysis

In **Table 1** the means and standard deviations of all model variables and their indicators are presented. The variables measuring age of walking and spatial language had each missing data from one child. Exploration through self-locomotion and Lexical and grammatical categories had data missing from three children each. Missing data were estimated, where possible, using single regression-based imputation (Schafer and Graham, 2002; Rubin et al., 2007). This method was chosen, rather than the standard listwise deletion, as it has been shown to be an appropriate method for small samples with a low percentage of missing. Moreover, imputing missing data is important with small samples, in order to prevent reduction in power of the analysis (Rubin et al., 2007). The final analyses were conducted with data of 30 children.

TABLE 1 | Descriptive statistics of model variables and indicators.

Variable	*N* before imputation	(imputed) *N*	*M*	*SD*
Age of independent walking	30	31	15.24	2.34
Exploration through self-locomotion 20 months	28	30	0.46	0.19
Total score productive spatial language 43 months[a]	30	31	−0.08	0.94
Spatial verbs productive 43 months	–	30	10.63	3.34
Spatial prepositions productive 43 months	–	28	5.83	2.14
Receptive vocabulary 43 months[b]	31	31	56.32	10.05
Total score grammatical and lexical categories 43 months[a]	28	31	0.09	0.94
Determiner omission 43 months	–	28	16.57	5.09
Subject omission 43 months	–	28	9.04	2.70
Auxiliary omission 43 months	–	28	9.89	2.62
Verbal prefix omission 43 months	–	28	11.00	1.19

Missing values were imputed at the level of total scores, therefore the total scores presented are after imputation but the raw scores still contain all missing values. [a]*This score is a mean of Z scores* [b]*Raw scores of the PPVT-III were used in the analysis.*

TABLE 2 | Correlations between all model variables ($N = 30$).

	1	2	3	4
(1) Age of independent walking				
(2) Exploration through self-locomotion	−0.46*			
(3) Total score productive spatial language	−0.06	0.42*		
(4) Receptive vocabulary	0.12	0.20	0.71***	
(5) Total score grammatical and lexical categories	−0.04	0.14	0.26	0.34†

†$p \leq 0.10$, *$p \leq 0.05$, ***$p \leq 0.001$.

As can be seen from **Table 1** the variable measuring the use of the verbal prefix in the sentence repetition task showed a ceiling effect as the maximum score on this variable was 12. Therefore, this variable was not used in the total score of grammatical and lexical categories. In addition, it should be noted that at age 20 months (the age at which exploration was measured) all children, but one, could already walk for at least 2 months. The child, who could not walk at age 20 months, was able to walk on her knees. **Table 2** presents the correlations between all the variables included in the analyses. **Table 2** shows that the two vocabulary measures (spatial vocabulary and general vocabulary) correlate strongly as can be expected. In addition, the total score of grammatical and lexical categories correlates moderately (though only marginally significant) with the score on general vocabulary, as can be expected. Finally, the indicators of the total score of spatial language correlated strongly with each other ($r = 0.70$, $p < 0.001$). The same was true for the indicators of the total score of grammatical and lexical categories (r ranges from 0.74 to 0.87, $p < 0.001$).

Factors Predicting Spatial Language

To test whether age of walking predicted spatial language at age 43 months and whether exploration through self-locomotion mediates this effect, a hierarchical regression analysis was conducted. The results are presented in **Table 3**. First, the age of walking was entered as a predictor of spatial language. As can be seen from **Table 3**, age of walking was not a significant predictor of spatial language. Next, the relation between age of walking and the mediator exploration through self-locomotion was examined. As can be seen from their correlation in **Table 2**, age of walking was a significant predictor of exploration through self-locomotion at age 20 months. The negative correlation coefficient indicates that an earlier age of walking predicts a higher level of exploration through self-locomotion at age 20 months. Finally, the mediator exploration through self-locomotion was added to the model (model 2 in the top panel of **Table 3**). The results show that this addition leads to a significant improvement of the model and exploration through self-locomotion significantly and positively predicts spatial language at age 43 months. This effect is medium sized. According to Kenny et al. (1998), there can be complete mediation even if the main effect (in this case the relation between age of walking and spatial language) is not significant. This is because the predictor and independent variable might be too far away in time. To test if this mediation is indeed significant the Sobel-Goodman test was performed. Results revealed that, in line with the hypothesis, exploration through self-locomotion indeed completely and significantly

TABLE 3 | Results of hierarchical regression analyses for factors predicting spatial vocabulary, receptive general vocabulary and grammatical and lexical categories ($N = 30$ for all analyses).

	Model 1			Model 2			
Predictors	***B (SE)***	**β**	***R*²**	***B (SE)***	**β**	***R*²**	**Δ*R*²**
Factors predicting spatial vocabulary							
Age of independent walking	−0.02 (0.08)	−0.06	0.004	0.07 (0.08)	0.17	0.20*	0.19*
Exploration through self-locomotion				2.47 (0.97)	0.49*		
Factors predicting receptive general vocabulary							
Age of independent walking	0.52 (0.81)	0.12	0.12	1.15 (0.89)	0.27	0.10	0.08
Exploration through self-locomotion				17.20 (10.94)	0.32		
Factors predicting lexical and grammatical categories							
Age of independent walking	−0.02 (0.06)	−0.04	0.002	0.01 (0.09)	0.03	0.02	0.02
Exploration through self-locomotion				0.74 (1.06)	0.15		

*$p \leq 0.05$.

mediated the effect of age of walking on spatial language ($Z = -2.25, p = 0.03$).

Factors Predicting General Vocabulary and Use of Grammatical and Lexical Categories

To test whether age of walking attainment predicted general vocabulary and grammatical and lexical categories and whether exploration through self-locomotion mediated these effects the same steps were followed as in the previous analysis. Two hierarchical regression analyses were conducted and the results are presented in the bottom part of **Table 3**. From **Table 3** it can be seen that age of walking did not significantly predict general vocabulary or the use of grammatical and lexical categories. Moreover, addition of exploration through self-locomotion to the model did not significantly increase the amount of explained variance as exploration did not significantly predict either outcome variable. Thus, in line with the hypotheses, the present study did not find evidence that age of walking attainment predicts general vocabulary or the use of grammatical and lexical categories. Moreover, also in line with the hypotheses, there was no evidence found that exploration through self-locomotion mediates the relation between walking attainment and these outcome variables.

DISCUSSION

The current study sought to examine whether previously reported relations between age of walking and general and spatial vocabulary are still evident when linguistic skills are measured at age 43 months. In addition, the study aimed to test whether the relations between age of walking and exploration through self-locomotion are specific for certain linguistic skills and not for others. To do so we studied whether age of walking predicts spatial vocabulary, general receptive vocabulary and use of grammatical and lexical categories at age 43 months and whether exploration through self-locomotion, observed at age 20 months, mediates these relations. The results show that the previously reported relations between age of walking and general and spatial vocabulary indeed disappear when linguistic skills are measured at age 43 months. In addition, we have replicated our previous finding (Oudgenoeg-Paz et al., 2015) showing that exploration through self-locomotion mediates the relation between age of walking and spatial vocabulary. However, unlike our previous work, in the current study the direct relation between age of walking and spatial language was no longer significant. Finally, we found no significant relation between age of walking attainment and exploration through self-locomotion and neither general vocabulary nor the use of grammatical and lexical categories. All these findings are in agreement with our hypotheses.

Long Term Effects of Attainment of Walking

Previous work with the current sample (Oudgenoeg-Paz et al., 2012) and work done by others (Walle and Campos, 2014; He et al., 2015) have shown that, early in life, attainment of walking is related to *general* receptive and productive vocabulary development. However, these studies measured language development relatively close to the age of attainment of walking. The current study extends this literature by showing that when vocabulary is measured later in life (at age 43 months) the initial relation found between walking attainment and vocabulary disappears. Similarly we also show that the relation between age of walking and *spatial* vocabulary previously found with this sample at age 36 months (Oudgenoeg-Paz et al., 2015) is no longer present when spatial language is measured at age 43 months. Other studies have shown that at school age there is only a link between motor skills and linguistic skills such as reading and writing in the case of significant motor delays (e.g., Viholainen et al., 2006). Taken together, these results suggest that over longer periods of time the effects of the age of attainment of motor milestones become smaller as most children eventually learn to walk. We do not think, however, that these findings mean that attainment of walking is not important for linguistic skills. At the short term it is clear that attainment of walking propels language development, as is shown by several studies. The decrease in the size of the effect over time is an example of a cascading effect on development. We return to this issue later in this discussion.

Unlike the relation between walking and linguistic skills, we were able to replicate our previous finding regarding the link between exploration through self-locomotion and spatial vocabulary. Exploration through self-locomotion is still significantly related to spatial vocabulary also when it is measured at age 43 months. Moreover, exploration through self-locomotion is also still related to the attainment of walking and thus mediates the initial effect of walking attainment on spatial vocabulary. Our current findings therefore provide additional empirical support for the role of exploration behavior as a mechanism underlying the relation between walking attainment and spatial language. This finding is similar to another study, where infant object exploration, measured using retrospective parental reports, but not the age of attaining motor milestones related to self-locomotion, predicted spatial memory at school age (Oudgenoeg-Paz et al., 2014). These findings suggest that attainment of walking sets in motion a series of processes that in turn contribute to language development. In this case, attainment of walking allows children to explore their environment in new ways and to extend the embodied knowledge basis that underlies language acquisition. Children that walk independently are able to move around and therefore to change their own location and perspective. They are also able to change the spatial arrangement of the environment. These enhanced exploration possibilities are especially related to walking, rather than to other forms of self-locomotion such as crawling, as the visual information acquired through walking is fundamentally different than the information acquired through crawling (Kretch et al., 2012). Exploration through walking enables children's learning about spatial concepts and eventually facilitates advances in spatial language, as shown in the current study.

Taken together, the results support the idea of a developmental cascade. Attainment of walking is important initially, as it facilitates ways of interacting with the environment which are important for linguistic development. The mechanisms through which walking propels the development of general vocabulary have not been studied in the current study. Possible underlying mechanisms discussed in the literature are an increase in gestures following the attainment of walking (for a review see Iverson, 2010) and changes in social interaction patterns which bring along changes in linguistic input (Gogate and Hollich, 2010; Clearfield, 2011; Karasik et al., 2011; Walle and Campos, 2014). Whatever the mechanisms are, the current study suggests that in the longer term, the initial relation between walking and linguistic skills diminishes and it is these underlying mechanisms that remain the important predictors of linguistic skills.

Specific Relations

According to the embodied view of development, the relations between motor skills, exploration and linguistic skills are specific as linguistic skills are grounded in specific sensorimotor interactions with the environment providing specific information. Our findings support this idea. We have shown that attainment of independent walking and exploration through self-locomotion are not related to all areas of linguistic development. Rather, their relation with spatial language (and the relation between walking and general vocabulary found at younger ages) is specific. Information obtained through exploration through self-locomotion, such as information about spatial relations in the larger space, is highly relevant for spatial language, but not for other domains of language.

Traditional approaches to cognitive development view relations between developmental domains as reflecting general maturation or some 'general developmental factor.' This general factor would explain why some children develop quicker than others. Some suggest that this domain general mechanism might involve maturational processes, processing speed, cognitive processes such as statistical learning, executive functions or environmental factors (for a review, see Rhemtulla and Tucker-Drob, 2011). Should such domain general mechanism underlie the relations found in the current study, one would expect a relation between the predictors (age of walking and exploration through self-locomotion) and all linguistic skills measured. However, the results seem to favor a situated model of cognition, as presented by the embodied-cognition approach. In this model, language (and any other cognition) is softly assembled in real-time from concrete real-life sensorimotor experiences (Thelen and Smith, 1994; Hockema and Smith, 2009). Therefore, relations between developmental domains are highly specific and intrinsically related to the specific types of information acquired through interaction with the environment.

An additional alternative explanation might be found in cross-sectional relations between motor and exploration skills and linguistic skills at age 43 months. Some studies indeed report such relations (e.g., Hill, 2001; Alcock and Krawczyk, 2010). The argument might be made that early motor and exploration skills predict current motor and exploration skills and these current skills, in turn, are related to current linguistic skills. In the present study no concurrent measures of exploration and motor skills were included. However, a cross-sectional relation between motor and exploration skills does not preclude a longitudinal relation nor contradicts the idea of a developmental cascade. Moreover, the decrease in the strength of relations between walking and linguistic skills implies that the experiences facilitated by the attainment of walking early in life, are the ones that, in turn, facilitate linguistic development.

Strengths and Limitations

The main limitation of the current study is the small sample size. However, based on previous work (e.g., Oudgenoeg-Paz et al., 2012; Walle and Campos, 2014) we expected to find medium to large effects. The current sample had sufficient power to detect such effects (Kelley and Maxwell, 2003; Tabachnik and Fidell, 2007). Moreover, the use of bootstrapping enabled us to obtain robust estimates despite the small sample size. A second limitation is the measurement of exploration behavior. While this is a good measure of the amount of self-locomotion in general, it does not differentiate between different types of self-locomotion such as crawling and walking. Given recent evidence suggesting that the type of visual information obtained from crawling is essentially different from that obtained through walking (Kretch et al., 2012), it would be interesting to code exploration through self-locomotion also in terms of type of self-locomotion in future studies. The question might also arise whether this measure is not confounded with attainment of walking. It is reasonable to assume that children who attained walking can engage more in exploration through self-locomotion (although crawling children can, of course, also engage in such exploration). However, we measured exploration at the age of 20 months, when all children, but one, were already walking for at least 2 months. Thus, while all children could engage in exploration through self-locomotion, children who attained walking at an earlier age more often chose to explore the objects while engaged in self-locomotion. Furthermore, the correlation between walking attainment and exploration through self-locomotion is medium sized, suggesting that while early walkers do engage more in exploration through self-locomotion at 20 months, other factors also play a role in determining the level of exploration at this age. This measure of exploration also forms a strength of the current study by being relatively context free. That is, while children's exploration was influenced by the specific context of the objects used, the coding is at the level of position and can therefore be also applied to other contexts using different objects. This will enable future studies to examine if the relations reported in the current study are also found in different contexts. An additional strength of the current study is the fact that the measurements were conducted at the children's home. While this offered less opportunity for standardization of the measures, it contributes to the ecological validity of this study, as compared to other work done in a lab setting. Finally, the use of multiple methods (parental reports, tests and observations) and the longitudinal design enabled us to study development over multiple domains and test hypotheses pertaining to developmental relations over time.

Future Directions

Future studies should further explore the specific and intrinsic relations between motor skills, exploration and language development. For example, studies could examine the different aspects of spatial language separately, rather than as a single one-dimensional skill as was done in the current study. An interesting question if whether the same pattern of results is found when verbs and prepositions are studied separately and if the same pattern of results will be found for all spatial words if these are considered individually. Similarly, a more detailed analysis of the general vocabulary data could also be interesting. In the current study, and in most studies in the field, general vocabulary is treated as a single one-dimensional skill. However, if the words in a test such as the PPVT are divided in subgroups representing for example verbs, nouns, prepositions and so forth, hypotheses regarding specific relations between certain linguistic categories and certain motor skills and forms of exploration could be tested. Another interesting direction is the study of the early predictors of grammatical development. Some work suggests that grammatical categories are learned early on through several types of language input such as book reading or asking questions that prompt conversations (Naigles and Hoff-Ginsberg, 1998; Hoff, 2006). The input is, however, not completely independent of the child. Children elicit certain kinds of input through their own actions on the environment (for a discussion of this idea, see Gogate and Hollich, 2010). Therefore future studies should seek for the aspects in children's interaction with the environment that are likely to elicit input that is relevant for the learning of certain grammatical forms.

CONCLUSION

The findings of the current study provide support to several hypotheses derived from an embodied view of development. First, we show that relations between attainment of walking and spatial and general vocabulary that are found at young ages decrease and even disappear with time. We also replicate previous findings showing that exploration through self-locomotion remains an important mediator of the relation between age of walking attainment and spatial language. Thus, results support the idea of cascading effects. While initial differences in motor skills are important for linguistic development early in life, over time individual differences in exploration behavior (which themselves are predicted by differences in the age of walking attainment) seem to be the important predictor of spatial language. Second, the results reveal that the relations between age of independent walking, exploration through self-locomotion and the linguistic skills included in the current study are specific as they were found to be limited to spatial language. This pattern of specific relations supports the embodied-cognition idea of situated language learning in which multiple real-life interactions with the environment provide the semantic basis for learning language.

AUTHOR CONTRIBUTIONS

OO-P took the leading role in conception and design and acquisition of the data. She also fulfilled the leading role in analysis and interpretation of the data. She also took the leading role in drafting and revising the article. MV participated in conception and design of the data and had a large role in analysis and interpretation of the data. He also took part in drafting and revising the article. PL participated in conception and design of the data and had a large role in analysis and interpretation of the data. He also took part in drafting and revising the article.

ACKNOWLEDGMENTS

Work on this article was supported by a grant from The Netherlands Organisation for Scientific Research (NWO).

REFERENCES

Adolph, K. E., Berger, S. E., and Leo, A. J. (2011). Developmental continuity? Crawling, cruising, and walking. *Dev. Sci.* 14, 306–318. doi: 10.1111/j.1467-7687.2010.00981.x

Alcock, K. J., and Krawczyk, K. (2010). Individual differences in language development: relationship with motor skill at 21 months. *Dev. Sci* 13, 677–691. doi: 10.1111/j.1467-7687.2009.00924.x

Baron, R. M., and Kenny, D. A. (1986). The moderator–mediator variable distinction in social psychological research: conceptual, strategic, and statistical considerations. *J. Pers. Soc. Psychol.* 51, 1173–1182. doi: 10.1037/0022-3514.51.6.1173

Berger, S. E., Theuring, C., and Adolph, K. E. (2007). How and when infants learn to climb stairs. *Infant Behav. Dev.* 30, 36–49. doi: 10.1016/j.infbeh.2006.11.002

Bodnarchuk, J. L., and Eaton, W. O. (2004). Can parent reports be trusted?: validity of daily checklists of gross motor milestone attainment. *J. Appl. Dev. Psychol.* 25, 481–490. doi: 10.1016/j.appdev.2004.06.005

Campos, J. J., Anderson, D. I., Barbu-Roth, M. A., Hubbard, E. M., Hertenstein, M. J., and Witherington, D. (2000). Travel broadens the mind. *Infancy* 1, 149–219. doi: 10.1207/S15327078IN0102_1

Clearfield, M. W. (2011). Learning to walk changes infants' social interactions. *Infant Behav. Dev.* 34, 15–25. doi: 10.1016/j.infbeh.2010.04.008

Cole, W. G., Robinson, S. R., and Adolph, K. E. (2015). Bouts of steps: the organization of infant exploration. *Dev. Psychobiol.* 58, 341–354. doi: 10.1002/dev.21374

Dunn, L. M., and Dunn, L. M. (2005). *Peabody Picture Vocabulary Test-III-NL Handleiding (L. Schlichting Trans.).* Amsterdam: Harcourt.

Gibson, E. J. (1988). Exploratory behavior in the development of perceiving, acting and the acquiring of knowledge. *Annu. Rev. Psychol.* 39, 1–42. doi: 10.1146/annurev.ps.39.020188.000245

Gibson, E. J., and Pick, A. D. (2000). *An Ecological Approach to Perceptual Learning and Development.* New York, NY: Oxford University Press.

Gibson, J. J. (1979). *The Ecological Approach to Visual Perception.* Hillsdale, NJ: Lawrence Erlbaum.

Gogate, L. J., and Hollich, G. (2010). Invariance detection within an interactive system: a perceptual gateway to language development. *Psychol. Rev.* 117, 496–516. doi: 10.1037/a0019049

He, M., Walle, E. A., and Campos, J. J. (2015). A cross-national investigation of the relationship between infant walking and language development. *Infancy* 20, 283–305. doi: 10.1111/infa.12071

Hill, E. L. (2001). Non-specific nature of specific language impairment: a review of the literature with regard to concomitant motor impairments. *Int. J. Lang. Commun. Disord.* 36, 149–171. doi: 10.1080/13682820010019874

Hockema, S. A., and Smith, L. B. (2009). Learning your language, outside-in and inside-out. *Linguistics* 47, 453–479. doi: 10.1515/LING.2009.016

Hoff, E. (2006). How social contexts support and shape language development. *Dev. Rev.* 26, 55–88. doi: 10.1016/j.dr.2005.11.002

Iverson, J. M. (2010). Developing language in a developing body: the relationship between motor development and language development. *J. Child Lang.* 37, 229–261. doi: 10.1017/S0305000909990432

Karasik, L. B., Tamis-Lemonda, C. S., and Adolph, K. E. (2011). Transition from crawling to walking and infant's actions with objects and people. *Child Dev.* 82, 1199–1209. doi: 10.1111/j.1467-8624.2011.01595.x

Kelley, K., and Maxwell, S. E. (2003). Sample size for multiple regression: obtaining regression that are accurate, not simply significant. *Psychol. Methods* 8, 305–321. doi: 10.1037/1082-989X.8.3.305

Kenny, D. A., Kashy, D., and Bolger, N. (1998). "Data analysis in social psychology," in *Handbook of Social Psychology*, 4th Edn, eds D. Gilbert, S. Fiske, and G. Lindzey (New York, NY: McGraw-Hill), 233–265.

Kretch, K. S., Franchak, J. M., Brothers, J., and Adolph, K. E. (2012). What infants see depends on locomotor posture. *J. Vis.* 12, 182–182. doi: 10.1167/12.9.182

Landau, B., and Jackendoff, R. (1993). "What" and "where" in spatial language and spatial cognition. *Behav. Brain Sci.* 16, 217–238. doi: 10.1017/S0140525X00029733

Landis, J. R., and Koch, G. G. (1977). The measurement of observer agreement for categorical data. *Biometrics* 33, 159–174. doi: 10.2307/2529310

Libertus, K., and Violi, D. A. (2016). Sit to talk: relation between motor skills and language development in infancy. *Front. Psychol.* 7:475. doi: 10.3389/fpsyg.2016.00475

Lobo, M. A., and Galloway, J. C. (2013). The onset of reaching significantly impacts how infants explore both objects and their bodies. *Infant Behav. Dev.* 36, 14–24. doi: 10.1016/j.infbeh.2012.09.003

Naigles, L. R., and Hoff-Ginsberg, E. (1998). Why are some verbs learned before other verbs? effects of input frequency and structure on children's early verb use. *J. Child Lang.* 25, 95–120. doi: 10.1017/S0305000997003358

Needham, A., Barrett, T., and Peterman, K. (2002). A pick-me-up for infants' exploratory skills: early stimulated experiences reaching for objects using 'sticky mittens' enhances young infrants' object exploration skills. *Infant Behav. Dev.* 25, 279–295. doi: 10.1016/S0163-6383(02)00097-8

Newcombe, N. S. (2002). "Spatial cognition," in *Cognition Volume, Stevens' Handbook of Experimental Psychology*, 3rd Edn, ed. D. Medin (New York, NY: Wiley), 113–163.

Oudgenoeg-Paz, O., Leseman, P. P. M., and Volman, M. J. M. (2014). Can infant self-locomotion and spatial exploration predict spatial memory at school age? *Eur. J. Dev. Psychol.* 11, 36–48. doi: 10.1080/17405629.2013.803470

Oudgenoeg-Paz, O., Leseman, P. P. M., and Volman, M. J. M. (2015). Exploration as a mediator of the relation between the attainment of motor milestones and the development of spatial cognition and language. *Dev. Psychol.* 51, 1241–1253. doi: 10.1037/a0039572

Oudgenoeg-Paz, O., Volman, M. J. M., and Leseman, P. P. M. (2012). Attainment of sitting and walking predicts development of productive vocabulary between ages 16 and 28 months. *Infant Behav. Dev.* 35, 733–736. doi: 10.1016/j.infbeh.2012.07.010

Pruden, S. M., Hirsh-Pasek, K., Maguire, M. J., and Meyer, M. A. (2004). "Foundations of verb learning: Infants form categories of path and manner in motion events," in *Proceedings of the 28th Annual Boston University Conference on Language Development*, (Somerville, MA: Cascadilla press), 461–472.

Rhemtulla, M., and Tucker-Drob, E. M. (2011). Correlated longitudinal changes across linguistic, achievement, and psychomotor domains in early childhood: evidence for a global dimension of development. *Dev. Sci.* 14, 1245–1254. doi: 10.1111/j.1467-7687.2011.01071.x

Rubin, L. H., Witkiewitz, K., St. Andre, J., and Reilly, S. (2007). Methods for handling missing data in the behavioral neurosciences: don't throw the baby rat out with the bath water. *J. Undergrad. Neurosci. Educ.* 5, A71–A77.

Saffran, J. R. (2001). The use of predictive dependencies in language learning. *J. Mem. Lang.* 44, 493–515. doi: 10.1006/jmla.2000.2759

Schafer, J. L., and Graham, J. W. (2002). Missing data: our view of the state of the art. *Psychol. Methods* 7, 147–177. doi: 10.1037//1082-989X.7.2.147

Schuetze, P., Lewis, A., and DiMartino, D. (1999). Relation between time spent in daycare and exploratory behaviors in 9-month-old infants. *Infant Behav. Dev.* 22, 267–276. doi: 10.1016/S0163-6383(99)00006-5

Sheya, A., and Smith, L. B. (2011). "Development through sensorimotor coordination," in *Enaction: Toward a New Paradigm for Cognitive Science*, eds J. Stewart, O. Gapenne, and E. A. Di Paolo (Cambridge, MA: MIT Press), 123–144.

Shi, R., Morgan, J. L., and Allopenna, P. (1998). Phonological and acoustic bases for earliest grammatical category assignment: a cross-linguistic perspective. *J. Child Lang.* 25, 169–201. doi: 10.1017/S0305000997003395

Smith, L. B., and Gasser, M. (2005). The development of embodied cognition: six lessons from babies. *Artif. Life* 11, 13–29. doi: 10.1162/1064546053278973

Soska, K. C., and Adolph, K. E. (2014). Postural position constrains multimodal object exploration in infants. *Infancy* 19, 138–161. doi: 10.1111/infa.12039

Tabachnik, B. G., and Fidell, L. S. (2007). *Using Multivariate Statistics*, 5th Edn. Boston, MA: Allyn and Bacon.

Thelen, E., and Smith, L. B. (1994). *A Dynamic Systems Approach to the Development of Cognition and Action.* Cambridge, MA: MIT Press.

Viholainen, H., Ahonen, T., Lyytinen, P., Cantell, M., Tolvanen, A., and Lyytinen, H. (2006). Early motor development and later language and reading skills in children at risk of familial dyslexia. *Dev. Med. Child Neurol.* 48, 367–373. doi: 10.1017/S001216220600079X

Walle, E., and Campos, J. J. (2014). Infant language development is related to the acquisition of walking. *Dev. Psychol.* 50, 336–348. doi: 10.1037/a0033238

Weisler, A., and McCall, R. R. (1976). Exploration and play: resume and redirection. *Am. Psychol.* 31, 492–508. doi: 10.1037/0003-066X.31.7.492

Wilsenach, A. C. (2006). *Syntactic Processing in Developmental Dyslexia and in Specific Language Impairment: A Study on the Acquisition of the Past Participle Construction in Dutch.* Ph.D. dissertation, NARCIS, The Hague.

Wilson, M. (2002). Six views of embodied cognition. *Psychon. Bull. Rev.* 9, 625–636. doi: 10.3758/BF03196322

Conflict of Interest Statement: The authors declare that the research was conducted in the absence of any commercial or financial relationships that could be construed as a potential conflict of interest.

10

Curling Up With a Good E-Book: Mother–Child Shared Story Reading on Screen or Paper Affects Embodied Interaction and Warmth

Nicola Yuill and Alex F. Martin*

Children and Technology Laboratory, School of Psychology, University of Sussex, Falmer, UK

This study compared changes in cognitive, affective, and postural aspects of interaction during shared mother and child book reading on screen and on paper. Readers commonly express strong preferences for reading on paper, but several studies have shown marginal, if any, effects of text medium on cognitive outcomes such as recall. Shared reading with a parent is an engaging, affective and embodied experience across time, as well as a cognitive task, so it is important to understand how paper vs. screen affects broader aspects of these shared experiences. Mid-childhood sees a steep rise in screen use alongside a shift from shared to independent reading. We assessed how the medium of paper or screen might alter children's shared reading experiences at this transitional age. Twenty-four 7- to 9-year-old children and their mothers were videotaped sharing a story book for 8 min in each of four conditions: mother or child as reader, paper, or tablet screen as medium. We rated videotapes for interaction warmth and child engagement by minute and analyzed dyadic postural synchrony, mothers' commentaries and quality of children's recall, also interviewing participants about their experiences of reading and technology. We found no differences in recall quality but interaction warmth was lower for screen than for paper, and dropped over time, notably when children read on screen. Interactions also differed between mother-led and child-led reading. We propose that mother – child posture for paper reading supported more shared activity and argue that cultural affordances of screens, together with physical differences between devices, support different behaviors that affect shared engagement, with implications for the design and use of digital technology at home and at school. We advocate studying embodied and affective aspects of shared reading to understand the overall implications of screens in children's transition to independent reading.

Edited by:
Joanne Tarasuik,
Swinburne University of Technology, Australia

Reviewed by:
Ruth Ford,
Anglia Ruskin University, UK
Susan K. Fenstermacher,
University of Vermont, USA

***Correspondence:**
Nicola Yuill
nicolay@sussex.ac.uk

Specialty section:
This article was submitted to Developmental Psychology, a section of the journal Frontiers in Psychology

Keywords: shared-reading, tablets, embodied cognition, synchrony, affect, human–computer interaction (HCI)

INTRODUCTION

When children share reading with their parents, on the road to becoming independent readers, does it matter whether they share stories using a traditional paper book or a tablet screen? Intense media interest surrounds the question of whether reading on screen differs from reading on paper, and there is now a small but growing literature on the topic. Many adults express a preference for paper (Pew Research Center, 2016) and sales of paper books have recently shown a small rise as e-book sales have slightly declined (Publishers Association, 2015). Where children are concerned, there has been strong concern about the amount of 'screen time', with fears that children reading from screens may not derive the same benefits as those reading from paper, and that digital devices will discourage children from reading for pleasure. In one recent report, 74% of parents said they would rather their child read a print book than an e-book, and 50% of parents of 5- to 7-year-olds worry about their child's excessive use of screens (Egmont, 2013). Conversely, a report from the National Literary Trust suggested that using e-books may increase the motivation and reading skills of young readers, particularly poorer performing boys (Picton and Clark, 2015). These questions have practical importance because parental involvement in reading influences children's later language and literacy development (e.g., Bus et al., 1995; Senechal and LeFevre, 2002) and is entwined with the attachment relationship of parent and child (Bus and van Ijzendoorn, 1995). Shared reading is a potent environment for the sort of positive parent–child interaction that can contribute to socio-emotional development, as well as literacy (Aram and Aviram, 2009).

As technology becomes increasingly pervasive in children's lives, the question of how digital technology affects their literacy and enjoyment of stories becomes more pressing. Figures from the UK communications regulator Ofcom (2015) show that the use of digital technology for entertainment is now something that even the youngest toddler encounters. The use of technology is also widespread in schools, so children's experience of reading, both at home and at school, is increasingly through the medium of a screen.

Research on children's reading from screens has focused, understandably, on young children who are just learning to decode text, and most of these studies therefore involve adult-led shared reading. Children's early experiences of books, whether on paper or on screen, are thus typically triadic interactions – reading device, child and adult. An increasingly influential approach in the field of human–computer interaction (HCI) is that of 'embodied interaction', 'the creation, manipulation, and sharing of meaning through engaged interaction with artifacts' (Dourish, 2004, p. 126), emphasizing the everyday social practices and physical reality through which people interact with technology, involving shared awareness, construction of meaning and emotions. Joint book-reading fundamentally involves the shared construction of meaning between adult and child, with the different opportunities and constraints provided by books or screens, both in terms of their physical properties and their social significance. Studying shared reading with this perspective in mind can help us see the contribution of different aspects of the natural situations in which joint reading happens. Potential differences in cognitive outcomes, such as comprehension, are without doubt important, but research also needs to investigate affective, interactional, and embodied factors that are central to the experience of early shared reading: child engagement in the story, interaction warmth and postural synchrony, as evidenced by how the two readers physically position themselves in relation to each other and the device. This wider compass is important because typical early reading involves triadic interaction in existing close relationships, in a cultural context, rather than being ahistorical, individual encounters between brains and words.

For traditional paper books, the typical transition period from shared reading to reading independently and alone usually occurs around the age of 7 to 9. At this point, children become able to choose books for themselves, to develop preferences, to start reading 'chapter books' independently, and to decide how much time they wish to spend reading. This age also marks a gradual shift from parent-led to child-led reading, with parents in a Book Trust survey reporting a drop in reading bedtime stories to their children, from 86% at 5-years-old, to just 38% at 11-years-old (Book Trust, 2016). Taking a school book home for shared reading is standard practice in the UK and elsewhere, supporting both literacy development and shared enjoyment through parent–child interaction. The significance of this phase in literacy development is demonstrated through statistics on book and computer use; book reading drops sharply at about the same rate as digital media consumption rises: (Egmont, 2013). This period of concurrent transitions, from shared to independent reading, and from reading for pleasure to multi-media usage, makes this age group of particular interest in investigating differences in reading experience between paper and screen.

In this study, we addressed potential differences between shared reading of digital and paper texts, when children are reading and being read to, in four inter-related areas:

Cognitive: Do children differ in the quality of their descriptive and structural recall for texts read on screen and on paper? Do they differ in their attentional engagement with the story between the two media, when reading and when being read to?

Interactive and affective: Are there differences in the warmth of mother-child interactions between screen and paper media, and depending on who is reading? Do mothers provide different kinds of verbal support according to medium and reader?

Postural synchrony: Are there coherent differences in the physical positioning of mother and child when reading from screens vs. paper?

Attitudinal: do mothers and children have different experiences with, and attitudes to shared and independent reading on screen and on paper?

The literature on reading traditional paper books with children ranging from toddlerhood to around age 10 focuses mainly on cognitive factors, and shows that shared reading aids children's learning, e.g., of vocabulary (for a meta-analysis see Flack, Field, and Horst, 2016, under review). Dialogic reading styles, where the adult engages in conversation about the story, are particularly helpful for learning and engagement (e.g., Reese and Cox, 1999), and for engendering a love of reading (Bus, 2001). Most comparative studies with e-books involve digital devices designed to support independent reading through audio, multimedia content, and games (e.g., see Bus et al., 2015). These enhanced e-books are generally not designed for shared reading, and can hence become frustrating for adult reading partners (see Chiong et al., 2012). Although there is less evidence comparing children's reading from paper to more basic e-books (text on screen with minimal extra features), there is some agreement within the existing studies: Chiong et al. (2012) found lower story comprehension in 3- to 5-year-olds reading a science-themed book with a parent from an iPad than from a paper book, and Krcmar and Cingel (2014) found a small but significant drop in comprehension for pre-schoolers reading with a parent on an iPad compared with paper. In both cases, the screen reading prompted more conversation about the processes of reading, likely at the expense of story-relevant comments. Similar findings about conversation type and comprehension were reported for 3- to 5-year-olds co-reading with adults (Parish-Morris et al., 2013), and also in a comparison of parents reading stories on paper vs. laptop with 4-year-olds (Lauricella et al., 2014), although this last study found no significant difference in comprehension. The 'traditional' books in these studies were generally unornamented paper books, although books aimed at younger children in particular often have features such as texture, sound, pop-ups or flaps: books with flaps were compared to e-books by Moody et al. (2010) although no comment was made specifically on the role of these interactive paper features.

There is an abiding feeling expressed by many adults that reading an e-book provides a different 'feel' and sense of engagement from reading on paper. There are some cognitively helpful affordances of paper, such as for note-taking and studying, that are not well-replicated in electronic media (O'Hara and Sellen, 1997) but could there also be differences in the child's engagement with narrative during shared reading on paper vs. on screen? As noted above, some studies have included measures of engagement. Lauricella et al. (2014) compared parent-led shared reading of a print book and a laptop e-book in parents of 4-year-olds, and coded parent–child engagement (a broad measure combining video ratings of active vs. passive parent involvement, mutuality of communication, parental success in engaging their child, and degree of conversational turn-taking). They found higher engagement for the e-book than for the paper book, similar to findings by Chiong et al. (2012) on children's engagement with paper vs. tablet books in 3- to 6-year-olds. However, engagement as measured in these studies included physical interaction, such as page-turning processes, using a mouse or touching hotspots, which would likely be required more for touchscreens or computer mice than for paper, and it is possible that heightened excitement because of novel technology use might also be seen as greater engagement. Measures of engagement that focus more on attentional engagement with the story than on physical interaction with a device may not find the same advantages for e-books. In fact, Chiong et al. (2012) measured 'overall engagement' including parent-child interaction and enjoyment, and found more such engagement for a print book than an e-book. It is therefore unclear whether a child's engagement with a story differs between parent-led shared reading on paper and on screen. We address this issue in our study by using a measure of child engagement based not on physical movement prompted by the device, but on the child's attentional engagement with the story.

The link between affect and shared reading has been recognized in research into early (pre-school) literacy, primarily in relation to mother-child attachment security (Bus and Van Ijzendoorn, 1988; Frosch et al., 2001; Daly et al., 2015). Despite this recognition, assessment of affective aspects of shared reading in print and on screen seems to have been neglected, particularly in studies beyond infancy. Techniques to measure characteristics such as warmth are easily available in the well-established literature on family interactions involving young children, so we adapted a measure of warmth (positive affect) from the widely used Parent–Child Interaction System, PARCHISY (Deater-Deckard et al., 1997). Given the lack of previous research that focuses on warmth independently of other aspects of general interaction, we did not make predictions about differences in interactional warmth by medium, or by reader. We note in respect of reader, though, that the adult tends to have a different role when reading or listening to a child read. While the adult is in both situations in a didactic, expert role, we would expect the focus in child-led reading to be more on supporting the child's decoding than on story discussion, and this might make for lower warmth.

Warmth and attunement to the needs of the child are underlying features of the dialogic reading style, so analyzing the ways that mothers talk with their children during shared reading should illuminate ways that the type of medium and reader influence shared reading. Several previous studies of e-books have analyzed the nature of adults' comments during shared reading. Perhaps unsurprisingly, adults make more comments about the mechanics of reading (e.g., about page turns or touching screens), and fewer comments about the story itself, such as vocabulary, for e-books than paper (Chiong et al., 2012; Krcmar and Cingel, 2014; Lauricella et al., 2014). Because we looked at both mother and child as reader, we separated out mothers' comments about specific vocabulary and about the story more generally. We expected that mothers would give more support for vocabulary when the child was reading, and this might be at the expense of broader story-related comments.

Physical positioning and interactional synchrony are intrinsic, but largely ignored, aspects of shared reading. We know that more broadly, dyadic synchrony is fundamentally involved in cognitive, social and emotional development (Harrist and Waugh, 2002) and exerts a fundamental influence on the tenor and warmth of interactions. We could find little or no evidence on the role of posture and synchrony in shared reading, but we predicted that postural synchrony would have an important role to play in shared reading interactions, with the potential to illuminate differences in the experiences of reading on screen and paper. Lauricella et al. (2014) described parent–child interaction for paper and screen in terms of how parents arranged the seating. However, the use of a laptop for the e-book affected positioning in a specific way, because the laptop generally had to be placed on a table, and since there was one mouse, control could not be shared. They found that half the children controlled the mouse in the e-book condition, increasing those children's physical engagement. In the present study we aimed to reduce variation introduced by device demands by using a tablet and book with similar dimensions, which could be held and controlled in similar ways, allowing the assessment of differences in dyadic posture and synchronization between the parent and child. We also compared child-led and parent-led shared reading: given that tablet use tends to be primarily individual, we expected that shared reading with a tablet might pose challenges in sharing the device.

In summary, we compared shared reading of illustrated chapter books between mothers and their 7- to 9-year-old children, on paper or on screen, with the child or the mother as reader, to investigate four aspects of the interactions: cognitive (recall and engagement), interactive warmth and dialog, postural synchrony, and attitudes to and experience with technology.

MATERIALS AND METHODS

Participants

Participants were recruited from 10 classes in four primary schools in a semi-rural region of south-east England, where flyers were put in the book-bags of all 7- to 9-year-old children, inviting them to take part. Twenty-eight families responded to the advert, of whom 26 agreed to take part. Two children were excluded from the final sample; one with dyslexia and one who did not meet the age criterion. Parents gave written, informed consent, children gave assent, and the study was approved by the University ethics committee. In addition, parents gave written consent to use images in training or publications. When the images herein were selected, as a courtesy we obtained additional written consent from the parents.

The final sample consisted of 24 mother-child dyads, all White-British, reflecting the local population. There were 15 boys and 9 girls, with ages ranging from 7.04 to 9.89 years ($M = 8.60$, $SD = 0.91$). All of the mothers were the biological parent. Mothers' ages ranged from 30.13 to 51.53 years ($M = 41.66$, $SD = 4.61$).

To assess representativeness, parental education and household income were compared with UK Census data (2011): 83.3% of the mothers held a degree level qualification or higher, which is greater than the national average (33.9% of women). Household incomes in the sample covered the whole range, from £0-14,999 to more than £100,000. The median was £55-74,999, greater than the national average (£46,500).

Design

We used a repeated-measures design, with each pair reading one book progressively through each of the four conditions (Mother–Paper, Child–Paper, Mother–Digital, Child–Digital) for 8 min in each condition. The order of conditions was counter-balanced in such a way that the medium of reading was blocked together, as follows: two paper conditions (mother reads then child reads, or vice versa) followed by two digital conditions (in the same order of who reads), or the digital conditions followed by paper conditions. This design allowed the comparison of overall recall between reading media without the disruption of repeated changes of device.

Materials

We gave children a choice of two books, both humorous fiction works recommended for children of 7 and over: '*You're a Bad Man, Mr Gum*' (Stanton, Jelly Pie, London, 177 PP) and '*Barry Loser: I am Not a Loser*' (Smith, Jelly Pie, London, 239 pages). The first chapter of 'Mr Gum' had a Flesch reading ease score of 79.3 and the first chapter of 'Barry Loser' scored 85.8, on a 1–100 scale with 100 as easiest. The book was presented as a paperback book, measuring 260 mm × 190 mm when open, and on a Microsoft Surface RT, with a reading area of 235 mm × 132 mm. The Surface RT compared with other tablets has low reflectance and a wide viewing angle (DisplayMate Technologies, n.d.). These features are helpful in supporting shared visual access in dyadic reading. The tablet presentation used the Book Bazaar e-reading application, using the 'Publisher's Settings' option which presented the text in Tahoma typeface, providing a visual appearance very similar to the paper format. Both formats provided text and illustrations in black and white on most pages, although the ways illustrations were positioned in text varied because of different reading area sizes and automated formatting by the e-reader. The two formats differed in weight, with the book at 196 g and the Surface, including case, notably heavier at 1,020 g. The participants had all used tablets, though to different extents (see Results), but were equally unfamiliar with the Surface RT.

Measures

Cognitive

Reading accuracy

Children's reading errors were coded for the first 100 words of the child-reading condition in the digital and paper conditions. Because order of presentation varied, the words read were not identical across children, but the books did not differ systematically in readability through the book, so the accuracy over 100 words would not be expected to differ systematically across books. A reading error was defined as a: failed or non-attempt to read a word; mispronunciation; missing or inserted word; or hesitation followed by mother's intervention.

Recall

The experimenter, who was absent during the reading, checked recall at the end of reading in each medium, i.e., after both partners had read on screen, or on paper. The child was asked, 'Since you've been reading the paper/digital book, can you tell me what's happened in the story?' This meant that each reader provided recall data twice, once after the two digital conditions and once after the two paper conditions. In order to discourage parental help, the parent was presented with a questionnaire (see below) during the child recall. Any subsequent parent-assisted recall was not included in the child's recall score.

Given our design, which aimed to support an informal and natural reading experience, children were recalling from different texts and for different amounts of input, depending on the book choice and the natural reading speed of the readers. We therefore did not score recall in terms of amount of information. We instead used 3-point scales to code descriptive detail and narrative coherence independently of the amount recalled, since the latter would depend on reading speed and fluency:

Richness of descriptive detail: 1 = no or very little information with little or no descriptive detail (two or fewer descriptive terms); 2 = some information, with three to four descriptive terms; 3 = more than four descriptive terms or details.

Narrative coherence: 1 = events or ideas not linked temporally or causally (e.g., listing unconnected ideas) no causal links; 2 = events or ideas linked as lists or with simple temporal terms (e.g., 'and then'), two or fewer causal links; 3 = More than two causal links between events or ideas.

Two raters blind to condition double-coded 10 (21%) of the recalls, achieving a satisfactory reliability, $\kappa = 0.71, p < 0.01$.

Video coding

Videos were coded by a researcher blind to the aims of the study and double-coded by a second coder for a randomly selected 25% of video sessions. Resulting reliability Kappa statistics are given below.

Interactive and Affective

Child engagement

Designed to capture child interest in the story, independently of differences that might occur as a consequence of different affordances of the reading device and reader. Engagement was judged from child visual attention, gesture, expression, and verbalization, and coded every minute on a scale from 1 = child distracted from story to 5 = highly engaged with story ($\kappa = 0.93$, $p < 0.001$).

Interaction warmth

The warmth of the interaction between mother and child was coded every minute on a 5-point scale, adapted from the PARCHISY coding scheme (Deater-Deckard et al., 1997), from 1 = no positive affect expressed to 5 = continuous positive affect ($\kappa = 0.82, p < 0.001$).

Mother comments

All mother verbalizations were coded into one of five categories:

Mechanical: referring to the digital or paper book itself, e.g., 'turn the page' 'tap there to turn'.

Vocabulary: Giving the meaning of a word, asking the child what a word means, helping the child decode a word, providing the correct pronunciation of a word.

Story: Explaining what is happening in the story, asking the child what is happening, extending the story, commenting on the story

Motivation: Encouraging child, e.g., 'well done' 'that was tricky!', keeping the child on task, e.g. 'concentrate' 'pay attention', 'you're here [pointing]' or re-reading the last sentence the child read, linking to the child's own experience, e.g., 'that sounds like your grandad!'.

Unrelated: Any utterance unrelated to the story or task.

Postural

We inspected screen shots of how participants positioned themselves with the device in each of the four conditions.

Attitudinal

Interview

Children were asked about their reading preferences and technology use at the end of the reading task. Mothers completed a paper questionnaire on the same topics which also included demographic questions.

Procedure

Families were visited at home on a single occasion by the same female researcher and assessed in as naturalistic a way as possible. Visits took place over a 5-week period at the end of the summer term and the first week of the summer holiday. Seven took place during the day, and 17 after school: we inspected the data for differences but did not see a markedly different pattern for children tested in the day. All participants were seated on comfortable sofas in their living room, except for two pairs who sat on chairs at a table. All except five children were seated on the left of the mother: it is likely that this reflected children's dominant hand preference but we did not check this. The study was explained, and parent consent and child assent gained, before the children were asked to choose which book they wanted to read, and then the pairs were asked to read aloud as they would normally. The tablet was briefly demonstrated just before the relevant reading conditions and there were no serious misunderstandings about its use or operation. The device was offered to the pair, with no instructions as to who should hold it or how they should arrange their positions. Occasionally other family members were present (a sibling as silent onlooker once, a family pet on six occasions) but no other adult humans were present. Participants were randomly allocated to one of the four orders of condition. The four conditions were completed in sequence, with a verbal recall task for the child after the second and fourth conditions. After the reading task the mother completed a paper questionnaire while the child was interviewed orally by the researcher.

Eleven children distributed roughly evenly between conditions and gender wore light activity monitors on a wrist and an ankle, and of these, three also wore a GoPro headcam, as part of a separate study. We could not detect systematic influences of wearing this equipment on behavior, other than occasional reporting of mild discomfort of a headcam and one child remaining relatively still in all conditions when wearing the activity monitors. These variables are not mentioned further.

RESULTS

Reading Choice and Accuracy

Book choices were almost evenly divided (13 Barry Loser, 11 Mr. Gum) with no significant gender or age bias in choice. In general, we found no effects of gender, book choice or condition order, and we do not report further on these variables.

Reading errors varied from 5 to 9% of words, indicating that the books were at the appropriate level, and showing no significant differences between book choice or medium of reading, both $Fs(1,16) < 1$. Children tended to progress further through Barry Loser (average progress to page 76) than Mr. Gum (average to page 57), as there were fewer words per page on average in Barry Loser.

Story Recall

There were no significant differences either in richness or coherence of recall according to text medium, each $F(1,16) < 1$, as shown in **Table 1**. There was no significant difference between the two book choices in either score, both $Fs(1,16) < 1$. The design did not enable separation of recall data by reader.

Child Story Engagement

An analysis of variance (ANOVA) for mean scores of child engagement showed a main effect of reading medium, $F(1,16) = 4.88$, $p < 0.05$. There was a small but significant difference, with higher engagement for reading from paper, $M = 3.50$, $SD = 0.16$, than from screen, $M = 3.31$, $SD = 0.19$. There was also a difference by identity of reader, $F(1,16) = 8.31$, $p < 0.01$, with higher engagement when the child was reading, $M = 3.64$, $SD = 0.19$, than when the mother was, $M = 3.17$, $SD = 0.19$. There was no significant interaction of medium and reader, $Fs(1,16) < 1$.

Interaction Warmth

A repeated-measures ANOVA on interaction warmth rating by medium and reader and by minute across the 8 minutes (using Greenhouse–Geisser *Fs* to correct for sphericity where required) showed a main effect of reading medium, $F(1,20) = 5.60$, $p < 0.05$, with a slight but significant lower overall warmth for screen reading ($M = 3.10$, $SD = 0.18$) than for paper ($M = 3.57$, $SD = 0.20$). There were no effects for mother vs. child as reader, $F(1,20) < 1$, and a main effect of time, $F(7,92) = 2.60$, $p < 0.05$. These effects were moderated by a significant interaction between medium, reader and time, $F(7,96.5) = 3.63$, $p < 0.005$. The changes in warmth across the sessions are shown in **Figure 1**. There appears to be a marked change for screen reading around halfway through the 8-min session, particularly when children read from screen. We examined the trends over time for the different conditions by running ANOVAs with trend analysis for each condition. There were no significant effects of time on interactive warmth for children reading on paper or for mothers on screen, $Fs < 1$. For children reading from screen, there was a main effect of time, $F(4.4,92.6) = 2.62$, $p < 0.05$, with a significant downward linear trend, $F(1,21) = 6.41$, $p < 0.02$, as shown in **Figure 1**. For mothers reading on paper there was also a significant effect of time, $F(3.78,75.63) = 2.96$, $p < 0.05$, with both a linear trend $F(1,20 = 5.99$, $p < 0.02)$ and a 5th order trend, $F(1,20) = 11.13$, $p < 0.005$) which we did not seek to interpret.

Maternal Commentaries

There were very few 'unrelated' comments (fewer than 3% in each condition), so we excluded these from analysis. We computed commentaries as a proportion of the total number of maternal comments, to control for differences in verbosity between conditions, as shown in **Figure 2**, and compared the effects of medium and reader using ANOVA, for each comment type. As we anticipated, mechanical comments were confined almost entirely to reading from screens rather than books, $F(1,23) = 25.70$, $p < 0.001$, with no influence of who was reading and no interaction, $Fs < 1$. Again as we would expect, mothers provided more commentary on vocabulary when the child was reading than when she read herself, $F(1,23) = 76.08$, $p < 0.001$. There was no difference between paper and screen for such comments, and no interaction between medium and reader, both $F < 1$.

Commentary about the story was reasonably frequent overall, but differed according to condition: there was a main effect of who was reading, $F(1,23) = 26.65$, $p < 0.001$, with more comments on the story when mother, rather than child, was the reader. Although not significant, we should note that the main effect of medium yielded $F(1,23) = 3.50$, $p < 0.07$, with more story comments for paper than for digital.

There were no significant effects of medium or reader for motivational comments, $Fs < 1$.

TABLE 1 | Mean and SD in recall richness and coherence (max = 3) following digital and paper shared reading.

Condition	Recall richness	Recall coherence
Paper	1.33 (0.82)	1.67 (0.82)
Screen	1.50 (0.84)	1.67 (0.52)

Postural Synchrony

All but two sessions involved mother and child sitting side-by-side on a sofa, holding the reading device either jointly or singly. Despite this uniformity, there was a range of ways that pairs divided the work of holding the device, turned pages, shared attention between text and partner, made themselves comfortable, and arranged themselves in relation to the device and their partner. These factors also changed between the different conditions, with partners altering their positions as device or reader shifted. We did not find a single method of coding these different features, since each pair had their own means of altering their differing postural relationships, but inspection of stills of the typical posture in each separate condition for each pair shows that the main contrast was between children reading on screens and mothers reading on paper. When children read from a screen they tended to hold the tablet in a 'head-down' posture typical of solo uses such as one-player games or surfing the internet (**Figure 3**, top left and top right). Temporal analysis of the videotapes shows that this 'head-down' starting position meant that mothers found it hard to share the screen, leading them to curl round behind the child in order to 'shoulder-surf' the screen, rather than adopting the 'curled up' position common when reading the paper book (**Figure 3**, bottom right). In contrast, when a mother read from paper, she often held the book between herself and the child, with the child very close to her, either tucked under her arm to facilitate visual sharing (**Figure 3**, bottom right) or in a very relaxed posture with audio sharing but little sight of the book (**Figure 3**, bottom left).

Mothers were seen to shift their positions between 'curled up with paper' and 'shoulder-surfing with tablet' or finding other ways to stretch to see the screen, to accommodate the different ways that children negotiated use of the reading device. We should note that this 'curling up' with the paper book, compared to 'shoulder-surfing' with a screen, was common but not universal, with one pair atypically closer together when the child was reading from the tablet, and more separate with mother reading the paper book. (**Figure 4**). However, this child was one of the youngest and therefore needed more help when reading.

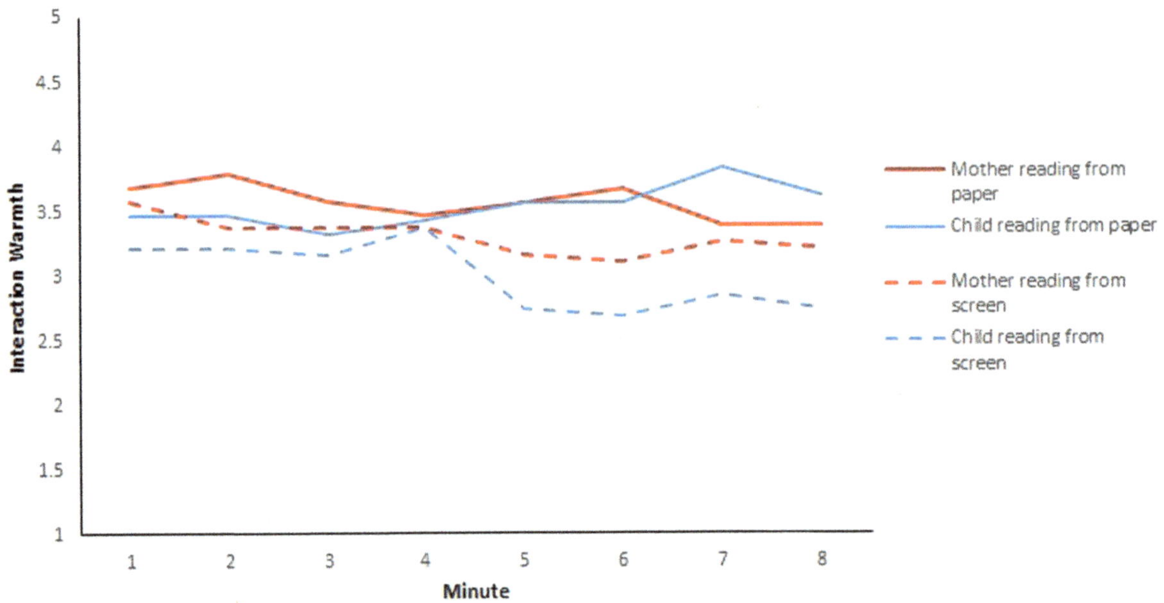

FIGURE 1 | Interaction warmth per minute for paper vs. screen with mother or child as reader (max = 5).

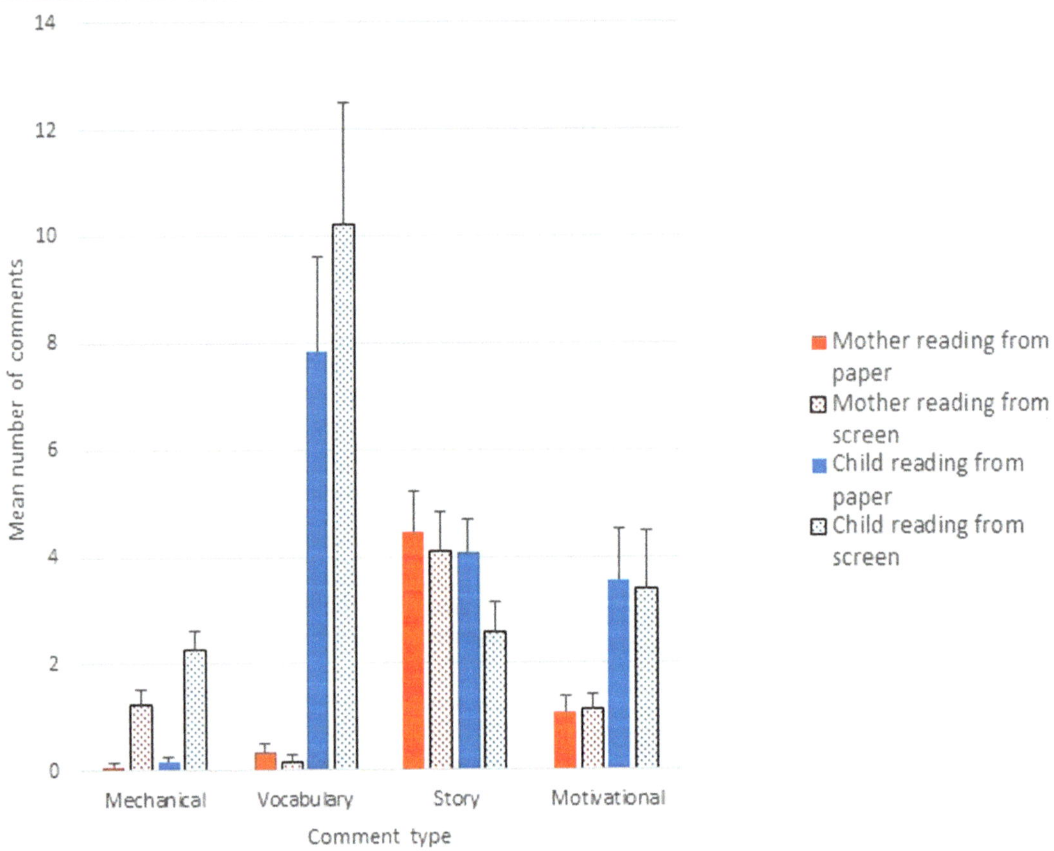

FIGURE 2 | Proportion of mother comments of each type for reading from paper and screen, with mother or child as reader.

FIGURE 3 | Curling up with paper, shoulder-surfing with screen: postures for mother reading from paper (bottom) to child reading from screen (top). Consent was obtained for use of these images.

Attitudes and Digital Experience

Mothers overwhelmingly expressed a preference for reading on paper, whether this was for reading themselves or for their child as reader, as shown in **Table 2**. Children were more mixed in their opinions, being fairly evenly split regardless of reader. Of the children, seven consistently preferred screen and nine consistently chose paper, and there was a slight tendency for paper to win out when the child was reading, with four children preferring paper for their own reading and screen for their mother reading and only one showing the reverse pattern. There were no marked gender differences in these figures.

All children (except 1 non-responder) reported having access to a tablet or computer plus television at home, and most had more devices than these. Twenty-two of 24 children used at least 1 available digital device for games, but only one child mentioned use of such a device for reading, despite all children reporting reading every day. Ten of the children reported reading at home with a parent, all using paper, not screens. Sixteen children reported reading mostly fiction, and only one child reported exclusively reading factual books.

For children's reported activity at school, 16 of 24 reported reading there every day, and all but one of these was exclusively on paper. Tablets (largely iPads) and/or laptops were in reported use at school for 19 of the 24 children, largely for educational games. No child reported shared story reading on a tablet either at school or in the home.

DISCUSSION

Many studies have investigated differences in children's experience of shared reading from screens vs. paper, but primarily addressing only individual cognitive factors. Furthermore, the majority focus only on parent-led shared reading, where the child is being read to by the adult, rather than both parent-led and child-led shared reading. We observed both types of shared reading to examine not just cognitive measures of recall and story engagement, but also measures designed to capture other aspects that we believed were important to the child's experience of shared reading: interaction warmth, parent commentary, postural synchrony, habits and attitudes to technology. We summarize the main findings of our study, and their novelty, and then discuss each of these aspects in turn, followed by remarks about design and questions for further research.

We found that reading interactions involving a screen showed slightly but significantly lower warmth than those with a paper book, and warmth dropped over time for screens, particularly when children rather than mothers took the role of reader. Further, children showed higher story engagement with paper than with screen, and there was suggestive evidence that mothers also made more story-relevant comments with paper books. The two media were associated with different positioning for mother and child: a qualitative analysis suggested that child readers held and used tablets in ways more typical of individual use, so that mothers had to 'shoulder-surf' the screen, whereas mothers read paper books in ways that supported shared visual attention, enabling the child to adopt a range of curled-up postures. We found no differences in narrative and descriptive aspects of story recall for stories shared on paper or screen, whether the mother or child was reading.

Child-led shared reading showed different patterns from mother-led reading: children were more engaged with the story when they read themselves rather than when their mothers read, and mothers provided differentiated commentary, with more

FIGURE 4 | Atypical pattern of surfing with paper, curling up with screen. Consent was obtained for use of these images.

vocabulary support and less story-focused commentary when the child was reading than when reading herself. Mothers almost exclusively preferred reading from paper, for themselves and for their child, while the results for children's preferences were more mixed. Despite this, in their everyday practice parents and children reported almost always reading on paper, whether alone or during shared reading.

Our study demonstrates the value of using a broader array of measures based on a wider appreciation of the factors that influence children's experience of naturalistic shared reading in everyday settings. In the interests of providing a reading experience as typical, smooth, and motivating as possible, we allowed children a choice of books and had them read in each condition with the same book, meaning that we did not control for content or amount read across the sample. However, the identity of the book did not appear to have any systematic influence on the results, and we believe that the choice and freedom of movement provided for participants enabled us to see an illuminating variety of physical synchrony between mother, child and reading device that informed our analysis. However, our sample was small, very homogeneous and in a narrow age-range, so deserves replication and extension with a more diverse range of groups, settings, and texts.

TABLE 2 | Expressed preferences for paper or screen by reader, for mothers and children. ($N = 24$, with remainder of participants expressing no preference).

	Mother reading		Child reading	
Medium	**Paper**	**Screen**	**Paper**	**Screen**
Respondent				
Mother	22	0	21	2
Child	11	11	13	10

The context of early reading is a shared one during which children gradually develop into independent readers. Our results demonstrate that, in light of this, it is important to consider not just the potential cognitive influences of paper vs. screen (e.g., recall), but also whether the reading medium influences wider cognitive properties such as engagement with the story, and interactional aspects such as warmth. We suggested that the affective differences we found were linked to the different physical positioning of mother and child in paper and screen reading. Our results demonstrate the validity of this approach, given that reliable and significant differences were identified in the extended measures, while we found no difference in standard cognitive aspects of recall.

We now turn to discussing each aspect of the interaction by medium: recall, attentional engagement, interaction warmth, maternal commentary and postural synchrony, and previous experiences with technology and reading. We also comment on differences between mother- and child-led shared reading and discuss possible implications for design.

Previous studies have shown varying results for the cognitive factors of children's story recall and comprehension when reading from paper or screen: for example, De Jong and Bus (2002) found better learning of content for pre-schoolers being read to by an adult from a paper book than from an e-book, but Takacs et al. (2014) noted that e-books can support word learning and story comprehension just as well as print stories when they use well-designed multi-media extras. Our study used digital texts with no multimedia extras, in order to compare paper to screens more directly in relation to recall, and yielded no difference by reading medium. Mothers provided fairly frequent commentary about the stories in all conditions, and this high level of support might have reduced any differences in recall that might otherwise have occurred. In our study, we used only a 1 to 3 scale of narrative coherence and descriptive richness, to allow comparison of children who had read different amounts of text. It may be that more nuanced measures, and measures across longer time periods, would pick up subtler differences in qualities of recall than recall counts alone. For example, Mangen and Kuiken (2014) found that adults reading text on an iPad self-reported lower narrative coherence than readers on paper. Given the mixed results on recall for screen reading, it seems that any such differences are neither simple nor compellingly large.

Our results on interactive warmth are novel. Although we did not predict the lower warmth for screen reading, it was consistent with the pattern of results from our other measures.

Reading on screens was associated with lower engagement of the child with the story and elicited a higher proportion of maternal comments about the mechanics of reading. There was a hint (not significant) of fewer maternal story-related comments for shared screen reading, a pattern also suggested by results of some previous studies. We suggested that the different postural arrangements of mother and child with the different media might support these different qualities of interaction. These findings deserve further research.

Our observations of the reading sessions suggested that posture, and how readers held the reading device, influenced the tenor of the interaction. The typical posture for an adult when children read on screen was a 'shoulder-surfing' one, which seems to be a consequence of the fact that when children are actively engaged with reading from the screen, their body position tends to be perched, head down, over the screen in a way that makes it difficult for the adult to see or join in – even in the present study where we used a device in landscape format with similar dimensions to the paper book. From our own observations and experience working with children sharing devices, we have found that children are often reluctant to cede control of a digital device, perhaps because they justifiably see themselves as 'digital natives', an impression supported in this study both by mothers' comments about their children's use of screens and by children's commonly expressed preference for reading from screen (see also Yuill et al., 2013 on children sharing iPads). Books seem not to present the same impulse for control: when the pair read a paper book, it seemed natural to open the pages wider to invite the listener to curve inwards and share. When the adult read on paper, we observed that children sometimes adopted a more passive back-seat role, curling up under the mother's arm or stretching out, sometimes not even in view of the book, but listening, with their upper limbs no longer poised to hold the book or to act, e.g., to turn pages. It may be that these postures more closely reflect their role if shared reading happens at bedtime, with the child lying in bed, distant from the book. Such behaviors will reflect both the cultural practices and habits tied to the reading device – for example, the primarily individual use of tablets – but also the physical properties of the device in relation to its use. Thus, the tablet we used was considerably heavier than the book, and so some children found it easier to hold it in both hands, so a child who needed a hand free to run a finger under the line of text had to manage the device differently. We propose that differences in posture reflect both physical properties of the devices and the powerful cultural practices and habits tied to the devices. The way the device is held has implications for how easy the device is to share, and this can influence the closeness of the interaction.

We now turn to implications for design and further research. Our study is novel in addressing child-led shared reading, a context that is common during children's extended transition to independent reading. It is notable that children showed more engagement with the story when they were reading themselves than when being read to, although our design did not enable us to see whether this difference was associated with differences in recall or comprehension. It seems plausible that story memory might be better when the adult reads, given the effort required by these emerging readers when required to decode the text themselves. This is a question for future research. As we might expect, mothers gave different verbal support when the child was reading than when she read herself: children were given help with vocabulary and decoding when they read, perhaps leading to a relatively small number of comments about the story content itself. Thus, the identity of the reader taps different requirements, even though, for paper at least, interactions appear equally warm with either reader. Our sample all volunteered for the study, so are likely to be families comfortable with shared reading, and results might be different with other samples, and indeed with other family members, such as fathers.

The number of parents reading to their children seems to reduce sharply during the transition to independent reading, and adult reading is generally a solo activity. Designing e-books for sharing has therefore not been a primary focus. E-books can provide digital traces of previous readers, such as text items highlighted and definitions checked, unlike print books, but e-books do not capitalize on the interactive processes that are typically part and parcel of children's shared book reading experience when they curl up to read a good book.

Children in our study, in common with many other children, used tablets and laptops very extensively both at home and at school. They also generally read on paper daily, and with enthusiasm, both alone and with their parents, sharing reading roles. However, the use of digital technology and the activity of reading seemed to exist in two somewhat separate spheres. Children were fairly evenly divided between how much they reported enjoying their experiences of reading on screen and on paper during the study. However, this did not reflect their customary reading practices, for which they overwhelmingly reported preferring paper. These self-reported preferences are reflected in our child engagement findings: children were rated as more engaged in shared reading from paper than from screens, and when they were reading rather than being read to. This may suggest that, because digital devices are so often used in solo situations (in contrast to the typically shared use of books in the early years), reading books on digital devices moves from a potentially shared activity to a more individual, private activity.

If digital texts are to be used for shared reading, then their features could be designed to support this more effectively. Krcmar and Cingel (2014) report some frustration experienced by adults using e-books for shared reading, and several studies (e.g., Lauricella et al., 2014), including our own, report more parental talk about the mechanics of reading for screen than for paper. Our e-reader was not designed with the needs of emerging readers in mind. In particular, children's imperfect control and coordination of eye movements means that they often find it helpful to run their finger below the line of text they are reading: clearly this can prove frustrating with many e-readers, as it will produce unintended effects such as accidental page-turns. Even basic digital features can prove distracting: for example, some children were intrigued by the electronic page-turning effects, with a child in our pilot work becoming particularly engaged with playing with the page turn function to produce interesting shapes on the screen. Page-turning was mentioned by some children as a feature they enjoyed, and by others as a source of frustration. Mothers' views were less variable, with many reporting that the automatic page turn function hampered their child when decoding unfamiliar words. Thus, features that were designed to remain in the background can become unexpectedly foregrounded. Their visibility can be exacerbated by the fact that there is no single standard for how e-texts operate.

The way readers arranged themselves physically round a reading device may affect how easily an adult can support young readers' word decoding. For example, an adult sitting side by side with a child can observe the child's finger traversing the words, see head posture, share the visual field and hear attempts to sound out a word, enabling them to provide help that is sensitive to the child's particular difficulty. E-readers could perhaps be designed to underpin adult support better, or to provide audio-visual cues to support synchronization of adult help in shared reading.

Children reading to adults is a typical part of early literacy development but has been rarely examined in the context of digital books, given that most research has involved younger and less accomplished readers. Comparison of children sharing paper and digital books at the transitional age of 7 to 9 is of practical import, as children in the immediately foreseeable future will need to gain independent literacy skills, even if they have access to audio-provided e-books for individual reading. Given that shared reading can clearly provide a warm and comfortable context for parent-child interaction, its potential role in fostering collaborative activity and shared emotional experience is worth considering, particularly in a context where digital media could reduce face-to-face sharing. Where everyone has their own device, there is less opportunity for co-watching and co-experiencing, but shared reading, for example, with the traditional bedtime story, provides such an opportunity.

Comparison of digital and print media is not a one-dimensional experimental variable defined by the physical properties of books or touchscreens. Each medium comes with its own set of affordances and cultural practices: for example, the models of how we acquire, archive and share digital vs. print media are quite distinct. We can lend paper books to as many friends as we like, while we may be restricted to a single loan with electronic media; we need to take a trip to the library to borrow a paper book, but can just log in to our account to borrow an e-book; a paper book tends to have a single purpose (being read, maybe being used as a paperweight or door wedge) while an e-book is often only one app on a highly multi-functional device that can also be used to book tickets, play games, work on spreadsheets, and watch films. Further, there are physical differences between books and screens, such as weight, that we can expect to influence the embodied experience of shared reading. The role of such differences is increasingly recognized in embodied approaches to cognition and interaction (Thelen and Smith, 1994).

The cultural significance of devices is a useful reminder that studies of children's e-reading are being carried out during a time of very rapid technological change: for example, light, flexible screens will change reading postures markedly, altering shared reading in new ways. In earlier studies of e-readers, the technology has tended to be novel, and hence perhaps motivating, and this novelty factor may be less compelling in more recent studies. Our sample, for example, were all very familiar with tablets: indeed, some parents commented on how pleasant novelty of sharing a paper book with their children. In line with previous studies (e.g., Lauricella et al., 2014), we found greater frequency of 'mechanical' comments about the process of reading in the screen condition, and this is to be expected when operation of the technology, e.g., of page-turning, is familiar, but less stable than the equivalent mechanism in a paper book. It is important to consider specific design of the technology in studies of digital literacy: for example, mouse interfaces (as in Lauricella et al., 2014) provide very different mechanisms of shared control than touchscreens.

Our findings of differences in warmth over time for paper versus screen reading, and the suggested influence of physical properties and cultural affordances of screens shows the value of considering shared reading and digital text in terms broader than just the cognitive. In particular, differences in warmth are of interest given the powerful role of parent–child relationship quality for a whole range of cognitive and social outcomes (O'Connor and Scott, 2007). Studying shared reading in terms of cognition, affect, posture and embodied interaction, with an eye to the cultural practices of reading devices, should help us understand and design better reading experiences as part of children's development into independent reading in the context of their family relationships.

ETHICS STATEMENT

This study was carried out in accordance with the recommendations of the University of Sussex Sciences and Technology C-REC with written informed consent for adult and child from all adult participants and assent from their children. Adult participants gave written informed consent in accordance with the Declaration of Helsinki. The protocol was approved by the University of Sussex Sciences and Technology C-REC.

AUTHOR CONTRIBUTIONS

NY planned the main research questions and methods, analyzed the data and drafted the paper. AM planned the precise details of method, was responsible for recruitment, data collection, data input, video coding schemes and reliability, and provided material and commentary for drafts.

ACKNOWLEDGMENTS

We are very grateful to the participants and schools involved in this research, to Egmont Publishing for providing the e-book content, Zoe Flack, and Georgia Leith for pilot testing, Kate Appleby and Lauren Rowse for coding support, ChaTLab, Yvonne Rogers and Matt Jaquiery for constructive comments.

REFERENCES

Aram, D., and Aviram, S. (2009). Mothers' storybook reading and kindergartners' socioemotional and literacy development. *Read. Psychol.* 30, 175–194. doi: 10.1080/02702710802275348

Book Trust (2016). *Book Trust Press Release: Time to Read: National Campaign.* Available at: http://fileserver.booktrust.org.uk/usr/resources/1434/time-to-read-press-release-080916.pdf

Bus, A. G. (2001). Joint caregiver-child storybook reading: a route to literacy development. *Handb. Early Lit. Res.* 1, 179–191.

Bus, A. G., Takacs, Z. K., and Kegel, C. A. T. (2015). Affordances and limitations of electronic storybooks for young children's emergent literacy. *Dev. Rev.* 35, 79–97. doi: 10.1016/j.dr.2014.12.004

Bus, A. G., and Van Ijzendoorn, M. H. (1988). Attachment and early reading: a longitudinal study. *J. Genet. Psychol.* 149, 199–210. doi: 10.1080/00221325.1988.10532153

Bus, A. G., and van Ijzendoorn, M. H. (1995). Mothers reading to their 3-year-olds: the role of mother-child attachment security in becoming literate. *Read. Res. Q.* 30, 998–1015. doi: 10.2307/748207

Bus, A. G., Van Ijzendoorn, M. H., and Pellegrini, A. D. (1995). Joint book reading makes for success in learning to read: a meta-analysis on intergenerational transmission of literacy. *Rev. Educ. Res.* 65, 1–21. doi: 10.3102/00346543065001001

Chiong, C., Ree, J., Takeuchi, L., and Erickson, I. (2012). *Print Books vs. E-Books: Comparing Parent-Child Co-Reading on Print, Basic, and Enhanced E-Book Platforms.* New York, NY: The Joan Ganz Cooney Center.

Daly, M., Delaney, L., Egan, M., and Baumeister, R. F. (2015). Childhood self-control and unemployment throughout the life span: evidence from two british cohort studies. *Psychol. Sci.* 26, 709–723. doi: 10.1177/0956797615569001

De Jong, M. T., and Bus, A. G. (2002). Quality of book-reading matters for emergent readers: an experiment with the same book in a regular or electronic format. *J. Educ. Psychol.* 94:145. doi: 10.1037/0022-0663.94.1.145

Deater-Deckard, K., Pylas, M. V., and Petrill, S. A. (1997). *The Parent-Child Interaction System (PARCHISY).* London: Institute of Psychiatry.

DisplayMate Technologies (n.d.). *Surface RT Display Technology Shoot-Out.* Available at: http://www.displaymate.com/Surface_RT_ShootOut_1.htm

Dourish, P. (2004). *Where the Action is: The Foundations of Embodied Interaction.* Cambridge, MA: MIT Press.

Egmont (2013). *Reading Street ch.1-3.* Available at: https://www.egmont.co.uk/reading-fun/reading-street/

Frosch, C. A., Cox, M. J., and Goldman, B. D. (2001). Infant-parent attachment and parental and child behavior during parent-toddler storybook interaction. *Merrill Palmer Q.* 47, 445–474. doi: 10.1353/mpq.2001.0022

Harrist, A. W., and Waugh, R. M. (2002). Dyadic synchrony: its structure and function in children's development. *Dev. Rev.* 22, 555–592. doi: 10.1016/S0273-2297(02)00500-2

Krcmar, M., and Cingel, D. P. (2014). Parent–child joint reading in traditional and electronic formats. *Media Psychol.* 17, 262–281. doi: 10.1080/15213269.2013.840243

Lauricella, A. R., Barr, R., and Calvert, S. L. (2014). Parent–child interactions during traditional and computer storybook reading for children's comprehension: implications for electronic storybook design. *Int. J. Child Comput. Interact.* 2, 17–25. doi: 10.1016/j.ijcci.2014.07.001

Mangen, A., and Kuiken, D. (2014). Lost in an iPad: narrative engagement on paper and tablet. *Sci. Study Lit.* 4, 150–177. doi: 10.1075/ssol.4.2.02man

Moody, A. K., Justice, L. M., and Cabell, S. Q. (2010). Electronic versus traditional storybooks: relative influence on preschool children's engagement and communication. *J. Early Child. Lit.* 10, 294–313. doi: 10.1177/1468798410372162

O'Connor, T. G., and Scott, S. (2007). *Parenting and Outcomes for Children.* York: Joseph Rowntree Foundation.

Ofcom (2015). *Children and Parents: Media Use and Attitudes Report.* London: Ofcom.

O'Hara, K., and Sellen, A. (1997). "A comparison of reading paper and on-line documents," in *Proceedings of the ACM SIGCHI Conference on Human Factors in Computing Systems,* (New York, NY: ACM), 335–342.

Parish-Morris, J., Mahajan, N., Hirsh-Pasek, K., Golinkoff, R. M., and Collins, M. F. (2013). Once upon a time: parent–child dialogue and storybook reading in the electronic era. *Mind Brain Educ.* 7, 200–211. doi: 10.1111/mbe.12028

Pew Research Center (2016). *Book Reading 2016.* Available at: http://www.pewinternet.org/files/2016/08/PI_2016.09.01_Book-Reading_FINAL.pdf

Picton, I., and Clark, C. (2015). *The Impact of Ebooks on the Reading Motivation and Reading Skills of Children and Young People: A Study of Schools Using RM Books, London: National Literacy Trust.* Availble at: http://www.literacytrust.org.uk/assets/0002/9076/The_Impact_of_Ebooks_final_report.pdf

Publishers Association (2015). *PA Statistics Yearbook.* London: The Publishers Association.

Reese, E., and Cox, A. (1999). Quality of adult book reading affects children's emergent literacy. *Dev. Psychol.* 35:20. doi: 10.1037/0012-1649.35.1.20

Senechal, M., and LeFevre, J.-A. (2002). Parental involvement in the development of children's reading skill: a five-year longitudinal study. *Child Dev.* 73, 445–460. doi: 10.1111/1467-8624.00417

Takacs, Z. K., Swart, E. K., and Bus, A. G. (2014). Can the computer replace the adult for storybook reading? A meta-analysis on the effects of multimedia stories as compared to sharing print stories with an adult. *Front. Psychol.* 5:1366. doi: 10.3389/fpsyg.2014.01366

Thelen, E., and Smith, L. B. (1994). *A Dynamical Systems Approach to the Development of Action and Perception. GEN.* Cambridge, MA: MIT Press.

Yuill, N., Rogers, Y., and Rick, J. (2013). "Pass the iPad: collaborative creating and sharing in family groups," in *Proceedings of the 2013 ACM annual conference on Human factors in computing systems,* (New York, NY: ACM), 941–950.

Conflict of Interest Statement: NY received financial support from Egmont Publishing for a separate pilot study using 3 texts provided by Egmont, which was carried out otherwise as independent research. The method of the current study was informed by that study and used two of the same texts, but the work reported in the current paper was carried out entirely independently. The other author declares that the research was conducted in the absence of any commercial or financial relationships that could be construed as a potential conflict of interest.

11

Neural systems and hormones mediating attraction to infant and child faces

*Lizhu Luo, Xiaole Ma, Xiaoxiao Zheng, Weihua Zhao, Lei Xu, Benjamin Becker and Keith M. Kendrick**

Key Laboratory for NeuroInformation of Ministry of Education, Center for Information in BioMedicine, University of Electronic Science and Technology of China, Chengdu, China

We find infant faces highly attractive as a result of specific features which Konrad Lorenz termed "Kindchenschema" or "baby schema," and this is considered to be an important adaptive trait for promoting protective and caregiving behaviors in adults, thereby increasing the chances of infant survival. This review first examines the behavioral support for this effect and physical and behavioral factors which can influence it. It then provides details of the increasing number of neuroimaging and electrophysiological studies investigating the neural circuitry underlying this baby schema effect in parents and non-parents of both sexes. Next it considers potential hormonal contributions to the baby schema effect in both sexes and the neural effects associated with reduced responses to infant cues in post-partum depression, anxiety and drug taking. Overall the findings reviewed reveal a very extensive neural circuitry involved in our perception of cuteness in infant faces, with enhanced activation compared to adult faces being found in brain regions involved in face perception, attention, emotion, empathy, memory, reward and attachment, theory of mind and also control of motor responses. Both mothers and fathers also show evidence for enhanced responses in these same neural systems when viewing their own as opposed to another child. Furthermore, responses to infant cues in many of these neural systems are reduced in mothers with post-partum depression or anxiety or have taken addictive drugs throughout pregnancy. In general reproductively active women tend to rate infant faces as cuter than men, which may reflect both heightened attention to relevant cues and a stronger activation in their brain reward circuitry. Perception of infant cuteness may also be influenced by reproductive hormones with the hypothalamic neuropeptide oxytocin being most strongly associated to date with increased attention and attraction to infant cues in both sexes.

Keywords: baby schema, infant face, neural circuitry, parental behavior, hormones

Edited by:
Andrea Hildebrandt, Ernst-Moritz-Arndt-Universität Greifswald, Germany

Reviewed by:
Marta Borgi, Istituto Superiore di Sanità, Italy
Jennifer Streiffer Mascaro, Emory University, USA

****Correspondence:***
Keith M. Kendrick, Key Laboratory for NeuroInformation of Ministry of Education, Center for Information in BioMedicine, University of ElectronicScience and Technology of China, No.2006, Xiyuan Ave., West Hi-Tech Zone, Chengdu, Sichuan 611731, China
k.kendrick.uestc@gmail.com

Specialty section:
This article was submitted to Perception Science, a section of the journal Frontiers in Psychology

Introduction

The faces of both infants and young children are potent cross-cultural emotive stimuli that adults find both very cute and highly likeable and evoke feelings of protectiveness and care which thereby serve to aid survival of these vulnerable individuals (Brosch et al., 2007; Luo et al., 2011, 2014; Proverbio et al., 2011a; Borgi et al., 2014). Konrad Lorenz (1943) has defined this as the so-called "baby schema" or "Kindchenschema" effect.

Baby schema are considered to be a set of prominent infantile facial physical features, including large head, round face, high and protruding forehead, big eyes, small nose, small mouth, etc., that evoke rapid cognitive, affective and behavioral responses in adults. This may serve as an innate releasing mechanism, a fundamental social instinct which serves to initiate and maintain a parent/carer-infant relationship, particularly during the period of early development when a child is unable to care for itself and is therefore highly vulnerable (Parsons et al., 2010). As such this mechanism helps infant individuals develop secure and cooperative relationships, improves their adaptation to the society and thereby enhances offspring/species survival (Darwin, 1872; Parsons et al., 2010). A number of studies have also reported correlations between perceived cuteness of infant faces and health (Yamamoto et al., 2009), including across cultures (Volk and Quinsey, 2002; Volk, 2009; Golle et al., 2015). Since adult facial attractiveness has often been associated with having "good genes" (Weeden and Sabini, 2005; Rhodes, 2006), it is possible that prominent baby schema may also signal that infants are genetically healthy. Thus, as has been proposed by Golle et al. (2015), cute babies by being perceived as more healthy may promote greater protective and nurturing responses in carers, thereby serving to strengthen a community gene pool.

It is well established that viewing infant and child faces produces positive effects in adult observers both within and across different cultures in terms of automatically and rapidly capturing their attention (Brosch et al., 2007, 2008; Proverbio et al., 2011a), evoking smiling (Schleidt et al., 1980), protective reactions (Alley, 1983), close approach and exaggerated greeting responses (Eibl-Eibesfeldt, 1989). Studies demonstrating increased attentional allocation to infant faces have used a wide variety of paradigms, including a "key-press," or "wanting" task (as in Parsons et al., 2014), an attentional capture task (as in Thompson-Booth et al., 2014), eye-tracking (as in Borgi et al., 2014), and the dot-probe task (Brosch et al., 2007).

Adult Caucasian observers presented with a choice between a cute and less cute infant face exhibit a preference for giving a toy to, or adopting, the cute infant irrespective of whether the infant is Caucasian or African, or even a dog puppy (Golle et al., 2015). A recent study has also shown that faces with baby schema not only evoke positive emotions and caring behaviors in adults but can even evoke enhanced ratings of cuteness in young children aged 3–6 years old (Borgi et al., 2014). Overall, children whose faces display strong baby schema features are perceived as being cuter, friendlier, healthier, more attractive, trustworthy, and adoptable (Karraker and Stern, 1990; Ritter et al., 1991; Chin et al., 2006; Glocker et al., 2009a; Little, 2012; Golle et al., 2015). A recent study using an infrared thermography technique revealed that in both Italian and Japanese subjects facial temperature, a physiological index of arousal, was significantly increased during perception of infant faces from both in-group and out-group cultures, whereas with adult faces this was only the case for those from in-group members (Esposito et al., 2014). Finally, in terms of a potential direct influence of baby schema on parental behavior, a study has reported that mothers with cute infants showed greater affection and playfulness toward them than did mothers with infants who were less cute (Langlois et al., 1995).

While it was originally thought that the effects of baby schema on perceivers were limited to young infants of <1 year of age, it is now clear that they can also extend to faces of children of up to 4.5 years of age (Luo et al., 2011). Indeed, even adult faces with "babyish," immature features are considered more attractive, lovable, warm, submissive, physically weak and naive (McArthur and Apatow, 1984; Berry and McArthur, 1986). Imagined interactions with individuals exhibiting these babyish features are also associated with an increased feeling of social belonging in observers (Sacco et al., 2014). Thus findings suggest a generalization of attractiveness of infantile face features across both children and adults (Zebrowitz et al., 2009). The baby schema effect also appears to extend to our perception of cuteness in the young of other species (Golle et al., 2013, 2015; Lehmann et al., 2013; Borgi et al., 2014), and exhibits high level perceptual "after effects" similar to observations for a number of key features in adult faces (i.e., prolonged perception of cute infant faces lowers attraction ratings given to less cute ones presented subsequently and vice versa- Golle et al., 2013).

The baby schema effect is not just dependent upon the presence of the relevant salient physical facial features (Glocker et al., 2009b; Komori and Nittono, 2013) and can, for example, be weakened by the presence of some form of facial disfigurement (Baeken et al., 2010a). A study has also investigated the influence of temperament on attractiveness of neutral expression infant faces by pairing them with happy or sad facial expressions and equivalent vocalizations. Infant faces paired with mostly happy faces and vocalizations are perceived as even cuter and adult observers are prepared to exert greater effort to view them. On the other hand observers of infant faces paired with mostly sad face expressions and vocalizations don't rate them as cuter and are less prepared to make an effort to view them (Parsons et al., 2014). Thus an infant's temperament can enhance or decrease their perceived attractiveness.

The baby schema effect can also be influenced by an observer's social experience. Adults raised together with siblings like infant and child faces more than those who were not, and the smaller the mean age difference between them and their siblings the greater this effect is (Luo et al., 2014). Similarly, Caucasian children with older siblings had a higher accuracy in recognizing unfamiliar Caucasian child faces relative to Asian ones, while those without them didn't show any such recognition difference between the faces (Macchi Cassia et al., 2014). Parental experience is also influential since mothers in an attention capture paradigm showed longer reaction times to infant vs. adult faces, suggesting that they were more attentive toward infant faces. Reaction times were also negatively correlated with self-reported parental distress in mothers (Thompson-Booth et al., 2014). However, another study did not find significant reaction time differences in mothers and non-mothers in judging infant face expressions (Nishitani et al., 2011).

Personality of the observer can also influence the effects of baby schema. Individuals with higher levels of trait empathy, interpersonal closeness and needing to belong rate infant faces more positively, while personality attributes such as narcissism and insecure attachment have no influence (Lehmann et al., 2013). Finally, degree of resemblance of a child's face to that of the observer has also been reported to increase their perceived attractiveness in both men and women (DeBruine, 2004).

In recent years there has been increasing interest in establishing the neural (Nitschke et al., 2004; Glocker et al., 2009b; Malak et al., 2015) and hormonal influences (Bhandari et al., 2014; Hahn et al., 2014) underlying attraction to baby schema in infant and child faces. There is also an increasing focus on understanding changes in the early post-partum period which are crucial for the formation of mother-infant bonds and factors which may contribute to the development of post-partum depression. For example, studies suggest that an appraisal bias might underlie some of the difficulties mothers with post-partum depression have in responding to cues from their own infant's signals, since they are more likely to rate less cute infant faces negatively (Stein et al., 2010), and rate even average ones more negatively than other mothers (Gil et al., 2011). Substance abuse has also been associated with altered behavioral and neural responses to infant cues (Landi et al., 2011). In the present review we will therefore summarize and discuss the various neural and hormonal influences on infant and child facial processing and attraction established in healthy observers and also clinical research findings in disorders where there is some impairment involved.

Neural Responses to Infant Faces: Baby Schema

As would be expected, emotive and salient social stimuli such as infant faces provoke widespread activation in brain systems involved in face perception, attention, emotion, empathy, memory, reward and attachment, theory of mind and also control of motor responses (see **Table 1**). The question of whether there is something special about brain processing of infant faces is therefore difficult to address given the involvement of so many different systems. Very few studies have investigated the influence of baby schema *per se* but have simply investigated neural responses to infant or child faces either alone or in comparison to adult human faces or young and adult faces from other species (Barrett et al., 2012; Caria et al., 2012; Stoeckel et al., 2014). The experimental protocols used in these studies are summarized in **Table 1** where it can be seen that the majority use a simple face viewing paradigm, although some have also used a one-back working memory task with faces, an oddball task design, face expression judgments or an affect rating task. Only Glocker and her colleagues have objectively quantified and parametrically manipulated the impact of baby schema content on patterns of brain activations (Glocker et al., 2009a,b). Thus, conclusions drawn from the present review are primarily based on the majority of findings reporting differences in neural responses between viewing infant as opposed to adult faces, or between viewing the faces of own as opposed to other infants.

In general neuroimaging studies, primarily using functional magnetic resonance imaging (fMRI), have shown that there is a degree of overlap in neural processing of infant and adult faces since both activate primary visual processing areas as well as those more specifically associated with face perception, such as the fusiform face area (FFA) (for abbreviations of brain regions see **Table 2**) (Kringelbach et al., 2008; Glocker et al., 2009b; Baeken et al., 2010a; Stoeckel et al., 2014). However, infant faces generally elicit more rapid responses and greater activity changes in these brain areas and additionally recruit other regions (Parsons et al., 2010; Caria et al., 2012; Hahn et al., 2014). In regions showing activation in response to both adult and infant faces stronger responses to infant/child faces have been reported in the fusiform gyrus [FFG—Brodmann area (BA) 41/37/19] (Leibenluft et al., 2004; Kringelbach et al., 2008; Caria et al., 2012; Stoeckel et al., 2014), middle occipital gyrus (MOG—BA 19/37) (Ranote et al., 2004; Caria et al., 2012), medial temporal gyrus (MTG—BA 21/37/39) (Leibenluft et al., 2004; Ranote et al., 2004; Caria et al., 2012) and superior temporal gyrus (STG—BA 38) (Ranote et al., 2004; Stoeckel et al., 2014) (**Figure 1A**). Of these regions, the right FFG in particular is of key importance to face processing (see Leopold and Rhodes, 2010) and may play a vital role in encoding baby schema facial features (Hoffman and Haxby, 2000; Glocker et al., 2009b; Stoeckel et al., 2014). These visual cortical areas may serve as an entry node to forward the processed baby face information to other brain regions associated with attention, emotion and memory for further processing and control of behavioral responses (Glocker et al., 2009b).

Infant and child faces also enhance attention and this is reflected in stronger activation of parietal areas involved both bottom up and top down processing of attention orientation (Shomstein, 2012) including the intraparietal sulcus (IPS—BA 19/7) (Leibenluft et al., 2004), precuneus (PCU—BA 7/31) (Leibenluft et al., 2004; Glocker et al., 2009b), and posterior cingulate cortex (PCC—BA 23) (Leibenluft et al., 2004) (**Figure 1B**). Greater activation of these parietal regions selectively help allocate more automatic and cognitive attentional resources to faces with baby schema features resulting in an attentional bias toward the infant faces (Brosch et al., 2007; Glocker et al., 2009b; Caria et al., 2012). An evoked-related potential (ERP) study has also reported stronger activation in response to neutral expression faces of unfamiliar infants at central-frontal (P3a) and occipital-lateral (N170) sites providing further support for increased attention toward infant cues (Weisman et al., 2012c).

There is also evidence that infant faces elicit strong activation in brain regions associated with core aspects of emotion processing (see Lindquist et al., 2012) including the anterior cingulate cortex (ACC—BA 33/24) (Glocker et al., 2009b) and medial cingulate cortex (MCC—BA 31/23/24) (Caria et al., 2012), insula (INS—BA 48/47/13) (Leibenluft et al., 2004; Glocker et al., 2009b; Caria et al., 2012; Stoeckel et al., 2014), amygdala (AMY; Lenzi et al., 2009; Barrett et al., 2012; Wan et al., 2014), orbitofrontal cortex (OFC—BA 11/47) (Leibenluft et al., 2004; Nitschke et al., 2004; Kringelbach et al., 2008; Minagawa-Kawai et al., 2009; Kuo et al., 2012; Wan et al., 2014) (**Figure 1C**). The OFC also plays an important role in learning the emotional value of information and tracking changing emotions (Goodkind et al., 2012), as well as with judgments of pleasantness (Bartels and Zeki, 2004). Thus, the left OFC (BA 11) is more strongly activated by happy vs. neutral infant faces while the right OFC (BA 11) to sad vs. neutral faces (Montoya et al., 2012; Stoeckel et al.,

TABLE 1 | Neural responses to infant and child faces.

Study	Participants (Age; N: M/F)	Face age	Stimuli	Design	Face duration	Paradigm	Contrasts	Findings: activated brain regions (Brodmann area)	Corrections
FUNCTIONAL MAGNETIC RESONANCE IMAGING (fMRI) STUDIES									
Bartels and Zeki, 2004	Healthy mothers (27–49 years; 20:0/20)	9 months to 6 years	Child face pictures	Block	2.5 s	View	Own > acquainted child	Middle INS (14)* Dorsal ACC (24)* Ventral ACC (24) dorsal CAU* medial PUT/GP* Lateral THA R SNi* Lateral OFC	$p < 0.001$ (uncorrected) *$p < 0.05$ (SVC corrected)
							Acquainted > own child	STS (39, 40)* PCC (29, 30)* Medial PCU (7/31)* MTG (21)* AMY*	
							(Own > acquainted child) > (loved partner > friends)	Lateral OFC	
Leibenluft et al., 2004	Healthy mothers (20–40 years; 7:0/7)	5–12 years	Pictures (friend, unfamiliar child, and unfamiliar adult)	Event	1.5 s	One-back memory	Own > familiar child	L ACC (32) L preCG SFG (6) L pSTS (39) R STG (22) MTG (21) R PCC (23) R PCU (31) L SMG (40) R AMY L INS THA GP R PUT Cerebellum	$p < 0.025$ (uncorrected)
							Familiar > unfamiliar children	R ACC (32) R SFG (8) MFG (46/9/47) L posterior OFC (11) L pSTS (39) R MTG (21) L PCC-PCU (39) SMG (40) IPS (40) R MOG (18) R FFG (37) L AMY INS THA L CAU Cerebellum	
							Unfamiliar children > unfamiliar adults	L posterior OFC (11) R pSTS (39) L MTG (21) L PCC-PCU (23/31) R SMG (40) L FFG (37) L INS R THA	

(Continued)

TABLE 1 | Continued

Study	Participants (Age; N: M/F)	Face age	Stimuli	Design	Face duration	Paradigm	Contrasts	Findings: activated brain regions (Brodmann area)	Corrections
Nitschke et al., 2004	Healthy mothers (-; 6: 0/6)	3–5 months	Happy faces neutral images	30-s block design	6 s	Mood rating	Own infants > baseline (blank screen)	Lateral OFC (all 6 subjects)	$p < 0.05$ (uncorrected)
							Unfamiliar infants > baseline	Lateral OFC (only 2 subjects)	*$p < 0.001$ (corrected)
							Own > unfamiliar infants	Lateral OFC (11/47)* Cerebellum*	
							Unfamiliar > own infants	ATC (20/21) *	
Ranote et al., 2004	Healthy mothers (19–35 years; 10: 0/10)	4–8 months	Video stimuli	Block	40s	View	Infants > neutral	Cerebellum MOG (19) L MTG (21/37/39) STG (38) postCG (4)	$p < 0.001$ (uncorrected) *$p < 0.05$ (SVC corrected)
							Own > unknown infants	R MOG (19) L AMY*	
							Unknown > own infants	lateral OFC (47) R MTG (21) L PCU (18) L postCG (7)	
Noriuchi et al., 2008	Healthy mothers (31.1 ± 2.2 years; 13:0/13)	16.5 ± 3.8 months	Video stimuli (smile, cry)	Block	32 s	View	Own > other infant	OFC (47)* R MTG (39) R anterior INS* L PCC (30) L THA* L PUT	$p < 0.001$, (uncorrected) *$p < 0.05$ (FWE corrected)
							Other > own infant	R STG (22) L IPS (40) L PCU (7) L FFG (36) L HIPP (37) PUT*	
							Own infant: separation > play situation	SL CAU* IPS (40) L PCC (31) L SNi* R MTG (21) L OFC (47) PCU (7/31) PREC (4) R ACC (32) SFG (6) STG (22/39/42) STS (21/22) THA*	
							own infant: play > separation situation	R MTG (22/41) SMG preCG (4) L hypothalamus*	

(Continued)

TABLE 1 | Continued

Study	Participants (Age; N: M/F)	Face age	Stimuli	Design	Face duration	Paradigm	Contrasts	Findings: activated brain regions (Brodmann area)	Corrections
Strathearn et al., 2008	Healthy first-time mothers (20–42 years; 28:0/28)	5–10 months	Baby face pictures (happy, neutral, sad)	Event	2 s	View	Own > unknown baby	L lateral OFC (47) R preCG (4) postCG MTG (21/38) STG (22/21) PUT dorsal CAU THA Lateral superior AMY HIPP (36) INS ACC (24/32) MCC (24) PCC (31/17) VTA SNi Cerebellum	$p < 0.05$ (FDR corrected)
							Own > unknown happy infant faces	PUT L SNi R THA L AMY	
							Own > unknown neutral infant faces	R PUT R medial dorsal/ventrolateral THA L dorsal PUT	
Glocker et al., 2009b	Healthy mothers (20–28 year; 16:0/16)	7–13 months	Baby schema pictures (high, low, original)	Event	3 s	Cuteness rating	Infant faces > cross	THA INS (13) SFG (6) Cerebellum PCU (7) postCG (2) preCG (6)	$p < 0.05$ (FWE corrected)
							High baby schema > unmanipulated & low baby schema	L ACC L PCU L FFG R NAcc	
Caria et al., 2012	Healthy adult non-parents (28.06 ± 5.66 years; 16:7/9)	–	Infant and adult human and animal face pictures	Event	4 s	View	Infant > adult	SMA (6) FFG (37/19) preCG (6) MCC (31/24) L anterior INS (48) THA	$p < 0.01$ (FWE corrected)
Montoya et al., 2012	Healthy nulliparous women (19–29 years; 17:0/17)	5–10 months	Unknown infant face pictures (happy, sad, neutral)	Event	1 s	One-back memory	Happy > neutral	L OFC (11)	$p < 0.05$ (FWE corrected)
							Neutral > happy	R STG (22) L INS (13) L preCG (4)	
							Sad > neutral	R PCU (31) R MTG (39) L preCG (6) R SFG (10) R OFC (11)	

(Continued)

TABLE 1 | Continued

Study	Participants (Age; N: M/F)	Face age	Stimuli	Design	Face duration	Paradigm	Contrasts	Findings: activated brain regions (Brodmann area)	Corrections
							Neutral > sad	L INS (13) R STG	
							Sad > happy	R FFG (19) R STG (39) R preCG (6) R FFG (19)	
Baeken et al., 2010a	Healthy females (26.6 ± 6.9 years; 20:0/20)	5.5 ± 4 months	Baby face pictures (neutral, positive, negative)	Block	3.6 s	view	Positive > neutral	FFG (37/19)	$p < 0.001$ (uncorrected)
							Negative > neutral	FFG (18/37/19)	
Barrett et al., 2012	Healthy mothers (25–35 years; 22:0/22)	~3 months	Baby face pictures (positive, negative)	Block	3 s	Affect-rating task (ART)	Positive: own > unfamiliar	Cerebellum STG (38) MTG (21) AMY TH	$p < 0.001$ (uncorrected)
							Negative: own > unfamiliar	PUT postCG (3) STG (38) Cerebellum	
Lenzi et al., 2009	Healthy mothers (23–42 years; 16:0/16)	6–12 months	Baby face pictures (joy, distress, ambiguous, neutral)	Block	2 s	View/imitate	Imitation: emotive > neutral	STS AMY	$p < 0.05$ (FWE, SVC corrected)
							Observation: emotive > neutral	IPS INS AMY	
							Observation: own > other child	IPS Anterior INS STS	
Strathearn et al., 2009	Primiparous mothers (N/A; 30:0/30)	~11 months	Infant face pictures (happy, neutral, sad)	Event	2 s	View	Own > unknown (secure > insecure)	Hypothalamus	$p = 0.0001$
							Own > unknown (insecure > secure)	anterior INS (13)	
							Own happy faces: secure > insecure	OFC (10/45/46)	
							Own happy faces: insecure > secure	dlPFC (9/46) SCG	
							Own sad faces: secure > insecure	lPFC (9) Ventral Striatum / NAcc	
							Own sad faces: insecure > secure	anterior INS (13)	
Zebrowitz et al., 2009	Healthy subjects (21–36 years;17:8/9)	5–9 months	Babies, babyfaced/maturefaced men pictures	Block	200 ms	View	Baby faces > mature faced adults	AMY	$p < 0.05$

(Continued)

TABLE 1 | Continued

Study	Participants (Age; N: M/F)	Face age	Stimuli	Design	Face duration	Paradigm	Contrasts	Findings: activated brain regions (Brodmann area)	Corrections
							Baby faced adults > mature faced adults	AMY	
Landi et al., 2011	Substance-using mothers (26:0/26); non-using mothers (28:0/28); 17–42 years;	5–10 months	Infant faces (happy, neutral, sad)	Event	1 s	One-back memory task	Happy infant faces: non-using>substance-using mothers	R postCG L SFG R HIPP/ parahippocampus L cerebellum	$p < 0.05$ (corrected)
							Happy infant faces: substance-using>non-using mothers	L. posterior parahippocampal gyrus	
							Sad infant faces: non-using>substance-using mothers	medial OFC MTG/STG PCC R AMY Parahippocampal gyrus	
Kuo et al., 2012	Healthy fathers (28–44 years; 10:10/0)	8–19 weeks	Videos stimuli (neutral or slight positive)	Block	15 s	View	Own > other infant	R SFG CAU R OFC	$p < 0.05$ (FDR corrected)
							Other > own infant	FFG	
Laurent and Ablow, 2013	Primiparous mothers (24.1 ± 4.1 years; 22:0/22) Half with depressive symptoms	15–18 months	Infant face pictures (joy, distress)	Block	6 s	View	Own > other infant joy faces (mothers with lower current self-reported depressive symptoms)	R INS L inferior OFC (11)	$p < 0.05$ (FDR corrected)
							Own > other infant distress faces (non-depressed > depressed mothers)	L dorsal ACC (32)	
							Own infant joy > distress faces (mothers with lower current self-reported depressive symptoms)	L INS- PUT L dorsal ACC-SMA (24/6) L SMG (40)	
Strathearn and Kim, 2013	Healthy primiparous mothers (28.5 ± 0.8 years; 39:0/39)	6.8 ± 0.3 months	Infant face pictures (happy, neutral, sad)	Event	2 s	View	Own > unknown happy infant faces	R preCG (4) R SFG (6) L postCG (3) R STG (38) R PUT L AMY / Dorsal striatum R Dorsal CAU R Dorsal PUT SNi/VTA	$p < 0.005$ (FDR corrected)

(Continued)

TABLE 1 | Continued

Study	Participants (Age; N: M/F)	Face age	Stimuli	Design	Face duration	Paradigm	Contrasts	Findings: activated brain regions (Brodmann area)	Corrections
Stoeckel et al., 2014	Healthy mothers (22–45 years; 14:0/14)	2–10 years	Dog and child pictures	Block	4s	View	Own > unfamiliar child	FFG (37)* PUT* SNi/VTA THA*	$p < 0.05$ (FWE corrected) *$p < 0.01$ (FWE corrected)
							Own child > fixation	AMY* FFG* R HIPP* Medial OFC* PUT* SNi/VTA* THA*	
Wan et al., 2014	Healthy mothers (20–43 years; 20:0/20)	4–9 months	Own and unfamiliar infant videos with neutral to mildly positive affect, and emotionally neutral stimuli (moving traffic)	Block	30 s	View (Infant video activation paradigm)	Infants > moving traffic	L Cerebellum (19)* R MTG (39)* R FFG (37)*	$p < 0.001$ (uncorrected) *$p < 0.05$ (FDR corrected) **$p < 0.05$ (SVC, FWE corrected)
							Own > unknown infant	Cerebellum PCU (7) R STG (38) R IPS (40) R postCG (1) preCG (4/6) L AMY**	
							Unknown > own infant	MTG (21); Cerebellum	
							Own > unknown infant (correlates with maternal nondirectiveness)	FFG (18) PUT	
							Own > unknown infant (correlates with infant interactive behavior)	preCG (4) THA	
							Own > unknown infant (correlates with mothers' perceived warmth of her infant)	PCU (7) INS (13)	
MAGNETOENCEPHALOGRAPHY (MEG) STUDIES									
Kringelbach et al., 2008	Healthy subjects (29.5 years; 12:5/7)	3–12 months	Positive, negative, neutral	Block	300 ms	View	Specially found on infant faces, not adult faces	L mOFC: 10–15 Hz, 130 ms R FFG: 20–25 Hz, 165 ms	
EVENT-RELATED POTENTIALS (ERP) / ELECTROENCEPHALOGRAPH (EEG) STUDIES									
Doi and Shinohara, 2012	Healthy mothers (33.7 ± 4.3 years; 16: 0/16)	$M = 5.6 \pm 0.8$ years	Children face pictures (eyes closed, gaze straight, gaze averted)	Block	1000 ms	Oddball paradigm (Respond to a face with its eyes open)	Straight > averted gazes	Own child (but not an unfamiliar child): N170	
							Unfamiliar >own child	Straight gaze: P3	
Proverbio et al., 2011b	Healthy subjects (19–27 years; 40:20/20)	N/A	Adults, children, infants, objects, landscape pictures	Event	800 ms	An implicit task with key press only to landscape pictures	Infants > adults	N1	
							Infants > children	Female: anterior N2	
							Children > adults	Male: anterior N2	

(Continued)

TABLE 1 | Continued

Study	Participants (Age; N: M/F)	Face age	Stimuli	Design	Face duration	Paradigm	Contrasts	Findings: activated brain regions (Brodmann area)	Corrections
Weisman et al., 2012c	Healthy parents (19–33 years; 24:13/11) Healthy lovers (19–33 years; 19:10/9) Healthy singles (19–33 years; 22:12/10)	6 months	Infant face pictures (neutral); standard landscape stimuli	Event	300 ms	Oddball paradigm (Press a key whenever an infant's face appeared on screen)	Unfamiliar infant faces: parents & lovers > singles (subjects)	Occipital–lateral (N170); central–frontal (P3a) sites;	
							Own > unfamiliar	Parietal-distributed P300 component	
Esposito et al., 2015	Healthy primiparous mothers (32.06 ± 4.66 years; 21:0/21)	3–6 months	Infant faces pictures (neutral)	Event	500 ms	View	Own > unfamiliar	Midline occipital (Oz) cluster;	
							Unfamiliar > own	Right temporal (Tr) cluster; left temporal (Tl) cluster;	
Malak et al., 2015	Mothers (28 ± 5.7 years; 47:0/47)	1–23 months	Unfamiliar infant faces pictures (neutral, distressed)	Event	1500 ms	View	Distressed > neutral	↑ LPP - The degree of late Positive potential (LPP) amplitude elicited by neutral infant faces was positively correlated with state anxiety.	
NEAR-INFRARED SPECTROSCOPY (NIRS) STUDIES									
Minagawa-Kawai et al., 2009	Healthy mothers (28–42 years; 18:0/18)	9–13 months	Video stimuli (neutral, smile)	Block	30 s	View	Own > unfamiliar	OFC	
Nishitani et al., 2011	14 healthy mothers (20–42 years; 14:0/14); 14 healthy non-mothers (20–42 years; 14:0/14)	9–36 months	Infant and adult face pictures (happy, angry, sad, fearful, surprised, neutral)	Event	N/A	Expression judgment	N/A	↑ R PFC activity (discriminating infant facial emotions but not adult facial emotions)	

N, numbers of subjects; M, male; F, female; L, left; R, right. Abbreviations of brain regions: see ***Table 2****.*

2014). Finally, a repetitive transcranial magnetic stimulation (rTMS) study has found that a single high frequency session with stimulation applied to the left dorsolateral prefrontal cortex enhanced processing of positive emotions on baby faces and reduced that for negative emotions (Baeken et al., 2010b). Thus infant faces elicit stronger responses in emotional brain circuitry involved with processing both valence and arousal. This would suggest that overall infant faces evoke both stronger arousal and enhanced responses to both positive and negative cues from the infant. The OFC and dorsolateral prefrontal cortex in particular appear to play a key role in mediating differential responses to positive and negative valence infant faces.

Many of the core brain regions engaged in emotion processing are also involved with core processing of empathy, notably the MCC, INS, and OFC (Fan et al., 2011), and other regions in the empathy network also show strong activation in response to infant faces, notably the posterior superior temporal sulcus (pSTS; Leibenluft et al., 2004), supplementary motor area (SMA—BA 6) and precentral gyrus (preCG; Caria et al., 2012), STG (Ranote et al., 2004; Stoeckel et al., 2014), PCU (Leibenluft et al., 2004; Glocker et al., 2009b), right supramarginal gyrus (SMG—BA 40) (Leibenluft et al., 2004), and also cerebellum (Ranote et al., 2004; Glocker et al., 2009b) (**Figure 1C**). Overall this pattern of enhanced activity in empathy processing regions suggests that it may contribute to better identification of emotions being expressed (cognitive empathy) and enhanced empathic feelings toward the infant (affective empathy). Furthermore, increased activity in preCG and SMA

TABLE 2 | The abbreviations and full names of activated brain regions.

Abbreviations	Full names
ACC	Anterior Cingulate Cortex
AMY	Amygdala
ATC	Anterior Temporal Cortex
ATP	Anterior Temporal Pole
APC	Anterior Paracingulate Cortex
CAU	Caudate
dlPFC	Dorsal Lateral Prefrontal Cortex
FFG	Fusiform Gyrus
GP	Globus Pallidus
GM	Gray Matter
HIPP	Hippocampus
IFG	Inferior Frontal Gyrus
INS	Insula
IPL	Inferior Parietal Lobule
IPS	Intraparietal Sulcus
lPFC	Lateral Prefrontal Cortex
MCC	Medial Cingulate Cortex
MFG	Medial Frontal Gyrus
MOG	Middle Occipital Gyrus
MTG	Middle Temporal Gyrus
mPFC	Medial Prefrontal Cortex
MTG	Medial Temporal Gyrus
NAcc	Nucleus Accumbens
OFC	Orbitofrontal Cortex
PAG	Periaqueductal Gray
PCC	Posterior Cingulate Cortex
PCU	Precuneus
PFC	Prefrontal Cortex
PHG	Parahippocampal Gyrus
preCG	Precentral Gyrus
postCG	Postcentral Gyrus
pSTS	Posterior Superior Temporal Sulcus
PUT	Putamen
SCG	Subcallosal Gyrus
SFG	Superior Frontal Gyrus
SMA	Supplementary Motor Area
SMG	Supramarginal Gyrus
SNi	Substantia Nigra
SPL	Superior Parietal Lobe
STG	Superior Temporal Gyrus
TC	Temporal Cortex
THA	Thalamus
VTA	Ventral Tegmental Area

might lead to increased motor empathy in terms of mimicry of facial expressions. Interestingly, a recent paper has shown that 18 month old infants exposed to a higher level of mimicry by their mothers exhibited increased prosocial behavior (Carpenter et al., 2013).

Enhanced activity changes in response to infant faces in the pSTS, PCU and PCC (Leibenluft et al., 2004; Glocker et al., 2009b) may also reflect an impact on core processes for theory of mind (Schurz et al., 2014). Theory of mind refers to the capacity to attribute mental states to oneself or others, and to predict and account for other people's behavior based upon understanding of their intentions and mental states (Premack and Woodruff, 1978; Leibenluft et al., 2004). Greater activation in these areas may therefore help adults utilize previous memorized experience and all the skills they have to better understand and respond toward the infant and successfully manage their social communication and relationship. Linked to this there is also evidence that infant faces evoke greater activation in regions associated with episodic memory including the hippocampus (HIPP; Stoeckel et al., 2014), PCU (Leibenluft et al., 2004; Glocker et al., 2009b) and thalamus (THA; Leibenluft et al., 2004; Caria et al., 2012; Stoeckel et al., 2014) (**Figure 1D**). Enhanced activation in FFG (BA 41/37/19) (Leibenluft et al., 2004; Kringelbach et al., 2008; Caria et al., 2012; Stoeckel et al., 2014) and STG (Ranote et al., 2004; Stoeckel et al., 2014) may additionally contribute through their role in social cognition.

A number of studies have addressed the question of whether infant faces are particularly rewarding. Findings have consistently shown that infant faces appear to evoke greater activation of regions involved in reward and attachment, including the OFC (Leibenluft et al., 2004; Nitschke et al., 2004; Kringelbach et al., 2008; Minagawa-Kawai et al., 2009; Kuo et al., 2012; Stoeckel et al., 2014; Wan et al., 2014), substantia nigra/ventral tegmental area (SNi/VTA; Stoeckel et al., 2014), nucleus accumbens (NAcc)/ventral striatum (Stoeckel et al., 2014), caudate (CAU; Glocker et al., 2009b; Kuo et al., 2012; Stoeckel et al., 2014), putamen (PUT) (Glocker et al., 2009b; Stoeckel et al., 2014), globus pallidus (GP) (Glocker et al., 2009b; Stoeckel et al., 2014) and the THA (Leibenluft et al., 2004; Caria et al., 2012; Stoeckel et al., 2014) (**Figure 1E**). Although the OFC is also involved in emotion processing, its contribution to enhanced rewarding properties of infant faces has been particularly emphasized. The NAcc and VTA are key interconnected regions in the dopaminergic brain reward system (Bourdy and Barrot, 2012) which are selectively activated during both overt perception and mental imagery of rewarding and reinforcing stimuli, especially pleasant and emotionally arousing ones such as infant faces (Costa et al., 2010). Furthermore, lesions in NAcc have been reported to impair the baby schema effect (Numan, 2007). The NAcc and VTA are important for reward-mediated attachment and affiliation (Stoeckel et al., 2014) and also appear to be important targets whereby prosocial hormones such as oxytocin and vasopressin exert their effects on social reward (Scheele et al., 2013).

One of the most notable effects of infant faces is that they evoke stronger activation in brain motor areas than adult faces, including the SMA (BA 6) (Caria et al., 2012), precentral gyrus (preCG—BA 6) (Caria et al., 2012; Glocker et al., 2009b), postcentral gyrus (postCG—BA 2/3/4) (Glocker et al., 2009b; Ranote et al., 2004), superior frontal gyrus (SFG—BA 6) (Glocker et al., 2009b; Caria et al., 2012; Kuo et al., 2012; Wan et al., 2014), THA (Leibenluft et al., 2004; Caria et al., 2012; Stoeckel et al., 2014) and cerebellum (Ranote et al., 2004; Glocker et al., 2009b) (**Figure 1F**). These interconnected areas form the core motor

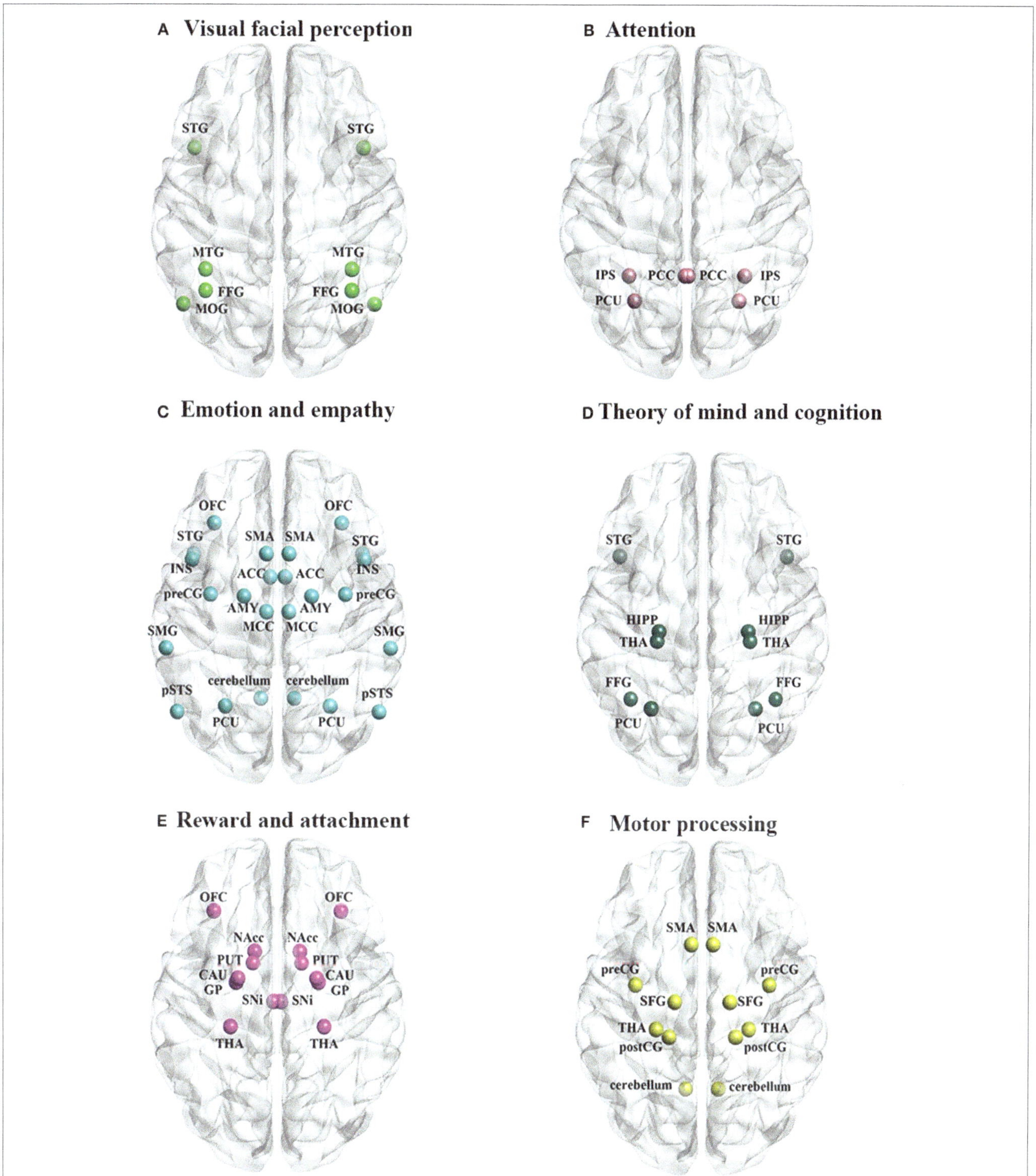

FIGURE 1 | The neural circuitry activated by perception of infant faces in parents and non-parents of both sexes associated with: (A) visual facial perception, (B) attention, (C) emotion and empathy, (D) theory of mind and cognition, (E) reward and attachment, and (F) motor processing.

circuit for preparation and planning and execution of intentional movements and speech (Goldberg, 1985; Caria et al., 2012). The SFG contains a number of different sub-regions with different patterns of connectivity with regions involved in motor control, working memory and attention and self-awareness (Li et al., 2013), and may play an important role in integrating perception and action (Goldberg et al., 2006). Overall the extensive pattern of activation in motor control circuitry seen in response to infant faces may be particularly important in mediating unconscious, intuitive and virtually unavoidable patterns of approach behavior in adults to protect infants and promote both physical and language interactions with them (Ackermann and Ziegler, 2010; Caria et al., 2012). As already discussed above in relation to motor empathy, adult observers may also show a greater propensity to mimic infant face expressions thereby aiding infant prosocial development (Carpenter et al., 2013).

Only a small number of studies have specifically investigated the impact of the intensity of baby schema features in infant faces either by comparing responses to the faces of infants (high baby schema) and children (low baby schema) or through direct manipulation of baby schema features in specific face stimuli. From these studies there is evidence that intensity of baby schema does influence neural responses in visual and face processing regions as well as in regions controlling emotional responses, attention and memory, theory of mind and reward. An ERP study found that N1 amplitude localized in the FFG was increased in response to infant faces compared to adult, although not child faces, in both males and females. On the other hand N2 amplitude localized in the medial occipital cortex and FFG, uncus and medial OFC was increased in response to infant compared with child and adult faces, although only in females (Proverbio et al., 2011b). An fMRI study which specifically manipulated the intensity of baby features found that infant faces with high baby schema features, and which were rated to be very cute, produced stronger activation than ones with low baby schema features in the right NAcc, left ACC (BA 24), left PCU (BA 7), and left FFG (Glocker et al., 2009b). Interestingly, another fMRI study showed that adult faces with a baby-faced appearance and infant faces evoked greater activation in the same brain regions (AMY and FFA) than more mature looking adult faces, and also stimulated greater functional connectivity between them (Zebrowitz et al., 2009). However, it should be noted that the enhanced impact of baby faces on AMY and OFC responses is disrupted if the infant face has physical anomalies, which disrupt the baby schema (Baeken et al., 2010a; Parsons et al., 2013). Overall therefore evidence from these studies indicates that infant faces with high baby schema are more likely to evoke greater responses in brain regions processing faces, attention, emotion and positive reward than those with low baby schema.

Specific Neural Responses to Own Infant Faces: Parental Love

In addition to the general impact of baby schema on neural processing discussed above there is widespread evidence for further enhanced effects when parents view their own as opposed to other infants. Thus, when mothers view their own infants there is greater activation observed in many of the same brain areas discussed above associated with visual processing, emotion, empathy, theory of mind, reward processing, social cognition and motor control (Bartels and Zeki, 2004; Leibenluft et al., 2004; Nitschke et al., 2004; Noriuchi et al., 2008; Minagawa-Kawai et al., 2009; Laurent and Ablow, 2013; Stoeckel et al., 2014; Wan et al., 2014; Esposito et al., 2015).

There are also some additional brain areas activated when mothers view their babies, including visual processing regions such as the occipital and temporal cortices (BA 17/18/19/37) (Nitschke et al., 2004), the right anterior temporal pole (ATP—BA 38) (Ranote et al., 2004) involved in emotional processing, periaqueductal gray (PAG) (Bartels and Zeki, 2004; Noriuchi et al., 2008), lateral OFC and lateral prefrontal cortex (lPFC—BA 11/47/46/45) (Bartels and Zeki, 2004) involved in maternal responses and emotion/reward processing and anterior paracingulate cortex (APC—BA 9) (Leibenluft et al., 2004) involved in theory of mind and cognitive processing. Moreover, ERP studies have found that both amplitudes of the parietal-distributed P300, involved in attention, and the temporal N170 component implicated in face encoding, were increased during viewing of own infant/child but not of unfamiliar infants/children (Doi and Shinohara, 2012; Weisman et al., 2012c). These specific neural responses toward own infant/child faces may represent components of maternal love/attachment which are clearly very important for the socio-emotional and cognitive development of infants, especially during the early post-partum period.

One of the most consistent findings in terms of an own infant-specific neural response in mothers is increased activation in the OFC which plays a key role both in emotion and reward processing (Bartels and Zeki, 2004; Nitschke et al., 2004; Kringelbach et al., 2008; Stoeckel et al., 2014). The OFC includes medial (BA 25/14/10) and lateral (BA 47/12/11/10) areas and in accordance with its anatomy and connectivity the lateral portion has been further subdivided into another three sub-regions: anterior, posterior and caudal (Elliott et al., 2000). The medial portion is particularly involved in monitoring reward value and making stimulus-reward associations while the lateral portion is more related to stimulus-outcome associations and reward-related response suppression (Elliott et al., 2000; Walton et al., 2010). Overall, studies have found that maternal love (in terms of maternal responses to own babies) is mostly associated with increased activation of the lateral OFC. Thus bilateral lateral OFC (BA 11/47) activation occurs when mothers passively view images of their own as opposed to another familiar infant (Bartels and Zeki, 2004); happy faces of their own compared to another unfamiliar happy infant (Nitschke et al., 2004) or video clips of their own compared to unknown infants (Noriuchi et al., 2008; Minagawa-Kawai et al., 2009). Another study has also reported greater activation in the left inferior OFC (BA 11) with own vs. other joyful infant faces in mothers with low self-reported current depressive symptoms (Laurent and Ablow, 2013). Finally there is also a study showing increased activations in response to viewing an own infant in the anterior portion of the OFC (Minagawa-Kawai et al., 2009).

An increasing number of studies have investigated the neural substrates of paternal love in recent years (Atzil et al., 2012; Lamb and Lewis, 2013; Leidy et al., 2013; Mascaro et al., 2014). Neuroimaging studies on fathers viewing own infant/child faces have found increased activity in brain areas including medial and lateral frontal cortex (IFG, MFG, SFG, OFC), SMG, MTG,

INS, cingulate, striatum (CAU) and AMY (Atzil et al., 2012; Kuo et al., 2012; Mascaro et al., 2014). All of these regions also show increased activation in mothers viewing their own infant/child faces. The only study to directly compare neural responses in mothers and fathers to videos of their own as opposed to other young infants also reported a considerable similarity between them (Atzil et al., 2012). However, this study also found significantly greater activation in mothers in a number of regions in the right hemisphere (STG, PostCG, FFG, MTG, AMY, lentiform nucleus, Cuneus, and CAU). On the other hand in fathers greater activation was found in the left MFG, inferior parietal gyrus, superior occipital gyrus and precuneus and in part of the right MTG and STG. This possibly suggests more right hemisphere dominated responses in mothers and left hemisphere dominated ones on father. Further evidence for differences between fathers and mothers has also been reported in response to own vs. other infant laughing of crying. In this case a deactivation response in the ACC, which is an important region in the control of emotion, was only found to occur in mothers (Seifritz et al., 2003). Somewhat surprisingly one study has reported that greater parental sensitivity and reciprocity in fathers was negatively associated with the activation in the right OFC for own compared with other infants (Kuo et al., 2012). This seems to imply that more responsive fathers may find all infants more rewarding, not just their own. However, only 10 subjects were included in this study and so some caution should be attached to interpreting this finding. Another a recent study has also investigated changes in regional gray matter (GM) volume in fathers from 2–4 to 12–16 weeks postpartum as an indication of potential neural plasticity changes. Results showed increased GM volume in the hypothalamus, AMY, striatum and lateral frontal cortex although a decrease in the OFC, PCC, and INS (Kim et al., 2014).

In summary, all the neuroimaging and electrophysiological findings described above support the conclusion that baby faces contain highly salient, affective and rewarding information that particularly engages the extensive neural processing systems involved in these functions in adult observers. These systems in turn mediate changes in motor preparation and response circuitry to promote approach, protection and nurturing behavior and the whole system undergoes plasticity changes to further strengthen the social bond with the infant and facilitate subsequent behavioral responses. Evidence to date suggests that the neural circuitry involved in maternal and paternal responses to own infants/children appears to be very similar, although there is some evidence for differential responses in some frontal, temporal, limbic, and brain reward regions. However further studies are clearly needed provide more extensive evidence for such parental sex differences.

Hormonal Correlates of Attraction to Infant Faces

A number of cultural, experiential and physiological factors could potentially contribute to observed sex differences in responses to infant and child faces. In particular, differential responses in men and women as a result of cultural norms and expectations may play a significant role (Lytton and Romney, 1991), although this has not been systematically investigated in the context of the baby schema effect. However, there is also a growing amount of evidence for hormonal influences on responses to infant cues in terms of sex differences, effects of puberty, the menstrual cycle and pregnancy, sex hormones and also neuropeptides, such as oxytocin and vasopressin, involved in the control of parental behavior and social bonds.

There is increasing behavioral and neural evidence for sex differences in response to infant faces. Behavioral findings have shown that while both males and females find infant faces cute, females tend to be more sensitive to the cuteness of infant faces than males (Glocker et al., 2009a; Lehmann et al., 2013), have stronger reactions and attentional bias toward them (Seifritz et al., 2003; Cárdenas et al., 2013), exhibit a higher preference for and liking of them (Maestripieri and Pelka, 2002; Parsons et al., 2011; Charles et al., 2013) and make more effort and have a stronger motivation to view them (Hahn et al., 2013). However, it should be noted that one study has failed to find a gender difference in attraction to infant faces, although this might possibly reflect the young age of the male participants or possibly the rather limited 5-point Likert scale used (Sprengelmeyer et al., 2013).

This observed gender difference in the perceived attractiveness of infant faces may to some extent be attributed to increased responsiveness in brain reward regions in mothers compared to fathers (Atzil et al., 2012), and also to the larger size of the OFC in females relative to males (Gur et al., 2002; Proverbio et al., 2011b). Indeed, support for a bias in women finding infant faces more rewarding, rather than being more sensitive to recognizing them, comes from a study showing that females were only better than males at choosing which of a pair of infant faces was cuter, but not when deciding which was the younger or the happier one (Lobmaier et al., 2010).

Preferences for infant faces also vary in women across their life cycle, and particularly with regard to their reproductive status. Two studies have reported that while females overall exhibit an overall higher preference for infant faces than males this preference varies with age. The first of these studies reported that during childhood (6–10 years) and adolescence (11–15 years) females exhibited the highest preference, but that this declined thereafter during early (19–35 years) and later (46–75 years) adulthood. Interestingly males showed a relatively constant preference across all four age groups (Maestripieri and Pelka, 2002). A second study reported that young women (19–26 years) are more sensitive to infant cuteness than men aged 19–26 and 53–60 years old. Women aged 45–51 years were the same as younger women whereas those aged 53–60 years old showed a reduced cuteness sensitivity that was equivalent to men (Sprengelmeyer et al., 2009). Thus both studies suggest that female reproductive hormones may play an important role in increasing perceived cuteness of infant faces. This explains the sex difference between young women and men and the decline seen in older women who are likely to have undergone menopause.

Puberty and age of puberty have also been shown to influence perception of infant cuteness. Post-menarcheal girls have a higher preference for infant faces and rated them more positively than pre-menarcheal peers and boys, suggesting that the onset of menstruation may increase attention toward infantile features (Goldberg et al., 1982). Furthermore, girls who had an early menarche also exhibited a greater subsequent preference for infant faces than those who had a later onset menarche (Maestripieri, 2004; Maestripieri et al., 2004). This latter finding is perhaps a little surprising given that early puberty is generally more associated with a negative impact in terms of increased likelihood of depression and behavioral problems (Copeland et al., 2010). However, it was also found that both early menarche and increased perception of cuteness were associated with early paternal absence from the home and so it is argued that this may represent an adaptation in terms of an earlier readiness for reproduction and parenting (Maestripieri et al., 2004).

Two studies to date have investigated potential differences in responses to infant faces across the menstrual cycle. One of these did not find any effects (Sprengelmeyer et al., 2013), however the other using a forced-choice paradigm where subjects indicated which of two infant faces was cuter, found that women were more likely to choose the cuter baby during their ovulatory than luteal phase of the cycle (Lobmaier et al., 2015). Nevertheless, cuteness discrimination was not associated with saliva concentrations of oestradiol, progesterone or testosterone, leading the authors to speculate that this menstrual cycle phase effect might be associated with other relevant hormones which change during the cycle, such as oxytocin or prolactin. To date no studies have looked at changes across pregnancy. However, overall findings do suggest some potential links between female reproductive hormones and their sensitivity to the cuteness of infant faces and that this can therefore contribute to facilitation of parental caregiving in individuals who have the reproductive potential to produce children (Sprengelmeyer et al., 2010).

In fathers two studies have reported correlations between blood testosterone concentrations and neural responses to infant cues. Testosterone concentrations were found to be decreased in fathers compared to non-fathers, and negatively associated with activation of the MFG in response to pictures of young children (Mascaro et al., 2014). On the other hand a study has also reported a positive association between testosterone concentrations in fathers and activation of a brain reward area, the left CAU, following interaction with an infant (Kuo et al., 2012). Thus the relationship between testosterone and neural responses to infant cues in fathers is somewhat unclear.

Effects of Sex Hormones on Attraction to Infant Faces

While no studies have systematically investigated the effects of exogenous treatments with either estradiol or progesterone on sensitivity to cuteness in infant faces one has reported that women using oral contraceptives (which contain estrogen and progesterone) are more sensitive compared to those who do not (Sprengelmeyer et al., 2009). However, the same group in a subsequent study failed to find an effect of oral contraceptives on the aesthetic and incentive salience of cute infant faces (Sprengelmeyer et al., 2013).

Another important sex hormone which influences parenting behaviors is testosterone (Bos et al., 2010; Kuo et al., 2012). Testosterone may play a role in regulating females' reward sensitivity since it has been shown to increase the reward value of financial incentives through testosterone administration (Hermans et al., 2010). While no studies to date have investigated effects of testosterone administration on viewing baby faces several have attempted to find any associations with salivary testosterone concentrations. Thus higher salivary testosterone concentrations in women were associated with greater reward scores given to cute infant faces and this effect was independent of progesterone and estradiol concentrations (Hahn et al., 2014). Higher salivary testosterone concentrations in fathers during interactions with infants have also been associated with greater activation in brain reward regions such as the CAU when processing own vs. other infant faces (Kuo et al., 2012).

Effects of Oxytocin and Vasopressin on Attraction to Infant Faces

There has been considerable interest in the role of the evolutionary conserved hypothalamic neuropeptides oxytocin and vasopressin in recent years and a large number of studies have investigated their importance for a wide range of human social and emotional behaviors. The majority of studies have focused on oxytocin (OXT) and its effects on trust, cooperation, face emotion recognition, empathy, in-group preferences and also on social bonds and maternal attachment (Bartz et al., 2011; Kemp and Guastella, 2011; Striepens et al., 2011; Weisman et al., 2012a,b; Scheele et al., 2014; Wigton et al., 2015). Oxytocin may play an important role in human parental responses, with higher plasma concentrations of maternal oxytocin across pregnancy being predictive of higher quality of postpartum maternal care (Feldman et al., 2007). Increased plasma concentrations of oxytocin across the first 6 months following the birth of a child have also been correlated with various, although differing, positive aspects of parental responsiveness in both mothers and fathers (Gordon et al., 2010). Associations between oxytocin receptor polymorphisms (Riem et al., 2011b; Feldman et al., 2012) and the vasopressin V1a receptor (Bisceglia et al., 2012) and sensitive parenting have also been reported. Oxytocin released during breast-feeding may also have stress-reducing effects (Heinrichs et al., 2001, 2002). In the context of the current review associations between oxytocin and vasopressin and attraction to infant faces have been shown by demonstrating correlations between plasma or saliva concentrations or associations with receptor polymorphisms or neural and behavioral responses to exogenous treatment using intranasal application.

Salivary oxytocin concentrations have been found to be positively correlated to mood ratings of happy but not sad infant faces in women (Bhandari et al., 2014). In an ERP study, urinary oxytocin concentrations in foster mothers following a cuddle interaction with their infants were also shown to be positively correlated with P300 amplitude in response to viewing all infant faces (Bick et al., 2013). However, another recent study which failed to demonstrate differences in responses to infant compared with adult faces in a facial visual research task found that urinary oxytocin concentrations were positively correlated with performance on both types of faces (Saito et al., 2014). Higher concentrations of plasma oxytocin have also been found to be related with stronger maternal response in terms of increased gaze toward the infant face in postpartum mothers (Feldman et al., 2007; Gordon et al., 2010), and greater activation in brain reward regions such as the ventral striatum, OFC and medial frontal cortex as well as in hypothalamic/pituitary regions in first-time mothers viewing own vs. unknown infant faces (Strathearn et al., 2009). Furthermore, those mothers with lower plasma oxytocin concentrations when viewing their own vs. unknown infant faces were found to be more likely to have insecure attachment and also reduced activation of the mesocorticolimbic dopamine reward system in response to infant face cues (Strathearn et al., 2008, 2009; Strathearn, 2011).

Thus while plasma, salivary and urinary concentrations of oxytocin may not necessarily always accurately reflect those in the brain (see Striepens et al., 2011) there does seem to be some association between higher endogenous concentrations of the peptide and enhanced responses to infant face cues, at least in post-partum mothers. In line with the potential role of oxytocin in influencing social reward and modulating activity in brain reward systems (Scheele et al., 2013; Striepens et al., 2014), increased peripheral concentrations also seem to be associated with greater responses to own vs. other infant faces and cues in dopaminergic reward pathways (Rilling, 2009; Strathearn et al., 2009; Strathearn, 2011). However, this relationship between oxytocin and enhanced activation in brain reward systems is not specific to parent-infant bonds since it has also been reported for romantic bonds in terms of men viewing the face of their female partner compared with another either familiar or unfamiliar woman (Scheele et al., 2013).

Intranasal oxytocin administration has been found to enhance responses to important infant cues such as crying (Riem et al., 2011a, 2014) and laughing (Riem et al., 2012). Oxytocin administration has also been reported to increase preference for infant faces in homozygous GG allele carriers for the rs53576 polymorphism of the oxytocin receptor, whereas rs53576A allele carriers showed the opposite pattern (Marsh et al., 2012). An ERP study has linked the rs53576 polymorphism with sensitivity to infant cues since in both mothers and nulliparous women who were GG allele carriers an early (~100 ms) differential frontal ERP response to strong intensity infant face expressions was associated with faster emotion recognition performance (Peltola et al., 2014). The same study found that mothers exhibited modulation of the early posterior negativity component (EPN) by negative valence faces. Intranasal OXT administration has also been shown to enhance subjective arousal ratings for infant photos in nulliparous women, and their ratings were positively correlated with their AMY activation in the oxytocin but not placebo treatment group (Rupp et al., 2013). Another study using the Infant Facial Expressions of Emotions from Looking at Pictures (IFEEL) task showed that oxytocin increased activation in empathy-related brain regions such as the left inferior frontal gyrus (IFG), MTG, and STG when women judged the emotion vs. gender of the infant faces. However, surprisingly it decreased behavioral performance on the face emotion recognition task independent of the difficulty level (Voorthuis et al., 2014). Oxytocin has also been reported to increase activity in the VTA, but not accumbens, of both nulliparous women and post-partum mothers during viewing of infant faces (Gregory et al., 2015). Studies investigating both neural and behavioral effects of intranasal oxytocin on responses to infant faces are summarized in **Table 3**.

While fewer studies have been carried out on men/fathers, one has reported the intranasal oxytocin treatment actually reduced activation in reward- and attachment-related brain regions, such as the left GP, when biological fathers passively viewed their own vs. an unfamiliar child (3–6 years) or an unfamiliar vs. familiar child. Oxytocin also decreased functional connectivity within a fronto-pallido-hippocampal network for own vs. unfamiliar child (Wittfoth-Schardt et al., 2012). Therefore, oxytocin may have differential effects on mothers and fathers by selectively modulating functional brain responses and connectivity to infant faces in regions associated with emotion, attachment, novelty and reward processing (Wittfoth-Schardt et al., 2012). Another study has also reported different associations between plasma oxytocin concentrations in mothers and fathers and brain regions showing greater responses to videos of own vs. other infants (Atzil et al., 2012). Thus, while higher AMY activation in mothers was positively associated with plasma oxytocin concentrations, this was not the case in fathers. In mothers oxytocin concentrations were positively associated with activity in the left INS, left inferior parietal lobule (IPL), bilateral temporal cortex (TC), left ventral ACC and left NAcc. In fathers on the other hand activation in the left IFG, SFG and medial prefrontal cortex (mPFC), left postCG and left ACC was negatively associated with oxytocin concentrations. These findings again support the possibility that oxytocin may be influencing brain regions associated with attention, emotion, reward and even motor processing differently in mothers and fathers, although obviously some caution needs to be applied to such simple correlational analyses of this kind.

A number of studies have reported effects of intranasal oxytocin on reducing AMY responses to negative emotional faces (see Striepens et al., 2011) and also to both laughing (Riem et al., 2012) and crying (Riem et al., 2011a) infants. However despite the fact that greater AMY activation has been reported in response to own infant faces in mothers (Atzil et al., 2012; Strathearn and Kim, 2013), effects of oxytocin on AMY responses to infant faces have so far not been found.

Vasopressin, which is closely associated with oxytocin, has also been shown to influence social behaviors (Hammock, 2015; Patel et al., 2015). In rats, for example, it plays a potent role in facilitating maternal behavior, independent of trait anxiety (Bosch and Neumann, 2008). However, to date few studies have investigated potential effects of vasopressin on the attractiveness of infant cues. One study has reported some overlapping but also different patterns of negative associations between plasma vasopressin concentrations and activity in brain regions responding more strongly to videos of own vs. other infants (Atzil et al., 2012). In mothers, associations were found in bilateral SFG, right MFG and right middle temporal gyrus (MTG), whereas in fathers they were found in the right IPL,

TABLE 3 | The effect of oxytocin administration on brain response to infant and child faces.

Study	Participants	Face age	OXT dose	Face presentation	Behavior task	Contrasts	WB/ROI	Neural effect of OXT
Voorthuis et al., 2014	50 nulliparous women: 18–27 years	N/A	16 IU	5 s	Adapted version of the Infant Facial Expressions of Emotions from Looking at Pictures (IFEEL pictures) task: to indicate the child's emotional state or the gender	Emotion > gender judgment	ROI ROI	↑L STG ↑L MTG
Wittfoth-Schardt et al., 2012	21 Fathers: 39.3 ± 6.2 years	3–6 years	24 IU	2 s	Implicit facial processing	Own > familiar child	ROI	↓ L GP
						Unfamiliar > familiar child	ROI WB ROI WB WB WB	↓ L GP (PUT) ↓ L preCG ↓ L HIPP (AMY) ↓ L/R MTG ↓ L STG ↓ L SMG (IPS)
						Own > unfamiliar child	WB	↑ L CAU
						Own > familiar child (functional connectivity)	ROI/WB ROI/WB ROI/WB ROI/WB	↓ L GP, R GP ↓ L GP, L MFG ↓ L GP, L HIPP ↓ L GP, R SPL
Gregory et al., 2015	30 nulliparous female; 29 postpartum female (16 primiparous, 13 multiparous); 20-40 years	N/A	24 IU	2s	One-back matching task: A sexually explicit, crying infant, smiling infant and neutral photos.	Crying infant > fixation	ROI	↓VTA

OXT, oxytocin; IU, international unit; WB, whole brain analysis; ROI, regions of interest analysis; L, left; R, right; ↑, increased; ↓, decreased. Abbreviations of brain regions: see ***Table 2****.*

right inferior and medial frontal gyri, left INS and right temporal lobe. Thus, as with oxytocin, there may be different responses to vasopressin in maternal and paternal brains, although this clearly needs more detailed confirmation. While at this stage it is unclear whether vasopressin may play an important role in influencing responses to infant cues by either males or females, one speculation might be that it could serve to enhance empathic responses, particularly in those individuals whose parental response sensitivity is high. For example, a recent study has reported that intranasal vasopressin, but not oxytocin, increased empathic concern in both male and female subjects. Interestingly this effect was strongest in individuals who had received higher levels of paternal warmth during their childhood (Tabak et al., 2014).

Altered Responses to Infant Cues in Post-partum Depression and Substance Abuse

Post-partum depression affects between 6.5 and 8.5% of mothers (Yonkers et al., 2001) and is associated with reduced positive interest and responses to infant cues, which in turn can lead to weakening the relationship between a mother and her child. Studies have shown that mothers suffering from postnatal depression are more likely to rate negative emotion infant faces more negatively (Stein et al., 2010), and even neutral expression ones more negative than controls (Gil et al., 2011). Mothers with post-partum depression are also less accurate when identifying unfamiliar happy infant faces than healthy mothers, although there were no differences found when identifying sad faces (Arteche et al., 2011). While paternal postpartum depression is also moderately and positively correlated with maternal depression (Paulson and Bazemore, 2010), no study to date has investigated altered responses of fathers with depression to infant cues. This should be an important area for future studies.

Neuroimaging and electrophysiological studies have found evidence for a reduced effect of infant faces in a number of the same brain regions involved in attention, emotional and empathic responses and reward discussed above. Thus, depressed mothers compared to healthy controls showed a slower response in the dorsal ACC when viewing the distressed face of their own infant. Also, those with higher levels of current symptomatology showed reduced responses in the OFC and INS toward their own infant's joyful faces. Symptom severity could also predict lower responses to their own infant in left prefrontal and insula/striatal regions (Laurent and Ablow, 2013). On the other hand an ERP study has reported that the face-sensitive N170 component elicited in response to infant face stimuli was positively related with depression symptom severity (Noll et al., 2012). This perhaps implies an increased initial automatic perceptual sensitivity to infant faces in mothers with a greater severity of post-partum depression, but a subsequent suppression of responses in brain regions controlling positive attentional, emotional and reward responses to infants.

Anxiety disorders can also impact negatively on maternal responses to infants and one study has shown that mothers with generalized anxiety disorder are inclined to rate the intensity of happy infant faces lower than controls (Arteche et al., 2011). Furthermore, the babies of anxious mothers appear to be less willing to look at their face since maternal anxiety scores have been shown to be negatively correlated with the amount of time babies looking at their mother's face (Jones et al., 2013). Thus babies also appear to be sensitive to reduced interest in them by anxious, and probably also depressed mothers, thereby further increasing the potential threat to the parent-infant bond.

Key regions exhibiting altered responses to negative emotional stimuli in patients with anxiety and depression disorders notably include those involved in responses to infant faces, such as the ACC, INS, and AMY (Jaworska et al., 2014; Oathes et al., 2015).

Drug addiction has also been shown to influence responses to infant faces. The National Survey on Drug Use and Health (NSDUH) in 2007 found that 5.2% of pregnant women reported using illicit drugs during pregnancy; and an additional 11.6% reported using alcohol and 16.4% tobacco. Mothers using cocaine during pregnancy have been found to respond more passively and in a more disengaged way to their babies (Gottwald and Thurman, 1994), and similar patterns of reduced responsivity in substance-using mothers have been reported in terms of parenting children even beyond infancy (Johnson et al., 2002; Molitor and Mayes, 2010). An fMRI study has shown that mothers using drugs during pregnancy (tobacco, heroin, marijuana, opiates, cocaine, and alcohol) had reduced responses to neutral and emotional infant faces in many of the regions discussed above which show enhanced responses to infant faces. For happy faces reduced responses were found in frontal regions involved in attention, salience and reward (ventromedial, dorsolateral and dorsomedial frontal cortex) as well as in early visual processing (occipital gyrus). For sad faces similar reductions were seen in frontal regions (dorsolateral frontal cortex, inferior and medial frontal gyri and medial OFC), although additionally in sensorimotor regions, MTG, STG, and PCC, as well as the AMY and parahippocampal gyrus (PHG). For neutral expression faces again there were extensive frontal reductions in responses (ventromedial, dorsomedial, and dorsolateral frontal cortex and inferior frontal gyrus) as well as in sensorimotor regions, PCC, GP, AMY, and PHG. There was also reduced responsiveness a primary visual processing region, the cuneus (Landi et al., 2011). Thus overall, drug taking appears to have an even more pronounced effect in reducing responsiveness in brain circuitry to infant faces than either post-partum depression or general anxiety.

Conclusions and Future Directions

In line with the potent impact of facial baby schema on adult attraction, protection and caregiving behaviors, neuroimaging and electrophysiological studies reveal an extensive neural circuitry involved in our perception of infant faces. Enhanced activation in response to infant compared to adult faces is found in cortical and sub-cortical brain regions involved in face perception, attention, emotion, empathy, memory, reward and attachment, theory of mind and also control of motor responses. Both mothers and fathers also show evidence for enhanced responses in these same neural systems when viewing their own as opposed to another child. Importantly post-partum depression, anxiety and drug-taking all tend to reduce responsivity in this neural circuitry involved in processing and responding to infant face cues, with the most extensive changes in this respect appearing to occur in women taking addictive drugs during pregnancy.

Reproductively active women tend to rate infant faces as cuter than men and this may be mainly a reflection of both heightened attention to relevant cues and a stronger activation in their brain reward circuitry. In both sexes perceived cuteness of infant faces is influenced by reproductive hormones, with women in particular showing an ovulatory peak in interest during their cycle and an apparent decline post-menopause. To date evidence does not support major roles for the gonadal hormones estradiol, progesterone and testosterone in influencing responsivity to infant faces, although there is increasing evidence linking oxytocin with facilitation of attention toward and attractiveness of infant cues in both sexes.

Future studies need to explore in more detail the functional relevance of specific components of the widespread neural circuitry associated with the enhanced responses to infant faces. To date, for example, only one study has demonstrated the functional importance of the dorsolateral prefrontal cortex in the processing of emotional baby faces using rTMS (Baeken et al., 2010b). A particular focus should be on the circuitry involved with face processing, attention, emotion, empathy and reward processing since this would appear to be affected in reduced responses observed in post-partum depression, anxiety and drug use. It is also important to establish the functional roles of the neuropeptides oxytocin and vasopressin in mediating enhanced neural and behavioral responses to infant faces and other salient cues since they could in future represent potential therapeutic agents.

References

Ackermann, H., and Ziegler, W. (2010). "Brain mechanisms underlying speech motor control," in *The Handbook of Phonetic Sciences, 2nd Edn.*, eds W. J. Hardcastle, J. Laver, and F. Gibbons (Oxford: Blackwell Publishing Ltd), 202–250. doi: 10.1002/9781444317251.ch6

Alley, T. R. (1983). Infantile head shape as an elicitor of adult protection. *Merrill-Palmer Q.* 29, 411–427.

Arteche, A., Joormann, J., Harvey, A., Craske, M., Gotlib, I. H., Lehtonen, A., et al. (2011). The effects of postnatal maternal depression and anxiety on the processing of infant faces. *J. Affect. Disord.* 133, 197–203. doi: 10.1016/j.jad.2011.04.015

Atzil, S., Hendler, T., Zagoory-Sharon, O., Winetraub, Y., and Feldman, R. (2012). Synchrony and specificity in the maternal and the paternal brain: relations to oxytocin and vasopressin. *J. Am. Acad. Child Adolesc. Psychiatry* 51, 798–811. doi: 10.1016/j.jaac.2012.06.008

Baeken, C., Van Schuerbeek, P., De Raedt, R., Bossuyt, A., Vanderhasselt, M. A., De Mey, J., et al. (2010a). Passively viewing negatively valenced baby faces attenuates left amygdala activity in healthy females scoring high on 'Harm Avoidance.' *Neurosci. Lett.* 478, 97–101. doi: 10.1016/j.neulet.2010.04.073

Baeken, C., Van Schuerbeek, P., De Raedt, R., DeMey, J., Vanderhasselt, M. A., Bossuyt, A., et al. (2010b). The effect of one left-sided dorsolateral prefrontal cortical HF-rTMS session on emotional brain processes in women. *Psychiatria Danubina* 22, S163.

Barrett, J., Wonch, K. E., Gonzalez, A., Ali, N., Steiner, M., Hall, G. B., et al. (2012). Maternal affect and quality of parenting experiences are related to amygdala response to infant faces. *Soc. Neurosci.* 7, 252–268. doi: 10.1080/17470919.2011.609907

Bartels, A., and Zeki, S. (2004). The neural correlates of maternal and romanticlove. *Neuroimage* 21, 1155–1166. doi: 10.1016/j.neuroimage.2003.11.00

Bartz, J. A., Zaki, J., Bolger, N., and Ochsner, K. N. (2011). Social effects of oxytocin in humans: context and person matter. *Trends Cogn. Sci.* 15, 301–309. doi: 10.1016/j.tics.2011.05.002

Berry, D. S., and McArthur, L. Z. (1986). Perceiving character in faces: the impact of age-related craniofacial changes on social perception. *Psychol. Bull.* 100, 3–18. doi: 10.1037/0033-2909.100.1.3

Bhandari, R., Bakermans-Kranenburg, M. J., van der Veen, R., Parsons, C. E., Young, K. S., Grewen, K. M., et al. (2014). Salivary oxytocin mediates the association between emotional maltreatment and responses to emotional infant faces. *Physiol. Behav.* 131, 123–128. doi: 10.1016/j.physbeh.2014.04.028

Bick, J., Dozier, M., Bernard, K., Grasso, D., and Simons, R. (2013). Foster mother–infant bonding: associations between foster mothers' oxytocin production, electrophysiological brain activity, feelings of commitment, and caregiving quality. *Child Dev.* 84, 826–840. doi: 10.1111/cdev.12008

Bisceglia, R., Jenkins, J. M., Wigg, K. G., O'Connor, T. G., Moran, G., and Barr, C. L. (2012). Arginine vasopressin 1a receptor gene and maternal behavior: evidence of association and moderation. *Genes Brain Behav.* 11, 262–268. doi: 10.1111/j.1601-183X.2012.00769.x

Borgi, M., Cogliati-Dezza, I., Brelsford, V., Meints, K., and Cirulli, F. (2014). Baby schema in human and animal faces induces cuteness perception and gaze allocation in children. *Front. Psychol.* 5:411. doi: 10.3389/fpsyg.2014.00411

Bos, P. A., Hermans, E. J., Montoya, E. R., Ramsey, N. F., and Van Honk, J. (2010). Testosterone administration modulates neural responses to crying infants in youngfemales. *Psychoneuroendocrinology* 35, 114–121. doi: 10.1016/j.psyneuen.2009.09.013

Bosch, O. J., and Neumann, I. D. (2008). Brain vasopressin is an important regulator of maternal behavior independent of dams' trait anxiety. *Proc. Natl. Acad. Sci. U.S.A.* 105, 17139–17144. doi: 10.1073/pnas.0807412105

Bourdy, R., and Barrot, M. (2012). A new control center for dopaminergic systems: pulling the VTA by the tail. *Trends Neurosci.* 35, 681–690. doi: 10.1016/j.tins.2012.06.007

Brosch, T., Sander, D., Pourtois, G., and Scherer, K. R. (2008). Beyond fear: rapid spatial orienting toward positive emotional stimuli. *Psychol. Sci.* 19, 392–370. doi: 10.1111/j.1467-9280.2008.02094.x

Brosch, T., Sander, D., and Scherer, K. R. (2007). That baby caught my eye... attention capture by infant faces. *Emotion* 7, 685–689. doi: 10.1037/1528-3542.7.3.685

Cárdenas, R. A., Harris, L. J., and Becker, M. W. (2013). Sex differences in visual attention toward infant faces. *Evol. Hum. Behav.* 34, 280–287. doi: 10.1016/j.evolhumbehav.2013.04.001

Carpenter, M., Vebel, J., and Tomasello, M. (2013). Being mimicked increases prosocial behavior in 18-month-old infants. *Child Dev.* 84, 1511–1518. doi: 10.1111/cdev.12083

Caria, A., de Falco, S., Venuti, P., Lee, S., Esposito, G., Rigo, P., et al. (2012). Species-specific response to human infant faces in the premotor cortex. *Neuroimage* 60, 884–893. doi: 10.1016/j.neuroimage.2011.12.068

Charles, N. E., Alexander, G. M., and Saenz, J. (2013). Motivational value and salience of images of infants. *Evol. Hum. Behav.* 34, 373–381. doi: 10.1016/j.evolhumbehav.2013.06.005

Chin, S. F., Wade, T. J., and French, K. (2006). Race and facial attractiveness: individual differences in perceived adoptability of children. *J. Cult. Evol. Psychol.* 4, 215–229. doi: 10.1556/JCEP.4.2006.3-4.2

Copeland, W., Shanahan, L., Miller, S., Costello, E. J., Angold, A., and Maughan, B. (2010). Outcomes of early pubertal timing in young women: a prospective population-based study. *Am. J. Psychiatry* 167, 1218–1225. doi: 10.1176/appi.ajp.2010.09081190

Costa, V. D., Lang, P. J., Sabatinelli, D., Versace, F., and Bradley, M. M. (2010). Emotional imagery: assessing pleasure and arousal in the brain's reward circuitry. *Hum. Brain Mapp.* 31, 1446–1457. doi: 10.1002/hbm.20948

Darwin, C. (ed.). (1872). *The Expression of the Emotions in Man and Animals.* Chicago, IL: University of Chicago Press.

DeBruine, L. M. (2004). Resemblance to self increases the appeal of child faces to both men and women. *Evol. Hum. Behav.* 25, 142–154. doi: 10.1016/j.evolhumbehav.2004.03.003

Doi, H., and Shinohara, K. (2012). Electrophysiological responses in mothers to their own and unfamiliar child's gaze information. *Brain Cogn.* 80, 266–276. doi: 10.1016/j.bandc.2012.07.009

Eibl-Eibesfeldt, I. (1989). *Human Ethology.* Hawthorne, NY: Aldine de Gruyter.

Elliott, R., Dolan, R. J., and Frith, C. D. (2000). Dissociable functions in the medial and lateral orbitofrontal cortex: evidence from human neuroimaging studies. *Cereb. Cortex* 10, 308–317. doi: 10.1093/cercor/10.3.308

Esposito, G., Nakazawa, J., Ogawa, S., Stival, R., Kawashima, A., Putnick, D. L., et al. (2014). Baby, You Light-Up My Face: culture-general physiological responses to infants and culture-specific cognitive judgements of adults. *PLoS ONE* 9:e106705. doi: 10.1371/journal.pone.0106705

Esposito, G., Valenzi, S., Islam, T., Mash, C., and Bornstein, M. H. (2015). Immediate and selective maternal brain responses to own infant faces. *Behav. Brain Res.* 278, 40–43. doi: 10.1016/j.bbr.2014.09.018

Fan, Y., Duncan, N. W., de Greck, M., and Northoff, G. (2011). Is there a core neural network in empathy? An fMRI based quantitative meta-analysis. *Neurosci. Biobehav. Rev.* 35, 903–911. doi: 10.1016/j.neubiorev.2010.10.009

Feldman, R., Weller, A., Zagoory-Sharon, O., and Levine, A. (2007). Evidence for a neuroendocrinological foundation of human affiliation plasma oxytocin levels across pregnancy and the postpartum period predict mother-infant bonding. *Psychol. Sci.* 18, 965–970. doi: 10.1111/j.1467-9280.2007.02010.x

Feldman, R., Zagoory-Sharon, O., Weisman, O., Schneiderman, I., Gordon, I., Maoz, R., et al. (2012). Sensitive parenting is associated with plasma oxytocin and polymorphisms in the OXTR and CD38 genes. *Biol. Psychiatry* 72, 175–181. doi: 10.1016/j.biopsych.2011.12.025

Gil, S., Teissèdre, F., Chambres, P., and Droit-Volet, S. (2011). The evaluation of emotional facial expressions in early postpartum depression mood: a difference between adult and baby faces? *Psychiatry Res.* 186, 281–286. doi: 10.1016/j.psychres.2010.06.015

Glocker, M. L., Langleben, D. D., Ruparel, K., Loughead, J. W., Gur, R. C., and Sachser, N. (2009a). Baby schema in infant faces induces cuteness perception and motivation for caretaking in adults. *Ethology* 115, 257–263. doi: 10.1111/j.1439-0310.2008.01603.x

Glocker, M. L., Langleben, D. D., Ruparel, K., Loughead, J. W., Valdez, J. N., Griffin, M. D., et al. (2009b). Baby schema modulates the brain reward system in nulliparous women. *Proc. Natl. Acad. Sci. U.S.A.* 106, 9115–9119. doi: 10.1073/pnas.0811620106

Golle, J., Lisibach, S., Mast, F. W., and Lobmaier, J. S. (2013). Sweet puppies and cute babies: perceptual adaptation to babyfacedness transfers across species. *PLoS ONE* 8:e58248. doi: 10.1371/journal.pone.0058248

Golle, J., Probst, F., Mast, F. W., and Lobmaier, J. S. (2015). Preference for cute infants does not depend on their ethnicity or species: evidence from hypothetical adoption and donation paradigms. *PLoS ONE* 10:e0121554. doi: 10.1371/journal.pone.0121554

Goldberg, G. (1985). Supplementary motor area structure and function: review and hypotheses. *Behav. Brain Sci.* 8, 567–588. doi: 10.1017/S0140525X00045167

Goldberg, I. I., Harel, M., and Malach, R. (2006). When the brain loses its self: prefrontal inactivation during sensorimotor processing. *Neuron* 50, 329–339. doi: 10.1016/j.neuron.2006.03.015

Goldberg, S., Blumberg, S. L., and Kriger, A. (1982). Menarche and interest in infants: biological and social influences. *Child Dev.* 53, 1544–1550.

Goodkind, M. S., Sollberger, M., Gyurak, A., Rosen, H. J., Rankin, K. P., Miller, B., et al. (2012). Tracking emotional valence: the role of the orbitofrontal cortex. *Hum. Brain Mapp.* 33, 753–762. doi: 10.1002/hbm.21251

Gordon, I., Zagoory-Sharon, O., Leckman, J. F., and Feldman, R. (2010). Oxytocin and the development of parenting in humans. *Biol. Psychiatry* 68, 377–382. doi: 10.1016/j.biopsych.2010.02.005

Gottwald, S. R., and Thurman, S. K. (1994).The effects of prenatal cocaine exposure on mother-infant interaction and infant arousal in the newborn period. *Topics Early Child. Spec. Educ.* 14, 217–231. doi: 10.1177/0271121494014 00206

Gregory, R., Cheng, H., Rupp, H. A., Senelaub, D., and Heiman, J. R. (2015). Oxytocin increases VTA activation to infant and sexual stimuli in nulliparous and postpartum women. *Horm. Behav.* 69, 82–88. doi: 10.1016/j.yhbeh.2014.12.009

Gur, R. C., Dixon, F. G., Bilker, W. B., and Gur, R. E. (2002). Sex differences in temporo-limbic and frontal brain volumes of healthy adults. *Cereb. Cortex* 12, 998–1003. doi: 10.1093/cercor/12.9.998

Hahn, A. C., DeBruine, L. M., Fisher, C. I., and Jones, B. C. (2014). The reward value of infant facial cuteness tracks within-subject changes in women's salivary testosterone. *Horm. Behav.* 67, 54–59. doi: 10.1016/j.yhbeh.2014.11.010

Hahn, A. C., Xiao, D., Sprengelmeyer, R., and Perrett, D. I. (2013). Gender differences in the incentive salience of adult and infant faces. *Q. J. Exp. Psychol.* 66, 200–208. doi: 10.1080/17470218.2012.705860

Hammock, E. A. (2015). Developmental perspectives on oxytocin and vasopressin. *Neuropsychopharmacology* 40, 24–42. doi: 10.1038/npp.2014.120

Heinrichs, M., Meinlschmidt, G., Neumann, I., Wagner, S., Kirschbaum, C., Ehlert, U., et al. (2001). Effects of suckling on hypothalamic-pituitary-adrenal axis responses to psychosocial stress in postpartum lactating women. *J. Clin. Endocrinol. Metab.* 86, 4798–4804.

Heinrichs, M., Neumann, I., and Ehlert, U. (2002). Lactation and stress: protective effects of breast-feeding in humans. *Stress* 5, 195–203. doi: 10.1080/1025389021000010530

Hermans, E. J., Bos, P. A., Ossewaarde, L., Ramsey, N. F., Fernández, G., and Van Honk, J. (2010). Effects of exogenous testosterone on the ventral striatal BOLD response during reward anticipation in healthy women. *Neuroimage* 52, 277–283. doi: 10.1016/j.neuroimage.2010.04.019

Hoffman, E. A., and Haxby, J. V. (2000). Distinct representations of eye gaze and identity in the distributed human neural system for face perception. *Nat. Neurosci.* 3, 80–84. doi: 10.1038/71152

Jaworska, N., Yang, X. R., Knott, V., and MacQueen, G. (2014). A review of fMRI studies during visual emotive processing in major depressive disorder. *World J. Biol. Psychiatry*. doi: 10.3109/15622975.2014.885659. [Epub ahead of print].

Johnson, A. L., Morrow, C. E., Accornero, V. H., Xue, L., Anthony, J. C., and Bandstra, E. S. (2002). Maternal cocaine use: estimated effects on mother-childplay interactions in the preschool period. *J. Dev. Behav. Pediat.* 23, 191–202.

Jones, R., Slade, P., Pascalis, O., and Herbert, J. S. (2013). Infant interest in their mother's face is associated with maternal psychological health. *Infant Behav. Dev.* 36, 686–693. doi: 10.1016/j.infbeh.2013.07.002

Karraker, K. H., and Stern, M. (1990). Infant physical attractiveness and facial expression: effects on adult perceptions. *Basic Appl. Soc. Psychol.* 11, 371–385. doi: 10.1207/s15324834basp1104_2

Kemp, A. H., and Guastella, A. J. (2011). The role of oxytocin in human affect a novel hypothesis. *Curr. Dir. Psychol. Sci.* 20, 222–231. doi: 10.1177/0963721411417547

Kim, P., Rigo, P., Mayes, L. C., Feldman, R., Leckman, J. F., and Swain, J. E. (2014). Neural plasticity in fathers of human infants. *Soc. Neurosci.* 9, 522–535. doi: 10.1080/17470919.2014.933713

Komori, M., and Nittono, H. (2013). Influence of age-Independent facial traits on adult judgments of cuteness and infantility of a child's face. *Procedia-Soc. Behav. Sci.* 97, 285–291. doi: 10.1016/j.sbspro.2013.10.235

Kringelbach, M. L., Lehtonen, A., Squire, S., Harvey, A. G., Craske, M. G., Holliday, I. E., et al. (2008). A specific and rapid neural signature for parental instinct. *PLoS ONE* 3:e1664. doi: 10.1371/journal.pone.0001664

Kuo, P. X., Carp, J., Light, K. C., and Grewen, K. M. (2012). Neural responses to infants linked with behavioral interactions and testosterone in fathers. *Biol. Psychol.* 91, 302–306. doi: 10.1016/j.biopsycho.2012.08.002

Lamb, M. E., and Lewis, C. (2013). "Father-child relationships," in *Handbook of Father Involvement: Multidisciplinary Perspectives*, Vol. 2, eds N. J. Cabrera and C. S. Tamis-Lemonda (New York, NY: Routledge), 119–135.

Landi, N., Montoya, J., Kober, H., Rutherford, H. J. V., Mencl, W. E., Worhunsky, P. D., et al. (2011). Maternal neural responses to infant cries and faces: relationships with substance use. *Front. Psychiatry* 2:32. doi: 10.3389/fpsyt.2011.00032

Langlois, J. H., Ritter, J. M., Casey, R. J., and Swain, D. B. (1995). Infant attractiveness predicts maternal behaviours and attitudes. *Dev. Psychobiol.* 31, 464–472. doi: 10.1037/DD12-1649.31.3.464

Laurent, H. K., and Ablow, J. C. (2013). A face a mother could love: depression-related maternal neural responses to infant emotion faces. *Soc. Neurosci.* 8, 228–239. doi: 10.1080/17470919.2012.762039

Lehmann, V., Huisin't Veld, E. M., and Vingerhoets, A. J. (2013). The human and animal baby schema effect: correlates of individual differences. *Behav. Process.* 94, 99–108. doi: 10.1016/j.beproc.2013.01.001

Leibenluft, E., Gobbini, M. I., Harrison, T., and Haxby, J. V. (2004). Mothers' neural activation in response to pictures of their children and other children. *Biol. Psychiatry* 56, 225–232. doi: 10.1016/j.biopsych.2004.05.017

Leidy, M. S., Schofield, T. J., and Parke, R. D. (2013). "Fathers' contributions to children's social development," in *Handbook of Father Involvement: Multidisciplinary Perspectives*, Vol. 2, eds N. J. Cabrera and C. S. Tamis-Lemonda (New York, NY: Routledge), 151–167.

Lenzi, D., Trentini, C., Pantano, P., Macaluso, E., Iacoboni, M., Lenzi, G. L., et al. (2009). Neural basis of maternal communication and emotional expression processing during infant preverbal stage. *Cereb. Cortex* 19, 1124–1133. doi: 10.1093/cercor/bhn153

Leopold, D. A., and Rhodes, G. (2010). A comparative view of face perception. *J. Compar. Psychol.* 124, 233. doi: 10.1037/a0019460

Lindquist, K. A., Wager, T. D., Kober, H., Bliss-Moreau, E., and Feldman Barrett, L. (2012). The brain basis of emotion: a meta-analytic review. *Behav. Brain Sci.* 35, 121–202. doi: 10.1017/s0140525x11000446

Little, A. C. (2012). Manipulation of infant like traits affects perceived cuteness of infant, adult and cat faces. *Ethology* 118, 775–782. doi: 10.1111/j.1439-0310.2012.02068.x

Li, W., Qin, W., Liu, H., Fan, L., Wang, J., Jiang, T., et al. (2013). Subregions of the human superior frontal gyrus and their connections. *Neuroimage* 78, 46–58. doi: 10.1016/j.neuroimage.2013.04.011

Lobmaier, J. S., Probst, F., Perrett, D. I., and Heinrichs, M. (2015). Menstrual cycle phase affects discrimination of infant cuteness. *Horm. Behav.* 70, 1–6. doi: 10.1016/j.yhbeh.2015.02.001

Lobmaier, J. S., Sprengelmeyer, R., Wiffen, B., and Perrett, D. I. (2010). Female and male responses to cuteness, age and emotion in infant faces. *Evol. Hum. Behav.* 31, 16–21. doi: 10.1016/j.evolhumbehav.2009.05.004

Lorenz, K. (1943). Die angeborenen Formenmöglicher Erfahrung. *Zeitschrift für Tierpsychologie* 5, 235–409.

Luo, L. Z., Kendrick, K. M., Li, H., and Lee, K. (2014). Adults with siblings like children's faces more than those without. *J. Exp. Child Psychol.* 129, 148–156. doi: 10.1016/j.jecp.2014.09.003

Luo, L. Z., Li, H., and Lee, K. (2011). Are children's faces really more appealing than those of adults? Testing the baby schema hypothesis beyond infancy. *J. Exp. Child Psychol.* 110, 115–124. doi: 10.1016/j.jecp.2011.04.002

Lytton, H., and Romney, D. M. (1991). Parent's differential socialization of boys and girls: a meta-analysis. *Psychol. Bull.* 109, 267–296. doi: 10.1037/0033-2909.109.2.296

Macchi Cassia, V., Luo, L., Pisacane, A., Li, H., and Lee, K. (2014). How race and age experiences shape young children's face processing abilities. *J. Exp. Child Psychol.* 120, 87–101. doi: 10.1016/j.jecp.2013.11.016

Maestripieri, D. (2004). Developmental and evolutionary aspects of female attraction to babies. *Psychol. Sci. Agenda* 18, 1–3.

Maestripieri, D., and Pelka, S. (2002). Sex differences in interest in infants across the lifespan: a biological adaptation for parenting. *Hum. Nat.* 13, 327–344. doi: 10.1007/s12110-002-1018-1

Maestripieri, D., Roney, J. R., DeBias, N., Durante, K. M., and Spaepen, G. M. (2004). Father absence, menarche and interest in infants among adolescent girls. *Dev. Sci.* 7, 560–566. doi: 10.1111/j.1467-7687.2004.00380.x

Malak, S. M., Crowley, M. J., Mayes, L. C., and Rutherford, H. J. (2015). Maternal anxiety and neural responses to infant faces. *J. Affect. Disord.* 172, 324–330. doi: 10.1016/j.jad.2014.10.013

Marsh, A. A., Henry, H. Y., Pine, D. S., Gorodetsky, E. K., Goldman, D., and Blair, R. J. R. (2012). The influence of oxytocin administration on responses to infant faces and potential moderation by OXTR genotype. *Psychopharmacology* 224, 469–476. doi: 10.1007/s00213-012-2775-0

Mascaro, J. S., Hackett, P. D., and Rilling, J. K. (2014). Differential neural responses to child and sexual stimuli in human fathers and non-fathers and their hormonal correlates. *Psychoneuroendocrinology* 46, 153–163. doi: 10.1016/j.psyneuen.2014.04.014

McArthur, L. Z., and Apatow, K. (1984). Impressions of baby-faced adults. *Soc. Cogn.* 2, 315–342. doi: 10.152/soco.1984.2.4.315

Minagawa-Kawai, Y., Matsuoka, S., Dan, I., Naoi, N., Nakamura, K., and Kojima, S. (2009). Prefrontal activation associated with social attachment: facial-emotion recognition in mothers and infants. *Cereb. Cortex* 19, 284–292. doi: 10.1093/cercor/bhn081

Molitor, A., and Mayes, L. C. (2010). Problematic dyadic interaction among toddlers and their polydrug- cocaine-using mothers. *Infant Ment. Health J.* 31, 121–140. doi: 10.1002/imhj.20248

Montoya, J. L., Landi, N., Kober, H., Worhunsky, P. D., Rutherford, H. J., Mencl, W. E., et al. (2012). Regional brain responses in nulliparous women to emotional infant stimuli. *PLoS ONE* 7:e36270. doi: 10.1371/journal.pone.0036270

Nishitani, S., Doi, H., Koyama, A., and Shinohara, K. (2011). Differential prefrontal response to infant facial emotions in mothers compared with non-mothers. *Neurosci. Res.* 70, 183–188. doi: 10.1016/j.neures.2011.02.007

Nitschke, J. B., Nelson, E. E., Rusch, B. D., Fox, A. S., Oakes, T. R., and Davidson, R. J. (2004). Orbitofrontal cortex tracks positive mood in mothers viewing pictures of their newborn infants. *Neuroimage* 21, 583–592. doi: 10.1016/j.neuroimage.2003.10.005

Noll, L. K., Mayes, L. C., and Rutherford, H. J. (2012). Investigating the impact of parental status and depression symptoms on the early perceptual coding of infant faces: an event-related potential study. *Soc. Neurosci.* 7, 525–536. doi: 10.1080/17470919.2012.672457

Noriuchi, M., Kikuchi, Y., and Senoo, A. (2008). The functional neuroanatomy of maternal love: mother's response to infant's attachment behaviors. *Biol. Psychiatry* 63, 415–423. doi: 10.1016/j.biopsych.2007.05.018

Numan, M. (2007). Motivational systems and the neural circuitry of maternal behavior in the rat. *Dev. Psychobiol.* 49, 12–21. doi: 10.1002/dev.20198

Oathes, D. J., Patenaude, B., Schatzberg, A. F., and Etkin, A. (2015). Neurobiological signatures of anxiety and depression in resting-state functional magnetic resonance imaging. *Biol. Psychiatry* 77, 385–393. doi: 10.1016/j.biopsych.2014.08.006

Parsons, C. E., Young, K. S., Bhandari, R., van Ijzendoorn, M. H., Bakermans-Kranenburg, M. J., Stein, A., et al. (2014). The bonnie baby: experimentally manipulated temperament affects perceived cuteness and motivation to view infant faces. *Dev. Sci.* 17, 257–269. doi: 10.1111/desc.12112

Parsons, C. E., Young, K. S., Kumari, N., Stein, A., and Kringelbach, M. L. (2011). The motivational salience of infant faces is similar for men and women. *PLoS ONE* 6:e20632. doi: 10.1371/journal.pone.0020632

Parsons, C. E., Young, K. S., Mohseni, H., Woolrich, M. W., Thomsen, K. R., Joensson, M., et al. (2013). Minor structural abnormalities in the infant face disrupt neural processing: a unique window into early caregiving responses. *Soc. Neurosci.* 8, 268–274. doi: 10.1080/17470919.2013.795189

Parsons, C. E., Young, K. S., Murray, L., Stein, A., and Kringelbach, M. L. (2010). The functional neuroanatomy of the evolving parent–infant relationship. *Prog. Neurobiol.* 91, 220–241. doi: 10.1016/j.pneurobio.2010.03.001

Patel, N., Grillon, C., Pavletic, N., Rosen, D., Pine, D. S., and Ernst, M. (2015). Oxytocin and vasopressin modulate risk-taking. *Physiol. Behav.* 139, 254–260. doi: 10.1016/j.physbeh.2014.11.018

Paulson, J. F., and Bazemore, S. D. (2010). Prenatal and postpartum depression in fathers and its association with maternal depression: a Meta-analysis. *J. Am. Med. Assoc.* 303, 1961–1969. doi: 10.1001/jama.2010.605

Peltola, M. J., Yrttiaho, S., Puura, K., Proverbio, A. M., Mononen, N., Lehtimäki, T., et al. (2014). Motherhood and oxytocin receptor genetic variation are associated with selective changes in electrocortical responses to infant facial expressions. *Emotion* 14, 469–477. doi: 10.1037/a0035959

Premack, D., and Woodruff, G. (1978). Does the chimpanzee have a theory of mind? *Behav. Brain Sci.* 1, 515–526. doi: 10.1017/S0140525X00076512

Proverbio, A. M., De Gabriele, V., Manfredi, M., and Adorni, R. (2011a). No race effect (ORE) in the automatic orienting toward baby faces: when ethnic group does not matter. *Psychology* 2, 931. doi: 10.4236/psych.2011.29140

Proverbio, A. M., Riva, F., Zani, A., and Martin, E. (2011b). Is it a baby? Perceived age affects brain processing of faces differently in women and men. *J. Cogn. Neurosci.* 23, 3197–3208. doi: 10.1162/jocn_a_00041

Ranote, S., Elliott, R., Abel, K. M., Mitchell, R., Deakin, J. F. W., and Appleby, L. (2004). The neural basis of maternal responsiveness to infants: an fMRI study. *Neuroreport* 15, 1825–1829. doi: 10.1097/01.wnr.0000137078.64128.6a

Rhodes, G. (2006). The evolutionary psychology of facial beauty. *Annu. Rev. Psychol.* 57, 199–226. doi: 10.1146/annurev.psych.57.102904.190208

Riem, M. M., Bakermans-Kranenburg, M. J., Pieper, S., Tops, M., Boksem, M. A., Vermeiren, R. R., et al. (2011a). Oxytocin modulates amygdala, insula, and inferior frontal gyrus responses to infant crying: a randomized control trial. *Biol. Psychiatry* 70, 291–297. doi: 10.1016/j.biopsych.2011.02.006

Riem, M. M. E., Pieper, S., Out, D., Bakermans-Kranenburg, M. J., and van Ijzendoorn, M. H. (2011b). Oxytocin receptor gene and depressive symptoms associated with physiological reactivity to infant crying. *Soc. Cogn. Affect. Neurosci.* 6, 294–300. doi: 10.1093/scan/nsq035

Riem, M. M. E., van Ijzendoorn, M. H., Tops, M., Boksem, M. A. S., Rombouts, S. A. R. B., and Bakermans-Kranenburg, M. J. (2012). No laughing matter: intranasal oxytocin administration changes functional brain connectivity during exposure to infant laughter. *Neuropsychopharmacology* 37, 1257–1266. doi: 10.1038/npp.2011.1313

Riem, M. M. E., Voorthuis, A., Bakermans-Kranenburg, M. J., and van Ijzendoorn, M. H. (2014). Pity or peanuts? Oxytocin induces differential neural responses to the same infant crying labeled as sick or bored. *Dev. Sci.* 17, 248–256. doi: 10.1111/desc.2014.17.issue2/issuetoc

Ritter, J. M., Casey, R. J., and Langlois, J. H. (1991). Adults' responses to infants varying in appearance of age and attractiveness. *Child Dev.* 62, 68–82. doi: 10.1111/j.1467-8624.1991.tb01515.x

Rilling, J. K. (2009). A potential role for oxytocin in the intergenerational transmission of secure attachment. *Neuropsychopharmacology* 34, 2621–2622. doi: 10.1038/npp.2009.136

Rupp, H. A., James, T. W., Ketterson, E. D., Sengelaub, D. R., Ditzen, B., and Heiman, J. R. (2013). Lower sexual interest in postpartum women: relationship to amygdala activation and intranasal oxytocin. *Horm. Behav.* 63, 114–121. doi: 10.1016/j.yhbeh.2012.10.007

Sacco, D., Wilson, J. P., Hugenberg, K., and Wirth, J. (2014). Overgeneralizing belonging: limited exposure to baby-faced targets increases the feeling of social belonging. *J. Soc. Psychol.* 154, 273–277. doi: 10.1080/00224545.2014.901286

Saito, A., Hamada, H., Kikusui, T., Mogi, K., Nagasawa, M., Mitsui, S., et al. (2014). Urinary oxytocin positively correlates with performance in facial visual search in unmarried males, without specific reaction to infant face. *Front. Neurosci.* 8:217. doi: 10.3389/fnins.2014.00217

Scheele, D., Wille, A., Kendrick, K. M., Stoffel-Wagner, B., Becker, B., Güntürkün, O., et al. (2013).Oxytocin enhances brain reward system responses in men viewing the face of their female partner. *Proc. Natl. Acad. Sci. U.S.A.* 110, 20308–20313. doi: 10.1073/pnas.1314190110

Scheele, D., Kendrick, K. M., Khouri, C., Kretzer, E., Schläpfer, T. E., Stoffel-Wagner, B., et al. (2014). An oxytocin-induced facilitation of neural and emotional responses to social touch correlates inversely with autism traits. *Neuropsychopharmacology* 39, 2078–2085. doi: 10.1038/npp.2014.78

Schleidt, M., Schiefenhövel, W., Stanjek, K., and Krell, R. (1980). "Caring for a baby" behavior: reactions of passersby to a mother and baby. *Man-Environ. Syst.* 10, 73—82.

Schurz, M., Radua, J., Aichhorn, M., Richlan, F., and Perner, J. (2014). Fractionating theory of mind: a meta-analysis of functional brain imaging studies. *Neurosci. Biobehav. Rev.* 42, 9–34. doi: 10.1016/j.neubiorev.2014.01.009

Seifritz, E., Esposito, F., Neuhoff, J. G., Lüthi, A., Mustovic, H., Dammann, G., et al. (2003). Differential sex-independent amygdala response to infant crying and laughing in parents versus nonparents. *Biol. Psychiatry* 54, 1367–1375. doi: 10.1016/S0006-3223(03)00697-8

Shomstein, S. (2012). Cognitive functions of the posterior parietal cortex: top-down and bottom-up attention control. *Front. Integr. Neurosci.* 6:38. doi: 10.3389/fninf2012.00038

Stein, A., Arteche, A., Lehtonen, A., Craske, M., Harvey, A., Counsell, N., et al. (2010). Interpretation of infant facial expression in the context of maternal postnatal depression. *Infant Behav. Dev.* 33, 273–278. doi: 10.1016/j.infbeh.2010.03.002

Stoeckel, L. E., Palley, L. S., Gollub, R. L., Niemi, S. M., and Evins, A. E. (2014). Patterns of brain activation when mothers view their own child and dog: an fMRI study. *PLoS ONE* 9:e107205. doi: 10.1371/journal.pone.0107205

Strathearn, L., Li, J., Fonagy, P., and Montague, P. R. (2008). What's in a smile? Maternal brain responses to infant facial cues. *Pediatrics* 122, 40–51. doi: 10.1542/peds.2007-1566

Strathearn, L., Fonagy, P., Amico, J., and Montague, P. R. (2009). Adult attachment predicts maternal brain and oxytocin response to infant cues. *Neuropsychopharmacology* 34, 2655–2666. doi: 10.1038/npp.2009.103

Strathearn, L. (2011). Maternal neglect: oxytocin, dopamine and the neurobiology of attachment. *J. Neuroendocrinol.* 23, 1054–1065. doi: 10.1111/j.1365-2826.2011.02228.x

Strathearn, L., and Kim, S. (2013). Mothers' amygdala response to positive or negative infant affect is modulated by personal relevance. *Front. Neurosci.* 7:176. doi: 10.3389/fnins.2013.00176

Striepens, N., Kendrick, K. M., Maier, W., and Hurlemann, R. (2011). Prosocial effects of oxytocin and clinical evidence for its therapeutic potential. *Front. Neuroendocrinol.* 32, 426–450. doi: 10.1016/j.yfrne.2011.07.001

Striepens, N., Matusch, A., Kendrick, K. M., Mihov, Y., Elmenhorst, D., Becker, B., et al. (2014). Oxytocin enhances attractiveness of unfamiliar female faces independent of the dopamine reward system. *Psychoneuroendocrinology* 39, 74–87. doi: 10.1016/j.psyneuen.2013.09.026

Sprengelmeyer, R. H., Perrett, D. I., and Young, A. W. (2010). Reproductive hormones modulate cuteness processing. *Psychol. Sci.* 21, 753–753. doi: 10.1177/0956797610368065

Sprengelmeyer, R. H., Lewis, J., Hahn, A. C., and Perrett, D. I. (2013). Aesthetic and incentive salience of cute infant faces: studies of observer sex, oral contraception and menstrual cycle. *PLoS ONE* 8:e65844. doi: 10.1371/journal.pone.0065844

Sprengelmeyer, R. H., Perrett, D. I., Fagan, E. C., Cornwell, R. E., Lobmaier, J. S., Spren-gelmeyer, A., et al. (2009). The cutest little baby face: a hormonal link to sensitivity to cuteness in infant faces. *Psychol. Sci.* 20, 149–154. doi: 10.1111/j.1467-9280.2009.02272.x

Tabak, B. A., Meyer, M. L., Castle, E., Dutcher, J. M., Irwin, M. R., Han, J. H., et al. (2014). Vasopressin, but not oxytocin, increases empathic concern among individuals who received higher levels of paternal warmth: a randomized controlled trial. *Psychoneuroendocrinology* 51, 253–261. doi: 10.1016/j.psychneuen.2014.10.006

Thompson-Booth, C., Viding, E., Mayes, L. C., Rutherford, H. J., Hodsoll, S., and McCrory, E. J. (2014). Here's looking at you, kid: attention to infant emotional faces in mothers and non-mothers. *Dev. Sci.* 17, 35–46. doi: 10.1111/desc.12090

Volk, A. A. (2009). Chinese infant facial cues. *J. Evol. Psychol.* 7, 225–240. doi: 10.1556/JEP.7.2009.3.3

Volk, A. A., and Quinsey, V. L. (2002). The influence of infant facial cues on adoption preferences. *Hum. Nat.* 13, 437–455. doi: 10.1007/s12110-002-1002-9

Voorthuis, A., Riem, M. M., Van IJzendoorn, M. H., and Bakermans-Kranenburg, M. J. (2014). Reading the mind in the infant eyes: paradoxical effects of oxytocin on neural activity and emotion recognition in watching pictures of infant faces. *Brain Res.* 1580, 151–159. doi: 10.1016/j.brainres.2013.10.051

Walton, M. E., Behrens, T. E., Buckley, M. J., Rudebeck, P. H., and Rushworth, M. F. (2010). Separable learning systems in the macaque brain and the role of orbitofrontal cortex in contingent learning. *Neuron* 65, 927–939. doi: 10.1016/j.neuron.2010.02.027

Wan, M. W., Downey, D., Strachan, H., Elliott, R., Williams, S. R., and Abel, K. M. (2014). The neural basis of maternal bonding. *PLoS ONE* 9:e88436. doi: 10.1371/journal.pone.0088436

Weeden, J., and Sabini, J. (2005). Physical attractiveness and health in western societies: a review. *Psychol. Bull.* 131, 635–653. doi: 10.1037/0033-2909.131.5.635

Weisman, O., Feldman, R., and Goldstein, A. (2012c). Parental and romantic attachment shape brain processing of infant cues. *Biol. Psychol.* 89, 533–538. doi: 10.1016/j.biopsycho.2011.11.008

Weisman, O., Zagoory-Sharon, O., and Feldman, R. (2012a). Intranasal oxytocin administration is reflected in human saliva. *Psychoneuroendocrinology* 37, 1582–1586. doi: 10.1016/j.psyneuen.2012.02.014

Weisman, O., Zagoory-Sharon, O., and Feldman, R. (2012b). Oxytocin administration to parent enhances infant physiological and behavioral readiness for social engagement. *Biol. Psychiatry* 72, 982–989. doi: 10.1016/j.biopsych.2012.06.011

Wigton, R., Radua, J., Allen, P., Averbeck, B., Meyer-Lindenberg, A., McGuire, P., et al. (2015). Neurophysiological effects of acute oxytocin administration: systematic review and meta-analysis of placebo-controlled imaging studies. *J. Psychiatry Neurosci.* 40, E1–E22. doi: 10.1503/jpn.130289

Wittfoth-Schardt, D., Gründing, J., Wittfoth, M., Lanfermann, H., Heinrichs, M., Domes, G., et al. (2012). Oxytocin modulates neural reactivity to children's faces as a function of social salience. *Neuropsychopharmacology* 37, 1799–1807. doi: 10.1038/npp.2012.47

Yamamoto, R., Ariely, D., Chi, W., Langleben, D. D., and Elman, I. (2009). Gender differences in the motivational processing of babies are determined by their facial attractiveness. *PLoS ONE* 4:e6042. doi: 10.1371/journal.pone.0006042

Yonkers, K. A., Ramin, S. M., Rush, A. J., Navarrete, C. A., Carmody, T., March, D., et al. (2001). Onset and persistence of post-partum depression in an inner-city maternal health clinic system. *Am. J. Psychiatry* 158, 1856–1863. doi: 10.1176/appi.ajp.158.11.1856

Zebrowitz, L. A., Luevano, V. X., Bronstad, P. M., and Aharon, I. (2009). Neural activation to babyfaced men matches activation to babies. *Soc. Neurosci.* 4, 1–10. doi: 10.1080/17470910701676236

Conflict of Interest Statement: The authors declare that the research was conducted in the absence of any commercial or financial relationships that could be construed as a potential conflict of interest.

12

The Attachment Doll Play Assessment: Predictive Validity with Concurrent Mother-Child Interaction and Maternal Caregiving Representations

Carol George[1]* and Judith Solomon[2]

[1] Department of Psychology, Mills College, Oakland, CA, USA, [2] School of Clinical Medicine, University of Cambridge, Cambridge, UK

Attachment is central to the development of children's regulatory processes. It has been associated with developmental and psychiatric health across the life span, especially emotional and behavioral regulation of negative affect when stressed (Schore, 2001; Schore and Schore, 2008). Assessment of attachment patterns provides a critical frame for understanding emerging developmental competencies and formulating treatment and intervention. Play-based attachment assessments provide access to representational models of attachment, which are regarded in attachment theory as the central organizing mechanisms associated with stability or change (Bowlby, 1969/1982; Bretherton and Munholland, 2008). The Attachment Doll Play Assessment (ADPA, George and Solomon, 1990–2016; Solomon et al., 1995) is a prominent established representational attachment measure for children aged early latency through childhood. This study examines the predictive validity of the ADPA to caregiving accessibility and responsiveness assessed from mother-child interaction and maternal representation. Sixty nine mothers and their 5–7-year-old children participated in this study. Mother-child interaction was observed during a pre-separation dyadic interaction task. Caregiving representations were rated from the Caregiving Interview (George and Solomon, 1988/1993/2005/2007). Child security with mother was associated with positive dyadic interaction and flexibly integrated maternal caregiving representations. Child controlling/disorganized attachments were significantly associated with problematic dyadic interaction and dysregulated-helpless maternal caregiving representations. The clinical implications and the use of the ADPA in clinical and educational settings are discussed.

Edited by:
Silvia Salcuni,
University of Padua, Italy

Reviewed by:
Rita B. Ardito,
University of Turin, Italy
Sergio Facchini,
National Health Service, Italy

***Correspondence:**
Carol George
george@mills.edu

Specialty section:
This article was submitted to Psychology for Clinical Settings, a section of the journal Frontiers in Psychology

Keywords: assessment, play, attachment, caregiving, representation, synchrony

INTRODUCTION

Attachment has been associated with developmental and psychiatric health across the life span, especially emotional and behavioral regulation of negative affect when stressed (Schore, 2001; Schore and Schore, 2008). The synergy of children's emotional, social, cognitive, and language development beginning around age 4 years poises play to be a rich and reliable methodology for assessing attachment (Solomon et al., 1995; Bretherton and Munholland, 2008). Attachment theory posits that internal representational models of attachment are derived from real experience with attachment figures. They are modulated and regulated by patterns of defensive exclusion and thus influence procedural scripts, memories, evaluations of self and attachment figures; as such, knowing children's representational "rules" enable us to understand how they view their world and make predictions about their development (Bretherton, 2005; Waters and Waters, 2006). Representations are the central organizing mechanism associated with stability or change, and provide a critical frame of reference for child treatment and family intervention (Bowlby, 1969/1982, 1980; Hodges and Steele, 2000; Hodges et al., 2003; Hoffman et al., 2006; Oppenheim and Goldsmith, 2007; Bretherton and Munholland, 2008).

Attachment researchers have developed a range of play-based methods to assess children's attachment patterns in which children "play out" attachment themes. Research findings support theoretically derived predictions regarding the associations between attachment security children's emotional and behavior adjustment in community and risk samples (Oppenheim, 1997; Verschueren and Marcoens, 1999; Goldwyn et al., 2000; Rydell et al., 2005; Goodman et al., 2007, 2012, 2013; Green et al., 2007; Venet et al., 2007; Bureau and Moss, 2010; Stievenart et al., 2011; Webster and Hackett, 2011; Torres et al., 2012; Miljkovitch et al., 2013; Salari et al., 2016). Research findings also support predictions of a disproportionate amount of attachment insecurity (especially disorganized children) in risk samples (e.g., divorce, maltreatment, adoption, foster care, institutionalized) (Gloger-Tippelt and König, 2007; Katsurada, 2007; Román et al., 2012; Torres et al., 2012; Bovenschen et al., 2016).

Caregiver accessibility and responsiveness to the child is the central explanatory mechanism of attachment security (Bowlby, 1969/1982; Ainsworth et al., 1978). Demonstration of an association between attachment security and the attachment-caregiving relationship is therefore considered to be a core construct, essential to validating any measure of attachment. Such studies are sparse, however (Solomon and George, 2016). The present study examines the validity of the Attachment Doll Play Assessment (ADPA, George and Solomon, 1990–2016; Solomon et al., 1995), reporting on two aspects of this core construct: mother-child interactive synchrony and maternal caregiving representation. We begin with an overview of attachment play-based assessments so as to provide an interpretive frame for this study.

Attachment Assessments Using Play

The field of attachment uses "doll play" to tap children's symbolic play around attachment themes. Doll play procedures follow Bretherton's original approach to studying symbolic representation in the preschool period using the Attachment Story Completion Task (ASCT, Bretherton et al., 1990). The ASCT was originally developed to assess attachment security in 4 year olds. Over several decades, a range of different protocols have appeared in the literature, most of which follow Bretherton et al.'s (1990) approach. The assessment is administered in a private setting, such as a laboratory or clinical office. The play materials are family dolls and props that create a symbolic "house." Houses range from using minimal props, such as the ASTC (Bretherton et al., 1990) to an elaborately configured Victorian style doll house (e.g., Green et al., 2000). The procedure used to determine the core play family varies across methods. The most common procedure follows the ASCT, whereby the adult (the researcher or clinician) creates a doll family comprised of two dolls and two children, a doll designated as the self and a sibling of the same gender. By contrast, some researchers ask the children to select the family. The ADPA procedure, for example, instructs the children first select the self and then select other family members (George and Solomon, 1990–2016). The majority of procedures then use the designated family for the entire assessment, with one exception – a procedure that asks children if they wish to reconfigure the family members before each story (Farnfield, 2015).

The administration technique is analogous across procedures. The goal is for the adult interviewer to systematically introduce story topics, termed story stems. Story stem scripts are followed exactly, and the interviewer's only interaction with children during their play is to use standardized scripted prompts to encourage children to describe and enact what happens in relation to the attachment topics. Topics are typically limited to four to five core themes conceived in attachment theory as activating the need for parental comfort and protection (Bowlby, 1969/1982): parent-child tension, mildly frightening events, parent separation, and parent reunion. A few procedures add extra topics, such as themes related to parental divorce (Page and Bretherton, 2003); others add a set of generalized stressful topics (e.g., parent loses keys; school bully) (Macfie et al., 2014; Farnfield, 2015). Doll play assessments frequently are used to establish attachment classification groups [secure/insecure; four attachment groups (Ainsworth et al., 1978; Cassidy et al., 1987–1992)]. Classification rubrics typically are developed using *a priori* intuitive extrapolation from other attachment measures or statistical composites based on summing rating dimensions (Bretherton et al., 1990; Green et al., 2000; Gloger-Tippelt et al., 2002). A different approach uses classification criteria based on attachment-expert opinions of essential representational elements (Miljkovitch et al., 2003). Some investigators also report the use of scales to augment or in lieu of classification (e.g., sensitivity, aggression, security, discourse coherency) (Green et al., 2000; Macfie et al., 2008; Webster and Hackett, 2011).

Despite procedural differences, the validity of the doll play method is fairly well established. Validity with other standard attachment measures (e.g., Strange Situation, Attachment Q-Sort) ranges from excellent to acceptable, depending on the method and if measurements were concurrent or administered at different ages. Associations tend to be strongest for comparisons of secure versus insecure attachment groups, for security scales, and associations with attachment disorganization (see Solomon and George, 2016). These procedures are reported to be valid for the use with children ages 3–12 years, although caution should be used when interpreting the doll play assessments of children under 4 years (R. S. Marvin, personal communication, November, 8, 2014). Doll play assessment has been used with English and non-English speaking children (Canada, France, Germany, Israel,

Japan, Spain) (Solomon et al., 1995; Goodman and Pfeffer, 1998; Goldwyn et al., 2000; Green et al., 2000; Gloger-Tippelt et al., 2002; Verschueren et al., 2006; Yamakawa, 2006; Katsurada, 2007; Dubois-Comtois and Moss, 2008; Dubois-Comtois et al., 2011; Román et al., 2012; Goodman et al., 2013; Miljkovitch et al., 2013; Farnfield, 2015; Bovenschen et al., 2016).

The Attachment Doll Play Procedure (ADPA, George and Solomon, 1990–2016; Solomon et al., 1995)

The ADPA is a doll play attachment assessment that follows the tradition of the ASCT (Bretherton et al., 1990). It uses the same basic attachment story stems: *Hurt Knee* (child's knee is hurt by falling off a rock), *Monster in the Bedroom* (child, when sent to bed, tells the parents that there is a monster in the bedroom), *Separation* (parents provide a babysitter to stay at home while they go on an overnight trip), and *Reunion* (parents return from their overnight trip).

There are several key elements in the procedure that differentiate the ADPA from the ASCT and other doll play procedures described in the literature. The most important of these is the classification scheme. The ADPA scheme is based on Bowlby's (1973, 1980) description of defensive processes related to separation and loss (George and Solomon, 1990–2016; George and Solomon, 1998, unpublished) and can also be detected in mothers' internal caregiving representations and in adult responses to free-response ("projective") attachment stimuli (Solomon and George, 1999b; George and West, 2011, 2012). Security is conceived in terms of the flexible integration of attachment-related thoughts and feelings, whereas strategies of defensive exclusion of information can be systematically brought into play as responses to anxiety regarding attachment figures. These processes include "deactivation" (prevention of attachment-related thoughts and feelings), associated with avoidant classifications, and "cognitive disconnection" (disconnection from awareness of the links between affect and thought), associated with ambivalent classifications. When attachment-related distress cannot be contained (assuaged), "dysregulation" of the attachment system (or, in Bowlby's 1980, terms, a "segregated system") is likely to be the result. Depiction of uncontained frightening and catastrophic events, as well as persistent constriction (refusal to play), are the single most defining indices of dysregulation and attachment disorganization (Solomon et al., 1995). The ADPA has demonstrated construct validity; there is significant concordance between the representation classifications and attachment classifications based on children's reunion behavior with the parent (Solomon and George, 2002; Yamakawa, 2006; Dubois-Comtois et al., 2011).

Concurrent evaluation of ADPA classifications demonstrated that the children's responses to the combination of the *Separation* and *Reunion* stories evaluated best predicted children's reunion classification (Solomon et al., 1995). Responses to other stories were more weakly associated with reunion classifications, suggesting that classification schemes that combine all story responses in an additive way are likely to introduce classification error (Solomon and George, 2002).

The ADPA offers some advantages over other doll play systems. The concurrent validation for the four-group classification system that is the most prominent rubric to evaluate attachment patterns in the field provides confidence in the ADPA classification that is not available for other methods, such as the ASCT for example. The MCAST does not differentiate among insecure classification patterns. Most other methods assess doll play in terms of security score (secure vs. insecure), and do not provide classification information (see Solomon and George, 2016 for overview). The examination of doll play against parent reunion also clarified that classification is not an additive process, a finding that is consistent with attachment theory. Attachment is activated differently in different children. Children who are secure in the Strange Situation, for example, may look like avoidant children if only observed during the first reunion with their attachment figure (Ainsworth et al., 1978). These children are thought to need more of a "push" so to speak to demonstrate the secure pattern and classification depends heavily on the observation of the second reunion (Ainsworth et al., 1978). In the same vein, we have noted the secure children, for example, develop stories in response to *Hurt Knee* or *Monster in the Bedroom* that would be associated with children with insecure classifications. Yet their *Separation-Reunion* sequence is the story material that fits their reunion with their mother (Solomon and George, 2002). For example, some children demonstrate sturdy independence in response to the injured knee, and tell a story that would be evaluated as avoidant. We also observed that separation stories do not differentiate among the stories of children in different attachment groups. In short, as in the Strange Situation, it is the representational reunion that provides the best classification information, and it remains an empirical question as to how to think about children's responses to the other story stems (Solomon and George, 2002).

The ADPA has been demonstrated to predict a range of theoretically expected variables in normative and high-risk samples (Dubois-Comtois and Moss, 2008; Stacks and Oshio, 2009; Bureau and Moss, 2010; Dubois-Comtois et al., 2011; Goodman et al., 2013; Salari et al., 2016).

The Association between Attachment Doll Play Assessments and Maternal Caregiving

As previously noted, the association between the children's attachment and parental caregiving is a core tenet of attachment theory. Yet there are only three published studies using attachment doll play procedures that report on these associations. All of these studies are of French-speaking children.

Two reports are from Moss et al. (1997) longitudinal study of attachment beginning in the preschool years. Dubois-Comtois and Moss (2008) and Dubois-Comtois et al. (2011) reported significant associations between children's attachment doll play representations and concurrent mother-child interactive behavior in a sample heterogeneous as to family background, income, including head of household, and education. Children's attachment classifications were assessed at age 8.5 years using the ADPA. Mother-child interaction and mother-child conversation were observed in two settings, 3 years earlier during snack time in the laboratory and concurrent assessment of family interaction. The results were similar for mother-child interaction at 5.5 years and family interaction at 8.5 years. The interactions of secure children were more coherent and reciprocal than the interactions of disorganized children, with patterns falling in the middle for avoidant and ambivalent-resistant children. Logistic regression results showed that concurrent interaction (family interaction) was a more powerful predictor, however, than mother-child interaction at age 5.5 years. Dubois-Comtois et al. (2011) also reported a significant association between children's representational classification at 8.5 years and mother-child conversation during snack time at age 5.5 years.

Miljkovitch et al. (2013) used the ACST to assess doll play representation in a sample of 3½-year-old children who were preterm and full term infants. The study goal was to examine associations between doll play representations and mother interaction. The study results showed significant associations between difficult and problematic mother-child interactions and disorganized attachment for the full-term children, but not for the preterm children. Although these results are consistent with previous research on attachment disorganization, conclusions about the association between doll play assessments and mother-child interaction may be constrained by infant development (Sameroff, 1993) and the age when the ACST was administered.

The Current Study

This study is the first to examine the concurrent associations between the attachment doll play classifications and parenting. The first set of hypotheses pertained to the association between ADPA attachment classifications and mother-child interaction. Interactions with dyads with secure children were expected to more balanced and harmonious than interaction in dyads with insecure children. Interaction in dyads with disorganized children was expected to be the least balanced and harmonious.

Two other sets of hypotheses examined the role of maternal caregiving representations as related to both ADPA attachment classifications and mother-child interaction. The attachment theory view of caregiving posits that it is guided by the caregiving behavioral system, following Bowlby's (1969/1982) ethological model of attachment. Caregiving system processes regulate representations of self, child, and evaluations of their relationship that are consolidated over time based on experiences with the child (George and Solomon, 1996, 2008; Solomon and George, 1996). Representations are conceived as reflecting mother-child interaction (Solomon and George, 1996; George and Solomon, 2008).

The evaluation of caregiving representation in this study is the same as was described for the ADPA. This approach follows Bowlby's (1980) model of defensive exclusion (see George and Solomon, 2008), defined as unconscious and automatic sorting and exclusion processes that guide and organize representation and behavior. When defensive processes are flexible and integrated, caregiving representations emphasize flexibility, synchrony, adjustment, and mutual enjoyment – qualities associated with maternal sensitivity and children's attachment security (Pasco Fearon and Belsky, 2016). Flexible integration supports secure base behavior and children's competence, and differentiates between mothers of children with secure and insecure attachment (George and Solomon, 1989, 1996, 2008; Solomon and George, 1999a). By contrast, when defenses are dysregulated, caregiving is at least to some degree disabled and the caregiving-attachment relationship may be said to be dysregulated as well (Solomon and George, 1996, 2011a; George and Solomon, 2008). In these cases, mothers are likely to be overwhelmed by their worst fears about self and child and report becoming flooded by feelings of being out of control, and vulnerable. In essence, these mothers are rendered *helpless* to care for and protect their children (George and Solomon, 2008). *Dysregulated-helplessness* is the term, we use for this dimension of defensive processing (George and Solomon, 2008; Solomon and George, 2011a). This dimension differentiates between mothers of children with disorganized/controlling and organized attachments (secure, avoidant, ambivalent-resistant) and has been shown to be positively associated with parental stress and child behavior problems in infancy and childhood (George and Solomon, 1996, 2008, 2011).

There is considerable support in the attachment literature for the association between mothers' mental processes (e.g., mentalization, reflective functioning) and dyadic interaction (see George and Solomon, 2008, for a complete discussion). This is the first study, however, to examine these associations from the perspective of the caregiving system and the caregiver's representations.

It was hypothesized that there would significant associations between maternal caregiving representations and children's representations of attachment and mother-child interaction. The mothers of children judged secure using the ADPA were expected to have significantly higher flexible integration ratings than mothers of insecure children; and mothers of disorganized-controlling children were expected to have significantly higher dysregulation-helplessness ratings than mothers of organized children (secure, avoidant, ambivalent). Similarly, flexibly integrated caregiving representation ratings were expected to be positively associated with balanced and harmonious mother-child interaction; and dysregulated-helpless caregiving representation ratings were expected to be inversely associated with balanced and harmonious interaction ratings, thus indicative of interaction problems.

MATERIALS AND METHODS

Participants

The participants were 69 mother-child dyads recruited through private and public kindergarten classrooms in the San Francisco Bay Area (Solomon et al., 1995). School principals and directors were first provided letters describing the study, following the guidelines of the institutions' internal review boards or school districts. All of the schools that were approached approved the study, and similar letters describing the study accompanied by administrators' support of the study were sent home in children's classroom packets. Families who were interested in participating returned the letter accompanied by contact information to classroom teachers. The researcher retrieved this information subsequently from the school and contacted families directly by telephone. The study was once again described, and mothers were provided an opportunity during that conversation to ask questions. The only inclusion criteria for schools and classrooms were that they served typically developing children and were within a 15 mile radius of the playroom to make it feasible for dyads to participate without undue travel.

The children (37 girls, 32 boys) were 6 years old ($M = 68.3$ months; range 57–85 months). Thirty five percent of the children were first born, 42% later born, and 23% were only children. Mothers' mean age was 37.4 years (range 21–49 years). Eight-one percent of the children were living with both parents, 4.3% were living with their mothers in a blended family, and 13% were living with a single head of household mother. Mothers were predominantly college educated (69.6%), Caucasian (80%), with moderate to high incomes.

Measures

Attachment

The child's attachment classification was assessed using the ADPA (George and Solomon, 1990–2016; Solomon et al., 1995). The doll play is administered to each child individually. The doll house is designed as a "single story," with furniture arranged on a large wooden board to designate the kitchen, living room, bedrooms (child and parent), and the backyard. In addition to basic furniture, props include kitchen and food items, children's toys, and a few household items (e.g., telephone). The adult interviewer asks the child to first select the doll to be the self and then select the other pretend family members from three sets of culturally diverse dolls (Caucasian, African American, and Asian). Each set includes a mother, father, female child, male child, and baby. The child is asked to put their pretend family in the house and play for 5 min as a warm up. Children are first asked to select the doll they want to be the self, and are then instructed to select the other dolls in their "pretend" family. They are never asked to select family members to represent real family members. Further, there is no requirements for doll selections that fill actual family roles, such as selecting a parent doll. Children are free to select a self as represented by a child or adult doll. As a result, it is not unusual when given this choice in family member selection for children to create families that have no mother or father or to select adult dolls to be the self. Indeed, these selection elements have been shown to be an index of attachment dysregulation and are prominent in children with disorganized attachments (George and Solomon, 1998, Unpublished).

The assessment is comprised of a set of story stems. Once a story stem is introduced, the interviewer asks the child to *"show me what happens next."* The first story, *Pets*, introduces animals into the play; the mother asks the family if they want to keep the puppy and kitten that have appeared at their door. The next story stems are: *Hurt Knee*, the child falls off of a high rock in the backyard and hurts their knee and can calls out to parents; *Monster in the Bedroom*, the parents tell the child to go to bed and the child cries out that there is a monster in the bedroom; *Separation*, the parents leave to go on an overnight trip and a babysitter stays with the children; and *Reunion*, the parents return the next day.

The attachment classification rubric designates five attachment groups based on children's responses to the combined evaluation of the *Separation* and *Reunion* stories (Solomon et al., 1995). Coding is done using verbatim transcripts that records the child's narration and actions. Children judged secure (B) demonstrate family or personal *integration*. Dangers or negative events (e.g., robbers come to the house) are resolved; parents are portrayed as committed and caring; reunions are complete and uninterrupted; or children demonstrate constructive agency during in the parents' absence. Children judged avoidant (A) demonstrate defensive deactivation. Stories include themes that describe complete shifts in attention that neutralize reunion distress, such as blocking the separation or family members asleep on reunion. Characters act non-chalant and casual. Children judged ambivalent (C) demonstrate defensive cognitive disconnection. Reunions are interrupted or incomplete. Ambivalent children often become mentally busy with small details (e.g., arranging dishes, sweeping the house). Children judged disorganized/controlling (D) demonstrate segregated systems processes that overwhelm other fears of their play, evidencing their underlying attachment fears. There are two forms of disorganized-controlling responses. Controlling punitive (D1) children respond with stories in which themes are frightening and uncontained. Characters are threatened or threatening, helpless, out of control, and the self and family are left at risk of *disintegration.* Controlling caregiving (D2) children are constricted. These children appear to be inhibited and extremely uncomfortable with the doll play task, frequently responding to prompts with only statements such as "I don't know," or "nothing happens." Solomon et al. (1995) showed that this was not due to an inability to play or refusal to play with dolls, and that this response pattern is not a form of avoidance. These children had no problem playing with family like toys (e.g., pretend people in a toy castle or space station) during the free play period. The association between constricted responses during assessment with attachment dysregulation has been confirmed in adult assessment using free response picture stimuli depicting people in attachment situations (George and West, 2012).

The ADPA attachment classification distribution was 16 B's, 17 A's, 18 C's, 18 D's (13 D1's; 5D2's). Classifications were completed by the first and second author. Inter-coder reliability, coded blind for the entire sample 71% (kappa = 0.62), with the highest agreement for disorganized versus organized (secure, avoidant, ambivalent combined) classifications, 95% (kappa = 0.85) (Solomon et al., 1995).

Mother-Child Interaction

Dyadic interaction was assessed using Moss et al. (1998) and Moss and St-Laurent (2001) scales for mother-child interaction affective quality, comprised of nine 7-point bipolar rating scales. One scale assesses the *overall* quality of interaction. A high *overall* score reflects balanced and harmonious interaction, with low scores indicating indifference or conflictual interaction. Eight additional subscales assess the components of balanced and harmonious interaction: *coordination* (smooth goal-oriented vs. unproductive flow of interaction), *communication* (verbal and non-verbal clarity vs. inconsistent or incongruous interchange), *partner roles* (appropriate parent-child role assumption vs. role reversal), *emotional expression* (balanced and shared positive and negative affective states vs. imbalanced, negative, or exaggerated expression), *responsivity/sensitivity* (interaction attunement vs. intrusiveness or ignoring), *tension/relaxation* (calm and comfortable vs. tense or anxious), *mood* (generally positive vs. negative), and *enjoyment* (sustained warmth and pleasure vs. displeasure). A principal-components factor analysis of the nine scales yielded a single factor explaining 83% of the variance (Moss and St-Laurent, 2001). Thus, only the overall scale score representing reciprocal, balanced, and harmonious interaction is used in data analysis (following Moss and St-Laurent, 2001).

Raters blind to all participant information rated dyadic interaction from videotape of mother and child "reading" a wordless story book. Rating and reliability were completed in two steps. Fifty one cases were rated by a reliable rater from the Moss lab. Inter-rater reliability between this rater and another trained rater from the Moss lab on 30% of these cases was 81% for the overall rating and ranged from 70 to 88% on the eight subscales. A third rater from our laboratory was trained to 80% reliability on this set of 51 cases and then rated the remaining 18 cases.

Scale validity has been established for children ages 3–7 years old. These scales distinguish mother-child interaction patterns associated with children's attachment patterns in cross-sectional and longitudinal studies, and have also demonstrated associations with behavior problem ratings and school performance (Moss et al., 1998, 2004a,b; Moss and St-Laurent, 2001). A correlation of 0.71 between the overall rating evaluated in the laboratory and the home observations demonstrated ecological validity for this measure (Dubois-Comtois and Moss, 2008).

Maternal Representation of Caregiving

Caregiving representation was assessed using the *Caregiving Interview*, an interview adapted by George and Solomon (1988/1993/2005/2007) from the *Parent Development Interview* (Aber et al., unpublished). The *Caregiving Interview* is a clinical-style interview designed to activate the caregiving system. The interview encourages mothers to describe memories of specific events, interactions, feelings, and their evaluations of these events using a series of open-ended questions about emotions associated with being a parent (e.g., joy, worry, guilt, confidence). Mothers are also asked to describe attachment-related events such as separations and, for this age of children, beginning school. The interview is relationship specific; that is, mothers are asked to focus on specific experiences and their relationship with a particular child rather than describing generic parenting situations.

This study focused on caregiving representations associated with attachment security and disorganization, utilizing two rating scales, *flexible integration* and *dysregulation-helplessness* (George and Solomon, 1988/1993/2005/2007). *Flexible integration* is characterized by descriptions of caregiving flexibility and self-other balance. High scores reflect an age appropriate commitment to the child's needs, neither at the expense nor indulgence of the mother's own needs; a capacity to support the child's competence and autonomy; sincere mutual enjoyment the desire and ability to seek repair relationship in response to tensions or ruptures and the desire to protect and buffer the child from unnecessary distress or risk. *Dysregulation-helplessness* is characterized by descriptions of behavioral and often also representational dysregulation. Situational examples and appraisals consistently demonstrate that attachment-caregiving situations are overwhelming, frightening, or out of control; mothers describe being helpless to find solutions to common childrearing challenges. These examples often also include descriptions of taking extreme measures, including prolonged and angry mother-child confrontations and battles of wills, freezing and being unable to take action, or failure to recognize children's vulnerability.

Rating is done from verbatim descriptions extracted from the interview of mother-child interaction, called biographical vignettes. All vignettes from a single case are combined into a single transcript and ratings are based on the overall evaluation of these vignettes using 7-point rating scales. High ratings (5–7) are assigned when the scale dimension is predominant. A midpoint rating (4) is assigned when there is clear evidence of that dimension but is not predominant. Ratings 3 and below are assigned when evidence is minimal to absent.

Two sets of raters blind to all information about the participants separately rated flexible integration and helplessness. The audio quality for six interviews was not of sufficient to transcribe, resulting in 63 interviews in the Caregiving Interview sample. Pearson correlations on 20% of the cases demonstrated interrater reliability that ranged from 0.79 to 0.90. Reliability checks between the raters and the first author on these same cases ranged from 0.78 to 0.85. The authors also rated dysregulation-helplessness using interviews for which case identifications were blinded. Correlations between the authors' ratings and those of trained raters on reliability sets from this sample and other samples ranged from 0.80 to 0.92.

These rating scales have been shown to distinguish among child attachment groups (George and Solomon, 1996, 2008). High ratings for flexible integration and dysregulation-helplessness were, respectively, associated with mothers of secure and disorganized/controlling child attachment (Solomon and George, 1999a, 2011b; George and Solomon, 2008). Flexible integration was associated with attachment security for high partner conflict divorced mothers (Solomon and George, 1999a). A significant positive association between dysregulation-helplessness was found for parenting stress and children's adjustment problems (George and Solomon, 2011).

Procedure

Dyads participated in a 90-min laboratory play room laboratory session. After signing consent forms, the dyad was introduced to the laboratory playroom. They were asked to select a book to "read" together from Mayer's (1976) *Four Frogs in a Box* "wordless" story books. When the story was completed, the mother was escorted to an adjacent room where she was given the

Caregiving Interview. The child remained in the playroom with a female adult stranger (child interviewer) who administered the ADPA and remained in the room while the child engaged in free play until the mother returned approximately 1 h later.

RESULTS

Preliminary Analyses

Pearson correlations among family demographic variables showed significant associations between maternal education and family income (r = 0.30, p < 0.05), and between marital status and family income (r = −0.42, p < 0.001). A composite score representing family configuration (i.e., maternal education, family income, marital status) was computed using mean standardized scores for these variables (Moss et al., 2004b). There were no significant associations between family configuration, birth order, and child age and the any of variables of interest. There was a significant association between gender and child attachment classification [$r(67) = 0.28$, $p < 0.05$] and maternal dysregulation-helplessness ratings [$t(61) = 2.71$, $p < 0.01$]. Mothers of boys were rated significantly more helpless than mothers of girls. There were significantly more boys in the disorganized/controlling classification groups than girls (see **Table 1**). Child gender was used as a covariate in analyses related to these variables. There were no significant differences on any study variables between the two disorganized-controlling subgroups. The results from these subgroups were combined for the purpose of analyses.

Children's ADPA Attachment Classification and Mother-Child Interaction

The first hypothesis addressed the associations between children's ADPA classifications and mother-child interaction. The means and standard deviations for all interaction scales are shown in **Table 2**. Only the overall rating was used for analysis; the means and standard deviations for all the interaction subscales are provided for descriptive purposes (following Moss et al., 1998; Moss and St-Laurent, 2001). As predicted, secure dyads demonstrated the highest levels of overall balanced and harmonious interaction and controlling-punitive dyads the least.

Analysis of covariance (ANCOVA, gender included as a covariate) showed a significant main effect for attachment [$F(4,65) = 7.02$, $p < 0.001$, partial $\eta^2 = 0.30$]. *T*-tests examining secure attachment dyads in relation to insecure dyads showed significant differences between secure and all insecure groups. Secure dyadic interaction was significantly more balanced and harmonious than the interaction in avoidant [$t(31) = 2.71$, $p < 0.01$], ambivalent [$t(31) = 2.65$, $p < 0.01$], and disorganized [$t(32) = 6.22$, $p < 0.001$].

TABLE 1 | Gender distribution of ADPA child attachment classifications.

Classification	Girls	Boys	Total
B	10	7	17
A	9	6	15
C	14	5	19
D1	4	7	11
D2	0	7	7
Total	37	32	69

Children's ADPA Attachment Classification and Maternal Caregiving Representation

The second set of hypotheses addressed the associations between children's attachment classifications assessed using the ADPA and maternal caregiving representation. The means and standard deviations for the caregiving representation rating scales for mothers of children in each attachment group are shown in **Table 3**. The results supported the predicted associations for both flexible integration and dysregulation-helplessness ratings.

MANCOVA results (gender included as a covariate) demonstrated a significant main effect for flexible integration [$F(3,60) = 37.16$, $p < 0.001$, partial $\eta^2 = 0.65$] and dysregulation-helplessness [$F(3,60) = 30.74$, $p < 0.001$, partial $\eta^2 = 0.66$]. *T*-tests between secure attachment dyads and the insecure dyads showed significant differences between secure and all insecure groups. The flexible integration ratings for mothers of secure children were significantly greater than the mothers of avoidant [$t(28) = 9.02$, $p < 0.001$], ambivalent [$t(30) = 8.39$, $p < 0.001$], and disorganized [$t(29) = 9.90$, $p < 0.001$] dyads.

T-tests between disorganized attachment dyads and organized dyads also showed significant differences between groups. The dysregulation-helplessness ratings for mothers of disorganized children were significantly greater than the mothers of secure [$t(29) = 8.22$, $p < 0.001$], avoidant [$t(29) = 10.48$, $p < 0.001$], and ambivalent [$t(29) = 12.46$, $p < 0.001$] dyads. There were no significant differences in dysregulation-helplessness ratings among the mothers of children with organized attachments.

Associations between Mother-Child Interaction and Maternal Caregiving Representation

The final set of hypotheses addressed the associations between mother-child interaction and maternal caregiving representation. Analyses using two-tailed Pearson correlations supported both hypotheses. Representational flexible integration was positively associated with balanced harmonious mother-child interaction [$r(63) = 0.49$, $p < 0.001$]. Representational dysregulation-helplessness was inversely associated with balanced harmonious interaction [$r(63) = -0.38$, $p < 0.01$].

DISCUSSION

This study was the first to examine the concurrent predictive validity of the ADPA and dimensions assessing mother-child interactive behavior and maternal representations of caregiving. Further, this study adds significantly to what is a sparse literature

TABLE 2 | Attachment Doll Play Assessment child attachment classification and mother-child interaction: means.

	Attachment classification				
Mother-child interaction	**B (*n* = 16)**	**A (*n* = 17)**	**C (*n* = 18)**	**D1 (*n* = 13)**	**D2 (*n* = 5)**
Overall	4.50	3.35	3.50	2.46	2.80
Coordination	4.38	3.24	3.44	2.38	2.60
Communication	4.44	3.29	3.33	2.96	3.60
Appropriate role assumption	4.25	3.12	3.33	2.23	3.40
Emotional expression	4.44	3.12	3.30	2.77	3.40
Responsivity/sensitivity	4.31	3.12	3.56	2.31	2.80
Tension/relaxation	4.00	2.94	3.11	2.54	3.00
Mood	4.50	3.41	3.56	2.85	3.40
Enjoyment	4.50	3.41	3.78	2.92	3.40

TABLE 3 | Attachment Doll Play Assessment child attachment classification and maternal caregiving representation: means.

	Child attachment				
Caregiving representation rating	**B (*n* = 15)**	**A (*n* = 15)**	**C (*n* = 17)**	**D1 (*n* = 12)**	**D2 (*n* = 4)**
Flexible integration	5.37	2.13	2.24	1.87	2.50
Dysregulation-helplessness	3.00	3.03	2.53	5.83	5.87

examining any doll play procedure in relation to core attachment theory constructs.

As predicted, the findings demonstrated that secure mother-child dyads, classified using the ADPA, engaged in significantly greater balanced and harmonious interactions than insecure dyads, with disorganized-controlling dyads showing the most interactive problems. This finding is consistent with longitudinal studies in which parent-child interaction and the ADPA doll play classification were evaluated several years apart (Dubois-Comtois and Moss, 2008; Dubois-Comtois et al., 2011). This finding is also consistent with the one other study of this kind, using the ACST (Miljkovitch et al., 2013) and studies demonstrating associations between mother-child interaction and attachment assessed using reunion procedures (e.g., Humber and Moss, 2005). Further, the results of the current study echo observations of the dyadic interaction breakdown that has been shown characteristic of disorganized toddlers under stress (Solomon and George, 1999a) and are consistent with a robust literature documenting mother-child interaction problems for disorganized and controlling children (Lyons-Ruth and Jacobvitz, 2016).

This study also found strong significant associations between mothers' caregiving system representations and children's attachment patterns. As predicted, mothers of secure children were differentiated from mothers of insecure children on the dimension of representational flexibility and integration. The interviews of mothers of secure children were characterized by descriptions of events with their children that expressed trust, cooperation, knowledge of self and child as individuals, and the joy of parenting. They described communicating clearly about caregiving and attachment goals, and thinking about a balanced solution when parents' and children's goals conflicted. These representational qualities contribute to sensitivity and the robust association in attachment literature between a range of "sensitive" parenting mental states and attachment security (see George and Solomon, 2008 for a literature review).

By contrast, ratings for dysregulated-helpless caregiving were highest in mothers of disorganized-controlling children. Representations of caregiving in these mothers were markedly out of balance, consistent with the controlling nature of their children on reunion (Solomon et al., 1995). Descriptions of events revealed the clear potential for *failed* protection, a phenomenon we have termed "abdication" of care (Solomon and George, 1996; George and Solomon, 2008). The descriptive vignettes of mothers of disorganized-controlling children mirrored their children's doll play stories. For mothers of punitive children, care and conflict with their children unleashed their worst fears. Mothers described themselves as being as out of control (e.g., acting like "maniacs," defiant, hysterical, threatening), and their children were often cast as antagonists, "devils" that rendered them helpless to combat or organize their children's behavior. Mothers of caregiving children often described themselves as psychologically or behaviorally frozen. They also had difficulty describing mother-child interaction vignettes, and could abruptly stop speaking in mid-sentence. They often described the need for absolute withdrawal from interacting with their children, sometimes associated with descriptions of becoming frightened that they could not maintain behavioral or emotional control if they remained in these situations. Their children tended to be described in the role of parental care, "angels" who did no wrong and were compassionate and sensitive not only to their mothers but had remarkable empathy for all living creatures. Lacking even a basic sense of "felt protection," it is no wonder that the doll play of punitive and caregiving children was, respectively, wild and out of control or frozen and constricted.

The results of this study also add to the literature demonstrating significant associations between mothers' representational states of mind and mother-child interaction for mothers of secure children. These include, for example, studies examining representational sensitivity and mind mindedness (e.g., Oppenheim and Koren-Karie, 2002; Grienenberger et al., 2005; Demers et al., 2010). There are no other studies to date that have examined the relation between maternal representation and mother-child interaction for disorganized-controlling children.

This study failed to find differences in any variables for the disorganized-controlling subgroups (punitive, caregiving). There were no differences in mother-child interaction between these two groups of children, suggesting that these mothers equally communicate a sense of failed protection and abandonment to their children. This finding stands in contrast, however, to the results reported by studies by Moss et al. (2004a,b), who found interaction differences between the D1 and D2 groups in both the preschool and childhood years. One explanation for the failure to find differences between the disorganized-controlling groups in this study may stem from the disproportionate number of boys with disorganized-controlling attachments in the current sample. Seventy four percent of the children in the disorganized/controlling group in the current study were boys, as were all of the children in the controlling-caregiving subgroup. Mothers of boys reported significantly higher helplessness ratings than mothers of girls. Although gender differences are not predicted by attachment theory, research is beginning to demonstrate that gender predicts divergent interactive behavior and child development outcomes as children grow beyond infancy (Hazen et al., 2011; Pasco Fearon and Belsky, 2016), with boys being more difficult than girls.

In addition to the gender composition of the disorganized-controlling attachment group, there are several other limitations to the current study that should inform future research. With regard to the ADPA, studies are needed to investigate test-retest reliability. Further, future research would benefit from including samples with children younger and older than this sample. Finally, the cross-sectional concurrent design cannot address questions of continuity and discontinuity in the associations reported here.

Clinical Importance of the ADPA

The inspiration to use semi-structured doll play to assess children's internal working models of their attachment relationships drew on the tradition of child psychotherapy, pioneered by early clinicians such as Anna Freud and Melanie Klein. The results of this study permit the field of attachment to repay that debt. First, it provides empirical validation for the clinical insight that such play is indeed a window into the child's inner world and it is indeed related to the observed quality of interaction patterns with attachment figures. Second, it demonstrates that the quality of the children's attachment to their mothers provides the framework for the *organization* of that play. Hence, it is advantageous to clinicians and educators to have a thorough understanding of attachment theory and of attachment-related defenses in order to make sense of the doll play of any particular child.

Variations in doll play associated with each of the attachment groups provide useful information about what is normative and what is potentially problematic. Most striking is the fact that similar "florid" symbolic content can be typical of both secure and disorganized children. Many secure children in this study created disaster scenarios in response to story probes, leading the naïve observer might feel concern about children's emotional regulation capacities or experiences. In fact, the rich narratives of secure children probably indicate an ability to express and flexibly integrate normative fears of separation and loss. Significantly, the failure to depict the successful resolution of their fears was the distinguishing feature of children in the disorganized group. Similarly, the placid stories or the party themes of some insecure children are likely perhaps to falsely reassure observers just as they probably do the children themselves. These stories, in fact, belie the significant anxieties of these children and the constraints they feel to express or experience them.

In a similar vein, it is important for observers to be aware that the content of doll play is indeed symbolic and strongly influenced by fantasy and associative processes. The children in this study—even the disorganized/controlling children—did not literally experience airplanes flying in the house, volcanoes, witches, getting lost and the like; probably none of them had in this sample experienced maltreatment in a formal sense. When doll play is observed among children who are clinically referred for behavior problems, clinicians in training or untrained observers have a tendency to take story content literally. Indeed, we have known observers to wish to make social services reports on the basis of the play or actually to do so. Just as the interpretation of dreams requires patient analysis of dream content based on knowledge of or interaction with an individual, we caution those new to this kind of work to maintain an open-minded stance regarding doll play assessments. Play content is best used to formulate hypotheses about the child's experience that can be confirmed or clarified over time.

In fact, if we view the doll play as essentially indicative of children's defenses, there is all the more reason for educators and observers to adhere to the usual unobtrusive stance of experienced play therapists, who refrain from interpretation or challenging children's defenses until a therapeutic alliance is well-established. The same should be said about children's failures to engage in symbolic play during the ADPA. "I don't know" in response to continued probes does not necessarily mean that task administration of the task has failed in some way or that children lack knowledge or desire to be difficult (though these may sometimes be the case). A more productive assumption is that these children are fearful of entertaining their own thoughts and emotions; such defenses require more, rather than less respect.

Access to the results of attachment security assessments *at a general level* can expand clinicians' and educators' understanding of children in their care by providing information about children's representation of self in relationships. Direct observation of children's doll play on attachment themes may help to clarify the emotional underpinnings of difficult or worrisome behavior of young children at home or in the classroom. For example, externalizing behavior is often, but not necessarily, associated with attachment disorganization. When doll play suggests secure attachment yet there is evidence of behavior problems, it may be wise to consider other sources of these problem behaviors. However, we strongly recommend against the use of such assessments as a way of formally assessing the mental health of particular young children or the quality of family life.

The ADPA is a demonstrated valuable and valid tool to use to unravel children's inner experience. It requires considerable training to administer and code reliably. Furthermore, classification information can have the unfortunate effect of labeling or pathologizing young children. Although attachment classifications appear to reflect different levels of developmental risk in a population, they do not convey specific diagnostic information for particular children. Considerably more research is required with respect to both the ADPA and other symbolic representational assessments to understand fully their predictive strengths and limitations.

AUTHOR CONTRIBUTIONS

CG and JS share equally the data set presented in this paper. CG was in charge of data analysis and was the primary author responsible for writing the paper. JS contributed ideas and editing to the paper.

FUNDING

This study was supported by a Mills College Faculty Development Grant awarded to the first author.

ACKNOWLEDGMENTS

We thank Chantal Cyr, Mary Campa, Karine Dubois-Comtois, Erica Greene, Amanda Jansen, Suzanne Lapidus, and Melissa Stewart-Kern for interaction and interview ratings. We also thank the mothers and their children who made this study possible.

REFERENCES

Ainsworth, M. D. S., Blehar, M., Waters, E., and Wall, S. (1978). *Patterns of Attachment: A psychological Study of the Strange Situation*. Hillsdale, NJ: Erlbaum.

Bovenschen, I., Lang, K., Zimmermann, J., Förthner, J., Nowacki, K., Roland, I., et al. (2016). Foster children's attachment behavior and representation: influence of children's pre-placement experiences and foster caregiver's sensitivity. *Child Abuse Negl.* 51, 323–335. doi: 10.1016/j.chiabu.2015.08.016

Bowlby, J. (1973). *Attachment and Loss: Separation: Anxiety and Anger*, Vol. 2. New York, NY: Basic Books.

Bowlby, J. (1980). *Attachment and Loss. Loss: Sadness and Depression*, Vol. 3. New York, NY: Basic Books.

Bowlby, J. (1969/1982). *Attachment and Loss: Attachment*, Vol. 1. New York NY: Basic Books.

Bretherton, I. (2005). "In pursuit of the internal working model construct and its relevance to attachment relationships," in *Attachment from Infancy to Adulthood: The major Longitudinal Studies*, eds K. E. Grossmann, K. Grossmann, and E. Waters (New York, NY): Guilford Press, 13–47.

Bretherton, I., and Munholland, K. A. (2008). "Internal working models in attachment relationships," in *Handbook of Attachment: Theory, Research, and Clinical Applications*, 2nd Edn, eds J. Cassidy and P. R. Shaver (New York, NY: Guilford Press), 102–127.

Bretherton, I., Ridgeway, D., and Cassidy, J. (1990). "Assessing internal working models of the attachment relationship: an attachment story completion task for 3-year-olds," in *Attachment in the Preschool Years*, eds M. T. Greenberg, D. Cicchetti, and E. M. Cummings (Chicago, IL: University of Chicago Press), 273–308.

Bureau, J.-F., and Moss, E. (2010). Behavioural precursors of attachment representations in middle childhood and links with child social adaptation. *Br. J. Dev. Psychol.* 28, 657–677. doi: 10.1348/026151009X468062

Cassidy, J., Marvin, R. S., and MacArthur Attachment Working Group. (1987–1992). *Attachment Organization in Preschool Children: Coding Guidelines*. State College, PA: Pennsylvania State University.

Demers, I., Bernier, A., Tarabulsy, G. M., and Provost, M. A. (2010). Mind-mindedness in adult and adolescent mothers: relations to maternal sensitivity and infant attachment. *Int. J. Behav. Dev.* 34, 529–537. doi: 10.1177/0165025410365802

Dubois-Comtois, K., Cyr, C., and Moss, E. (2011). Attachment behavior and mother-child conversations as predictors of attachment representations in middle childhood: a longitudinal study. *Attach. Hum. Dev.* 13, 335–357. doi: 10.1080/14616734.2011.584455

Dubois-Comtois, K., and Moss, E. (2008). Beyond the dyad: do family interactions influence children's attachment representations in middle childhood? *Attach. Hum. Dev.* 10, 415–431. doi: 10.1080/14616730802461441

Farnfield, S. (2015). The child attachment and play assessment (CAPA): validation of a new approach to coding narrative stems with children Ages 3–11 years. *Int. J. Play Ther.* doi: 10.1037/a0038726

George, C., and Solomon, J. (1988/1993/2005/2007). *The Caregiving Interview: Caregiving Representation Rating Manual*. Oakland, CA: Mills College.

George, C., and Solomon, J. (1989). Internal working models of parenting and security of attachment at age six. *Paper Presented at the Biennial Meeting of the Society for Research in Child Development*, Kansas City, MO.

George, C., and Solomon, J. (1990–2016). *Attachment Doll Play Assessment and Classification System*. Oakland, CA: Mills College.

George, C., and Solomon, J. (1996). Representational models of relationships: links between caregiving and attachment. *Infant Ment. Health J.* 17, 18–36. doi: 10.1002/(SICI)1097-0355(199623)17:3<198::AID-IMHJ2>3.0.CO;2-L

George, C., and Solomon, J. (2008). "The caregiving system: a behavioral systems approach to parenting," in *Handbook of attachment: Theory, research, and clinical applications*, 2nd Edn, eds J. Cassidy and P. R. Shaver (New York, NY: Guilford Press), 833–856.

George, C., and Solomon, J. (2011). "Caregiving helplessness: the development of a screening measure for disorganized maternal caregiving," in *Disorganized Attachment and Caregiving*, eds J. Solomon and C. George (New York, NY: Guilford Press), 133–163.

George, C., and West, M. (2011). The adult attachment projective picture system: integrating attachment into clinical assessment. *J. Pers. Assess.* 93, 407–416. doi: 10.1080/00223891.2011.594133

George, C., and West, M. (2012). *The Adult Attachment Projective Picture System: Attachment Theory and Assessment in Adults*. New York, NY: Guilford Press.

Gloger-Tippelt, G., Gomille, B., Koenig, L., and Vetter, J. (2002). Attachment representations in 6-year-olds: related longitudinally to the quality of attachment in infancy and mothers' attachment representations. *Attach. Hum. Dev.* 4, 318–339. doi: 10.1080/14616730210167221

Gloger-Tippelt, G. S., and König, L. (2007). Attchment representations in six-year-old children from one- and two-parent families in Germany. *Sch. Psychol. Int.* 28, 313–330. doi: 10.1177/0143034307078540

Goldwyn, R., Stanley, C., Smith, V., and Green, J. (2000). The Manchester child attachment story task: relationship with the parental AAI, SAT, and child behavior. *Attach. Hum. Dev.* 2, 71–84. doi: 10.1080/146167300361327

Goodman, G., Bartlett, R. C., and Stroh, M. (2013). Mothers' borderline features and children's disorganized attachment representations as predictors of children's externalizing behavior. *Psychoanal. Psychol.* 30, 16–36. doi: 10.1037/a0031068

Goodman, G., and Pfeffer, C. R. (1998). Attachment disorganization in prepubertal children with severe emotional disturbance. *Bull. Menninger Clin.* 62, 490–525.

Goodman, G., Sapp, M. S., Stroh, M., and Valdez, A. (2007). "Maternal depression, prepubertal children's representations of attachment disorganization, and the development of aggression and depression: a mediational model," in *Focus on Family Relations in the 21st*, ed. C. Yoon (New York, NY: century), 43–68.

Goodman, G., Stroh, M., and Valdez, A. (2012). Do attachment representations predict depression and anxiety distress in psychiatrically hospitalized prepubertal children? *Bull. Menninger Clin.* 76, 260–289. doi: 10.1521/bumc.2012.76.3.260

Green, J., Stanley, C., and Peters, S. (2007). Disorganized attachment representation and atypical parenting in young school age children with externalizing disorder. *Attach. Hum. Dev.* 9, 207–222. doi: 10.1080/14616730701453820

Green, J., Stanley, C., Smith, V., and Goldwyn, R. (2000). A new method of evaluating attachment representations in young school-age children: the manchester child attachment story task. *Attach. Hum. Dev.* 2, 48–70. doi: 10.1080/146167300361318

Grienenberger, J., Kelly, K., and Slade, A. (2005). Maternal reflective functioning, mother-infant affective communication, and infant attachment: exploring the link between mental states and observed caregiving behavior in the intergenerational transmission of attachment. *Attach. Hum. Dev.* 7, 299–311.

Hazen, N. L., Jacobvitz, D., Higgins, K. N., Allen, S., and Jin, M. K. (2011). "Pathways from disorganized attachment to later social-emotional problems," in *Disorganized Attachment and Caregiving*, ed. J. S. C. George (New York, NY: Guilford Press), 167–206.

Hodges, J., and Steele, H. (2000). Effects of abuse on attachment representations: narrative assessments of abused children. *J. Child Psychother.* 26, 433–455. doi: 10.1080/00754170010003674

Hodges, J., Steele, M., Hillman, S., Henderson, K., and Kaniuk, J. (2003). Changes in attachment representations over the first year of adoptive placement: narratives of maltreated children. *Clin. Child Psychol. Psychiatry* 8, 351–367. doi: 10.1177/1359104503008003006

Hoffman, K. T., Marvin, R. S., Cooper, G., and Powell, B. (2006). Changing toddlers' and preschoolers' attachment classifications: the circle of security intervention. *J. Consult. Clin. Psychol.* 74, 1017–1026. doi: 10.1037/0022-006X.74.6.1017

Humber, N., and Moss, E. (2005). The relationship of preschool and early school age attachment to mother-child interaction. *Am. J. Orthopsychiatry* 75, 128–141. doi: 10.1037/0002-9432.75.1.128

Katsurada, E. (2007). Attachment representation of institutionalized children in Japan. *Sch. Psychol. Int.* 28, 331–345. doi: 10.1177/0143034307078543

Lyons-Ruth, K., and Jacobvitz, D. (2016). "Attachment disorganization from infancy to adulthood: neurobiological correlates, parenting context, and pathways to disorder," in *Handbook of Attachment: Theory, Research, and Clinical Applications*, 3rd Edn, ed. P. R. S. J. Cassidy (New York, NY: Gilford Press), 667–695.

Macfie, J., Fitzpatrick, K. L., Rivas, E. M., and Cox, M. J. (2008). Independent influences upon mother-toddler role reversal: infant-mother attachment disorganization and role reversal in mother's childhood. *Attach. Hum. Dev.* 10, 29–39. doi: 10.1080/14616730701868589

Macfie, J., Swan, S. A., Fitzpatrick, K. L., Watkins, C. D., and Rivas, E. M. (2014). Mothers with borderline personality and their young children: adult attachment interviews, mother-child interactions, and children's narrative representations. *Dev. Psychopathol.* 26, 539–551. doi: 10.1017/s095457941400011x

Mayer, M. (1976). *Four Frogs in a Box*. New York, NY: Dial Press.

Miljkovitch, R., Moran, G., Roy, C., Jaunin, L., Forcada-Guex, M., Pierrehumbert, B., et al. (2013). Maternal interactive behaviour as a predictor of preschoolers' attachment representations among full term and premature samples. *Early Hum. Dev.* 89, 349–354. doi: 10.1016/j.earlhumdev.2012.11.006

Miljkovitch, R., Pierrehumbert, B., Karmaniola, A., and Halfon, O. (2003). Les representations d'attachement du jeune enfant. Développement d'un codage pour les histoires ácompléter (The attachment of the young child representations. Development of a code for stories.). *Devenir* 15, 143–177.

Moss, E., Bureau, J., Cyr, C., Mongeau, C., and St-Laurent, D. (2004a). Correlates of attachment at age 3: construct validity of the preschool attachment classification system. *Dev. Psychol.* 40, 323–334. doi: 10.1037/0012-1649.40.3.323

Moss, E., Cyr, C., and Dubois-Comtois, K. (2004b). Attachment at early school age and developmental risk: examining family contexts and behavior problems of controlling-caregiving, controlling-punitive, and behaviorally disorganized children. *Dev. Psychol.* 40, 519–532. doi: 10.1037/0012-1649.40.4.519

Moss, E., Gosselin, C., Parent, S., Rousseau, D., and Dumont, M. (1997). Attachment and joint problem-solving experiences during the preschool period. *Soc. Dev.* 6, 1–17. doi: 10.1111/1467-9507.ep11631667

Moss, E., Rousseau, D., Parent, S., St-Laurent, D., and Saintonge, J. (1998). Correlates of attachment at school age: maternal reported stress, mother-child interaction, and behavior problems. *Child Dev.* 69, 1390–1405. doi: 10.2307/1132273

Moss, E., and St-Laurent, D. (2001). Attachment at school age and academic performance. *Dev. Psychobiol.* 37, 863–874. doi: 10.1037/0012-1649.37.6.863

Oppenheim, D. (1997). The attachment doll-play interview for preschoolers. *Int. J. Behav. Dev.* 20, 681–697. doi: 10.1080/016502597385126

Oppenheim, D., and Goldsmith, D. F. (2007). *Attachment Theory in Clinical Work with Children Bridging the Gap between Research and Practice*. New York, NY: Guilford Press.

Oppenheim, D., and Koren-Karie, N. (2002). Mothers' insightfulness regarding their children's internal worlds: the capacity underlying secure childâ€ "mother relationships. *Infant Ment. Health J.* 23, 593–605. doi: 10.1002/imhj.10035

Page, T., and Bretherton, I. (2003). Gender differences in stories of violence and caring by preschool children in post-divorce families: Implications for social competence. *Child Adolesc. Soc. Work J.* 20, 485–508. doi: 10.1023/A:1022864614244

Pasco Fearon, R. M., and Belsky, J. (2016). "Precursors of attachment security," in *Handbook of Attachment: Theory, Research, and Clinical Applications*, 3rd Edn, ed. P. R. S. J. Cassidy (New York, NY: Gilford Press), 291–313.

Román, M., Palacios, J., Moreno, C., and López, A. (2012). Attachment representations in internationally adopted children. *Attach. Hum. Dev.* 14, 585–600. doi: 10.1080/14616734.2012.727257

Rydell, A.-M., Bohlin, G., and Thorell, L. B. (2005). Representations of attachment to parents and shyness as predictors of children's relationships with teachers and peer competence in preschool. *Attach. Hum. Dev.* 7, 187–204. doi: 10.1080/14616730500134282

Salari, R., Bohlin, G., Rydell, A.-M., and Thorell, L. B. (2016). Neuropsychological functioning and attachment representations in early school age as predictors of adhd symptoms in late adolescence. *Child Psychiatry Hum. Dev.* doi: 10.1007/s10578-016-0664-1

Sameroff, A. J. (1993). "Models of development and developmental risk," in *Handbook of Infant Mental Health*, ed. C. H. Zeanah (New York, NY: Guilford Press), 3–14.

Schore, A. N. (2001). Attachment and the regulation of the right brain. *Attach. Hum. Dev.* 2, 23–47. doi: 10.1080/146167300361309

Schore, J., and Schore, A. N. (2008). Modern attachment theory: the central role of affect regulation in development and treatment. *Clin. Soc. Work J.* 36, 9–20. doi: 10.1007/s10615-007-0111-7

Solomon, J., and George, C. (1996). Defining the Caregiving Systems: toward a Theory of Caregiving. *Infant Ment. Health J.* 17, 3–17. doi: 10.1002/(SICI)1097-0355(199623)17:3<183::AID-IMHJ1>3.0.CO;2-Q

Solomon, J., and George, C. (1999a). The caregiving system in mothers of infants: a comparison of divorcing and married mothers. *Attach. Hum. Dev.* 1, 171–190. doi: 10.1080/14616739900134221

Solomon, J., and George, C. (1999b). "The place of disorganization in attachment theory: linking classic observations with contemporary findings," in *Attachment Disorganization*, eds J. Solomon and C. George (New York, NY: Guilford Press), 3–32.

Solomon, J., and George, C. (2002). Understanding children's attachment representations in terms of defensive process. *Paper Presented at the 4th Annual Conference of the International Academy of Family Psychology*, Heidelberg.

Solomon, J., and George, C. (2011a). "The disorganized attachment-caregiving system: dysregulation of adaptive processes at multiple levels," in *Disorganized*

Attachment and Caregiving, eds J. Solomon and C. George (New York, NY: Guilford Press), 3–24.

Solomon, J., and George, C. (2011b). "Dysregulation of maternal caregiving across two generations," in *Disorganization of Attachment and Caregiving*, eds J. Solomon and C. George (New York, NY: Guilford Press), 25–51.

Solomon, J., and George, C. (2016). "The measurement of attachment security in infancy and childhood," in *Handbook of Attachment: Theory, Research, and Clinical Applications*, 3rd Edn, eds J. Cassidy and P. R. Shaver (New York, NY: Guilford Press), 366–396.

Solomon, J., George, C., and De Jong, A. (1995). Children classified as controlling at age six: evidence of disorganized representational strategies and aggression at home and at school. *Dev. Psychopathol.* 7, 447–463. doi: 10.1017/S0954579400006623

Stacks, A. M., and Oshio, T. (2009). Disorganized attachment and social skills as indicators of Head Start children's school readiness skills. *Attach. Hum. Dev.* 11, 143–164. doi: 10.1080/14616730802625250

Stievenart, M., Roskam, I., Meunier, J. C., and van de Moortele, G. (2011). The reciprocal relation between children's attachment representations and their cognitive ability. *Int. J. Behav. Dev.* 35, 58–66. doi: 10.1177/0165025410370790

Torres, N., Maia, J., Veríssimo, M., Fernandes, M., and Silva, F. (2012). Attachment security representations in institutionalized children and children living with their families: links to problem behaviour. *Clin. Psychol. Psychother.* 19, 25–36. doi: 10.1002/cpp.739

Venet, M., Bureau, J.-F., Gosselin, C., and Capauno, F. (2007). Attachment representation in a sample of neglected preschool age children. *Sch. Psychol. Int.* 28, 264–293. doi: 10.1177/0143034307078534

Verschueren, K., Dossche, D., Marcoen, A., Mahieu, S., and Bakermans-Kranenburg, M. (2006). Attachment representations and discipline in mothers of young school children: an observation study. *Soc. Dev.* 15, 659–675. doi: 10.1111/j.1467-9507.2006.00363.x

Verschueren, K., and Marcoens, A. (1999). Representation of self and socioecmotional competence in kindergartners: differential and combined effects of attachment to mother and father. *Child Dev.* 70, 183–201. doi: 10.1111/1467-8624.00014

Waters, H. S., and Waters, E. (2006). The attachment working models concept: among other things, we build script-like representations of secure base experiences. *Attach. Hum. Dev.* 8, 185–197. doi: 10.1080/146167306008 56016

Webster, L., and Hackett, R. K. (2011). "An exploratory investigation of the relationships among representation security, disorganization, and behavior in maltreated children," in *Disorganized Attachment and Caregiving*, eds J. Solomon and C. George (New York, NY: Guilford Press), 292–317.

Yamakawa, K. (2006). Assessing attachment representations in early childhood: validation of the attachment doll play. *Jpn. J. Educ. Psychol.* 54, 476–486. doi: 10.5926/jjep1953.54.4_476

Conflict of Interest Statement: The authors declare that the research was conducted in the absence of any commercial or financial relationships that could be construed as a potential conflict of interest.

13

Child–Computer Interaction at the Beginner Stage of Music Learning: Effects of *Reflexive Interaction* on Children's Musical Improvisation

Anna Rita Addessi[1]*, Filomena Anelli[1], Diber Benghi[1] and Anders Friberg[2]

[1] Department of Education Studies, University of Bologna, Bologna, Italy, [2] Department of Speech, Music and Hearing, KTH Royal Institute of Technology, Stockholm, Sweden

In this article children's musical improvisation is investigated through the "reflexive interaction" paradigm. We used a particular system, the MIROR-Impro, implemented in the framework of the MIROR project (EC-FP7), which is able to reply to the child playing a keyboard by a "reflexive" output, mirroring (with repetitions and variations) her/his inputs. The study was conducted in a public primary school, with 47 children, aged 6–7. The experimental design used the convergence procedure, based on three sample groups allowing us to verify if the reflexive interaction using the MIROR-Impro is *necessary* and/or *sufficient* to improve the children's abilities to improvise. The following conditions were used as independent variables: to play only the keyboard, the keyboard with the MIROR-Impro but with not-reflexive reply, the keyboard with the MIROR-Impro with reflexive reply. As dependent variables we estimated the children's ability to improvise in solos, and in duets. Each child carried out a training program consisting of 5 weekly individual 12 min sessions. The control group played the complete package of independent variables; Experimental Group 1 played the keyboard and the keyboard with the MIROR-Impro with not-reflexive reply; Experimental Group 2 played only the keyboard with the reflexive system. One week after, the children were asked to improvise a musical piece on the keyboard alone (Solo task), and in pairs with a friend (Duet task). Three independent judges assessed the Solo and the Duet tasks by means of a grid based on the TAI-Test for Ability to Improvise rating scale. The EG2, which trained only with the reflexive system, reached the highest average results and the difference with EG1, which did not used the reflexive system, is statistically significant when the children improvise in a duet. The results indicate that in the sample of participants the reflexive interaction alone could be sufficient to increase the improvisational skills, and necessary when they improvise in duets. However, these results are in general not statistically significant. The correlation between Reflexive Interaction and the ability to improvise is statistically significant. The results are discussed on the light of the recent literature in neuroscience and music education.

Keywords: reflexive interaction, children's music improvisation, child–computer interaction, assessment of children's performance, MIROR-Impro

Edited by:
Aaron Williamon,
Royal College of Music and Imperial College London, UK

Reviewed by:
André Klostermann,
University of Bern, Switzerland
Rafael Ramirez,
Pompeu Fabra University, Spain

****Correspondence:***
Anna Rita Addessi
annarita.addessi@unibo.it

Specialty section:
This article was submitted to Performance Science, a section of the journal Frontiers in Psychology

INTRODUCTION

In his book "The improvising mind. Cognition and creativity in the musical moment," Berkowitz (2010), explores the field of ability to improvise through an interdisciplinary approach (i.e., musical analysis, neuroscience, historical pedagogical methods on improvisation, interviews with musicians), showing the complexity of the phenomenon of improvisation and, at the same time, the complexity of studying music improvisation. In the field of music education, several scholars approached the problem from different perspectives and by means of different methodologies, giving rise to discussion about the definition of improvisation in children's musical experience, the relationships between improvisation and creativity, learning/teaching theories and social/familial contexts. Baroni (1997) describes several examples of children's improvisation in the context of expressive activities in a classroom setting (kindergarten and primary school); Brophy (2005) carried out a longitudinal study of selected characteristics of children's melodic improvisation; Delalande (1993) used the concept of "conduct" to observe the musical improvisation of children on the basis of the Piagetian concepts of sensory-motor, symbolic and rules games; Hickey and Lipscomb (2006) also offer a model of assessment of children's creative musical thinking; Kratus (1996) established several levels of improvisation: exploration, process-oriented improvisation with the presence of some micro-structures, product-orientated with four more levels of relationship between micro and macro-structures; McPherson (1993, 2005) elaborates a grid to assess the student's ability to improvise; Mialaret (1997) proposes a model to classify children's instrumental musical explorations; Tafuri (2006) describes several models of musical improvisation with children; Young (2004), introduces the interpersonal perspective on childrens' music improvisation together with the teacher; Webster (2002) studies children as creative thinkers in music and proposes a model of creative thinking in music.

In our study, we investigated this issue through the "reflexive interaction paradigm." This paradigm describes a particular kind of human–machine interaction where the users can interact with a virtual copies of themselves, through specific software called interactive reflexive musical systems (IRMS). The first prototype of IRMS, the Continuator (Pachet, 2003) was originally conceived for adult musicians. However, we decided to experiment it with children and the exploratory study (e.g., Addessi and Pachet, 2005, 2006) immediately showed that these systems can have a strong impact on the development of children's creative musical experiences, introducing a new perspective in the field of technology-enhanced learning In this field,, most studies deal with internet devices, teaching strategies, composition, performance, and music therapy: the new technology opens new scenarios on musical learning and teaching (e.g., Delalande, 2003; Brown, 2007; Webster, 2007; Williams and Webster, 2008; Finney and Burnard, 2009; Dorfman, 2013; Bauer, 2014). However, new technology can be considered not only as a "tool" to aid teaching, but also as providing languages and "brainframes" (Turkle, 1984; De Kerckhove, 1991) that deeply influence the processes of musical learning and the musical creativity of children. Recently, several studies have been realized to analyze human–machine interaction and the evaluation and design of interfaces for collaborative music making, focused on user experience, and affective and emotional behavior: these studies were mainly focused on adults and adolescents (cfr. Morgan et al., 2014).

Our study aims to investigate whether the reflexive interaction using the IRMS influences the children's skillfulness to improvise, at the beginner stage of musical learning. We used a particular IRMS, the MIROR-Impro, implemented in the MIROR project (EC-FP7), which is able to reply to the child playing a keyboard by mirroring (with repetitions and variations) her/his inputs (Pachet et al., 2011; Addessi et al., 2013). During a session with the MIROR-Impro, the user plays a (Midi) keyboard and, when she/he stops, the system immediately answers with a musical phrase similar to the input played by the user. A dialog then takes place between the user and the machine, in which the two partners repeat and vary the musical ideas. The user's inputs are analyzed by the MIROR-Impro to gradually build a model of the user. **Figures 1A,B** show how a simple musical input played by a child (**Figure 1A**) is continued by the MIROR-Impro (**Figure 1B**) with repetition and variation.

The Interactive Reflexive Musical Systems

Pachet (2003, 2004, 2006) considers reflexive interactive systems as a particular "class of interactive systems in which users can interact with virtual copies of themselves, or at least with agents that have a mimetic capacity and can evolve in an organic fashion" (2006, 360). He identified several features that characterized reflexivity but were to be considered "by no means exhaustive" (2006, p. 360):

- *Similarity or mirroring effect:* The IRMS "produces musical sounds similar to what the user is (...) able to produce. This similarity must be easily recognizable by the user, who must experience the sensation of interacting with a copy of her/himself" (2006, p. 360).
- *Agnosticism:* "The system's ability to reproduce the user's personality is learned automatically and agnostically, - i.e., without human intervention." In the case of the Continuator, "for instance, no pre-programmed musical information is given to the system" (2006, p. 360).
- *Scaffolding of complexity.* "Incremental learning ensures that the (IRMS) keeps evolving and consequently that the user will interact with it for a long time.... Incremental learning is a way to endow the system with an organic feel, typical of open, natural systems (as opposed to pre-programmed, closed-world systems)" (2006, p. 361).
- The turn-taking between the user and the system is the *basic playing mode* of the IRMS. It is organized on the basis of three principles: (1) "Automatic detection of phrase endings"; (2) Setting the duration of the phrase generated by the IRMS "to be the same as the duration of the last input phrase"; (3) Giving "priority to the user" (Pachet, 2004).

The principle of "similarity and mirroring" is particularly important for the definition of the IRMS: "the musical output must typically lie in between two extreme forms of

FIGURE 1 | Piano roll representation: A musical input played by a child (A) is continued by the MIROR-Impro **(B)**, with repetition and variation.

musical production: Repetition and Randomness. Repetition is obtained by echoing musical elements of the user, without any reorganization. Repetition creates a sense of mirroring, but does not exhibit any increase in complexity. Randomness can exhibit complexity but is not related to the user's personality (2006, p. 362)". The system's output is generated by means of the Markov probabilities calculated during the analysis of the musical input. In the framework of the MIROR project, Pachet et al. (2011) recently proposed using the Markov probabilities to generate musical sequences satisfying several constraints, such as the starting and the ending notes. According to this perspective, the system output does not imitate exactly what the musician is doing, but rather imitates her/his musical style. The notion of style of IRMS consists "of the statistical distribution of notes, chords and musical elements in general as well as their ordering" (Pachet, 2004, p. 3).

Observations and Theoretical Framework of Reflexive Interaction

In our previous work, we tried to explain the human behaviors during the interaction with a reflexive system, starting from the observation of the interaction between children and the IRMS (Addessi, 2014). Our aim was to examine the human reflexive behavior, both in human–machine and human–human interaction, to understand how reflexive interaction can support and enhance creativity and the learning/teaching processes. We suggested that the idea of mirroring originated in ancient Western culture and now resonates with contemporary theory of musical embodiments and the mirror system.

An example of micro-analysis featuring this mechanism and how it develops is provided by the interaction between the MIROR-Impro and a 7-year-old girl, video-recorded during the experiment introduced in this article:

The little girl plays two consecutive notes, C2 and A2, and then stops to wait for the response of the system. The system responds by repeating the same notes. The child then plays a single note, G2, and the system responds with a single note but this time introduces a variation: she plays C3, thus introducing a higher register. The girl, following the change introduced by the system, moves toward the higher register and plays a variant of the initial pattern, namely: D2-A2-E2-C3, and introduces a particular rhythm pattern. This "reflexive" event marks the beginning of a dialog based on repetition and variation: the rhythmic-melodic pattern will be repeated and varied by both the system and the child in consecutive exchanges, until acquiring the form of a complete musical phrase. At some point in the dialog, the child begins to accompany the system's response with arm movements synchronized with the rhythmic-melodic patterns, creating a kind of music-motor composition.

In this example, as well as several examples reported in our previous works (e.g., Addessi and Pachet, 2005; Addessi, 2014), it is possible to observe how:

- The attention of the young girl increases when the system imitates her musical sentences and decreases when the system's output become more varied;
- The interaction between the child and the machine is not predetermined by the machine, nor realized only by the child, but is co-constructed by the child along with the machine;
- The *co-regulation* (Fogel, 2000) is based on a continuous *repetition* and *variation* mechanism between input and output data from the child and the system;
- The partners are able to imitate each other and the child recognizes being imitated;
- The interaction is based on *turn-taking*: the child plays, then stops, waiting for the response of the system and when it comes she listens to it carefully, perceives its reflexive qualities and in turn the child responds by imitating and varying the system's response;
- The response of the system takes up the last input played by the child, giving rise to a *regular timing of turns*.
- The child dialogs with the system by means of sounds, which is an evident manifestation of *thinking in sound* (McPherson, 2005).

What it is interesting in this kind of child–machine interaction, is the creation of a dialog between the child and the system, which shows some *biological constraints* as described in Katayose (2014): physical fatigue, sensory error, and, above all, balancing between repetition and novelty. The repetition and variation mechanism is, in fact, the fundamental characteristic of reflexive interaction: the girl in the microanalysis starts to show an absolute attraction toward the system's reply precisely when she recognizes the system's repetition of her input. It is interesting to note that it is not merely a repetition, but rather a repetition that is constantly varied. The co-presence of repetition along with something different seems to attract and stimulate the user to become involved in the interaction. The topics of *mirror* and *sound mirror* are very ancient in Western culture: from the myth of Echo and Narcissus (Ovid, 43 B.C.-18, *Metamorphoseon libri XV*), to the antiphonal *echo* effects of renaissance and baroque music, to the power of music to reflect the human affects of the *Teoria degli affetti* and the *Affektenlehre* (Galilei, 1581; Kircher, 1650), More recently, the mechanism of repetition and variation is at the heart of the semiological paradigmatic analysis (Ruwet, 1966) and the theory of similarity perception in listening to music (Deliège, 2001; Toiviainen, 2007). The imitation of the behavior of others seems to be grounded on the non-conscious processing known as the *chameleon effect* (Lakin and Chartrand, 2003). Studies in neuroscience root these non-conscious mechanisms in the mirror neuron system (MNS), a network of neurons that becomes active during the execution and observation of actions, on the basis of a "resonance mechanism" (Rizzolatti et al., 2002). Recent studies in psychology and neurosciences increasingly suggest that the mechanisms of repetition and variation, imitation, recognition, and self-imitation, play an important role in infant musicality development and in the ontological fundamentals of human musicality (e.g., Bruner, 1983; Dissanayake, 2000; Meltzoff and Prinz, 2002; Stern, 2004; Imberty, 2005; Papoušěk, 2007; Gratier and Apter-Danon, 2009; Malloch and Trevarthen, 2009). The majority of this research refers to the ability of children to imitate, described by Meltzoff as the *like-me* mechanism: "persons are like-me entities in so far as they can do like me, and I can do like them" (Nadel, 2002, p. 46). Anzieu (1996) introduced the concept of *musical wrapping* of the Self, to describe the original infant-mother relationship, characterized by the presence of the most archaic forms of repetition: the *echo*. For this raison, reflexive interaction can also be described as a "*dynamic process*" (Addessi, 2014, p. 219): the experience of repetition and variation that the infant experiences during the vocal interaction with the adult in the 1st months of life, is realized in the framework of affective and emotional valence, that is the *amodal* experience that Stern (2004) calls *affective contours*. The fundamental role of the body in human musical activities is underlined also by the recent studies carried out in the field of embodied music cognition, which can explain the relationship between reflexive interaction and body perception. In particular way, it is important to underline the nearness of the reflexive interaction paradigm with the acoustic metaphor of "resonance mechanism," used by Rizzolatti et al. (2002, p. 253) to describe the correspondence between "observed and executed biological motion" in the framework of the mirror neurons system. Leman (2007, p. 91), underlines that "mirror neurons are amodal, in the sense that they can encode the mirroring of multiple sensory channels." Therefore, "reflexive interaction would stimulate a resonance mechanism in the child interacting with an IRMS. This resonance could have a neural basis in the MNS" (Addessi, 2014, p. 220). At the same time, interactive learning and the development of individual musical expressivity has been investigated in various studies that highlight the complex multi-modal character of these processes. Prinz (2008) described a *common coding* theory, which posits a shared representational domain for perception and action among individuals based on a mirroring mechanism, which can explain the neurobiological fundamental of reflexive interaction.

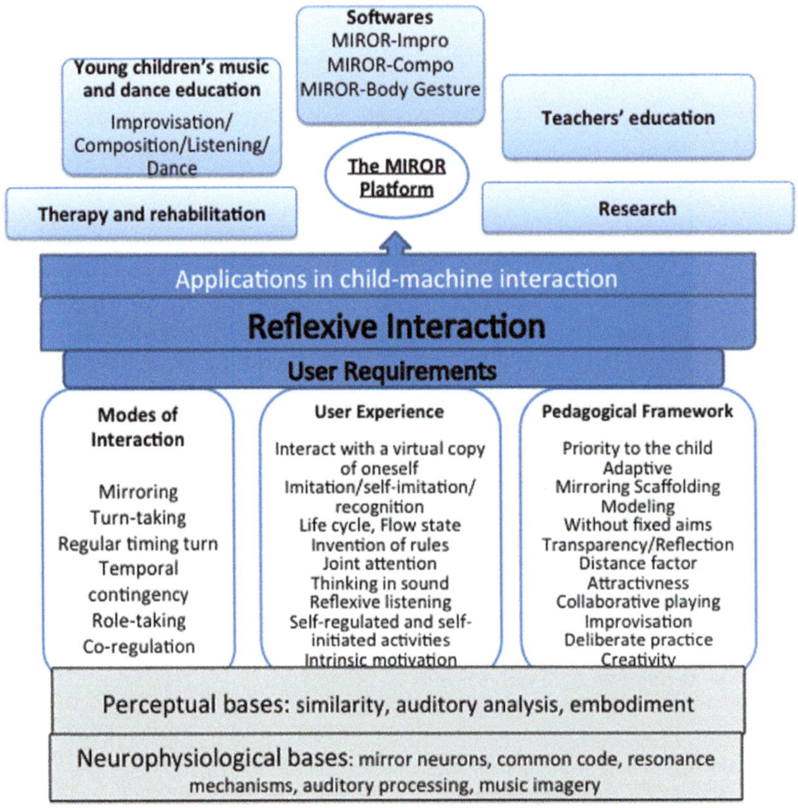

FIGURE 2 | Theoretical framework of reflexive interaction with implication for child–computer interaction (as from Addessi, 2014).

Is Reflexive Interaction Necessary and/or Sufficient to Improve Children's Ability to Improvise?

The basic hypothesis of our study is that reflexive interaction (in short RI) can "enhance music learning and musical creativity in young children (...). The pedagogical potential of reflexive interaction is based on the fact that it stimulates the subject to undertake a dialog during which the repetitions and variations enhance cognitive conflict that the child resolves during the course of the interaction, giving rise to a learning by problem finding and problem solving" (Addessi, 2014, p. 223). It was observed that the reflexive interaction using IRMS stimulated and reinforced children's exploratory conducts, characterized by the use of variations, in a variety of elements: melody, rhythms, gestures, registers, speed, dynamics, phrasing. The discovery that the system replies by imitating them, motivates the children to undertake a musical dialog with the system, which is the basis for the elaboration of particular sounds and musical ideas. It was possible to observe that each child expressed her/his individual musical style, in producing the sounds, handling the keyboard and the other equipment, and her/his style was supported and reinforced by the mirroring effect of the system's output. It is possible to affirm that, during the reflexive interaction, the musical invention is a collaborative experience of playing: the child/ren and the system, in a pair, improvise together like two musicians. It was observed that reflexive interaction using the IRMS increases the attention span, stimulates attentive listening, intrinsic motivation, musical creativity, and ability in collaborative improvisation (e.g., Addessi and Pachet, 2005, 2006; Addessi et al., 2013; Ferrari and Addessi, 2014; Rowe et al., 2015). The dialog with a "virtual" musician stimulates children to "think in sound," which is considered one of the main aims of music education (McPherson, 2005). IRMS establish an interaction between pairs, which exploits the Vygotskian concept of zone of proximal development (ZPD) (Vygotsky, 1962). The mirroring mechanism creates a balance between challenges and skills, which enables the MIROR application to create children's flow experiences and creative processes (Csikzsentmihalyi, 1990; Pachet, 2004; Addessi et al., 2015).

The pedagogical potential of IRMS was fully exploited in the framework of the MIROR project, to enhance children's collaborative playing, self-regulation, self-initiated activities, and a learner-centered approach. These pedagogical strategies are already used in some educational contexts, including music education (e.g., Custodero, 2005). But we underline that in the case of the MIROR applications, these strategies and behaviors occur between the children and the machine, a mechanism that is not very usual in the field of child–machine interaction and in the field of technology-enhanced learning. **Figure 2** shows the theoretical framework of reflexive interaction with implications for child–computer interaction.

The questions that lie at the basis of our study are as follows: does the reflexive interaction by means of the MIROR-Impro affect children's ability to improvise? In particular, does it affect the ability to improvise a musical dialog with a partner? Can the MIROR-Impro be used as a teaching device at the beginner stage of learning musical improvisation? In our pilot studies and investigations on children and IRMS, we observed several features of child–machine interaction, based on reflexive interaction, which led the children to improvise musical duets with the system (cfr. Addessi and Pachet, 2005). These "musical conversations" were based on the mechanism of repetition-variation, which is "at the heart of reflexive interaction" (Addessi, 2014, p. 2017). We observed and measured the flow emotional state (Csikzsentmihalyi, 1990) of children playing with the MIROR-Impro (Addessi et al., 2015). We showed that the flow experience increases when children play with the system and, in particular, when the system's reply is more reflexive. The experience of flow is often used to describe the sense of complete absorption in the act of improvising, in which the improviser seems to merge with the music and transcend everyday consciousness (Berkowitz, 2010, p. 127) and has been used as a tool to investigate human–machine interaction (Leman et al., 2010; Nijs et al., 2012). Therefore, we could argue that reflexive interaction is able to enhance the experience of musical creativity and improvisation. Further studies conducted in the framework of the MIROR project highlight the children's perspective on their own improvisation (e.g., Triantafyllaki et al., 2012; Cardoso de Araújo and Addessi, 2013; Rowe et al., 2015) and some musical patterns evident in their improvisations with the MIROR-Impro (Alexakis et al., 2013). Nevertheless, there are still no studies that show in a controlled experimental design that IRMS positively influence in a particular way the ability to improvise.

The aim of the present study is to investigate whether the use of reflexive interaction with the MIROR-Impro is "necessary" and/or "sufficient" to improve children's abilities to improvise, and, consequently, whether it could be useful to include the MIROR-Impro in a program of teaching improvisation. Moreover, in our study, we studied two specific conditions of improvisation: solo and duet performance.

MATERIALS AND METHODS

Participants

The study sample consisted of 47 children, aged 6–7, distributed in two natural classroom groups in the 1st year of a primary school. Participants were randomly divided into three sample groups: 16 children for the Control group (CG), 15 children for the Experimental Group 1, and 16 children for the Experimental Group 2. The children had not attended any formal course of instrumental education. They were used to carrying out general classroom activities in music education with the teachers.

Equipment

The software MIROR-Impro, a component of the MIROR Platform (v.3.14). Three different setups of the system's output were used: setup Nothing, the system did not reply; setup Similar, the system's outputs were similar to the input of the child; setup Very Different, the system's outputs were totally different from the child's input. As can be seen, only the setup Similar used reflexive interaction. In addition: music synthesizers KORG X50; notebooks; headphones; amplifiers M-AUDIO AV30; USB cables for the connection between the synthesizer and the notebook; video cameras (recording in HD).

Experimental Design

The convergence procedure (Campbell and Heller, 1979; Fiske, 1992) was used, based on three sample groups (one control group - CG - and two experimental groups -EG1 and EG2), allowing us to verify not only if the reflexive interaction using the MIROR-Impro affects the children's musical improvisation but also, more precisely, if it is "necessary" and/or "sufficient" to improve the children's abilities to improvise, in solos and in duets. This procedure is based on the comparison of three different experimental conditions, represented by three groups of participants: CG, Experimental Group number 1, and Experimental Group number 2. Each experimental condition represents a possible combination of different independent variables, one of which is reflexive interaction.

In our protocol the following three independent variables were considered:

(1) Playing the keyboard (v1): in this case, we used the MIROR-Impro system with the setup Nothing and, as a consequence, the system did not produce any output;
(2) Playing the keyboard with the MIROR-Impro but with not-reflexive reply (v2). In this case we used the MIROR-Impro system with the setup Very Different: in this setup the system's reply is very different from the input played by the children and there is no reflexive interaction. For example: the child plays a long cluster, loud, with the palms of the hands in the higher register, and the system replies with three short single notes in the low register.
(3) Playing the keyboard with reflexive interaction using the MIROR-Impro (v3): in this case we used the setup Similar in which the system repeats the child's input with variations and a reflexive interaction is thus started between child and system. For example: the child plays a long cluster, loud, with the palms of the hands, and the system replies with a short cluster in the same register followed by an ascending *arpeggio*.

The convergence procedure focuses the attention on one of these variables, which is manipulated in order to determine if the variable is *necessary* to enhance the dependent variables, and *sufficient* to enhance the dependent variables. In our protocol the independent variable to be controlled is variable no 3: playing the keyboard with the MIROR-Impro with reflexive reply. The aim is to observe if the reflexive interaction using MIROR-Impro is *necessary* and/or *sufficient* to improve the dependent variables.

The dependent variables are as follows: (1) the children's ability to improvise in solos, and (2) the children's ability to improvise in duets.

Procedure

The activities were carried out in a primary school. Several preliminary meetings were held with the teachers in order to introduce the MIROR Project, to discuss and share any issues, and to introduce and clarify the roles of the researchers and operators and the role of the teachers. A preliminary meeting was held with the children in order to assure a good relationship and positive attunement between researchers and children. The children were invited to participate freely. The observations were carried out in the school setting and the experimental activities were introduced in the daily routines of the children. The activities were carried out in a space in front of the class, so that the teacher could be present. Each child carried out a preliminary individual session to familiarize her/himself with the keyboard, the equipment, and the setting. This preliminary session lasted about 10 min for each child. After that, each child carried out the training activities (see the package of activities below), and then the Solo and the Duet tests. All sessions were video recorded.

Setting: for the training activities, three locations were prepared, one for each child. The children were accompanied two or three at a time to their personal location. Each location included a keyboard connected to a computer and provided with headphones. Each location was equipped with a video camera for video recording. The camera was attached to the keyboard in order to record the audio while the child listened through headphones. The child had the headphones in order to listen to her/his own productions, the productions of the system and, in the Duet task, those of the companion. In the Duet task, the setting included two keyboards and only one camera video-recorded both children. An assistant researcher managed the cameras and took note of the participants (names, ID number); the music teacher managed the keyboards and computers, and gave instructions to the children.

Package of Activities

Each child carried out a training program consisting of 5 weekly individual 12 min sessions. The CG played the complete package of independent variables (v1+v2+v3); EG1 played the keyboard and the keyboard with the MIROR-Impro with not-reflexive reply (v1+v2); EG2 played only the keyboard with the MIROR-Impro with the reflexive reply (v3).

The package of activities was organized as follows:

- *Control Group* (Complete package of activities): task 1- the child plays the keyboard (v1) (4 min); task 2 - the child plays the keyboard using the MIROR-Impro without reflexive reply (v2) (4 min); task 3 - the child plays the keyboard using MIROR-Impro with reflexive reply (v3) (4 min).
- *Experimental Group 1* (Package minus independent variable): task 1 - the child plays the keyboard (v1 = 6 min); task 2 - the child plays the keyboard using the MIROR-Impro without reflexive reply (v2) (6 min).
- *Experimental Group 2* (Independent variable minus Package): task 3 - the child plays the keyboard using MIROR-Impro with reflexive reply (v3) (12 min).

The different amount of time for each variable in each group is due to the fact that the convergence procedure is not used to verify which of the three independent variables considered is more effective, but rather to focus on only one variable which is manipulated in order to verify if the focused variable is sufficient and/or necessary for improving the dependent variable.

At each session, the child was asked to carry out the following tasks/games:

Control Group: "You can play three different games. One game is to play just the keyboard, another game is to play the keyboard with the system that will reply differently, another game is to play the keyboard with the system that will reply similarly. Each game lasts 4 min. After every 4 min we will ask you to change game. After 12 min we will ask you to stop. If you are tired you can stop and re-start when you want."

Experimental Group 1: "You can play two different games. One game is to play just the keyboard; another game is to play the keyboard with the system that will reply differently. Each game lasts 6 min. After every 6 min we will ask you to change game. After 12 min we will ask you to stop. If you are tired you can stop and re-start when you want."

Experimental Group 2: "You can play one game. You can play the keyboard with the system that will reply similarly. The game lasts 12 min. After 12 min we will ask you to stop. If you are tired you can stop and re-start when you want."

In the first session the task order was chosen by the child. In the following sessions, the music teacher set the task order in a balanced manner. All sessions were video recorded.

Test

After doing the package activities, all participants of the three groups were submitted to a test. The test consisted of two tasks: the Solo task (the child improvises alone) and the Duet task (the children improvise in pairs).

Each participant received the same instructions as follows:

Solo Task: "Create a short piece of music with a beginning, a development, and an end (like a story). You have 5 min to explore and invent the piece. After 5 min we will stop you and you will play your musical piece." Before starting the performance, the music teacher repeats: "Now you play the musical piece that you invented. It should have a beginning, a development, and an end. When you finish, you stop and I understand that the piece is finished." See **Figure 3** for an example of the Solo task setting.

During the 5 min available, the children had the possibility to explore some musical ideas, but did not write what they had created. Then, during the test, they performed their improvisation, in the sense that they elaborated in real-time the musical ideas previously explored (Kratus, 1996; McPherson, 2005; Tafuri, 2006). In the words of McPherson (2005, p. 10) they created "music aurally without the aid of notation".

FIGURE 3 | An example of the Solo task setting.

FIGURE 4 | An example of the Duet task setting.

Duet task: "You can play the keyboards like in a dialog. In this dialog you can only use sounds, and not words. You have 10 min. At the end of the time, we will stop you." See **Figure 4** for an example of the Duet task setting.

All sessions were video recorded.

In accordance with Campbell and Heller (1979), and Fiske (1992), we then compared:

(1) The results of the CG ("complete package" condition, v1+v2+v3) with the results of the Experimental Group 1 ("package minus" condition, v1+v2) to verify if the independent variable 3 (reflexive interaction using MIROR-Impro) is *necessary* to improve the dependent variables, that is the ability to improvise alone and in a duet: if CG > EG1 = independent variable 3 is *necessary* to improve dependent variables;

(2) The results of the CG ("complete package" condition"(v1+v2+v3) with the results of the Experimental Group 2 ("v2 minus package" condition, v3) to verify if the independent variable 3 (reflexive interaction using MIROR-Impro) is *sufficient* to improve the dependent variables, that is the ability to improvise alone and in a duet: if CG < EG2 = independent variable 3 is *sufficient* to improve dependent variables.

Table 1 shows a synthesis of the experimental design.

Interview with the Children and Questionnaire to the Teacher

Each child was interviewed in order to collect data about their musical activities (e.g., playing an instrument). Moreover, a questionnaire was given to the teacher in order to collect information about the classroom activities done during music education lessons.

Data Collected

The following data were collected:

- 47 individual preliminary sessions
- 47 × 5 individual sessions of the package activities
- Solo task: 47 individual improvisations lasting about 2 min each.
- Duet task: 23 duet improvisations lasting about 10 min each. Three cases were missed because of technical problems with the audio recordings and the setting. The following total number of duets were analyzed: eight duets with CG, six duets with Experimental Group number 1, six duets with Experimental Group number 2.

Data Analysis

Assessment of Solo and Duet Tasks

Three independent judges assessed the Solo and Duet task improvisations by means of a grid based on the TAI (Test for Ability to Improvise, by McPherson, 1993, 1995, 2005) rating scale. The TAI is one of the three measures implemented by McPherson to assess high school instrumentalists' ability to perform music (the other areas are the TAPFM-Test for Ability to Play From Memory, and the TAPE-Test for Ability to Play by Ear). In order to assess the ability to improvise (TAI), the students are asked to continue and conclude a musical sentence ("stylistically conceived" task) and to improvise a piece on their own that has a beginning, a middle, and an end ("freely conceived" task). The TAI includes four evaluative criteria: Instrumental Fluency (including Technical skill, Musical expression, and Musical fluency), Creativity (including Musical flexibility and Musical originality), Musical Syntax (including Ability to define style and Conception of logical response), and Musical Quality (see also McPherson, 1993).

TABLE 1 | The convergence procedure (Campbell and Heller, 1979; Fiske, 1992), based on three sample groups (Control Group, Experimental Groups 1 and 2), allowing to verify if the reflexive interaction using the MIROR-Impro is *necessary* and/or *sufficient* to improve the children's abilities to improvise, in solo and in duet.

Timeline	Control Group activity (complete package)	Experimental Group 1 activity (package minus v3)	Experimental Group 2 activity (v3 minus package)
5 weekly 12-min individual sessions	v1: playing only keyboard (4 min.) v2: keyboard with not reflexive reply (4 min.) v3: keyboard with MIROR reflexive reply (4 min.)	v1: playing only keyboard (6 min.) v2: keyboard with not reflexive reply (6 min.)	v3: playing keyboard with MIROR reflexive reply (12 min.)
1 week after: Test	Solo task Duet task	Solo task Duet task	Solo task Duet task

Test results: if CG > EG1 = independent variable 3 (reflexive interaction using the MIROR-Impro) is necessary to improve dependent variables; if CG < EG2 = independent variable 3 is sufficient to improve dependent variables.

Because the TAI was designed for high school instrumentalists, whereas in our study the participants were musically untrained children aged 6–7, it was necessary to introduce several modifications in order to adapt the TAI to the age and training level of the participants. Firstly, we only used the "freely conceived" task because the children were musically untrained and were at the beginner stage of musical learning, so they would not have been able to improvise on the basis of a particular musical style, as requested by the "stylistically conceived" task; for the same reason, the "Ability to define style" was excluded from the evaluative criteria of Musical Syntax: only the "Conception and logical response" was used, and we called this criterion Musical Organization. In conclusion, the evaluation grid of the study introduced in this article used the following four evaluative criteria: Instrumental Fluency, Creativity, Musical Organization, and Musical Quality. Some musical details were added for each criterion.

One other difference concerns the Duet task, because the TAI only foresees a solo improvisation task. Three new evaluative criteria were therefore added for the assessment of the Duet task, dealing with the ability of children to improvise in pairs: Musical Dialog, dealing with the children's ability to dialog with a friend by means of sounds; Reflexive Interaction, dealing with the children's ability to use reflexive interaction (repetition/variation, turn-taking, and co-regulation); and Attention Span, which is the duration of the dialog between the two children. In fact, some children stopped playing together and continued to play alone. Therefore, the judges were asked to indicate the time when the dialog between the children ended.

Finally, because the judges were asked to evaluate video recordings, instead of audio recordings as in the original TAI, they were also asked to consider the children's bodily movement and expression. In accordance with several experts in children's musical improvisation (for example: Delalande, 1993; Kratus, 1996; Mialaret, 1997; Sundin, 1998; Imberty, 2005), we considered the children's musical improvisation as an experience of production/listening in which the gesture is fundamental, for both the sound quality of the product, and the child's musical experience. In our specific case, for example, if the improvisation presented a repeated note, it was important for the judges to observe if the child was playing always with the same finger, or with several fingers, or with a lighter or harder touch, and observe the child's facial expressions, her/his tension of the arms, the body position, and so on. The observation of the motor behaviors was also crucial in the evaluation of the Duet test, particularly, but not exclusively, for the Quality of Musical Dialog: the children's motor behavior, for example, helped the judges to evaluate whether the child was stopping because she/he wanted to give the turn to her/his partner, or if she/he was tired of playing. In our study, the musical improvisation was considered an act of "production," including motor and bodily gestures, which is not the same as in the tradition of music theory studies, where the object of analysis is primarily the sound or the scores.

The judges of our study were three professors of music education at an Italian university and/or conservatory, all experts in children's music education. They worked together over several sessions. They first evaluated the Solo task and then the Duet Task. The Solo and the Duet tasks assigned to the children were communicated to the judges. The judges were required to watch the videos and to evaluate the children's musical performances using a 5-point scale (the same as used by McPherson, 1993, 2005). For the Attention Span, the judges were asked to indicate when the dialog between the children ended (time in seconds). The judges were given an observation grid with the definitions of each category to be evaluated. They received the following written instructions: "Circle a number from 1 to 5 that indicates your rating for each of the assessed categories. Use the *Flow Chart of Evaluative Dimensions* (as in McPherson, 1993) in order to define the assessment criteria. You may use the observation of the child's body movements, expressions, and gestures in order to better assess each category. Judgments should be made relative to one another and not according to absolute criteria. You may go back to the items already assessed and change your assessment. The videos can be watched as often as necessary, until each judge is satisfied with her/his assessment. Where appropriate, the videos can be stopped and re-watched if any of the judges want to re-hear/watch any performance. Generally the first 5–7 examples of the total performances should be used as consensus items, and to become familiar with the scoring methods for that particular item. The normal procedure then involves alternating between scoring up to five items in a row independently, followed by using another three or four items as consensus items. Where there is a break in the scoring, the judges again use the consensus approach adopted for the first three items at the commencement of the next session." The consensus items were used to become familiar with the evaluative criteria and to check that, during the procedure (which lasted several sessions of 5/4 h each), the evaluative criteria were always clear and applied by all the judges in a coherent way. The consensus items were therefore used by the judges in order to discuss and clarify any conflicts of interpretation and application of the criteria. Having reached a consensus on the evaluative criteria, each judge gave her/his individual score to the item. For the Duet task, the following sentence was added at the beginning of the Instructions: "In this questionnaire you will be asked to assess the ability to improvise of two children who are each playing a keyboard."

The judges received the following evaluative criteria used for both Solo and Duet tasks (see McPherson, 1993, pp. 139–141):

Instrumental Fluency: Ability to execute musical ideas clearly and accurately. This includes the ability of the child (children) to respond freely to musical ideas and to perform with technical skill and musical expression. The ability is demonstrated in the extent to which the child (children) can perform in a spontaneous manner, moving easily from one musical idea to another.[1]

Musical Organization: Ability to organize musical material in a freely conceived idiom. The task of the child (children) is to provide a performance that is inherently logical and which makes musical sense. Musical organization is demonstrated in the degree to which the improvisation demonstrates one or more organizational principles such as: imitation, repetition, variation, contrast, alternation, question/answer, beginning/development/closing, phrasing, etc.

Creativity: Ability to think divergently, as demonstrated in an original and imaginative product. This is evaluated through an analysis of: (1) *Musical flexibility*: the extent to which the child (children) can generate differing musical ideas, and manipulate/elaborate these ideas during the course of the improvisation. (2) *Musical originality*: the extent to which the child (children) can provide a musically unique or unusual response. A unique or unusual response may result from the manipulation and/or elaboration of pitch (e.g., use of sequence, etc.), or rhythm (e.g., diminution, augmentation, dotted vs. no dotted, metric vs. syncopated, etc.), or other musical elements (e.g., timbre, articulation, dynamics, etc.).

Musical Quality: (Overall Musical Appeal): Ability to fluently perform creatively conceived material in a freely conceived idiom. This is a global rating indicating your assessment of the overall musical appeal of the improvisation. It should indicate the extent to which a committed performance played expressively and in a musically meaningful and creative manner, was achieved.

Free comments: After completing the assessment, please write your free comment about the performance: write everything you found interesting and meaningful.

Furthermore, for the Duet task the judges also received the following three categories (which are not included in McPherson's TAI test):

Quality of Musical Dialog: Ability to dialog and interact with the partner by using the sounds: paying attention to the musical proposal (listening), the ability to reply in a way correlated to the friend's musical proposal (e.g., by repetition, variation, contrast, etc.), the presence of symmetries, co-regulation, sharing and co-production of musical ideas, the ability to show a global intentionality to dialog with the friend.

Reflexive Interaction: Ability to interact using repetition and variation, turn taking, and co-regulation.

Attention Span: The subjects' tendency to persist in their contact with the activities, in this case the musical dialog with the other child, irrespective of any underlying aim. In fact, in some performances you can observe that after a while, the children start to play by themselves. This implies that their attention toward the musical dialog with the friend has ended. In this case, indicate the duration (in seconds) of the dialog, from the beginning of the performance to the moment when the children start to play by themselves.

In accordance with McPherson (2005), the evaluative criteria of Instrumental Fluency, Musical Organization, Creativity, and Musical Quality were considered equally important. In the case of the Duet Task, we also considered Quality of Musical Dialog

[1] In accordance with the perspective of children's spontaneous improvisation (Delalande, 1993; Kratus, 1996; Baroni, 1997; Webster, 2002; Tafuri, 2006), the term technical skills was not intended as indicating the ability to perform particular instructions, but rather the ability of the children to control the keyboard in a spontaneous way, for example to play in different registers, to use different gestures and combination of gestures (with one finger, with all fingers, one hand, two hands, symmetrically or with alternation of the gestures). According to this perspective in children's improvisation a musical idea is, for example, a rhythmical pattern, or a sequence of sounds, preconceived or initially generated randomly, which is repeated and elaborated with variations.

TABLE 2 | Evaluation grid used by the judges to assess the children's musical performance.

	Hesitant and Labored				Spontaneous and Confident
Instrumental Fluency	1	2	3	4	5
	Illogical				Logical
Musical Organization	1	2	3	4	5
	No Uniqueness				Marked Uniqueness
Creativity	1	2	3	4	5
	Unappealing				Appealing
Musical Quality	1	2	3	4	5
	Little Dialog				Much Dialog
Musical Dialog	1	2	3	4	5
	Poor Reflexivity				Much Reflexivity
Reflexive Interaction	1	2	3	4	5

To evaluate the SOLO task the judges only used Instrumental Fluency, Musical Organization, Creativity and Musical Quality. To evaluate the Duet task the judges used all criteria.

equally important, on the basis of various perspectives on musical improvisation, which focused on the ability of the performers to dialog together (cfr. Sawyer, 2001; Gratier, 2008). The Reflexive Interaction was measured in order to verify if the use of the reflexive system "teaches" the children to use reflexive interaction during their improvised musical dialogs, and if there is some correlation with the ability to improvise.

Table 2 shows the evaluation grid used by the judges.

Data Analysis

After the scoring, one score for each of the behaviors was calculated for each child for each task (Solo and Duet). First, each final score of each behavior was obtained by averaging the three scores registered by the three judges for each behavior. Then the level of ability to improvise was obtained by averaging the means of the behaviors, that is, for the Solo task, Instrumental Fluency, Musical Organization, Creativity, and Musical Quality, and for the Duet task, also the Quality of Musical Dialog. The Attention Span was calculated by averaging the duration of the dialog between the children of each duet and the correlation with each behavior was calculated. We calculated the correlation between Reflexive Interaction and each group, and between Reflexive Interaction and the overall ability to improvise. The final scores were considered for the statistical analyses. In order to evaluate the effect of the different conditions we performed planned pair-wise comparisons between the CG and Experimental Group 1 (EG1); and between the CG and Experimental Group 2 (EG2). Furthermore, we performed the same comparisons between EG1 and EG2. This was done separately for all behaviors including the overall ability to improvise, the Reflexive Interaction, and the Attention Span in the Duet task. We used independent-samples t-test assuming equal variances, which were computed using the SPSS software. Considering the relatively large number of independent comparisons (10 in the Solo task, 16 in the Duet task) it may have been appropriate to compensate for family wise error. However, in this case, the different behaviors were not considered independent. This was also confirmed in the measurements. Therefore, a compensation for family wise error, for example using Bonferroni correction, was considered to be a too conservative estimation. The reliability of the mean estimation across judges was assessed using Cronbach's alpha. The judges' agreement was estimated by the average Pearson's correlation between all pairs of judges.

RESULTS

Below we report the results of the Solo and Duet tasks.

Solo Task

Agreement of the Judges

Both Cronbach's alpha and Pearson's correlation between all pairs of judges indicate high agreement, as shown in **Table 3**. The Cronbach's alpha was around 0.95, which is considered excellent according to a common rule-of-thumb. Thus, it indicates that the calibration procedure among the judges was efficient.

Total Score of the Solo Task

The total score of the Solo task (see **Table 4**; **Figure 5**) shows that the CG (3.39), which trained with the complete package of variables, that is to play only with the keyboard, with the reflexive system, and with the not reflexive system, obtained a slightly lower score compared to the EG1 (3.46), which did not play with the reflexive system. Following the experimental

TABLE 3 | Solo task: Agreement of the judges.

	Cronbach's alpha	pairwise corr
Instrumental Fluency	0.93	0.83
Musical Organization	0.96	0.88
Creativity	0.95	0.86
Musical Quality	0.95	0.86
Mean	**0.95**	**0.86**

TABLE 4 | Solo task: Score for each evaluative criteria (Instrumental Fluency, Musical Organization, Creativity, and Musical Quality), and the Total score of Ability to Improvise (means).

	Instrumental Fluency	Musical Organization	Creativity	Musical Quality	Total score of Ability to Improvise
Control Group	3.48 (±0.50)	3.13 (±0.53)	3.44 (±0.53)	3.52 (±0.53)	3.39 (±0.47)
Experimental Group 1	3.47 (±0.51)	3.38 (±0.54)	3.47 (±0.55)	3.51 (±0.55)	3.46 (±0.49)
Experimental Group 2	3.71 (±0.53)	4.00 (±0.56)	3.74 (±0.57)	4.00 (±0.57)	3.86 (±0.51)
*CG*EG1*	$p = 0.970$	$p = 0.527$	$p = 0.942$	$p = 0.981$	$p = 0.854$
*CG*EG2*	$p = 0.547$	$p = 0.039$	$p = 0.452$	$p = 0.221$	$p = 0.198$
*EG1*EG2*	$p = 0.499$	$p = 0.080$	$p = 0.453$	$p = 0.184$	$p = 0.207$
	CG > EG1 necessary	*CG < EG1 not necessary*	*CG < EG1 not necessary*	*CG > EG1 necessary*	*CG < EG1 not necessary*
	CG < EG2 sufficient	*CG < EG2 sufficient*	*CG < EG2 sufficient*	*CG < EG2 sufficient*	*CG < EG2 sufficient*

Numbers in parenthesis are 95% confidence intervals (means). According to the experimental design if the score of the Control Group is higher than the Experimental Group 1, then the independent variable of reflexive interaction with MIROR-Impro (v3) is necessary to improve the ability to improvise in solo performance; if the score of the Control Group is lower than the Experimental Group 2, then the independent variable reflexive interaction with MIROR-Impro (v3) is sufficient to improve ability to improvise in solo performance.

design, this result indicates that the independent variable of reflexive interaction (v3) may *not be necessary* to improve the dependent variable of ability to improvise (CG > EG1). The results also show that the CG obtained a lower score compared to the EG2 (3.86), which only played with the reflexive system. In this case, it could be said that the reflexive interaction could be *sufficient* to improve the ability to improvise (CG < EG2). However, it is not possible to generalize these results because the differences were not statistically significant (t-test, comparing CG and EG1, $p = 0.854$; CG and EG2, $p = 0.198$).

Results for Each Evaluative Criterion of the Solo Task

The analyses on each evaluative criterion confirm the overall trend (**Table 4**; **Figure 5**). Regarding the condition of "sufficiency," the comparison between EG2, which only played with the reflexive system, and the CG, which also played with the not reflexive system and only with the keyboard, shows that EG2 reaches higher scores in all evaluative criteria. This result shows, therefore, that the use of the reflexive system alone could be *sufficient* to improve both Instrumental Fluency, Musical Organization, Creativity, and Musical Quality. Regarding the condition of "necessity," the comparison between EG1, which never played with the reflexive system, and the CG, which also played with the reflexive system, shows that the score of EG1 is slightly lower in Instrumental Fluency and Musical Quality and slightly higher in Musical Organization and Creativity. These results show that, for the sample of participants, the use of the reflexive system could be *necessary* to improve Instrumental Fluency and Musical Quality in solo improvisation, but *not necessary* to improve Musical Organization and Creativity. However, as indicated by the p-values in **Table 4**, the differences between the CG and the Experimental Groups 1 and 2 are rarely significant and thus it is problematic to generalize these results. The only exception was Musical Organization that was significant and received a p-value of 0.039 comparing CG with EG2.

Moreover, it is worth noting that EG2, the group that trained only with the reflexive system, showed a higher score in all criteria.

In order to examine the differences between the groups in more detail we plotted each child rank-ordered within each group, see **Figure 6**. It is clear from the figure that the variation within each group is comparatively large but also that there is a (smaller) difference between the groups, in particular between CG and EG2.

Duet Task

Agreement of the Judges

Both Cronbach's alpha and Pearson's correlation between all pairs of judges indicate high agreement, as shown in **Table 5**. The Cronbach's alphas were in this case also excellent and even higher than for the solo task, and for two behaviors reached 0.99

Total Score of the Duet Task

The total score of the Duet task shows that the CG (3.31), which played the complete package of variables including the reflexive system, obtained a higher score compared to the EG1 (3.05), which did not play with the reflexive system (**Table 6**; **Figure 7**). Therefore, the total trend indicates that for the sample of participant the reflexive interaction using the MIROR-Impro (variable 3) could be *necessary* to improve children's ability to improvise. Comparing the CG with the EG2 (4.32), which only played with the reflexive system, the CG obtained a lower score. Therefore, the total trend indicates that for the sample of participants the reflexive interaction using the MIROR-Impro (variable 3) could be *sufficient* to improve children's ability to improvise. However, it is not possible to generalize these results because the differences are not statistically significant (t-test, comparing CG and EG1, $p = 0.707$; CG and EG2, $p = 0.124$).

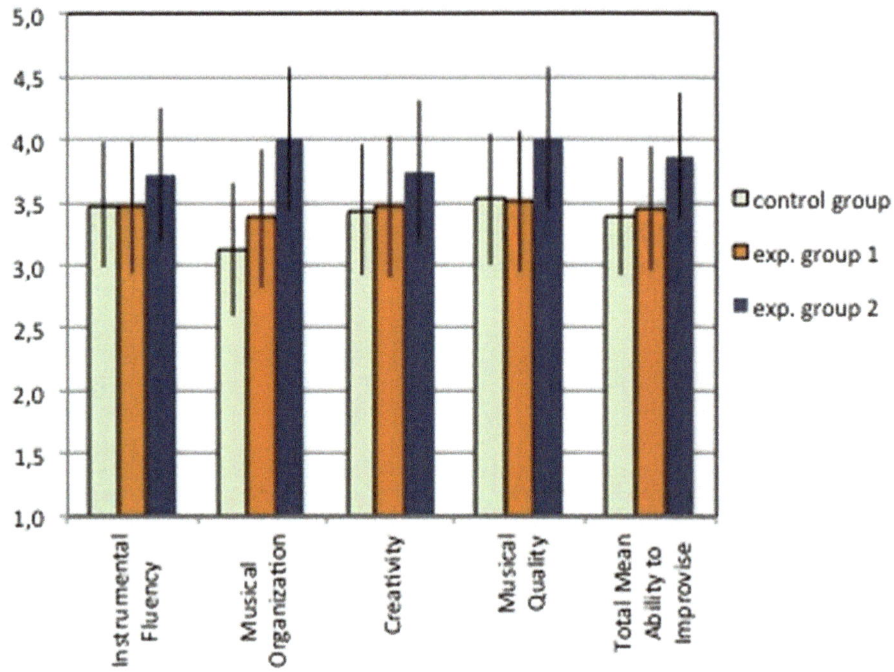

FIGURE 5 | Solo task: Scores for each evaluative criteria and the Total score of Ability to Improvise (means). The error bars indicate 95% confidence intervals.

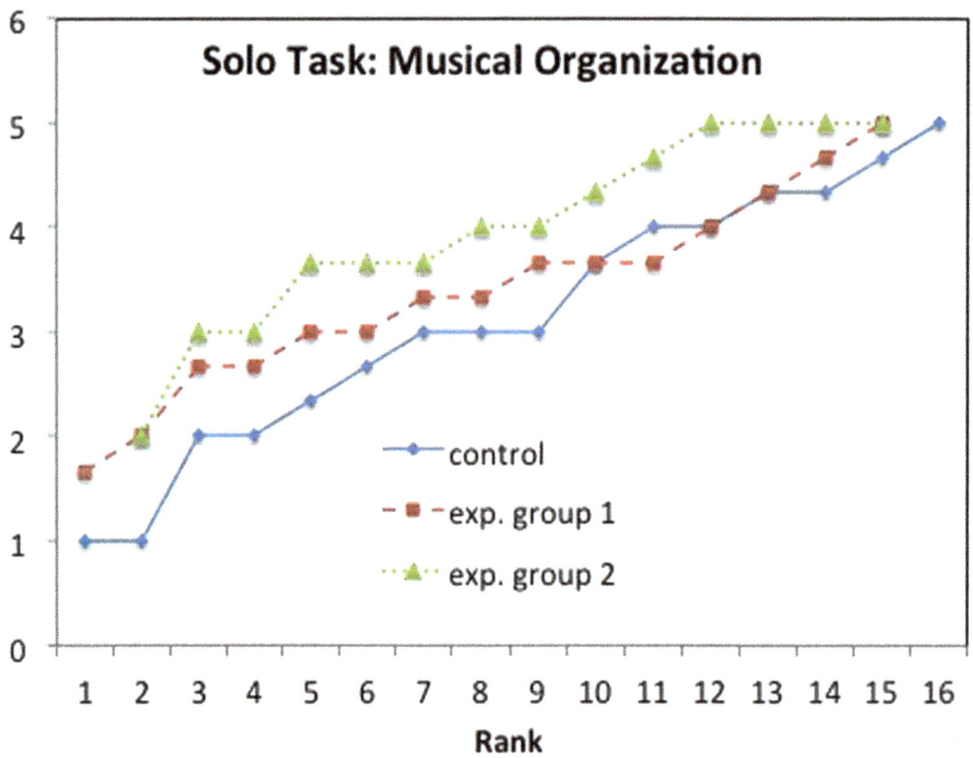

FIGURE 6 | Solo task, *Musical Organization*: Mean values rank-ordered in each group.

Results for Each Evaluative Criterion of the Duet Task

The analyses on each criterion of the Duet task confirm the total trend, with few exceptions; see **Table 6** and **Figure 7**. Regarding the condition of "sufficiency," the comparison between EG2, which only played with the reflexive system, and the CG, which also played with the not reflexive system and only the keyboard, shows that the EG2 reaches higher scores in all evaluative criteria. This trend shows, therefore, that the use of the reflexive system alone could be *sufficient* to improve all behaviors. Regarding the condition of "necessity," the comparison between EG1, which never played with the reflexive system, and the CG, which also played with the reflexive system, shows that the score of EG1 is lower in all criteria, excluding Musical Organization and Musical Quality. This trend shows that the use of the reflexive system could be *necessary* to improve Instrumental Fluency, Creativity, and Musical Dialog. Also in this case it is not possible to generalize these results because the p-values are not significant. However, note that the trend is close to significance with Musical Quality, in the *necessity* condition, ($CG = 3.08$; $EG2 = 4.33$; $p = 0.063$). It is important to note that, also in the Duet Task, EG2, which played just with the reflexive system, shows a higher score in all criteria in comparison with both CG and EG1. The difference between EG1 and EG2 is statistically significant ($p < 0.05$) for Creativity, Musical Quality, Musical Dialog, and for the overall ability to improvise, and close to the significance for Instrumental Fluency ($p = 0.059$).

Figure 8 gives the mean values rank-ordered for each group with Musical Quality, showing that the EG2 score is always above that of the other two groups. Note that the variation within groups is rather large and represents a possible source for the non-significant results between EG2 and CG.

Reflexive Interaction

The data of Reflexive Interaction show that the EG2 obtained the highest score (4.17), followed by the CG (3.33) and the EG1 (2.61); see **Table 6** and **Figure 7**. The difference between EG1, which only use the system with reflexive interaction, and EG2, which did not use the system with reflexive interaction, is significant ($p = 0.043$). Therefore, it could be said that the use of MIROR-Impro can enhance the use of the reflexive behaviors: mirroring, turn-taking, and co-regulation. We observed a statistically significant correlation between the Reflexive Interaction and the total score ($r = 0.937$; $p < 0.01$), and all other evaluative criteria, with correlations ranging from $r = 0.87$ ($p < 0.01$) for Musical Quality to $r = 0.92$ ($p < 0.01$) for Musical Organization. Thus, the higher the children's use of reflexive interaction, the better their results in each criterion and in the ability to improvise. This result can support the hypothesis that reflexive interaction is a fundamental component of musical improvised dialog. Instead, although the differences between the CG and the Experimental Groups 1 and 2 indicate that the use of the MIROR-Impro appears to be "necessary" (CG > EG1) and "sufficient" (CG < EG2) to improve the ability to improvise, we cannot generalize these results because the results are not statistically significant (t-test, comparing CG and EG1: $p = 0.388$; CG and EG2: $p = 0.285$).

Attention Span

The Attention Span indicates the subjects' tendency to persist in their contact with the activities, in this case the musical dialog with the other child, irrespective of any underlying aim. In fact, in some performances, after a while, the children started to play by

TABLE 5 | Duet task: agreement of the judges.

	Cronbach's alpha	pairwise corr
Instrumental Fluency	0.94	0,84
Musical Organization	0.97	0.91
Creativity	0.98	0.94
Musical Quality	0.96	0.91
Musical Dialog	0.99	0.97
Reflexive Interaction	0.99	0.97
Mean	**0.97**	**0.92**

TABLE 6 | Duet task: Score for each evaluative criteria (Instrumental Fluency, Musical Organization, Creativity, Musical Quality, and Musical Dialog), the Total score of Ability to Improvise, and the score of Reflexive Interaction (means).

Group	Instrumental Fluency	Musical Organization	Creativity	Musical Quality	Musical Dialog	Total score of Ability to Improvise	Reflexive Interaction
CG	3.75 (±0.64)	3.21 (±0.85)	2.96 (±0.96)	3.08 (±0.80)	3.54 (±1.03)	3.31 (±0.82)	3.33 (±1.02)
EG1	3.56 (±0.74)	3.28 (±0.98)	2.83 (±1.10)	3.17 (±0.93)	2.83 (±1.19)	3.13 (±0.95)	2.61 (±1.17)
EG2	4.50 (±0.74)	4.11 (±0.98)	4.22 (±1.11)	4.33 (±0.93)	4.56 (±1.19)	4.34 (±0.95)	4.17 (±1.18)
*CG*EG1*	$p = 0.702$	$p = 0.922$	$p = 0.877$	$p = 0.898$	$p = 0.427$	$p = 0.799$	$p = 0.388$
*CG*EG2*	$p = 0.135$	$p = 0.164$	$p = 0.087$	$p = 0.063$	$p = 0.126$	$p = 0.101$	$p = 0.285$
*EG1*EG2*	$p = 0.059$	$p = 0.152$	$p = 0.046$	$p = 0.039$	$p = 0.043$	$p = 0.047$	$p = 0.043$
	CG > EG1 necessary	*EG1 > CG not necessary*	*CG > EG1 necessary*	*CG > EG1 necessary*	*CG > EG1 necessary*	*CG > EG1 necessary*	*CG > EG1 necessary*
	CG < EG2 sufficient	*CG < EG2 sufficient*	*CG < EG2 sufficient*	*CG < EG2 sufficient*	*CG < EG2 sufficient*	*CG < EG2 sufficient*	*CG < EG2 sufficient*

Numbers in parenthesis are 95% confidence intervals. According to the experimental design if the score of the Control Group is higher than the Experimental Group 1, then the independent variable of reflexive interaction with MIROR-Impro (v3) is necessary to improve the ability to improvise in duet; if the score of the Control Group is lower than the Experimental Group 2, then the independent variable reflexive interaction with MIROR-Impro (v3) is sufficient to improve ability to improvise in duet.

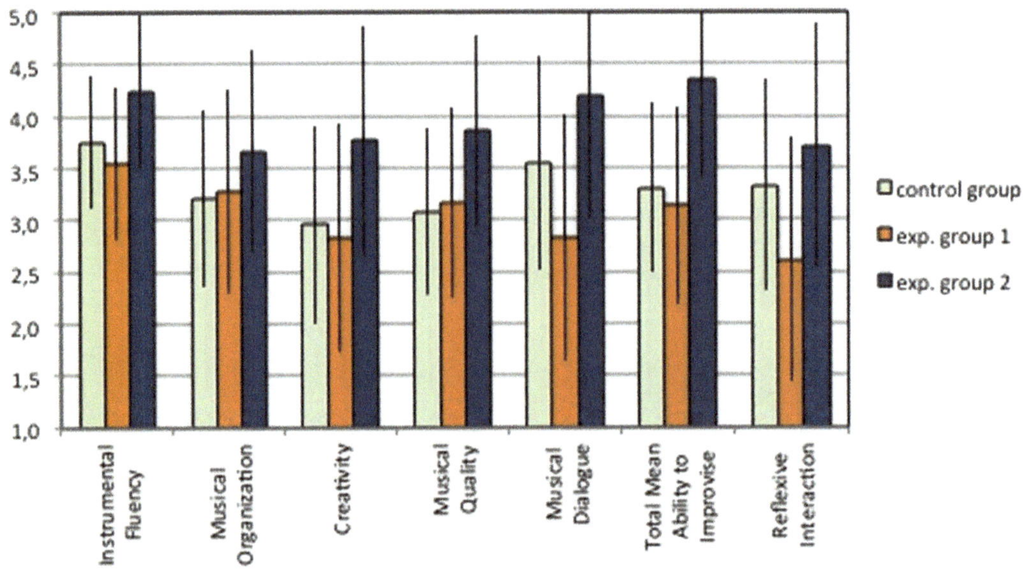

FIGURE 7 | Duet task: Scores for each evaluative criteria, Total score of Ability to Improvise, and score of Reflexive Interaction (means). The error bars indicate the 95% confidence intervals.

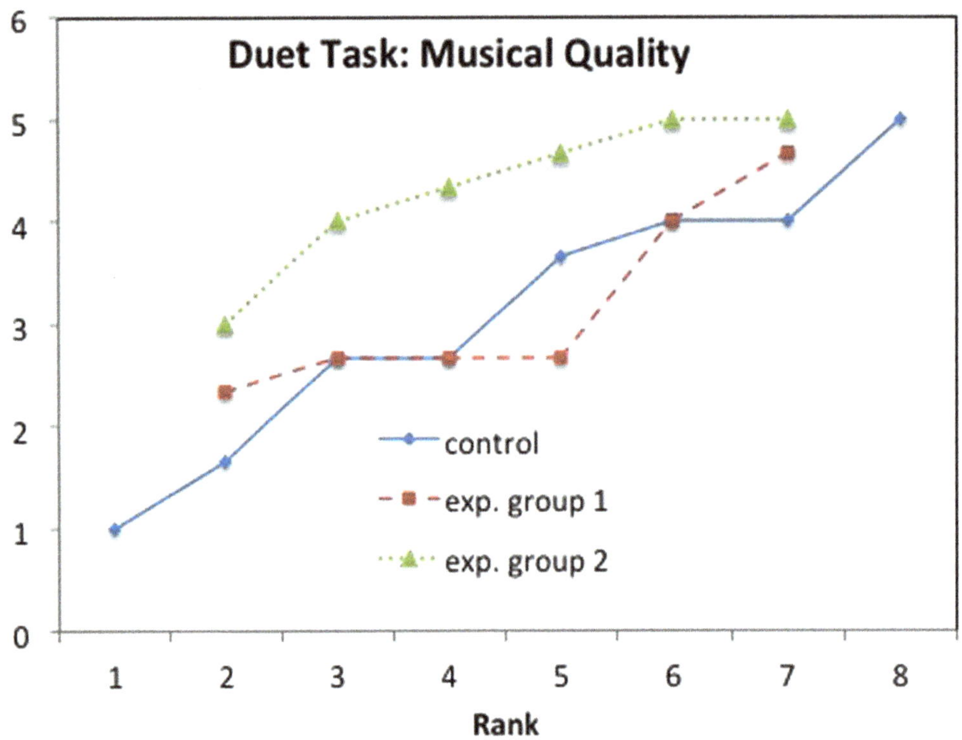

FIGURE 8 | Duet task: Mean values rank-ordered in each group for Musical Quality.

themselves. This means that their attention for the musical dialog with the friend had ended. The judges were asked to indicate the duration (in seconds) of the dialog, from the beginning of the performance to the moment when the children start to play by themselves. The results show that the EG2 (585 s), which trained only with the reflexive system, reaches the highest Attention Span, compared with the CG (428 s) and the EG1 (510 s) (see **Figure 9**). In particular, we observed a statistically significant

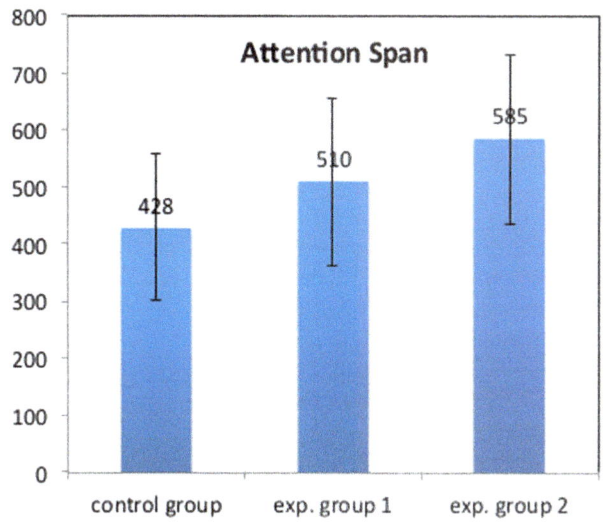

FIGURE 9 | Duet task: Plot of the attention span in each group. The columns indicate the duration of children's attention in seconds. The error bars indicate the 95% confidence intervals.

correlation between the Attention Span and all other evaluative criteria, with correlations ranging from $r = 0.52$ ($p < 0.05$) for Instrumental Fluency to $r = 0.63$ ($p < 0.01$) for Musical Quality. Thus, the longer their attention span, the better their results in all criteria.

DISCUSSION

In this article, we introduced a study about the effects of reflexive interaction with the software MIROR-Impro on the musical improvisation ability of children playing a keyboard. In the framework of the MIROR project and, more in general, in the field of studies on reflexive technology and children, this is the first study which assesses in a controlled way the effects of reflexive technologies on the children's ability to improvise. The study was conducted with 47 children aged 7 and 8 years, and used the experimental design of convergence procedure and the TAI-Test of Ability to Improvise (McPherson, 2005), partially adapted to the purposes of this study. Two conditions were observed: the condition of "sufficiency" (RI with MIROR-Impro is sufficient to develop the ability to improvise) and the condition of "necessity" (RI with the MIROR-impro is necessary to develop improvisational skills). The trend of the results with the sample of participants indicates that RI with MIROR-Impro alone can be *sufficient*, compared to the remaining two observed variables (playing only with the keyboard and playing with the same software but programmed with a non-reflexive response), to increase the improvisational skills of the subjects who participated in the study, both when improvising alone and in a duet. The trend also shows that RI using MIROR-Impro can be *necessary*, compared to the remaining two variables considered, to develop the ability to improvise in duets. However, the results of necessity and sufficiency are in general not statistically significant and they cannot be generalized. A greater number of subjects (to control the internal variance of subjects) and a longer training period (6 months rather than 5 weeks, and 1 h per session rather than 12 min), could have strengthened the experimental design, and then given a greater statistical significance. It is interesting to note that the trend is more evident in the Duet task, where some results and the correlation between Reflexive interaction and the ability to improvise are statistically significant or closer to the significance. The EG2, which trained only with the reflexive system, reached always the highest average results, both when the children improvise alone and in a duet. The difference between EG2 and EG1, which did not use the reflexive system, is statistically significant in the Duet task. Even though it was not part of the experimental design to test this, it indicates that the training with reflexive system was effective for the ability to improvise in pair. In conclusion, the results of the study are interesting and worth exploring the reflexive interaction paradigm further in the field of children's musical improvisation, creativity and education.

Reflexive Interaction, Musical Improvisation, and Creativity

In the Duet task, the behaviors characteristic of the Reflexive Interaction (mirroring, turn-taking, and co-regulation) were statistically correlated with the ability to improvise; furthermore, the children that used the interactive system alone during the training program showed the highest results for these behaviors. It seems that reflexive interaction using the MIROR-Impro enhances some processes of music dialog that the child learns during the interaction with the system and then uses even when the interaction occurs with a partner. Repetition in music takes on particular importance, both in improvisation and composition, as well as in listening, and concerns all aspects, from music analysis to the cognitive and neurobiological processes (cfr. Margulis, 2014). In the specific field of children's musical experience, it was observed how the repetition-variation action during the explorations of sound objects in early childhood allow the child to know a sound, to share it with others, to invent music and express emotions (Delalande, 1993; Kratus, 1996; Baroni, 1997), in children's musical improvisation with instruments, repetition and mirroring becomes the fundamental principle of invention (cfr. Young, 2004; Tafuri, 2006). In the practice of improvisation, the repetition and variation mechanism can structure the musical discourse over time, establishing the basic pillars for exploration and transformation, thereby paving the way for the creation of new musical ideas. Recent studies in neuroscience underline the neural and cognitive mechanisms that allow us to transform and manipulate existing musical representations. Zatorre (2012) suggests that the dorsal pathway of auditory processing performs equivalent operations on musical inputs. The results allow new hypotheses about how novel musical ideas may emerge from pre-existing musical images, by means of the mechanism of repetition and variation. This finding highlights the close link between improvisation, repetition and variation, and creative processes. Kleinmintz et al. (2014) points out that musical improvisation increases creativity. The link between improvisation and creativity was also emphasized in neurobiology, where it was found that the greater connectivity between brain regions sharing functional properties observed in professional improvisers may be due to a more efficient working of the associative networks of musical creativity (Pinho et al., 2014; see also Beaty, 2015). In our study, the Experimental Group 2, which only use the MIROR reflexive system, shows the highest score not only in Reflexive Interaction behaviors but also in the Creativity criterion. This result also reinforces our previous study, which showed the effectiveness of RI with MIROR-Impro in the development of creative processes, as described in the flow theory (Addessi et al., 2015).

Turn-taking is fundamental in reflexive interaction. Neurobiological studies have highlighted the close link between turn-taking and the processes of imitation and suggest that "simulation is a foundational mechanism underlying the temporal dynamics of joint action" (Hadley et al., 2015, p. 19516. Cfr. also Gratier et al., 2015). Another important mechanism of reflexive interaction is immediate feedback, which allows the child to have a perception of the relevance of its intervention in relation to that of the virtual partner. The importance of improvisation feedback is highlighted by Pressing when he writes "Feedback is a vital component in improvisation for it enables error correction and adaptation – a narrowing of the gap between intended and actual motor and musical effects" Pressing (1988).

Therefore, the rules of reflexive interaction (turn-taking, listening to the partner, repetition and variation, co-regulation), become musical rules. These rules help the children to listen to and invent musical improvisation based on turn-taking (musical phrasing), repetition, variation, contrast, dialog, etc. Some of these mechanisms are indicated by several scholars to be the basis of creativity and improvisation: e.g., Sawyer (2001) introduces improvisation in everyday discourse; Berkowitz (2010) describes various kinds of variations, recombination and combinatory procedures as pedagogical strategies for teaching music improvisation. Since reflexive interaction develops rules of interaction, the results of our study also support the idea that the collective performance cannot only be studied from a purely musical point of view but also on the basis of the interactive and communicative context between the partners (Schiavio and Høffding, 2015), and on the basis of social interaction characteristics (e.g., Sawyer, 2001; Littleton and Mercer, 2012; Pesquita et al., 2014; Kawase, 2015). In this regard, Moran et al. (2015) highlighted that the back-channeling cues during a free improvisation do not dependent on specific music skills but rather on a general human ability to communicate. In particular, the results of the Duet task in our study could be an efficient index of the effects of reflexive interaction, thanks to the presence of several characteristics of the co-performer interaction (e.g., Williamon and Davidson, 2002; Seddon, 2005; Gratier, 2008; Moran et al., 2015).

Child–Machine Interaction in a Reflexive Environment

In the field of child–machine interaction, the results of this study can acquire a particular interest for two reasons: the first is by presenting a new scientific paradigm, reflexive interaction, which proves to be empirically effective in developing creative and improvisational skills in children; the second concerns the type of methodology used, which started not from theoretical assumptions on child–machine interaction, but from the observation of the concrete and naturalistic context of such interaction. Our observation has given rise to hypotheses, empirical studies and theoretical explanations in the scientific literature. It has been possible to observe the child–machine interaction and note how RI develops between the child and the system without adult mediation. This issue is particularly important in the field of technology and children's education, because the presence of the adult as mediator between child and machine is generally considered fundamental. This is not to say that reflexive systems should replace the teacher (although they could do so when the teacher does not want or is not able to teach improvisation), but rather that they can have an important role in learning to improvise and, in general, in enhancing children's musical creativity. In the reflexive setting, the role of the teacher would be to create the context where the children, alone or in groups, can interact with the system, and to re-launch the more creative musical ideas of the children: in other words, to use the reflexive system as a "device," in the meaning that Delalande (1993) gave to it, that is a tool to motivate and reinforce the musical creativity of children (see Addessi, 2015).

Implication in Music Education

The results of this study contributes to the research on children's musical improvisation, highlighting new details about children's processes of musical improvisation. An important aspect of the results of this study is that they show how the reflexive interaction with the system also affects the intrinsic motivation of the child while playing. The results show in fact that the attention spans of children of Experimental Group 2, who have training only with MIROR-Impro, are higher than the Experimental Group 1 (which never played with MIROR-Impro) and the CG (which trained with MIROR-Impro with and without reflexive reply, and only the keyboard). This result, which confirms those of a previous study (Addessi and Pachet, 2006), shows that RI with MIROR-Impro develops intrinsic motivation, which is considered one of the most important conditions for learning (cfr. Austin et al., 2006). We consider it important to emphasize that the effectiveness of IR on the ability of improvisation derives from the fact that this develops an intrinsic motivation to participate in a musical dialog: children can express themselves by means of sounds, which is a fundamental need of children. As Baroni writes: "We believe it is possible to maintain a rigid position of principal, that is, the absolute necessity for the pre-eminence of expression over learning: and this is not only because the construction of expressive objects can be considered the principal goal, but also because it constitutes the only valid and persuasive motivation for learning activities" (1997, p. 141).

From a pedagogical point of view, we suggest that the child and the teacher can use the MIROR-Impro in order to support an improvisation teaching program by means of individual and collective "deliberate practice" (Ericsson,

1997; Kenny and Gellrich, 2002; McPherson, 2005) with the system. It is important in fact to emphasize that the training activities of our experiment were carried out as "deliberate practice": the children trained by themselves, out of their own choice, during normal educational activities. Such systems may have a use in basic schooling as a means of expression, to dialog through sounds, to invent music and build relationships among peers (Cardoso de Araújo, 2015; Ferrari and Addessi, 2015), as well as helping music improvisation classes to learn/teach techniques of improvisation (exploration, imitation, invention, dialog with sounds, listening) (cfr. Benghi and Addessi, 2015; Nijs and Leman, 2015). As the interaction is based mainly on sound, this interaction could be very important for the development of the child's *thinking in sound*, which has been identified as one of the most important aims for music education and music improvisation (cfr. Webster, 1994; Williamon, 2004; McPherson, 2005). They can also be used for teacher education to develop teachers' basic musical competences (making music, improvisation and composition, listening), teachers' professional competences related to child–machine interaction, children's musical development, children's musical creativity, and reflection about the role of teacher in reflexive environments. Finally, reflexive interaction can itself become a teaching technique, and the teachers can learn how to teach music improvisation: dialoguing with children by means of sounds, mirroring the musical ideas of children, using a repetition and variation approach, respecting turn-taking, co-regulating the dialog, etc.

Future Directions

The results of this study, and the video analysis of the training activities, will contribute to create a list of technical and pedagogical requirements to improve the reflexive technology to support children's ability to improvise: for example, the possibility to use special rhythmic-melodic patterns, or alternative setups (cfr. Regazzi and Benghi, 2015). The results can also contribute to better understand the reflexive interaction mechanism in human interactions, in particular in infant-adult interaction based on turn-taking and the mechanism of repetition-variation: with this aim, further studies are planned to observe the presence of reflexivity in infant-adult interaction. In the field of neurobiology, the reflexive technologies could represent an efficient tool to investigate the "resonance" (Rizzolatti et al., 2002) mechanism related to sound perception, and the neural and cognitive processes that allow us to transform and manipulate existing musical representations (Berkowitz, 2010; Zatorre, 2012). The midi data collected during sessions with the system could allow computational analysis of improvisation based on reflexive interaction. Some tentative steps have already been made (Anagnostopoulou et al., 2012; Alexakis et al., 2013) and this could also offer future perspectives on the basis of some positive experiences of computational analysis of musical dialog between therapist and patient (Luck et al., 2008; Erkkilä et al., 2012; Wigram, 2012). As we wrote, "the musical analysis of reflexive dialog should allow us to capture the aspects that characterize the presence of structural variation in repeated patterns, and to hypothesize how these variations are produced" (Addessi, 2014, p. 222). At this moment, the methodology of observation seems to be the most effective tool to study reflexive interaction in children's musical improvisation, as it captures aspects of improvisational behavior linked to the gestures, body communication, and intentionality of the subjects, which cover the full experience of musical improvisation, as also underlined by a recent study in music performance (King and Gritten, 2016). In this regard, the TAI-Test of Ability to Improvise (McPherson, 1993, 2005), including the changes made for this study, has proved to be an effective and flexible research tool (cfr. Thompson and Williamon, 2003) for the assessment of children's ability to improvise, not only for audio data, as in the original Test, but also for the video performance assessment. We are working in order to implement an observational grid for a more detailed analysis of the musical dialogs of the duets, also in collaboration with experts in computational video analysis and motion capture systems.

The reflexive interaction paradigm and reflexive technologies are relatively new in the field of music education and teaching improvisation. The MIROR project aimed to exploit this paradigm in the field of children's music and movement creativity and education, in terms of technology (three applications were implemented: MIROR-Impro, MIROR-Compo and MIROR-Body Gesture), empirical and theoretical research, and pedagogical practices. The process of spiral implementation of this kind of technology has not yet finished: the MIROR applications can be perfected on the basis of the empirical experiences that will continue to be carried out by children, teachers, researchers, and therapists. In this context, the study introduced in this paper indicated that reflexive interaction and the reflexive technologies can have a positive effect on children's ability to improvise and we suggest introducing this device in the program of teaching to improvise and as an exciting tool for children's "deliberate practice." A new longitudinal case-study has been planned to analyze the effects of reflexive interaction using the MIROR-Impro in deliberate practice, over a longer period of activities. The future challenge is to implement a new MIROR application based on reflexive interaction, called MIROR-MultiModal, which will also involve the visual perception of children, and to design and implement the MIROR platform, a learning/teaching environment with related architecture and technological tools, for children, teachers, and researchers.

ETHICS STATEMENT

The study has been approved by the Legal Office of Research Department of the University of Bologna, which took care of the legal and ethical aspects related to the Consent form, and by the Primary School of Casalecchio di Reno (Italy). All the children's parents gave their written informed consent in accordance with the relevant national, European and international data protection laws and regulations and personal data treatment obligations. Each judge signed a confidentiality undertaking. Specifically the consent form complied with the following laws and regulations:

- EC Data Protection Directive 95/46/EC of the European Parliament and of the Council of 24 October 1995 on the protection of individuals with regard to the processing of personal data and on the free movement of such data.
- Council of Europe Recommendation 83/10 Protection of personal data used for scientific research and statistics.
- Council of Europe Recommendation 97/18 Concerning the protection of personal data collected and processed for statistical purposes.
- Italian Legislative Decree No 196/2003.
- Attachment A4 to the Italian Legislative Decree No 196/2003 "Code of conduct and professional practice applying to processing of personal data for statistical and scientific purposes" (Published in the Official Journal no. 190 of August 14, 2004).

AUTHOR CONTRIBUTIONS

AA wrote the paper and is the principal investigator. AF collaborated in carrying out the experiment and in the statistical analysis. DB collaborated in the data collection. AF elaborated the statistical analyses and contributed in the corresponding text, figures, and tables. The final manuscript was supervised by all authors.

ACKNOWLEDGMENTS

This work was partially supported by the EU-ICT Project MIROR-Musical Interaction Relying On Reflexion (FP7, Grant agreement n° 258338, www.mirorproject.eu). We thank Prof. Gary McPherson for giving us access to his doctoral thesis (1993).

REFERENCES

Addessi, A. R. (2014). Developing a theoretical foundation for the reflexive interaction paradigm with implications for training music skill and creativity. *Psychomusicology* 2, 214–230. doi: 10.1037/pmu0000055

Addessi, A. R. (2015). "La piattaforma MIROR come "dispositivo" per la creatività musicale e motoria dei bambini," in *La Creatività Musicale e Motoria dei Bambini in Ambienti Riflessivi. Proposte Didattiche con la Piattaforma MIROR*, ed. A. R. Addessi (Bologna: Bononia University Press), 33–64.

Addessi, A. R., Anagnostopoulou, C., Newman, S., Olsson, B., Pachet, F., and Volpe, G. (2013). *MIROR-Musical Interaction Relying On Reflexion. Project Final Report*. Available at: www.mirorproject.eu/download/Final-Report_3rd-year.pdf

Addessi, A. R., Ferrari, L., and Carugati, F. (2015). The Flow Grid: a technique for observing and measuring emotional state in children interacting with a flow machine. *J. New Music Res.* 4, 129–144. doi: 10.1080/09298215.2014.991738

Addessi, A. R., and Pachet, F. (2005). Experiments with a musical machine. Musical style replication in 3/5 year old children. *Br. J. Music Educ.* 2, 21–46.

Addessi, A. R., and Pachet, F. (2006). Young children confronting the Continuator, an interactive reflective musical system. *Musicae Sci.* 10(Suppl.), 13–39. doi: 10.1177/1029864906010001021

Alexakis, A., Khatchatourov, A., Triantafyllaki, A., and Anagnostopoulou, C. (2013). "Measuring musical creativity advancement," in *Proceedings of the Sound and Music Computing Conference*, ed. R. Bresin (Berlin: Logos Verlag).

Anagnostopoulou, C., Alexakis, A., and Triantafyllaki, A. (2012). "A computational method for the analysis of musical improvisations by young children and psychiatric patients with no musical background," in *Proceedings of the 12th International Conference on Music Perception and Cognition and the 8th Triennial Conference of the European Society for the Cognitive Sciences of Music*, eds E. Cambouropoulos, C. Tsougras, P. Mavromatis, and K. Pastiadis (Thessaloniki: University of Thessaloniki), 64–68.

Anzieu, D. (1996). *Les Enveloppes Psychiques*. Paris: Dunod.

Austin, J., Renwick, J., and McPherson, G. E. (2006). "Developing motivation," in *The Child as Musician. A Handbook of Musical Development*, ed. G. E. McPherson (Oxford: Oxford University Press), 213–238.

Baroni, M. (1997). *Suoni e Significati. Attività Espressive nella Scuola*. Torino: Edizioni di Torino.

Bauer, W. I. (2014). *Music Learning Today: Digital Pedagogy for Creating, Performing, and Responding to Music*. Oxford: Oxford University Press.

Beaty, R. E. (2015). The neuroscience of musical improvisation. *Neurosci. Biobehav. Rev.* 51, 108–117. doi: 10.1016/j.neubiorev.2015.01.004

Benghi, D., and Addessi, A. R. (2015). "Insegnare ad improvvisare con il MIROR-Impro," in *La Creatività Musicale e Motoria dei Bambini in Ambienti Riflessivi: Pratiche Didattiche con la Piattaforma MIROR*, ed. A. R. Addessi (Bologna: Bononia University Press), 153–166.

Berkowitz, A. L. (2010). *The Improvising Mind. Cognition and Creativity in the Musical Moment*. New York, NY: Oxford University Press.

Brophy, T. S. (2005). A longitudinal study of selected characteristics of children's melodic improvisation. *J. Res. Music Educ.* 5, 120–133. doi: 10.2307/3345513

Brown, A. R. (2007). *Computer in Music Education. Amplifying Musicality*. New York, NY: Routledge.

Bruner, J. (1983). *Child's talk: Learning to Use Language*. New York, NY: Norton.

Campbell, W. C., and Heller, J. (1979). Convergence procedures for investigating music listening tasks. *Bull. Counc. Res. Music Educ.* 59, 18–23.

Cardoso de Araújo, R. (2015). "Improvvisazioni con la piattaforma MIROR," in *La Creatività Musicale e Motoria dei Bambini in Ambienti Riflessivi: Pratiche Didattiche con la Piattaforma MIROR*, ed. A. R. Addessi (Bologna: Bononia University Press), 79–86.

Cardoso de Araújo, R., and Addessi, A. R. (2013). "A study about children's musical improvisation in an interactive/reflexive musical context," in *Proceedings of the Anais do IX Simpósio de Cognição e Artes Musicais (Internacional)*, eds V. C. Marques and M. Moreira (Belém: Federal University of Pará), 21–31.

Csikzsentmihalyi, M. (1990). *Flow: The Psychology of Optimal Experience*. New York: Harper & Row.

Custodero, L. A. (2005). Observable indicators of flow experience: a development perspective on musical engagement in young children from infancy to school age. *Music Educ. Res.* 7, 185–209. doi: 10.1080/14613800500169431

De Kerckhove, D. (1991). *Brainframes: Technology, Mind and Business*. Baarn: Bosch & Keuning.

Delalande, F. (1993). *Le condotte musicali*. Bologna: Cooperativa Libraria Universitaria Edizioni Bolognesi.

Delalande, F. (2003). D'une technologie à l'autre. *Dossiers de l'Ingénierie Educative* 43, 6–10.

Deliège, I. (2001). Similarity perception < - > Categorization < - > Cue abstraction. *Music Percept.* 1, 233–243. doi: 10.1525/mp.2001.18.3.233

Dissanayake, E. (2000). "Antecedents of the temporal arts in early mother-infant interaction," in *The Origins of Music*, eds N. L. Wallin, B. Merker, and S. Brown (Cambridge, MA: Massachusetts Institute of Technology Press), 389–410.

Dorfman, J. (2013). *Theory and Practice of Technology-Based Music Instruction*. Oxford: Oxford University Press.

Ericsson, K. A. (1997). "Deliberate practice and the acquisition of expert performance. An overview," in *Does Practice Make Perfect? Current Theory and Research on Instrumental Music Practice*, eds H. Jørgensen and A. C. Lehmann (Oslo: Norges Musikkhogskole), 9–51.

Erkkilä, J., Ala-Ruona, E., Punkanen, M., and Fachner, J. (2012). "Creativity in improvisational, psychodynamic music therapy," in *Musical Immaginations*, eds D. Hargreaves, D. Miell, and R. McDonald (Oxford: Oxford University Press), 404–428.

Ferrari, L., and Addessi, A. R. (2014). A new way to play music together: the Continuator in a classroom setting. *Int. J. Music Educ.* 3, 171–184. doi: 10.1177/0255761413504706

Ferrari, L., and Addessi, A. R. (2015). "Il MIROR-Impro nella scuola dell'infanzia: scenari di esplorazione e improvvisazione musicale," in *La Creatività Musicale e Motoria dei Bambini in Ambienti Riflessivi: Pratiche Didattiche con la Piattaforma MIROR*, ed. A. R. Addessi (Bologna: Bononia University Press), 65–78.

Finney, J., and Burnard, P. (2009). *Music Education with Digital Technology*. London: Continuum International Publishing Group.

Fiske, H. E. (1992). "Experimental research," in *Some Approaches to Research in Music Education*, ed. A. E. Kemp (Reading: International Society for Music Education).

Fogel, A. (2000). "Oltre gli individui: un approccio storico – relazionale alla teoria e alla ricerca sulla comunicazione," in *Il Rapporto Madre-Bambino*, ed. M. L. Genta (Rome: Carocci), 123–161.

Galilei, V. (1581). *Dialogo Della Musica Antica et Della Moderna*. Firenze: Marescotti.

Gratier, M. (2008). Grounding in musical interaction: evidence from jazz performances. *Musicae Sci.* 12(Suppl.), 71–110. doi: 10.1177/1029864908012001041

Gratier, M., and Apter-Danon, G. (2009). "The improvised musicality of belonging: repetition and variation," in *Communicative Musicality. Exploring the Basis of Human Companionship*, eds S. Malloch and C. Trevarthen (Oxford: Oxford University Press), 301–330.

Gratier, M., Devouche, E., Guellai, B., Infanti, R., Ylmaz, E., and Parlato-Oliveira, E. (2015). Early development of turn-taking in vocal interaction between mothers and infants. *Front. Psychol.* 6:1167. doi: 10.3389/fpsyg.2015.1167

Hadley, L. V., Novembre, G., Keller, P. E., and Pickering, M. J. (2015). Causal role of motor simulation in turn-taking behavior. *J. Neurosci.* 3, 16516–16520. doi: 10.1523/JNEUROSCI.1850-15.2015

Hickey, M., and Lipscomb, S. (2006). "How different is good? How good is different? The assessment of children's creative musical thinking," in *Musical Creativity*, eds I. Deliege and G. Wiggins (Hove: Psychology Press), 97–110.

Imberty, M. (2005). *La Musique Creuse le Temps. De Wagner à Boulez: Musique, Psychologie, Psychoanalyse*. Paris: L'Harmattan.

Katayose, H. (2014). "Autonomously acquiring "human-like behaviors" of agents with biological constraints," in *Proceedings of 1st International Workshop Systems for Automatic Music Performance (SAMP14)*, (Padova: University of Padova).

Kawase, S. (2015). Relationships between performers daily social skills, social behaviors in ensemble practice, and evaluations of ensemble performance. *Musicae Sci.* 19, 350–365. doi: 10.1177/1029864915590171

Kenny, B. J., and Gellrich, M. (2002). "Improvisation," in *The Science and Psychology of Music Performance: Creative Strategies for Teaching and Learning*, eds G. McPherson and R. Parncutt (Oxford: Oxford University Press), 117–134.

King, E., and Gritten, A. (2016). "Dialogue and beyond: communication and interaction in ensemble performance," in *Musicians in the Making: Pathways to Creative Performance*, eds J. Rink, H. Gaunt, and A. Williamon (Oxford: Oxford University Press).

Kircher, A. (1650). *Musurgia Universalis*. Rome: Francesco Corbelletti [II Ludovico Grignani].

Kleinmintz, O. M., Goldstein, P., Mayseless, N., Abecasis, D., and Shamay-Tsoory, S. G. (2014). Expertise in musical improvisation and creativity: the mediation of idea evaluation. *PLoS ONE* 9:e101568. doi: 10.1371/journal.pone.0101568

Kratus, J. (1996). A developmental approach to teaching musical improvisation. *Int. J. Music Educ.* 1, 35–50.

Lakin, J. L., and Chartrand, T. L. (2003). Using nonconscious behavioral mimicry to create affiliation and rapport. *Psychol. Sci.* 14, 334–339. doi: 10.1111/1467-9280.14481

Leman, M. (2007). *Embodied Music Cognition and Mediation Technology*. Cambridge, MA: Massachusetts Institute of Technology Press.

Leman, M., Lesaffre, M., Nijs, L., and Deweppe, A. (2010). User-oriented studies in embodied music cognition research. *Musicae Sci.* 14(Suppl.), 203–224. doi: 10.1177/10298649100140S212

Littleton, K., and Mercer, N. (2012). "Communication, collaboration, and creativity: how musicians negotiate a collective "sound"," in *Musical Immaginations*, eds D. Hargreaves, D. Miell, and R. McDonald (Oxford: Oxford University Press).

Luck, G., Toiviainen, P., Erkkilä, J., Lartillot, O., and Rikkilä, K. (2008). Modelling the relationships between emotional responses to, and musical content of, music therapy improvisation. *Psychol. Music* 3, 23–45.

Malloch, S., and Trevarthen, C. (Eds) (2009). *Communicative Musicality. Exploring the Basis of(human)Companionship*. Oxford: Oxford University Press.

Margulis, E. H. (2014). *On Repeat. How Music Plays the Mind*. New York, NY: Oxford University Press.

McPherson, G. E. (1993). *Factors and Abilities Influencing the Development of Visual, Aural and Creative Performance in Music and Their Educational Implications*. Sydney, NSW: University of Sydney.

McPherson, G. E. (1995). The assessment of musical performance: development and validation of five new measures. *Psychol. Music* 23, 142–161. doi: 10.1177/0305735695232003

McPherson, G. E. (2005). From child to musician: skill development during the beginning stage of learning an instrument. *Psychol. Music* 3, 5–35. doi: 10.1177/0305735605048012

Meltzoff, A. N., and Prinz, W. (Eds) (2002). *The Imitative Mind. Development, Evolution, and Brain Bases*. New York, NY: Cambridge University Press.

Mialaret, J.-P. (1997). *Les Explorations Instrumentales Chez les Jeunes Enfants*. Paris: Presses Universitaires de France.

Moran, N., Hadley, L. V., Bader, M., and Keller, P. E. (2015). Perception of 'back-channeling' nonverbal feedback in musical duo improvisation. *PLoS ONE* 1:e0130070. doi: 10.1371/journal.pone.0130070

Morgan, E., Gunes, H., and Bryan-Kinns, N. (2014). "Instrumenting the interaction: affective and psychophysiological features of live collaborative musical improvisation," in *Proceeding of the International Conference of New Interfaces for Musical Expression, NIME14*, (Goldsmiths: University of London), 23–28.

Nadel, J. (2002). "Imitation and imitation recognition: functional use in preverbal infants and nonverbal children with autism," in *The Imitative Mind. Development, Evolution, and Brain Bases*, eds A. Meltzoff and W. Prinz (New York, NY: Cambridge University Press), 42–62.

Nijs, L., and Leman, M. (2015). "Improvvisare con e senza la componente MIROR-Impro della piattaforma MIROR: proposte di pratiche con i bambini secondo un approccio task-based," in *La Creatività Musicale e Motoria dei Bambini in Ambienti Riflessivi: Pratiche Didattiche con la Piattaforma MIROR*, ed. A. R. Addessi (Bologna: Bononia University Press), 121–138.

Nijs, L., Moens, B., Lesaffre, M., and Leman, M. (2012). The Music Paint Machine: stimulating self-monitoring through the generation of creative visual output using a technology-enhanced learning tool. *J. New Music Res.* 4, 79–101. doi: 10.1080/09298215.2011.650180

Pachet, F. (2003). The Continuator. Music interaction with style. *J. New Music Res.* 3, 333–341. doi: 10.1076/jnmr.32.3.333.16861

Pachet, F. (2004). "On the design of Flow Machine," in *A Learning Zone of One's Own: Sharing Representations and Flow in Collaborative Learning Environments*, ed. M. Tokoro (Amsterdam: IOS Press), 111–134.

Pachet, F. (2006). "Creativity studies and musical interaction," in *Musical Creativity*, eds I. Deliège and G. A. Wiggins (Hove: Psychology Press), 347–358.

Pachet, F., Roy, P., and Barbieri, G. (2011). "Finite-Length Markov processes with constraints," in *Proceedings of the Twenty-Second International Joint Conference on Artificial Intelligence IJCAI 2011*, Barcelona,

Papoušek, M. (2007). Communication in early infancy: an arena of intersubjective learning. *Infant Behav. Dev.* 30, 258–266. doi: 10.1016/j.infbeh.2007.02.003

Pesquita, A., Corlis, T., and Enns, J. T. (2014). Perception of musical cooperation in jazz duets is predicted by social aptitude. *Psychomusicology* 2, 173–183. doi: 10.1037/pmu0000047

Pinho, A. L., de Manzano, O., Fransson, P., Eriksson, H., and Ullén, F. (2014). Connecting to create: expertise in musical improvisation is associated with increased functional connectivity between premotor and prefrontal areas. *J. Neurosci.* 3, 6156–6163. doi: 10.1523/JNEUROSCI.4769-13.2014

Pressing, J. (1988). "Improvisation: methods and models," in *Generative Processes in Music: The Psychology of Performance, Improvisation, and Composition*, ed. J. A. Sloboda (Oxford: Clarendon Press), 129–178.

Prinz, W. (2008). "Mirrors for embodied communication," in *Embodied Communication in Humans and Machines*, eds I. Wachsmuth, M. Lenzen, and G. Knoblich (New York, NY: Oxford University Press), 111–128.

Regazzi, F., and Benghi, D. (2015). "Setup alternativi," in *La Creatività Musicale e Motoria dei Bambini in Ambienti Riflessivi: Pratiche Didattiche con la Piattaforma MIROR*, ed. A. R. Addessi (Bologna: Bononia University Press), 193–200.

Rizzolatti, G., Fadiga, L., Fogassi, L., and Gallese, V. (2002). "From mirror neurons to imitation: facts and speculations," in *The Imitative Mind. Development, Evolution, and Brain Bases*, eds A. N. Meltzoff and W. Prinz (New York, NY: Cambridge University Press), 247–266.

Rowe, V., Triantafyllaki, A., and Anagnostopoulou, C. (2015). Young pianists exploring improvisation using interactive music technology. *Int. J. Music Educ.* 3, 113–130. doi: 10.1177/0255761414540137

Ruwet, N. (1966). Méthodes d'analyse en musicologie. *Rev. BelgeMusicol.* 20, 65–90. doi: 10.2307/3686642

Sawyer, K. R. (2001). *Creating Conversations. Improvisation in Everyday Discourse.* Cresskil, NJ: Hampton Press, Inc.

Schiavio, A., and Høffding, S. (2015). Playing together without communicating? A pre-reflective and enactive account of joint musical performance. *Musicae Sci.* 1, 366–388.

Seddon, F. (2005). Modes of communication during jazz improvisation. *Br. J. Music Educ.* 2, 47–61. doi: 10.1017/S0265051704005984

Stern, D. (2004). *The Present Moment in Psychotherapy and in Everyday Life.* New York, NY: Norton.

Sundin, B. (1998). "Musical creativity in the first six years: a research project in retrospect," in *Children Composing, Research in Music Education*, eds B. Sundin, G. McPherson, and G. Folkestad (Malmö: Malmo Academy of Music), 35–56.

Tafuri, J. (2006). "Processes and teaching strategies in musical improvisation with children," in *Musical Creativity*, eds I. Deliège and G. A. Wiggins (Hove: Psychology Press), 134–158.

Thompson, S., and Williamon, A. (2003). Evaluating evaluation: musical performance assessment as a research tool. *Music Percept.* 2, 21–41. doi: 10. 3389/fnsys.2013.00030

Toiviainen, P. (Ed.) (2007). Similarity perception in listening to music [Special Issue]. *Musicae Sci.* 11(Suppl.).

Triantafyllaki, C., Anagnostopoulou, A., and Alexakis, A. (2012). "An exploratory study of young children's technology-enabling improvisation," in *Proceedings of the 12th ICMPC and the 8th Triennial Conference of ESCOM*, eds E. Cambouropoulos, C. Tsougras, P. Mavromatis, and K. Pastiadis (Thessaloniki: School of Music Studies, Aristotle University of Thessaloniki), 1009–1015.

Turkle, S. (1984). *The Second Self: Computer and the Human Spirit.* New York, NY: Simon-Schuster.

Vygotsky, L. S. (1962). *Thought and Language.* Cambridge, MA: Massachusetts Institute of Technology Press.

Webster, P. (1994). "Thinking in sound: studying children's improvisation," in *Proceedings of the 21st World Conference of the International Society for Music Education held at Tampa: Musical Connections: Tradition and Change, Florida*, ed. H. Lees (Dunedin North: Uniprint), 146–153.

Webster, P. R. (2002). "Creative thinking in music: advancing a model," in *Creativity and Music Education*, eds T. Sullivan and L. Willingham (Edmonton: Canadian Music Educators Association), 16–33.

Webster, P. R. (2007). "Computer-based technology and music," in *International Handbook of Research in Arts Education*, ed. L. Bresler (Dordrecht: Springer), 1311–1328.

Wigram, A. (2012). "Developing creative improvisation skills in music therapy. The tools for imaginative music-making," in *Musical Immaginations*, eds D. Hargreaves, D. Miell, and R. MacDonald (Oxford: Oxford University Press), 429–450.

Williamon, A., and Davidson, J. W. (2002). Exploring co-performer communication. *Musicae Sci.* 6, 53–72. doi: 10.1177/102986490200600103

Williamon, A. (Ed) (2004). *Musical Excellence: (Strategies)and Techniques to Enhance Performance.* Oxford: Oxford University Press.

Williams, D. B., and Webster, P. R. (2008). *Experiencing Music Technology.* Boston, MA: Clark Baxter.

Young, S. (2004). The interpersonal dimension: a potential source of musical creativity for young children. *Musicae Sci.* 7(Suppl.), 175–179.

Zatorre, R. J. (2012). Beyond auditory cortex: working with musical thoughts. *Ann. N. Y. Acad. Sci.* 1252, 222–228. doi: 10.1111/j.1749-6632.2011.06437.x

Conflict of Interest Statement: The authors declare that the research was conducted in the absence of any commercial or financial relationships that could be construed as a potential conflict of interest.

14

Parent-child math anxiety and math-gender stereotypes predict adolescents' math education outcomes

Bettina J. Casad[1]*, **Patricia Hale**[2] **and Faye L. Wachs**[2]

[1] Department of Psychological Sciences, University of Missouri-St. Louis, St. Louis, MO, USA, [2] Department of Mathematics and Statistics, California State Polytechnic University, Pomona, Pomona, CA, USA

Two studies examined social determinants of adolescents' math anxiety including parents' own math anxiety and children's endorsement of math-gender stereotypes. In Study 1, parent-child dyads were surveyed and the interaction between parent and child math anxiety was examined, with an eye to same- and other-gender dyads. Results indicate that parent's math anxiety interacts with daughters' and sons' anxiety to predict math self-efficacy, GPA, behavioral intentions, math attitudes, and math devaluing. Parents with lower math anxiety showed a positive relationship to children's math outcomes when children also had lower anxiety. The strongest relationships were found with same-gender dyads, particularly Mother-Daughter dyads. Study 2 showed that endorsement of math-gender stereotypes predicts math anxiety (and not vice versa) for performance beliefs and outcomes (self-efficacy and GPA). Further, math anxiety fully mediated the relationship between gender stereotypes and math self-efficacy for girls and boys, and for boys with GPA. These findings address gaps in the literature on the role of parents' math anxiety in the effects of children's math anxiety and math anxiety as a mechanism affecting performance. Results have implications for interventions on parents' math anxiety and dispelling gender stereotypes in math classrooms.

Keywords: math anxiety, gender stereotypes, gender, parents, math education

Edited by:
Erin Anne Maloney, University of Chicago, USA

Reviewed by:
Zhe Wang, The Ohio State University, USA
Macarena Suárez Pellicioni, University of Barcelona, Spain

***Correspondence:**
Bettina J. Casad
casadbj@umsl.edu

Specialty section:
This article was submitted to Cognition, a section of the journal Frontiers in Psychology

INTRODUCTION

The status of math education in the US is cause for concern. Standardized math test performance indicates the US is ranked 35th out of 64 countries (National Center for Education Statistics, 2012). Politicians, educators, and researchers may point the blame at the US system of higher education, but another source should share the blame: our math-phobic culture (Burns, 1998; Chew and Dillon, 2014). Many Americans report fear or anxiety about conducting math and many students shy away from math-intensive disciplines such as the sciences, technology (e.g., computer science), engineering, and of course, mathematics and statistics (STEM; Meece et al., 1990; Chipman et al., 1992). Many Americans report that they just do not like math and statistics. This is problematic as mathematics is a gateway field for STEM disciplines and societal advancement in technology and science (Roman, 2004). If the majority of Americans are afraid of math, as a country we face falling further behind our math-friendly counterparts.

This social problem leads researchers and educators to ask why, where does this math anxiety originate? Math anxiety can be defined as "feelings of fear, apprehension, or dread that many people experience when they are in situations that require solving math problems" (Maloney et al., 2014, p. 404). Research on adolescents' math anxiety has pointed to parents, teachers, and peers as major environmental sources (Wigfield and Eccles, 2000; Beilock et al., 2010; Gunderson et al., 2012). We learn our math phobia in part from important others who influence our early life development. Another potential source of math phobia that has received research attention is cultural stereotypes about gender and math (Steffens et al., 2010; Cheryan, 2012). Despite evidence that the gender gap in math performance in the US has disappeared (Hyde et al., 2008; Lindberg et al., 2010), cultural biases about the superiority of boys and men in math permeate our social consciousness. Media attention has proscribed disparaging comments about girls' and women's inferiority in math and science (e.g., former Harvard President Lawrence Summers and Nobel Laureate Tim Hunt; Bombardieri, 2005; Associated Press, 2015). Yet, these cultural influences have lasting effects and will likely remain pervasive for years to come, as research shows stereotype change is a slow process (Devine and Elliot, 1995) and public attitudes are slow to change following cultural shifts (e.g., Civil Rights Movement and school desegregation; Newport et al., 1999).

The purpose of the present studies is to further probe the social determinants of adolescents' math anxiety by examining the relationship between math anxiety from same and other-gender parents with children's math anxiety and how this relates to math education outcomes. Parents' math anxiety is conceptualized as a moderator, determining the strength and direction of the relationships between children's math anxiety and math education outcomes. A plethora of research has examined the relationship between parents' (primarily mothers') math-gender stereotypes and perceptions of their child's math abilities with children's math attitudes and math anxiety (Eccles and Jacobs, 1986; Yee and Eccles, 1988; Midgley et al., 1989; Eccles et al., 1990; Jacobs, 1991, 2005; Jacobs and Eccles, 1992); however, little research has examined parents' own math anxieties (Gunderson et al., 2012; see Maloney et al., 2015). Addressing this gap in the literature, this study examines parents' own math anxiety and how it interacts with children's math anxiety to predict math education outcomes. Further, the first study examines these relationships within same- and mixed-gender parent-child dyads to explore the gendered nature of the intergenerational transmission of math anxiety (e.g., see for example Gniewosz and Noack, 2012). Addressing a call for a mechanistic approach (Gunderson et al., 2012), the second study examines children's math-related gender stereotypes as a source of math anxiety and tests math anxiety as a mechanism through which math-gender stereotypes negatively influence math outcomes for *both* girls and boys. The math education outcomes examined herein include math self-efficacy, math attitudes, math devaluing, math education behavioral intentions, and classroom math performance (GPA).

Teachers and Parents as Sources of Math Anxiety

Eccles et al. (1983) developed an Expectancy-Value Theory of achievement motivation, originally in mathematics, that describes various cultural, social, interpersonal, and individual factors that influence children's motivations, task values, expectations for success, and achievement related choices. Included in the cultural milieu factors are cultural stereotypes about the subject and occupation (e.g., mathematics) and socializers' (e.g., parents) beliefs and behaviors, as well as children's own perceptions of socializers' beliefs and society's stereotypes about the domain. The Expectancy-Value Theory has received extensive support over the past few decades (see Wigfield and Eccles, 2000, for a review). Thus, the role of parents in influencing children's values, beliefs, expectations, performance, and choice in the math domain is well-known.

Both teachers and parents play a major role in socializing children's academic values and attitudes and an extensive body of research documents how parents' and teachers' expectations, gender stereotypes, and attributions impact children's math attitudes and performance (Yee and Eccles, 1988; Eccles et al., 1990; Tiedemann, 2000; Jacobs, 2005). Interestingly, however, little research has examined teachers' and parents' own math anxiety as an antecedent for children's math anxiety, attitudes, and achievement. A recent study found that female teachers' math anxiety impacted early elementary school girls', but not boys', math achievement and attitudes (Beilock et al., 2010). Specifically, girls whose teacher had higher math anxiety had lower math grades and learned less content at the end of the year compared to girls whose teacher had lower math anxiety, even after controlling for girls' math achievement in the beginning of the school year. It seems math-anxious teachers reinforced math-gender stereotypes as girls' endorsement of math-gender stereotypes mediated the effect of teacher anxiety on their math performance. A study with second grade elementary children examined parents' math anxiety in relationship to children's math anxiety, activities, and academic self-perceptions, but found no effects (Jameson, 2014). This work suggests the need for continued investigation of the role of parents' anxiety in children's anxiety in various developmental stages to determine when this effect begins. The only known study to find an effect of parents' math anxiety on their first and second grade child's math anxiety is a recently published study (Maloney et al., 2015). Thus, the present study focuses on parents' math anxiety as a socializing agent of children's math anxiety and the downstream effects on math education outcomes.

One reason researchers may have ignored the role of parents' anxiety in developing children's math anxiety and performance is a common (mis)perception that math learning is more likely to take place during school than at home and the role of parents may be less critical than teachers in math learning (Cannon and Ginsburg, 2008). However, just as teachers serve as role models for students, parents serve as long-term role models and their beliefs can influence their children as children develop their own identities, values, and efficacy (Yee and Eccles, 1988; Eccles et al., 1990; Tiedemann, 2000; Jacobs, 2005). Another potential reason for this gap in the literature is that people may not think about parents computing math, unless it is part of their occupation (e.g., accounting, banking). In contrast, school is the domain in which math is learned and regularly used and teachers perform mathematical problems publically in front of students and therefore seem to have more direct influence on children's math attitudes and anxiety. However, parents, regardless of their profession, likely perform more mundane mathematical computations on a regular basis such as making a household budget, balancing a checkbook, and calculating a tip at a restaurant, which can elicit math anxiety (Ashcraft, 2002). Parents' math anxiety may be subtly communicated to children through these mundane activities, or even more directly in their role of helping (or not helping) children with their math homework (Bhanot and Jovanovic, 2005; Maloney et al., 2015).

Does Parent Gender Matter?

Beilock et al. (2010) found that female teachers' math anxiety affected girls' math anxiety, performance, and amount of math learning over a school year, but it did not affect boys. This raises the question of the gender dynamics of math attitude, anxiety, and math-gender stereotype transmission between teachers and students and parents and children. Beilock et al. (2010) did not examine effects of male teachers, likely because more than 90% of elementary school teachers are female, and this is a new area of research, thus the effect of teacher gender remains a question for investigation. Likewise, only one published study has examined the effect of parents' math anxiety on children's math anxiety and achievement (Maloney et al., 2015), but sample demographics did not allow for a gender analysis, thus the question of parent gender is also yet to be addressed.

A great deal of the research using an expectancy-value framework focuses on the transmission of math-gender stereotypes from parents to children and how stereotypes influence children's achievement outcomes. This body of work has examined the gender of parents, particularly in the transmission of their math-gender stereotypes and math attitudes, but not specifically their math anxiety. This literature can inform questions and hypotheses about the gender composition of parent-child dyads in the intergenerational transmission of math anxiety. For example, is the influence of mothers to daughters and fathers to sons greater than mixed-gender transmission of mothers to sons and fathers to daughters? Research has mostly supported the same-gender dyad model such that mothers in particular communicate math-gender stereotypes to their daughters (O'Bryan et al., 2004), which subsequently predicts daughters' academic and career choices, even several years later (Bleeker and Jacobs, 2004). For example, if mothers endorse math-gender stereotypes that men are superior to women in math, they may communicate this (intentionally or unintentionally) to their daughters, who then may show less interest in math and choose other academic and career domains. Indeed, girls' and women's choices of academic and career trajectories is one explanation for the underrepresentation of women in STEM, rather than a lack of ability explanation (Wang et al., 2013). Many girls and women who show high aptitude in multiple domains choose academic and career paths outside of STEM in part because they have more opportunities available to them (Wang et al., 2013).

There are several reasons we hypothesize that same-gender parent-child transmission of math anxiety is more common than mixed-gender transmission. First, women and girls tend to experience greater math anxiety than men and boys (Hembree, 1990; Ramirez et al., 2013), regardless of their actual math ability (Hyde et al., 1990; Meece et al., 1990; Devine et al., 2012), and it begins as early as first and second grade (Harari et al., 2013; Ramirez et al., 2013) and increases as children get older (Hembree, 1990). Currently about 20% of the population is characterized as high in math anxiety (Eden et al., 2013). If women are more likely to suffer from math anxiety than men, then it is logical to predict that mothers experience greater math anxiety than fathers and likely communicate this to their children, particularly daughters, who also are more likely to have high math anxiety than sons. Second, gender role socialization most commonly occurs with same-gender caregivers (Bussey and Bandura, 1984). During development, daughters may be more likely to pick up on mothers' math anxiety than fathers', and sons from fathers rather than mothers. Of course there are children who strongly identify with other-gender parents and may more quickly adopt their beliefs, values, and attitudes (e.g., daddy's girl or mama's boy; Gniewosz and Noack, 2012). Finally, parents often hold gender stereotypes about their children's performance in math, believing that sons' have stronger math ability than daughters, even when there is no evidence to support this belief (Furnham et al., 2002). As a result, parents may expect daughters to perform more poorly in math, which may contribute to greater math anxiety for girls.

Antecedents and Effects of Math Anxiety

There is a large body of literature documenting the negative effects of math anxiety; however, there is still much we do not know. The majority of research focuses on negative consequences rather than antecedents and contexts in which math anxiety develops (Ashcraft and Ridley, 2005; Jameson, 2014; Maloney et al., 2015), and more research is needed with children (Jameson, 2014). Recent research has documented cognitive and biological antecedents of math anxiety including diminished working memory capacity, low math ability, attentional bias, and genetic factors (Wang et al., 2014; Suárez-Pellicioni et al., 2015).

The present studies examine an environmental factor, specifically parents' anxiety as a moderator of adolescents' math anxiety, thus helping to fill this gap in the literature.

Several negative consequences of math anxiety include avoidance of mathematics (e.g., math courses and math-intensive careers), less confidence, lower math self-efficacy, and more negative attitudes toward math (Hembree, 1990; Ashcraft et al., 1998; Ashcraft, 2002). Avoidance of math courses and math-intensive careers may be one explanation for the gender gap in STEM careers (Wigfield and Eccles, 2000; Gunderson et al., 2011; Cheryan, 2012). Math anxiety causes lower math performance, regardless of actual math ability (Hembree, 1990; Maloney and Beilock, 2012; Park et al., 2014).

Another negative consequence of math anxiety is low math self-efficacy. Self-efficacy is the confidence that one has the ability to succeed in the domain (Schunk, 1981, 1982a,b; Pajares, 1996). Although research clearly demonstrates the importance of math self-efficacy in math achievement and attitudes, few studies have examined how self-efficacy relates to math anxiety (Jameson, 2014). Two studies have found a negative relationship between math self-efficacy and math anxiety (Meece et al., 1990; Cooper and Robinson, 1991). Math anxiety was directly related to both boys' and girls' math ability perceptions, but interestingly, not to math grades (Meece et al., 1990). Given the importance of reducing students' math anxiety in order to promote positive math achievement and attitudes, many studies have examined ways that parents can help reduce children's math anxiety (e.g., Vukovic et al., 2013).

Overview of Studies

The current studies address different gaps in the literature by exploring antecedents of math anxiety: parents' math anxiety (Study 1) and math-gender stereotypes (Study 2), and a mechanistic (mediational) perspective of math anxiety (Study 2). Study 1 posits an interaction between parent and children's math anxiety in predicting several math education outcomes including math self-efficacy, math attitudes, math devaluing, math education behavioral intentions, and math GPA. These relationships are tested within the dyadic relationships of parents and children and the gender of parent and child dyad is examined for similar and different patterns in math education outcomes. Study 2 examines children's endorsement of math-gender stereotypes as an antecedent of math anxiety, and tests math anxiety as a mechanism through which math-gender stereotypes negatively influence math outcomes for *both* girls and boys.

STUDY 1

Hypotheses

Based on the literature reviewed we predict (1) main effects of child's math anxiety on the outcome variables. Specifically, greater math anxiety will predict (1a) lower math self-efficacy, (1b) lower math GPA, (1c) lower math education behavioral intentions, (1d) more negative math attitudes, and (1e) greater math devaluing. We predict (2) an interaction between parents' and children's math anxiety such that higher levels of children's math anxiety will be negatively correlated with math education outcomes, and the correlations will be strongest when parents also have higher math anxiety. Finally, we predict that (3) same-gender parent-math dyads are most likely to show significant relationships between math anxiety and education outcomes (both positive and negative), particularly (3a) mother-daughter dyads. Relatedly, (3b) we expect mothers and daughters to show patterns indicative of higher anxiety than other parent-child dyads. We expect (3c) few if any significant relationships for mixed-gender dyads including mother-son and father-daughter.

Method

Participants

A total of 1342 parents were recruited and 683 participated[1], resulting in a 51% response rate. Student participants included 377 (55%) girls and 306 (45%) boys in 6th (n = 157, 23%), 7th (n = 291, 43%), or 8th (n = 235, 34%) grade honors (n = 366, 55%) or standard math (n = 298, 45%) classes (e.g., Algebra Readiness, Pre-Algebra, or Algebra)[2]. Students' ages ranged from 11 to 14 reflecting ages in the 6th through 8th grades. There were 8 middle schools from southern California with 24 math teachers participating. Dyad types consisted of Mother-Daughter (n = 315, 46%), Mother-Son (n = 239, 35%), Father-Daughter (n = 62, 9%), and Father-Son (n = 67, 10%). The majority of students (n = 538, 88%) were born in the US. In contrast, the majority of parents were born outside the US (62%, n = 419). The majority of students and parents born outside the US were born in Mexico, South America, or an Asian country (e.g., China, Cambodia, Vietnam, Philippines). Students' self-reported race/ethnicity included 66% (n = 435) Latino/a or Hispanic, 10% (n = 62) Asian/Pacific Islander, 9% (n = 58) multiracial, and less than 5% each of Black/African American, Native American, White/Caucasian, or other. Parents' self-reported race/ethnicity included Latino/a or Hispanic 73% (n = 486), 10% (n = 65) Asian/Pacific Islander, 7% (n = 47) White/Caucasian, 7% (n = 45) Black/African American, and less than 5% of each group Native American, multiracial, or other. Parents' ages ranged from 22 to 63 (M = 42.20, SD = 6.73). Parents' education and household income are shown in **Table 1**.

TABLE 1 | Parents' education and household income.

Level of education	Mother $N = 525$	Father $N = 121$	Household income (in thousands)	Mother $N = 211$	Father $N = 72$
8th Grade or less	13.9%	8.3%	<5	20.4%	8.3%
9th–12th Grade	15.8%	14.0%	5–9999	5.2%	1.4%
HS Graduate	23.2%	20.7%	10–14,999	13.7%	11.1%
Some College	28.0%	26.4%	15–24,999	15.6%	5.6%
College Graduate	14.7%	22.3%	25–34,999	21.8%	13.9%
Post Graduate	4.4%	8.3%	35–49,999	9.5%	22.2%
Missing information (excluded from calculations)	5.2%	6.2%	50–74,999	8.1%	22.2%
			75 or more	5.6%	15.3%
			Missing Information (excluded from calculations)	61.9%	44.2%

Values are rounded to one decimal place for ease of reading. HS, High school education; Some College, attended college but did not complete a degree. Income is household income in thousands per year.

Materials

The students' questionnaires contained items assessing math anxiety, math self-efficacy, math education behavioral intentions, math attitudes, and math devaluing. Math class GPA was

[1] There were some marginal and significant differences in the characteristics and demographics of the students whose parent participated compared to students whose parent did not participate. Students without a participating parent had lower self-efficacy, and marginally greater endorsement of gender stereotypes and math. However, there were no significant differences for math anxiety, math attitudes, math devaluing, and math behavioral intentions. There was a marginal difference in the gender of the child such that females were more likely to have had a parent participate than males. There was a difference in the race of the child such that racial non-minority students, that is Caucasians or Asian Americans, were more likely to have had a parent participate than minority students. There were no differences for GPA, class type (honors/non honors) or grade level. See the Supplemental Results for the analyses.

obtained directly from the teacher. Parents' questionnaires contained a variety of similar measures, but only parents' math anxiety data are reported here.

Children's math anxiety was assessed by 3 items rated on a scale from 1 (*Very Strongly Disagree*) to 6 (*Very Strongly Agree;* based on Marx and Stapel, 2006). Items included "I often get nervous when I have to do math," "Many times when I see a math problem I just 'freeze up'," and "I have never been as good in math as I am in other classes." The items had acceptable internal consistency ($\alpha = 0.731$) and were averaged so that higher values represented greater anxiety.

Parents' math anxiety was assessed by 2 items rated on a scale from 1 (*Very Strongly Disagree*) to 6 (*Very Strongly Agree;* based on Marx and Stapel, 2006). Items included "Many times when I see a math problem I just 'freeze up'," and "I have never been as good in math as in other classes in high school." The items were moderately to highly correlated, $r_{(558)} = 0.548$, $p = 0.001$ and were averaged so that higher values represented greater anxiety.

Children's math self-efficacy was measured by 5 items rated on a scale from 1 (*Not at all Confident*) to 6 (*Very Confident;* based on Zimmerman and Martinez-Pons, 1988). Sample items included "How confident are you that you will pass your math class at the end of the term?" "How confident are you that you will pass math at the end of this term with a grade better than a B?" and "How confident are you that you will get an A?" The items had acceptable internal consistency ($\alpha = 0.898$) and were averaged so that higher values represented greater math self-efficacy.

Children's math education behavioral intentions were measured by 6 items rated on a scale from 1 (*Very Strongly Disagree*) to 6 (*Very Strongly Agree;* adapted from Sparks et al., 1997; Butler, 1999). Sample items included "I plan to take more math classes than I have to in high school," "I plan to complete all of my math homework on time," and "I plan to participate in school related activities about math (like competitions or projects)." The items had acceptable internal consistency ($\alpha = 0.749$) and were averaged so that higher values represented greater math education behavioral intentions.

Children's math attitudes were measured by 5 items rated on a scale from 1 (*Very Strongly Disagree*) to 6 (*Very Strongly Agree*; adapted from Sparks et al., 1997; Butler, 1999). Items included "I will use math a lot when I grow up", "I enjoy studying math," and "I think math is boring" (reverse-scored). The items had acceptable internal consistency ($\alpha = 0.761$) and were reverse scored and averaged so that higher values represented more positive math attitudes.

Finally, children's math devaluing (Major and Schmader, 1998) was assessed by 5 items rated on a scale from 1 (*Very Strongly Disagree*) to 6 (*Very Strongly Agree*). Sample items included "I always feel good about myself when I do well on a math test" (reverse-scored) and "Doing well on math tests is very important to me" (reverse-scored). The items had acceptable internal consistency ($\alpha = 0.770$) and were reverse-scored and averaged so that higher values represented greater math devaluing.

Procedure

Institutional Review Board approval was obtained from California State Polytechnic University, Pomona and permission was granted by the District Superintendent, each school principal, and each participating school teacher. Parents provided consent forms indicating whether their child could participate, and also signed a consent form if they participated in the questionnaire. Finally, students provided consent/assent forms in class if they chose to participate.

Researchers visited the classroom during the designated period and distributed the questionnaires, which were available in both English and Spanish. After students completed the questionnaires, they were each given a packet containing a consent form and questionnaire to take home to give to one of their parents. Completed parent questionnaires were typically mailed back to the researchers in a pre-paid enveloped or returned to the teacher and later collected by the researchers.

Analysis Strategy

Although all of the relationships of interest exist at the student and parent level, the data came from an inherently hierarchical structure of children/parents (Level 1) nested within classrooms (Level 2) with different teachers, nested within different schools (Level 3). This sort of hierarchical structure often results in correlations of residuals among nested units that can bias the outcome of an ordinary least squares (OLS) regression by underestimating standard errors (Snijders and Bosker, 2011). Multilevel modeling (Raudenbush and Bryk, 2002) offers an appropriate remedy for analyzing nested data and is able to accommodate a wide range of data structures, including circumstances where the focal variables of interest are all situated on one level and the clustering is only a nuisance that prevents the use of OLS regression. To that end, two-level random intercept models were computed using the restricted maximum likelihood estimation, which adjusts for unequal sample sizes and is ideal for smaller datasets, with variance components estimator in SPSS Mixed Models Version 21 (IBM Corp., 2012). We were not able to use a three-level model because the number of schools ($N = 8$) was too small for a cluster analysis. However, the number of teachers ($N = 24$) was adequate for a two-level model to capture the nested nature of the data.

In addition, the data are also dyadic and non-independent as parents of the children also completed the questionnaire. The data were organized using the standard dyadic design and analyses are computed within dyad rather than between individuals (Kenny et al., 2006). For dyadic data, the slopes (the effects of predictors on Y for each dyad) are fixed to be equal across all dyads (Kenny et al., 2006). Instead the data are modeled through variation in the intercept at the Level 2 variable (teacher) across dyads. Finally, the Satterthwaite approximation was used to calculate degrees of freedom (Kenny et al., 2002).

For each model, the student's grade level and type of math class (honors or standard) were treated as control variables. Dyad type, child's math anxiety, and parent's math anxiety were entered into the model as main effects. Dyad type was effects coded as 1, 0.5, −0.5, and −1 for Father-Son, Father-Daughter, Mother-Son, and Mother-Daughter, respectively. To facilitate interpretation, child and parent math anxiety were group mean centered. All possible two-way interactions between the three variables were also entered into the model, as was a three-way interaction between dyad type, child's math anxiety, and parent's math anxiety. Significant interactions were graphed depicting the continuous variables (child and parent math anxiety) at one standard deviation above, at the mean, and one standard deviation below the mean (Aiken and West, 1991). Results for non-significant analyses are reported in the Supplementary Materials.

Results

Descriptive statistics for all study variables are provided in **Table 2** and the correlation matrix is displayed in **Table 3**. None of the variables were skewed or kurtotic to the extent that transformations were required.

Math Self-efficacy

The model predicting child's math self-efficacy indicated main effects of grade level, dyad type, and child's math anxiety, as well as the predicted three-way interaction between dyad type, child's math anxiety, and parent's math anxiety [$F_{(3, 577.13)} = 3.311$, $p = 0.020$; see **Table 4**]. The main effect of grade level indicated sixth grade students had higher math self-efficacy than seventh or eighth grade students ($\beta = 0.291$, $p = 0.051$); however, this effect was marginal and not of theoretical interest. The main effect of dyad type showed marginally lower math self-efficacy in the Mother-Daughter dyad compared to the other dyads ($\beta = -0.312$, $p = 0.062$). The main effect of child's math anxiety indicated a negative relationship such that greater math anxiety is associated with lower math self-efficacy ($\beta = -0.472$, $p = 0.003$), supporting Hypothesis 1a. However, both these main effects are subsumed in the three-way interaction. The three-way interaction model showed a significant relationship only for the Mother-Daughter dyad, supporting hypothesis 3a ($\beta = 0.379$, $p = 0.037$; see **Figure 1**). Daughters with lower math anxiety had higher math self-efficacy than daughters with higher math anxiety, and this relationship was stronger at lower levels of mother's anxiety ($b = -0.512$, $p = 0.001$), supporting Hypothesis 2 (Moderate mother anxiety: $b = -0.380$, $p = 0.001$; Higher mother anxiety: $b = -0.248$, $p = 0.006$). However, daughters with higher math anxiety had lower math self-efficacy when mothers had lower math anxiety, contrary to Hypothesis 2. There were no three-way interactions for other Parent-Child dyads (see Supplementary Results).

TABLE 2 | Descriptive statistics of study variables.

	M	*SD*	Range	Skew	Kurtosis
Child math anxiety	2.932	1.039	1–6	0.037	−0.233
Parent math anxiety	3.124	0.929	1–6	−0.048	0.070
Math self-efficacy	4.523	1.107	1–6	−0.752	0.077
Math GPA	2.267	1.204	0–4.30	−0.213	−0.824
Math behavioral intentions	4.471	0.801	1.33–6	−0.350	0.387
Math attitudes	4.384	0.973	1–6	−0.324	−0.076
Math devaluing	2.032	0.816	1–5.60	0.742	0.572

For Child and Parent Math Anxiety, Math Behavioral Intentions, Math Attitudes, and Math Devaluing, 1 = Very Strongly Disagree and 6 = Very Strongly Agree. For Math Self-Efficacy, 1 = Not at all Confident and 6 = Very Confident.

Math Class GPA

The model predicting child's math class GPA indicated main effects of class type and child's math anxiety, a two-way interaction between parent and child math anxiety, as well as the predicted three-way interaction between dyad type, child's math anxiety, and parent's math anxiety [$F_{(3, 544.56)} = 3.940$, $p = 0.048$; see **Table 4**]. The main effect of class type indicated honors math students had higher math GPAs than standard math students ($\beta = 0.415$, $p = 0.001$). The main effect of child's math anxiety indicated a negative relationship such that greater math anxiety is associated with lower math GPAs ($\beta = -0.582$, $p = 0.001$), supporting Hypothesis 1b. The two-way interaction showed a negative relationship between the interaction of parent and child math anxiety and child's math GPA. When parents' math anxiety was lower, children with lower math anxiety had higher GPAs than children with higher anxiety ($b = -0.442$, $p = 0.001$). The same relationship held for parents with moderate ($b = -0.422$, $p = 0.001$) and higher ($b = -0.402$, $p = 0.001$) math anxiety, though the slopes are slightly lower as parent anxiety increases. The three-way interaction model showed a significant relationship only for the Father-Son dyad, supporting Hypothesis 3 ($\beta = -0.457$, $p = 0.026$; see **Figure 2**). When sons had lower math anxiety, their GPAs were higher compared to sons with higher math anxiety. Interestingly this relationship was strongest when fathers' had higher math anxiety, contrary to Hypothesis 2 (GPA around 3.5; $b = -1.01$, $p = 0.005$). There was a similar pattern when father's math anxiety was moderate (GPA around 3.2; $b = -0.629$, $p = 0.008$). The relationship was not significant when father's anxiety was lower. There were no three-way interactions for other Parent-Child dyads (see Supplementary Results).

Math Behavioral Intentions

The model predicting child's math behavioral intentions indicated main effects of class type and child's math anxiety, and a two-way interaction between dyad type and child's math anxiety, [$F_{(3, 574.65)} = 5.370$, $p = 0.021$; see **Table 5**]. The predicted three-way interaction was not significant. The main effect of class type indicated honors math students had lower math behavioral intentions than standard math students ($\beta = -0.158$, $p = 0.049$). The main effect of child's math anxiety indicated a negative relationship such that greater math anxiety is associated with lower math behavioral intentions ($\beta = -0.319$, $p = 0.008$), supporting Hypothesis 1c. The two-way interaction model showed a marginally significant relationship only for the Mother-Daughter dyad that indicated the lower daughters' math anxiety, the higher their math behavioral intentions particularly if their mothers had lower math anxiety ($\beta = 0.251$, $p = 0.054$, see **Figure 3**), providing some support for Hypotheses 2 and 3a. However, when daughters had higher math anxiety, their math behavioral intentions were lower, particularly when mothers' math anxiety was low, contrary to Hypothesis 2. There

TABLE 3 | Correlations among continuous variables.

	1	2	3	4	5	6	7
1. Child math anxiety	–						
2. Parent math anxiety	0.500***	–					
3. Math self-efficacy	−0.415***	−0.250***	–				
4. Math GPA	−0.371***	−0.210***	0.526***	–			
5. Math intentions	−0.200***	−0.050	0.416***	0.141***	–		
6. Math attitudes	−0.409***	−0.203***	0.441***	0.241***	0.483***	–	
7. Math devaluing	0.196***	0.099*	−0.379***	−0.134***	−0.598***	−0.486***	–

*$p < 0.05$, ***$p < 0.001$.

TABLE 4 | Three-way interaction predicting math self-efficacy and math GPA.

	Math self-efficacy			Math GPA		
	B	*SE*	*P*	*B*	*SE*	*P*
Intercept	4.751	0.185	0.001	2.126	0.282	0.001
Class type	−0.167	0.099	0.093	0.415	0.112	0.001
Grade level	−0.167	0.078	0.041	−0.201	0.145	0.178
Dyad type	0.106	0.048	0.029	−0.007	0.050	0.883
Child math anxiety	−0.472	0.156	0.003	0.582	0.160	0.001
Parent math anxiety	−0.300	0.165	0.069	−0.165	0.183	0.367
Parent × Child Math anxiety	−0.233	0.171	0.175	−0.395	0.196	0.044
Dyad type × Child math anxiety	−0.056	0.050	0.262	−0.074	0.052	0.155
Dyad type × Parent math anxiety	−0.076	0.054	0.162	−0.003	0.058	0.960
Three-way interaction	−0.140	0.049	0.005	−0.108	0.054	0.048

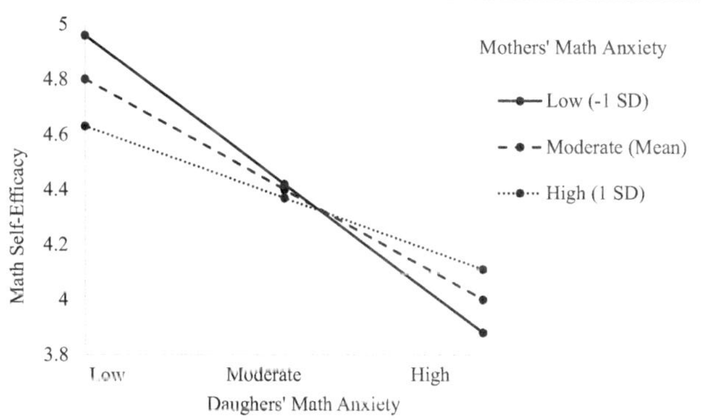

FIGURE 1 | Three-way interaction predicting math self-efficacy from Mother's and Daughter's math anxiety.

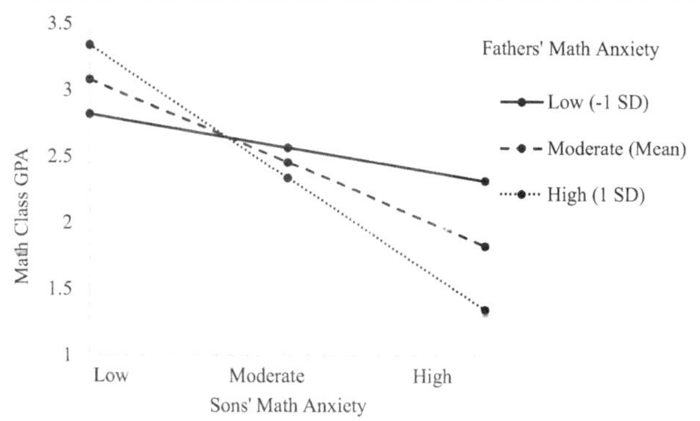

FIGURE 2 | Three-way interaction predicting math GPA from Father's and Son's math anxiety.

were no two-way interactions for other Parent-Child dyads (see Supplementary Results).

Math Attitudes

The model predicting child's math attitudes indicated main effects of grade level, dyad type, and child's math anxiety (see **Table 5**). There was a two-way interaction between parent and child math anxiety, as well as a three-way interaction between dyad type, child's math anxiety, and parent's math anxiety, [$F_{(3,\ 572.83)} = 4.580$, $p = 0.004$; see **Table 5**]. The main effect of grade level indicated math attitudes become more negative as children progress through middle school ($\beta = -0.259$, $p = 0.002$; 6th grade $M = 4.670$, $SD = 0.430$; 7th grade $M = 4.460$, $SD = 0.429$; 8th grade $M = 4.090$, $SD = 0.462$). The main effect of dyad type indicated significant differences between dyads such that son's in Father-Son dyads had significantly more positive math attitudes ($M = 4.690$, $SD = 0.530$) than sons and daughters in all other dyad types ($Ms = 4.240 - 4.470$, $SDs = 0.427$–0.510).

TABLE 5 | Interactions predicting math behavioral intentions and math attitudes.

	Math behavioral intentions			Math attitudes		
	B	*SE*	*P*	*B*	*SE*	*P*
Intercept	4.484	0.164	0.001	4.58	0.177	0.001
Class type	−0.158	0.080	0.049	−0.059	0.089	0.509
Grade level	−0.127	0.072	0.091	−0.259	0.072	0.002
Dyad type	0.061	0.037	0.097	0.195	0.042	0.001
Child math anxiety	−0.319	0.119	0.008	−0.467	0.134	0.001
Parent math anxiety	0.121	0.126	0.338	0.170	0.141	0.228
Parent × Child math anxiety	−0.021	0.131	0.870	−0.355	0.147	0.016
Dyad type × Child math anxiety	−0.088	0.038	0.021	−0.033	0.043	0.435
Dyad type × Parent math anxiety	0.032	0.042	0.438	0.054	0.047	0.247
Three-way interaction	−0.040	0.038	0.287	−0.135	0.043	0.002

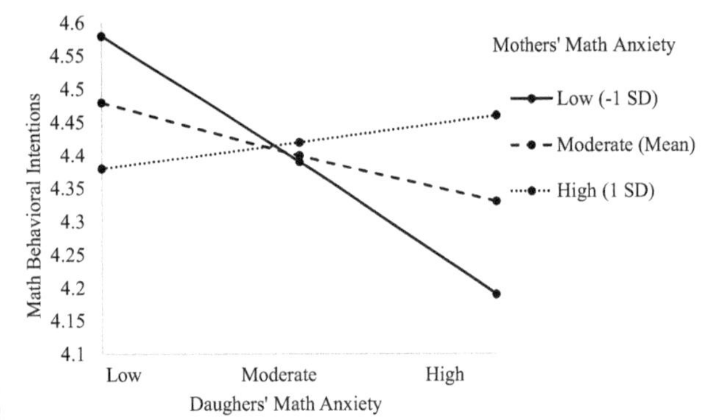

FIGURE 3 | Two-way interaction predicting math behavioral intentions from Mother's and Daughter's math anxiety.

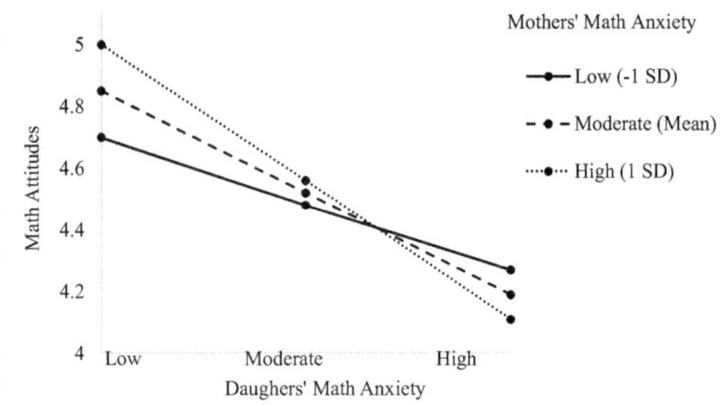

FIGURE 4 | Three-way interaction predicting math attitudes from Mothers' and Daughters' math anxiety.

This main effect is further explained by the three-way interaction and is described in more detail next. The main effect of child's math anxiety indicated a negative relationship such that greater math anxiety is associated with more negative math attitudes ($\beta = -0.467$, $p = 0.001$), consistent with Hypothesis 1d. The two-way interaction showed a negative relationship between the interaction of parent and child math anxiety and child's math attitudes ($\beta = -0.355$, $p = 0.016$). When children had lower math anxiety, their math attitudes were positive regardless of parent's math anxiety. However, when children's math anxiety was moderate to high, the higher parent's math anxiety, the lower children's math attitudes, supporting Hypothesis 2. This two-way interaction is subsumed by the three three-way interaction and is described in more detail next. The three-way interactions were significant for Mother-Daughter ($\beta = 0.453, p = 0.004$), Mother-Son ($\beta = -0.231$, $p = 0.005$), and the Father-Son dyad ($\beta = -0.453$, $p = 0.004$; see **Figures 4–6**). For the Mother-Daughter dyad, daughters with lower math anxiety had more positive math attitudes than daughters with higher math anxiety, and this relationship was strongest when mothers had higher anxiety ($b = -0.414$, $p = 0.001$) contrary to hypothesis 2, followed by moderate ($b = -0.339$, $p = 0.001$), followed by lower anxiety ($b = -0.264$, $p = 0.003$). For the Mother-Son dyad, sons with lower math anxiety had more positive math attitudes than sons with higher math anxiety, and this relationship was strongest when mothers had high anxiety ($b = -0.430$, $p = 0.001$) contrary to Hypothesis 2, followed by moderate ($b = -0.321$, $p = 0.001$), followed by low anxiety ($b = -0.212$, $p = 0.030$). For the Father-Son dyad, sons with lower math anxiety had more positive math attitudes than sons with higher math anxiety, and this relationship was strongest when fathers had high anxiety ($b = -0.796$, $p = 0.005$), contrary to Hypothesis 2, followed by moderate ($b = -0.494$, $p = 0.007$). This relationship was not significant when fathers had lower anxiety ($b = -0.193$, $p = 0.286$). There were no three-way interactions for other Parent-Child dyads (see Supplementary Results).

Math Devaluing

The model predicting child's math devaluing indicated main effects of grade level, dyad type, and child's math anxiety (see **Table 6**). There was a marginal three-way interaction between dyad type, child's math anxiety, and parent's math anxiety, [$F_{(3,\ 576.30)} = 2.330$; $p = 0.074$, see **Table 6**]. The main effect of grade level indicated math devaluing increases as children progress through middle school ($\beta = 0.120$, $p = 0.040$; 6th

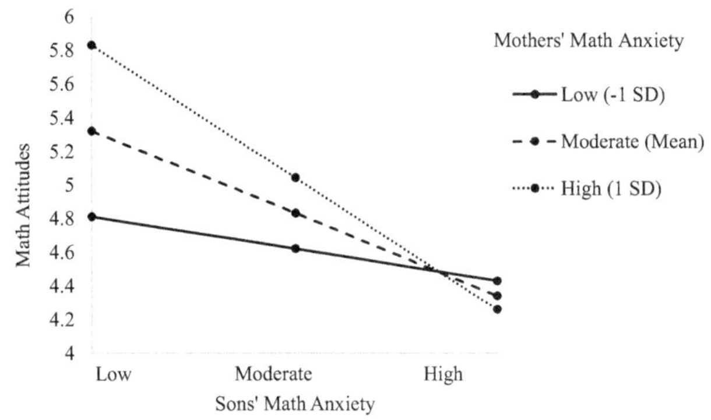

FIGURE 5 | Three-way interaction predicting math attitudes from Mothers' and Sons' math anxiety.

TABLE 6 | Three-way interaction predicting math devaluing.

	Math devaluing		
	B	***SE***	***p***
Intercept	1.846	0.146	0.001
Class type	0.003	0.079	0.968
Grade level	0.120	0.054	0.040
Dyad type	−0.099	0.039	0.011
Child math anxiety	0.253	0.125	0.043
Parent math anxiety	0.012	0.132	0.930
Parent × Child math anxiety	0.144	0.137	0.296
Dyad type × Child math anxiety	0.059	0.040	0.141
Dyad type × Parent math anxiety	−0.010	0.044	0.816
Three-way interaction	0.050	0.040	0.074

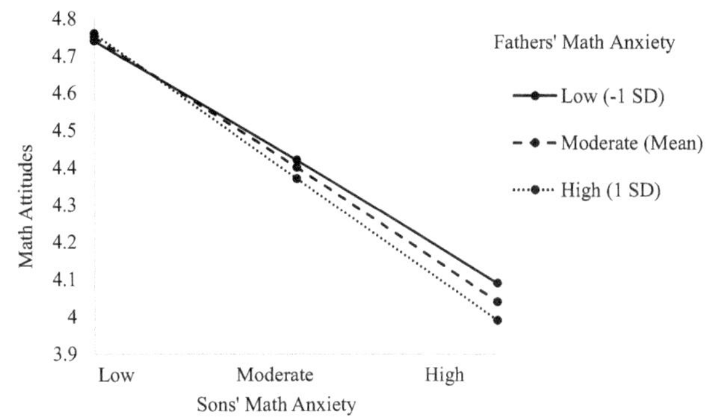

FIGURE 6 | Three-way interaction predicting math attitudes from Fathers' and Sons' math anxiety.

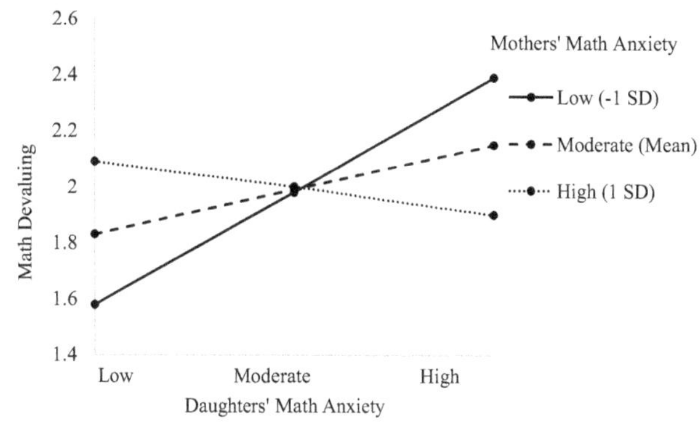

FIGURE 7 | Three-way interaction predicting math devaluing from Mothers' and Daughters' math anxiety.

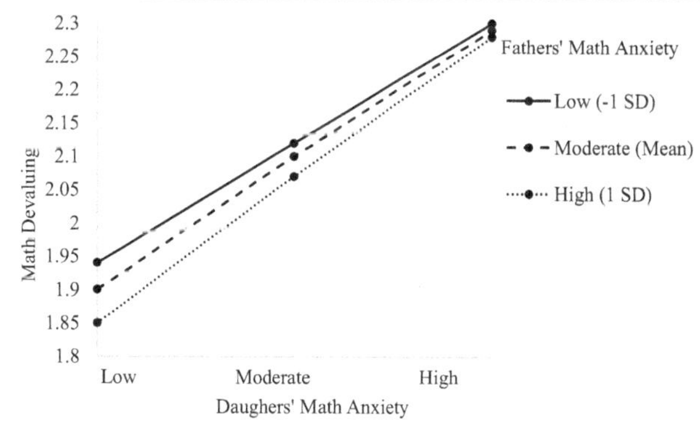

FIGURE 8 | Three-way interaction predicting math devaluing from Fathers' and Daughters' math anxiety.

grade $M = 1.880$, $SD = 0.224$; 7th grade $M = 2.040$, $SD = 0.220$; 8th grade $M = 2.150$, $SD = 0.206$). The main effect of dyad type ($\beta = -0.099$, $p = 0.011$) indicated significant differences between dyads such that children in mother dyads had significantly more math devaluing (M-D: $M = 2.070$, $SD = 0.184$; M-S: $M = 2.110$, $SD = 0.210$), consistent with Hypothesis 3b, than children in father dyads (F-D: $M = 1.880$, $SD = 0.314$; F-S: $M = 1.830$, $SD = 0.284$). This main effect is further explained next by the marginal three-way interaction. The main effect of child's math anxiety indicated a positive relationship such that greater math anxiety is associated with more math devaluing ($\beta = 0.253$, $p = 0.043$), supporting Hypothesis 1e. The marginal three-way interaction showed that in the Mother-Daughter dyad, daughters with lower anxiety with mothers also lower in anxiety had less math devaluing than daughters with higher anxiety ($b = 0.172$, $p = 0.015$), providing some support for Hypothesis 2. However, daughters with higher math anxiety had greater math devaluing, particularly when mothers had lower math anxiety, contrary to Hypothesis 2. The relationship between daughters' anxiety and mothers' with moderate or high anxiety was not significant. The greater daughters' math anxiety, the more they devalued math; see **Figures 7**, **8**). For the Father-Daughter dyad, fathers with lower math anxiety with daughters also low in anxiety had less math devaluing than daughters higher in anxiety ($b = 0.429$, $p = 0.008$), supporting Hypothesis 2b. The relationship between daughters' anxiety and fathers with moderate or high anxiety was not significant. The greater daughters' math anxiety, the more they devalued math. There were no three-way interactions for other Parent-Child dyads (see Supplementary Results).

A summary of all the Study 1 three-way interaction results are summarized in **Tables 7, 8**.

Discussion

The results generally support the prediction that parents' anxiety plays a role in children's math anxiety and the variables interact to predict several math education outcomes including math self-efficacy, math GPA, math behavioral intentions, math attitudes, and math devaluing. First, consistent with existing literature, there were five main effects (Hypotheses 1a–e) of child's math anxiety on all outcomes such that greater math anxiety was associated with lower math self-efficacy, lower math GPA, lower math behavioral intentions, more negative math attitudes, and greater math discounting. However, more interesting is the interaction of children's math anxiety with parents' math anxiety within gendered dyads. In support of Hypothesis 3, the same-gender parent-child dyads showed the most significant relationships, and more specifically in line with Hypothesis 3a, the Mother-Daughter dyad dominated the findings. The Mother-Daughter dyads' math anxiety predicted math self-efficacy, math behavioral intentions, math attitudes, and math devaluing, or four of the five hypothesized effects. The general pattern was consistent with the hypothesis that when both mothers' and daughters' math anxiety were low, daughters had more positive math outcomes compared to when mothers' and daughters' math anxiety were both high. For the cases when both mothers' and daughters' math anxiety were high, daughters had more negative math outcomes compared to when mothers' and daughters' math anxiety were both low for math attitudes. However, the simple effects for math self-efficacy, behavioral intentions, and math devaluing were contrary to Hypothesis 2 when daughters' math anxiety was high. In these cases, math outcomes were worst when mothers has lower math anxiety rather than higher math anxiety. A possible explanation is that mothers' involvement in

TABLE 7 | Patterns of simple effects in significant three-way interactions for math self-efficacy and math GPA.

	Math self-efficacy				Math GPA			
Dyad type		**H Par**	**M Par**	**L Par**				
Mother-Daughter	**H Chld**	Lower	Lower	*Lower	ns			
	L Chld	Higher	Higher	*Higher				
Mother-Son	ns				ns			
Father-Daughter	ns				ns			
Father-Son	ns					**H Par**	**M Par**	**L Par**
					H Chld	*Lower	*Lower	ns
					L Chld	*Higher	*Higher	ns

*H, High; M, Moderate; L, Low; Par, Parent; Chld, Child. Moderate is excluded for the child data because it reflects the mean and is more informative in graphic form. *Reflects the stronger relationship in the interaction.*

TABLE 8 | Patterns of simple effects in significant three-way interactions for math attitudes and math devaluing.

	Math attitudes				Math devaluing			
Dyad type		**H Par**	**M Par**	**L Par**		**H Par**	**M Par**	**L Par**
Mother-Daughter	**H Chld**	Lower*	Lower	Lower	**H Chld**	ns	ns	*Higher
	L Chld	Higher*	Higher	Higher	**L Chld**	ns	ns	*Lower
Mother-Son		**H Par**	**M Par**	**L Par**	ns			
	H Chld	Lower*	Lower	Lower				
	L Chld	Higher*	Higher	Higher				
Father-Daughter	ns					**H Par**	**M Par**	**L Par**
					H Chld	ns	ns	*Higher
					L Chld	ns	ns	*Lower
Father-Son		**H Par**	**M Par**	**L Par**	ns			
	H Chld	Lower*	Lower	Lower				
	L Chld	Higher*	Higher	Higher				

*H, High; M, Moderate; L, Low; Par, Parent; Chld, Child. Moderate is excluded for the child data because it reflects the mean and is more informative in graphic form. *Reflects the stronger relationship in the interaction.*

daughters' math education, e.g., helping with homework, may moderate these unexpected findings (see Maloney et al., 2015). It seems that daughters' level of math anxiety was a better predictor of math self-efficacy, behavioral intentions, and math devaluing such that if daughters' math anxiety was high, math outcomes were negative even when mothers' math anxiety was lower. Perhaps the sample is mixed with mothers who are more active in helping their daughters with homework and others who are less active. This moderating variable may help explain the mixed results and should be measured in future studies that examine effects of gendered parent-child dyads.

The other same-gender parent-child dyad Father-Son showed two significant effects of the five possible. Interestingly, the Father-Son dyad was the only one to show a significant relationship to GPA. When both fathers and sons had lower math anxiety, math GPA was higher. Fortunately, even when fathers' math anxiety was higher, if sons had lower math anxiety, GPA was higher. Only when both fathers and sons had higher math anxiety was GPA lower.

Consistent with predictions there not many effects for mixed-gender parent-child dyads. For the Father-Daughter dyad, fathers with lower math anxiety with daughters also low in anxiety had less math devaluing than daughters higher in anxiety. For the Mother-Son dyad, sons with lower math anxiety had more positive math attitudes than sons with higher math anxiety, and this relationship was strongest when mothers had high anxiety. This is contrary to hypotheses and suggests that sons are showing reactance against mothers' higher math anxiety. Alternatively, this might suggest that transmission of parents' anxiety might not occur to the same extent in mixed-gender dyads. Also, mothers' involvement in sons' math education (e.g., math homework) may be a moderator. Further research is needed to investigate these gendered patterns.

In sum, this study contributes to the existing literature by helping to address several gaps. First, there is only one known published study that found effects of parents' math anxiety on children's math education outcomes, particularly their math performance. Second, this study examined these relationships using a gendered lens and found support for the gender stereotype literature that the transmission of math anxiety seems most prevalent among same gender parent-child dyads, particular the Mother-Daughter dyad.

Since math anxiety is well-established as a correlate of many important math education outcomes, Study 2 sought to examine a second source of math anxiety, math-gender stereotypes. In addition, study 2 examines math anxiety as a potential mediator explaining the relationship between endorsement of math-gender stereotypes and math achievement.

STUDY 2

The purpose of study 2 is two-fold: first to address a call for examination of antecedents of math anxiety (Ashcraft and Ridley, 2005; Jameson, 2014; Maloney et al., 2015) and second to address the call for a more mechanistic approach to examine mediators in the math anxiety and achievement domains (Gunderson et al., 2012).

Gender Stereotypes as a Source of Math Anxiety

The Expectancy-Value Theory of achievement motivation describes the role of cultural and social factors that influence children's motivations, task values, expectations for success, and achievement related choices. In regards to mathematics achievement, the cultural milieu includes cultural stereotypes about math and gender roles appropriate in the math domain (Cheryan, 2012). Children are influenced by these cultural factors and also have their own perceptions of society's stereotypes about gender and math.

A great deal of the research using an expectancy-value framework work focuses on the transmission of math-gender stereotypes from parents to children and how stereotypes influence children's achievement outcomes. A logical extension of this work is that children's own endorsement of math-gender related stereotypes will affect their achievement outcomes. Indeed, research on stereotype threat shows that women who endorse stereotypes about women's inferiority in math are more susceptible to experiencing stereotype threat and subsequently show math performance decrements (Schmader et al., 2004). Anxiety is one mechanism through which stereotype threat negatively affects performance (Schmader et al., 2008). Stereotype threat is the fear of confirming a negative stereotype about one's social group (e.g., gender), and is particularly relevant in evaluative contexts (Steele and Aronson, 1995). Like math anxiety, stereotype threat also disrupts working memory capacity and depletes necessary cognitive resources to tackle complex problems (Schmader et al., 2008).

Taken together, the work on the expectancy-value model showing that parents' and teachers' gender stereotypes influence girls' math gender stereotypes, and work in stereotype threat showing stereotypes create anxiety that negatively impacts performance, the prediction of math-related gender stereotypes as a source of math anxiety seems logical.

Work by Beilock et al. (2010) found that math-anxious female teachers reinforced math-gender stereotypes and girls' endorsement of math-gender stereotypes mediated the effect of teacher anxiety on their math performance. Thus, teachers' anxiety affects gender math stereotypes not female students' anxiety, suggesting it works indirectly through stereotypes.

This finding provides further evidence that math-gender stereotypes can create math anxiety in girls.

Math Anxiety as a Mechanism

Existing research on the negative effects of math anxiety suggests that it can function as a mechanism influencing math achievement. Studies have found that math anxiety lowers math performance regardless of actual math ability (Hembree, 1990; Maloney and Beilock, 2012; Park et al., 2014). Research by Chipman et al. (1992) found that math anxiety was a mediator in students' career choice. As Gunderson et al. (2012) stated, children's stereotypes, self-perceptions, math anxieties, and math achievement are all interconnected, therefore it is critical to know which component of children's gendered math attitudes is affected by specific behaviors from parents or teachers. One way to address this question is to test math-gender stereotypes as a predictor of math anxiety.

Hypotheses

In Study 2 we argue that in addition to parents, math-related gender stereotypes are a source of math anxiety. We base this argument on research showing that math-gender stereotypes held by parents, teachers, and important others are linked to reports of higher math anxiety by females more so than males (Hembree, 1990). Further, students' endorsement of math-gender stereotypes mediated the effect of teacher anxiety on their math performance (Beilock et al., 2010). Additionally, we predict that math anxiety is a mechanism through which math-gender stereotypes negatively influence math outcomes for *both* girls and boys. Specifically we predict that (1) endorsement of math-gender stereotypes will predict math anxiety such that greater endorsement is associated with greater anxiety. Although we expect the variables to be correlated, and therefore bidirectional, we expect that (2) stereotypes are a stronger predictor of anxiety than vice versa. Further we predict that endorsement of math-gender stereotypes will be negatively related to (3a) math self-efficacy, (3b) math GPA, (3c) math behavioral intentions, (3d) math attitudes, (3e) and positively related to math devaluing. Finally, we predict that (4) math anxiety will fully mediate the relationship between math-gender stereotype endorsement and math outcomes. Although much of the focus on math-gender stereotypes has been on girls and women, (5) we predict these same relationships for boys, although the effects will be larger for girls. Boys who endorse math-gender stereotypes believe that boys and men *are* (descriptive stereotype) and *should be* (injunctive stereotype) superior to women in math. However, societal stereotypes of high math achievement reflects majority group members (Stephens et al., 2012), specifically males, Caucasians but also Asian Americans (Shih et al., 1999), and middle to upper middle class educated males. Not all males "benefit" from gender stereotypes about men's superiority math as we see in research on stereotype lift (Walton and Cohen, 2003). In our sample of racially diverse, low-income students, endorsing such stereotypes is likely to be threatening and remind male participants that they may not be high achieving in the math domain (Croizet and Claire, 1998).

Method

Participants

The sample included 1342 students ($n = 713$, 53% female; $n = 629$, 47% male) from the same project described in Study 1; however, the sample included all students who completed a questionnaire in the classroom, regardless of whether their parent participated in the study. Students came from the same 8 schools in southern California and were enrolled in 6th grade ($n = 361$), 7th grade ($n = 459$), or 8th grade ($n = 522$) honors ($n = 768$), or standard ($n = 574$) math classes with one of 24 teachers. Students self-reported their race/ethnicity and the largest group represented was Latino/a or Hispanic ($n = 910$, 68%) followed by 131 (10%) multiracial, 111 (8%) Asian/Pacific Islander, and less than 5% each of remaining groups including Native American, White/Caucasian, and Other. Nearly 5% of students ($n = 63$) did not report a race or ethnicity. Students' ages ranged from 11 to 14 reflecting ages in the 6th through 8th grades.

Materials

Participants completed a 9-item measure of endorsement of math-related gender stereotypes on a scale from 1 (*Very Strongly Disagree*) to 6 (*Very Strongly Agree*). Sample items included "Girls are worse at math than boys," "Girls are better at English, art, and history than math," "Girls can do just as well as boys in math" (reverse-scored) and "Girls who like studying math are nerds." The items had acceptable internal consistency ($\alpha = 0.803$) and were reverse scored and averaged so that higher values represented more endorsement of math-related gender stereotypes.

Participants' math anxiety was assessed with the same measure from study 1. The items had acceptable internal consistency ($\alpha = 0.727$) for this sample and were averaged so that higher values represented greater anxiety.

Participants' math self-efficacy was measured by the same 5-item measure reported in Study 1. The scale was internally consistent for this sample ($\alpha = 0.881$) and items were averaged so that higher values represented greater math self-efficacy.

Participants' math education behavioral intentions were measured by the 6 items used in study 1. The items were reliable for this sample ($\alpha = 0.753$) and items were averaged so that higher values represented greater math intentions.

Math attitudes were measure by the 5-item scale from study 1. The measure was reliable ($\alpha = 0.760$) and averaged so that higher values indicated more positive attitudes.

Finally, participants' math devaluing was assessed by the 5 items used in study 1. The scale was internally consistent for this sample ($\alpha = 0.793$) and items were averaged so that higher values represented greater math devaluing.

Procedure

The procedure was identical to Study 1. Participants completed the questionnaire during the assigned class time, which took 20–30 min, and the questionnaire was offered in both English and Spanish. The researchers collected the questionnaires and obtained the math class GPA roster from the teachers.

Analysis Strategy

Like Study 1, the data came from an inherently hierarchical structure of children (Level 1) nested within classrooms with different teachers (Level 2). Multilevel modeling (MLM; Raudenbush and Bryk, 2002) was used to analyze the nested data, in this case in which the focal variables of interest are all situated on one level. Two-level random intercept models were computed using the restricted maximum likelihood estimation, which adjusts for unequal sample sizes and is ideal for smaller datasets, with variance components estimator in SPSS Mixed Models Version 21 (IBM Corp., 2012). Mediation analyses were conducted following guidelines by Baron and Kenny (1986) within a MLM framework to account for the nested data. Path A tested the relationship between the predictor variable (gender stereotypes) and the mediator (math anxiety), path B tested the relationship between the mediator and the outcome variable (math self-efficacy, math GPA, math intentions, math attitudes, and math devaluing), and path C tested the relationship between the predictor variable and the outcome variable. To test the significance of C' we computed the path from the predictor to the outcome variable while controlling for the mediator. In cases of significant mediation, reverse mediation will be tested and a Sobel test will be used to determine significant differences in the size of beta values. To examine gender differences and similarities in the mediation models, models will be run separately by gender. Consistent with Study 1, in all models we controlled for grade level and math class type.

Results

For descriptive purposes, the means, standard deviations, and correlations for all study variables are provided in **Table 9**. All correlations are significant, except for one, and in the predicted direction, supporting Hypotheses 1 and 3a–e. There is a positive relationship between endorsement of math-gender stereotypes and math anxiety for both girls and boys. There is a negative relationship between math-gender stereotypes and math self-efficacy, math intentions, and math attitudes for both girls and boys and a negative relationship between math-gender stereotypes and math GPA for girls only. There is a marginal trend for boys, but it did not reach significance at the 0.05 level for a two-tailed test ($p = 0.076$). Math-gender stereotypes were positively correlated with math devaluing for both girls and boys. Math anxiety was negatively correlated with math self-efficacy, math GPA, math intentions, and math attitudes, and positively correlated with math devaluing for both girls and boys. Math self-efficacy was positively related to math GPA, math intentions, and math attitudes, and negatively related to math devaluing for both girls and boys. Math GPA was positively related to math intentions and attitudes, and negatively related to math devaluing for both girls and boys. Math intentions and math attitudes were positively related and both were negatively related to math devaluing for both gender groups.

Mediational Models for Girls

Math self-efficacy

The mediational models supported Hypothesis 4 that math anxiety mediates the effect of math-gender stereotypes on math self-efficacy, and the size of these relationship did not differ by gender, counter to Hypothesis 5. In support of the mediation models for girls, the more girls endorsed math-gender stereotypes, the greater their math anxiety ($\beta = 0.257, p = 0.001$; Path A, see **Table 10A**). Math anxiety was negatively related to math self-efficacy such that greater math anxiety predicted lower math self-efficacy ($\beta = -0.382$, $p = 0.001$; Path B, see **Table 10B**). The direct effect of math-gender stereotypes on math self-efficacy was negative, such that greater endorsement of stereotypes predicted lower math self-efficacy ($\beta = -0.125$, $p = 0.024$; Path C, see **Table 10B**). However, when math anxiety was entered into the model the effect of math-gender stereotypes on math self-efficacy was no longer significant (Path C', see **Table 10B**). Thus, math anxiety is a mediator of the relationship between math-gender stereotypes and math self-efficacy, supporting Hypothesis 4. Since the data are correlational and cross-sectional, a reverse mediation analysis was computed to rule out math-gender stereotypes as a mediator, particularly because the variables are correlated, $r_{(696)} = 0.191$, $p = 0.001$. The reverse mediation model showed the same pattern of relationships for math anxiety predicting gender stereotypes, although it was weaker ($\beta = 0.133$, $p = 0.001$). A sobel test confirmed that the beta for math-gender stereotypes predicting anxiety ($\beta = 0.257$) was significantly greater than the beta for anxiety predicting stereotypes ($\beta = 0.133$), $z = 2.120$, $p = 0.034$, supporting Hypothesis 2. Math-gender stereotypes also predicted self-efficacy ($\beta = -0.123$, $p = 0.026$), which was also weaker than the standard mediational model, $z = 3.910$, $p = 0.001$. However, when math-gender stereotypes was entered as the mediator, the direct relationship between math anxiety and self-efficacy did not change (C path $\beta = -0.382$, $p = 0.001$; C' path $\beta = -0.381$, $p = 0.001$), indicating math-gender stereotypes does not mediate the relationship between math anxiety and math self-efficacy, supporting Hypothesis 4.

Math GPA

The mediational models support Hypothesis 4 that math anxiety mediates the effect of math gender stereotypes on math GPA, and that the size of these relationship differs by gender, supporting Hypothesis 5. In support of the mediation models for girls, math anxiety was negatively related to math GPA such that greater math anxiety predicted lower math GPA ($\beta = -0.325, p = 0.001$; Path B, see **Table 10B**). The direct effect of gender stereotypes on math GPA was negative, such that greater endorsement of math-gender stereotypes predicted lower math GPA ($\beta = -0.137$, $p = 0.012$; Path C, see **Table 10B**). However, when math anxiety was entered into the model the effect of math-gender stereotypes on math GPA was no longer significant. Thus, math anxiety is a mediator for the relationship between math-gender stereotypes and math GPA. The same reverse mediation analysis was conducted and indicated the direct effect of anxiety on math GPA did not significantly change when math-gender stereotypes was added to the model, thus math anxiety is the mediator rather than math-gender stereotypes.

Math intentions

The mediational models testing math anxiety as a mediator of the effect of math-gender stereotypes on math intentions was not significant, contrary to Hypothesis 4; however the pattern of relationships were in the predicted directions (see **Table 11A**). For girls, math anxiety was negatively related to math intentions such that greater math anxiety predicted lower math intentions ($\beta = -0.108$, $p = 0.001$; Path B, see **Table 11B**). The direct effect of math-gender stereotypes on math intentions was negative, such that greater endorsement of stereotypes predicted lower math intentions ($\beta = -0.205$, $p = 0.012$; Path C, see **Table 11B**). However, when math anxiety was entered into the model the effect of math-gender stereotypes on math intentions was weaker ($\beta = -0.187$, $p = 0.001$; Path C', see **Table 11B**), but the difference was not statistically significant, $z = 0.322$, $p > 0.05$. This indicates that math anxiety does not mediate the relationship between math-gender stereotypes and math intentions.

TABLE 9 | Descriptive statistics and correlation matrix by gender for all variables.

	M	*SD*	1	2	3	4	5	6	7
1. Gender stereotypes	2.318	0.756	–	0.191***	−0.086*	−0.116**	−0.193***	−0.252***	0.287***
	2.567	0.861							
2. Math anxiety	3.051	1.068	0.180***	–	−0.365***	−0.385***	−0.154***	−0.367***	0.133***
	2.800	1.048							
3. Math self-efficacy	4.469	1.107	−0.106**	−0.351***	–	0.520***	0.369***	0.392***	−0.350***
	4.436	1.163							
4. Math GPA	2.369	1.156	−0.074^	−0.372***	0.550***	–	0.142***	0.231***	−0.183***
	2.088	1.228							
5. Math. intentions	4.511	0.808	−0.088*	−0.167***	0.440***	0.169***	–	0.504***	−0.584***
	4.381	0.829							
6. Matk attitudes	4.356	0.950	−0.156***	−0.336***	0.475***	0.305***	0.591***	–	−0.496***
	4.419	1.00							
7. Math devaluing	2.025	0.843	0.176***	0.182***	−0.383***	−0.157***	−0.626***	−0.594***	–
	2.089	0.891							

*Girls' values, are above the diagonal in bold and boys' values are below the diagonal in standard typeface.^p = 0.076, *p < 0.05, **p < 0.01, ***p < 0.001.*

TABLE 10 | Mediation model statistics for girls' math self-efficacy arid math GPA.

A		**Outcome: Math anxiety (M)**		
Antecedent	**Identifier**	**Coeff**	***SE***	***P***
Intercept	i_1	2.650	0.180	0.001
Grade level	Control	0.184	0.080	0.029
Class type	Control	−0.059	0.096	0.542
Math Anxiety (M)	–	–	–	–
Gender Stereotypes (X)	A	0.257	0.052	0.001
Model Summary	$F_{(1,\ 692)} = 24.289, p = 0.001$			

B		**Outcome: Math Self-Efficacy (Y)**				**Outcome: Math GPA (Y)**		
Antecedent	**Identifier**	**Coeff**	***SE***	***P***	**Identifier**	**Coeff**	***SE***	***P***
Intercept	i_2	5.734	0.199	0.001	i_2	3.400	0.278	0.001
Grade level	Control	−0.032	0.073	0.680	Control	−0.102	0.145	0.488
Class type	Control	−0.127	0.095	0.182	Control	0.320	0.097	0.001
Math Anxiety (M)	b	−0.382	0.037	0.001	b	−0.325	0.096	0.001
Gender Stereotypes (X)	c	−0.125	0.055	0.024	c	−0.137	0.055	0.012
	c′	−0.034	0.053	0.524	c′	−0.043	0.052	0.406
Model summary	$F_{(1,\ 690)} = 101.69, p = 0.001$				$F_{(1,\ 639)} = 106.60, p = 0.001$			

Math attitudes

The mediational models testing math anxiety as a mediator of the effect of math-gender stereotypes on math attitudes was not significant, contrary to Hypothesis 4; however, the pattern of relationships were in the predicted directions. For girls, math anxiety was negatively related to math attitudes such that greater math anxiety predicted lower math attitudes ($\beta = -0.309$, $p = 0.001$; Path B, see **Table 11B**). The direct effect of math-gender stereotypes on math attitudes was negative, such that greater endorsement of stereotypes predicted lower math attitudes ($\beta = -0.314$, $p = 0.001$; Path C, see **Table 11B**). However, when math anxiety was entered into the model the effect of math-gender stereotypes on math attitudes was weaker ($\beta = -0.248$, $p = 0.001$; Path C', see **Table 11B**), but the difference was not statistically significant, $z = 1.049$, $p > 0.05$. This indicates that math anxiety does not mediate the relationship between math-gender stereotypes and math attitudes.

Math devaluing

The mediational models testing math anxiety as a mediator of the effect of math-gender stereotypes on math devaluing was not significant, contrary to Hypothesis 4; however the pattern

TABLE 11 | Mediation model statistics for girls' math intentions, attitudes, and devaluing.

A	Outcome: Math Anxiety (M)			
Antecedent	Identifier	Coeff	*SE*	*P*
Intercept	i_1	2.650	0.180	0.001
Grade level	Control	0.184	0.080	0.029
Class type	Control	−0.059	0.096	0.542
Math anxiety (M)	–	–	–	–
Gender stereotypes (X)	a	0.257	0.052	0.001
Model summary	$F_{(1,\ 692)} = 24.289, p = 0.001$			

B	Outcome: Math intentions (Y)				Outcome: Math Attitudes (Y)			
Antecedent	**Identifier**	**Coeff**	**SE**	***p***	**Identifier**	**Coeff**	**SE**	***P***
Intercept	i_2	4.760	0.132	0.001	i_2	5.119	0.145	0.001
Grade level	Control	0.164	0.116	0.178	Control	−0.161	0.062	0.015
Class type	Control	−0.035	0.073	0.630	Control	0.021	0.080	0.794
Math anxiety (M)	b	−0.108	0.028	0.001	b	−0.309	0.031	0.001
Gender stereotypes (X)	c	−0.205	0.039	0.001	c	−0.314	0.045	0.001
	c'	−0.187	0.040	0.001	c'	−0.248	0.044	0.001
Model summary	$F_{(1,\ 689)} = 8.857, p = 0.001$				$F_{(1,\ 691)} = 33.651, p = 0.001$			

C	Outcome: Math Devaluing (Y)			
Antecedent	**Identifier**	**Coeff**	***SE***	***p***
Intercept	i_2	0.826	0.377	0.043
Grade level	control	0.131	0.054	0.029
Class type	control	−0.052	0.074	0.478
Math anxiety (M)	b	0.098	0.030	0.001
Gender stereotypes (X)	c	0.322	0.040	0.001
	c′	0.313	0.041	0.001
Model summary	$F_{(1,\ 691)} = 15.967, p = 0.001$			

of relationships were in the predicted directions. For girls, math anxiety was positively related to math devaluing such that greater math anxiety predicted greater math devaluing ($\beta = 0.098$, $p = 0.001$; Path B, see **Table 11C**). The direct effect of math-gender stereotypes on math devaluing was positive, such that greater endorsement of stereotypes predicted greater math devaluing ($\beta = 0.322$, $p = 0.001$; Path C, see **Table 11C**). However, when math anxiety was entered into the model the effect of math-gender stereotypes on math devaluing was weaker ($\beta = 0.313$, $p = 0.001$; Path C', see **Table 11C**), but the difference was not statistically significant, $z = 0.122$, $p > 0.05$. This indicates that math anxiety does not mediate the relationship between math-gender stereotypes and math devaluing.

Mediational Models for Boys

Math self-efficacy

In support of Hypothesis 4, the mediational model for math self-efficacy was significant. In support of the mediation models for boys, the more boys endorsed math-gender stereotypes, the greater their math anxiety ($\beta - 0.214$, $p = 0.001$; Path A, see **Table 12A**). Math anxiety was negatively related to math self-efficacy such that greater math anxiety predicted lower math self-efficacy ($\beta = -0.383$, $p = 0.001$; Path B, see **Table 12B**). The direct effect of math-gender stereotypes on math self-efficacy was negative, such that greater endorsement of stereotypes predicted lower math self-efficacy ($\beta = -0.128$, $p = 0.017$; Path C, see **Table 12B**). However, when math anxiety was entered into the model the effect of math-gender stereotypes on math self-efficacy was no longer significant. Thus, math anxiety is a mediator of the relationship between math-gender stereotypes and math self-efficacy. Reverse mediation was not significant, indicating math-gender stereotypes is not a mediator of the relationship between math anxiety and math self-efficacy.

Math GPA

In partial support of Hypothesis 4, there was an indirect effect of math-gender stereotypes on math GPA; however, the mediational model was not significant due to the marginal trend between

TABLE 12 | Mediation model statistics for boys' math self-efficacy and Math GPA.

A		Outcome: Math anxiety (M)		
Antecedent	**Identifier**	**Coeff**	**SE**	**p**
Intercept	i_1	2.283	0.185	0.001
Grade level	control	−0.010	0.086	0.912
Class type	control	−0.070	0.099	0.477
Math anxiety (M)	–	–	–	–
Gender stereotypes (X)	A	0.214	0.048	0.001
Model summary	$F_{(1, 613)} = 19.861, p = 0.001$			

B		Outcome: Math self-efficacy (Y)				Outcome: Math GPA (Y)		
Antecedent	**Identifier**	**Coeff**	**SE**	**P**	**Identifier**	**Coeff**	**SE**	**p**
Intercept	i_2	5.518	0.222	0.001	i_2	3.05	0.261	0.001
Grade level	Control	−0.184	0.010	0.081	Control	−0.230	0.129	0.089
Class type	Control	−0.118	0.105	0.258	Control	0.244	0.108	0.023
Math anxiety (M)	b	−0.383	0.041	0.001	b	−0.405	0.043	0.001
Gender stereotypes (X)	c	−0.128	0.054	0.017	c	−0.092	0.056	0.101
	c′	−0.051	0.051	0.323	c′	−0.006	0.053	0.910
Model summary	$F_{(1, 612)} = 74.888, p = 0.001$				$F_{(1, 564)} = 80.958, p = 0.001$			

math-gender stereotypes and math GPA for boys. The model paths showed the same pattern, that math-gender stereotypes was positively related to math anxiety, and math anxiety was negatively related to math GPA such that greater math anxiety predicted lower math GPA ($\beta = -0.405$, $p = 0.001$; Path B, see **Table 12B**). The direct effect of math-gender stereotypes on math GPA was negative but marginal ($\beta = -0.092$, $p = 0.101$); however, accounting for math anxiety reduced this effect substantially ($\beta = -0.006$, $p = 0.91$; Path C, see **Table 12B**), indicating an indirect effect of gender stereotypes. A reverse mediation model is not plausible given the lack of a significant direct relationship between math-gender stereotypes and math GPA for boys. Since the mediational model for girls was significant but not for boys, this provides support for Hypothesis 5 that the size of the relationship differs by gender.

Math intentions

Contrary to Hypothesis 4, the mediational model for math intentions was not significant; however the pattern of relationships were in the predicted directions (see **Table 13A**). Math anxiety was negatively related to math intentions such that greater math anxiety predicted lower math intentions ($\beta = -0.148$, $p = 0.001$; Path B, see **Table 13B**). The direct effect of math-gender stereotypes on math intentions was negative, such that greater endorsement of stereotypes predicted lower math intentions ($\beta = -0.096$, $p = 0.017$; Path C, see **Table 13B**). When math anxiety was entered into the model the effect of math-gender stereotypes on math intentions remained significant ($\beta = -0.082$, $p = 0.040$; Path C', see **Table 13B**) and the reduction in the beta value was not significant, $z = 0.0247$, $p > 0.05$. Thus, math anxiety is a not a mediator of the relationship between math-gender stereotypes and math intentions.

Math attitudes

Contrary to Hypothesis 4, the mediational model for math attitudes was not significant; however the pattern of relationships were in the predicted directions. Math anxiety was negatively related to math attitudes such that greater math anxiety predicted lower math attitudes ($\beta = -0.325$, $p = 0.001$; Path B, see **Table 13B**). The direct effect of math-gender stereotypes on math attitudes was negative, such that greater endorsement of stereotypes predicted more negative math attitudes ($\beta = -0.191$, $p = 0.007$; Path C, see **Table 13B**). When math anxiety was entered into the model the effect of math-gender stereotypes on math attitudes remained significant ($\beta = -0.134$, $p = 0.002$; Path C', see **Table 13B**) and the reduction in the beta value was not significant, $z = 0.895$, $p > 0.05$. Thus, math anxiety is a not a mediator of the relationship between math-gender stereotypes and math attitudes.

Math devaluing

Contrary to Hypothesis 4, the mediational model for math devaluing was not significant; however the pattern of relationships were in the predicted directions. Math anxiety was positively related to math devaluing such that greater math anxiety predicted greater math devaluing ($\beta = 0.165$, $p = 0.001$; Path B, see **Table 13C**). The direct effect of math-gender stereotypes on math devaluing was positive, such that greater endorsement of stereotypes predicted greater math devaluing ($\beta = 0.1731$, $p = 0.001$; Path C, see **Table 13C**). When math anxiety was entered into the model the effect of math-gender

TABLE 13 | Mediation model statistics for boys' math intentions, attitudes, and devaluing.

A — Outcome: Math anxiety (M)

Antecedent	Identifier	Coeff	*SE*	*p*
Intercept	i_1	2.283	0.185	0.001
Grade level	Control	−0.010	0.086	0.912
Class type	Control	−0.070	0.099	0.477
Math anxiety (M)	–	–	–	–
Gender stereotypes (X)	a	0.214	0.048	0.001
Model summary	$F_{(1,\ 613)} = 19.861, p = 0.001$			

B

Antecedent	Outcome: Math intentions (Y)				Outcome: Math attitudes (Y)			
	Identifier	**Coeff**	***SE***	***p***	**Identifier**	**Coeff**	***SE***	***p***
Intercept	i_2	5.87	0.499	0.001	i_2	6.73	0.475	0.001
Grade level	Control	−0.131	0.071	0.081	Control	−0.195	0.067	0.011
Class type	Control	−0.176	0.078	0.024	Control	−0.038	0.085	0.658
Math anxiety (M)	b	−0.148	0.031	0.001	b	−0.325	0.036	0.001
Gender stereotypes (X)	c	−0.096	0.040	0.017	c	−0.191	0.046	0.001
	c′	−0.082	0.040	0.040	c′	−0.134	0.044	0.002
Model summary	$F_{(1,\ 607)} = 8.818, p = 0.001$				$F_{(1,\ 612)} = 20.241, p = 0.001$			

C — Outcome: Math devaluing (Y)

Antecedent	**Identifier**	**Coeff**	***SE***	***p***
Intercept	i_2	0.653	0.571	0.267
Grade level	Control	0.142	0.081	0.096
Class type	Control	0.032	0.083	0.703
Math anxiety (M)	b	0.165	0.034	0.001
Gender stereotypes (X)	C	0.173	0.041	0.001
	c′	0.140	0.041	0.001
Model summary	$F_{(1,\ 612)} = 8.657, p = 0.001$			

stereotypes on math devaluing remained significant ($\beta = 0.140$, $p = 0.001$; Path C', see **Table 13C**) and the reduction in the beta value was not significant, $z = 0.569$, $p > 0.05$. Thus, math anxiety is a not a mediator of the relationship between math-gender stereotypes and math devaluing.

Discussion

Results from Study 2 supported the hypotheses that endorsement of math-gender stereotypes was negatively related to two math outcomes including math self-efficacy and math GPA for both girls and boys. Math anxiety fully mediated the relationship between endorsement of math-gender stereotypes and math self-efficacy and math GPA. Thus, the persistence of math-based gender stereotypes in the US are not only inaccurate, but they are harmful for both girls' and boys' math achievement.

Results support the argument that endorsement of math-gender stereotypes may serve as an antecedent to math anxiety. Although the variables are correlated, regression analyses indicate the stronger relationship is from stereotypes to anxiety for two math outcomes: self-efficacy for girls and boys, and math GPA for girls. Further, mediational analyses indicate that math anxiety, not math gender stereotypes, mediate the relationship between endorsement of math-gender stereotypes and negative math achievement. Interestingly, although the predicted patterns of relationships emerged, math anxiety did not mediate the relationship between math-gender stereotypes and math attitudes, intentions, or devaluing. It may be that gender stereotypes have a stronger relationship with more achievement outcomes (e.g., self-efficacy and GPA) and math anxiety serves as a mediator of these relationships, but not for more attitudinal variables. Future research is needed to better understand the conditions under which math anxiety serves as a mediator between math-gender stereotypes and math outcomes.

This study provided initial evidence that the socialization of, and endorsement of math-gender stereotypes among girls and boys is related to negative math achievement. Further, math anxiety serves as a mechanism for lower math self-efficacy and math performance but not math attitude related variables.

GENERAL DISCUSSION

The purpose of this research was to further probe the social determinants of adolescents' math anxiety by examining the relationship between same and other-gender parents' math anxiety with their child's math anxiety, and the downstream effects of math anxiety on math education outcomes. The first study addressed a gap in the literature by examining parents' own math anxieties (Gunderson et al., 2012; see Maloney et al., 2015). Results confirmed expectations that parents' anxiety is related to children's anxiety and these two variables interact to predict math education outcomes. In doing so, the first study also advances our knowledge of the gendered nature of the intergenerational transfer of math anxiety (Gniewosz and Noack, 2012). The results for mother-daughter dyads were mixed, supporting the hypothesis when daughters' and mothers' math anxiety were both low, but not consistently supporting hypotheses when daughters' and mothers' math anxiety were both high. Future research should further examine the mixed results by measuring possible moderating variables such as the extent to which mothers are involved in daughters' math education, such as helping with homework (see Maloney et al., 2015). It may be the case that for daughters whose mother does not help much, daughters' own math anxiety is a better predictor of math self-efficacy, behavioral intentions, and math devaluing. However, when mothers are actively involved in helping daughters with math homework, the predicted interaction of low-low and high-high parent-child math anxiety may reflect the hypothesized relationships.

Results from study 1 indicate that parents' anxiety plays a role in children's math anxiety and the variables interact to predict several math education outcomes including math self-efficacy, math GPA, math behavioral intentions, math attitudes, and math devaluing. Consistent with existing literature, children with greater math anxiety had lower math self-efficacy, lower math GPA, lower math behavioral intentions, more negative math attitudes, and greater math discounting. However, more interesting was the interaction of children's math anxiety with parents' math anxiety within gendered dyads. The same-gender parent-child dyads showed the most significant relationships, and more specifically the Mother-Daughter dyad dominated the findings. The Mother-Daughter dyads' math anxiety predicted math self-efficacy, math behavioral intentions, math attitudes, and math devaluing. The general pattern was consistent with the hypothesis that when both mothers' and daughters' math anxiety were low, daughters had more positive math outcomes compared to when mothers' and daughters' math anxiety were both high, with exceptions as discussed previously.

Interestingly, the Father-Son dyad was the only one to show a significant relationship to GPA. When both fathers and sons had lower math anxiety, math GPA was higher. Fortunately, even when fathers' math anxiety was higher, if sons had lower math anxiety, GPA was higher. Only when both fathers and sons had higher math anxiety was GPA lower. This finding is novel and should be replicated in future studies. Mothers' anxiety did not predict daughters' GPA, thus there may be other variables intervening in this relationship that are not present in the Father-Son dyad. This likely reflects the gendered nature of math stereotypes and the fact that girls and women are more negatively impacted by cultural biases.

Study 2 addressed a call for a mechanistic approach (Gunderson et al., 2012), and demonstrated that math anxiety is a mechanism through which math-gender stereotypes negatively influence performance related math outcomes for *both* girls and boys. Further, the results suggest that endorsement of math-gender stereotypes may be an antecedent for developing math anxiety for both boys and girls.

In sum, two studies contributed to the existing literature by helping to address several gaps. First, there is only one known published study that found effects of parents' math anxiety on children's math education outcomes, particularly their math performance (Maloney et al., 2015). Second, this study examined these relationships using a gendered lens and found support for the gender stereotype literature that the transmission of math anxiety seems most prevalent among same-gender parent-child dyads, particularly the Mother-Daughter dyad. Further, the results provided initial evidence that the socialization of, and endorsement of math-gender stereotypes among girls and boys is related to negative math achievement.

Limitations

Although the studies make novel contributions to the literature, they are not without weaknesses. First, the data are correlational and cross-sectional. Longitudinal data over at least a full school year would be more informative regarding potential causal relationships. Although the mediational analyses for performance outcomes held after testing for reverse mediation, a stronger case for causality and direction of effects can be made with longitudinal data.

A drawback of Study 1 is that only one parent completed the questionnaire, limiting the full test of the gender of parent who might be most influential on daughters and sons. It can be argued that the parent completing the questionnaire may be the one most involved in the child's math education, but this assumption is tenuous. Further, the sample size of fathers was smaller, which perhaps made the analysis of Father-Daughter and Father-Son dyads underpowered. The fathers who did participated may be particularly good in math and therefore the results with fathers may not be representative of the full spectrum of Father-Daughter and Father-Son relationships regarding math education.

The response rate in Study 1 was 51%, thus the sample of parents who participated is likely different in some ways than parents who did not participate. Without data on non-participating parents, this is difficult to know. We do know that the children whose parents participated did vary in some systematic ways from children whose parents did not participate[2]. Further, the sample of parents reflects racial,

[2]In the United States, grades in school reflect the level of one's education. Sixth grade is either the final year of elementary school education, or the first year of middle school education. Seventh and eighth grades are typically offered in middle schools, which is the educational period before high school where students earn their diploma. Honors math classes indicate the students are high achieving and are over-qualified for the math classes offered to most students. In the United States, students are often tracked into higher level math classes, such as ones to prepare

ethnic, and national diversity. There may be cultural differences in norms regarding parental involvement in children's math education that are not captured in this study[3].

Implications

Despite these limitations the studies provide several contributions to the literature and the data can be used to inform school-based interventions. For example, stereotype busting interventions for teachers, parents, and students may be helpful. Given that several meta analyses show there is no longer a gender gap in math performance (Hyde et al., 2008; Lindberg et al., 2010), educators need to spread awareness to break down gender stereotypes as a barrier to math achievement. Further, anti-math anxiety training seems to be critical for math teachers and parents, particularly mothers. Such training can help boost math self-efficacy, which can be transmitted to students (Hendel and Davis, 1978; Tooke and Lindstrom, 1998; Gresham, 2007). Similarly, parents need to know about the subtle effects they may have on their children in communicating their own math anxiety. It is well known that parental involvement in students' education influences academic outcomes (Jeynes, 2007). Educational campaigns to promote parental involvement and educate parents on the importance of math education for all students might help encourage parents to support their children's math education endeavors. Specifically, educating parents on the impact that their beliefs and actions may have on their children's academic success would be of benefit.

Finally, schools should implement math anxiety reducing workshops for students. All students, girls and boys, will benefit from lower math anxiety. Perhaps what is ultimately needed is an overhaul of the US education system to focus less on competition and testing and more on collaboration and learning. Research has shown that when there is less focus on getting the right answers, and providing students with social support, students show less math anxiety (Turner et al., 2002). Also, when teachers emphasize incremental intelligence, working hard and making mistakes to learn, students have better academic achievement (Dweck, 2006).

them for college, and these courses are often called "honors" courses or advanced placement.

[3]We thank an anonymous reviewer for pointing this out.

AUTHOR NOTE

Bettina J. Casad, Department of Psychological Sciences, University of Missouri-St. Louis; Patricia Hale, Department of Mathematics and Statistics, California State Polytechnic University, Pomona; Faye L. Wachs, Department of Psychology and Sociology, California State Polytechnic University, Pomona. The work in this manuscript was supported by the National Science Foundation under Grant No. 0734124. Any opinions, findings, and conclusions or recommendations expressed in this paper are those of the authors and do not necessarily reflect the views of the National Science Foundation. The authors would like to thank Brandon Nakawaki for consultation on data analysis and members of the Cal Poly Pomona STEPS to Math Success research team for their assistance with data collection. Thank you to the school district administrators, teachers, parents, and students who participated and allowed us to conduct this study during school time.

REFERENCES

Aiken, L. S., and West, S. G. (1991). *Multiple Regression: Testing and Interpreting Interactions*. Thousand Oaks, CA. Sage.

Ashcraft, M. H. (2002). Math anxiety: personal, educational, and cognitive consequences. *Curr. Dir. Psychol. Sci.* 11, 181–185. doi: 10.1111/1467-8721.00196

Ashcraft, M. H., Kirk, E. P., and Hopko, D. (1998). "On the cognitive consequences of mathematics anxiety," in *The Development of Mathematical Skills: Studies in Developmental Psychology*, ed C. Donlan (Hove, UK: Psychology Press), 175–196.

Ashcraft, M. H., and Ridley, K. S. (2005). "Math anxiety and its cognitive consequences: a tutorial review," in *Handbook of Mathematical Cognition*, ed J. I. D. Campbell (New York, NY: Psychology Press) 315–327.

Associated Press (2015). *Nobel Laureate Sees Science Education Career Collapse in Wake of Sexist Comments*. Associated Press. Retrieved from: http://www.nydailynews.com/news/world/nobel-laureate-sees-career-collapse-sexist-comments-article-1.2258310 (June 15, 2015).

Baron, R. M., and Kenny, D. A. (1986). The moderator-mediator variable distinction in socialpsychological research: conceptual, strategic, and statistical considerations. *J. Pers. Soc. Psychol.* 51, 1173–1182. doi: 10.1037/0022-3514.51.6.1173

Beilock, S. L., Gunderson, E. A., Ramirez, G., and Levine, S. C. (2010). Female teachers' math anxiety affects girls' math achievement. *Proc. Natl. Acad. Sci. U.S.A.* 107, 1860–1863. doi: 10.1073/pnas.0910967107

Bhanot, R., and Jovanovic, J. (2005). Do parents' academic gender stereotypes influence whether they intrude on their children's homework? *Sex Roles* 52, 597–607. doi: 10.1007/s11199-005-3728-4

Bleeker, M. M., and Jacobs, J. E. (2004). Achievement in math and science: do mothers' beliefs matter 12 years later? *J. Educ. Psychol.* 96, 97–109. doi: 10.1037/0022-0663.96.1.97

Bombardieri, M. (2005). *Summers' Remarks on Women Draw Fire Boston Globe*. Retrieved from http://www.boston.com/news/education/higher/articles/2005/01/17/summers_remarks_on_women_draw_fire/?page=full

Burns, M. (1998). *Math: Facing an American phobia*. Sausalito, CA: Math Solutions Publications.

Bussey, K., and Bandura, A. (1984). Influence of gender constancy and social power on sex-linked modeling. *J. Pers. Soc. Psychol.* 47, 1292–1302. doi: 10.1037/0022-3514.47.6.1292

Butler, M. B. (1999). Factors associated with students' intentions to engage in science learning activities. *J. Res. Sci. Teach.* 36, 455–473.

Cannon, J., and Ginsburg, H. P. (2008). "Doing the math": maternal beliefs about early mathematics versus language learning. *Early Educ. Dev.* 19, 238–260. doi: 10.1080/10409280801963913

Cheryan, S. (2012). Understanding the paradox in math-related fields: why do some gender gaps remain while others do not? *Sex Roles* 66, 184–190. doi: 10.1007/s11199-011-0060-z

Chew, P. K., and Dillon, D. B. (2014). Statistics anxiety update refining the construct and recommendations for a new research agenda. *Perspect. Psychol. Sci.* 9, 196–208. doi: 10.1177/1745691613518077

Chipman, S. F., Krantz, D. H., and Silver, R. (1992). Mathematics anxiety and science careers among able college women. *Psychol. Sci.* 3, 292–295. doi: 10.1111/j.1467-9280.1992.tb00675.x

Cooper, S. E., and Robinson, D. A. (1991). The relationship of mathematics self-efficacy beliefs to mathematics anxiety and performance. *Meas. Eval. Couns. Dev.* 24, 4–11.

Croizet, J. C., and Claire, T. (1998). Extending the concept of stereotype threat to social class: the intellectual underperformance of students from low socioeconomic backgrounds. *Pers. Soc. Psychol. Bull.* 24, 588–594. doi: 10.1177/0146167298246003

Devine, A., Fawcett, K., Szucs, D., and Dowker, A. (2012). Gender differences in mathematics anxiety and the relation to mathematics performance while controlling for test anxiety. *Behav. Brain Funct.* 8, 2–9. doi: 10.1186/1744-9081-8-33

Devine, P. G., and Elliot, A. J. (1995). Are racial stereotypes really fading? The Princeton trilogy revisited. *Pers. Soc. Psychol. Bull.* 21, 1139–1150. doi: 10.1177/01461672952111002

Dweck, C. (2006). *Mindset: The New Psychology of Success.* New York, NY: Random House.

Eccles, J. S., Adler, T. F., Futterman, R., Goff, S. B., Kaczala, C. M., Meece, J. L., et al. (1983). "Expectancies values and academic behaviors," in *Achievement and Achievement Motivation,* ed J. T. Spence (San Francisco, CA: Freeman), 75–146.

Eccles, J. S., and Jacobs, J. E. (1986). Social forces shape math attitudes and performance. *Signs* 11, 367–380. doi: 10.1086/494229

Eccles, J. S., Jacobs, J. E., and Harold, R. D. (1990). Gender role stereotypes, expectancy effects, and parents' socialization of gender differences. *J. Soc. Issues* 46, 183–201. doi: 10.1111/j.1540-4560.1990.tb01929.x

Eden, C., Heine, A., and Jacobs, A. M. (2013). Mathematics anxiety and its development in the course of formal schooling—a review. *Psychology* 4, 27–35. doi: 10.4236/psych.2013.46A2005

Furnham, A., Reeves, E., and Budhani, S. (2002). Parents think their sons are brighter than their daughters: sex differences in parental self-estimations and estimations of their children's multiple intelligences. *J. Genet. Psychol.* 163, 24–39. doi: 10.1080/00221320209597966

Gniewosz, B., and Noack, P. (2012). Mamakind or papakind?[Mom's child or Dad's child]: parent-specific patterns in early adolescents' intergenerational academic value transmission. *Learn. Individ. Differ.* 22, 544–548. doi: 10.1016/j.lindif.2012.03.003

Gresham, G. (2007). A study of mathematics anxiety in pre-service teachers. *Early Child. Educ. J.* 35, 181–188. doi: 10.1007/s10643-007-0174-7

Gunderson, E. A., Gripshover, S. J., Romero, C., Dweck, C. S., Goldin-Meadow, S., and Levine, S. C. (2011). "Naturalistic variation in parents' praise and the formation of children's theories about trait stability," in *Paper presented at the Biennial Meeting of the Society for Research in Child Development, Montreal, Canada* (Montreal, QC).

Gunderson, E. A., Ramirez, G., Levine, S. C., and Beilock, S. L. (2012). The role of parents and teachers in the development of gender-related math attitudes. *Sex Roles* 66, 153–166. doi: 10.1007/s11199-011-9996-2

Harari, R. R., Vukovic, R. K., and Bailey, S. P. (2013). Mathematics anxiety in young children: an exploratory study. *J. Exp. Educ.* 81, 538–555. doi: 10.1080/00220973.2012.727888

Hembree, R. (1990). The nature, effects, and relief of mathematics anxiety. *J. Res. Math. Educ.* 21, 33–46. doi: 10.2307/749455

Hendel, D. D., and Davis, S. O. (1978). Effectiveness of an intervention strategy for reducing mathematics anxiety. *J. Couns. Psychol.* 25, 429–434. doi: 10.1037/0022-0167.25.5.429

Hyde, J. S., Fennema, E., Ryan, M., Frost, L. A., and Hopp, C. (1990). Gender comparisons of mathematics attitude and affect. *Psychol. Women Q.* 14, 299–324. doi: 10.1111/j.1471-6402.1990.tb00022.x

Hyde, J. S., Lindberg, S. M., Linn, M. C., Ellis, A. B., and Williams, C. C. (2008). Gender similarities characterize math performance. *Science* 321, 494–495. doi: 10.1126/science.1160364

IBM Corp. (2012). *IBM SPSS Statistics for Windows, version 21.0.* Armonk, NY.

Jacobs, J. E. (1991). Influence of gender stereotypes on parent and child mathematics attitudes. *J. Educ. Psychol.* 83, 518–527. doi: 10.1037/0022-0663.83.4.518

Jacobs, J. E. (2005). Twenty-five years of research on gender and ethnic differences in math and science career choices: what have we learned? *New Dir. Child Adolesc. Dev.* 110, 85–94. doi: 10.1002/cd.151

Jacobs, J. E., and Eccles, J. S. (1992). The impact of mothers' gender-role stereotypic beliefs on mothers' and children's ability perceptions. *J. Pers. Soc. Psychol.* 63, 932–944. doi: 10.1037/0022-3514.63.6.932

Jameson, M. M. (2014). Contextual factors related to math anxiety in second-grade children. *J. Exp. Educ.* 82, 518–536. doi: 10.1080/00220973.2013.813367

Jeynes, W. H. (2007). The relationship between parental involvement and urban secondary school student academic achievement a meta-analysis. *Urban Educ.* 42, 82–110. doi: 10.1177/0042085906293818

Kenny, D. A., Bolger, N., and Kashy, D. A. (2002). "Traditional methods for estimating multilevel models," in *Modeling Intraindividual Variability with Repeated Measures Data: Methods and Applications,* eds S. L. Hershberger and D.S. Moskowitz (Mahwah, NJ: Lawrence Erlbaum Associates), 1–24.

Kenny, D. A., Kashy, D. A., and Cook, W. L. (2006). *Dyadic Data Analysis.* New York, NY: Guilford.

Lindberg, S. M., Hyde, J. S., Petersen, J. L., and Linn, M. C. (2010). New trends in gender and mathematics performance: a meta-analysis. *Psychol. Bull.* 136, 1123–1135. doi: 10.1037/a0021276

Major, B., and Schmader, T. (1998). "Coping with stigma through psychological disengagement," in *Prejudice: The Target's Perspective,* eds J. Swim and C. Stangor (San Diego, CA: The Academic Press), 219–241.

Maloney, E. A., and Beilock, S. L. (2012). Math anxiety: who has it, why it develops, and how to guard against it. *Trends Cogn. Sci.* 16, 404–406. doi: 10.1016/j.tics.2012.06.008

Maloney, E. A., Ramirez, G., Gunderson, E. A., Levine, S. C., and Beilock, S. L. (2015). Intergenerational effects of parents' math anxiety on children's math achievement and Anxiety. *Psychol. Sci.* 26, 1480–1488. doi: 10.1177/095679761 5592630

Maloney, E. A., Sattizahn, J. R., and Beilock, S. L. (2014). Anxiety and cognition. *Wiley Interdiscipl. Rev. Cogn. Sci.* 5, 403–411. doi: 10.1002/wcs.1299

Marx, D. M., and Stapel, D. A. (2006). Distinguishing stereotype threat from priming effects: on the role of the social self and threat-based concerns. *J. Pers. Soc. Psychol.* 91:243. doi: 10.1037/0022-3514.91.2.243

Meece, J. L., Wigfield, A., and Eccles, J. S. (1990). Predictors of math anxiety and its influence on young adolescents' course enrollment intentions and performance in mathematics. *J. Educ. Psychol.* 82, 60–70. doi: 10.1037/0022-0663.82.1.60

Midgley, C., Feldlaufer, H., and Eccles, J. S. (1989). Change in teacher efficacy and student self-and task-related beliefs in mathematics during the transition to junior high school. *J. Educ. Psychol.* 81, 247–258. doi: 10.1037/0022-0663.81.2.247

Newport, F., Moore, D. W., and Saad, L. (1999). *Long-term Gallup Poll Trends: A Portrait of American Public Opinion Through the Century.* Retrieved from: http://www.gallup.com/poll/3400/longterm-gallup-poll-trends-portrait-american-public-opinion.aspx (June 24, 2015).

National Center for Education Statistics (2012). *National Assessment of Education Progress Nations Report Card.* Retrieved from: https://nces.ed.gov/nationsreportcard/

O'Bryan, M., Fishbein, H. D., and Ritchey, P. N. (2004). Intergenerational transmission of prejudice, sex role stereotyping, and intolerance. *Adolescence* 39, 407–426.

Pajares, F. (1996). Self-efficacy beliefs in academic settings. *Rev. Educ. Res.* 66, 543–578. doi: 10.3102/00346543066004543

Park, D., Ramirez, G., and Beilock, S. L. (2014). The role of expressive writing in math anxiety. *J. Exp. Psychol. Appl.* 20, 103–111. doi: 10.1037/xap0000013

Ramirez, G., Gunderson, E. A., Levine, S. C., and Beilock, S. L. (2013). Math anxiety, working memory, and math achievement in early elementary school. *J. Cogn. Dev.* 14, 187–202. doi: 10.1080/15248372.2012.664593

Raudenbush, S. W., and Bryk, A. S. (2002). *Hierarchical Linear Models: Applications and Data Analysis Methods, Vol. 1.* Thousand Oaks, CA: Sage.

Roman, H. T. (2004). Why math is so important. *Tech. Dir.* 63, 16–18.

Schmader, T., Johns, M., and Barquissau, M. (2004). The costs of accepting gender differences: the role of stereotype endorsement in women's experience in the math domain. *Sex Roles* 50, 835–850. doi: 10.1023/B:SERS.0000029101.74557.a0

Schmader, T., Johns, M., and Forbes, C. (2008). An integrated process model of stereotype threat effects on performance. *Psychol. Rev.* 115:336. doi: 10.1037/0033-295x.115.2.336

Schunk, D. H. (1981). Modeling and attributional effects on children's achievement: a self-efficacy analysis. *J. Educ. Psychol.* 73, 93–105. doi: 10.1037/0022-0663.73.1.93

Schunk, D. H. (1982a). Effects of effort attributional feedback on children's perceived self- efficacy and achievement. *J. Educ. Psychol.* 74, 548–556. doi: 10.1037/0022-0663.74.4.548

Schunk, D. H. (1982b). Progress self-monitoring: effects on children's self-efficacy and achievement. *J. Exp. Educ.* 51, 89–93. doi: 10.1080/00220973.1982.11011845

Shih, M., Pittinsky, T. L., and Ambady, N. (1999). Stereotype susceptibility: identity salience and shifts in quantitative performance. *Psychol. Sci.* 10, 80–83. doi: 10.1111/1467-9280.00111

Snijders, T. A. B., and Bosker, R. J. (2011). *Multilevel Analysis: An Introduction to Basic and Advanced Multilevel Modeling.* Thousand Oaks, CA: Sage Publications.

Sparks, P., Guthrie, C. A., and Shepherd, R. (1997). The dimensional structure of the perceived behavioral control construct. *J. Appl. Soc. Psychol.* 27, 418–438. doi: 10.1111/j.1559-1816.1997.tb00639.x

Steele, C. M., and Aronson, J. (1995). Stereotype threat and the intellectual test performance of African Americans. *J. Pers. Soc. Psychol.* 69, 797–811. doi: 10.1037/0022-3514.69.5.797

Steffens, M. C., Jelenec, P., and Noack, P. (2010). On the leaky math pipeline: comparing implicit math-gender stereotypes and math withdrawal in female and male children and adolescents. *J. Educ. Psychol.* 102, 947–963. doi: 10.1037/a0019920

Stephens, N. M., Fryberg, S. A., Markus, H. R., Johnson, C. S., and Covarrubias, R. (2012). Unseen disadvantage: how American universities' focus on independence undermines the academic performance of first-generation college students. *J. Pers. Soc. Psychol.* 102, 1178–1197. doi: 10.1037/a0027143

Suárez-Pellicioni, M., Núñez-Peña, M. I., and Colomé, À. (2015). Math anxiety: a review of its cognitive consequences, psychophysiological correlates, and brain bases. *Cogn. Affect. Behav. Neurosci.* doi: 10.3758/s13415-015-0370-7. [Epub ahead of print].

Tiedemann, J. (2000). Parents' gender stereotypes and teachers' beliefs as predictors of children's concept of their mathematical ability in elementary school. *J. Educ. Psychol.* 92, 144–151. doi: 10.1037/0022-0663.92.1.144

Tooke, D. J., and Lindstrom, L. C. (1998). Effectiveness of a mathematics methods course in reducing math anxiety of preservice elementary teachers. *Sch. Sci. Math.* 98, 136–139. doi: 10.1111/j.1949-8594.1998.tb17406.x

Turner, J. C., Meyer, D. K., Anderman, E. M., Midgley, C., Gheen, M., Yongjin, K., et al. (2002). The classroom environment and students' reports of avoidance strategies in mathematics: a multimethod study. *J. Educ. Psychol.* 94, 88–106. doi: 10.1037/0022-0663.94.1.88

Vukovic, R. K., Roberts, S. O., and Green Wright, L. (2013). From parental involvement to children's mathematical performance: the role of mathematics anxiety. *Early Educ. Dev.* 24, 446–467. doi: 10.1080/10409289.2012.693430

Walton, G. M., and Cohen, G. L. (2003). Stereotype lift. *J. Exp. Soc. Psychol.* 39, 456–467. doi: 10.1016/S0022-1031(03)00019-2

Wang, M. T., Eccles, J. S., and Kenny, S. (2013). Not lack of ability but more choice individual and gender differences in choice of careers in science, technology, engineering, and mathematics. *Psychol. Sci.* 24, 770–775. doi: 10.1177/0956797612458937

Wang, Z., Hart, S. A., Kovas, Y., Lukowski, S., Soden, B., Thompson, L. A., et al. (2014). Who is afraid of math? Two sources of genetic variance for mathematical anxiety. *J. Child Psychol. Psychiatry* 55, 1056–1064. doi: 10.1111/jcpp.12224

Wigfield, A., and Eccles, J. S. (2000). Expectancy–value theory of achievement motivation. *Contemp. Educ. Psychol.* 25, 68–81. doi: 10.1006/ceps.1999.1015

Yee, D. K., and Eccles, J. S. (1988). Parent perceptions and attributions for children's math achievement. *Sex Roles* 19, 317–333. doi: 10.1007/BF00289840

Zimmerman, B. J., and Martinez-Pons, M. (1988). Construct validation of a strategy model of student self-regulated learning. *J. Educ. Psychol.* 80, 284–290. doi: 10.1037/0022-0663.80.3.284

Conflict of Interest Statement: The authors declare that the research was conducted in the absence of any commercial or financial relationships that could be construed as a potential conflict of interest.

15

Mother–Child Communication: The Influence of ADHD Symptomatology and Executive Functioning on Paralinguistic Style

Elizabeth S. Nilsen[1], Ami Rints[1], Nicole Ethier[1] and Sarah Moroz[2]*

[1] Centre for Mental Health Research, Department of Psychology, University of Waterloo, Waterloo, ON, Canada,
[2] Department of Psychology, University of Western Ontario, London, ON, Canada

Paralinguistic style, involving features of speech such as pitch and volume, is an important aspect of one's communicative competence. However, little is known about the behavioral traits and cognitive skills that relate to these aspects of speech. This study examined the extent to which ADHD traits and executive functioning (EF) related to the paralinguistic styles of 8- to 12-year-old children and their mothers. Data was collected via parent report (ADHD traits), independent laboratory tasks of EF (working memory, inhibitory control, and cognitive flexibility), and an interactive problem-solving task (completed by mothers and children jointly) which was coded for paralinguistic speech elements (i.e., pitch level/variability; volume level/variability). Dyadic data analyses revealed that elevated ADHD traits in children were associated with a more exaggerated paralinguistic style (i.e., elevated and more variable pitch/volume) for both mothers and children. Mothers' paralinguistic style was additionally predicted by an interaction of mothers' and children's ADHD traits, such that mothers with elevated ADHD traits showed exaggerated paralinguistic styles particularly when their children also had elevated ADHD traits. Highlighting a cognitive mechanism, children with weaker inhibitory control showed more exaggerated paralinguistic styles.

Keywords: paralinguistic, parent–child, executive functioning, inhibitory control, communication, pragmatic language, ADHD, dyadic analyses

Edited by:
Jessica S. Horst,
University of Sussex, UK

Reviewed by:
Natalie Ann Munro,
The University of Sydney, Australia
Nancie Im-Bolter,
Trent University, Canada

Correspondence:
Elizabeth S. Nilsen
enilsen@uwaterloo.ca

Specialty section:
This article was submitted to Developmental Psychology, a section of the journal Frontiers in Psychology

INTRODUCTION

The phrase, 'Use your inside voice!' is frequently uttered within homes, and highlights our expectations for individuals to communicate in a particular manner. An individual's style of speaking includes several paralinguistic features (e.g., pitch, tempo, and sound intensity; Cutler et al., 1997), and is implicated in several aspects of communicative competence (i.e., pragmatic language skills) including conveying sensitivity to situational context and/or listener characteristics (e.g., Ferguson, 1964; Kemper et al., 1995; Biersack et al., 2005) and providing important information about one's intended meaning (Berman et al., 2010, 2013). Moreover, style of speech is a cue listeners rely on to form impressions about the personality characteristics of the speaker (Hecht and LaFrance, 1995). While a number of studies have sought to explicate children's sensitivity to, or production of, particular speech styles (e.g., Morton and Trehub, 2001, Tomasello and Mannle, 1985; Weppelman et al., 2003), the degree to which individual differences in cognitive and behavioral traits relate to manner of speech has been neglected. As such, the present work assessed the degree to which child and maternal ADHD traits related to their paralinguistic style during an interactive problem-solving task – and whether children's executive function skills accounted for any potential effects.

From an early age, children show sensitivity to the paralinguistic aspects of language. For example, 7-month-olds are able to discriminate sounds based on their frequency and harmonic structure (Clarkson and Clifton, 1985) and young infants prefer to listen to infant-directed speech that has increased prosodic qualities over adult-directed speech (Fernald, 1985; Cooper and Aslin, 1990). Mothers use different paralinguistic styles to convey different intentions, including to comfort and to show affection or approval (Fernald, 1993; Kitamura and Burnham, 2003), which infants can detect (Kitamura and Lam, 2009). Children's interpretations of statements favor paralinguistic cues over lexical cues within the first year of life. Lexical cues are increasingly relied on during the mid-school years, and then, following this period, paralinguistic cues are privileged over lexical information once more (Friend, 2001; Morton and Trehub, 2001). With respect to the production of various paralinguistic cues, using a naturalistic observation, Tomasello and Mannle (1985) found that preschoolers used infant-directed intonation when interacting with their infant siblings, providing some evidence that preschoolers modify their paralinguistic behavior. However, Weppelman et al. (2003), using computer software to extract paralinguistic information, found that 4-year-olds did not modify their pitch or volume depending on their communicative partner (adult or child; Weppelman et al., 2003).

The ability to monitor and regulate one's paralinguistic cues is viewed as a reflection of communicative competence (O'Neill, 2007). Moreover, research in the interpersonal domain suggests that paralinguistic behavior has been identified as a major contributor to how individuals form judgments and impressions about others. For instance, exposure to even 5 s of audio allows individuals to form personality (Hecht and LaFrance, 1995) and psychopathology ratings (Friedman et al., 2006; Fowler et al., 2009). These "thin slice" studies present audio clips that are too short to offer any kind of meaningful speech content; thus, one can infer that ratings are based primarily on paralinguistic cues. Given the importance of this aspect of language for children's communicative development as well as for individuals' interactions generally, it would be of interest to examine potential cognitive and behavioral factors that relate to particular speech styles.

Recently, there has been a growing emphasis on elucidating the cognitive mechanisms and behavioral traits that underlie communicative competence, broadly construed. For example, research has suggested that several aspects of communicative behavior are supported by underlying executive functioning (EF). EF refers to higher order processes that aid in the monitoring and control of thoughts/actions and facilitate goal-directed behavior (Burgess, 1997). Though different conceptualizations of EF exist (e.g., Jurado and Rosselli, 2007), core EF skills include inhibitory control (i.e., the ability to suppress dominant responses), working memory (i.e., actively holding important information in mind), and cognitive flexibility/shifting (i.e., considering simultaneous representations of an object or event and/or flexibly alternating between tasks), which are separable yet inter-related (e.g., Miyake et al., 2000; Huizinga et al., 2006). Individual differences in EF have been found to relate to the comprehension and production of communicative utterances in both pediatric (Nilsen and Graham, 2009, 2012; Gillis and Nilsen, 2014; Nilsen et al., 2015) and adult populations (Brown-Schmidt, 2009; Wardlow, 2013). Related to paralinguistic behavior more specifically, deficits in the *comprehension* of paralinguistic elements, such as prosody, have been associated with impairments in EF in various clinical samples, including those with depression (Uekermann et al., 2008) and traumatic brain injury (Struchen et al., 2008). However, the role of EF in the *production* of various paralinguistic features has not been clearly delineated and presents an important avenue for the present research.

The role of EF for communication poses important implications for individuals who show weaknesses in EF, such as amongst those with diagnoses of Attention-Deficit/Hyperactivity Disorder (ADHD; Barkley, 1997, 2006; Nigg, 2001; Martinussen et al., 2005; Willcutt et al., 2005), as well as those whose ADHD traits are at a sub-clinical threshold (Sonuga-Barke et al., 2002; Thorell and Wåhlstedt, 2006). That is, it may be that individuals with elevated ADHD traits show communicative styles that differ from those with low levels of ADHD traits due to differences in EF. Certainly, elevated levels of ADHD traits have also been associated with communicative difficulties across both parent-report (e.g., Bishop and Baird, 2001; Geurts et al., 2010) and performance-based communicative tasks (e.g., Purvis and Tannock, 1997; Nilsen et al., 2013). For example, children with elevated ADHD traits tend to provide insufficient information for listeners (Purvis and Tannock, 1997; Nilsen et al., 2015) and show difficulty with moderating the content of their utterances to fit the social context (Whalen et al., 1979; Landau and Milich, 1988). Critically, theoretical accounts have posited an underlying role of EF in accounting for these associations (e.g., Geurts et al., 2010; Nilsen and Fecica, 2011; Green et al., 2014). To date, however, little research has specifically examined the association of ADHD traits and paralinguistic aspects of speech. In addition, the available research has been limited to children's detection of affect from paralinguistic cues (e.g., Uekermann et al., 2010; Oerlemans et al., 2014) or has examined this aspect as part of a broader constellation of other communicative abilities (e.g., Kim and Kaiser, 2000). Resultantly, little is presently known about the specific qualities of speech that may differ for individuals with elevated ADHD traits, and more specifically, the extent to which EF may be implicated in any association between these factors.

Attempting to fill gaps in the literature, this study focused specifically on examining the paralinguistic styles of mothers and children during an interactive task. We isolated paralinguistic qualities, including the features of volume mean (the general volume at which one is speaking); volume variation (which can be thought of as vocal emphasis where greater volume variation suggests that a person is using punctuated bursts of volume in order to emphasize certain statements or words);

pitch mean (the average fundamental frequency at which one speaks); and pitch variation (the degree to which an individual's pitch rises and falls over time). We chose to assess these speech qualities during a mother–child interaction as previous work has highlighted the degree to which ADHD traits, in either a mother or a child, impact content of the interpersonal exchange. For example, mothers with increased ADHD symptoms demonstrate less corrective feedback to their children and use shorter, less complex, and less elaborate language with their children (Kryski et al., 2010; Griggs and Mikami, 2011), while children with increased ADHD symptoms tend to have parents who use more negative-reactive and less positive parenting strategies, and are more directive, controlling, and negative (Mash and Johnston, 1982; Johnston, 1996; Gadeyne et al., 2004). In the present study, our first research aim was to examine whether children's and mothers' ADHD traits related to their paralinguistic style. In particular, we wondered whether elevated ADHD traits would result in a more exaggerated style (i.e., higher and more variable pitch and volume) given that there may be less regulation of vocal behavior. Dyadic data analyses (i.e., Actor-Partner Interdependence Model; APIM) were used to examine and account for the extent to which one's ADHD traits would relate to one's own paralinguistic style, as well as the paralinguistic style of one's partner (Kenny et al., 2006). Such an approach is important as it allowed for us to account for the interdependence in the relationship between mothers and their children when assessing the relations between ADHD and paralinguistic style (Cook and Kenny, 2005). We also examined the extent to which child and maternal ADHD traits may interact to impact either or both partners' paralinguistic style (as per previous work suggesting that social interactions differ depending on the degree of similarity/difference between parent and child symptomatology; e.g., Psychogiou et al., 2007, 2008; Wymbs et al., 2015). That is, we questioned whether having both a parent and child with elevated ADHD traits could lead to a differential paralinguistic style (relative to when only one member had elevated traits).

The second research aim was to determine whether, for children, EF accounted for a more exaggerated paralinguistic style. Accordingly, regression analyses were conducted to assess the degree to which children's performance on EF tasks (assessing working memory, inhibitory control, and cognitive flexibility) related to a paralinguistic style that was more exaggerated (i.e., using ADHD traits and EF as predictors of the paralinguistic composite). Note that while we were interested in assessing whether children's EF skills may be responsible for the relation between ADHD, mediation analyses were not conducted due to the assumption of causality that is implicit within mediation analyses. That is, mediation analysis implies that the mediator is 'caused' by the predictor (Baron and Kenny, 1986). Recent theoretical accounts posit that executive deficits may give rise to ADHD symptoms, rather than being a consequence of the disorder (Crosbie et al., 2008). In addition, other work shows that, while relations do exist, there is much variability in the degree of EF impairment for youth with ADHD (Lambek et al., 2011). Thus, we looked at these factors concurrently rather than assuming one was a downstream effect of another.

MATERIALS AND METHODS

Participants

Participants consisted of 68 pairs of community-recruited mothers and children (aged 8–12 years). Forty-three children were reported to be typically developing, while 25 were reported to have received a previous diagnosis of ADHD from a physician (2), pediatrician (9), or psychologist (16; participants were allowed to select more than one option). As ADHD traits operate on a continuum and exist within non-clinical samples (e.g., Bignell and Cain, 2007), children with and without a previous diagnosis of ADHD were able to participate. Participants were recruited from a community reflecting typically middle class families using flyers and advertisements posted at local community centers and internet sites promoting child-focused programs. The majority of participants were Caucasian (85%) with all participants reporting fluency in English and English reported as the primary language for 96% of participants (other languages included Mandarin, Urdu, and Taiwanese). Nine dyads were excluded from analyses due to a microphone malfunction and two dyads due to statistical outliers (i.e., $>3SD$; one on the cognitive flexibility task and another on the child's paralinguistic data). This resulted in a final sample of 57 dyads (24 females, *M*age = 10 years; 4 months [*SD* = 14.58 months]; see **Table 1**). Twenty-two of the remaining children had previous diagnoses, and 20 of these children were prescribed stimulant medication for

TABLE 1 | Demographic information and executive function task performance.

	M (SD)
Age	10 years; 4 months (14.58 months)
Gender	Males: 57.9% (*n* = 33); Females: 42.1% (*n* = 24)
Percentage of children with a previous diagnosis of ADHD	38.6% (*n* = 22)
Percentage of previously diagnosed children on medication at time of testing	50% (*n* = 11)
Children's SNAP scores	Inattention: 1.15 (0.86; range: 0–3)
	Hyperactivity: 0.76 (0.77; range: 0–2.89)
Mothers' CAARS scores (*T*-scores)	Inattention: 52.38 (12.54; range: 36.00–88.50)
	Hyperactivity: 50.07 (9.64; range: 35.50–73.50)
Correct responses on Stroop Task	77.28 (17.72; range: 41–110)
Correct responses on Reading Span Task	19.11 (2.04; range: 14–25)
Response Time on Trails Letter–Number	127.96 s (68.96 s; range: 46–358)
Errors on Trails Letter–Number	1.12 (1.46; range: 0–6)

ADHD traits (with 11 taking their medication on the day of testing[1]).

Materials and Procedures

The present research was part of a larger study on children's communicative behavior and consisted of one 90-min session for each dyad. This study was approved through the Office of Research Ethics at the University of Waterloo. Mothers completed questionnaires independently while children completed the EF tasks with a researcher in a separate room. All tasks were presented in a fixed order, a standard practice when assessing individual differences that ensures that individuals are exposed to identical stimulus contexts. Subsequently, the mothers and children participated in an interactive task together.

ADHD Traits

Children's ADHD traits were assessed via parent-report using the Inattention and Hyperactivity-Impulsivity subscales of the SNAP-IV Teacher and Parent Rating Scale (SNAP-IV; Swanson, 1992). Mothers rated the extent to which children demonstrated 18 behaviors from (0) *Not At All* to (3) *Very Much.* The SNAP-IV has acceptable internal consistency, item selection, and factor structure, all consistent with the constructs of ADHD put forth in the *Diagnostic and Statistical Manual of Mental Disorders, Fourth Edition* (*DSM-IV*; Bussing et al., 2008). Mothers' ADHD traits were assessed through mothers' self-report on the Conners Adult ADHD Rating Scale - Short version (CAARS-S; Conners et al., 1999). Mothers rated the frequency with which they exhibited 26 behaviors related to ADHD on a scale from (0) *Not At All* to (3) *Very Much/Very Frequently.* The Conners scale demonstrates good internal consistency and predictive validity (Erhardt et al., 1999; Kooij et al., 2013).

In the present study, strong positive correlations emerged between the inattentive and hyperactive subscales of the SNAP-IV ($r = 0.79$, $p < 0.001$) and the CAARS-S ($r = 0.47$, $p = 0.02$). Given this, and consistent with current factor analytic studies supporting the use of a general factor of ADHD (e.g., Normand et al., 2012), scores across inattentive and hyperactive-impulsive traits were averaged to create a single estimate of ADHD traits for children and mothers. For all analyses, ADHD traits were treated continuously, consistent with research suggesting that ADHD traits fall on a continuum in community samples (Bignell and Cain, 2007).

Executive Function

Developmentally appropriate tasks to capture each aspect of EF (inhibitory control, working memory, cognitive flexibility were selected.

Inhibitory control

Children's inhibitory control, specifically the interference control aspects of inhibitory control, was assessed using a Stroop task (Stroop, 1935). This task asked children to first read words from a list of colors with congruent font colors and then identify the colors of the font from a list of words with incongruent font colors. Stroop tasks have been found to load onto an inhibition factor in factor analytic studies (Miyake et al., 2000). The task discontinued after 2 min for all children. Interference control was calculated by regressing the incongruent color-word naming scores on the congruent color naming scores and saving the unstandardized residuals wherein higher scores reflect better performance.

Working memory

Children's working memory was assessed using the reading span task from the Stanford–Binet intelligence scales (Roid, 2003). This task has demonstrated acceptable reliability and strong correlations with other measures of working memory (Conway et al., 2005). Children were asked to answer sets of yes/no questions (asked by the examiner) and recall the last word in each question (with the number of questions in each set increasing over trials). Scores reflect the number of errors made, ranging from 0 (two or more errors) to 2 (no errors). Per task instructions, testing discontinued when two consecutive scores of 0 were obtained. Participants' total score was included in the analyses.

Cognitive flexibility

The Trail Making Test (Reitan and Wolfson, 1985) was used to examine children's cognitive flexibility (Sánchez-Cubillo et al., 2009). Performance on this task has been shown to correlate with other measures of set-switching (Arbuthnott and Frank, 2000). Children began by connecting circles of sequential numbers on paper; they then switched to connecting alternated numbers and letters, again in sequential order, with this latter task reflecting children's ability to flexibly switch sequences. Ratio scores were calculated to index children's time to complete the second task controlling for time to complete the first task, and were entered into the analyses (Strauss et al., 2006).

Mother–Child Interaction

After the questionnaires and EF tasks were completed, the mother joined her child in a second testing room where they sat side-by-side (positioning in terms of left/right was randomly chosen by dyads). Dyads were provided with a relatively open-ended collaborative problem-solving task based on a task used by youth groups (Scouting Web, 2013), and which required dyads to imagine they were survivors of an airplane crash in freezing temperatures and 20 miles from the nearest town. They were informed that in the plane wreckage they would find 10 items (shown by pictures, i.e., a compass, gun, cooking oil, lighter, heavy-duty canvas, map, ax, steel wool, chocolate bars, and newspaper), and were asked to work together to generate one list rating the items from most to least important. Pairs were given 15 min to complete the task, and were asked to converse in their typical fashion if they finished early. The interaction was recorded by way of a microphone, placed in a designated position on the table between the dyad, connected wirelessly to a video camera located behind a one-way mirror.

[1]It was requested that children not take their medication on the day of testing, but it was made clear the decision was up to the parent/child and would not affect their ability to participate in the study. Medication status was not significantly related to the dependent measures (i.e., when comparing the performance of those individuals with a previous diagnosis of ADHD who were taking versus not taking medication; $p = 0.25$) and, as such, was not included in further analyses.

Extraction of auditory data

To obtain measures of paralinguistic styles for children and their mothers, each video was converted into an auditory file using the VLC media player (VideoLAN, 2012). Researchers then selected samples of interactants' speech from a 10-min window of the interaction during which mothers and children worked on the task. The researcher compiled a selection of 10 speech clips using the program Audacity (Audacity Team, 2011), using a standardized sampling procedure: one clip from each of the first 10 min of the interaction was extracted, beginning from 30 s after the experimenter left the room (i.e., 30 s, 1 min 30 s, 2 min 30 s, etc.). To be viable, an audio clip had to involve the participant speaking and be least 2 s long, to a maximum of 10 s. An audio clip was deemed unusable when it involved a participant reading from the information sheet (i.e., not producing spontaneous speech), when it was interrupted by the partner's voice, and when it contained audible background noise. The voice clips were then compiled to form a 30–60 s sample of the participant's paralinguistic style. If the resulting compilation did not exceed 30 s, the researcher sampled the 11th and 12th minutes of the interaction, under the condition that the mother and child were still working on the task. Failing this, the researcher re-sampled the first 10 min (i.e., using a second clip within the minute time frames), until at least 30 s of material could be obtained. These paralinguistic samples were compiled for both the mother and the child, separately by two different researchers. The computer program Praat (Boersma and Weenink, 2011) was then used to determine the mean and standard deviation of both pitch (in Hertz) and volume (in decibels) of the paralinguistic sample. The various indices (i.e., pitch and volume mean and standard deviation) were standardized due to differences in the scaling and then aggregated to provide an index of exaggerated paralinguistic styles (i.e., wherein higher scores were reflective of a communicative style evidenced by elevated and more variable pitch and volume). Intercorrelations among children and mothers' paralinguistic qualities, as well as their relation to the overall composite are provided on **Table 2**. Cronbach's alpha for the exaggerated paralinguistic composite was 0.69 for children and 0.60 for mothers.

TABLE 2 | Intercorrelations amongst paralinguistic qualities in children's and mothers' speech.

	Pitch Mean	Pitch *SD*	Volume Mean	Volume *SD*
Children				
Pitch Mean	–			
Pitch *SD*	0.14	–		
Volume Mean	0.45**	0.15	–	
Volume *SD*	0.54**	0.30*	0.44**	–
Exaggerated Composite	0.79**	0.42**	0.76**	0.83**
Mothers				
Pitch Mean	–			
Pitch *SD*	0.30*	–		
Volume Mean	0.40**	0.36**	–	
Volume *SD*	0.24†	0.13	0.24†	–
Exaggerated Composite	0.69**	0.62**	0.76**	0.63**

†$p < 0.10$, *$p < 0.05$, **$p < 0.01$ (all two-tailed).

RESULTS

Preliminary Analyses

Table 1 provides the demographic characteristics of the sample. The ratings of mothers' and children's ADHD traits showed a wide range that was normally distributed and within acceptable limits for skew/kurtosis. Mean levels of ADHD were within the non-clinical range. There were no significant correlations between children's age and ADHD traits ($p = 0.83$), but age was correlated with exaggerated paralinguistic style, $r = -0.30$, $p = 0.03$, and as such was controlled in further analyses. A *t*-test revealed no significant difference between male and female children on the exaggerated paralinguistic aggregate, $p = 0.82$, nor was gender significantly associated with any other key variables included in the study, *ps* > 0.09. As such, gender was not included in further analyses.

The bivariate correlation between the mothers' and children's paralinguistic behavior was significant, $r = 0.40$, $p = 0.003$ ($r = 0.43$, $p = 0.001$ when controlling for child's age), suggesting that a dyadic approach to the analyses is important given the influence that mother/child paralinguistic behaviors have on each other.

Relation between Paralinguistic Style and ADHD Traits

Actor-Partner Interdependence Model analyses (using AMOS Graphics 22.0; Arbuckle, 2013) were used to examine the association between paralinguistic style and ADHD traits. Such analyses allow for investigating both actor effects (i.e., how one's ADHD traits predict their own paralinguistic style, shown in **Figure 1** as horizontal lines representing the standardized regression weights), and partner effects (i.e., how one's ADHD traits predict one's partner's paralinguistic style, shown as diagonal lines in **Figure 1**) (Kenny et al., 2006), as well as to assess the effects of an interaction between mothers' and children's ADHD traits on each partner's respective paralinguistic style. Moreover, this model allowed us to examine the correlation between maternal and child ADHD traits (i.e., the arc on the left of the model represents the covariation between mothers' and children's ADHD traits) and the correlation between maternal and child paralinguistic styles (i.e., the arc on the right of the model represents the covariation between the residual variance of mothers' and children's paralinguistic styles) controlling for the predictors. All predictor variables were mean centered prior to analyses.

Addressing our first research question, the analyses revealed a significant actor effect for children, such that increased ADHD traits were significantly associated with a more exaggerated paralinguistic style, $\beta = 0.45$, $p = 0.001$. In addition, a significant partner effect emerged for mothers, such that increased ADHD traits in children were significantly associated with a more exaggerated paralinguistic style in mothers, $\beta = 0.35$, $p = 0.012$. Thus, increased child ADHD traits related to

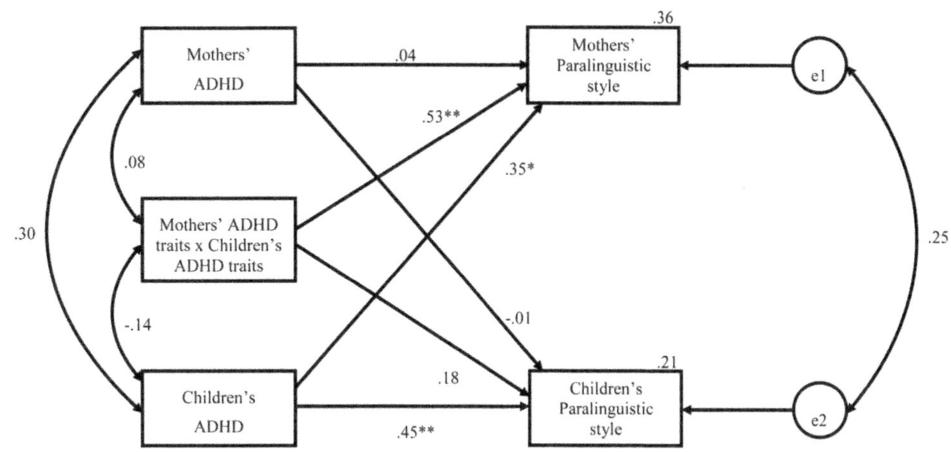

FIGURE 1 | APIM: ADHD traits predicting exaggerated paralinguistic style (standardized estimates).

more exaggerated paralinguistic styles in both children and mothers.

The pattern for maternal ADHD traits showed a more complex pattern. That is, we did not find that the ADHD traits of mothers related to the paralinguistic style of their children ($\beta = -0.01$, $p = 0.97$), nor was the interaction term a significant predictor of children's paralinguistic aggregates ($\beta = 0.18$, $p = 0.28$). However, a significant interaction effect emerged with respect to mother's paralinguistic style, $\beta = 0.53$, $p < 0.001$ (**Figure 2**). Tests of the simple slopes suggested that when mothers' ADHD traits were low, children's ADHD traits did not influence mothers' paralinguistic style ($\beta = -0.18$, $p = 0.42$). However, when mothers' ADHD traits were high, having a child who demonstrated low levels of ADHD traits was associated with a more subdued paralinguistic style in mothers, while having children with higher levels of ADHD traits was associated with a more exaggerated paralinguistic style in mothers ($\beta = 0.86$, $p = 0.002$).

The percentage of variance in the paralinguistic aggregate explained by ADHD traits (i.e., including children's ADHD traits, maternal ADHD traits, and the interaction of the two) was 21% for children and 36% for mothers. In terms of other findings, we did not find a significant correlation between ADHD traits in mothers and children ($r = 0.30$, $p = 0.14$), suggesting that mothers did not tend to report comparable levels of ADHD traits for themselves and their children. In addition, once controlling for ADHD traits, the correlation between mothers' and children's paralinguistic aggregates was not significant ($r = 0.25$, $p = 0.14$).

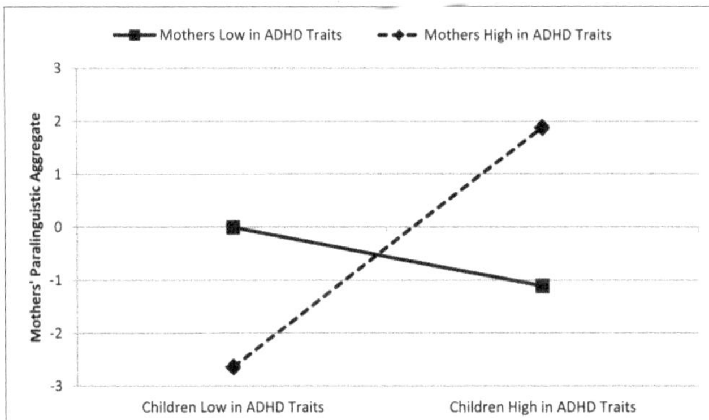

FIGURE 2 | Mothers' and children's ADHD traits predicting mothers' exaggerated paralinguistic style.

Children's Executive Functioning and Paralinguistic Style

Correlations between children's ADHD traits, EF, and the paralinguistic aggregate are shown in **Table 3**. Children's ADHD traits were related to their inhibitory control skills ($r = -0.37$, $p = 0.005$), but not working memory or cognitive flexibility ($ps > 0.54$).

Addressing the second research question, hierarchical regression analyses were conducted to examine the extent to which EF was related to paralinguistic style. At the first step of the regression, ADHD traits were a significant predictor of paralinguistic style ($\beta = 0.41$, $p = 0.001$), as was age ($\beta = -0.29$, $p = 0.02$). The regression model with these two predictors accounted for a significant amount of variance in children's paralinguistic style, $R^2 = 0.26$. When inhibitory control was entered alongside age and ADHD traits in the second step, there was a significant increase in the variance explained by the model, where the change in $R^2 = 0.08$ (together accounting for 34% of the variance). Both ADHD traits and inhibitory control were significant predictors of children's paralinguistic style (inhibitory control, $\beta = -0.34$, $p = 0.01$; ADHD traits, $\beta = 0.29$, $p = 0.02$). Thus, children with elevated ADHD traits, as well as those with weaker inhibitory control, show a more exaggerated paralinguistic style, with both characteristics accounting for unique variance. (Of note, Fischer's z-tests were conducted to examine whether there were significant differences between ADHD traits and each specific paralinguistic feature (controlling for age). Volume variability was found to have a stronger

TABLE 3 | Bivariate correlations between children's ADHD traits, executive functioning, and paralinguistic style (partial correlations controlling for age in months are in parentheses).

	ADHD traits	Inhibitory control	Working memory	Cognitive flexibility	Exaggerated paralinguistic Style
Age (months)	−0.03	0.44**	0.21	0.10	−0.30*
ADHD traits		−0.37** (−0.40)**	−0.08 (−0.06)	−0.08 (−0.09)	0.42** (0.43**)
Inhibitory control			0.36** (0.32*)	0.03 (0.01)	−0.51** (−0.44**)
Working memory				−0.14 (−0.12)	−0.11 (−0.06)
Cognitive flexibility					0.01 (−0.03)

$^{*}p < 0.05$, $^{**}p < 0.01$ (all two-tailed).

relation with ADHD traits than all other paralinguistic features ($ps < 0.02$), which did not differ from each other ($ps > 0.36$). In addition, Fisher's z-tests revealed no significant differences in the strength of the relations between inhibitory control and each paralinguistic feature, controlling for age ($ps > 0.19$)).

Similar regression analyses were conducted that included both working memory and cognitive flexibility in the place of inhibitory control, yielding non-significant results. That is, working memory and cognitive flexibility did not significantly improve the model containing just ADHD traits and age (consistent with the non-significant bivariate correlations between these measures and paralinguistic style).

DISCUSSION

Given the relevance of paralinguistic style for both communicative development and impression formation, it is important to understand individual differences that may contribute to variability in speech styles. The present study provides insight into the degree to which maternal and child ADHD traits, and children's EF skills, related to their paralinguistic style.

First, we found that elevated ADHD traits in children related to the production of a more exaggerated paralinguistic style; that is, speaking in a louder, higher-pitched, and more variable fashion (which was particularly characterized by greater volume variability). This was true even after controlling for mothers' paralinguistic style (i.e., to account for possible phonetic-acoustic convergence effects; Pardo, 2013). These findings suggest that in addition to affecting the *content* of children's utterances (e.g., Purvis and Tannock, 1997; Nilsen et al., 2015), children's ADHD traits also relate to their manner of speaking. Past work has found that elevated ADHD traits result in worse detection of affective prosody recognition (albeit in a sample of children with Autism Spectrum Disorder; Oerlemans et al., 2014). As such, it may be that the children in our study with elevated ADHD traits are less sensitive to their own paralinguistic style, thereby having more difficulty with regulating their communicative behavior. While previous work has found that children with elevated traits show differential communicative behavior, this research has either not isolated paralinguistic style from other communicative behavior (Kim and Kaiser, 2000) or has relied on global parent report measures of communication (Leonard et al., 2011), which limits conclusions about how ADHD traits impact paralinguistic styles specifically (though certainly, examining the relation between paralinguistic style and other communicative behavior would be an interesting extension of this work). Moreover, in the present work, we used an objective computerized coding system to isolate and capture the paralinguistic style. By doing so, we could ensure that the measures were not impacted by the overt behavior of the child (which poses problems for interpreting communicative skills based on observer data).

In addition to an actor effect, children's ADHD traits were associated with a more exaggerated paralinguistic style in mothers, which adds to our understanding of features which characterize communication between children with traits of ADHD and others in their social worlds. That is, even when the mother's own style and behavioral profile were controlled, we found that the behavioral traits of the child related to a maternal paralinguistic style that was more exaggerated. The impact of child symptomatology on a parents' behavior has been explored previously, showing that elevated ADHD traits negatively impact parents' parenting styles (e.g., Mash and Johnston, 1982; Johnston, 1996; Gadeyne et al., 2004). What is unique about the present findings is that we find that child ADHD traits influence a very basic, yet important, component of a mother's interaction style. A more stringent extension of these findings would be to determine whether mothers vary their paralinguistic style when interacting a child who has ADHD versus another child who does not.

Second, we found an interaction effect, such that mothers' ADHD traits had a differential relation to their own paralinguistic style depending on the level of ADHD traits exhibited by their children. More specifically, it seems that when mothers' ADHD traits were low, children's ADHD traits did not seem to impact mothers' paralinguistic style. In contrast, when maternal ADHD traits were high, there was an impact of children's ADHD traits on maternal paralinguistic style. More specifically, for mothers with high ADHD traits, when children's ADHD traits are low, the paralinguistic style was more subdued, whereas when children's ADHD traits are high, mothers' paralinguistic style was more exaggerated (i.e., increased and more variable prosody and volume). Thus, it seems as though mothers with elevated ADHD traits are more impacted by the behavioral styles of their children, which are manifest through their paralinguistic styles. These findings are interesting to consider in the context of past work examining the "similarity-fit hypothesis" which posits that parents and children may have better interactions when there is a similarity in ADHD symptomatology. Conflicting support for such hypotheses have been yielded, whereby some studies, supporting the similarity-fit predictions, have found that high maternal traits ameliorate the negative effects of child ADHD on parenting (e.g., Psychogiou et al., 2007, 2008). In contrast, others have found evidence in support of "similarity-misfit" predictions such that parent and child ADHD symptoms operate together to predict negative parenting styles and communicative patterns (Wymbs et al., 2015). In the present work, we find that there is indeed an interaction between maternal and child ADHD traits for mothers' paralinguistic style. That is, mothers with elevated ADHD traits, when interacting with a child with elevated ADHD traits, are showing a similar exaggerated paralinguistic style. However, the current data do not allow for determining whether reciprocity in the exaggerated paralinguistic style is beneficial (e.g., sharing a similar exuberant style) or maladaptive (e.g., both engaging in a less regulated style). That is, while reciprocity in other aspects of interaction (e.g., affiliation) is seen as resulting in more satisfying and positive interactions (e.g., Tracey, 2004; Locke and Sadler, 2007), it is difficult to know how similarly matched exaggerated paralinguistic styles would be experienced by the interlocutors.

Third, we found that inhibitory control contributed to children's manner of speaking. That is, children with weaker inhibitory control (but not working memory or cognitive flexibility) showed a more exaggerated paralinguistic style. Such a finding suggests that an individual's paralinguistic style is something that is, at least in part, reliant on cognitive resources. Moreover, such a finding allows for speculation about the meaning of the exaggerated style - that is, that it may reflect a less controlled, more chaotic manner of speaker as opposed to a controlled, but more exuberant or excited style. However, as noted above, the impact for such a paralinguistic style for impression formation or interpersonal interactions cannot be determined from our data and will be an important avenue for future research. Regardless, findings add to a growing body of work highlighting the role of inhibitory control for other aspects of communication, such as suppressing one's own perspective in order to take the perspective of a conversational partner (Nilsen and Graham, 2009, 2012). Interestingly, we found that although ADHD traits and inhibitory control were related (as has been demonstrated previously, Sonuga-Barke et al., 2002; Thorell and Wåhlstedt, 2006), each characteristic accounted for unique variance in children's paralinguistic style. Thus, it could be the case that children who behaviorally exhibit ADHD traits and/or cognitively show difficulties with suppressing dominant reactions would show a paralinguistic style that is more exaggerated than other children.

The present work advances the understanding of the role of ADHD traits and inhibitory control in communicative behavior. However, a number of limitations should be noted. First, the functional impact of an exaggerated paralinguistic style, and more specifically how it may impact one's social functioning, cannot be ascertained from this study. That is, it would be of interest for future work to examine how others interpret an exaggerated paralinguistic style and whether such a style impacts the reaction of one's communicative partner. Certainly, there is some emerging work suggesting that paralinguistic styles influence adults' ratings of speakers' socio-communicative competency (Varghese and Nilsen, 2015). Moreover, an important extension of this work would be to determine whether ADHD traits or inhibitory control relate to the extent to which individuals are able to appropriately modify their paralinguistic styles across contexts (Ellis and Ure, 1969). Second, we did ask about nor conduct an examination of the hearing abilities of our sample. Third, our findings are limited to mothers and mother-child interactions and may not generalize to father-child dyads given significant variability in vocal qualities across genders (e.g., Warren-Leubecker and Bohannon, 1984). Fourth, EF skills of mothers, as well as their age, were not examined, and thus the role of inhibitory control in the paralinguistic style of adults and the possible influence of maternal age has been left for future work to explore. Finally, to minimize the length of the study we had only included one task of EF for each component; however, such a decision prevented us from analyzing the data using latent variables for the various EF constructs.

In sum, the paralinguistic features of one's speech represent an important aspect of one's communicative approach. The present work highlights the role of ADHD traits and inhibitory control for a paralinguistic style that is more exaggerated and unrestrained. While previous studies have found that these individual factors relate to the *content* of communication, this is the first to show their importance in predicting an individual's manner of speech. Findings have implications for theoretical models of communication, which identify executive functions as an important factor in the development of children's communicative skills, as well adding to the growing literature as to how ADHD traits relate to one's own as well as others' communicative behavior.

AUTHOR CONTRIBUTIONS

EN participated in/supervised the design, data collection, analyses, and manuscript-writing; AR analyzed the data and contributed to the conceptual framework in writing the manuscript; NE designed the study, collected data, and contributed to the writing of the manuscript, SM collected data as part of her honors thesis and contributed to the writing of the manuscript.

FUNDING

This research was funded by an Ontario Mental Health Foundation New Investigator Grant awarded to EN.

ACKNOWLEDGMENTS

We thank the children and parents who participated in the study, as well as the community organizations that assisted us in recruiting participants. The authors also thank T. Kung for her assistance with this research as well as E. Woody for his consultation on statistical analyses.

REFERENCES

Arbuckle, J. L. (2013). *Amos (Version 22.0) [computer program]*. Chicago: SPSS.

Arbuthnott, K., and Frank, J. (2000). Trail making test, part B as a measure of executive control: validation using a set-switching paradigm. *Clinical and Experimental Neuropsychology* 22, 518–528. doi: 10.1207/S15324826AN0902_5

Audacity Team (2011). *Audacity (Version 1.3 beta) [computer software]*. Available from http://audacity.sourceforge.net/

Barkley, R. A. (1997). Behavioral inhibition, sustained attention, and executive functions: Constructing a unifying theory of ADHD. *Psychol. Bull.* 121, 65–94. doi: 10.1037/0033-2909.121.1.65

Barkley, R. A. (2006). *Attention-Deficit Hyperactivity Disorder: A Handbook for Diagnosis and Treatment*, 3rd Edn. New York, NY: Guilford Press.

Baron, R. M., and Kenny, D. A. (1986). The moderator-mediator variable distinction in social psychological research: conceptual, strategic, and statistical considerations. *J. Pers. Soc. Psychol.* 51, 1173–1182. doi: 10.1037/0022-3514.51.6.1173

Berman, M. J., Chambers, C. G., and Graham, S. A. (2010). Preschoolers' appreciation of speaker vocal affect as a cue to referential intent. *J. Exp. Child Psychol.* 107, 87–99. doi: 10.1016/j.jecp.2010.04.012

Berman, M. J., Graham, S. A., and Chambers, C. G. (2013). Contextual influences on children's use of vocal affect cues during referential interpretation. *Q. J. Exp. Psychol.* 66, 705–726. doi: 10.1080/17470218.2012.713367

Biersack, S., Kempe, V., and Knapton, L. (2005). "Fine-tuning speech registers: a comparison of the prosodic features of child-directed and foreigner-directed speech," in *Proceedings of the 9th European Conference on Speech Communication and Technology: Interspeech*, Lisbon, 2401–2404.

Bignell, S., and Cain, K. (2007). Pragmatic aspects of communication and language comprehension in groups of children differentiated by teacher ratings of inattention and hyperactivity. *Br. J. Dev. Psychol.* 25, 499–512. doi: 10.1348/026151006X171343

Bishop, D. V. M., and Baird, G. (2001). Parent and teacher report of pragmatic aspects of communication: use of the children's communication checklist in a clinical setting. *Dev. Med. Child Neurol.* 43, 809–818. doi: 10.1017/S0012162205000435

Boersma, P., and Weenink, D. (2011). *Praat (Version 5.3) [Computer Software]*. Available from http://www.fon.hum.uva.nl/praat/

Brown-Schmidt, S. (2009). The role of executive function in perspective taking during online language comprehension. *Psychon. Bull. Rev.* 16, 893–900. doi: 10.3758/PBR.16.5.893

Burgess, P. W. (1997). "Theory and methodology in executive function and research," in *Methodology of Frontal and Executive Function*, ed. P. Rabbitt (Hove: Psychology Press), 81–116.

Bussing, R., Fernandez, M., Harwood, M., Hou, W., Wilson Garvan, C., Eyberg, S. M., et al. (2008). Parent and teacher SNAP-IV ratings of attention deficit hyperactivity disorder traits. *Assessment* 15, 317–328. doi: 10.1177/1073191107313888

Clarkson, M. G., and Clifton, R. K. (1985). Infant pitch perception: evidence for responding to pitch categories and the missing fundamental. *J. Acoust. Soc. Am.* 77, 1521–1528. doi: 10.1121/1.391994

Conners, C. K., Erhardt, D., and Sparrow, E. P. (1999). *Conners' Adult ADHD Rating Scales: Technical Manual*. New York, NY: Multi-Health Systems.

Conway, A. R. A., Kane, M. J., Bunting, M. F., Hambrick, D. Z., Wilhelm, O., and Engle, R. W. (2005). Working memory span tasks: a methodological review and user's guide. *Psychon. Bull. Rev.* 12, 769–786. doi: 10.3758/BF03196772

Cook, W. L., and Kenny, D. A. (2005). The actor-partner interdependence model: a model of bidirectional effects in developmental studies. *Int. J. Behav. Dev.* 29, 101–109. doi: 10.1080/01650250444000405

Cooper, R. P., and Aslin, R. N. (1990). Preference for infant-directed speech in the first month after birth. *Child Dev.* 61, 1584–1595. doi: 10.2307/1130766

Crosbie, J., Pérusse, D., Barr, C. L., and Schachar, R. J. (2008). Validating psychiatric endophenotypes: inhibitory control and attention deficit hyperactivity disorder. *Neurosci. Biobehav. Rev.* 32, 40–55. doi: 10.1016/j.neubiorev.2007.05.002

Cutler, A., Dahan, D., and van Donselaar, W. (1997). Prosody in the comprehension of spoken language: a literature review. *Lang. Speech* 40, 141–201.

Ellis, J., and Ure, J. (1969). "Language varieties: Register," in *Encyclopedia of Linguistics: Information and Control*, ed. A. R. Meetham (London: Pergamon), 251–259.

Erhardt, D., Epstein, J. N., Conners, C. K., Parker, J. D. A., and Sitarenios, G. (1999). Self-ratings of ADHD traits in auts II: reliability, validity, and diagnostic sensitivity. *J. Atten. Disord.* 3, 153–158. doi: 10.1177/108705479900300304

Ferguson, C. A. (1964). Baby talk in six languages. *Am. Anthropol.* 66, 103–114. doi: 10.1525/aa.1964.66.suppl_3.02a00060

Fernald, A. (1985). Intonation and communicative intent in mothers' speech to infants: is the melody the message? *Child Dev.* 60, 1497–1510. doi: 10.2307/1130938

Fernald, A. (1993). Approval and disapproval: infant responsiveness to vocal affect in familiar and unfamiliar languages. *Child Dev.* 64, 657–674. doi: 10.2307/1131209

Fowler, K. A., Lilienfeld, S. O., and Patrick, C. J. (2009). Detecting psychopathology from thin slices of behavior. *Psychol. Assess.* 21, 68–78. doi: 10.1037/a0014938

Friedman, J. N. W., Oltmanns, T. F., Gleason, M. E. J., and Turkheimer, E. (2006). Mixed impressions: reactions of strangers to people with pathological personality traits. *J. Res. Pers.* 40, 395–410. doi: 10.1016/j.jrp.2005.01.005

Friend, M. (2001). The transition from affective to linguistic meaning. *First Lang.* 21, 219–243. doi: 10.1177/014272370102106302

Gadeyne, E., Ghesquière, P., and Onghena, P. (2004). Longitudinal relations between parenting and child adjustment in young children. *J. Clin. Child Adolesc. Psychol.* 33, 347–358. doi: 10.1207/s15374424jccp3302_16

Geurts, H. M., Broeders, M., and Nieuwland, M. S. (2010). Thinking outside the executive functions box: theory of mind and pragmatic abilities in attention deficit/hyperactivity disorder. *Eur. J. Dev. Psychol.* 7, 135–151. doi: 10.1080/17405620902906965

Gillis, R., and Nilsen, E. S. (2014). The role of cognitive flexibility in children's ability to detect communicative ambiguity. *First Lang.* 34, 58–71. doi: 10.1177/0142723714521839

Green, B. C., Johnson, K. A., and Bretherton, L. (2014). Pragmatic language difficulties in children with hyperactivity and attention problems: an integrated review. *Int. J. Lang. Commun. Disord.* 49, 15–29. doi: 10.1111/1460-6984.12056

Griggs, M. S., and Mikami, A. Y. (2011). The role of maternal and child ADHD traits in shaping interpersonal relationships. *J. Abnorm. Child Psychol.* 39, 437–449. doi: 10.1007/s10802-010-9464-4

Hecht, M. A., and LaFrance, M. (1995). How (fast) can I help you? Tone of voice and telephone operator efficiency in interactions. *J. Appl. Psychol.* 25, 2086–2098. doi: 10.1111/j.1559-1816.1995.tb02389.x

Huizinga, M., Dolan, C. V., and van der Molen, M. W. (2006). Age-related change in executive function: developmental trends and a latent variable analysis. *Neuropsychologia* 44, 2017–2036. doi: 10.1016/j.neuropsychologia.2006.01.010

Johnston, C. (1996). Parent characteristics and parent-child interactions in families of nonproblem children and ADHD children with higher and lower levels of oppositional-defiant behaviour. *J. Abnorm. Child Psychol.* 24, 85–104. doi: 10.1007/BF01448375

Jurado, M. B., and Rosselli, M. (2007). The elusive nature of executive functions: a review of our current understanding. *Neuropsychol. Rev.* 17, 213–233. doi: 10.1007/s11065-007-9040-z

Kemper, S., Vandeputte, S., Rice, K., Cheung, H., and Gubarchuk, J. (1995). Speech adjustments to aging during a referential communication task. *J. Lang. Soc. Psychol.* 14, 40–59. doi: 10.1177/0261927X95141003

Kenny, D. A., Kashy, D. A., and Cook, W. L. (2006). *Dyadic Data Analysis*. New York, NY: Guilford.

Kim, O. H., and Kaiser, A. P. (2000). Language characteristics of children with ADHD. *Commun. Disord. Q.* 21, 154–165. doi: 10.1177/152574010002100304

Kitamura, C., and Burnham, D. (2003). Pitch and communicative intent in mother's speech: adjustments for age and sex in the first year. *Infancy* 4, 85–110. doi: 10.1207/S15327078IN0401_5

Kitamura, C., and Lam, C. (2009). Age-specific preferences for infant-directed affective intent. *Infancy* 14, 77–100. doi: 10.1080/15250000802569777

Kooij, S. J. J., Conners, K. C., Goto, T., Tanaka, Y., Williams, D., Allen, A. J., et al. (2013). Validity of Conners' adult attention-deficit/hyperactivity disorder rating scale investigator rated: screening version in patients from within and outside of Europe. *Psychiatry Res.* 208, 94–96. doi: 10.1016/j.psychres.2012.12.003

Kryski, K. R., Mash, E. J., and Ninowski, J. E. (2010). Maternal symptoms of attention-deficit/hyperactivity disorder and maternal language: implications for infant language and development. *J. Child Fam. Stud.* 19, 270–277. doi: 10.1007/s10826-009-9294-6

Lambek, R., Tannock, R., Dalsgaard, S., Trillingsgaard, A., Damm, D., and Thomsen, P. (2011). Executive dysfunction in school-age children with ADHD. *J. Atten. Disord.* 15, 646–655. doi: 10.1177/1087054710370935

Landau, S., and Milich, R. (1988). Social communication patterns of attention-deficit-disordered boys. *J. Abnorm. Child Psychol.* 16, 69–81. doi: 10.1007/BF00910501

Leonard, M. A., Milich, R., and Lorch, E. P. (2011). The role of pragmatic language use in mediating the relation between hyperactivity and inattention and social skills problems. *J. Speech Lang. Hear Res.* 54, 567–579. doi: 10.1044/1092-4388(2010/10-0058)

Locke, K. D., and Sadler, P. (2007). Self-efficacy, values, and complementarity in dyadic interactions: integrating interpersonal and social-cognitive theory. *Pers. Soc. Psychol. Bull.* 33, 94–109. doi: 10.1177/0146167206293375

Martinussen, R., Hayden, J., Hogg-Johnson, S., and Tannock, R. (2005). A meta-analysis of working memory impairments in children with attention-deficit/hyperactivity disorder. *J. Am. Acad. Child Adolesc. Psychiatry* 44, 377–384. doi: 10.1097/01.chi.0000153228.72591.73

Mash, E. J., and Johnston, C. (1982). A comparison of the mother-child interactions of younger and older hyperactive and normal children. *Child Dev.* 53, 1371–1381. doi: 10.2307/1129028

Miyake, A., Friedman, N. P., Emerson, M. J., Witzki, A. H., and Howerter, A. (2000). The unity and diversity of executive functions and their contributions to complex "frontal lobe" tasks: a latent variable analysis. *Cogn. Psychol.* 41, 49–100. doi: 10.1006/cogp.1999.0734

Morton, J. B., and Trehub, S. E. (2001). Children's understanding of emotion in speech. *Child Dev.* 72, 834–843. doi: 10.1111/1467-8624.00318

Nigg, J. T. (2001). Is ADHD an inhibitory disorder? *Psychol. Bull.* 127, 571–598. doi: 10.1037/0033-2909.127.5.571

Nilsen, E. S., and Fecica, A. M. (2011). A model of communicative perspective-taking for typical and atypical populations of children. *Dev. Rev.* 31, 55–78. doi: 10.1016/j.dr.2011.07.001

Nilsen, E. S., and Graham, S. A. (2009). The relations between children's communicative perspective-taking and executive functioning. *Cogn. Psychol.* 58, 220–249. doi: 10.1016/j.cogpsych.2008.07.002

Nilsen, E. S., and Graham, S. A. (2012). The development of preschoolers' appreciation of communicative ambiguity. *Child Dev.* 83, 1400–1415. doi: 10.1111/j.1467-8624.2012.01762.x

Nilsen, E. S., Mangal, L., and MacDonald, K. (2013). Referential communication in children with ADHD: the role of a listener. *J. Speech Lang. Hear Res.* 56, 590–603. doi: 10.1044/1092-4388(2012/12-0013)

Nilsen, E. S., Varghese, A., Fecica, A., and Xu, Z. (2015). Children's production of referential statements. An examination of the role of ADHD traits and executive functioning. *J. Cogn. Dev.* 36, 68–82. doi: 10.1017/S0305000911000432

Normand, S., Flora, D. B., Toplak, M. E., and Tannock, R. (2012). Evidence for a general ADHD factor from a longitudinal general school population study. *J. Abnorm. Child Psychol.* 40, 555–567. doi: 10.1007/s10802-011-9584-5

Oerlemans, A. M., van der Meer, J. M., Steijn, D. J., de Ruiter, S. W., Bruijn, Y. G., Sonneville, L. M., et al. (2014). Recognition of facial emotion and affective prosody in children with ASD (+ADHD) and their unaffected siblings. *Eur. J. Child Adolesc. Psychiatry* 23, 257–271. doi: 10.1007/s00787-013-0446-2

O'Neill, D. K. (2007). The language use inventory for young children: a parent-report measure of pragmatic language development for 18- to 47-month-old children. *J. Speech Lang. Hear Res.* 50, 214–228. doi: 10.1044/1092-4388(2007/017)

Pardo, J. S. (2013). Measuring phonetic convergence in speech production. *Front. Psychol.* 4:559. doi: 10.3389/fpsyg.2013.00559

Psychogiou, L., Daley, D., Thompson, M., and Sonuga-Barke, E. (2007). Testing the interactive effect of parent and child ADHD on parenting in mothers and fathers: a further test of the similarity-fit hypothesis. *Br. J. Dev. Psychol.* 25, 419–433. doi: 10.1348/026151006X170281

Psychogiou, L., Daley, D. M., Thompson, M. J., and Sonuga-Barke, E. J. S. (2008). Do maternal attention-deficit/hyperactivity disorder symptoms exacerbate or ameliorate the negative effect of child attention-deficit/hyperactivity disorder symptoms on parenting? *Dev. Psychopathol.* 20, 121–137. doi: 10.1017/S0954579408000060

Purvis, K. L., and Tannock, R. (1997). Language abilities in children with attention deficit hyperactivity disorder, reading disabilities, and normal controls. *J. Abnorm. Child Psychol.* 25, 133–144. doi: 10.1023/A:1025731529006

Reitan, R. M., and Wolfson, D. (1985). *The Halstead-Reitan Neuropsychological Test Battery: Theory and Clinical Interpretation.* Tucson, AZ: Neuropsychology Press.

Roid, G. H. (2003). *Stanford-Binet Intelligence Scales, (SB5).* Rolling Meadows, IL: Riverside.

Sánchez-Cubillo, I., Periáñez, J. A., Drover-Roig, D., Rodríguez-Sánchez, J. M., Ríos-Lago, M., Tirapu, J., et al. (2009). Construct validity of the trail making test: role of task-switching, working memory, inhibition/interference control, and visuomotor abilities. *J. Int. Neuropsychol. Soc.* 15, 438–450. doi: 10.1017/S1355617709090626

Scouting Web (2013). *Survival: A Simulation Game.* Available at: http://www.epilogsys.com/scoutingweb/SubPages/SurvivalGame.htm

Sonuga-Barke, E. J. S., Dalen, L., Daley, D., and Remington, B. (2002). Are planning, working memory, and inhibition associated with individual differences in preschool ADHD traits? *Dev. Neuropsychol.* 21, 255–272. doi: 10.1207/S15326942DN2103_3

Strauss, E., Sherman, E. M. S., and Spreen, O. (2006). *A Compendium of Neuropsychological Tests: Administration, Norms, and Commentary*, 3rd Edn. New York, NY: Oxford University Press.

Stroop, J. R. (1935). Studies of interference in serial verbal reactions. *J. Exp. Psychol.* 18, 643–662. doi: 10.1037/h0054651

Struchen, M. A., Clark, A. N., Sander, A. M., Mills, M. R., Evans, G., and Kurtz, D. (2008). Relation of executive functioning and social communication measures to functional outcomes following traumatic brain injury. *NeuroRehabilitation* 23, 185–198.

Swanson, J. M. (1992). *School-Based Assessments and Interventions for ADD Students*. Irvine, CA: KC Publishing.

Thorell, L. B., and Wåhlstedt, C. (2006). Executive functioning deficits in relation to symptoms of ADHD and/or ODD in preschool children. *Infant Child Dev.* 15, 503–518. doi: 10.1002/icd.475

Tomasello, M., and Mannle, S. (1985). Pragmatics of sibling speech to one-year-olds. *Child Dev.* 56, 911–917. doi: 10.2307/1130103

Tracey, T. J. G. (2004). Levels of interpersonal complementarity: a simplex representation. *Pers. Soc. Psychol. Bull.* 30, 1211–1225. doi: 10.1177/0146167204264075

Uekermann, J., Abdel-Hamid, M., Lehmkämper, C., Vollmoeller, W., and Daum, R. (2008). Perception of affective prosody in major depression: a link to executive functions? *J. Int. Neuropsychol. Soc.* 14, 552–561. doi: 10.1017/S1355617708080740

Uekermann, J., Kraemer, M., Abdel-Hamid, M., Schimmelmann, B. G., Hebebrand, J., Daum, I., et al. (2010). Social cognition in attention-deficit hyperactivity disorder (ADHD). *Neurosci. Biobehav. Rev.* 34, 734–743. doi: 10.1016/j.neubiorev.2009.10.009

Varghese, A., and Nilsen, E. (2015). Prosody influences children's judgments of appropriate communication styles. *Poster presented at Society for Research in Child Development (SRCD) Biennial Meeting*, Philadelphia, PA.

VideoLAN (2012). *VLC Media Player (Version 2.0.0) [computer software]*. Available from http://www.videolan.org/vlc/

Wardlow, L. (2013). Individual differences in speakers' perspective taking: The roles of executive control and working memory. *Psychon. Bull. Rev.* 20, 766–772. doi: 10.3758/s13423-013-0396-1

Warren-Leubecker, A., and Bohannon, J. N. (1984). Intonation patterns in child-directed speech: mother-father differences. *Child Dev.* 55, 1379–1385. doi: 10.2307/1130007

Weppelman, T. L., Bostow, A., Schiffer, R., Elbert-Perez, E., and Newman, R. S. (2003). Children's use of the prosodic characteristics of infant-directed speech. *Lang. Commun.* 23, 63–80. doi: 10.1016/S0271-5309(01)00023-4

Whalen, C. K., Henker, B., Collins, B. E., McAuliffe, S., and Vaux, A. (1979). Peer interaction in a structured communication task: comparisons of normal and hyperactive boys and of methylphenidate (Ritalin) and placebo effects. *Child Dev.* 50, 388–401. doi: 10.2307/1129414

Willcutt, E. G., Doyle, A. E., Nigg, J. T., Faraone, S. V., and Pennington, B. F. (2005). Validity of the executive function theory of attention-deficit/hyperactivity disorder: a meta-analytic review. *Biol. Psychiatry* 57, 1336–1346. doi: 10.1016/j.biopsych.2005.02.006

Wymbs, B. T., Wymbs, F. A., and Dawson, A. E. (2015). Child ADHD and ODD behavior interacts with parent ADHD symptoms to worsen parenting and interparental communication. *J. Abnorm. Child Psychol.* 43, 107–119. doi: 10.1007/s10802-014-9887-4

Conflict of Interest Statement: The authors declare that the research was conducted in the absence of any commercial or financial relationships that could be construed as a potential conflict of interest.

Permissions

All chapters in this book were first published in FPSYG, by Frontiers; hereby published with permission under the Creative Commons Attribution License or equivalent. Every chapter published in this book has been scrutinized by our experts. Their significance has been extensively debated. The topics covered herein carry significant findings which will fuel the growth of the discipline. They may even be implemented as practical applications or may be referred to as a beginning point for another development.

The contributors of this book come from diverse backgrounds, making this book a truly international effort. This book will bring forth new frontiers with its revolutionizing research information and detailed analysis of the nascent developments around the world.

We would like to thank all the contributing authors for lending their expertise to make the book truly unique. They have played a crucial role in the development of this book. Without their invaluable contributions this book wouldn't have been possible. They have made vital efforts to compile up to date information on the varied aspects of this subject to make this book a valuable addition to the collection of many professionals and students.

This book was conceptualized with the vision of imparting up-to-date information and advanced data in this field. To ensure the same, a matchless editorial board was set up. Every individual on the board went through rigorous rounds of assessment to prove their worth. After which they invested a large part of their time researching and compiling the most relevant data for our readers.

The editorial board has been involved in producing this book since its inception. They have spent rigorous hours researching and exploring the diverse topics which have resulted in the successful publishing of this book. They have passed on their knowledge of decades through this book. To expedite this challenging task, the publisher supported the team at every step. A small team of assistant editors was also appointed to further simplify the editing procedure and attain best results for the readers.

Apart from the editorial board, the designing team has also invested a significant amount of their time in understanding the subject and creating the most relevant covers. They scrutinized every image to scout for the most suitable representation of the subject and create an appropriate cover for the book.

The publishing team has been an ardent support to the editorial, designing and production team. Their endless efforts to recruit the best for this project, has resulted in the accomplishment of this book. They are a veteran in the field of academics and their pool of knowledge is as vast as their experience in printing. Their expertise and guidance has proved useful at every step. Their uncompromising quality standards have made this book an exceptional effort. Their encouragement from time to time has been an inspiration for everyone.

The publisher and the editorial board hope that this book will prove to be a valuable piece of knowledge for researchers, students, practitioners and scholars across the globe.

List of Contributors

Jill Vaughan, Gillian Wigglesworth and Deborah Loakes
School of Languages and Linguistics, University of Melbourne, Parkville, VIC, Australia

Samantha Disbray
Northern Institute, Charles Darwin University, Alice Springs, NT, Australia

Karin Moses
Student Learning, La Trobe University, Bendigo, VIC, Australia

Yvette R. Harris and Seham Almutairi
Department of Psychology, Miami University, Oxford, OH, USA

Shannon K. Bennetts and Elizabeth M. Westrupp
Department of Paediatrics, The University of Melbourne, Parkville, VIC, Australia
Murdoch Childrens Research Institute, Parkville, VIC, Australia
Judith Lumley Centre, La Trobe University, Melbourne, VIC, Australia

Fiona K. Mensah
Department of Paediatrics, The University of Melbourne, Parkville, VIC, Australia
Murdoch Childrens Research Institute, Parkville, VIC, Australia
The Royal Children's Hospital, Parkville, VIC, Australia

Naomi J. Hackworth
Murdoch Childrens Research Institute, Parkville, VIC, Australia
Judith Lumley Centre, La Trobe University, Melbourne, VIC, Australia

Sheena Reilly
Department of Paediatrics, The University of Melbourne, Parkville, VIC, Australia
Murdoch Childrens Research Institute, Parkville, VIC, Australia
The Royal Children's Hospital, Parkville, VIC, Australia
Menzies Health Institute Queensland, Griffith University, Gold Coast, QLD, Australia

Claudia Catani and Iris M. Sossalla
Department of Psychology, Bielefeld University, Bielefeld, Germany

Erin K. Martin and Peter H. Silverstone
Department of Psychiatry, University of Alberta, Edmonton, AB, Canada

Adelina Brizio
Department of Psychology and Center for Cognitive Science, University of Turin, Turin, Italy
Faculty of Communication Science, Università della Svizzera Italiana, Lugano, Switzerland

Ilaria Gabbatore
Faculty of Humanities, Child Language Research Center, University of Oulu, Oulu, Finland

Maurizio Tirassa and Francesca M. Bosco
Department of Psychology and Center for Cognitive Science, University of Turin, Turin, Italy
Department of Psychology and Neuroscience Institute of Turin, Turin, Italy

Cándido J. Inglés
Department of Health Psychology, Miguel Hernandez University of Elche, Elche, Spain,

José Manuel García-Fernández, María Vicent, Carolina Gonzálvez and Ricardo Sanmartín
Department of Developmental Psychology and Didactics, University of Alicante, Alicante, Spain

Elisabeth M. de Jong, Francine C. Jellesma, Helma M. Y. Koomen and Peter F. de Jong
Research Institute of Child Development and Education, University of Amsterdam, Amsterdam, Netherlands

Ora Oudgenoeg-Paz, M(Chiel). J. M. Volman and Paul P. M. Leseman
Department of Child, Family and Education Studies, Utrecht University, Utrecht, Netherlands

Nicola Yuill and Alex F. Martin
Children and Technology Laboratory, School of Psychology, University of Sussex, Falmer, UK

Lizhu Luo, Xiaole Ma, Xiaoxiao Zheng, Weihua Zhao, Lei Xu, Benjamin Becker and Keith M. Kendrick
Key Laboratory for NeuroInformation of Ministry of Education, Center for Information in BioMedicine, University of Electronic Science and Technology of China, Chengdu, China

Carol George
Department of Psychology, Mills College, Oakland, CA, USA

Judith Solomon
School of Clinical Medicine, University of Cambridge, Cambridge, UK

Anna Rita Addessi, Filomena Anelli and Diber Benghi
Department of Education Studies, University of Bologna, Bologna, Italy

Anders Friberg
Department of Speech, Music and Hearing, KTH Royal Institute of Technology, Stockholm, Sweden

Bettina J. Casad
Department of Psychological Sciences, University of Missouri-St. Louis, St. Louis, MO, USA

Patricia Hale and Faye L. Wachs
Department of Mathematics and Statistics, California State Polytechnic University, Pomona, Pomona, CA, USA

Elizabeth S. Nilsen, Ami Rints and Nicole Ethier
Centre for Mental Health Research, Department of Psychology, University of Waterloo, Waterloo, ON, Canada

Sarah Moroz
Department of Psychology, University of Western Ontario, London, ON, Canada

Index